John Courtney Murray, Time/Life, and the American Proposition:

HOW THE CIA'S DOCTRINAL WARFARE PROGRAM CHANGED THE CATHOLIC CHURCH

VOLUME II

NEW EDITION
WITH FORWARD BY
DR. JOHN RAO

David Wemhoff

JOHN COURTNEY MURRAY, TIME/LIFE AND THE AMERICAN PROPOSITION: HOW THE CIA'S DOCTRINAL WARFARE PROGRAM CHANGED THE CATHOLIC CHURCH - Volume II

Published by Wagon Wheel Press of Presence LLC in South Bend, Indiana

Book formatting and book cover provided by Trisha Fuentes

Printed and bound in the United States of America.

ISBN: 978-1-7379573-3-1

This book is dedicated

to a better understanding

of what happened to all of us

CONTENTS

PART XXIII
NADIR AND RENEWAL

SUMMARY OF PARTS XV
THROUGH XXIII

PART XV - HARRY, CLARE, AND JOHN STAY TOGETHER (1959-1960)

At the height of the Cold War, during the 1960 presidential election, and while the Catholic Church readied itself for Vatican II, the power trio was threatened with dissolution. That bode ill for Murray who counted on the Luces so much for his credibility in the Church. The Luces in turn held credibility with the Catholics as Clare was a Catholic married to a Presbyterian. Should that union dissolve or appear publicly to rupture, then the answer to the important question of "can a Catholic be an American," would be cast into doubt.

Harry, Clare and John stayed together due to the efforts of Murray and LSD. The latter came into their lives through Gerald Heard, one of the most influential men of twentieth century culture. Heard focused modern man on himself and he espoused the idea that the businessman is the ultimate authority of modern life. This cultural philosophy was perfect for advancing the American Proposition.

PART XVI - UNCONDITIONAL SURRENDER (1960)

As 1959 wound down and the Presidential election year began, Luce, who was supporting JFK, presented the real issue of the 1960 election: Can a Catholic be an American? The answer to the question was yes if the Catholic accepted Murray's "American interpretation" of church and state. This meant repudiating the Catholic doctrine on church and state which Blanshard called "the most important issue." This meant accepting as good in principle, and hence not subject to change, the First Amendment with its disestablishment of the Catholic Church, and all churches for that matter, as well as the repudiation of religion as the basis of public policy. This meant accepting the American ideology before the doctrines of the Catholic Faith.

During the first half of 1960, it was not clear whether the Catholics had sufficiently accepted the "American interpretation" of the First Amendment, or the American ideology. The Protestants pressured the Catholics to submit. Across the ocean, statements from Church leaders encouraged the Catholics to submit while theologians like Fr. Connell and prelates like Archbishop Egidio Vagnozzi, Papal nuncio to the US, admitted that the American system of church and state need not change. By late summer, the Catholic leadership in the US gave an unconditional pledge of support to the American system of church and state relations. Prominent Catholics in academe, the press, theology, business and civic life signed a statement endorsing the American system of church and stae relations. Catholic and Presidential candidate John F. Kennedy, gave a speech in Houston, and Jesuit Gustave Weigel's important September 27 talk said that Catholics could hold one view in private and another in public. Weigel gave cover to Mario Cuomo and others who publicly supported abortion while privately opposing it.

The 1960 presidential election confirmed that a good Catholic could be an American and could advance in society provided that he or she was loyal to the American ideology before Catholic doctrine and agreed to not work for either the Catholic confessional state or, as

John Cardinal Wright had explained earlier, to Catholicize the fatherland. This sent a powerful message to Catholics in Latin America where the Catholic Church grew more Americanist. America taught that a Catholic could serve both God and Mammon, and the Church leadership approved by endorsing the American system of social organization.

Murray's book, *We Hold These Truths,* was published, and in December he was on the cover of *Time.* The book sanctified America as good and acceptable to Catholicism in principle. Catholics had a duty to defend and advance American foundational principles, the most important of which was religious liberty as contained in the "Establishment Clause" and the "Free Exercise Clause" of the First Amendment. Catholics were to accept an ill-defined natural law as the basis of state actions while serving another equivocal concept called freedom. The American Proposition became the ideal in the Catholic mind. It was an important victory for the American elites and their doctrinal or ideological offensive. Its effect is felt to this day as Catholics hold key positions in Government, in finance, and in industry.

The Catholic prelates helped to bring about the Catholic surrender. First, they provided rhetorical ammunition for use by the Americans against the Catholics. Second, the prelates spoke so as not to offend the Americans and so were equivocal at best. Third, the actions by the prelates were such that they signified support for the American ideology. The reason for the prelates' failure is perhaps best summed up in a letter from John LaFarge, SJ to his confrere, Murray, in 1955. LaFarge wrote: "Coupled with the functional view of the laity in general comes, in too many cases, a subservience to the wealthy layman, when such occurs. Where the Church should be inspiring the wealthy to moral leadership in meeting squarely our great social problems, we are too apt to fear offending them, and are often quasi driven to this attitude."[1]

PART XVII - PREPARING FOR VATICAN II (1960-1962)

Pope John XXIII announced an ecumenical council to "correspond to the needs of the present times."[2] The needs seemed to be twofold – to respond to the persecution in Communist countries and to strengthen the spiritual dimension of life. The latter indicated a concern over a growing materialism that was destroying the life of faith. This was a direct response to what CD Jackson had remarked was the "Revolution of Expectations" brought about by the US and the USSR during the Cold War. While the Pope did not intend to promulgate new doctrine, he sought to present the Church's doctrine in accordance with "new means."[3] This lent itself to manipulation and mischief by the American media. Throughout 1959 and 1960, the Vatican went about soliciting comments and proposed topics for discussion. Catholic bishops, professors, and heads of religious orders submitted topics to be considered by the preparatory committees for submission to the Council. Fr. Connell submitted a number of topics, with one of the more important being the clear statement that every society had a responsibility to the Divine Positive Law of Jesus Christ. With such, every society had an obligation to recognize and establish the Catholic Church and the Catholic Faith. This was in direct contravention of Murray's position and repudiated The American Proposition.

Fenton was called to Rome to assist in preparing issues for consideration by the Council. He saw a rot in the Vatican that consisted of careerism and Americanism. Materialism and worldliness were infusing the hierarchy. There was more of a concern for not offending "separated brethren" than for the welfare of the faithful or defense of the truth. It was there that Fenton realized Catholic doctrine was undergoing a world-wide assault which consisted not only in the propagation and promotion of false or erroneous doctrines, but also the use of vague and ambiguous language that failed to clarify and caused confusion. Indeed, a general sense of confusion increased with Papal declarations and statements. John XXIII's words gave rhetorical ammunition to the American media who watched the whole matter quite closely.

CIA agent and Time, Inc. employee Dohrn in one of his regular reports to CD Jackson wrote "I have established a rather close contact with Guzzardi who told me that he had been in conversation with back home and that it had been brought to our friend's attention. Whatever the fate of the Ecumenical council (so far rather an improvisation) will be, that will be a spot of increasing importance in the future."[4] In June, 1960 Dohrn reported that an upcoming Eucharistic Congress provided German and Polish prelates to gather for discussions of liturgy, but that was not unimportant he intimated, as these could have bearings on the upcoming Ecumenical Council.[5] In a Motu Proprio from June, 1960, John XXIII sounded an Americanist tone when he called for the forthcoming Council to promote the "growth of the Catholic Faith and the renewal along right lines of the habits of Christian people and the adapting of ecclesiastical discipline to the needs and conditions of the present time."[6]

In November, the Pope seemed to switch and sounded an anti-materialist theme when he said "In the present era the face of the world is much altered, with its strenuous development amind the attractions and the dangers of quest almost entirely after material goods, and a forgetfulness or great weakening of the principles fo the spirutal and supernatural order which characterized the penetration and expansion fothe Christian civilization during the centuries." He decried the "deviations of the human spirit, drawn or driven towards enjoyment of this world's goods alone…." In a statement that heartened the Americans, the Pope mentioned "great sorrow" for "dear brother Bishops, of excellent priests and fervent laity who… endure loss of human and religious freedom, and sometimes of physical and moral freedom as well." It was not to be a doctrinal council, and he said "Oecumenical Councils in the past dealt for the most part with expressions which evoked anxiety on the score of doctrinal accuracy…."[7]

If the Council was to be about a new expression of truths, then Americanism was implicated. This, along with intimations of a desire for unity with non-Catholics, made the Council a way to quickly turn the Church Americanist. Luce's magazine could more easily divide Catholics into different camps – good guys and bad guys just like in the then popular American Western movies. The events in Rome were to be cast as an American morality play. On one side were the liberals or progressives who sought to make the Church like America. These favored American style church and state organization. These were the good guys. On the other side were reactionaries, conservatives, authoritarians who favored the establishment of the Catholic religion and church in societies as the ideal. These were the bad guys.

PART XVIII - VATICAN II – 1962

The Catholic Church was both an obstacle and an asset to the Americans. Its doctrine was a potent counter weight to the American ideology, and the most important part of that doctrine was that which pertained to church and state relations as Paul Blanshard observed in the late 1940s. The American ideology re-engineered societies to the service of wealth and subjugated those societies to the American economic and financial elites. The Church's world-wide presence and hierarchical structure offered the Americans an asset to be used to spread the American ideology around the world. The Vatican II Council provided an opportunity for the Americans to harness the Catholic Church for their purposes of world dominion which FDR first announced in modern times with his Four Freedoms speech in January, 1941. Essential to exploiting that opportunity presented by the Council was the American media, most notably Henry Luce's *Time* magazine with its proven ability to shape the issues and influence thoughts as well as action.

The Catholic bishops, and leaders like Msgr. Fenton, knew that the American media was a problem, not the least of which was to raise the expectations of the laity and the world on the upcoming Council. While preparing for the Council, the Central Preparatory Committee acknowledged the need to establish norms for the use of the media and limit its power to distort. The Pope also established a media commission for the Council to try and assist with the proper understanding of the events of the Council. These and other actions were taken in good faith by the Catholics, but they miscalculated because the Americans were not acting in good faith. Another miscalculation was the growing Modernist and Americanist threat within the Church. Fenton observed repeatedly the desire of theologians to use figurative and flowery language so as not to offend non-Catholics. He also observed the flagrant, and subtle, subversion of Catholic doctrine and the refutation of truths held for centuries by the Catholics in the Catholic universities.

Consistent with pronouncements prior to the start of the Council, Pope John emphasized there would not be any doctrinal changes. However, his statements were twisted by the American media. One was that the Church sought a renewal, which was translated by the media as meaning a modernization. Another was that the Church was hoping for unity with other religions, notably Christian sects, and that was twisted by the media to mean that the Catholic Church had been wrong and was seeking unity on any term possible. Finally, the Pope stressed repeatedly the need to present old truths in new ways. This invited innovation and the use of epeidictic language, both of which served Americanism which had centered with the prelates and priests from France and Germany, ground zero of American psychological warfare to destroy the European peoples for the benefit of the titans of Mammon. The Church was divided between Catholics and Americanists on the even of the Council. The Pope unfortunately set the stage for a Council to be hijacked in service to American geopolitical interests.

Klaus Dohrn noted that a revolution occurred almost from the beginning of the Council. It initially manifested itself in the Council's procedures and then spread to the liturgy and from there to the rest of Catholic doctrine. *Time* depicted the struggle as one between liberals versus reactionaries, or pastoralists and progressives versus conservatives who tried to block progress. The good guys were trying to make the Church like America and have the Church accept American ideas as good, and the bad guys resisted.

PART XIX - VATICAN II - 1963

As the year started, the Americans were optimistic. CD Jackson wrote an old source, Dr. Vittorio Vaccari who resided in Rome, positively crowing about the ongoing ecumenical council: "Ever so many thanks for the perfectly marvelous `panettone' – as well as for the reports and the copy of the `Osservatore Romano'. The Catholic Church really seems to be making tremendous strides these days."[8]

An American media barrage followed every session of the Council so as to tell the world how to understand or interpret the session's events. The Catholic bishops grew upset over this situation, denouncing the inaccuracies of the reporting and the conflict that the reporting was creating. The Council Fathers moved quickly on a declaration calling the media to account. The result of that labor was *Inter Mirifica* which was vigorously condemned by the Americans including John Courtney Murray and Michael Novak, an ambitious young Catholic writer.

This did not slow down the American media, especially Luce's *Time* magazine. A number of prelates gave interviews or made statements that were used against the Church to advance the American agenda and Americanist interests. The efforts to keep a number of dissident theologians, to include Kung and Murray, from speaking at Catholic University of America was given great play in *Time* which continued to depict the Church as undergoing a revolution for freedom. The morality play continued even after the death of John XXIII who was praised as a revolutionary, while Cardinal Ottaviani, and all who stood by him, were condemned as reactionaries. Paul VI succeeded to the Papal throne with the high hopes of the Americans,[9] but these hopes were dashed.

Americanists gained ground at the Council. Their successes were not in the doctrinal arena but in the presentation of doctrine in the documents, or the "pastoral" arena. Msgr. Fenton captured the dynamic, which was Americanism: "The statement of the Council is not a theological text book. At the same time, however, a declaration by a council can cause confusion or finally can actually be harmful when, even though there is no error about faith or morals in it, the statement passes over truths which are, and which have long generally been recognized as, assertions of Catholic doctrine."[10]

By Autumn, Murray was at the Council as a periti of Francis Cardinal Spellman, a long-time friend of the Luces. The US bishops increased their efforts to obtain a declaration on religious liberty. Ottaviani could not delay the onslaught any more. Fenton's health failed and he resigned as editor of *American Ecclesiastical Review*. The Catholic press in the US grew increasingly pro-American ignoring *Inter Mirifica*.

PART XX - VATICAN II – 1964

At the start of the Vatican II Council, ex priest Carlo Falconi observed, as had others, "the leadership of the Roman church belongs to the USA in the same way that the political leadership of the Western world is in its hands." He wrote accurately that some in the American episcopate held "for the good of the Church," it should be injected "with new blood from the most modern and powerful country in the world." These churchmen held, according to Falconi, the Americans had the "technical equipment" and the know how to train the forces to "guarantee the dynamism" of the Church in the modern world. Falconi concluded the American approach, was "lacking in idealism" and combined "crude commercialism" along with "childish programmes of technical reform."[11]

The Americans made their play for religious liberty in the Third Session of the Council. Murray had the plan, and Richard Cardinal Cushing was the general according to *Time* magazine. The goal was for a statement from that approved "the concept of religious freedom" in its "commonly accepted sense." That meant an "immunity" to practice one's own religion as one chose, which meant belonging to the religious denomination, or none, of one's choice and attending worship services as one chose. This endorsed the American ideology and the First Amendment as good in principle.

During the third session, the famous phrase, "the spirit of Vatican II," was coined and first appeared in the pages of *Time* magazine. This phrase represents the efforts to remake the Church in the image of America, and is akin to the spirit of rebellion or the "spirit of '76." To advance this spirit, the Church was told it had to "catch up" with the modern world or lose relevancy when the reality was, and is, that once it did "catch up," it became irrelevant. That is because once the Church becomes like America, it is no longer needed as it is just a reaffirmation of America which then becomes the teacher of the nations.

It looked as though the Americans, and their allies in the Church, the Americanists, might carry the day, but Pope Paul VI stopped them. The Americans were furious. *Time,* the American media, and its echo chamber, the Catholic media, kept up the steady drumfire of words to make the Church like America. The morality play of good guy versus bad guy, liberal versus conservative or reactionary, both continued and intensified. The Church leadership struck back as well as it could but they were gradually losing control of their own institutions. The historical milieu (post World War II and Cold War) suppressed any criticism of America and Americans, by name, and so the Catholics were hampered in their efforts to defend themselves. Churchmen like Cardinal Bea were elevated by the Americans to pre-eminence for their work in breaking down barriers to the capitalist spirit in the name of ecumenism or unity. The Catholics did not have a media as strong as did the Americans.

PART XXI - VATICAN II – 1965

Time told people what to think, and one of those things was that the Church had to become "an open society." The December 25, 1964 edition of the magazine referred to the Second Vatican Council as having "unleashed a passion for aggiornamento in the most tradition-encrusted of churches." This meant that the Church was reconfiguring itself to be like America: "Catholicism's vitality shows in the new liturgy, and in the zest with which a generation of 'open church' priests and laymen are calling for more reforms of outdated rules (clerical celibacy, for example), institutions (the Index of Forbidden Books) and teachings (birth control)...."[12]

Another change was in the area of church and state relations, and religious liberty was the epitome of that change. Archbishop John Krol of Philadelphia made that clear in the *Camden Star Herald* early in 1965. He said the Declaration on Religious Liberty would be the "first thing" taken up by the Council when it returned in September.[13] It was, and by the end of the Council there issued the Declaration on Religious Liberty, or *Dignitatis Humanae*. The Church did not change doctrine, but the language of the Declaration lent itself to manipulation, misunderstanding, and misinterpretation by the Americans and Americanists all of which was to put Catholics and the Church in service to America. The Declaration, as Fr. Connell explained, justified theologically the role of freedom in religious matters. It emphasized the duty of man to seek truth and hold to it. That truth is found in the Catholic Faith. *Inter Mirifica* and *Gaudium et Spes* set out the central portions of Connell's efforts – that all societies, regardless of how organized, are to base their policies on the Divine Positive Law and not Liberalism.

Sociologists noted the perception by Catholic prelates that they were under pressure, and they were striving to survive in the Cold War world. There existed "other powerful institutions" that were pressuring the episcopates to "demonstrate organizational legitimacy."[14] Establishing a stable relation with the societies of the world drove much of the deliberations. The Council documents sought to "improve relations with Protestants." The "focus on Protestants was a key dividing line among four distinct types of organizational fields. The first group, bishops from religiously diverse but stable countries (e.g., Germany and the United States), was the friendliest to Protestants. Such countries had a strong ecumenical movement, providing an organizational arena in which religious leaders, primarily Protestants, sought to better relations among all Christians."[15]

The opposition to this group came from the "monopolistic Catholic countries, such as Italy and Spain, who constituted the second major group. These bishops were openly antagonistic to ecumenism and even to Protestants in general." However, because "these two groups' agendas were so diametrically opposed, passing any particular reform whether ecumenically oriented or not, depended on winning a majority of the votes from the two remaining groups: monopolistic countries in Latin America, where the Church was in decline and whose bishops were progressive but not ecumenical, and missionary countries in Africa and Asia, where the Church was growing and whose bishops were generally supportive of all change...."[16] All of this was occurring during a time that a materialist spirit was spreading though the World as CD Jackson observed, and societies were changing to accommodate that spirit with the changes often reflecting those brought by accepting Liberalism in one form or another.

Msgr. Rudolph Bandas gave a homily in Summer, 1965 printed in *The Wanderer*. He reminded the faithful the purposes for the Council were three fold: renewal of the internal life of the Church, the "penetration of the modern world with the principles of the Gospel", and "a dialogue with all men of good will." There would not be any doctrinal change he indicated, a reference that unmistakably referred to the pending discussions of religious liberty. He said there would be a "bleak Winter" that will "precede the bright Spring when the Church will emerge in new strength and vigor."[17] How long that bleak Winter would last, he did not say, but the "spirit of Vatican II" announced the season.

PART XXII - AFTER VATICAN II

The Church descended into anarchy with the close of the Council. The doctrine was corrupted by priests and discipline collapsed. Despite the statements of Paul VI, the Vatican II documents were interpreted as giving rise to a change in doctrine. The faithful were cut off from nineteen centuries of teaching and wisdom.

The anarchy escalated during the summer of 1966 with the increase of dissenters and the paralysis of the Catholic hierarchy who avoided appearing authoritarian and hence un-American. Allied with this was Murray's view that theologians knew better than the bishops. He also said cool and calm discussion is the way to truth. And, he taught that America was the ideal for it allowed these discussions amidst freedom. *Dignitatis Humanae's* prohibition of coercion in civil society came to be applied to the Church. The rebellion against Church teaching and authority commenced by Murray, Weigel, and others and fanned by the American media went to its next logical step --deconstruction of Church doctrine in the area of sexual ethics. The Spirit of Vatican II exploded within the Church. It was an American and Americanist spirit, and the prelates accepted it. The leadership let America teach the Church, and about 50 years later, Pope Francis publicly repudiated Catholic doctrine on the proper relation of church and state. A Catholic President, a largely Catholic Supreme Court of the United States, and a Catholic Speaker of the House of Representatives kept in place not only the American ideology but advanced things like abortion.

After the Council, Murray advanced the interests Luce represented. He made clear, especially to Archbishop John Dearden, that barriers to the capitalist spirit had to be torn down. Murray lent his name and support to the dissenters in the Church who sought to have it approve of the agenda of the plutocrats – legalized contraception and abortion. Connell relentlessly fought the forces of dissolution despite his advancing years, but by early 1967, Rome had surrendered.

Within four years of the end of the Council, the main characters in this drama were dead: Gustave Weigel (January 3, 1964), C.D. Jackson (September 18, 1964), Henry Luce (February 28, 1967), Fr. Francis Connell (May 12, 1967), John Courtney Murray (August 16, 1967), Francis Cardinal Spellman (December 2, 1967), and Msgr. Joseph C. Fenton (July 7, 1969).

The fires of destruction were fanned by *Time,* the rest of the American media, and the Catholic press that turned pro-American. Americanism had indeed taken over the thinking of the Catholic leadership, which saw the world in terms of American constructs. This meant that the Catholic Church became the carrier of the

American ideology, just as Henry Luce, the interests he represented, and the US Government wanted. The bishops relinquished their duties of protecting the flock and suppressing error and instead adopted the "medicine of mercy" which lead to the propagation of false ideas and heterodoxy. This was part of the remaking of the Church into the image of America, another goal of the Americans. This was the beginning of the Church's American Captivity, and the faithful as well as the societies in which they live, feel the effects to this day.

PART XXIII - NADIR AND RENEWAL

The acceptance of The American Proposition is the acceptance of the secular state and the rejection of the Catholic Confessional State with all that entails. In 2016, the leader of the Roman Catholic Church publicly rejected the Catholic Confessional State and thereby gave the Church, and the peoples of the entire world, over to the will of the plutocrats. Despite this, there are signs of hope as the Catholics stir themselves to confront the greatest issue of the day – the proper organization of society. Intellectuals are critiquing The American Proposition and the *Catechism of the Catholic Church* makes clear the purpose of society and the civil authorities. The foundations are being laid for renewal.

PART XV

HARRY, CLARE, AND JOHN STAY
TOGETHER (1959-1960)

CHAPTER 65
MURRAY SAVES THE LUCE MARRIAGE

Murray did not have a relationship with Mr. & Mrs. Luce; he had one relationship with Henry Luce and a very different one with Clare. After a long listening session with Harry, Murray concluded his report on their meeting by telling Clare "that I am fond of him and I love you."[1] The three of them, nonetheless, formed a team, an American trinity if you will, that had to work together to accomplish its goal of bringing Catholics around to accepting America as the ideal, leading the Church into its American Captivity. Their effectiveness would lessen if they broke up, and each stood to lose if the trinity fell apart. The most serious risk to the ongoing existence of that trinity of wealth, power and ideas, occurred during the crucial period of 1959 and 1960 when, as the Church prepared for another Ecumenical Council, Harry announced that he wanted a divorce.

Murray understood the danger of divorce better than either of the parties to it. Murray discussed the divorce issue with Clare after having a "long transcendental talk" with Harry, who was recuperating from heart problems. The couple was "moving to, a crisis," which was made more serious by the "absence, on both sides, of all angry passion, etc. All is calm, but certainly not bright."

3

Harry's indifference concerned Murray, who explained "the danger lest this process of disassociation (if that is the word) go on to the point of a break. I cannot think that that could possibly be a good thing – for either of you. Things are a whole lot less than ideal, or even satisfactory, the way they are. But something worse can always happen...."[2]

Harry and Clare's marital problems intensified beginning in September, 1959 when Harry traveled to Paris to see Lady Jeanne Campbell. During his absence, Clare put her thoughts, emotions, and the history of the marriage into a journal called "By Love Possessed," which she wrote "to intuit why I knew he would ask for a divorce" but also to give an account of their lives together.[3] Clare never wanted to be his mistress and did not counsel divorce from Lila in 1935. However, Harry was driven by lust for her, even though his family was against marrying Clare. Mack Ingersoll, who became a *Life* editor, was angry at Clare for taking Harry away from the publications and he accused Clare of ruining Harry's editorial abilities. As a result of a bitter scene, Clare abandonded the editorial limelight at *Life* magazine and resolved at that point not to be part of Harry's publishing work. Instead, Clare engaged in creative writing and wrote a successful play, "The Women." By 1940, after Clare's third hit play, Harry lost sexual interest in Clare. Matters worsened when Clare was unable to get pregnant despite three operations and Harry lied about his impotence.[4]

By this point in their marriage, Clare concluded Harry was hoping she would find someone else and divorce him. When Clare became a Catholic, Harry hoped that a divorce would end the marriage "for a higher cause." After Clare had a hysterectomy, Harry sent a lawyer to her while she was recovering to convince her that the Church would view it as her duty to divorce Harry. However, instead of agreeing to a divorce, Clare discussed the matter with Archbishop Spellman, who said that the couple could live as brother and sister and not be committing adultery. In reality, Harry was using his "impotence" the cover for a number of sexual liaisons over the years. When Clare found out about the affair, the couple discussed the possibility of divorce, but, in the end, Clare decided that she did not want a divorce and opted to stay in the sexless relationship for friendship and companionship.[5]

The two stayed together distracted for a while from their marital problems by the Eisenhower presidential campaign and Clare's role of US ambassador to Italy. After Clare's term as ambassador ended and she returned to the United States in 1957, all of the suppressed marital problems resurfaced. Harry threw himself back into his old life, dedicated to "making a better and richer America – The American Proposition," maintaining the "Luce Dynasty" (keeping faith with his ancestors was important to Harry),[6] and buying a new house in Phoenix. During one of their stays at that house, Clare saved Harry's life by happening into the room when Harry was having a heart attack. Then in September, 1959, Harry told Clare that he wanted a divorce so that he could marry Lady Jeanne. During the course of the next seven months, Harry told Clare that he would not fight for a divorce and that they must both agree to it.[7]

It was during this period of emotional turmoil that Clare and Murray took their first LSD trip together.

CHAPTER 66

LSD – MURRAY'S PATH TO SAINTHOOD

In the midst of her marital crisis, Clare turned to LSD to find either solace or a cure. After noticing that LSD made the marriage and its difficulties "a little mellower" by 1959,[1] Clare introduced Murray to LSD, who seemed to enjoy the experience. But the one who brought LSD into both their lives was Gerald Heard. Ironically, Murray was a good friend of Heard and had known him long before Heard turned Clare on to LSD.

Gerald Heard was one of the most influential, but least well-known, people of the Twentieth Century and a friend, confidant, and advisor to many of the luminaries of his day, especially those involved with shaping thought and opinion. As "one of Hollywood's first celebrity gurus, as he counted James Dean and Tyrone Power among his readers,"[2] he had a great influence on Bill Wilson, co-founder of Alcoholics Anonymous. Heard may even have written the twelve steps for which Alcoholics Anonymous became so famous.[3] Heard influenced Michael Murphy and Richard Price, the founders of Esalen; Professor Evelyn Hooker, the psychologist instrumental in removing homosexuality as a disorder from the American Psychological Association's classification of mental disorders; Dave Brubeck, musician; Steve Allen, actor and opinion-shaper; James C.

Ingebretsen, leader of the Spiritual Movement; and Henry and Clare Luce.[4] Heard had the power to get people recognized and start them on their way to stardom. One of these people was Ray Bradbury, science fiction writer, whose work, *The Martian Chronicles*, caught Heard's eye.[5]

Heard himself had been introduced to LSD in December, 1955 by Dr. Sidney Cohen and became thereafter a regular user of the substance, to the point of being on a "ninety day cycle."[6] Heard, who was very outgoing and engaging,[7] found that the most effective way to promote his views was by not putting his name to any of the ideas that he sought to propagate.[8] He told one of the members of his "inner circle" that he played with words "an awful lot," and admitted at one point that he could not write his autobiography because he admitted that he could not tell the truth.[9] Heard was, like Murray, a typical example of the sort of writers and thinkers the Luces enjoyed, held in their confidence, and promoted. LSD was in many ways the culmination of American materialism, because both the philosophy and the drug were based on the material world of chemicals and not the spiritual world of truth.

Heard was born and raised in Northern Ireland as the son, grandson, and brother of Anglican ministers. At an early age he rebelled against "both his conservative family upbringing and his culture's outdated world view." At Cambridge, Heard earned a degree in history and undertook postgraduate work in the philosophy of religion though he "specialized in unspecialization" and he came to embody a "youthful open spirit of creative versatility" or "neotony." He became the personal secretaries of Lord Robson of Jesmond, Attorney General to Prime Minister Asquith, and later Sir Horace Plunkett who was instrumental in founding the agricultural cooperative movement in Ireland and championed Irish cultural renaissance. It was there that Heard came to know the intellectual class of Britain, Ireland, and the United States.[10] Heard also became associated with British scientific socialist reformers,[11] and in 1929 he was introduced to Aldous Huxley by Raymond Mortimer, an English man of letters.[12]

7

After Lord Plunkett died in 1932, Heard was appointed the administrator of his estate. In 1937, Heard and his by-then good friend, Aldous Huxley, along with Huxley's first wife, moved to the United States, eventually settling in Southern California, where he pioneered what became known as the Human Potential movement, a form of therapy that included a mix of mysticism, psychadelics, and intellectualism along with mind-body transformation. As part of that effort, Heard founded a monastic community that could pursue these lines of thought in Trabuco Canyon in the 1940s, but the community eventually failed and Heard handed the property over to the Vedanta movement. In the late 1940s and throughout the 1950s, Heard, who had been an active homosexual since at least the 1920s,[13] started writing under the nom de plume of D.B. Vest to expound on the "evolutionary and spiritual significance of homosexuals."[14] At the same time he emphasized the importance of human freedom and religious practice thereby joining in the endorsement of America as opposed to Soviet communism.[15]

During the late 1940s, Heard met Clare, and the two became close, sharing an interest in theater and the arts. At one point Clare and Heard made a pact that they would care for each other after the other's companion died.[16] In one of the many letters they exchanged over the years, Heard thanked Clare for sending an article by Thomas Merton published in *Commonweal* and he wrote: "I am looking forward to your letting me see the final forms of the articles you wrote on your conversion."[17] Heard and his assistant and confidant Michael Barrie spent a considerable amount of time with the Luces at their homes in New York, Connecticut, Phoenix, and Hawaii, and it was on one of these visits that Heard introduced Clare to LSD.[18] Heard explained the "sacramental" nature of the LSD experience to Clare in 1959:

"the LSD experience...is a death-deliverance experience and those that share it can have a rapport which is a profound communion.... Because [LSD] is in this respect `sacramental' it can only be wholly therapeutic and lastingly efficacious if it is given in that complete freedom of charity which alone is possible if those present are motivated by nothing but profound living kindness, the compassion that can have no desire but to serve and the realization that they themselves can give nothing but this the free gift of God which He may mediate through them and they themselves may receive from Him as His supreme reward."[19]

When Murray expressed a desire to take a trip, Clare wrote to Heard inviting him to Phoenix to set up the adventure. Together, Clare and Heard made plans to initiate Murray.[20] Addressing her as "Dear Darling," Heard described that first meeting with Murray in a letter to Clare:

"It was pain to leave you while you were in it, but it was a relief to know that before we left you had been able to let us repeat how dearly we love you and prize you. You can feel that we are your family and that you can confide in a love that is understanding and faithful. Thank you too for letting us come to know Father John. It was his concern for all of us (and too small a dose considering his deep exercises in intellectual awareness) that kept him, as he put it, `on the verge.'"[21]

When Murray took LSD with Clare and Heard, he was "on the verge" in a number of different ways. LSD, according to James Ingebretsen, "works by removing the barriers which are necessary for us to operate in ordinary working day consciousness, opening what William Blake called the 'doors of perception' to other phenomenon; in order to engage in any rational discussion, those gates have to be closed."[22] Its use caused an "upsurge in libido."[23]

Murray enjoyed the LSD experience and encouraged Clare to engage in LSD trips to enhance her ability to write. In one letter addressed to "Clare dearest," Murray wrote "I wrote to Sid [Cohen] this morning, asking that he somehow manage to come over to see you, for an LSD session and also to discuss with you the possibilities of something better than this one-shot sort of proposition....The big thing would be to solidify the `compositional' effects of the drug so that you may have the `composure' to get on to the work you want to do." He concluded with "Your only problem is to get over the threshold. Then you will find the energies beginning to flow. LSD will surely help in that initial step." Murray signed the letter, "Dearest & most abundant love – John".[24]

Murray discussed his LSD trips with TV personality Steve Allen on one occasion. Allen, a protégé of Heard, visited Heard's center in Santa Barbara on a number of occasions in the early 1960s after his first marriage dissolved. It was here that Allen met Murray, who visited Heard there on several occasions. In his conversation with Murray, Allen admitted LSD research was funded by the CIA but that did not stop the luminaries from "tripping." Murray commented favorably on LSD and its effects saying that it amounted to a religious experience which gave him a "love for the whole universe." If he could maintain that high, Murray told Allen, it would make him a saint, but he would have to take LSD daily. Murray said that with LSD he could be himself because we all had to live with a type of social mask, usually.[25] On at least one occasion, he talked his way out of a faculty meeting to fly to Los Angeles to visit Heard.[26]

Dr. Sidney Cohen, an advocate for the use of LSD, praised Murray's apparent understanding of the value of LSD, but he disagreed on its value for Clare. "It is just two weeks since Clare had LSD," Cohen wrote:

"It was almost to be expected that this experience would be similar to, and yet different from the others when Gerald was present. In addition to the exterior beauty and order, there appeared to be some degree of encounter, which you described so well in your letter. That which was encountered, was, I am sure, not novel; the difference was in the eye of the beholder. The encounter was by no means complete, but it was sufficient unto the day. Certainly, it would be naïve to expect that the corrective experience that may come forth through LSD will, of itself, be sufficient to alter the rutted pathways of thought and response of a lifetime...."[27]

Writing to Clare the following day, Cohen discussed the morality of taking LSD and bemoaned the fact "LSD isn't and it looks like it won't become a legal escape. It's a bit of a shame that this most serious of drugs has been scrubbed by the escapists who want to escape." He traced his own involvement with LSD back to "Ross Adey, a neurophysiologist at UCLA who gave large doses of LSD to cats and noted ` unusual behavior' that persisted for weeks."[28]

Ross Adey, or Dr. William Ross Adey, was an Australian who arrived at UCLA in 1957 to study "membrane biophysics" and "complex behavior in man." This included work at the Jerry Pettis VA Hospital and at UCLA especially into "Cell membrane organization and intercellular communication" and "Electromagnetic field interactions with biological tissues."[29] After studying how to use electronics and biochemical means to control behavior, Adey became associated with the CIA as a researcher for advancing the use of ELF as means to control people through their thoughts.[30] The CIA was also involved in using LSD as a form of control.[31]

Cohen praised Murray to Clare, and said he "found uncanny...its [Murray's letter] understanding of the LSD process, and what it can and cannot do. He has a wisdom, that man. I hope that one day we shall all be able to meet and describe the part of the elephant that we subtend in the hope that a whole animal will emerge...."[32]

Because LSD trips are, in the words of one well-known researcher who performed foundational research into the matter, "very visual, not verbal" and because one does not feel like writing when undergoing such a trip,[33] Clare's "babysitters" or as Heard called them, "invigitators"[34] kept journals describing her trips. Most of her trips began after she ingested anywhere from 100 to 175 micrograms of LSD and lasted anywhere from about three to seven hours. Her first acid trip took place on March 11, 1959 in Phoenix, Arizona with Heard and his secretary, Michael Barrie, present.[35] The next was on April 4, 1959, again with Barrie and Heard present, this time at the Fairmont Motel, in Nob Hill, San Francisco, California, when the US Senate was considering her for an Ambassadorship to Brazil.[36] On May 16, 1959 she had another trip with Heard and Barrie present.[37] Then on December 8, 1959 in Phoenix with Heard and Barrie she again dropped acid.[38] An undated entry in Harry's handwriting indicated that he took 100 micrograms of LSD in his study at their Phoenix home at 11:45 a.m. and kept notes until 3:40 p.m., when he apparently dozed off.[39] An entry dated April 16, 1960 described how Clare ingested 100 micrograms at 11:45 a.m. at their home in Phoenix. She received an additional 25 micrograms at 2:57 p.m. and then apparently mused about how different Harry and Murray would be "if they had only the aesthetic experience."[40] On August 8, 1960 Clare tripped at Ridgefield, Connecticut again with Heard and Barrie.[41] An undated diary entry mentioned her taking 75 micrograms of LSD at 11:30 a.m. at the Waldorf before getting into the car to be driven to dinner in Ridgefield.[42]

After taking Communion at Mass on the Feast of the Holy Family, Sunday, January 8, 1961, Clare took 100 micrograms of LSD at their house in Phoenix. During the three and a half hours the trip lasted, Clare said things like "picks up suwara growth cactus – monstrous baby. That's the way Harry will look me too one eye burned out" and "death decay damnation scar tissue. But when it's also very beautiful (sees beauty in death) death reveals all the layers – more than life. Then her fingers tingle and she asks to touch – we do and the current passes through."[43] On Valentine's Day in Phoenix, Clare took 175 micrograms again with Heard and Barrie at 11:20 a.m. When Harry came home at 1:20 p.m. Heard, Barrie and Harry went to lunch leaving Clare alone until 2:00 p.m. The final entry was 3:45 p.m.[44]

Aside from the March, 1960 acid trip they took together, Murray shared another trip with Clare in June, 1962 after ingesting 190 micrograms of LSD, nearly twice the dosage of Clare's first trip three years earlier. Over the course of four hours, ending at 3:30 p.m., Murray recorded all of Clare's statements. At 11:50 she said, "one regrets not having loved enough; cannot love when mind is full of inhibitions and compulsions." At 12:15 she said, "poor John (repeated); call John Father & vice-versa." At 1:15 p.m., "not to be loved is to be dead" and "how lucky I am – found someone to love me" and "love is a pretty gutsy thing" which is "so simple" and "in guts – or not at all." Then at 1:40 she opined that she was "no giant brain she – like Murray for want of better comparison" and "I try to like you; I'm happy" and "all those years; stupid; my fault". At 2:50 p.m., she said: "get back to find out who you are; potentialities; want to love and be loved; no substitute…everything else is silly." Then, "when I'm not with you, darling, enough fall over to make beautiful thump – and lay at your feet" and "to you I leave reason". Then she spoke of the house. "Am I bored in this house?..I'm bored… Demanding to know who loves me around here… I know I'm old, dying…. All years of pain this house vindicated by looking at this…." Then the final entry at 3:00 p.m., "should have known long ago, none of us loved each other around here."[45]

As his incongruous relationship with Clare indicated, Heard exercised enormous influence over America's cultural elite. He inspired Price and Murphy to start Esalen in the early 1960s by telling them that a "huge transformation of the human species" was about to take place and that Esalen was needed to help make that happen.[46] Humanity was at a turning point needed a new vision for mankind, a "psychological revolution"[47] if it were to continue in existence. Esalen's belief system echoed the spirit of Jesuit Teilhard de Chardin which was that mankind was on an "onward and upward path."[48] De Chardin had read many of Heard's works during the 1940s,[49] which explains the similarities between Heard's beliefs and de Chardin's, for at "the core of Teilhard's doctrine…he held that, through men, the cosmos was struggling towards a further stage of complexity and consciousness."[50] What Esalen offered, in addition to a stay at a beautiful resort in California's Big Sur, was permission to indulge in self-absorption. Described as a process of gaining "self-awareness, self-discovery, self-actualization, self-expression" all of which are the "lifeblood of personal growth, qualities essential to the make up of the healthy individual – and also clearly the stuff of which narcissists are made."[51]

Heard is credited with guiding the well-connected lawyer, businessman, and Libertarian James C. Ingebretsen after the latter's spiritual awakening in 1955.[52] Ingebretsen explained that he had been baptized into the Congregationalist Church, and that he joined the leadership of Spiritual Mobilization, an organization he described was "devoted to the future role of the Protestant Church in America,"[53] to mobilize Protestants for a Libertarian viewpoint.[54] His mission was to fight "the forces which wanted to abolish the free enterprise system...not promoting Christ" and after meeting Heard he worked to "extract the elements which are common to most religious traditions" to create a new way.[55] One of Ingebretsen's disciples was business management guru Peter Drucker.[56] Drucker's work, like Ingebretsen's, was conflated business and moral interests and ideas that "unified humanity rather than fragment[ing] it, starting with large assumptions about the nature and meaning of life."[57] It was perfect for knocking down barriers to the capitalist spirit. As Fanfani explained, an essential first step in this regard is to focus on the material world, the earthly world, and the best way to do that was to focus on oneself.

Heard devised plans for a "New Man" that would join the brightest minds in "growing-edge sciences" to explore how there could be developed a "greater religious understanding of life for everyone" because, as Ingebretsen quoted Heard, `Our crisis today is at base due to the fact that we have made our knowledge of the outer world experimental, tested, scientific, while we are leaving our knowledge of the inner world traditional, vague, confused....."[58] To bring this about, Heard wrote *AE: The Open Persuader.*[59] Billed as "A Science Fiction," the book contained homo-erotic images, an attack on the Holy Eucharist, which was called a "horror,"[60] and a derogation of Catholics and Germans because they did not engage in "psychophysical panaesthetic Religion" and denied themselves "psychophysical ecstasy."[61] Heard's homoerotic fantasy fostered "total uprightness,"[62] wherein man was to achieve "a new degree of freedom" that will come about when man will "be made by himself into a completely free creature."[63]

Heard saw homosexuality as a "creative evolutionary force." He persuaded Dr. Evelyn Hooker to do the research that lead to the American Psychological Association's *Diagnostic and Statistical*

Manual of Psychiatric Disorders (DSM-II) to expunge homosexual behavior as a pathological sexual deviation.[64]

Heard's most influential work, *The Five Ages of Man*, advanced what he called a "psycho-spiritual thesis" that held the "key to history's meaning is the evolution of consciousness, which is tending toward a utopian transformation of the human mind-body: `In brief, the really possible Utopia would be this world experienced by a psychophysique at full aperture.'"[65] Funding for *The Five Ages of Man*, which was released in 1963, came from the Bollingen Trust,[66] a foundation established for "educational purposes" in 1945 by Paul Mellon, heir to the great Mellon fortune that had been created by the efforts of Thomas and Andrew Mellon. Mankind, like the individual human being, passes through five ages or life-cycle stages, and Heard proposed five therapies to assist with each of these transitions.

Heard's view man could mutate as a result of his own efforts was tailor made to serve the newly awakening post-war economic libertarianism and political conservatism noted his biographer:

"Heard's career reflects the intersection of spiritualized psychology, religion, and conservatism in postwar America. He became a religious counselor to several libertarian businessmen as well as to Clare Boothe Luce, the writer, diplomat, and Republican Congresswoman. Although he advocated self-transcendence, he ultimately entrenched individual selfhood with its spiritual prescriptions of yoga, meditation, and LSD. Although he subverted the individual in his theology, he affirmed individualism by putting his spiritual system at the service of libertarianism. As a postwar Californian prophet, Heard helped shape the cultural and intellectual climate of conservatism and spiritualized psychology."[67]

Heard dispelled any doubt about who was going to hold the power in Heard's Brave New World in a lecture he gave in Idylwild, California on August 16, 1956. There he said clearly, "We must look to the businessman for contemporary leadership." Heard went on to say that the "operation of business can be considered in relation to the laws of nature" and "business is an organism streamlined for natural selection." According to Heard, business was the instrument which would bring about the evolution of the human race because "business is an evolving social pattern. Business must every day prove the reason for its existence….. Business must always shear and cut these non-useful growths." Heard endorsed economic Libertarianism. The business environment must be "Laissez faire – must be free, let the thing do; means exercise, the leaving of room. When your faculties cannot be exercised then comes hypertrophy and death. Must always choose ease of enterprise, thus preventing disease."[68]

At a lecture entitled "Ethics in Business," which he delivered at Harvard, Heard claimed that morality was unnecessarily complicating the life of the businessman. "Morality thereafter [from the time of Amos] seems to have spent its time, in the name of Heaven thinking up ways of making the business man's business harder than the practical conditions of Earth had anyhow already made it."[69] The "great universal religions" were to blame for making the "lot of the money makers increasingly difficult." Heard singled out Buddhism, with the monks who begged to live, and Catholicism, with the writings of St. Thomas Aquinas who "set the seal of condemnation on any kind of interest-bearing loan" as especially harmful to business. After all, "Had not Aristotle (whom Aquinas was persuading the Church to accept as the Philosopher)… ruled that any interest on a loan was unnatural and so a sin, the sin of usury, because money was barren: it did not and could not 'breed' and so produce saleable offspring."[70] Protestantism came to the rescue when Henry VIII decreed that "interest was to be permitted but controlled… [and] dissolved the monasteries (and so put much specie and real estate into circulation), favored merchants and established legal interest rates." God blessed those who made profits due to industry and skill such that Dr. Johnson could exclaim "Sir, a man is seldom so innocently employed as when he is making money!"[71]

Heard explained the psycho-social dynamics causing guilt feelings in the businessman, and he proposed a solution. He said "money gain is a valid criterion of success" and the "great professional class whose morality is neither Law nor Love but Equity, finds itself with its ultimate aim not to be gainfully but <u>giftfully</u> employed."

Heard proclaimed "we can . . . have a business morality which is contemporary, realistic. This morality is a valid morality for the businessman because it is the conduct deducible from the actual pivotal condition of the man who is, par excellence, the middleman. For he is neither the saint whose frame of reference is Eternity and so whose behavior deduced from the Everlasting can (and it alone can) be Love. But neither is he that `average sensual man' whose appetites are his prime movers and their satisfaction his aims.... But he does work for and dedicates himself to the future. These simple principles, this recognition of this central morality can restore accurate thinking in basic values in the business mind, give back to the businessman, with the enhanced status of full rationality, the figure of himself as one of the great modern patterns of social prestige and, not least, by giving him an inner and complete consistency, grant him a new measure of psychosomatic health, a way of life that is `healthy, wealthy and wise.'"[72]

In other words, the businessman creates his own morality with Heard providing the psychological, spiritual, and philosophical justification for the lifting of all restrictions on economic activity. The only moral restrictions come from by the businessman himself, whose ultimate and only goal is profitability. Hence, the more profitable one is, the more moral one is. Heard, in other words, repackaged what Weber called the Protestant Ethic in the language of the New Age Movement, and so it should come as no surprise that Heard was the rage during the 1950s and 1960s. The interest of the public in matters spiritual was burgeoning, and Heard was undoubtedly a powerful speaker.[73] Since Heard scholar John V. Cody was of the opinion that all of Heard's writings were in the natural law tradition,[74] it was hardly surprising that Heard and Murray traveled in the same circles, took LSD together and were promoted by Luce venues in spreads like the one featuring the iconic "brains of southern California" photo, which appeared in the December 26, 1959 edition of *Life* magazine. The *Life* photographer just happened to drop in for lunch at Aldous Huxley's house, where he found Linus Pauling, along with other crafters of the smog that came to be used to define the "modern man". These were Heard, Julian Huxley, Aldous Huxley, Christopher Isherwood, Buckminster Fuller, and Richard Neutra, now considered one of the most important architects of modernism.[75] Luce provided a platform for Heard's spiritualism and its support for economic and political libertarianism that would reach millions of readers.

CHAPTER 67
A GREAT DECISION

In one letter from March, 1960 postmarked Phoenix, and about the time Clare introduced Murray to his first LSD trip with Heard and Michael Barrie, Clare revealed that she would never consent to a divorce. The "worst kind of a marriage seemed preferable to that." She proposed a "concordat – suggestions of a specific nature from him (I would give mine, too)…." Harry read the note in his own room and then came to her room with a bottle of whiskey and spoke to her until 6:30 a.m. Clare wrote that "it was the most extraordinary performance I have ever witnessed, the most alarming of all his extraordinary performances." Harry's general attitude during the talk was "'Well, I knew that is what you would finally do – but why didn't you say so in September? I knew I could never get a deal out of you; that's why I knew all your talk and John Murray's about `freedom' was rubbish." [1]

Despite that, Harry seemed "relieved…cheerful. Several times he announced he loved me, and never wanted to leave me…because he knew my problems better than anyone; he swore he was not going to be grim and unhappy about it; we would make the best of it." Clare would ask Harry to get on his knees with her and pray to God for the strength to deal with it all, and they did. Harry kissed her, went to his room, and returned in about five minutes to ask if Clare knew about Mary Bancroft, which she did not."[2]

Mary Bancroft, whose family once owned Dow Jones & Company, spied for the OSS during World War II and in that capacity became the lover of Allen Dulles, who assigned her to work with Hans Gisevius on the plot to murder Hitler. After the war, she became a novelist and eventually one of Luce's lovers. Luce was one of Bancroft's 43 lovers. We have no idea where he ranked other than that her favorite was Allen Dulles. During the course of their affair, Bancroft told Harry that "his salvation lay in divorcing me [Clare]: I was ruining him." He said about Bancroft "'She's a Catholic, if she's anything. Homely. The map of Ireland is all over her face.'" His relationship with Bancroft proved that sex was not important to him though he believed that "'affairs left me disgusted with myself'. Only love was good enough." Harry said "what had ruined our marriage was that I [Clare] thought sex, not love, important. Jeannie understood this fact that sex wasn't so important.'" Harry went on describing his miserable youth and how much he was a genius. And, when Clare asked why he did not take the divorce that she offered when becoming a Catholic he said 'a penitential marriage at that time spoke to my psychological condition. I was sick of all the women I had slept with until then. But I think I have done my penance. Only three since that time. And the last was Jeannie....The way I saw it...when you consider the women I could have had, I think you must admit I have been a very moral man, even by Catholic standards.'"[3]

Then Harry mentioned Murray. "'I love Father Murray. I love John. He is a fool, because he does not understand human nature. You will admit, he doesn't understand you at all, or he wouldn't have gone thru all that theological hocus pocus about 'freedom' in September. And he wouldn't have made a pitch to convert me, on the grounds of truth. But I love him. Yes I love him.'"[4]

Clare then told Murray about a book by Tim Matthews that claimed "the most over-powering impression Harry left on those he worked with was that he was a man with a <u>very</u> guilty conscience about God.

A hypocrite who knew he was a hypocrite…." Clare explained that Harry, in spite of the Presbyterianism he invariably fell back on, did not know right from wrong. Harry, she wrote:

"will never (as T. Matthews says) give up the faith of his Fathers. But -- he needs someone to tell him about `right' and `wrong.' . . . He's as fuzzy about right and wrong in his personal relations with Jeanne and me, as he is about `God's truth'…. If he is incapable, and I fear he is, of Christian charity – of filia and agape, then at least let him be a Christian stoic: bad tempered, irritable, self-regarding, but not a silly, dirty little boy, sniveling because he can't emerge in the eyes of the world as a Great Lover, as well as a Giant of Journalism."[5]

Clare never agreed to a divorce. In April, 1960 with Harry in Europe to meet again with Jeanne, Clare said she would fight any move by Harry for a divorce because she "could not agree it was a good thing for either him or myself." Harry returned in May, when they discussed the situation further, rehashing a lot of history. After Harry told Jeanne that Clare did not want a divorce, Jeanne responded by saying that she still wanted to go on seeing Harry in New York when it was convenient for the two of them. Harry said that between May and September, 1959 he decided that he wanted to marry Jeanne, and in June he was contemplating asking Clare for a divorce, but did not. At around this time, Harry told his son he was going to divorce Clare and proceeded to sell the New York apartment at 450 without telling Clare. After pocketing the money from the sale, Harry asked Clare to set forth what she would like if anything happened to him, which could have served as the basis for a divorce settlement, though such had not been discussed by the Summer of 1959. As tension built in late Summer after Harry's return from Paris, he asked Clare for a divorce. As he told Murray, Harry's sister, and Harry's brother-in-law, it was Clare's outburst that prompted his request. The outburst, in Harry's mind, "convinced me that you were finished with me and would welcome a divorce." Harry did not tell Clare at the time, nor did he tell Murray who had been called in as a "reliable witness," that he was seeing Jeanne. Harry viewed the two problems as separate.[6]

Word of Harry's intentions to marry Jeanne eventually got out when Igor Cassini telephoned their Ridgefield, Connecticut home, which Harry had put up for sale without telling Clare, asking about the details of the sale. It was during this phone call that Clare discovered the name of her husband's lover, something she found doubly upsetting because of Jeanne's bad reputation as someone "over thirty, who had not married, who drank heavily, and had a reputation for sleeping about, even with your own employees, including your religion editor, Douglas Auchincloss...." Jeanne, Clare wrote, "would not make you very happy in the end, and ...I intended to fight to keep you from marrying her, as hard as I could." Harry said though that he married the loves of his life and Jeanne was the third one. Harry also told Murray that Clare was a "pitiful woman" and so he rethought divorcing her for Jeanne. From September to April, the situation was in a state of constant flux. Clare said that she would grant a divorce if Harry thought that was best for him and he initiated it, but if that were the case she would fight for her interests in the settlement. Harry, for his part, was telling Jeanne that he loved her and was trying to bring Clare around. Then, Harry suggested a legal separation for Clare's health.[7]

Eventually, Harry concluded that he did not want a divorce because of various considerations which included the thought that Clare still loved him, their 25 year history, the public image impact (business associations did not think it was a good idea), and Harry's feeling about the Presbyterian Church. He had been seeing Jeanne since 1957 and it was only after Clare's nomination to the Brazil mission collapsed in May 1959 that Jeanne suggested that Harry marry her. Harry's sister and brother-in-law tried to persuade Clare to grant a divorce to Harry, but she refused. Their talks, combined with the drinking, the smoking that invariably accompanied them, all took a toll on the health of both of them. Harry wanted Clare to be happy with his decision, which she was not. By early April, 1960, Clare refused a divorce, either then or ever, and Harry, upset over what he called a "unilateral decision" proposed a "concordat" or written agreement about what each might expected of the other. Harry, who accepted the decision as final, expected that Clare to allow him to continue seeing Jeanne.[8]

During the late Spring and early Summer of 1960, it was Murray's job to keep the Luces together. In his capacity as a "qualified witness" to the discussions between Clare and Harry, it was Murray's job to get Harry out of trouble with Clare: "Now it is his habit, whenever he gets 'in trouble' with me, to appeal to Father Murray, and his 'religious insights' and 'intellectual categories' for help in managing the situation...."[9] Clare kept handwritten notes of a lengthy exchange in mid-June 1960 at the Ridgefield Connecticut house between the three of them concerning the marriage.[10] During the course of this difficult weekend, Murray confirmed that Harry had on two occasions proposed a separation to "end Clare's and my emotional involvement" and to allow Harry to "see the Jeanne problem clearly." Clare refused such an arrangement, claiming that the issue of their marriage had to be resolved first. Harry told Clare that he loved Jeanne, though he had doubts that a marriage with Jeanne was a good thing. Murray tried to dissuade Harry from a "final confrontation" with Jeanne for some reason. Clare also thought that such a marriage would be a bad thing and would harm Harry."[11] According to Harry, Clare would not divorce him if he ran away with Jeanne ("no divorce, now or ever"). This, according to Harry was a unilateral decision by Clare, but he wanted a "mutual decision" – either to stay married or to get a divorce. There was a "concordat" between Harry and Clare by which he had the freedom to have an affair with Jeanne but could not marry her. Harry said that he believed Clare saw herself as housekeeper and "legal wife," or second best.[12]

Eventually, Harry decided that "divorce is wrong for both of us," and that he no longer wanted to continue his affair with Jeanne. Harry agreed to write a letter to Clare explaining the reasons he would "go on with the marriage," what he expected from her as his wife, a "job description" if you will, and assurances she would not encounter the same situation months down the line. He had not written the letter as of the meeting with Murray, but he did say that he would not divorce her because, after 25 years together, it was morally wrong (or, quoting the "prayer book," that it was not "right or proper"). As prudential or secondary reasons, Luce listed the fact his family was opposed, business associates were opposed, the Church was against it, and Harry's age during the latest trip proved he did not have the same level of vitality given his heart condition. Harry concluded saying Clare knew he loved her as much as he can love anyone.[13]

After weeks of acrimonious dialogue, Murray concluded a separation was inhuman, dangerous, and selfish on Harry's part. The only way to end the seemingly endless dialogue was "a 'concordat,'" which put in writing what Harry expected and wanted while serving as a practical agreement to reduce the conflicts of life. It was to be a statement of Harry's wishes as to "times and places for being together and apart," the "rules for communication" which would occur when Harry was "accessible" and did not want to be disturbed, and setting out the times for "discussion of concrete problems, for advice, etc." along with the "forbidden times" for such. Finally, it was to contain an understanding of just what Harry expected of Clare.[14]

Clare's motivation for all of this, Murray wrote Harry, was four-fold: need, friendship, a desire to do good by Harry, and a history. Murray described the first three elements as a type of love using the Latin words eros, philia, and agape. There was a desire also by Clare to end all of the "dialogue" and to look forward and not backwards. The basis of any conflict or quarrelling between the two, Murray concluded, was that there was a quarrel or conflict within each of them. Murray concluded that each Clare and Harry bring something good to each other. Harry brought to Clare "things that are not of the order of the material or of the merely convenient", and as to Clare, Murray wrote that "it might be possible for her to say, with Othello, 'I have done the state some service....'" Harry had to consider whether another relationship would be good for him, and whether losing Clare might just not be bad for him.[15]

The result of the interminable back and forth was "The Great Decision" of June 19, 1960, according to which Harry agreed to transfer certain property to Clare and stay married to her. The property included "$200,000 (its equivalent in securities)" for a New York residence; joint ownership of the Luces' home in Phoenix; joint ownership of the Luces' home in Ridgefield, Connecticut; and transfer of legal ownership of certain paintings.[16]

Nearly eighteen months later, Clare, indignant that Harry had not lived up to his promises made in "The Great Decision," asked Murray to "establish that you were a witness to the fact that these promises were made by me to Harry, apparently in good faith." She told Murray she "did not have the faintest idea what sort of provision Harry has made about anyone, much less myself, in the event of his death…. despite all Harry's promises at the time of 'the Great Decision,' I am less able to take care of myself, if he should die – or of my friends, if I should die – than I was before it all happened."[17]

Murray quickly responded to Clare's urgent request by writing it was a "distressful occasion at Ridgefield over the weekend of June 18, 1960, when I performed my final task as 'qualified witness'… was far too painful for me to have forgotten the details." He agreed to confirm what Harry promised, but "I ask you to promise that you will not use this document directly against Harry during his lifetime. It so happens that he is my friend, and I haven't many. I was your advocate during the whole miserable business; and I was, and am willing to be such—but not against him. Love you, John."[18]

PART XVI
UNCONDITIONAL SURRENDER (1960)

CHAPTER 68
CAN A CATHOLIC BE PRESIDENT?

The December 21, 1959 edition of *Life* contained an article entitled "Should a Catholic be President?" by the California Episcopal bishop, James A Pike, who was listed as the chairman of the "clergyman's national advisory committee of the Planned Parenthood Federation of America." The editors printed the article because "In recent months, largely because of Senator Kennedy of Massachusetts, the possibility of a Roman Catholic running for President has caused much discussion." *Life* "invited Roman Catholic authorities to offer their views."[1]

Pike was uniquely qualified to talk about Catholicism and public life. Raised Catholic, he rejected Catholicism in college, became an agnostic, met and married his first wife and later had the Episcopal Church annul that marriage. Pike then became a lawyer, joined the Securities and Exchange Commission at its headquarters in Washington, DC, and then served in Naval Intelligence during World War II, where he met and married his second wife, Esther Yanofsky. He started going to Episcopalian services, which led him to undertake studies to become a deacon, then a minister, which led to his ordination at New York's Union Theological Seminary in 1946.[2]

From there he went to Columbia where he assumed leadership of the religion department and served as university chaplain. Within three years, he took a department with no courses and built up a "full complement of 32 courses" that sported the likes of popular Protestant theologians such as Paul Tillich. At the Cathedral of St. John the Divine he became involved in desegregation and the civil rights movement. In 1958, he was consecrated the Bishop of California and moved to San Francisco, where he raised funds to finish the Grace Cathedral. With Presbyterian Eugene Carson Blake he proposed the "Protestant unification plan that has since become the nine-church Consultation on Church Union."[3]

Pike found even the attenuated dogma of Episcopalianism too constraining, and by 1964 was referring to the concept of the Trinity as so much "excess baggage." After he announced that there should be "more belief, fewer beliefs" and that the credo should be reduced to "the importance of imitating Christ...as `the man for others,'" Pike was accused of heresy. He won that battle by avoiding a trial as a consequence of John Courtney Murray's consultation during the run-up to the trial. With his acquittal, the entire idea of heresy disappeared from the Episcopal Church. [4]

In 1966, Pike resigned as Bishop of California, and then started another career as a fellow with the Center for the Study of Democratic Institutions in California, a think tank that served the American economic and cultural elites. After his son committed suicide in the same year, Pike became interested in parapsychology, psychic research, and spiritualism, eventually authoring a book entitled *The Other Side* with the help of his 28 year-old secretary, Diane Kennedy, whom he married after divorcing his second wife. Together, they founded the Foundation for Religious Transitions for those, who, like themselves, had left "organized religion." Earlier, Pike called the Episcopalian Church a "dying institution." Searching for the "historical Jesus," Pike suffered a bizarre death walking in the desert east of Jerusalem on the way to Qumran during a desert sojourn in 1969 with his third wife.[5] After Pike's death, Diane went on to head up the Teleos Institute supporting those "choosing the individualizing process" of their "awakening."[6]

But all of this was years in the future. In 1959, Pike, as leader of institutional Protestantism, was intent on subjugating the Catholics. Pike's article began with a question: "A Roman Catholic for President?" which he answered by writing: "It depends on *which* Roman Catholic.... The question of where a President's first allegiance will lie is far too important to be evaded. So is the question of where a President stands on the relationship between Church and State." The controversy over birth control brought this issue to the fore. Pike noted that on November 25, 1959, 200 Catholic bishops joined in Washington DC to denounce the paying for birth control in foreign countries with public funds. JFK and Edmund Brown, both Catholics, were asked if the bishops' policy would be binding on them, and they replied "not necessarily." While paying lip-service to the proposition that a "man's religion [is] his private business," Pike stated nonetheless, that "the matter of Roman Catholic allegiance belongs among the real questions."[7]

Like Paul Blanshard, Pike claimed that the defining issue was where a Catholic stood on the matter of Church and State relations. Pike wrote there is an official Catholic Church position that is at variance with the "ideals of most Americans" but that this position is seldom asserted by Roman Catholics in the United States. He examined two major theories of Church State relations both of which the reader could surmise as evil or anti-American. The first was the State over the Church which was the situation in Nazi Germany, and now in the Soviet Union which was also using the Orthodox Church for its purposes. The second theory was the Church over the State, and there the Catholic Church still maintained authority over civil rulers as evidenced by the recent elections in Sicily. The "Sicilians were ordered by ecclesiastical authority not to support a particular party. The party may not have been a good one... but that is not the point. The question is: Is the modern Roman Catholic restricted in making political decisions?" Pike's answer was "yes" in Italy and Spain and any other country where the Catholic

Church had preferential status. In the US, that was not the case, but "then we must ask ourselves: Is this church content to find itself in a non-preferential status in *any* country?" Pike concluded his article by claiming that both theories of Church and State must be opposed, and Luther's approach had to be followed. This was that the individual with his conscience and God stood against all earthly institutions including the state and the church because, quoting from Paul Tillich, these institutions are *"under judgment."*[8]

Pike admitted that the Bill of Rights essentially protects the Protestant view of Church-State relations or the "priority of conscience over institutions." According to Pike, there were two Catholic viewpoints so it was important that voters knew which view was held by a Catholic candidate. The one was the "official view" and the other was the "American Interpretation." The former was the creation of Pius IX and most prominently and recently is held by Cardinal Ottaviani and Fr. Connell, who espoused the view that the state "has the right of repression" whenever error may harm the spiritual interests of Catholics. The other view was held by John Courtney Murray, the "distinguished American Jesuit theologian," who "insisted that the traditional American position on the separation of Church and State can be supported within Roman Catholic dogma." Pius IX's position was meant to apply only to European liberalism and not the situation that presented itself in America.[9]

According to Pike, Murray framed the issue in the following way: "Is the Church in America to be allowed to travel her own historical pattern and forward her own particular solutions to the Church-State problems, remaining faithful to essential Catholic principles and to the specific character of the political traditions within which her institutional life has been lived? Or, on the other hand, is the Church in America to repudiate the history of America and what is most unique about it – its installation of a political tradition sharply in contrast to that of modern continental Europe?"[10]

Pike supported his claim on a 1948 declaration by the US Catholic bishops in support of Murray's position. They affirmed as good "our original American tradition of free cooperation between government and religious bodies – cooperation involving no special privilege to any group and no restriction on the religious liberty of any citizen."[11]

When Senator Eugene McCarthy, a Catholic, was asked his opinion on all of this, he opined that while that some Catholics probably hold to the traditional view, most probably hold to the American view. If Catholics would become a majority, he continued, the Constitution could still serve as a defense for minority religions. The fact that the Vatican had issued no excommunications allowed Pike to "answer our initial question more precisely: a Roman Catholic for President? If he holds the 'official' view (in the manner of Pius IX, Pius XII, Father Connell, *Civilta Catolica* and Cardinal Ottaviani), *No* – unless the other candidate is very unsuitable indeed. This 'No' would hold for any voter who believes in the freedom of dissent, i.e., that what some groups may deem 'error' *does* have a right to 'existence, propagation or action.'" And, "if the Roman Catholic candidate holds to the American interpretation (as stated by father Murray, and the American bishops), the answer would be *Yes*. This would of course assume that he is otherwise the best candidate." In sum the question has to be asked of candidates, because religion does matter wrote Pike. He asked, "is Father Murray right? Or is Pope Pius XII right?"[12]

There were five issues that tested a Catholic's allegiance to America. These were: "official United States representation at the Vatican, federal subsidies to parochial schools, censorship freedom in the distribution of contraceptive information (now focused on the question of our willingness to aid other nations wanting it), and certain matters of foreign policy involving the Roman Catholic Church." JFK took the American position on aid to parochial schools and an ambassador to the Vatican, so he appeared acceptable. Distrust of Catholics flared when a report found the US military in Spain required US servicemen to comply with Catholic teaching when they married by agreeing to raise their children Catholic if parents were of different religions.[13]

Connell wrote Pike a letter shortly after the magazine came out asking the source of the quote "The State has the right of repression 'when error is doing harm to the spiritual interests of Catholic citizens.'"[14] Pike replied that he quoted Connell from the June 19, 1949 edition of the *Catholic Register – National Edition* and that the quote was taken from an article by Paul Hallatt called "Keeping Up With Events.[15] Connell then contacted Hallatt who provided the entire quote, and Connell stated Pike misrepresented Connell's position. Connell told Hallatt that he wrote a letter to *Life* approving of the Bishops' statement.[16]

Connell wanted to clear up a misconception which the Pike article presented – namely, that it appeared that he opposed the bishops – by stating "The Catholic citizens of the United States have always approved the policy of religious freedom as established by the first amendment to the Constitution for our country." Connell denied that Catholics were "obliged by their principles to give special favor to the Catholic Church and to impose restrictions on the religious activities of their Non-Catholic fellow citizens" should Catholics come to power. [17] Quoting a previous piece refuting Pike's charge that Catholics in the majority would overturn the First Amendment, Connell continued:

"This charge is utterly erroneous. Catholics have no obligation to seek special privileges for their Church in a land where the bad results of such a procedure would surpass the good effects; and certainly if there is any land where that would be the case, it is the United Sates, even if a very great proposition of our people eventually became Catholics. Such a radical change of a policy that has worked out successfully since the birth of our nation would inevitably cause grave harm to the unity of our people….In view of all these considerations, Catholics in the United States can assert without any hesitation or mental restriction that, as far as they are concerned the policy of complete religious freedom and of full governmental impartiality toward all religious groups will continue, whatever the future may bring in the way of an increase of the Catholic population in our land."[18]

"Thank you for your recent letter," the Editors of *Life* tersely responded. "In order to share your comments with our readers we have decided to publish a part of your letter in the Letters Column of the issue which will appear on the newsstands this Thursday. We are mailing to you a copy with our compliments."[19]

Connell continued to keep Rome informed of the happenings in the US concerning the issues Pike presented. His chief contact was Cardinal Ottaviani, recently elevated to Secretary of the Sacred Congregation of the Holy Office by Pope John XXIII on October 21, 1959. The appointment, according to *The New York Times*, came when Cardinal Pizzardo, who was 82 years of age, asked to be released from his duties.[20]

Earlier that year, Ottaviani traveled to the United States, where on June 7 he gave the commencement address at the Catholic University of America and received an honorary doctorate of laws. Ottaviani stressed that "Faith and learning have their common chair: the chair of truth, the harmony and the dignity of Christian knowledge." He exhorted the university and the bishops who were its trustees to persevere in defending truth even when "some seem to think that Christian truth may be rendered more palatable to others if it is seasonal with a little error."[21]

Echoing Leo XIII, Ottaviani called Catholics to their primary loyalty when he said:

I come from Rome and I cannot pass over in silence the help and support which you so generously give to the See of Peter. Love for Rome is not a mere ornament or parade of high-sounding words. If the great Newman (Cardinal John Henry Newman), in the maturity of his years, did not hesitate to receive from Rome, not only his priesthood, but also her pious practices and devotions, this must surely mean that, loving Rome, one must not lag behind in the ways of goodness and truth. Newman, as you know, was a man who loved to remember Rome, as one remembers one's mother and the bright years of youth. You must forgive me for speaking so much about Rome, but I feel that we are all Romans in our Faith and devotion, like Patrick of Ireland and Boniface of Germany and Augustine of Canterbury; Romans like your great cardinals and bishops; Romans like your first saint, Mother Cabrini. When in Rome, one is loath to leave, and away from her, one wishes to return, to the Rome of Peter and Paul, and of so many saints and all the popes. It alone, among the cities of the world, has received, like Jerusalem in the Old Testament, the name and dignity of Holy City."[22]

Ottaviani reported to Pope John upon his return to Rome later in June, and on the 25th of that month he gave a statement to the NCWC News Service. In it, Ottaviani admired the "great growth which in the last 70 years has brought the Church in the US to the forefront of the most flourishing Catholic groups" as the Church in the US passed from a missionary system to one that gives "powerful help" to missions of the Holy See. The bishoprics in the US Catholic church were well organized and growing, and they had direction over Catholic activities at the pastoral, educational and financial levels." The universities were also growing and developing, and with the increasing number of students, it showed the "trust the people place in the universities."[23]

Despite the gloom and doom which Ellis had exhibited just four years earlier, Ottaviani "saw the perfect crowning of the forces which the Church has in the field of education, beginning in the elementary and high schools and then carried out in the colleges and finally in the universities. I believe I am able to affirm that in this field the Catholics of the U.S have no rivals who are able to equal them."[24]

After his return to Rome, which he characterized as the "center of Catholicism," Ottaviani assured "the august Pontiff" that "notwithstanding the dangers which Catholicism meets even in America, (as in every nation) of temptations of indifferentism, one can be certain of America's constant love for Christ, Church and Pope."[25]

Connell wrote Ottaviani of the American efforts to divide Catholics and corrupt doctrine:

"I am enclosing an article from the magazine LIFE, by a Protestant bishop (formerly a Catholic layman) [Pike] centered around the Church-State controversy. You will note that the writer says that the Vatican is aware of the view proposed by Father Murray but has not condemned it, and that it is held by the majority of Catholics in this land. I do not believe that this last is true, but I am sure that the `American view' will continue to spread unless an official statement is made. As I wrote to Your Eminence on December 15, 1955: `I believe that until the Holy See issues a public statement on the doctrine of Father Murray, there will be many in our land who will continue to uphold this view, and I fear that it will gradually spread and be accepted by many Americans.' I am not a pessimist, but I fear that today there are many American Catholics who would leave the Catholic Church rather than give up their `American view'."[26]

Senator John F. Kennedy seemed intent on running for president, and so the church state issue became pressing. "I would also like to see a statement on the Catholic's loyalty to the principles of U.S. citizenship in view of all the attacks on us that are coming from Protestant groups," Connell wrote to Bishop Lawrence Shehan of Bridgeport, Connecticut. Connell said such a statement "should not be an apparent attempt to get a Catholic in the White House. For example, it should contain the principle that a Catholic President would consider the law of God, as his Church proclaims it, as the supreme norm of his conduct. Of course, when the statement comes out the elections will be ended. I don't think that John Kennedy has as much chance as I have to be President. And I certainly would not vote for him, in view of his weak statements."[27]

Connell kept Ottaviani informed of how he was being portrayed in the press. In a January 12, 1960 letter, Connell mentioned the quotes attributed to him concerning communist dictators.[28] When Connell heard that Pike, who "was formerly a Catholic layman, and is divorced with a second wife," was writing a book entitled *A Catholic in the White House,* he notified Ottaviani that: "The most unfortunate feature of this is not its direct attack on Catholics, but rather the assertion that there are two views among American

Catholics of the Church-State question. I am supposed to represent the 'official' opinion, and Fr. Murray is cited as representing the 'American' opinion. The article states that the Holy See is showing a tacit approval of this second opinion by its silence. I fear that many of our Catholic people are being led astray by these statements."[29]

Connell advised Ottaviani that Pike and his publishers wanted to publish some of Connell's statements. Connell balked as "evidently the intention of Bishop Pike is to take statements out of the context."[30] The *America* editor in chief was both downplaying religion in the upcoming election and forecasting the significance of the election. *The New York Times* quoted Fr. Thurston N. Davis as saying that "the religion of a political candidate did not mean as much today as it did ten years or a generation ago." The US, he said, was in a "'post-Protestant era' in which the image of the President was 'no longer that of an Anglo-Saxon with a Masonic background.'" Nonetheless, Davis believed that "the bid by the Senator from Massachusetts for the Presidency is 'filled with immense sociological and cultural meaning'"[31]

CHAPTER 69

LUCE SUPPORTS; VAGNOZZI CONFUSES

As in Luke 11:33, Catholic leadership over the generations devised an elaborate strategy to keep their Catholicism private and the light of the gospel under a bushel whenever it conflicted with the American Proposition. No one was more skilled at this than Joseph Kennedy, the father of the man who was thinking of becoming the first Catholic President of the United States. Clare felt that Joe's son Jack was "worried about the high visibility of the cross on his back" as he entered the 1960 race for president. "Old Joe," as a result, called Clare to ask for her assistance with a vexing problem that occurred whenever Jack showed up at a campaign stop:

"It seems that his appearance at rallies…signals for the emptying of the convents…. The early bird nuns zoomed in, and settled down in the front rows, were clicking their rosaries…and dentures, [so] they could see, really see, this beloved political apostle. Joe said "Will you go see Spellman, and tell him—the little SOB hates me (something about a real estate deal). Ask him if he really wants a Catholic up there. If he does, tell him Jack is coming into New York, and will he keep those goddamn nuns out of the front rows? He's running for the White House, not for crucifixion."[1]

Jack ended up getting crucified, but not in the way that Joe imagined. More surprising than Kennedy's untimely end less than four years later was the fact that Henry Luce supported JFK's run for president. Luce, who had written the introduction to JFK's Harvard senior year thesis, was a staunch Republican, and Clare simply could not understand why Luce would support JFK, a Democrat, for President. Clare was not concerned that the Catholic Church was being targeted by the American elites and had long ago accepted the view that one can be both American and Catholic. Even accepting that premise, Clare wrote "Harry, for reasons which baffle me, has aided Jack from the beginning." JFK was "a friend, and a Catholic, and a damned attractive, able, intelligent fellow." She recognized that Harry was "pleased, excited by Jack's forthcoming nomination (and all he has written and printed to bring it about.)" Harry apparently knew that both JFK and Joe Kennedy were either interested in or had been romantically involved with Harry's current paramour "Lady Jeanne,"[2] but in this instance simple jealousy would have militated against Harry supporting Kennedy. Luce's support was even more puzzling given the fact that Joe Kennedy held Harry in contempt, and Harry knew it. Harry had a long-standing fascination with Catholic politicians that went back to 1928 when he endorsed Al Smith's bid for the presidency.[3]

Ultimately, it was not Clare but Nicolo Macchiavelli who came up with the best explanation of Luce's support for JFK's presidential bid: "When men receive favours from someone they expected to do them ill, they are under a greater obligation to their benefactor." When those benefactors are the wealthy and the noble in society, "it is impossible to satisfy the nobles honourably, without doing violence to the interests of others."[4] With the support of Luce and the American elites, JFK became beholden to them. He was expected to do their bidding, and that included destroying the very people who were most likely to vote for him, namely, the Catholics. The first step in that process was the Presidential Campaign of 1960.

VAGNOZZI CONFUSES

In December, 1958 Archbishop Egidio Vagnozzi became the Apostolic Delegate to the USA, replacing Amleto Cicognani. During World War II, Vagnozzi worked closely with Martin Quigley, Jr., an OSS agent and Hollywood executive.[5] In the middle of March, 1960, Vagnozzi gave an address at a symposium entitled "Leo and the Modern World" which marked the 150th birthday of Leo XIII at Loyola University in Chicago which about 500 clerics and lay people attended. Even with Connell helping him draft the talk, Vagnozzi seemed bent more on not offending the Americans than in giving a clear, unequivocal statement of Catholic doctrine understandable to the observer.

The New York Times covered the event in a small article that ran in its following Sunday edition in a way that emphasized Americanism by quoting Vagnozzi as saying:

"In the practical field of relations with civil powers the Catholic Church shows with reciprocal international agreements called concordats, a considerable variety of positions in particular questions, depending on local traditions, customs and practices. As fare [sic] as the United States is concerned, I feel that it is a true interpretation of the feelings of the hierarchy and of American Catholics in general to say that they are well satisfied with their Constitution, and pleased with the fundamental freedom enjoyed by their church. Whether they remain a minority, or become a majority, I am sure that American Catholics will not jeopardize their cherished religious freedom in exchange for a privileged position."[6]

Vagnozzi drew a fine distinction – the practical value of the First Amendment as opposed the doctrinal necessity of it. Nuanced distinctions quickly got lost in the news accounts of the talk, though. A Boston newspaper reported that the "Apostolic Delegate also contributed a persuasive paragraph on the Constitutional provisions of church-state separation." This was a positive thing, because "we still hear from some sources that it impinges in some manner on Catholic teaching. How refreshing to hear the Delegate of the Holy See quote with clear approval the long-standing American tradition and even go further to insist that Catholics would not exchange the present system, even were they a majority, for any position of special privilege for the Church." In addition, "Archbishop Vagnozzi has pointed out how the papal tradition of Leo was continued in the famous text of Pius XII to the Italian Jurists where the late Pontiff indicated that there is not and never has been ‘an absolute and universal command’ that religious and moral error cannot be tolerated for some good reason."[7]

Connell helped draft Vagnozzi's talk, "Pope Leo XIII and the Problem of Human Liberty." Connell's main contribution was to change the line in which Vagnozzi claimed that Pope Leo XIII "taught, too, that in certain circumstances a Catholic government might lawfully restrict the activities of those who would endeavor to persuade the Catholic citizens to abandon their faith, for this would be a grave spiritual misfortune." Connell believed that this should be re-written so that Leo XIII's teaching could be better presented, and to "avoid any criticism from at least reasonable non-Catholics. For they know that these same measures are used against Catholics in some non-Catholic countries." Connell felt that Vagnozzi's statement should be changed to a more positive formulation, namely: "'He taught... too, that in certain circumstances a Catholic government might lawfully preserve and protect the Catholic religion as a prudential measure for the good of the community.'"[8]

Vagnozzi explained Leo XIII's condemnation of false liberty and the explanation of true liberty contained in his 1888 encyclical *Libertas*. True liberty meant following God's eternal law and recognizing Him. According to Vagnozzi, the American founders recognized this principle, but the atheistic Communists did not. The Americans were enjoying "peace with freedom" as Eisenhower said, but the Communists had neither. However, in the US "true liberty" was under attack by some promoting "salacious writings, obscene shows... [and] loose manners." In sum, they denied the "existence of any divine authority to which obedience is due, and proclaim that every man is the law to himself...." In this context, Vagnozzi explained that the state had a duty to protect the true religion. He said the state could use coercion or force to protect religion. The state could not force people to convert to Catholicism, but it could prevent certain people from undermining the Catholic faith. Vagnozzi made that distinction with Connell's help.[9]

Unfortunately, approval of the American Founders' ideas got mixed in with the Catholic position, causing confusion in the speech's most-quoted part, which, in the draft, bore the handwritten comments of either Connell or Vagnozzi:

"Certainly those who claim that whenever the Catholics of a nation attain the power to grant special privileges to their Church, they will inevitably do so, are disproved by the Independent Irish State, where more than 90% of the citizens are Catholics, yet where every form of religion is equally free and where the Catholics have elected to high office Protestants and Jews. As far as America is concerned, every intelligent person should realize, that, however much the proportion of Catholics may increase with the passing of the years, American Catholics will never be obliged to contradict the Constitutional principle of the civil equality of all religions by which they themselves have profited so much. It would be well for Catholics, if charged with attempts to change the principle of religious equality, to ask their questioners what other particular religious group could give as strong a guarantee that they would not modify the American principle of religious equality if they ever acquired the power to do so."[10]

Vagnozzi ended his speech saying an endorsement of "the American principle of religious equality" was "the teaching on the important subject of human liberty" propounded by Leo XIII in *Lumen de Coele.* This message "was not contingent on the particular time in which he lived. It was the logical conclusion from fundamental truths of reason and faith, applicable to every generation."[11]

Vagnozzi thanked Connell for his "valuable assistance" in delivering the talk that "was very well received, by clergy and laity alike."[12] He had no idea of how the Americans were using the talk to further their ends. Media accounts, for example, invariably focused on the final part of Vagnozzi's speech as it pertained to America and the First Amendment or "freedom of religion" and ignored Vagnozzi's claim that the state must conform its laws to the law of God, making it appear that Vagnozzi endorsed the American view of the separation of church and state.

Shortly after the talk, Connell advised Vagnozzi of a growing split among Catholics in the area of sexual ethics. After reviewing the book, *Counseling the Catholic,* Connell warned of a move afoot to "create a casual and lenient attitude toward sins of impurity." The book threatened even "priests who are supposed to know the principles of Catholic doctrine." The authors were Fr. George Hagmaier, who later became a member of the Board of SIECUS and advanced the idea of sex education before committing suicide, and Fr. Robert Gleason, SJ, a professor of theology at Fordham.[13] If Catholics split on the most important relationship – the one with God – then they were certainly going to be split on the second most important – relationships with their fellow man.

CHAPTER 70
PROTESTANT PRESSURE; MURRAY'S BOOK; LUCE AND FREEDOM

If Vagnozzi thought he was going to turn the anti-Catholic tide by being conciliatory, he was mistaken. With the full force of America's massive media establishment on their side, the Protestants continued to apply pressure. On May 10, 1960, *Look* published "A Protestant View of a Catholic for President" written by the well-known anti-Catholic agitator, Methodist Bishop G. Bromley Oxnam, and Dr. Eugene Carson Blake, a Presbyterian minister on the executive committee of the World Council of Churches and the Stated Clerk (chief permanent officer) of the General Assembly of the United Presbyterian Church of the USA. Both were officers in the rabidly anti-Catholic organization known as Protestants and Other Americans United for the Separation of Church and State (POAU) which they claimed was "committed to the clear and constructive purpose of preserving the separation of church and state."[1]

Beginning with a tendentious rhetorical question that set the tone for what was to come, the article was an attack on Catholics and Catholicism:

"How do you feel about a Catholic candidate for President? Uneasy. This uneasiness arises from a feeling, widespread among American Protestants, that the election of a roman catholic [sic] to the Presidency would both symbolize and strengthen the growing and direct political influence that the Roman Catholic Church exerts on our government and our society.

"It seems clear to us that at every level, from school boards to Congress, the Roman Catholic Church today uses its influence to block legislation that is contrary to its desires, and to stimulate action that it wants. The candidacy of a Roman Catholic, or his occupancy of the White House, cannot help but increase the concern of Protestants about the role his church will play in a great many matters of crucial importance to Americans."[2]

Blake and Oxnam exhibited the fears of the American Founders, who did not want religion informing the policies of the state. While the two ministers thought the first Catholic President might "lean over backward to follow the Constitution, as interpreted by the Supreme Court," Protestants "can hardly be expected to relish the picture of a President of the United States under *the authority of any other person* with respect to his duties as President." That "other person" was a bishop or cardinal, and according to Blake and Oxnam, most Americans and Catholics, "no doubt, will find it difficult to accept the picture of the chief executive of our nation kneeling before a cardinal or an archbishop and kissing his ring. We feel an American President should kneel before no one but God...."[3]

Blake and Oxnam then brought up the double standard. Religion was a private matter when Protestants imposed it, but it was disqualifying issue when Catholics tried to live their faith, or as they put it, "when any citizens honestly worry about how the religious affiliation of a candidate may *affect his fulfillment of his official duties.*" In particular, the two Protestant ministers worried about "the bearing of a man's religion on issues such as public education, planned parenthood, freedom of medical information on birth control and – most fundamentally – on the relations between church and state, on the rights of people who conscientiously disagree with the majority" and on foreign affairs.[4] JFK, they noted, was attacked by Catholics for taking positions approved by the Protestants:

"We think that two of Senator Kennedy's answers – concerning the use of public money for parochial schools and the appointment of an ambassador to the Vatican – were candid and fearless. We praise him for speaking out in this way. He said flatly that the payment of Federal funds to sectarian schools was unconstitutional, and he opposed the appointment of an ambassador to the Vatican. We also praise him for voting against a recent Senate amendment to a school-aid bill, introduced in February, which would have used public money to build nonprofit private schools, including parochial schools."[5]

Blake and Oxnam believed the Catholic Church would oppose JFK were he elected because the "Roman Catholic Church has generally used its influence to try to get public funds for its own institutions – whether schools, colleges or hospitals…. Roman Catholics generally believe that, as far as possible, education and welfare *should* be operated by the churches publicly and at government expense."[6]

The next two issues were crucial for in raising birth control and church state relations, Blake and Oxnam linked the Protestant position in America to opposition to the Divine Positive Law as the basis of civil law and policy. Once again the issue was framed in a tendentious rhetorical questions:

"What do you think of Senator Kennedy's statement opposing government support for information on birth control to the peoples in overpopulated countries that are getting U.S. aid? We think it was inadequate. So was President Eisenhower's position….We believe that both the President and Senator Kennedy showed typical political timidity in not wanting to risk the Catholic Church's displeasure."[7]

As of 1960, Protestant support for birth control was a moral imperative and politically a non-negotiable demand for any candidate seeking public office. "Any candidate for the Presidency," Blake and Oxnam continued:

"should be required by the force of public opinion to face the birth-control issue squarely – especially a Roman Catholic, we believe, since it is Catholic political power that continues to deny birth-control information, even to non-Catholics, in Massachusetts and Connecticut. The population explosion of our time and the continuing advance in the populations of poor and already overcrowded countries make a sensible and realistic policy on birth-control information absolutely necessary as an integral part of programs of long-range economic aid all over the world."[8]

The "natural" or "rhythm" method of birth control approved by the Catholics was the least effective method according to the Protestants. This was based on the view of Alan F. Guttmacher, chief of obstetrics and gynecology at New York's Mt. Sinai Hospital.[9]

The second main issue was whether the Catholic Church supported the American doctrine of the separation of church and state. Once again, the Protestant ministers answered their own rhetorical questions by saying: "No. Certainly not consistently. We say this despite the undoubted sincerity of Father O'Brien and many other American Catholics who claim that the traditional and `official' Roman Catholic view does *not* represent the Roman Catholic position in the United States." The priest mentioned was Father John O'Brien, a professor of theology at the University of Notre Dame, who took the Americanist position in the debate that spilled into *Look* and attacked the "high-ranking Catholic theological journal, *The American Ecclesiastical Review.*" [10] O'Brien would later be instrumental in arranging the secret Rockefeller funded birth control conferences at Notre Dame.

As the election neared, the Americans were starting to sense a split in Catholic thinking that could be exploited. According to Dr. A. F. Carrillo de Albornoz of the World Council of Churches, the Catholic "policy on the question of church-state separation" is not "necessarily frozen to the position laid down by Pope Pius IX." American Catholics should be aware of this difference in doctrine because in Spain and Colombia, "Protestants are harassed and persecuted" and the Supreme Court in 1947 set out the principle that there was a "wall of separation between church and state."[11]

Oxnam and Blake condemned the attitude of Catholic states towards non-Catholic religions as hypocritical, claiming "No Catholic can deny that a great many official documents, produced with the approval of the very highest authorities of the Catholic Church, argue that in a completely Catholic state, *freedom may rightly be denied non-Catholics, under Catholic law.* This concept, derived from Leo XIII's encyclical *Christian Constitution of States,* is taught to American Catholic students today. It is taught in the important Catholic textbook *Catholic Principles of Politics,* by Msgr. John A Ryan and Father Francis J. Boland, a book copyrighted by the National Catholic Welfare Conference and published under the imprimatur of Cardinal Spellman."[12]

"Both Monsignor Ryan and Father Boland," according to Blake and Oxnam:

"declare, in the 1958 edition (page 316): 'The State should officially recognize the Catholic religion as the religion of the commonwealth;..' They pose the question (page 317) whether 'no other religion should be tolerated,' and answer it by saying: 'Much depends upon circumstances and much depends on what is meant by toleration.' They oppose outright conversion of non-Catholics by physical coercion, but in discussing freedom for Protestant doctrines, which they call 'false doctrine,' and non-Catholic forms of worship, which they consider 'false religious worship,' they say: If these are carried on within the family, on in such an inconspicuous manner as to be an occasion neither of scandal nor of perversion to the faithful, they may properly be tolerated by the state…. Quite distinct from the performance of false religious worship and preaching to the members of the erring sect is the propagation of false doctrine among Catholics. This could become a source of injury, a positive menace, to the religious welfare of true believers. Against such an evil, they have a right of protection by the Catholic state....*there exists no right to indulge in this practice... Error has not the same rights as truth.*"[13]

When asked if they thought Catholics wanted to make Catholicism the religion of the US, Blake and Oxnam responded: "good Catholics want to spread their religion, just as good Protestants do... But the difference is that American Protestants generally do not believe in using the power of any state to favor them in their evangelistic task. Some Catholics believe it is right to use *political power as a means of implementing what they believe is the truth.*" Religious freedom came about because of the efforts of "secular power and Protestantism, plus anti-clerical feeling among Roman Catholics themselves, that won the battle for the freedom of the state."[14]

Except for Murray, the Catholic hierarchy, intellectuals, and lay leadership remained silent in the face of this assault. Then in the spring of 1960, Sheed & Ward published Murray's pseudo-theological apologia for America, *We Hold These Truths: Catholic Reflections on the American Proposition.* The timing for its release was perfect and was "most surely instrumental in helping to clear some of the popular confusion which played so great a role in the controversy that preceded the election." JFK's election was a "turning point in the history of American Catholicism" and Murray's book helped to "clear the air" as "it answered many questions about the still thorny Church-State issue." Murray had by that time become one of JFK's advisors. In fact, according to Arthur Schlesinger, Jr., author of *A Thousand Days,* JFK's "'basic attitude was wholly compatible with the sophisticated theology of Jesuits like Father John Courtney Murray, whom he greatly admired."[15]

Perhaps the greatest significance of all of this was transmission of the book's central message that the Catholics had to defend and promote America. In other words, America was Catholic and the Catholics had a duty to advance its organizing principles around the globe. Murray wrote this in the context of there coming a day when there would be "dissent from the political principles which emerge from natural law" and in that situation then the

"Catholic community would still be speaking in the ethical and political idiom familiar to them as it was familiar to their fathers, both the Fathers of the Church and the fathers of the American Republic. The guardianship of the original American consensus, based on the Western heritage, would have passed to the Catholic community, within which the heritage was elaborated long before America was. And it would be for others, not Catholics, to ask themselves whether they still shared the consensus which first fashioned the American people into a body politic and determined the structure of its fundamental law."[16]

In the aftermath of the book's publication, money began to flow into Murray's pocket via Woodstock College, which received both royalties and contributions after the book came out. John de Menil, American businessmen, patron of modern arts as well as supporter of worldwide human rights, gave Murray shares of stock in Schlumberger Limited. Paul Tishman, a Jewish real estate developer from a long line of developers and, like Menil, a promoter of modern art, paid Murray to have *Theological Studies* publish the selected works of Dr. Gregory Zilboorg, the Jewish convert and psychoanalyst who treated Thomas Merton, but whom Murray would not personally recommend for Clare.[17]

LUCE AND FREEDOM

As Luce's marital problems subsided, Harry re-emerged as a public figure, testifying before Senator Henry (Scoop) Jackson's subcommittee and bringing out a nine-issue series in *Life* magazine on the "National Purpose" that featured articles by a number of prominent Americans to include JFK and Richard Nixon, the two Presidential contenders. "National Purpose" was on Jackson's mind when he convened his subcommittee hearings, and Luce was determined to help him formulate the issue. Luce knew "Once it is clearly established what the national purpose is, then means to carry it out can be more readily devised, and men and resources can be dynamically mobilized."[18]

"What is the American national purpose?" Luce asked with a flourish: "In my view, the United States was founded for a purpose and it can endure only so long as that purpose is its highest law. The founding purpose of the United States was to make men free, and to enable them to be free and to preach the gospel of freedom to themselves and to all men."[19] This was the same purpose he articulated during the height of World War II when he claimed that the national purpose that was not a "mere nationalistic revolt against an empire." Rather, the American purpose stood "for the freedom of the world," which is a "uniquely appropriate mission of the political state."[20]

Nothing really changed from World War II to the Cold War other than the name of the enemy. The aims were the same but the methods were radically different as Luce told the Senate:

"What should be our purpose in the cold war? Very simple: we must win it, and the sooner the better.... A minimum definition of victory in the cold war would be: to sever the state power of Russia and Red China from the mission of their present Communist rulers to Communize the world.... Our objective is to reduce the threat of organized Communism. If this is described as a negative aim, it is no less valid. Yet we all realize that you can't beat something with nothing. If we do not want Communist governments or Communist chaos to prevail, then what do we provide in its place?.... Our national purpose must be to promote, by every honest means, the establishment of constitutional governments – that is, governments which respond to man's dream of freedom by giving him freedom under law. In 1917, President Wilson expressed this purpose by saying we must make the world safe for democracy. For me, that is still the best one-phrase definition of our national purpose. But I would add the correlative: that we must also make democracy safe for the world. Democracy becomes actual only when it exists in and through constitutional governments."[21]

Many of these nations did not have a "background of history and tradition conducive to constitutional government." They lacked experience, competent people, and were divided. However, the goal had to be to "promote and support constitutional governments."[22]

That meant accepting limited government with its corollary of American-style church and state relations.

CHAPTER 71
JULY, 1960

The Church and State Controversy continued to simmer through the Summer of 1960. For its Independence Day issue, *Life* ran a story about religion and politics written by Robert Coughlan, a long-time contributor to the magazine, which started by mentioning Pike's December,1959 article and that not one Catholic voice had responded to its charges. Coughlan mentioned Article VI of the Constitution, the First Amendment, and the fact that representatives of all Christian denominations as well as one rabbi attended Washington's inauguration. Liberty, Coughlan opined, had a "nonsectarian spirit."[1]

As the only non-Protestant presidential candidate in the history of the United States, JFK sought to allay the fears of Protestant voters when, announcing his candidacy in the Winter of 1959-1960, he said: "I would think that there is really only one question involved in the whole question of a candidate's religion. That is, does a candidate believe in the Constitution, does he believe in the First Amendment, does he believe in the separation of church and state? When the candidate gives his views on that question, and I have given my views fully, then I think the subject is exhausted."

That this was not the case was unmistakably clear. The Wisconsin primary caused fears, even among "open-minded" columnists like Walter Lippmann, of a Protestant-Catholic split. The Southern Baptists, who were notoriously not open-minded when it came to Catholics, openly questioned whether a Catholic should be president. When the northern American Baptists endorsed the right of any US citizen to run for president, these fears abated somewhat.[2]

America, said Coughlan, echoing Thomas Paine's statements in *The Rights of Man,* was different because it was formed by those seeking to escape from religious persecution.[3]

Because America was unique in this regard, the Church adapted its policies to accommodate American circumstances. Coughlan then played divide and conquer with the Catholics. He pitted Archbishop John Hughes (and other unspecified "earlier Irish Catholic fanatics"), who proclaimed the Church's divine mission "'to convert all pagan nations, and to convert all Protestant nations...to convert the world including the inhabitants of the United States'," against Americanists like Ireland and Gibbons. Hughes, *Life* claimed, represented the forces of "aggressive Catholicism," and that the Know-Nothings and other anti-Catholic groups were a reaction to Catholic aggression.[4]

Bishops Ireland and Gibbons, on the other hand, were portrayed as men of "humane and liberal beliefs, tolerant of others, friendly toward the public school system, and squarely on record as favoring – for America – the separation of church and state." According to *Life,* "Gibbons had almost done as much good as Hughes had done harm." Recognized in 1911 as a great American, Gibbons laid the groundwork for Al Smith's presidential run in 1928. But the Ku Klux Klan was powerful in that day and instrumental in Smith's defeat. The KKK conflated old lies such as immoralities going on in convents with historical truths about the Inquisition. In an attempt to placate the same anti-Catholic bigotry of his day, Smith issued what sounded like a secular parody of the Apostles' Creed that was published in the *Atlantic* and became a model for JFK's campaign 32 years later:

"I believe in the worship of God in accordance with the faith and practice of the Roman Catholic Church. I recognize no power in the institutions of my church to interfere with the operations of the Constitution of the United States or the enforcement of the law of the land. I believe in the absolute freedom of conscience of all men, and in equality of all churches, all sects and all beliefs before the law as a matter of right and not as a matter of favor. I believe in the absolute separation of Church and State and in the strict enforcement of the provisions of the Constitution that Congress shall make no law respecting an establishment of religion or prohibiting the free exercise thereof... I believe in the support of the public school as one of the cornerstones of American liberty... I believe in the principle of noninterference by this country in the internal affairs of other nations and that we should stand steadfastly against any such interference by whomsoever it might be urged. And I believe in the common brotherhood of man under the common fatherhood of God."[5]

JFK's statement was similar to Smith's. At its core was the idea that the Constitution and the "laws of the land" somehow operated according to principles higher than those a religion could offer. Things were a little different in 1960, because Protestant leaders like Pike and Dean John C. Bennett of the Union Theological School gave voters a litmus test to apply to Catholic candidates: "'What sort, kind, and variety of Catholic is he?' Is he a Catholic in the tradition of Archbishop Hughes, or in that of Cardinal Gibbons?"[6]

Connell wrote to Coughlan to offer his assistance "with any future articles" on the subject. Connell pointed out that the article failed to make any mention of the "discrimination against Catholics found <u>on the state level</u> for many years. Certainly, this must be regarded as an important factor in every historical presentation of the religious issue in our land." The second comment condemned the reference to Archbishop Hughes of New York as a "fanatic because he proclaimed it the Church's divine mission to convert all non-Catholics." The Americans could not forget the man who more than 100 years earlier had the courage to call them to their duties. Connell calmly wrote, "Now, what Archbishop Hughes stated is simply Catholic doctrine which must be admitted by everyone. It is the Church's conviction that this is her proper end, given her by Jesus Christ Himself."[7]

VOICES FROM SPAIN

Latin Catholics were vocal in their disagreement, something used as evidence by the Americans that there was a split in the Church on the important issue of church and state relations. Archbishop Ildebrando Antoniutti, the Apostolic Nuncio to Spain, recalled how Spanish Catholics saved Christian civilization during the Civil War (1936 to 1939) and resulted in the deaths of one million persons of which 7,000 were religious. Because of "their heroic resistance, sufferings and martyrs, the Spanish Catholics saved their country and preserved their priceless religious and cultural heritage."[8] The fact that these heroes were forgotten in the West indicated especially since the Catholic Church "has always worked to assure for all the treasure of the true freedom of the sons of God," something "foreign periodicals" have "presented inexactly and – permit me to say – in a slanted way with news taken from rather doubtful sources of information…."[9]

A little more than a week later in London, the Spanish Foreign Minister, Fernando Castiella y Maiz, delivered a speech to the House of Commons entitled "Protestantism and Religious Freedom in Spain" in response to questions raised by British Foreign Secretary Selwyn Lloyd. Castiella y Maiz said there was "no Protestant problem" in Spain though "'an imaginary Protestant problem' still engages attention abroad." There were about 30,000 Protestants in a country of 30,000,000 Catholics, and their worship was tolerated. Article 6 of the Spanish Charter of 1945 stated that "nobody shall be molested for his religious beliefs nor in the private practice of his form of worship." The 1953 Vatican-Spain Concordat, Article 53, permitted the excuse of children from Catholic education upon the mere request of the parents. Non-Catholics could be married despite some delays in issuing instructions from the Spanish Government.

In April, 1958, the British and Foreign Bible Society was awarded about $2,000 to indemnify them for unjustified confiscation of their property. The Protestants had more than 118 churches and chapels and 117 clergymen, which meant there was a higher proportion of Protestant clergy to congregants and places of worship to congregants than with Catholics.[10]

In conclusion, Castiella y Maiz said "'There is therefore no real Protestant problem in Spain, although many abroad would have it otherwise. However, an immense Catholic majority and 2,000 years of history closely bound up with Catholicism must result in an undeniable social pressure or weight on small and dispersed Protestant nuclei. In general then, this is the cause of difficulties of a practical order – since there is no legal discrimination—encountered on occasion by Spanish Protestants.'"[11] These sentiments were repeated most notably by Generalissimo Francisco Franco himself.

COGLEY EXPLAINS THE TERMS OF UNCONDITIONAL SURRENDER

Later that same busy month of July, 1960, Connell and John Cogley of the Center for the Study of Democratic Institutions, the Fund for the Republic, Inc., exchanged letters. The topic was Church state relations and the occasion was a talk Cogley gave at Rosary College, in which he claimed that Protestants, who were Christians like Catholics, were justified in asking their fellow Catholic citizens:

"Can the principles of pluralism and religious freedom be secure when a vast religious body in America, superbly organized and notably docile, still flirts with such ideas [limiting freedom of religion and denying the separation of church and state]? The answers their Catholic fellow-citizens give them it must be admitted, are not wholly reassuring, for the Catholics can only acknowledge that the 'thesis' not only exists in theological textbooks but is put in practice in a few Catholic countries."[12]

Backing up his claim, Cogley cited:

"Father Connell: `(The American system) is not per se preferable to the system in which the one true Church would be acknowledged and specially favored….' "Msgr. Ryan and Father Boland: `If there is only one true religion, and if its possession is the most important good in the life for states as well as individuals, then the public profession, protection and promotion of this religion and the legal prohibition of all direct assaults upon it, must become one of the most obvious and fundamental duties of the state.'

"Civilta Cattolica: `The Roman Catholic Church…must demand the right of freedom for herself alone, because such a right can only be possessed by truth, never error. As to other religions, the church will never draw the sword, but she will require that by legimitimate [sic] means they shall not be allowed to propagate false doctrine…'"[13]

Connell responded that Cogley misrepresented the thesis "in a nation overwhelmingly Catholic, the Church should be formally recognized by the government, its claim to uniqueness should be respected, etc." by describing "the situation merely in terms of numbers." This misrepresentation was "brought about by the enemies of the Church."[14]

Connell undercut his own position when he wrote:

"For example, in our country, even though Catholics constituted 99% of the citizens, I would not favor any special privilege for the Catholic Church, any union of Church and State, any repression of false doctrine. But at the same time, as a Catholic I must hold the so-called thesis. I myself believe that the best solution of this problem today would be to have complete separation of Church and State in every land. Of course, that would include England and the Scandinavian countries where there is such a union between the state and a Protestant church."[15]

Cogley responded to Connell:

"You say that you would not be for the application of the thesis in our own country even if 99% of the people were Catholic. We can certainly agree on that. You add that you think the best solution of the problem today would be to have complete separation of Church and State in every land, including the Protestant countries of England and Scandinavia, and, I presume, Israel. Again, ideally, I would agree, provided that the word `complete' were not understood too radically. And, incidentally, in the Rosary paper I drew attention to the fact that there was union of Church and State in these countries, with more or less tolerance granted to non-conformists. In practice, then, we are in agreement, it seems to me."[16]

If Cogley had left it at that, there would have been no division among Catholics on the Church state ssue, but Cogley demanded unconditional surrender from the Catholics, who had to relinquish in principle the desirability of the Catholic confessional state. Connell's comments show that he was unwilling to accept such terms. Cogley advised Connell that "I simply reject" the Catholic State Thesis and that "even if by some miracle the U.S. became overwhelmingly Catholic, religious liberty would be secure because any imposition of the Catholic State would mean subversion from within and attack from without." This was "extremism" that even the Church rejected he claimed. However, "as long as the Catholic State thesis is even abstractly defended by American Catholics, relations between Catholics and non-Catholics will not be secure in the U.S."[17]

Cogley admitted he "held a different view of the State than was held by those who devised the theory in the first place." The State, according to Cogley who was reading from the same "script" as Murray, "is a conceptual being which is only remotely related to the Thing we call the United States of America, where authority is divided, powers are withheld by the people to themselves and the centers of governmental powers are numerous and varied." Catholic theologians had not kept up "with the development of political doctrine and therefore misunderstand the second half of the Church-State problematic." As a result, Cogley did not believe that Catholics had to hold to the Catholic State Thesis, especially when "it would appear that something is wrong with a theory that is universally undesirable when put into effect." Cogley held the issue of the Catholic State thesis an "open theological question." He expressed sympathy for the theologians wanting to justify "religious tolerance on the part of the State which we all seem to accept as a desirable political development, in fact if not in theory."[18]

About the same time as this exchange, Vagnozzi signaled a strategic retreat from the Catholic position when he told Americans that the institutional Church would not direct the actions of a US President. In Dallas he said that there is "'no instance of interference from the Church' in those republics which today have a Catholic as president." He also said that the "Catholic Church is not concerned about the so-called religious issue in the presidential race. Catholic voters have their individual preferences among candidates, but the Church itself does not take sides in such matters…. In illustration of the fact that the Church does not interfere with the exercise of their duties by Catholics who are presidents…Vagnozzi cited President Charles De Gaulle of France, whom he described as 'a very good Catholic.'"[19]

CHAPTER 72

SURRENDERS IN SEPTEMBER

In August, 1960, the Americanists got support from an unsuspected quarter when Jesuit Augustin Cardinal Bea urged Catholics to support America as the only alternative to Communism. In a speech he gave at a formal reception in Freiburg, his native archdiocese, Bea was quoted as saying that "all who are baptized are members of the one Mystical Body of Christ even though divided by historical events for which they are not guilty. Although Christians may differ on faith, he said, they are called to cooperate in all fields not directly concerned with faith. Such cooperation should extend to the political, economic and social fields...." In an August 15, 1960 NCWC News Service release, Bea said the Church was engaged in a "present struggle against organized atheism and the enticements of materialism are more difficult than the struggles and persecutions of past centuries. 'Today,' he said, 'all who are baptized in Christ must cooperate in defending the values of Christianity and culture and join in warding off the onslaught of atheism.'" [1]

Connell wrote to Ottaviani explaining that Bea's comments concerning baptism and the "one Mystical Body of Christ" would "cause confusion here in the United States, and even may lead some to believe that the doctrine of <u>Mystici Corporis</u> on membership in the Church can now be rejected."[2]

PROTESTANT PRESSURE

Emboldened by doctrinal defections within the Catholic ranks, the Protestants intensified their attack using secularist arguments. Norman Vincent Peale organized a national conference of Citizens for Religious Freedom (CRF) which brought together 150 Protestant Ministers and laymen representing 37 different sects and issued a statement that expressed serious concern about a Catholic candidate for President. He portrayed the Church as a political and authoritarian entity that compelled compliance with its demands and threatened the "American brotherhood" which held all to be one, but not in Christ. America, to the Protestants, was the new basis of unity and not belief in Christ. The CRF statement reiterated all of the old complaints, claiming that the Roman Catholic Church "has specifically repudiated on many occasions the principle sacred to us that every man shall be free to follow the dictates of his conscience in religious matters". While some Catholics disagreed with their own hierarchy, "The Roman Catholic Church in the United States has repeatedly attempted to break down the wall of separation of church and state by a continuous campaign to secure public funds for the support of its schools and other institutions." Given these and other facts, the CRF was forced to conclude that the views of a particular candidate were irrelevant because the problem "is created by the nature of the Roman Catholic Church which is, in a very real sense, both a church and also a temporal state."[3]

Caught unawares by the anti-Catholic bigotry his conference issued, Peale began backtracking furiously, claiming that the meeting had been taken over by conservatives and evangelicals. On the following day, he issued a statement that essentially rebuked the group and stated that "'public agitation of religion as an issue can only be divisive and therefore in the long run harmful to our country.'" Dr. John C Bennett, Dean of the Union Theological Seminary and Reinhold Niebuhr, a Vice President Emeritus of UTS accused Peale's group of "blind prejudice," claiming that Peale and his associates showed "no understanding of the developments within Roman Catholicism in many democratic countries which are favorable to religious liberty to all.'"[4] The moment of truth was fast approaching for the Catholic leadership in the US.

Later in the Summer, the Americanists put together "A Statement on Religious Liberty in Relation to the 1960 National Campaign," whose purpose was to oppose the Peale group's statement by bringing "basic American principles of religious liberty in a democracy into a dispassionate focus, so that all citizens, irrespective of their religious affiliations, may function reasonably and with foresight in an area that too often lends itself to emotion."[5] This Statement, which was signed by about 100 churchmen and theologians representing the Catholic Americanist point of view, including John Courtney Murray, SJ, Reinhold Neibuhr, Richard Cardinal Cushing, Archbishop Robert Lucey of San Antonio, Bishop Robert Dwyer of Reno, Nevada, Fr. Thurston N. Davis, SJ of *America* magazine, Robert F Drinan SJ, John LaFarge SJ, G. Bromley Oxnam, James A Pike, Dr. George N. Shuster, Edward Skillin editor of *The Commonweal*, Jerome G Kerwin Professor from the University of Chicago, and a number of Rabbis to include Morris Adler (Detroit), Charles Weinberg (Malden, Mass.), and Bernard Bamberger (New York)[6] was a veritable who's who of religious apologists for the American experiment and its preamble was clear in its endorsement of American religious liberty and the American ideology:

"We reaffirm our loyalty to the Constitution of the United States and its provision that 'no religious test shall ever be required as a qualification to any office or public trust under the United States,' and the declaration in the American Bill of Rights that 'Congress shall make no law respecting an establishment of religion or prohibiting the free exercise thereof.' We affirm that religious liberty is basic, both historically and philosophically to all our liberties and that religious and civil liberties are interdependent and indivisible. It is our conviction that man's freedom is an essential attribute of human nature. The sacredness of this truth has long been recognized as fundamental to Western society. The founders of this nation, in emancipating themselves from tyranny, asserted their right to life, to liberty, and to the pursuit of happiness. These rights are guaranteed in our Constitution to each of us as citizens, and also to the associations, societies, and religious faiths to which we belong. Freedom is fundamental to faith. Freedom is fundamental to the exercise of conscience. It is necessary, therefore, to the essence of our faith that we respect the diversity of religious viewpoints and their freedoms. We believe that it is the responsibility of the members of our various religious organizations to oppose vingorously [sic] all attempts to make religious affiliation the basis of the voter's choice of candidates for public office. It is a vicious practice and repugnant to all honorable Americans to set class against class, race against race, and religion against religion."[7]

The signatories felt that they were being tested at a "particular moment in history" and that they "must act according to our principles, or be found wanting." The reason was the religion of JFK during the Presidential election, and the concern that "40,000,000 of our fellow-citizens should be made to feel that they are barred from full and free participation in our national life" because of their "religious affiliation."[8] Catholic auspices aside, the Statement espoused a false (and Protestant) dichotomy when it claimed that religious institutions should not "seek to influence and dominate public officials for" their "own institutional advantage" since the "exercise of public office must always be in the public interest, and serve the welfare of the whole community." [9]

The most important points were the sixth and the tenth. The sixth claimed that "Every person of every faith must be accorded full religious liberty, and no person should be coerced into accepting any religious belief or practice. No religious group should be given special preference or advantage by the state, nor allowed to use state agencies for the restriction of other faiths." The tenth held that "Every public official who is a member of a religious group should, of course, take into consideration the spiritual and moral principles of his faith in confronting the decisions he must make. But in our pluralistic society he will recognize that the values in historic faiths other than his own must be brought to bear upon the problems of the day. He alone, under the judgment of God, can fully appraise the force and applicability of all such values and advice for his situation, and he should seek to apply all in such a way as to enhance and undergird the best interests of the nation."[10]

The Statement was signed and released at around the same time JFK was in Houston giving his famous speech to the Houston Ministerial Association. According to Theodore Sorensen, JFK's campaign manager, Murray approved the speech, in which Kennedy claimed that he would not allow his religious beliefs to have any impact on his public decisions, after it was read to him over the telephone. Sorensen considered this speech not only very important but the "best speech" that Kennedy gave during his campaign, and JFK was applauded for it,[11] but it didn't go far enough to satisfy the Protestants.

In spite of what the Protestants thought, JFK's Houston speech received wide-spread support from America's Catholics. Within about three weeks, a group of 165 of the most prominent Catholics in America signed a statement endorsing American church and state separation in principle. The statement, according to *The New York Times* affirmed "its belief today in the separation of church and state and in full religious freedom for all. In a five-point statement, the group said a Catholic was `bound in conscience to promote the common good and to avoid any seeking of a merely sectarian advantage' in his public acts. `He is bound also...to recognize the proper scope or independence of the political order.'" The constitutional separation of church and state, according to the Statement was "`the best guarantee both of religious freedom and cicvic [sic] peace.'"[12] *The New York Times* surmised that a purpose for the statement was to "allay doubts that Senator John F. Kennedy's beliefs on church-state relations were widely shared by fellow Catholics in the United States." One of the signers, William Clancy the education director and the editor of *Worldview,* said "'Senator Kennedy's stand is typical of American lay Catholicism rather than atypical.'" JFK promised to "make every decision, if elected, 'without regard to outside religious pressures or dictates.' He does not speak for the church on public matters 'and the church does not speak for me.'"[13]

Clancy and other signers held a news conference in New York on October 5, at which they claimed that their statement represented the "'modern' Catholic position on separation of church and state as opposed to the 'traditional' one accepted in such countries as Spain." The "modern view" stressed religious freedom. Clancy claimed that since "there was 'no official' church position, that Catholics were free to accept either one." The American Catholic bishops, Clancy added just to be safe, backed the modern position in a 1948 statement and the majority of American Catholics were for the modern position also.[14] The group's director of Operations and Policy Research, William J. Nagle, noted that "no member of the hierarchy was contacted about the statement before it was issued" and none of the signers thought of themselves as being "'revolutionary in any sense.'"[15] Clancy added, "'There is a common misconception that Catholic laymen are afraid to open their mouths without consulting the priests and we just went ahead on our own to show that this is not true. We are confident of our orthodoxy and we saw no reason to consult with the Bishops.'"[16]

The signers were a "representative sampling" of "Catholic leaders" from the arts, education, business, science, politics, and labor according to Clancy and crew. Some of the signers were Clare Boothe Luce; Daniel J. Callahan a teaching fellow at Roman Catholic Studies at the Harvard Divinity School; A Robert Caponigri a Professor of Philosophy at the University of Notre Dame; General J. Lawton Collins, retired US Army general; John G Deedy, Jr. editor of the *Pittsburgh Catholic*; Senator Thomas Dodd of Connecticut; Thomas F Doyle Catholic editor of *Religious News*

Service; David Host, director of the Institute of the Catholic Press; Thomas B Kennedy, editor of *The Official Catholic Directory;* Jerome G Kerwin Professor of Political Science at the University of Chicago; Senator Eugene McCarthy of Minnesota; J. Norman McDonough, Dean of the School of Law for Saint Louis University; Thomas H. Mahoney, former chair of the Catholic Commission of Intellectual and Cultural Affairs; Vernon X. Miller, Dean School of Law CUA; Joseph O'Meara Dean University of Notre Dame Law School; William O'Brien Chairman of the Institute of World Polity at Georgetown; Thomas O'Toole Director of the Institute of Church and State Villanova; Harold Gill Reuschlein Dean of the School of Law of Villanova; Heinrich Rommen Professor of Government at Georgetown; Miriam Theresa Rooney Dean Seton Hall Law School; Philip Scharper editor for Sheed & Ward; and George N Shuster of the Center for Democratic Institutions.[17] The invitations were sent by Rommen, Shuster, O'Meara, Clancy, Kerwin, and Francis G Wilson a Professor of Political Science at the University of Illinois.[18]

Faced with such an impressive list of prominent Catholics, backing "freedom of conscience," deploring and denial of religious freedom in any country, and praising US constitutional provisions regarding separation of Church and State as "'the best guarantee both of religious freedom and civic peace,'"[19] the Catholic hierarchy fell silent. This was so despite the fact that 200 of the nearly 350 Catholics who had been asked to lend their names to the statement did not sign it. The Protestants were quick to notice the absence of episcopal names on the petition, causing Glenn L. Archer of the Protestants and Others United for the Separation of Church and State to remark he "wished it 'could be shared by the Roman Catholic clergy who actually manage the church's affairs.'"[20]

When the October 7, 1960 edition of the official diocesan paper of the Archdiocese of San Francisco covered the story, it opined that "the Church provides certain general principles to guide Catholics as citizens, but it is as individual citizens and office-holders, not as a religious bloc, that Catholics apply these principles. 'Here we function not as "Catholic citizens," but as citizens who are

Catholics'."[21] It was a reversal of loyalty to place the earthly Caesar before Jesus Christ. This had enormous consequences on Catholics and societies in which they lived, it was perfectly consistent with US doctrinal warfare, and it served to preserve and enhance the real power held by the private monied interests who really ran America.

CHAPTER 73

WEIGEL

On September 27, Weigel gave a talk at the Shrine of the Most Blessed Sacrament in Washington DC on "A Theological Consideration of the Relations Between Church and State." According to John W. Finney, author of the story for *The New York Times,* the talk was "regarded as an authoritative exposition of the Catholic hierarchy's views on the 'religious issue' raised by the Presidential candidacy of Senator John F. Kennedy." Weigel said that the "Roman Catholic Church would not attempt to interfere in the political activities of a Catholic President nor would the President be bound by Catholic morality in deciding public issues." According to Weigel, a politician led a "double life" because he worships "as he pleases in his private life, but in his public role 'he is a man of the law which is framed for practical purposes and canonizes no philosophy or theology.'"[1] With one stroke, Weigel came up with an argument that would have terrible consequences for America, by giving Catholic Democratic politicians like Teddy Kennedy and Mario Cuomo the theoretical justification for being "personally opposed to abortion, but publicly supportive of a woman's right to choose." Weigel provided the theoretical framework that allowed Catholic politicians to espouse every and any form of immorality, thus destroying what little leverage the Church had in maintaining the moral order as the basis of the social order which Murray claimed was an indispensable part of the American experiment.

Weigel assured the audience that neither the Pope nor the bishops would interfere if a Catholic President was elected. Catholic doctrine distinguished between the sacral or divine law that pertained to man's relation "with his divinity" and the human or secular law that concerned itself with "man's associations with his community." The state was "'autonomous, free and authoritative in its decisions'" when it came to secular matters. The real source of the problem, according to Weigel, was not Catholic theology, but theologians like Connell, Fenton, and Ottaviani promoting an extraneous "third principle of Catholic doctrine, which demands 'the greatest possible concord between the sacral and the secular.'"[2]

"Human law," according to Weigel, "is for the human community"; it is not "a religious profession of faith nor even a prolongation of divine law." In some instances, the state may tolerate actions that are intolerable under the moral law in order to hold the community together. According to Weigel's interpretation, "the morality of divorce, birth-control, liquor traffic and the like are one thing," while "civil legislation about them is quite another. Morality is categorical and obliges by inner consent. Legislation is conditioned and works by some kind of external coercion." Weigel claimed that it would be wrong for a Catholic official to "push Catholic moral precepts into our laws." Weigel said "it would be immoral for him to impose on the community what he thinks immoral."[3]

Weigel tackled the issue of religious freedom. When speaking in the name of American Catholics, if not in the name of the American Catholic Church, Weigel claimed "officially and really American Catholics do not want now or in the future a law which would make Catholicism the favored religion on this land. They do not want the religious freedom of American non-Catholics to be curtailed in any way…They sincerely want the present Frist [sic] Amendment to be retained and become ever more effective."[4]

Finney, the author of the article, opined that the "speech seemed designed to answer questions and objections that have been raised by certain Protestant groups about a Catholic's occupying the White House." This included concerns over what the Church might impose on the individual or require of the person who occupied the office. While Protestants found JFK's September 12 speech in Houston reassuring, the Protestants wanted to know what the position of the Catholic hierarchy would be, and, sensing what the moment required, Weigel presumed to speak for the hierarchy. [5] They collaborated in his effrontery by remaining silent, and by remaining silent the American episcopate allowed Weigel to set Church policy for US Catholic politicians to this day.

Not only did the American bishops not contradict Weigel when he contradicted Church teaching, they allowed him to give the talk at the heart of Catholicism in the US – the Shrine of the Most Blessed Sacrament, Washington DC. They then allowed the National Catholic Welfare Conference, the secretariat of the Catholic Bishops in the US, to distribute the talk in its entirety. Articles on Weigel's talk appeared in diocesan newspapers and gave the impression that the Catholics were "fighting back" when in reality Catholics were surrendering.[6]

Weigel made clear that his presentation could be use to justify Catholic refusal to resist the legalization of abortion and contraception when he added at the end of his talk that a Catholic politician leads "a double life":

"In his public role he is a man of the law which is framed for practical purposes and canonizes no philosophy or theology. I can conceive of a highly moral man who in his interior conscience considers traffic in liquor to be immoral and yet could refuse to make a law about it, or vote for the removal of such existing legislation. He is being highly moral in his political action if he judges that such a law would do more public harm than good." [7]

If the Catholic politician went to his confessor, he would learn, according to Weigel "The confessor's service to the public figure would be exclusively private, moral and religious. He has no competence in political matters which belong not to the order of morality and piety but to the order of law...."[8]

In order to foster the illusion he was promoting Catholic doctrine, Weigel cited the writings of various Americanist prelates, like John Carroll, who said "Freedom and independence, acquired by the united efforts, and cemented with the mingled blood of Protestant and Catholic fellow citizens, should be equally enjoyed by all." He cited Bishop McNicholas of Cincinnati, who claimed in 1948:

"We deny absolutely and without any qualification that the Catholic bishops of the United States are seeking a union of Church and State by any endeavors whatsoever, either proximate and remote. If tomorrow Catholics constituted a majority in our country, they would not seek a union of Church and State....In complete accord with the Catholic doctrine, we hold firmly that our own constitutional provisions are the best for our country. Even had we the authority to do so, we would not change one iota of them."[9]

Archbishop Vagnozzi contributed to the rout of Catholic principle by adding:

"As far as the United States is concerned, I feel that it is the true interpretation of the feelings of the hierarchy and of American Catholics in general to say that they are well satisfied with their Constitution and pleased with the fundamental freedom enjoyed by their Church; in fact, they believe that this freedom is to a large extent responsible for the expansion and consolidation of the Church in this great country. Whether they remain a minority, or become a majority, I am sure that American Catholics will not jeopardize their cherished religious freedom in exchange for a privileged position."[10]

Weigel's speech was a direct attack on Connell's 1946 book *Morals in Politics and Professions: A Guide for Catholics in Public Life,* which stated a Catholic politician must be aided in "making decisions and in passing legislative measures by the definite and comprehensive norms of right and wrong proposed by" the Church, and not the "flexible standards of expediency" that was accepted by many political leaders. The Catholic official had to render an account to God of his official conduct, as well as his private conduct. Connell explained that the moral and social teachings of Catholicism, lucidly set forth in the encyclicals, were beneficial to every society and could be defended by "natural reason, even independently of divine revelation as interpreted by the Church."[11]

Recognizing the grave scandal that the wide dissemination of Weigel's talk caused, Connell told Ottaviani in a letter that: "I cannot see how the opinions proposed by Fr. Weigel can be reconciled with the doctrine of the Church and the common teaching of theologians. Surely, we have always believed and taught that a Catholic in public office must speak and act in accordance with the law of God as interpreted by the Catholic Church, though at times he can tolerate evil. But the impression given in the article is that a Catholic ruler in his official conduct can positively approve and do things which are contrary to God's law as the Church proclaims it."[12]

Connell quoted Weigel with particular alarm: "In America any elected official is a citizen designated by the people for some temporary function of state. This man has a double life. He has his own and that of a civil servant. If in his own life he wishes to worship in one way or in none, this is no political concern of the civic community. By our laws he is free in the matter. In his public role he is a man of the law, which is framed for practical purposes and canonizes no philosophy or theology."[13]

After citing Weigel's claim that a confessor "has no competence in political matters, which belong, not to the order of morality and piety, but to the order of law,"[14] Connell noted, "the average person reading such statements will conclude that a Catholic public official would be permitted to give positive approval to laws favoring birth control, euthanasia, abortion, etc." Weigel was basing his theories on Murray's view of Church and state, something that became obvious when Weigel wrote: "States are natural things because they have their origin in human nature. They are therefore non-sacral....The state has as its purpose the worldly welfare of the community. It is not religious in its preoccupations."[15]

American Catholics were coming to accept these ideas as Church teachings. Wrote Connell: "Fr. Weigel's statement is regarded as `an authoritative exposition of the Catholic hierarchy's views on the religious issue raised by the presidential candidacy of Senator John F. Kennedy. And many persons are now saying that these ideas have the approval of the Holy See, because the Holy See has been silent regarding the teachings of Fr. Murray and Fr. Weigel." Once again Connell concluded his letter by asking Ottaviani to refute Weigel's errors publically. Connell feared "the faith of Catholics is being undermined by `liberal' views in America, and that eventually a schism for the formation of an `American Church' would not be improbable."[16]

CHAPTER 74
OCTOBER SURPRISE

I n October, the Protestants pulled out all the stops in a media campaign whose goal was preventing JFK from winning the election. On October 4, 1,000 delegates to the United Pentecostal Church convention in Dallas adopted a resolution opposing the election of a Catholic as president, stating: "We do not believe that a member of the Roman Catholic Church can be loyal to his Church and still faithfully carry out the demands of the Constitution." The Greenville County (South Carolina) Baptist Pastors' Conference issued a statement that held "a Catholic who became President would be under tremendous pressure from the Roman Catholic authorities."[1] The American Council of Christian Churches in Washington, D.C. issued a statement in which they claimed there was an "'inconsistency'" between the Catholics' loyalty to the Church as opposed to the "'the historic American tradition.'"
[2]

Reaction among Protestants varied. Referring to President Eisenhower's opposition US Government participation in the dissemination of birth control,[3] Episcopalian Bishop Pike complained that President Eisenhower "yielded more to Catholic influence than Sen. John Kennedy could possibly afford to" and concluded, the Catholic Church "might exert more pressure on a Protestant President than on a Catholic one." After Dr. Harold A Bosley of the First Methodist Church in Evanston was criticized for saying in a homily that he opposed the election of a Catholic to the Presidency, his students demanded a retraction, claiming that "the religious issue is of relatively minor importance in this campaign, and that a position such as yours does not allow rational appraisal of other issues."'[4]

On October 18, after the Pentecostals and the American Council of Christian Churches asked: How could Catholics be true to the "demands of the Constitution" which was not guided by the Faith, and the Church which taught fidelity to the Faith?, the NCWC dragged Murray into the fray. Its news service published an article based on Murray's book, *We Hold These Truths,* which reinforced Weigel's comments as the authoritative voice of the Church by quoting Murray as saying: "The American Catholic is entirely prepared to accept our constitutional concept of freedom of religion and the policy of no establishment" of religion. "The American thesis is that government is not juridically omnipotent. Its powers are limited, and one of the principles of limitation is the distinction between State and Church....To describe the U.S. Catholic attitude on Church and State as mere expediency...is altogether to misunderstand the moral nature of the community and its collective moral obligation towards its own common good."[5]

Murray taught the U.S. Constitution was binding in conscience, reasoning that because the "origins of our fundamental law are in moral principle; the obligations it imposes are moral obligations, binding in conscience. One may not, without moral fault, act against these articles of peace." The US Constitution was morally binding because the United States was different and because the situation created "a turning point in the long and complicated history of Church-State relations." The "Catholic Church has benefited by our free institutions, by the maintenance, even in exaggerated form, of the distinction between Church and State."[6] Any arrangement in the US other than separation of Church and

State would be "disruptive, imprudent, unpractical, indeed impossible." Additionally, "questioning whether 'Catholicism is compatible with American democracy' is both 'invalid' and 'impertinent.'" "An affirmative answer to" that impertinent question "is one of the truths I hold." The Catholic must "reckon with his own tradition of thought" and "he must recognize that a new problem has been put to the universal church by the American doctrine and project in the matter of pluralism, as stated in the First Amendment."[7]

SOME BISHOPS DEFEND DOCTRINE

Bishop John Mussio of Steubenville, Ohio was one of the few Catholic leaders in the US who refused to surrender. In an October 16 statement to the local Knights of Columbus, he struck back at Weigel, Murray and the Americanists, by warning Catholics to "avoid compromise in their attempts to square Catholicism with other people's interpretations of America. It seems to me that some writers are going so far in their protestations of loyalty that they give the impression that it would be unpatriotic even to listen to the admonitions and instructions of the Supreme Pontiff.... If this ever creeps into our thinking then we have fallen victim to a pernicious error, election or no election."[8]

Connell commended the bishop by letter a few days later, stating that he was "glad that a member of the hierarchy has come out so definitely" in support of Church teaching. Connell then told Mussio that he was "planning to publish an article on this subject in the AMERICAN ECCLESIASTICAL REVIEW in the near future. Above all, I hope to bring out the fact that the Catholic Church has the right to direct the moral life of Catholics in public as well as in private life. I shall wait until after the elections."[9]

In another letter, Connell pleaded with Vagnozzi to do something about the flood of false doctrine that the 1960 Presidential election was generating "concerning the relation between Church and State, the obligations and rights of a Catholic in civil office, etc. I believe that some of these statements are very ambiguous, to say the least; and certainly they give a false impression of the teaching of the Church to many readers and hearers. If Your Excellency wishes a written statement about this in greater detail, I shall be glad to present it. Or, if a personal interview would be more desirable, I am at your service. I believe it would be better to wait until after the elections before making any public statement because it would surely be regarded as an attempt to sway the balloting, and I would be accused of causing trouble unnecessarily. But I do believe that Americans, both Catholic and non-Catholic, should be given a correct and clear statement of the Church's position in regard to the duties of a Catholic in high office.[10]

Vagnozzi responded, but only after the outcome of the battle was a foregone conclusion.

THE PRELATES OF PUERTO RICO GET SERIOUS

On October 21, at around the same time that Connell traveled to Puerto Rico for a series of lectures at the Catholic University, the Catholic Bishops of Puerto Rico spoke to their flock and, out of deep concern for their souls and the welfare of society, told them how to vote. Archbishop James P. Davis of San Juan, installed just the week before by Cardinal Spellman, Bishop James E McManus of Ponce and Bishop Luis Aponte Martinez Lares, just consecrated by Spellman, all signed a pastoral letter that forbade island Catholics from voting for Gov. Luis Munoz Marin's Popular Democratic party. JFK immediately denounced the bishops saying it was "'wholly improper' for clergymen to tell church members how to vote" but despite this attempt to seem more American than Catholic, considerable damage was done to his bid for election.[11]

The Protestant press was irate. An editorial by David Lawrence entitled "Free Speech and Church Disputes: Prelate's Political Advice Held All Right Except Where Penalty is Threatened" explained that the Puerto Rico Governor had been encouraging birth control. The Catholic bishops complained for years that

Marin's policies were "promoting abortion and tolerating common-law marriages" and they condemned a recent law that allowed sterilization and taught birth control. Marin refused to let 500,000 public school children "take time off for religious observance" as the United States Supreme Court had authorized public authorities to do. Spellman said that violating the bishops' pastoral letter was not a sin worthy of confession to a priest, which was similar to what many Protestant clergy said when they advised their flocks. However, pastors were, and are, influential people. Presbyterian chief executive Rev. Eugene Carson Blake of the United Presbyterian Church, USA recognized so much in a talk at the Colgate-Rochester Divinity School. His talk concerned the church in politics and he mentioned that what is said in the pulpits is more influential than all the pronouncements from synods, councils, and such. He decried the attempts of people to limit or marginalize the churches in the political realm, or to say that they were incompetent in that regard. The "real dilemma" arose when church members believe they will be punished for not following their bishops and clergy.[12]

Connell wrote a congratulatory note to Bishop McManus, who was visiting Brooklyn at the time, complaining that it was "sad to see so many Catholics, including prelates, trying to cover the Church's doctrine that the bishop has the right to declare what is right or wrong, particularly when there is question of a sinful political measure. I am sure that St. Athanasius and St. John Chrysostom didn't worry about prestige and worldly prudence when they proclaimed the true doctrine. Keep it up."[13]

Meanwhile, Governor Marin fired off a telegram of outrage to his mentor, Walter Lippmann, informing him that he was "calling [a]press conference this afternoon to condemn before the American people this incredible medieval interference in political campaign [sic] under the American flag as well as under the Puerto Rican Constitution."[14]

Three weeks later, Marin cabled Lippmann to report with great relief "the people of Puerto Rico have shown democratic maturity of great quality in being able, as a Catholic people, to vote against very strict and very explicit and specific orders of all their bishops."[15]

Marin had long been an ardent admirer of America. He wrote an article for the July, 1954 edition of *Foreign Affairs* entitled "Puerto Rico and the U.S., Their Future Together" in which he discussed Puerto Rico's future with the US. While Governor, he gave a talk at Harvard on June 16, 1955 in which he laid out his efforts to deal with the poorest people. At the same time he was leading the Puerto Ricans "further into political freedom – not a freedom of narrowness and isolation, but one of genuine brotherhood with free men everywhere" and improving the economic situation overall by increasing production.[16] Marin was also a favorite of Time, Inc. and C.D. Jackson, who identified himself as "a Munoz-Marin enthusiast from way back" as his way of arranging an interview with "my good friend and colleague John Scott, of TIME."[17]

In an October 27 interview which he gave while visiting in Mobile, Alabama, Vagnozzi distanced himself from the statement of the Puerto Rican Bishops, saying that "the Catholic bishops of the United States have never taken any position similar to that taken by the bishops of Puerto Rico. I am confident, also, no such action would ever be taken by the hierarchy in this country."[18] Cardinal Cushing reinforced the idea there was a difference between American Catholicism and a Latin Catholicism by shamelessly condemning his fellow prelates from Puerto Rico as "totally out of step." While not mentioning the Puerto Rican situation, he did say that "all church leaders" had an obligation to speak out against evils like Nazism and Communism. Cushing went on to say: "With all this said, however, we must repeat that whatever may be the custom elsewhere, the American tradition of which Catholics form so loyal a part is satisfied simply to call to public attention moral questions with their implications and leave to the conscience of the people the specific political decision which comes in the act of voting."[19]

Professor and Dean of Students, Jerome Kerwin, of the University of Chicago wrote that the Puerto Rican bishops had a legitimate complaint against Marin, whose actions were in the area in which morals and politics meet. Dean Kerwin said the separation of church and state was not violated. By opposing the outlawing of birth control and sterilization, recognizing common law marriages, and refusing to give students time off for religious training, Marin went against Catholic doctrine.[20] To his credit, Kerwin saw that Marin's actions were not based on the moral or Divine Positive Law and so were not in accord with Catholic doctrine.

Predictably, *America* attacked the Puerto Rican bishops. In the November 5, 1960 edition, its editors commented that "the U.S. Catholic remains profoundly confused and bewildered – not to say embarrassed – by the action of the bishops of Puerto Rico. In a joint pastoral read in all their churches on October 23, they forbade Catholics to vote, in that Commonwealth's November 8 elections, for the Popular Democratic Party [PDP] headed by Gov. Luis Munoz Marin."[21] The article proceeded to differentiate Latin Catholics from American Catholics. The Latin temperament and Latin politics were different from those in the US and other Anglo-Saxon countries, whose prelates stand in the best position to evaluate the moral nature of various activities and the morality of certain policies. The PDP had "consistently advanced public policies offensive to the moral sense of Catholics and alien to the traditions of the Puerto Ricans." No "Catholic should presume to pass definitive judgment on actions taken by responsible Church leaders in distant regions under circumstances difficult to evaluate." In France, the prelates issued a statement concerned with the "grave declaration on the moral problems posed by the continuing conflict between the Government of France and the Algerian nationalists" and the French listened respectfully.[22]

America then wondered: "Is the attempt to use Church authority to determine, by formal prohibition, how a man votes, an action that is necessary or desirable in this country?" In France, information was given on how one may inform one's conscience. In Puerto Rico, a "suggestion of coercive action by ecclesiastical spokesmen" was presented in "that very area of civic life, the voting booth, which a democratic state necessarily surrounds with a maximum of privacy and independence." The voting booth was supposedly where the "individual citizen is presumed to be able to come to a free decision – a choice enlightened, it may be, by the guidance of those he trusts and reveres, but a choice responsibly made by himself." The events in Puerto Rico were regrettable, *America* held, because the Church's prestige was at stake, and there was a threat of embittering that commonwealth.[23]

The editorial assured its readers, and the world, that these events affect American Catholicism, which held an "unquestioning conviction – inculcated, by the way, in the parochial schools now flourishing in this free country – that human dignity and the freedom of the Church have been and will remain best guaranteed by the wholehearted and unswerving support all Americans pledge to the democratic rules that lie at the core of our most cherished civic institutions."[24]

CHAPTER 75
"YOU CAN'T BE A LOYAL AMERICAN AND A LOYAL CATHOLIC"

Robert G. Hoyt, the editor of *Catholic Reporter*, the Kansas City-St Joseph diocesan weekly newspaper, and founder in 1964 of the *National Catholic Reporter*, wrote an editorial in *America* in which he reviewed the US presidential campaign. The election was not "one between religion and irreligion, nor is it concerned with the broad relationship of Catholicism and the social order. Insofar as it can be rationally formulated, it is focused on the narrower issue of religious freedom." The issue, put simply, is that "'Catholics can't believe in the First Amendment,' or more crudely: 'You can't be a loyal American and a loyal Catholic.'"[1] The group responsible for formulating the question this way--"Protestants, clergymen, and the fundamentalist and evangelical 'sects' to a much greater extent than from the older Protestant denominations—was composed of bigots and the psychologically disturbed, who had used the same phrases in 1628 to refuse the franchise to Catholics in Massachusetts Bay."[2]

In spite of the bigots, key Protestants endorsed JFK, most notably Reinhold Niebuhr and John C. Bennett, who in 1958 wrote *Christians and the State* which "supplied the community of Protestant scholars with sympathetic insights into Catholic views on

Church and State." The list of Protestant Kennedy supporters included Martin Marty, an editor of the *Christian Century*; Lutheran theologian Dr. Jaroslav Pelikan; Episcopalian Bishop Arthur Lichtenberger; Dr. Listen Pope, Dean of Yale University Divinity School; and Robert McAfee Brown. Noted publications supporting JFK were *Living Church* (Episcopalian), *Christianity and Crisis* (with Niebuhr and Bennett), *Presbyterian Life,* and *World Outlook* (Methodist). The Jews, according to Leo Pfeffer, stated that the "establishment of pluralism was demonstrated 32 years ago by the nomination of Al Smith." Sociologist Will Herberg stated "Protestants themselves interiorly think of their faith as one of the `three great religions of democracy,' rather than as a national American religion."[3]

Protestants, according to Hoyt, were sympathetic to JFK "because religious conflict is socially disruptive and economically wasteful." Those who opposed a Catholic in the White House, were, according to Hoyt, most identified with opposition to the "social gospel, the ecumenical and liturgical movements, the World Council of Churches, the welfare state and political negotiation with Russia." They feel "that the national Council of Churches (representing, for the most part, the historic Protestant denominations) is heavily infiltrated with Communist agents or fellow travelers." [4]

Catholics reacted to anti-Catholic rhetoric with a combination of anger, bewilderment, and inner disturbance because the average Catholic:

"knows that he has never heard his teachers or his pastors attack democracy or the American system – on the contrary, he has recited the Pledge of Allegiance thousands of times, he has been taught to honor George Washington and Abraham Lincoln, to revere the Declaration of Independence and the constitution, to see America as a land of opportunity not only for himself but for the Church – and strictly on American terms. If he has encountered a textbook like Ryan and Boland' s *Catholic Principles of Politics* at all, he regards its theories for what they are: ideas out of a textbook without practical present or future application to the circumstances he knows. If he has heard anything at all about political matters from the pulpit of his parish church, it has been either generalized and platitudinous, or directed to an immediate moral issue, that sort of thing almost all American churches feel licensed to comment upon."[5]

Overall, Hoyt believed that the Church "does not stand to gain or lose greatly from the election itself. The general trend toward the integration of Catholics into the life of the country was not begun by Kennedy" and his success or failure was not determinative. "The important question," Hoyt wrote was "not whether this trend continues, but whether Catholics will be able to preserve and deepen their Catholicity as they assume the responsibilities and privileges of full civic and social acceptance. The question is not only what Catholics stand to gain, but what they have to offer." One of the beneficial effects of the election was to increase "the degree of theological sophistication among American Catholics." This was good because "too many have been content with a catechism knowledge of the faith, with a concept of Catholic truth as a set of verbal propositions unaffected by changing realities, demanding assent but not understanding."[6]

CHAPTER 76
WE HOLD THESE TRUTHS

On November 8, 1960, John F. Kennedy was elected president of the United States by the narrowest margin of the Twentieth Century. His opponent, Richard Nixon, actually won more states than Kennedy, but Kennedy won the states with larger populations and therefore more electoral votes. Many attributed his narrow margin to the efforts of big city machines in places like Chicago, which had large Catholic populations, fueling renewed fears of Catholic political power. In analyzing the outcome, the NCWC News Service ran a piece which held that Kennedy got elected because his religion won votes in the industrial states of the northeast and east, in the big cities where Catholics were concentrated, and because the anti-Catholic protest vote of "vast proportions…failed to materialize." The Catholic press called it a "defeat for bigotry" while *Time* magazine wrote that "in many Protestant areas….Kennedy's Catholicism seems not to have worked against him."[1]

Arthur Krock and John Wickleim of *The New York Times* wrote that the election proved that "Catholic voters have greater influence on the electoral result than Protestants." Secular publications called Kennedy's election a blow against bigotry and a victory for religious tolerance. The *New York Catholic News* wrote the election "made it impossible for the anti-Catholics to boast that they have the power to violate the Constitution and apply the religious test to a Catholic candidate for the White House." The *Pittsburgh Catholic* stated the election "dramatized that Protestant clericalism is as outmoded as Catholic clericalism would be out of order." The *Catholic Review* from Baltimore wrote "Catholics no longer have the excuse that the fear of prejudice and misunderstanding has denied them a full share in American government." And the Davenport, Iowa *Catholic Messenger* wrote the election of JFK was an indication "'an unwritten religious test for the presidency has been abolished.'"[2]

WE HOLD THESE TRUTHS

Fr. Connell sent JFK a letter a week after the election advising him that a president should greet Catholic prelates with "a simple handshake."[3] A couple of weeks later when *Time* asked for copies of *American Ecclesiastical Review* and his photo, Connell realized *Time* magazine was doing a story on Murray and his views on church-state relations. In a note to the Apostolic Nuncio, Connell presumed

"the purpose of the article will be to extol the doctrine of Fr. Murray as truly 'American' in that Msgr. Fenton and myself (and perhaps Cardinal Ottaviani) as outmoded and 'un-American.' I am more and more fearful that in the United States we are developing an 'American church,' that some day may go into schism or heresy. I shall let Your Excellency know if there are any further developments. In any event, I hope to see beforehand what TIME plans to publish from my writings, with the hope that they will be correctly presented."[4]

The December 12, 1960 *Time* magazine did indeed feature a cover story on Murray's book, *We Hold These Truths*, with an idealized portrait of Murray on the cover and a banner in the upper right hand corner that read "Catholics and the State." *Time* was telling the Catholics America was organized in accordance with Catholic doctrine, and Murray was the guy who figured it out. At the same time, Murray was calling America back to its roots.

The seven-page article was largely written by Douglas Auchincloss, the religion editor for *Time* and occasional paramour of Harry's lover, Lady Jeanne Campbell. Auchincloss's article gave a glowing exposition of Murray's thought and elevated him to a position of pre-eminence among Catholic theologians, from which Murray was now "telling his fellow Catholics that they must become more intellectually aware of their `coexistence' in a pluralist, heavily Protestant society."[5]

The article began with a bit of flattery by claiming America needed Catholics because they could make a "decisive contribution" to "an American society in spiritual crisis."[6] The article proceeded to divide Catholics and play them against each other by portraying Murray as the good guy in a drama that was playing out in the Catholic world. He was "liberal and eloquent," presented "lucid, well-modulated" arguments, and had risen to "eminence among the *cognoscenti*" for his learned work. He argued for government funding of parochial schools, but said "Catholic pressure for it should be confined to argument and slow persuasion." When it came to movies and books, or "censorship," he upheld "the right of the church to guide its own faithful and to convince others with its moral judgments, but by persuasion, not boycotts." Murray was "generally in favor of the U.S. version of church-state separation" which permitted the government to look after the "earthly well-being" of people while the churches were "guiding them toward salvation." Murray claimed that church state separation was a Christian principle and the only reason that Pope Leo III crowned Charlemagne in 800 AD was "because it was 800 AD."[7]

The church state issue in the 1960 presidential election brought out the need for an "American public philosophy, which must provide a kind of spiritual charter by which all Americans can live together." It must be based on "constitutional consensus whereby the people acquires its identity as a people and the society is endowed with its vital form...its sense of purpose as a collectivity organized for action in history." This consensus, in turn, was based on "right reason" which leads one to discover "self-evident truths" which were "ultimate, universal truths" that could be "perceived by human reason." These included the need for virtue to guarantee freedom, individual and inward governance by the moral law, limited government, the guidance from laws, and reliance on God. *Time* asked the critical question: "Whose reason is right?" To this Murray with "an urbane, engaging smile…popes it: natural law." "Natural law," *Time* explained, was a "law of man's nature" existing prior to the laws men enact in society, and per Murray, it was "the meeting place" of power and morality so that a moral solution could be reached for the big issues of the day.[8]

The catch came when Auchincloss wrote the "content of natural law may change with time and circumstance" and cited as an example the lending of money at interest or usury. Condemned by the Church as being against natural law in the Middle Ages, with the rise of Calvinism and the proliferation of middle-class lenders it was no longer condemned by the Church. The American Founders got their idea of the natural law from John Locke, whose emphasis on the individual was far different from that of the Catholic view. Murray did not like Locke's natural law but "when pressed . . . concedes that Locke's natural law is better than no natural law at all, and throughout much of US history, the concept, appeared in the courts and in government." Somehow, the US and the Bill of Rights were products of "Christian history" having sprung out of the Christian Middle Ages and bypassed 250 years of Protestant history.[9]

Unfortunately, the concept of natural law fell into decline with the rise of Protestant theology and "modern rationalist philosophy." Both Protestants and Jews rejected St. Paul's statement in Romans 2:14-15 that justified the idea of a natural law knowable by men. This coupled with the rejection of the Scholastic tradition which "keeps man from direct contact with God by interposing an artificial structure of reason" meant that most Americans no longer believed that the natural law could be the basis of the American consensus.

Catholics were to restore that consensus because "contents of this consensus – the ethical and political principles drawn from the tradition of natural law – approve themselves to the Catholic intelligence and conscience." Catholics were the "true custodians of the American consensus," and so "a new era has begun for Catholics in America, a country that in itself represents a new era in the history of church and state."[10]

Time needed Murray as its expert because he could claim the Catholics were the inventors of the principle of the separation of church and state. According to Murray, the "idea that religion and government are different – let alone separate – is a relatively new one," which the Catholics under Pope Gelasius I discovered in 494. According to Murray, the Gelasian principle established a "freedom of the Church" in the spiritual sphere by limiting the power of the government and bringing "moral consensus of the people to bear upon the King." This broke up beginning in the 1500s with what *Time* called the "'heresy'" of Protestantism. St. Robert Bellarmine, a Jesuit Cardinal, developed the idea that the papal jurisdiction over heads of state was only indirect and spiritual, and according to *Time,* he earned the hatred of "ecclesiastical conservatives."[11]

This led to another important dichotomy. Whereas the French Revolution led to a monism where the state was all powerful and a moral end in itself with the state's control over the church, the American Revolution was a "conservation, in that it revived the old freedom of the church" according to Murray. The Church in America, since 1783, was "free to work and witness as it saw fit, without special privileges but also without requiring a whole chain of consent from secular government." The US system established a "nation under God" that allowed people to worship as they saw fit because "God is best honored by free men." *Time* admitted that Catholics were bound to "acknowledge the One True Church," but American Catholics saw that the situation in the US gave then "unprecedented freedom to grow." Catholics were growing at a rate faster than the rest of the country, and, according to Murray, contributing to the "civic machinery and the need for consensus beneath it." Reinhold Niebuhr commented Murray could think as a Catholic theologian and in accordance with American tradition all at the same time.[12]

Time portrayed Murray as an American voice which the Catholic conservatives were trying to silence. After mentioning briefly the circumstances of his birth and entry into the Jesuit order, *Time* noted Murray "is still the debater (and more subtly the actor)....Theologian Murray makes effective use of his long, well-manicured hands and his well-pitched baritone, which is as clear as his well-organized thought." *Time* then adverted to Murray's confrontation in the early 1950s with Father Connell and Msgr. Fenton in the pages of the *American Ecclesiastical Review*, after which Murray was told "henceforth he would have to clear all his writings on this particular subject with Jesuit headquarters in Rome."[13]

By putting Murray on its cover, *Time* declared Murray the victor in that confrontation and simultaneously anointed Murray as America's pre-eminent Catholic theologian. So powerful was *Time's* endorsement that the Catholic press could do nothing but say "Amen" and reiterate what *Time* had said. The message was clear to Catholics – think and talk like Murray if you want worldly success and acceptance. And without a moment's hesitation the chattering classes—Protestant, Catholic, and Jew—joined in the chorus of praise that Murray received after the *Time* article. Secular publications such as *Harper's*, the *Yale Review*, and *The Saturday Review* joined *Commonweal* and *America* in effusive praise of Murray and his doctrine. In particular, *Commonweal* noted that "whatever the final judgment of history, there can be no doubt that Murray's theological work represents the most profound attempt yet made to establish the compatability [sic] of American pluralism and Catholicism." George Shuster remarked that Murray's work was a "development of American Catholic thinking about the social order at which this thinking came of age."[14]

The fact that Murray was still under censure from the Holy Office did nothing to stem the flood of invitations to speak before Catholic audiences coming in the wake of the *Time* article. On January 6,

1961 the *St Louis Review* reported Murray was scheduled for an appearance on the "Catholic Hour" Series on KSD-TV. He was to "give his reflections on the American experience and the national purpose,"[15] and his appearance was promoted by the National Council of Catholic Men.[16]

Honors soon followed from Catholic organizations equally oblivious to the Holy Office's censure. In the Spring of 1961 Murray's high school, Xavier High School in Manhattan, New York, recognized Murray's achievements by awarding him its Insignis Medal at the Annual Alumni Dinner in May. The announcement mentioned Murray was "a renowned theologian whose most widely read book is `We Hold These Truths'…is a sweeping review of state-church relationships and was published during the Presidential campaign. It was generally considered a clear statement of the Catholic position on responsibility of voters toward a Catholic candidate."[17]

During the same month, Murray received the Manhattan College St. John Baptist De La Salle Medal, an honor which was awarded "each year by the board of trustees at Manhattan College to a person who has made outstanding contributions to the education of American youth." Murray was "widely recognized as an authority on Catholic theology." In addition to listing his various academic achievements, the article noted that Murray "is a departmental editor for `Encyclopedia Britannica,' and is a consultant to the Center for the Study of Democratic Institutions Fund for the Republic, and the Institute of Ethics at the Jewish Theological Seminary of America." Murray received the Catholic Theological Association's Cardinal Spellman award for "contributions to theological scholarship."[18]

FENTON AND CONNELL RESPOND

Fenton was in Rome preparing for the upcoming Ecumenical Council when the *Time* article on Murray appeared. In a letter dated December 7, 1960, Fenton told Connell that he would not let *Time* take his picture for the article because "had no desire to be dragged behind J. Courtney's chariot wheels." Fenton also refused to answer any of *Time*'s questions and hoped Connell would "deal with the matter in AER as soon as possible," promising that "I shall write an article on it, if God lets me, when I return."[19]

Five days later, Fenton dined with Ottaviani, who, after asking Fenton to "write a Latin summary of the history of this discussion in the USA," opined "something must be done on this topic very soon. I told him that something must be done also on the dogma of the necessity of the Church for salvation. And I told him how the Catholics in the USA, as a group, are convinced that the Church has changed or softened its teaching on this point as a result of the uncontradicted stories in the papers."[20]

A few days after dinner with Ottaviani, while still at work on the Pontifical Theological Commission in preparation for the upcoming Council, Fenton received two letters on the *Time* article which convinced him that Murray "has gotten away with an open insult to the Holy Office and its Cardinal. And he has profited from it."[21] Fenton had doubts about Vagnozzi, and, indeed, doubts about the entire leadership of the Church. These doubts deepened as time passed and the assault against the Church and its doctrine around the world became more apparent.

In a letter to Connell dated January 23, 1961, Fenton wrote "It is now apparent that Romeo is right, and that there is…[a] world-wide movement against orthodoxy in the Church." The Jesuits seemed to be in forefront of the attack as Fenton wrote "It is tough on the Jebbies that their men happened to be the ones who were caught."[22]

In the meantime, Vagnozzi asked Connell to review Murray's book. The book consisted of thirteen chapters, each of which was an article that Murray had written between 1950 and 1958. Editor Scharper assembled the book with Murray's concurrence. Murray included in the book was his article "The Problem of Pluralism in America" which appeared in the Summer, 1954 edition of *Thought* Magazine. Lippmann glowingly referenced this article in his 1955 book, *Essays on the Public Philosophy*, and that recognition further signaled the approval of Murray's work by the Americans. The book contained a chapter condemning Communism which comported with the Americans' doctrinal warfare program, provided an argument in favor of public aid for parochial schools which was a popular topic with the American Catholic hierarchy, and discussed the Catholic doctrine on the conditions needed for just war.

Connell found the review of Murray's book difficult because he "had to read and reread the book several times in order to find out just what the author means and to give a fair, objective judgment." After apologizing for the delay in doing the review, Connell summarized the essential problem with Murray's position. Murray "still holds that the government of a state is bound only by the natural law, not by the law of Christ. Such a view is not only opposed to Catholic tradition, but would also lead to disastrous consequences, such as the denial of the Church's authority over the marriages of all baptized persons, including non-Catholics." Connell concluded his review by hoping that "the Holy See will make a public statement on this matter in the near future, for many American Catholics are accepting Father Murray's theory, which is so closely in accord with American ideas of separation of Church and State."[23] Connell's

"chief objection to this book is the fact that it undoubtedly gives the average reader the impression that the American system of separation of Church and State and the absence of special preference for the true Church of Jesus Christ is per se the ideal, in contradistinction to the traditional Catholic doctrine, according to which some form of union between the State and the Catholic Church is per se the ideal (thesis), so that complete equality of all religions must be regarded as something which per accidens can be merely tolerated in order to avoid greater evils (hypothesis). Such surely was the doctrine of Pope Leo XIII [who claimed]: 'In...truth, though the Church judges that it is not lawful to grant the various types of divine cult the same rights as the true religion, it does not condemn those civil rulers who, for the sake of attaining some good or of preventing some evil, tolerate in custom and use that they all have a place in the state.'"[24]

Connell explained that Murray's position had not changed since the publication of his 1948 paper, "The Governmental Repression of Heresy":

"Fr. Murray held that the government of any state, even of a Catholic state, is bound only by the natural law, not by the positive law of Christ. In fact he says, the state 'knows nothing' of the basic source of the Church's power to teach all truth (p. 73). Of course, if the government cannot recognize the unique right of the Catholic Church to preach divine truth, there can be no acknowledgment of the Church as the true Church of Jesus Christ, the essential feature of Church-State union. But surely, the persons who govern a state can recognize the Church in their official capacity just as easily as they can recognize it as private individuals....And that civil rulers are bound per se to recognize the Catholic Church and to acknowledge its prerogatives and rights as surely a traditional Catholic doctrine, which can be demonstrated by convincing arguments."[25]

Murray's position resulted in a contradiction that Murray could not explain away:

"One argument, which was brought up against Fr. Murray's view when he read his paper in Chicago in 1948 was this: 'The Church claims to possess by divine-positive law from Jesus Christ the right to make impediments for the marriages of all baptized persons. If the state is bound only by the natural law, the state has a right to reject this claim of the Church. In such an event a marriage could be valid by the natural law and invalid by the Church's application of the divine-positive law. Thus, there could be a contradiction between the natural law of God and the divine-positive law of Jesus Christ.' He could give no satisfactory answer."[26]

Murray, Connell continued, mentions "Nowhere in this book . . . that per se there should be any form of union between the State and the Catholic Church." Nor does he mention that "'the Church cannot approve the complete separation between the two Powers (Church and State)' (Essa per principio, ossia in tesi, non puo approvare la complete separazione fra i due Poteri) (AAS, 1953,

802)." Nor did Murray mention Pius XII's statement that "'That which does not correspond to the truth and to the moral norm has not objectively any right to exist, to be spread or to be activated' (AAS, 1953, p. 799)." Murray ignored the Papal statement as he had since the beginning of the debate claimed that the statement "Error has no rights" was "meaningless" and "hardly a `principle' from which to draw any conclusions with regard to the powers of the state..."[27]

One of the most important statements that Murray omitted was from Leo XIII, specifically paragraph 6 of the encyclical *Longinqua Oceani* which statement is that while "although all this is true, it would be erroneous to conclude that from America is to be sought the example of the best condition of the Church, or that it is universally lawful and expedient for civil and religious matters to be dissociated, as in America.'" [28]

Ignoring some Papal statements, either Murray made up others or provided interpretations that were not warranted. Such was the situation with Pius XII's *Ci riesce* in which the pope said "objective truth and the obligation of conscience toward that which is objectively true and good...can hardly be made the object of discussion and ruling among the individual states and their communities, especially in the case of a plurality of religious confessions." Murray wrote this meant "Government is not a judge of religious truth; parliaments are not to play the theologian" when in reality the pope meant the government still has the right and ability, albeit difficult, "to distinguish a false religion from the true religion." Murray invented meaning with Pius IX's *Syllabus of Errors* and Leo's various pronouncements, claiming these popes' various condemnations of Continental ideologies and not "freedom of religion and of separation of Church and State." Connell made clear the "documents in question made no such distinction as Fr. Murray attributes to them; hence, they should be understood in their literal sense as rejecting separation of church and state as per se the most desirable system." [29]

However, despite his objective, and scathing critique, Connell made a curious comment that must have resonated in the mind of Vagnozzi and the Church hierarchy. Connell wrote Murray's "assertion that the Catholics of the United States are fully in accord with the actual modus vivendi of their land, whereby all religious groups receive freedom and equal treatments, represents the mind of the hierarchy and of all intelligent Catholics."[30] While Murray's doctrine was contradictory and at odds with Catholic doctrine, it really did not matter since the hierarchy and "all intelligent Catholics" were not willing to implement Catholic doctrine.

As Murray's erroneous positions remained constant, so did Luce's support. With *Time's* massive publicity engine behind it, Murray's book was having a dangerous impact. Connell noted that *We Hold These Truths* was "acclaimed the Catholic book of the year" and it was exerting "an influence among millions of...Catholics and non-Catholics." Positive reviews had appeared in *Time, The Saturday Review, Information, Ave Maria,* and *The Critic.* Additionally, J. B. O'Neill gave Murray's book a positive review in the "Notice of the Catholic Book Club." Not one of the Catholic reviewers mentioned the sections of the book dealing with Church state relations that may have caused concern in Rome, but *Time, Life,* and *Theological Digest* did. The Winter 1961 issue of *Theological Digest* proclaimed Murray's "line of reasoning will prevail 'since it is abreast of current social and political developments, whereas the older line is antiquated'" and *We Hold These Truths* sets out the "rules of the game for inter-faith relations."[31]

Connell concluded his memorandum to the Apostolic Delegate with a plea for a "clear and public decision from the Holy See . . . to settle the doctrinal problem that is now causing such confusion among Catholics in the United States." If Murray's doctrine was upheld, then those holding to the traditional view of the Church would obey though "there will be in that case great exultation among the enemies of the Church, because they will declare that the Church has at last changed its teachings." Should the "Holy See pronounce... the doctrine of Fr. Murray erroneous, I believe it should be done as soon as possible, so that no further harm may come. Whatever pronouncement the Holy See makes, will be the voice of Christ."[32]

A week after this memorandum, Connell sent to Vagnozzi another letter in which he included other reviews of *We Hold These Truths*. The reviews confirmed Connell's suspicion Murray was "proposing a doctrine contrary to the traditional Catholic notion of the relation between Church and State." Again, Connell urged the Holy See to issue "a definite and public statement . . . either for or against Fr. Murray's doctrine. . . . " As if to add emphasis, Connell cited a review which appeared in *The Commonweal* written by Daniel Callahan. He wrote Murray "brilliantly brings together very diverse intellectual gifts – theological, political, judicial – to show that the famous papal condemnations of the separation of Church and State which appeared regularly in the second half of the 19th century simply do not apply to the American situation."[33]

PART XVII
PREPARING FOR VATICAN II (1960-1962)

CHAPTER 77
GOING INTO A PERIOD OF DOCTRINAL ANARCHY

On the morning of October 26, 1960, Msgr. Joseph Fenton, along with the other members of the Pontifical Theological Commission and the theological preparatory committee, took the oath of secrecy. They were told when the various commissions and committees were meeting. Fenton described in his diary the first meeting of the Commission as "by far the most solemn affair I have ever attended." Fenton describe the first session:

"clearly the most important meeting I have ever entered and . . . in some ways the most important meeting of the 20th century. I pray God that I shall not fail His cause during the weeks of terribly hard work that lie ahead. The Cardinal President made it clear that during the course of our discussions some of the secrets of the Holy Office will have to be revealed to us.... I shall never forget the evening with Bishop Griffith. And of course I shall never forget the first meeting of the Pontifical Theological Commission."[1]

Fenton was clearly humbled by the call to serve in Rome. "It still seems like a dream," he wrote in his diary, "that I should have been chosen for the theological commission and then for the subcommittee. God has been exceptionally good to me. I hope I shall not show myself recreant to His gracious kindness."[2] His sense of God's kindness was undoubtedly tempered by the fact that earlier in the year he suffered a heart attack and spent the summer recovering. In July he was "officially notified through NCWC that I was a member of the Pontifical Theological Commission for the forthcoming Second Ecumenical Vatican Council,"[3] and Connell congratulated him promptly.[4]

Fenton's committee came about through the Papal Bull, *Superno Dei Nutu*, which established ten commissions, a central coordinating commission devoted to "study of the matters which it will be possible to have discussed at the council," a secretariat to field questions from the media, and a secretariat concerned with questions of Christian duty.[5] By the Autumn of 1960, the list of members and consultors for the commissions and secretariats was complete. The Central Preparatory Commission, which set procedural rules, "consisted of 74 cardinals, bishops, patriarchs, archbishops, and heads of religious orders." It was busy "completing large volumes of proposals for subjects to be discussed at the council." The volumes of proposals, one from each country or geographic area, were "restricted to the various commissions" and were "not be made public until the council is in progress." This central commission included Spellman, James Cardinal McIntyre of Los Angeles, Aloisius Cardinal Muench from the central administrative offices in Vatican City, Archbishop Karl Alter of Cincinnati, and Archbishop Lawrence Graner, CSC of Dacca, Pakistan. The Theological Commission included Bishop John J Wright of Pittsburgh, Auxiliary Bishop James H. Griffiths of New York, and Fenton. Archbishop O'Boyle of Washington was a consultor for the Commission for Studies and Seminaries, and Bishop Fulton J. Sheen was a member of the Commission of the Lay Apostolate. A consultor for the Secretariat for Christian Unity was Gustave Weigel, SJ. [6]

DOCTRINAL ANARCHY

Fenton came to Rome highly esteemed by Vagnozzi, who "praised me highly when he was over here, and had mentioned my work to the Pope" but "not particularly popular with [Cardinal] Pizzardo and with [Bishop] Staffa,"[7] the leaders of the Sacred Congregation of the Seminaries and Universities. Fenton knew for some time that things were not right in Rome. Earlier in the year while suffering from influenza, Fenton told Connell that "some of the recent views of the New Testament do not seem to be reconcilable with statements by Pope Pius X in regard to Modernism."[8] Connell so advised Ottaviani, who also felt that "certain scholars are not so much using, as abusing the freedom and encouragement to study given them by His Holiness, Pope Pius XII." Ottaviani urged Connell to "collect some of these recent and questionable views so that an eventual study might be made of them."[9]

Shortly after starting work on the preparatory commissions, Fenton saw the depth of the problems. The council was becoming a circus run by "clowns" and heretical Jesuits. The result was "low morale" among the faithful who were "convinced that some of these men are actually trying to change the Church...." [10] One week after his arrival in Rome, Fenton was asking Connell for help, in person if possible. "Your presence [in Rome]," he wrote to Connell, "would be providential" because "we are going into a period of doctrinal anarchy."[11] A deadly materialist and worldly spirit that was leading to a loss of faith had infected the leadership of the Church, which "is being run by men who have no concern whatsoever for the purity or the integrity of Catholic doctrine." But in spite of everything, Fenton remained optimistic because "when the chips are down, the doctrine of Christ always comes through."[12]

Over the short haul, however, there was reason for concern. While attending a party thrown by Cardinal Ottaviani, Fenton was approached by someone he identified as a "Count (or Commendatore), who whispered to me that the keys of St. Peter open everything." The count, who was evidently a Mason, "was astonished and a little frightened" when Fenton, the earnest American, "answered severely that they were for the kingdom of heaven only and that to use them is an abuse." The incident left Fenton shaken. "There does not seem to be too much real faith over here," he concluded gloomily.[13] Even those who understood the value of Catholic doctrine, like "the Oriental Congregation, over which Chick [Cardinal Cicognani] presides" seemed to value it "only for the sake of making an impression on those outside the Church." Fenton found that attitude particularly appalling, and he referred to it as "the unhealthiest symptom apparent over here. If we really believe that the teaching of the Church is the salutary doctrine of Christ, as the First Vatican Council says, then this teaching is worthwhile for its own sake."[14]

In the midst of his bewilderment, Fenton received a ray of clarity about the political undercurrents at the council from Msgr. DiMeglio, who told him that "a great many very distinguished people had protested against my inclusion on the Commission, and that one of those who had protested most bitterly was Spellman. I never realized that the old boy was that dirty." Spellman's betrayal "explains a good deal, and it is obviously behind the behavior of [Sebastian] Tromp."[15] Even more disconcerting revelations were coming:

"DiMeglio was quite astonished to find that Weigel and Tavard are consultors on the Bea secretariats. And he did not know about the new book by Murray. He is going to see the Cardinal now. He told me that in 1958 he was working on the elaboration of an encyclical on Church & State, but that the death of the Pope broke up all those plans. He thought that old Chick was weak in his handling of the Church in the USA. And he was aware of the fact that Vagnozzi is unpopular with the American Bishops. He is also aware of the fact that the real trouble in the Church in our country is due to a faulty choice of bishops. Perhaps he can do something about it. I do not know. I hope he can."[16]

Fenton concluded his entry by writing "This was one of the most enlightening conversations I have ever had in my life. One thing is certain. I definitely have the power of arousing the antipathy of the liberal Catholics. And my position on this Commission is a more precious thing than perhaps I realized. Now I am not in such a rush to get back to Washington."[17]

Fenton tried to rehabilitate the Jesuit, Fr. Feeney. He emphasized the importance of the doctrine, "*extra ecclesium nulla salus*," in a meeting with Ottaviani on November 15, after which he observed to Jesuit Father Edouard Dhanis "that there is no mention of the necessity of the Church in the report of the Caysino subcommission. And I told him that the Council should speak out on that point for the good of souls in the USA." Once again, Fenton was disappointed by the Jesuits, finding Dhanis "woefully misinformed on the whole situation, and none too sturdy on the doctrine itself. The American Jebbies have really done a publicity job on this case. I told him that, thanks to the mishandling of the entire case, many if not most of our American Catholic people are honestly convicted that the Church has in some way abandoned the dogma that there is no salvation outside the Church."[18]

Fenton found sympathetic ears at the Holy Office. After telling one official "the cause of Christ in the world will be harmed rather than advanced if the council does not come out forcefully on the necessity of the Church for salvation," Fenton was told "God has put me on this Theological Commission and on this particular subcommission"[19] to make clear the necessity of the Church for salvation.[20]

But *extra ecclesiam nulla salus* was not the only doctrine concerning Fenton. Heavy on his mind and in his heart were the four secret propositions Apostolic Delegate to the US Archbishop Cicognani handed to both him and Connell on October 28, 1954. Fenton made frequent references to these "*Proposizioni Dottrinali Erronee*" which condemned the following propositions:

"a) The catholic confessional state, professing itself as such is not an ideal to which organized political society is universally obliged; b) Full religious liberty can be considered as a valid political idea in a truly democratic State; c) The state organized on a genuinely democratic basis must be considered to have done its duty when it has guaranteed the freedom of the church by a general guarantee of liberty of religion; d) It is true that Leo XIII has said: `...*civitates... debent eum in colendo nomine morem usurpare quo coli se Deus. Ipse demonstravit velle.' (Enc. Immortale Dei).* Words such as these can be understood as referring to the state considered as organized on a basis other than that of the perfectly democratic state."[21]

Fenton was determined to submit "the teaching embodying the contradictions to these four condemned propositions" to the forthcoming council, so that the true Catholic position on Church state relations and religious liberty could be "set forth by the Council itself." "I shall try my best," Fenton wrote in his diary on January 28, 1961, "to get this doctrine into the schema on the Church. At the moment I would not bet much on my chances for success."[22] In spite of the fact that Ottaviani asked Fenton to "write a brief schema of the things that should be treated," his pessimism was justified. Another theologian was asked to write the *votum*, and Fenton's 78 theses were ignored.[23]

CHAPTER 78
INFECTED WITH AMERICANISM

As a member of the Theological Preparatory Commission, Fenton came in close contact with the "great minds" of the day. Fenton observed the intellectual firepower of the Church had gone "liberal," rendering him and Connell a beleaguered minority. Perhaps a better way to put it was that Connell and Fenton remained Catholic, while the rest of the Church's intellectual and episcopal leadership had become Americanists. The Vatican was inordinately concerned about what others thought, a dangerous dynamic in an institution that so highly prized the pursuit of truth. Rumors were "circulating that the Council is going to be a `Fenton Ottaviani Council and nothing will be done.'" During one of the many parties that punctuated work on the council commissions, Fenton met "a typical left-wing theologian," an admirer of Teilhard de Chardin, Karl Rahner, and Yves Congar. Congar informed Fenton "the whole weight of European scholarship is with our opponents," and Fenton was forced to admit it was true. Fenton wrote "The crowd that likes Ottaviani in Europe and in the USA is indeed a very small minority, if we restrict ourselves to the so-called intelligentsia. But my point is that the great majority of the Catholic laity, confused though they may be in many ways, is with us all the way"[1] (his emphasis).

Fenton heard the same thing from Msgr. Jim Tucek and Msgr. Romeo, who told Fenton Ottaviani was "literally hated, by many of the men in high posts on the curia," forcing Fenton to conclude he and Connell were the only two Americans priests who "write and work like Ottaviani for doctrinal reasons."[2] Fenton knew the divide between the Ottaviani-Fenton camp and the "liberals" was so great that "Humanly speaking there is no possibility at all that we will convert any of the men opposed to us. Things have gone too far by this time." Fenton kept working despite these odds hoping to reach the "great majority of the Catholic laity" and gain their support because "otherwise it would be hard to see why we should continue the struggle."[3]

Fenton was aware of the antipathy against him and Ottaviani. The Americanists, led by Cardinal Spellman, exhibited "frightful hatred against me both here and in America." Spellman, was "one of those who had protested against my appointment, as a member of the theological commission,"[4] was indebted to Luce, both of whom were backing Murray. Americanism was just as big in Europe, according to the Bishop of Besancon, who "warns against Americanism." After working with Congar (whom Fenton described as "a little fellow with bulging eyebrows and the murky blue eyes of a fanatic"[5]) and reviewing various theologians' texts on the Church, Fenton concluded "the Americanism condemned by Leo XIII in Testem benevolentiae still lives on, and not only in America."[6]

VANITY, CAREERISM AND MORE AMONGST THE LEADERS

Fenton concluded the Church was "being run by vain and money-hungry cowards who are afraid of the manifest opponents of the true faith within the ranks." Such a situation allowed Americanism to flourish. In discussions with another priest assisting him in reviewing the various comments from bishops around the world, Fenton wrote

"We agreed that we had both made sacrifices to become priests, and that the disgrace and the danger of the Roman Church is to be found in the fact that many of the priests here are priests to improve their own social position. When they arrive, they are men without faith and without honor."[7]

The one person who could change all of this was the Pope himself, but the more Fenton contemplated the situation, the more troubled he became:

"I am quite discouraged myself.... Romeo made one remark to which I must make a great 'Amen.' He said that, where the faith is gone, there is no such thing as justice. Of course that is perfectly true as far as the infused virtues of justice is concerned. But I must not allow myself to forget that even the most mendacious liberal Catholic is obligated by the laws of justice, and that people like Cardinals, bishops, and delegates have no excuse for violating justice. Neither has the Pope. After all he could straighten all this mess out in a short time if he really wanted to. And he is the only one who can. The rest of them, especially the gang here in the curia, are absolutely hopeless."[8]

At the root of the Curia's problems Fenton discerned a love of the world, pride of the flesh, and the pride of life:

"The inner circle here lives on a diet of steady promotion....They go to foreign lands as diplomats mixing with and living like the richest of the rich. They occupy archbishoprics or fill-in posts. Then they return and drive around Rome in super-sized chauffeur driven German cars, and, at the top of the ladder, there is always the big prize.... Here are members of the Church who are obviously in a state of mortal sin. Some of them do not believe Our Lord's message at all...What nonsense!"[9]

As time passed, Fenton gradually lost faith in allies like Vagnozzi, who came to symbolize the careerism and self-serving nature of so many in the Church hierarchy. "What utterly disgusts me," he wrote in his diary, "is the cowardice of the men who claim to be working for the faith but who are, as a matter of fact, only working to gain promotion and money for themselves. And, from the way he talked, I am afraid that Vagnozzi is one of these" and after helping Vagnozzi's relative, when Fenton attracted enemies, then Vagnozzi treated him as a "persona non grata." Ottaviani was not "one of these," but age and the burdens of the council were starting to take their toll:

"The old boy's memory seems to be slipping badly. He told me once that he was quite anxious to have me write a judgment on Murray's latest book. He seems to have forgotten it entirely. He said that he was going to take me with him for that audience so that I could give some of my writings to the Pope. He seems to have forgotten all about that. And there are a lot of other things he has forgotten. There was a time when the old boy's word was as good as his bond. Those days are gone. He is obviously up to his neck in work, and too much of that work is political rather than religious."[10]

AN ASSAULT ON ORTHODOXY

Two months after sounding the warning about the impending doctrinal anarchy in the Church, Fenton concluded the assault on doctrine was being lead by the Jesuits. Msgr. Romeo's article in *Divinitas* "blasts off against two Jesuits from the Biblicum who are guilty of the same thing you caught Murray and Parsons doing years ago. They were teaching the error that the entire content of scripture studies was changed after the appearance of the Divino afflante spiritu." He added "All Rome is discussing the thing."[11] The Biblicum, where the Jesuits held sway, according to Fenton, "has become a center for anti-Catholic teaching here in Rome."[12] As a result, the faith of many seminarians was being undermined in devious ways[13] not the least of which included a tactic of writing something "bad on one page" but then correcting the error "several pages later" or calling the Modernist a "learned man even at the very moment that he is blundering most stupidly."[14]

Fenton took special aim at the movement that held "in order to know the literal meaning of a writing, it is necessary to know clearly [to be clearly aware of] the form or type of expression that the writer wished to use...." The reason for this "fever...about the literary forms of the various books that have been inspired by God, including the Gospels" came about in part "by a hyper-critical spirit which prescinds completely from the traditional teaching of the Church and from the conviction of believing Catholics which convictions are the faithful echo of the Church's traditional teaching. So it comes about that some, and too often even ecclesiastics, more or less explicitly eliminate from the historical plan accounts that are most important, as for example the narration of the first chapters of Genesis and of the Gospels."[15]

Fenton was not concerned about how the constitution on the Church was developing. It needed to implement *Humani Generis* and refute "errors in the field we are discussing today. One is the error of those who refuse to admit that the thing called the body of Christ in the Pauline epistles is exactly the same as the thing called the Roman Catholic Church. The other error is made by those who deny that the Roman Catholic Church is really necessary for the attainment of eternal salvation."[16] In refuting these errors, the constitution needed to be:

"based on the actual statements of the ecclesiastical magisterium, and not on some questionable inference that has been read into some statement of the magisterium. Furthermore it should be clear....Ambiguity is precisely what we must avoid. Definite errors are being taught, and it is the business of the Council to set forth the teaching of Christ in such a way that the faithful will no longer be in danger of falling into these errors."[17]

One of those involved in spreading those errors was a friend of Jacques Maritain, Charles Cardinal Journet, whom Fenton described as a "poor old half dead deaf man." Journet made a "fool of himself" when he said the "doctrine of the Church should be a corollary on the mystery of the Incarnation." Journet was one of those in favor of allowing the statement that "non-Catholics are members of the Church."[18]

Another was the Jesuit Sebastian Tromp with whom Fenton was at odds because of Tromp's pride and self-assurance that he alone could explain the nature of the Church. Tromp was a devotee of Murray, Fenton concluded, and so that made him and his motives subject to suspicion: "I know that Tromp is definitely a hostile person. He is manifestly of the J. Courtney Murray group, and would do anything to get me in trouble."[19] Fenton surmised that Tromp wanted to write the "de ecclesia schema and he wants to make it a simple recapitulation of his own books – This would be a disaster. Tromp, while learned in his own particular and extremely narrow field, is not able to co-operate. His whole attitude is built around the much-advertised fact that he 'wrote' the Mystici Corporis. He wants to be the man who 'wrote' the section on the Church for the Second Ecumenical Vatican Council."[20] Fenton did agree with Tromp that "the Council is not called upon to write a treatise in ecclesiology."[21] He also agreed with another subcommission member, Fr. Marie-Rosaire Gagnabet, OP, that the section on the Church was "simply to bring out those truths that are most misunderstood and most denied in this particular field. If we merely turn in a rewrite of Mystici Corporis with some of Tromp's later production, we shall definitely not be doing what we have been told to do."[22]

The votum on the Church was submitted by a priest Fenton did not consider to be a very good theologian. The votum had a number of deficiencies one of which was that the "teaching of the Church on membership within itself. Lattanyi gives his version of this teaching on a causal clause. It is not clear, and, to my mind it is dangerously ambiguous." Fenton concluded that parts were not even Catholic:

"We do not teach that those who are baptized and who have an implicit desire to enter the Church are necessarily closer to the Church than the unbaptized. The nearness obviously depends on the strength of the desire, the faith and the charity….It is not proper to speak of those who have an implicit and only an implicit desire to enter the Church as our brothers any more than anyone else. Our brothers in Christ, properly speaking, are all and only our fellow Catholics. There is a wider sense in which all men may be called

114

brothers. This notion that baptized people with an implicit desire to enter the Church are our brothers is a theological monstrosity."[23]

The votum, which became known as the Lattanyhi votum:

"does not mention faith or the profession of faith, which must be given, particularly in these days, in any accurate and adequate statement about the Church....St. Pius X in his Oath against the Modernists said that Our Lord had founded the Church 'while He was dwelling among us,' and had founded it 'immediately and directly.' Lattanyi does not touch on that." Fenton noted that "There is a bad ambiguity in the last sentence. He speaks of the 'Prophet, Priest, and King' mission and says that the successors of the Apostles exercise these functions under the Pope 'collegialite. [sic]' This is bad thinking. The ordinary priest with no Episcopal orders is not a successor of the Apostles and yet he exercises the power of a priest, and he does not do it collegiality [sic]."[24] Fenton insisted "The Council should obviously state again the dogma, set forth in Mystici Corporis and in Humani Generis, to the effect that the Catholic Church alone is the Mystical Body...."[25]

CHAPTER 79
BISHOPS, MORE TROUBLING LANGUAGE, AND DOUBT

During his work on the preparatory committee, Fenton dealt with the national agendas that were often at odds with each other and with the unity of the Church. The Germans made many good points about St. Augustine's ecclesiology and the unity and Catholicity of the Church, "but as usual they spoil it with their endless references to the separated brethren."[1] The Spaniards were not interested in placating the separated brethren. On the contrary, they knew they were under attack from the Americans, who were using Protestant sects to undermine the traditional teaching on Church state relations. As a result, the "Bishops of Spain want a new statement of public ecclesiastical law, and others want a statement on the confessional character of the State."[2]

The American bishops also wanted a statement on the relationship between Church and state, but one that was diametrically opposed to the statement the Spaniards wanted. After reviewing the documents from North America, Fenton was forced to conclude he had more in common with the Spaniards because "Alter and Dick Cushing are certainly against us on Church and State...."[3] Because of America's geopolitical pre-eminence after the war, the American bishops were in a position to intimidate Rome, a position the Americanists exploited by showing their determination to force through a statement on religious liberty. It was no secret the American episcopate was a potential threat to the center of the Church. "Our Maltese friend Micheloff," Fenton wrote in a diary entry, "came over for the daily gossip…We discussed the fact that, in general, Rome is afraid of strong American bishops."[4]

All the bishops seemed to have parochial and personal agendas because they seemed interested in "maintaining and improving their own positions in the Church. All the Bishops want more control over exempt religious communities. The Superior Generals of these communities want to keep their exemption, and for the most ridiculous reasons that I have ever seen."[5] Fenton was the first American theologian to read the book containing the responses of the bishops to Tardini's request during the antepreparatory days. He noted "It is interesting to see just how dissatisfied many of the bishops of the world are with the situation here."[6] This later comment suggested the presence of an organizational dynamic that pitted the edges, or the field, against the center, or the Curia. This dynamic could be exploited by the powerful American media.

Fenton felt that there were bright spots. There was an awareness of the need for discipline in the ranks. At one gathering on November 13, 1960 during the preparation for the Council, Archbishop Pietro Parente of the Holy Office, and also the "ghost-writer" of *Humani Generis,* "gave a magnificent paper on the need of authority in present-day theology…."[7] The Bishop of Agen spoke of the "subordination of theologians with reference to the Church's magisterium should be explained, especially with regard to the actual practice of the Church." And the bishop of Angouleme (Bishop Megnin) wanted a condemnation of laicism and progressivism.[8]

But the bright spots grew dim whenever Fenton contemplated the shadow that the American presence cast over the Council. He understood the power of the American media with its ability to exploit divisions and ambiguities to create novelty, and he knew the US episcopal leadership was sympathetic to the message put out by this media. Given this situation, Fenton understood the importance of the Council speaking clearly and in accord with Catholic Tradition. The Council Fathers had to confine themselves to an objective presentation of magisterial texts accompanied by "the requisite theological explanation and demonstration." The Council "should really follow the magisterium, and not go into any conjectures on what a Pope or Council might have meant." It should avoid "figurative language" at all costs.

To be pastoral in the true meaning of the term, the Council Fathers had to protect the faith of Catholics, and the proper language was essential: "*They must have a reference to Catholic life and devotion. This involves the question of figurative language. These must be clearly stated. They must take cognizance of the Church as God actually dwells in it; and as God actually made it. Again, we must take cognizance of how it looks. We will not gloss over the fact that very frequently it makes a very bad appearance.*"[9]

In order to be truly pastoral and missionary, the Council had to: "take cognizance of the actual errors now being taught to Catholics on the subject of the Church" by proposing the traditional formulae and using the basic definitions set out by Popes. For example, *extra ecclesiam nulla salus* was "objectively true, and not merely statements of our point of view." So this would "make men of good will see that the Catholic Church is the one kingdom of God on earth." The Council Fathers "should insist upon the fact that this always has been the teaching of the Church." Essence was more important than qualities.[10] Fenton was adamant the metaphorical language be minimized since "this is the age of science":[11]

"I must insist that figurative language be used as little as possible in setting forth the divine teaching on the Church and, when it must be used, the meaning of the figure of speech must immediately be made clear. There is definitely a danger that the men of our time will consider teaching presented in figurative or metaphysical language as non-objective."[12]

Fenton was appalled at the use of figurative language which crept into official Church documents like the Lattanyi votum on the Church, which he characterized as "a mess":

"The whole thing is a mess. Now I am faced with the necessity of going up to the Holy Office in an hour or so and having to make some kind of a report to the Cardinal. I shall tell him, if he asks me, that, as I stands, the votum 1) has no order at all, 2) that it lacks clarity, and that 3) it proposes as the content of a conciliar constitution doctrine that is not even theologically probable. As I analyze the matter now, the votum of Latanyi will have to be done over again entirely. And the play seems to be that it will be done by Tromp.

If it is, the votum submitted by the subcommission will be precisely what the Church of our times does not want. It will be a wordy document meaningless or even confusing to the ordinary Catholic. The language will be poetic and metaphorical at the very time when we need above everything else to get away from such figurative language in our teaching."[13]

One of the main sources of the flowery and vague language, poor organization, and bad thinking disfiguring the council's preliminary documents was the writing of French theologian Yves Congar, OP. Congar's troubling theological positions invariably reinforced Murray's position on religious liberty and Church state relations. Congar gave aid to the Americanists by his willingness to alienate those presently in the Church in the name of reaching out to the "separated brethren." After plowing through eight closely typed pages of Congar's full votum, Fenton reached the summary in which "the old fanatic" exposed his "weakness as a theologian" by citing passages from sacred scripture which actually undermined his point:

"Here Congar cites a passage from the prayer after the 4th prophecy in the old Holy Saturday liturgy -- `Ut in Abrahae filios et in israeliticam dignitatem totius mundi transeat plenitodo.' This is a marvelous citation…And, in my opinion, it is absolutely fatal to the position of Congar himself. The true Church of the N.T. is the true

Israel, the continuation of the true and supernatural kingdom of God that existed in this world under the dispensation of the O.T. and it is the only true Israel." [14]

When Congar attempted to explain how the Church fulfilled its secondary mission, which was "influence society in the temporal order so that this society may turn itself to God as much as possible," he opened the door "for poor Murray's 'pluralism,' a situation in which many religions (including the Catholics) agree to coexist peacefully on the assumption that they are outgoing and try to raid each other's ranks, and likewise on the assumption that each agrees to go its own individual way....." [15]

Congar's terminology was "figurative and ambiguous," contained "mixed metaphors," was "always fuzzy," and ruined whatever was good in his writing. Congar like the other "liberals," or more properly Americanists, "advocate all kinds of gentleness for 'separated brethren' but they seethe with uncharity towards the Catholics they regard as 'integrists.' They are a queer lot." [16] Congar's concern for the separated brethren ignores the fact that "the Church is a team, and that the first thing required is the co-operation of the members of the team for the attainment of their common purpose. Again, Congar shies away from that bond of charity within the Church." [17]

Congar also ignored the fact that the "whole human race is divided into the kingdom of God and the kingdom of Satan, and that these two kingdoms have been fighting against each other and will continue to do so until the end of time" as Leo XIII wrote in *Humanum Genus.* It was a strange refusal because Fenton found Congar to be "one of the few who seems to realize that the efforts against the Church, by members as well as by non-members of the Church, are ultimately directed by Satan." [18]

DOUBT IN THE CHURCH

Sensing the direction the documents were taking under the direction of Congar's "fuzzy and ambiguous" prose, Fenton "objected to the practice of making every speech a plea for not being offensive to non-Catholics. I said that no one at all wanted or could be offensive to non-Catholics, and that it was about time we took this for granted."[19]

Ottaviani agreed with Fenton, telling the commission they were not to advance their own ideas, they were to use "few words," and be brief in writing the various documents.[20] However, in a most troubling statement, Fenton believed Tromp had "swung Ottaviani behind him" in regards to the view "that there is never definitive teaching in the ordinary magisterium."[21]

After watching document after document consistently head off in the wrong direction, Fenton began to suspect something larger than simple human stupidity was a work shaping the Council. Unaware the power of America's newly created departments of psychological and doctrinal warfare were behind public figures like Jesuit John Courtney Murray and shadowy double agents like the Dominican Felix Morlion, Fenton attributed the malaise at the council to self-doubt. Many Church leaders were consumed by the nagging doubt that the Church had gotten it wrong and that figures like Teilhard de Chardin, who had been condemned and even been the subject of a document written during the preparatory phase revealing his errors, had gotten it right. This was especially the case among the Jesuits, who still secretly considered Teilhard one of their own. "As far as I can see," Fenton wrote in his diary, the supporters of doctrinal innovation "are working to make Catholicism a kind of Teilhard religion. And the authorities are deathly afraid that what the Church has been teaching over the course of all these centuries may turn out to be wrong after all. The martyrs may have died in vain (according to them) and men like Saint Athanasius may have been mistaken."[22]

Fenton dealt with the growing sense that the Church had gotten it all wrong in his article "Rome and the Status of Catholic Theology" published the previous December in *American Ecclesiastical Review.* He explained doctrine could not change; it could only be clarified, and presented more accurately or effectively. Doctrine and dogma could not change or evolve or become self-contradictory, nor was doctrine or dogma "in some way inadequate to the needs of the day." Faith cannot be at odds with reason, and vice versa. Those charged with defending the Faith have to know of the attacks on the Faith carried out in the name of "science and philosophy." Theology is a science subject to improvement so as to more accurately and clearly state the truths "defined and taught by the ecclesiastical magisterium."[23]

The great danger among those tasked with writing council documents was "Contempt for terms and notions habitually used by scholastic theologians." That, Fenton wrote, "leads of itself to the weakening of what is known as speculative theology" as Pius XII taught in *Humani Generis* in 1950. The new theologians, who were willing "to utilize an entirely metaphorical terminology, and, indeed, to replace perfectly familiar proper terms with words and expressions of a definitely figurative character," were in error. True progress in theology was accomplished when from figurative language could be drawn in "proper terms, truths." Turning from clarity by using metaphoric language lead to "vagueness and confusion" thereby harming "theological investigation."[24]

Despite the truth of Fenton's words, the Americanists were winning the battle for the Council's mind because they could count on the superior fire power provided by the American media. By the time Fenton was ready to depart back to the US in February, 1961, Ottaviani was feeling the effects of the negative attacks on him. Fenton mentioned "liberals," but the term's vagueness disguised the fact that he was effectively referring to Americanists and Americans. Fenton told Connell that:

"The old boy [Romeo] was here to see me last night again. I think that he is being affected by the things that are being said against him. He was complaining about insulting letters and things of that sort. And, of all things, he was trying to convince me that I should be afraid of the liberal Catholics. I told him that I fear Our Lord, but that I have been singularly fortunate in that I had never been seriously hurt by the liberal Catholics who have had it in for me. Here I am, an old time, editor or [sic] AER and an ordinary professor of theology in spite of them. And of course there is the appointment to the commission as a member. As enemies, the liberals have shown themselves quite inept. I talked that way, not because I discount the force of the people arrayed against us, but because I wanted to cheer him up."[25]

During the Summer of 1961, both the intensity of the preparations as well as the expectations for the Council grew. After four months of work, there were "four volumes of the *Acta* and documents of the Antepreparatory Commission were published for use" by the various commissions. The meetings of the various preparatory commissions began June 12 and lasted until June 20, 1961. The Central Preparatory Commission held seven weeks of meetings.[26]

Pope John addressed the Central Preparatory Commission on June 12, 1961. Expressing "still greater hope for the best outcome (of the council)," the Pope remarked the "expectation of the council is widespread and has been serenely and courteously received not only by our beloved sons but also by those outside the Church." The Preparatory Commission was to study the "different doctrinal and practical points" derived from the bishops, Curia, and universities. [27] Latin was the official language of the council, though expression in one's native language was permitted. Journalists and others were thanked. He recognized the "whole world is interested in the preparation of the ecumenical council." The language must be "serene and calm, must enlighten, dispel misunderstandings and remove errors with the force of truth" and matters must be presented with "prudence and simplicity." The council would be "sensitive" to the "ever beloved, but separated, brother" and "embraces the whole world" but the purpose of the council was:

"that the clergy should acquire a new brilliance of sanctity, that the people he instructed efficaciously in the truths of the Faith and Christian morals, that the new generations, who are growing like a hope of better times, should be educated properly; that attention be given to the social apostolate and that Christians should have a missionary heart, that is to say, brotherly and friendly toward all and with all...."[28]

CHAPTER 80

MOTHER AND TEACHER

On May 15, 1961, Pope John issued his famous encyclical, *Mater et Magistra*. It came about a year after Murray's *We Hold These Truths*, and about five months after *Time* published its cover story on Murray, both of which told the world that America had a better idea than the Church. Pope John begged to differ and told the world the Church has the better idea thereby correcting the Americans. The forcefulness of this statement was not lost on the Americans, as evidenced by the reaction of Catholics Gary Wills and William Buckley, Jr., a former CIA agent and editor of *National Review*.[1]

After reading the encyclical, Wills and Buckley chatted. Both disliked it. Wills coined the phrase "Mater? Si. Magistra? No." Buckley liked it so much that he ran it that summer in an edition of *National Review*."[2] Pope John XXIII went to the heart of the Americans' attempt to conquer the Catholic mind by restating at the beginning of *Mater et Magistra* Christ's command in Matthew 28:19-20 to "teach all nations." In paragraph 1, Pope John wrote:

"Mother and Teacher of all nations – such is the Catholic Church in the mind of her Founder, Jesus Christ; to hold the world in an embrace of love, that men, in every age should find in her their completeness in a higher order of living, and their ultimate salvation. She is `the pillar and ground of the truth.' To her was entrusted by her holy Founder the twofold task of giving life to her children and of teaching them and guiding them – both as individuals and as nations – with maternal care."[3]

Pope John emphasized the role of the Church as teacher of nations in the encyclical as well as the role of the Church in properly structuring societies in accordance with doctrine. When the pope wrote that the Church has *"'the indisputable competence' to `decide whether the bases of a given social system are in accord with the unchangeable order which God our Creator and Redeemer has shows us through the Natural Law and Revelation"*[4] it sounded as if he were siding with Fenton, Connell, and Ottaviani in their battle with Murray, the Americanists, and American media by claiming that society's organizing principles and the State's enactments must be based on the Divine Positive Law. This requirement, with the corollary duties of the State towards the Church and the Faith, was made clear elsewhere in the encyclical, especially when the pope said in paragraph 253: "In the name of God, therefore, and for the sake of the material and spiritual interests of men, We call upon all, public authorities, employers and workers, to observe the precepts of God and His Church and to remember their grave responsibilities before God and society."[5]

The Americanists found troubling the parts setting out responsibilities to the poor and underprivileged and limits on the gaining of wealth. John XXIII re-iterated Leo XIII's attack on "the idols of liberalism" when he validated the positive role of the state in forming the economy:

"As is well known, the outlook that prevailed on economic matters [during the time of Leo XIII] was for the most part a purely naturalistic one, which denied any correlation between economics and morality. Personal gain was considered the only valid motive for economic activity. In business the main cooperative principle was that of free and unrestricted competition. Interest on capital, prices –

whether of goods or of services – profits and wages, were to be determined by the purely mechanical application of the laws of the market place. Every precaution was to be taken to prevent the civil authority from intervening in any way in economic matters."[6]

After the economic collapse of the 1930s, "Pius XI [over]saw the re-establishment of the economic world within the framework of the moral order and the subordination of individual and group interests to the interest of the common good as the principal remedies for these evils. This, he taught, necessitated an orderly reconstruction of society, with the establishment of economic and vocational bodies which would be autonomous and independent of the State. Public authority should resume its duty of promoting the common good of all. Finally, there should be co-operation on a world scale for the economic welfare of all nations."[7]

The purpose of the economy was not the enrichment of the few, but rather to "promote production in a way best calculated to achieve social progress and the well-being of all citizens" and the state had an affirmative role to play to make that happen.[8] Pope John criticized both the liberal West (namely, the Americans) and the Communist countries for encouraging materialism or, as what CD Jackson would have called the "Revolution of Expectations." This materialism served to increase consumption, but Pope John claimed that the capitalist spirit which encouraged this consumption, and hence materialism, was choking the life of the spirit in people though American psychological manipulation was encouraging it in societies all for the purpose of extending the power of the commercial banks. Taken together, this ensemble of interlocking ideas and institutions combined with "pernicious" practices collaborated "in the absurd attempt to reconstruct a solid and fruitful temporal order divorced from God, who is, in fact, the only foundation on which it can endure. In seeking to enhance man's grates, men fondly imagine that they can do so by drying up the source from which that greatness springs and from which it is nourished. They want, that is, to restrain and, if possible to eliminate the soul's upward surge toward God…. There is, alas, a spirit of hedonism abroad today which beguiles men into thinking that life is nothing more than the quest for pleasure and the satisfaction of human passions. This attitude is disastrous. Its evil effects on soul and body are undeniable."[9]

In Summer, 1961, Fenton published an article rebutting the sentiment among American Catholics the Council was going to lead to some major changes in Catholic teaching. The occasion for his article was a story in *Our Sunday Visitor* entitled "Priest Journalist Says…Revolution Under Way in Catholic Attitudes." It discussed an address by the president of the Australian Catholic Press Association, Fr. James Murtagh, who said:

"'The Church has entered the Age of Dialogue and the Age of Public Relations – dialogue with non-Catholic Christians and public relations with the community at large…I don't think it an exaggeration to say that we are on the threshold of a revolution in Catholic attitudes and policies in the Church's confrontation with the world. The revolution has already begun. It may well be signed and sealed and directed at the Second Vatican Council and will mark the end of the Reformation era.'" [10]

One of the issues the Council was sure to "clarify" was "the relationship between the Church and State in pluralist secular democracies like ours," and when it did, the Council "may well call for a considerable readjustment of attitudes and ideas and the deliberate re-setting of editorial sights."[11] Fenton had high expectations also as he wrote "There is a kind of revolution (a better word is `conversion')," he wrote, "which the Church rightly expects to result from the coming Council." The Council expects "a new brilliance of sanctity" among the clergy. It expects the people be instructed effectively in the truths of the Faith and of Christian morals; that new generations arising as a hope of better times be educated properly; that care be given to the social apostolate; that Christians have a missionary heart.'" The goal of the council based on the intentions of the Pope, was that there be "an increase in holiness within the Church, especially within the ranks of the clergy....and thus of such a renewal of Catholic life and holiness."[12]

Fenton discredited the view of those, many of whom were in the Catholic press in the US, there would be a "softening of Catholic teaching or directives with reference to religious societies and religious doctrines other than the Catholic." First, the Church could never change or modify the truth as set forth by the magisterium to include those of the Sovereign Pontiffs. The teachings of the First Vatican Council, Leo XIII, and St. Pius X could not be changed especially as to the condemnations of Modernism and the descriptions of Modernism. Any doctrinal statements from the council would make a truth clearer and remove or avoid ambiguity. Statements by the council on doctrinal matters "will be the more effective and adequate restatements of the divine message which the Catholic Church has taught since the beginning of its existence. They will neither order nor imply any revolution or any readjustment of Catholic attitudes and ideas."[13]

As to the claims of "dialogue" and "pluralism" and the allegations the "Church is inaugurating [sic] a new set of attitudes with reference to non-Catholic religious bodies," Fenton summarily dismissed these by writing that the terms will pass out of usage with time. The term "dialogue" connoted "artificiality" much like what is found in a play. The term is based on the presumption of friendliness with each side not trying to convince the other of the rightness or correctness of its position. "Pluralism" was a word used "to designate a situation in which many religious beliefs and organizations coexist in one country or district, in such a way that they are presumed to agree to differ as peacefully as possible among themselves." In such a situation, the Catholic is "presumed to believe" that he should not forcefully assert Catholic dogmas that the Faith and the Church are necessary for one to attain eternal salvation. The members of the Church should "get along as well as possible with non-Catholics" so as to "achieve that objective by not trying to make converts to the Catholic Church and the Catholic faith, at least on any large scale...."[14]

Fenton predicted "certain modifications of positive ecclesiastical law" just as in the past, and the Pope and the Church "expects from the Second Ecumenical Vatican Council exactly what it expected from every other Council that was ever called." He attacked Murtagh's comment about the Church reaching "the end of the Reformation era." Fenton called erroneous the idea the Church since the time of the 1500s adopted a "state of siege" approach which was an "extraordinary and unnatural defensive posture," and for some reason in the last 50 to 60 years that mentality was all coming to an end. The Church had always opposed the errors taught by the Protestant revolutionaries, just as it had always taught against the Arian heresy. The Church "is not going to modify its doctrine, and it is not going to admit at long last that the doctrines it denounced as heretical in times past are now acceptable in any way as Catholic doctrine…..It is not going to say that, after all, there is some truth in the propositions condemned in the *Lamentabili,* the *Pascendi,* and the *Sacrorum antistitum.*" The fundamental ecclesiological error of the Protestant "Reformers was the teaching that the true Church of Jesus Christ according to the dispensation of the New Testament is an invisible Church, that is to say, a social unit which is not an organized society with purely visible requisites for membership. During the long and glorious reign of Pope Pius XII, the Church… had to insist upon the fact that there can be no attainment of eternal salvation outside of this same Roman Catholic Church."[15] Fenton stressed *extra ecclesium nulla salus.*

Concluding with the discussion of Fr. Charles Davis' introduction to the English translation of Father Durrwel's treatise, *The Resurrection,* Fenton criticized Davis' comment that the treatise did not contain the "rich matter and profound thought they expected." He claimed Davis' comments were inept and revealed a lack of comprehension. Indeed, "the only Catholics who imagine that there will be or can be any doctrinal revolution in the Church are those who do not know the teaching of the Church. The only Catholics who liked such a revolution are the individuals who have not grasped the meaning of Catholic doctrine and of Catholic theology." In claiming any change was to occur by the "force of the truth and the love of Jesus Christ" and "this will be brought about only in and through the teaching of the Church,"[16] Fenton showed he was determined to defend the Faith.

CHAPTER 81
FENTON GOES BACK TO ROME

F enton was distressed by what he read coming out of the Theological Commission over the Spring and Summer of 1961. In September, upon returning to Rome, he wrote in his diary "There is one schema on the membership in and the necessity of the Church. It is disastrously bad. I shall work as effectively as I can for its elimination. I have enough faith to realize that God will never allow a mess like that to come out of a Council."[1]

While in Rome, Fenton received word that the Catholic Biblical Association (CBA) condemned him, Connell and the *American Ecclesiastical Review* during its summer, 1961 meeting. *Time* showed an interest in this condemnation and one of its Roman correspondents tried repeatedly to get a statement from Fenton, who refused to say anything until he had an opportunity to read the CBA's statement.[2]

The controversy began in June, according to Robert Blair Kaiser, *Time* correspondent to the Council during its first two sessions, when Apostolic Delegate Vagnozzi, during a talk at Marquette University given at the request of Pope John, "expressed 'a necessary caution to those who allow themselves to be overcome by the glamour of that which is new and by the allurement of that which is calculated to startle rather than to enlighten.'" When Catholic laymen and intellectuals wrote an open letter objecting to his warning, Vagnozzi replied that "the layman has not been constituted as teacher of the magisterium nor as admonitor of the hierarchy. When, after mature deliberation, one wishes to inform those in authority of the problems and inspirations of the people, he can do it directly, rather than by sending critical letters to the press." The Holy Office issued a Monitum thereafter on biblical studies, which was interpreted as a reprimand to bible scholars though some saw in it a "reasonable and restrained call for all biblical teachers and writers to exercise due prudence and reverence." Vagnozzi followed up his warning by reprimanding the University of Notre Dame in August, advising the university that students and clerics "pursue their studies in a spirit of humble faith, not vain rationalism or self-seeking... forming for your institute religious who are strangers to the self-assurance of subjectivism...."[3]

Once he was back in Rome, Fenton discussed the entire matter with Archbishop Pietro Parente of the Holy Office. The discussion revealed not only how widespread and serious the Modernist threat was in the Church but also the Pope's own vacillation in dealing with it. "Archbishop Parente," Fenton wrote, "told me that they ran into great difficulty about the Monitum. It was meant to appear here months before it actually came out. The Modernists (and he used the word frequently) thought that they had it blocked. Finally, when it appeared, it came as a sad surprise to the Modernists."[4]

During the discussion of the Monitum, Parente argued with the Pope, during which he told the Pope that the rampant corruption in Biblical scholarship "was not some little unimportant detail." It concerned the very nature of the Petrine office and its role in preserving the Church from doctrinal error. Exasperated at Pope John's lax attitude toward doctrinal orthodoxy, Parente told the pope "that if Our Lord had not given that promise to Peter, that he and the Pope should take off their pectoral crosses and quit."[5]

Shrugging off the CBA's censure, Fenton praised Parente for being "forthright"[6] in dealing with the doctrinal crisis spreading through Biblical scholarship, especially at Catholic universities, where traditional biblical interpretation were attacked and derided.[7] At Ottaviani's request, Fenton wrote a letter to Msgr. William McDonald, the rector of CUA, summarizing the position of the Holy Office. In a letter to *Time*, Fenton made many of the same points, emphasizing the traditional understanding of the doctrine on the Annunciation, the establishment of the Church by Christ in Matthew 16:17, and the truth of the Ascension, all of which had been attacked by the Modernists,[8] whom Fenton described as vicious hypocrites, whose language was "cryptic in the extreme" and who dismissed anyone "not in accord with their own teachings" as guilty of "gross ignorance" and "malicious perversion of the truth."[9]

Undaunted by the CBA's censure, which accused them of "unwarranted attacks" on Bible scholars and *Time,* which depicted their efforts as an attack on the teaching of Pius XII contained in *Divino Afflante Spiritu,* Fenton, Msgr. Francesco Spadafora, and Cardinal Ruffini fought back. [10] That autumn, Fenton's review of Murray's book, *We Hold These Truths* appeared in the *American Ecclesiastical Review,* refuting Murray's claim that "when the *magisterium* condemned the separation of Church and state, it acted in the line of policy or tactic." Fenton also rejected Murray's claim that the popes had limited their condemnation to the Jacobin version of separation of Church and state. Fenton disproved Murray's claim that the Jacobin idea, or Continental Liberalism, had been rejected by the popes because it assumed the juridical omnicompetence of the state, and he supported his position by citing to a number of papal writings from Gregory XVI to Leo XIII that condemned the separation of church and state on doctrinal grounds and not on policy grounds based on the omnicompetence of the state.[11]

Fenton mentioned Pius IX's *Acerbissmum,* delivered September 27, 1852, and referenced as the source of item 55 of the *Syllabus of Errors* published by Pius IX in 1864. Item 55 of the *Syllabus* stated as error the proposition "The Church is to be disjoined from the state and the state from the Church." In the *Syllabus,* Pius IX made reference to *Mirari Vos* issued by Gregory XVI in 1832 as the first document to condemn the separation of Church from the State. Fenton concluded that *"Acerbissimum,* like the Syllabus itself, did not condemn the doctrine" of "separation of Church and state" solely or primarily on the basis "this teaching in some way involves or is connected with the doctrine of the omnicompetence or the omnipotence of the state."[12] In other words, the condemnation was not limited to Continental Liberalism. According to *Acerbissmum,* the separation of the Church from the state is "completely (*omnino*) opposed to the irreformable doctrine of the Catholic Church and to its most sacred rights." The proposed laws of Colombia which prompted the papal teaching were "completely opposed to the unchangeable doctrine of the Catholic Church and to its most sacred rights." The Pope's condemnation of the proposed laws was not "on the assumption that such a separation would bring with it interference by the state in ecclesiastical affairs, but on the grounds that such a separation, under the circumstances was wrong in itself." Therefore, the condemnation of the thesis of the separation of church and state was not based on tactical or political considerations. The rejection of the separation of Church and state whereby the "Church was to be set apart from the state" was rejected by the Church's *magisterium.*[13]

Leo XIII reiterated this teaching explicitly in *Immortale Dei* and *Longinqua Oceani,* when he wrote: "Since. . . it is a public crime to act as though there were no God. It is therefore a sin for the State not to have care for religion, as a something beyond its scope, or as of no practical benefit; [or] of out of many forms of religion to adopt that one which chimes in with the fancy; for we are bound absolutely to worship God in that way which He has shown to be His will." Society, therefore, was bound to worship God by the Catholic religion and "not such religion as they may have a preference for."[14]

In *Longinqua Oceani,* Leo XIII emphasized the same doctrine in the context of the situation in the US, when he wrote "it would be very erroneous to draw the conclusion that in America is to be sought the type of the most desirable status of the Church, or that it would be universally lawful or expedient for State and Church to be, as in America, dissevered and divorced….His Church….would bring forth more abundant fruits if, in addition to liberty, she enjoyed the favor of the laws and the patronage of the public authority." Fenton pointed out the "Sovereign Pontiff…was quite well aware of the fact that, in the United States at least, separation of Church and state did not involve any omnicompetence of the state, or any domination of the Church by the state." Indeed, he specifically wrote: "the example of the best condition of the Church is not to be sought from America," a position consistent with *Immortale Dei.*[15] Leo XIII realized the "American separation of Church and state is predicated upon a condition which definitely is not good in itself….Furthermore, even considered in itself, the failure of this, the greatest of the nations of history, to thank God according to the rite of the one true religion cannot be considered as objectively anything other than undesirable."[16]

The state, according to Fenton, had the affirmative duty to "give public worship to God and to Christ according to the rite of the one true religion, and . . . should recognize the Catholic Church for what it is, the one and only supernatural kingdom of God in this world." The Church could not accept separation of church and state (i.e., disestablishment) "as a thesis" as it was objectively wrong regardless of whether that separation occurred in the context of an organizing ideology limiting the powers of government or one in which the state was omnicompetent. The Church was bound to preach the truth for the salvation of souls, and this truth, as well as the truths of the faith, could not be obscured due to fear or out of sympathy for "the liberalism of the day."[17]

Finally, Fenton discredited the claim that "the truly democratic state need never concern itself in any way or under any circumstances about any obligation to worship God according to the rite of true religion, and to acknowledge Jesus Christ Our Lord as God." Such "would be a rejection of the Church's own commission and obligation. It would be a contradiction of basic truths the Church is meant to teach and to guard until the end of time."[18] Fenton was attacking the four erroneous propositions given him years earlier by the Apostolic Delegate at the time, Cardinal Cicognani.

As Fenton hammered out the traditional position, tension with the Protestants continued to escalate. In late 1961, Cardinal Cicognani, now the Vatican's Secretary of State, said that "Protestant missionaries . . can expect oppression" if they try to proselytize in predominantly Catholic countries. Cicognani made his remarks in response to a statement from the Baptist General Convention of Texas, which had complained that "some Baptist missions...have met with uncooperative reception by some governments where Catholicism has been entrenched for generations on an undivided church-state basis." In the same interview, Cicognani claimed profits should be shared and a form of social security put in place.[19]

On Christmas Day, 1961 Pope John announced the Second Vatican Council, which was scheduled to begin in 1962, would address "a crisis under way within society" by "bringing the modern world into contact with the vivifying and perennial energies of the Gospel." The modern world was attempting to create "a temporal order [from] which some have wished to reorganize excluding God. . . modern society is earmarked by a great material progress to which there is not a corresponding advance in the moral field. Hence there is a weakening in the aspiration toward the values of the spirit. Hence an urge for the almost exclusive search for earthly pleasures, which progressive technology places with such ease within the reach of all. And hence there is a completely new and disconcerting fact: The existence of a militant atheism which is active on a world level."[20]

The Church, which he implied, was also infected with materialism and a spiritual decline needed, to be "transformed and renewed... strengthened itself socially in unity...reinvigorated intellectually... interiorly purified and is thus ready for trial." The Church, "still so vibrant with vitality," was to be given "the possibility to contribute more efficaciously to the solution of the problems of the modern age."[21]

To do that, the Council needed to promote "doctrinal clarity and of mutual charity that will make still more alive in our separated brothers the wish for the hoped for return to unity and will smooth the way." She could only accomplish this, and real peace, through the magisterium, which he described as "the most authoritative voice, interpreter and affirmer of the moral order, and champion of the rights and duties of all human beings and of all political communities" in a way that was sure to rankle the Americanists and the Americans.[22]

CHAPTER 82

CONNELL GETS TO GO TO ROME

I
n January, 1962, Bishop McManus, a Redemptorist prelate in Puerto Rico, asked Fr. Connell to be his peritus at the council. Connell accepted, and, while waiting for Francis X. Murphy (the Xavier Rhynne of future and *New York Times* fame) to arrange accommodations in Rome and his departure, spent his time lecturing American bishops on what to expect from the upcoming council.[1] On February 6, he told a Serra Club luncheon that this extraordinary event, only one of three Church councils since 1563, could not change doctrine. Specifically, neither the doctrines of papal infallibility nor the immorality of contraception could be changed. The "principal object of this coming council is not the reunion of all Christians" but rather "to guide and direct the members of the Catholic Church to a deeper understanding and appreciation of the faith which they already possess." Any non-doctrinal proclamations must be "accepted without hesitation by Catholics, for they too are based on the authority which Jesus Christ communicated to His bishops...."[2]

Connell's message, no matter how consoling, was the exception and not the rule as American Catholics suffered a barrage of disinformation whose main purpose was to unsettle them by giving the impression that once the Council started everything was on the table. During Summer, 1961, Fr. Riccardo Lombardi, SJ, the founder of the Movement for a Better World in 1946 with the encouragement of Pope Pius XII, and a prominent opponent of the Communists in Italy during the 1948 election, arrived in America and called for "sweeping changes in the Church's administrative staff, the Roman curia, including the establishment of a `world senate' of Catholic laymen."[3] The Pope rebuked Lombardi saying commentators on the forthcoming council had to speak with "prudence and objectivity." To his credit, Lombardi admitted his error, announced his public submission to Church authorities, and stated his proposals for the council were of only personal value.[4]

Aware the Council would be conducted in a hostile media environment, the Pope called for "a greater development of the press office so that public opinion may be suitably informed." The pope encouraged "free discussion…for the good of the free assembly." He recognized the Council offered Christ's enemies an opportunity to engage in psychological manipulation. He quoted St. Paul who "reminds us that `difficulties are almost inseparable from the announcement of good doctrine.'"[5] Subsequent events would prove both St Paul and the Pope right. The American media was about to cover the Council with a blanket of disinformation, and *Time* played a leading role.

CHAPTER 83
IDENTIFYING THE ISSUES FOR THE COUNCIL

By the time the Central Commission handed in its third report on January 23, 1962, it appeared that over the course of the preceding seven months the Catholics had beaten the Americanists in formulating the issues for discussion at the Council. In its document on the moral order, the Commission concluded that "the world of fashion, movies, and the press" were involved in a concerted effort "to shake the foundations of Christian morality . . . as if the Sixth Commandment should be considered outmoded and free reign should be given to all passions, even those against nature." The Church would have to refute these "most diverse errors [which] multiply, favored by the conditions of the modern world: by its technical progress, its modes of life, and its growing means of propaganda ad publicity" and "indicate the practical and sure ways that lead to salvation."[1]

As though speaking to Henry Luce and the US Government, the Commission at its Fifth Session in March, 1962 recognized the enormous power held by the media:

"These instruments, collectively or separately, have an incalculable power of penetration and persuasion. As news and pictures are transmitted, so are opinions, doctrines, and principles also diffused. These rapidly modify the habits and mores, as well as ways of thinking and living. These, then, directly touch the minds and consciences of men. Does the church, therefore, have the right to intervene, if only to safeguard the fundamental rights of man with his Christian dignity and immutable principles of truth and goodness, in the case of attempts to corrupt or to propagate error?"[2]

The answer was, of course, yes. The Church, according to the Commission which referred to encyclicals and statements from Pius XI, Pius XII, and John XXIII:

"condemns in the press and theaters what offends God, mutilates or deforms truth, weakens moral principles, promotes corruption, teaches or counsels evil and spreads hatred, she does not impede liberty but tries only to restrain license, whatever its form might be....There are those who work in and with these media: journalists, directors, producers, actors, etc. They cannot dispense themselves from the moral law that regulates all human action. There are others who use these media: lecturers, auditors, and spectators. For these also, there are laws that cannot be violated without grave moral danger. Certain others have the duty of being vigilant and of guiding the use of these media: these are parents, masters, educators, and priests. Finally, civil authority itself has the duty to defend and protect the good morals and common good of its citizens, while respecting their liberty."[3]

The Pope opened the Commission meeting on April 3 with an admission that "In modern society, there is hardly anyone who is not influenced more or less, often in an unconscious manner, by the lectures and performances which they attend. Youth especially are the most easily taken in due to their lack of knowledge, their curiosity, or imprudence."[4]

Pope John then quoted Pius XII from the 1957 encyclical *Miranda prorsus*: "'These technical media which, we can say, are now available to all, exercise an extraordinary power on man. They lead him to the kingdom of light, nobility, and beauty as well as to the domain of darkness and deprivation. He is open to the influence of the nature of the scenes proposed to his senses.'"[5]

Faced with a challenge like this, the Church responded in a way that was not "purely negative" because "condemnation was useless."[6] Acting on Pius XII's exhortation, the

Commission urged that a "permanent national office be established in every country," which "would encourage good films and establish a moral standard that would be publicized for both the clergy and faithful." The Pope made the Pontifical Commission for the Cinema a "permanent and stable character as an office of the Holy See for the examination, support, and direction of the diverse activities in the area of cinema, radio, and television," and he appointed as its first director Bishop O'Connor, the president of the Pontifical Secretariat for the Press and Entertainment.[7] It was an acknowledgement the media was the decisive battleground on which the Church had to fight its enemies.

On June 18-19, the seventh and final session, the Commission discussed the role of theologians, the Church's authority, relations of Church and state, religious liberty, church unity, and ecumenism—in short, all of the issues which fueled the Murray-Fenton and Murray-Connell debates of the early 1950s. First the role of the theologian had to be defined as theologians considered and clarified Catholic doctrines. The Commission decided, quoting from Pius XII, "'theologians exercise their functions, not by divine right but from a delegation of the church; they remain, therefore, subject to the authority and vigilance of the legitimate magisterium....What is decisive for the knowledge of truth is the *Sensus ecclesiae,* not the opinion of theologians." Otherwise, theologians would be a "kind of *magistri magisterii*...an obvious error."[8]

In the area of Church and state, the Commission began the discussion by defining its first principle: everything in human affairs has a moral component, or, as Leo XIII indicated in *Immortale Dei,* "Everything in human affairs is sacred by some title, either bearing on the salvation of souls or on divine cult by its nature or in relation to its purpose." Two powers govern human affairs: the ecclesiastical and the civil with the former over divine affairs and the latter over human affairs, and each exercises "its action by its own right." But, the civil powers are to respect the rights and ends of the Church, safeguard the divine law, be neither opposed nor indifferent to religion, not rule as if God did not exist, and to "honor God in the way he himself showed he wanted to be honored."[9]

Cardinal Bea, of the Secretariat for Christian Unity, presented the question of religious liberty, claiming that it was "not only freedom of opinion or the free performance of religious ceremonies; it is, rather, the ability to practice and proclaim all the private and public duties concerning God and men."[10]

Cardinal Ottaviani proposed a comprehensive and simple restatement of Catholic doctrine with a document entitled "On the Relations Between the Church and the State and On Religious Tolerance." It consisted of seven parts.[11]

Part 1 stated these two societies – the civil and the Church or Caesar and God – "cannot ignore each other" because they "exercise their power over the same persons and often with regard to one same object." They were each established or instituted "for the usefulness of man" and by implication by the same authority – God Himself. While the civil society exists for the temporal happiness of man, the "end of civil Society must never be sought by excluding or by endangering the ultimate end, namely, eternal salvation."[12] Part 2 explained that the Church brings "great benefits...for civil Society while accomplishing its mission," as it imposes on citizens the "obligation of complying with legitimate orders" not out of fear but out of a "motive of conscience." The Church serves to check the ambitions of those in government so they work for "the good of the citizens" as they must "render an account to God." It teaches those in government that real peace, justice, and right order within and between nations comes about by observance of the natural laws and the supernatural laws.[13]

Part 3 set out the relation between the government, or civil authority, and the Catholic Church, and essential to that relation was the principle the government "cannot be indifferent with regard to religion." Since God is the "author of Civil Society and the source of all the goods which flow down through it to all its members," then Civil Society must "honor and serve God" in the manner that He has determined "as obligatory, in the true Church of Christ." This service must not be "only in the person of the citizens, but equally in that of the Authorities who represent civil Society." The obligation was to be by the civil authorities as well as the populace, and that meant to "recognize the true Church of Christ" as such is "clear from the manifest signs of its divine institution and mission, signs given to the Church by its divine Founder." Most notably, the Civil Authorities were to accept the "Revelation proposed by the Church itself. Likewise, in its legislation, it must conform itself to the precepts of the natural law and take a strict account of the positive laws, both divine and ecclesiastical, intended to lead men to supernatural happiness." As if to remove any doubt, the proposed document stated the Civil Authority is to "exclude from legislation, government, and public activity everything which it would judge to be capable of impeding the Church from attaining its eternal end." Further, it must facilitate the "life which is founded on principles that are Christian and consistent" to achieve the end for which men were created.[14]

Parts 5 through 7 addressed the applicability of the general principle of doctrine thus set forth. There was the issue of application in a Catholic City and the application of these principles in a Non-Catholic City. As to the former, no one was to be compelled to accept the Faith, and a "just tolerance, even sanctioned by laws...be imposed onto the civil Authority." Such would avoid a greater evil such as "scandal or civil war, a hindrance to conversion to the true faith, and other evils...." Such tolerance could "obtain a greater good, like civil cooperation and the peaceful coexistence of citizens of different religions, a greater freedom for the Church, and a more effective accomplishment of its supernatural mission...." In the "Non-Catholic City," the civil Authority had to "conform at least to the precepts of the natural law" which meant giving "civil liberty to all the forms of worship that are not opposed to natural religion." This suits the welfare of the Church and the State, and "Catholic citizens have above all the duty to bring it [that is, the profession of the Catholic religion] about, through their virtues and civic actions." In conclusion, a "false laicism" could not be allowed to obscure these principles "even under pretext of the common good." For these principles, as set out above, are based on the "firm rights of God," the "unchangeable constitution and mission of the Church," and the "social nature of man."[15]

The Commission showed an awareness of the threat posed by the Protestant, or American, version of uniting churches and different belief systems, and it recounted a long line of the various meetings of the major Protestant sects beginning with Edinburgh in 1910 through the World Council of Churches November, 1961 gathering. Hearkening to Pius XII's warnings in *Orientalis Ecclesiae,* the union proposed by the Protestants was not to be countenanced by the Catholics since the Protestants sought union based on agreement, not truth.[16]

At the closing day for the seventh and final session of the Preparatory Commission, on June 20, the Pope spoke again. He said the agenda would be sent to the Fathers of the Council throughout the world and they would be able to review it and provide further written comments to the Secretary of State. The "intentions are forthright and clear. This Holy Church, founded by Jesus as a City of God, rises peacefully among the towers built by men. The latter do not tend to seek the glory of the Lord…and they tend instead to become a source of anxiety and permanent danger for the peace of the world."[17]

That summer, the US Bishops' news agency publicized a number of statements inflating expectations. In one report by Msgr. Tucek, the agenda was discussed in a general way with 67 proposed topics approved by the Pope but these were not a "rigid program for the council Fathers." Tucek explained the products of the Council would be either a decree which was defined as "generally an ordinance which, coming from a council, [that] has universal binding force" or a constitution which was defined as "a statement of position on a given question."[18]

On August 19, Cardinal Spellman's Administrative Board of the NCWC, the governing arm of the US bishops, issued a statement on the Council referrencing a growing "religious expectancy" in the Church since the announcement of the Council. The statement distinguished the forthcoming Council, which was for the "direct and conscious purpose" of the "internal renewal of the Church," from the previous twenty councils which dealt with doctrinal issues or heresies. Spellman's statement acknowledged "external conditions and pressures" (such as "long-standing disunity among Christians, the menace of atheistic communism, the materialism which engulfs so much of the modern world and infects so many of its people") which "lend special timeliness" to the calling of the Council. The statement then incongruously went on to discuss the advantages to the Church "from living and growing in an atmosphere of religious and political freedom" in the US, and it praised the American situation as "responsible in large measure for the vitality" of the Church in American society where it could grow to maturity "unaided by political preference but unimpeded by political ties." This vitality was reflected in Mass devotions, the flowering of vocations and "contemplative vocations," missionary activities, charitable works, and a "love for our brothers of all races and nations."[19] It was a subtle and powerful endorsement of the American system of church and state relations on the eve of the Council.

Archbishop O'Boyle asked Connell to educate the faithful about the Council and write a homily for presentation on September 30. "What is the chief purpose of this Second Vatican Council?" Connell asked in his homily: "The Administrative Board of Bishops of the United States, speaking as representative of all our Bishops, tell us that the chief aim of this coming council is 'the internal renewal of the Church' and they quote Pope John as saying that he hopes the Council will restore 'to full splendor the simple and pure lines that the face of the Church had at its birth…presenting it as its Divine Founder made it.'[20]

Connell was "managing expectations," and at this point Connell had reason for optimism. Given how the Preparatory Commission framed the issues, the Council might actually achieve the end for which it was intended. Even though there was talk "of the possibility that the Council will bring about a union between the Catholic Church and the many other Christian religious bodies," Connell assured the faithful the Church could not "make any compromises in its efforts toward Christian unity." This meant there would not be any changes in the infallible doctrines the "Church has solemnly proclaimed…even though thereby millions of conversions to the Church could be obtained." No, the "non-Catholics who seek unity with the Catholic Church must accept all the Church's teachings without any qualification, otherwise they can never be united to the Catholic Church."[21]

The Council's principal goals were to "arouse to greater fervor the members of the Church, to guide Catholics on the way that leads to eternal life, to apply the age-old principles of Catholic faith to modern problems." Connell concluded by hoping the Council's deliberations would bring "many benefits . . . to Catholics throughout the entire world."[22]

As some indication Divine help was needed to bring about the Council's objectives, a novena was ordered for the period of October 3 through 11, 1962.[23] The prayers were needed.

PART XVIII
VATICAN II – 1962

CHAPTER 84
THE SECOND MOST IMPORTANT FACTOR AT THE COUNCIL

I f, as Catholics believe, the Holy Spirit was the most powerful force at the Council, insuring that error would not arise, then the second most powerful force was the American media, which under the leadership of Henry Luce and *Time* magazine, arrived at the Council to insure that error had rights after all.

Robert Blair Kaiser, *Time's* first reporter to cover the Council, said "*Time* took sides. We were encouraged to tak sides....*Time* reporters were reporters as well as participant-observers to influence the schemas [of Vatican II]...Murray was a member of the conspiracy."[1]

The context which best explains the Second Vatican Council is World War II. "The clouds and dust of the Second World War," Carlo Falconi, former priest and an observer at the Council, acutely observed, "had not yet dispersed sufficiently for the future to be seen in perspective."[2] In an address he gave on September 9, 1962 or about one month before the start of the Council, Pope John pointedly said: "The Ecumenical Council is about to assemble, seventeen years after the end of the Second World War. For the first time in history the Fathers of the Council belong in reality to all peoples and nations, and each of them will bring his contribution of intelligence and experience, to cure and heal the wounds of the two conflicts which have changed profoundly the face of all countries. The mothers and fathers of families detest war."[3] The horror of that European war was still fresh in the memories of the participants at the Council, who also knew who won that war. On the eve of the Council, the United States was basking in universal acclaim as the defender of the West. America was prosperous, good, and optimistic, and, thanks largely to American media, Hollywood, and doctrinal warfare, it was the embodiment of the ideal state in the minds of millions of the world's inhabitants.

The Council took place during the height of the Cold War, something everyone connected with it knew, but it also took place during the era of psychological warfare, something which very few people knew and which even fewer understood. The main battlefield of psychological warfare was the human mind, with its thoughts, perceptions, and emotions, which could be shaped or manipulated, in a way that the target or victim was unaware he or she was under attack. Like the atom bomb, but more powerful, psychological warfare changed the nature of warfare forever, and it was more effective because no one was aware of its use. The American mass media – television, movies, magazines, newspapers, radio—worked in tandem with the US Government to change the social environments of targeted societies, thereby enabling a societal reengineering whose primary beneficiary was the American financial elites. In order to bring about the needed change, the psychological warriors changed the targeted population's understanding of social organization, and they first changed the relationship between Church and state, or the spiritual to the material. This was done by elevating the individual's desires, which were easily manipulated by the media, to be the final arbiter of every conflict. The magic word which made an individual's will sovereign was "freedom." America used this word to target societies around the globe, especially the "Free World" as the beneficiaries of a social engineering that would remain invisible to the targeted peoples. A free press was essential to all of this, and the idea of a free press was also enshrined in the sacred First Amendment. This innovation helped the plutocrats to control societies by giving people the illusion that what was published or broadcast was of, by and for the people – the exalted civil society of Thomas Paine and other American Founders. The Americans sought to accomplish two main objectives in regards to all societies in the Free World: 1) a short term goal of having the target societies grow sympathetic to US policies as well as Americans and their institutions in general; and 2) a longer term goal of re-organizing the target society along American principles, or, in other words, to make the target society like America, the ideal society.

The Catholic Church was an important target of American efforts during much of the Cold War. As to the Catholic Church, the Americans worked to accomplish a third important objective which was to use its vast international organization as a means to spread American ideas and ideals. This required the Catholics change their doctrine, or at least their policies, to bring them in line with American principles, trends, and actions which then became morally superior to the principles proposed by the Church. If the Church could be colonized by new ideas about the relationship between freedom and truth, to give just one example, the Church's world-wide infrastructure could be used to inculcate American ideas throughout the world. The vehicle for all of those ideas, including the Protestant spirit of capitalism, was The American Proposition, as developed by Henry Luce and John Courtney Murray. It became the basic weapon in the ideological offensive against societies around the globe – especially the Catholic Church—to turn them into cultural and economic colonies of America.

Vatican Council II provided the Americans, working mainly through the CIA and Time, Inc., and their allies within the Church, the Americanists, with an opportunity to re-make the Church in the image of the ideal society, that is America, and then use the Americanized Church to spread The American Proposition around the globe. In order to do this, *Time* first had to take over the interpretation of the Council and become the sole arbiter of the Council's real meaning. *Time* did this through a number of techniques, all of which were in accordance with tried and true principles of psychological warfare.

First, *Time* divided the Catholics into good guys and bad guys, much like the American movie Westerns of the day, using terms that imparted emotional responses favorable to the Americans. The former were termed liberal or democratic or progressive. The latter were termed conservative or authoritarian or reactionary. The former were depicted in positive tones such as intelligent or compassionate, and the latter as ignorant or oppressive. The former were like the Americans, the latter were not. Those like the Americans were the good guys, the others were not. The Council was an attempt by those like the Americans to bring the Church "up to date," or make it like America, which was good, the ideal. The name given to that effort and the spirit that infused it was "the Spirit of Vatican II" coined by *Time* magazine during the Council while Catholic writer Michael Novak, who took the place of Robert Blair Kaiser as *Time's* correspondent, was covering the events of the Council. The "spirit of Vatican II" was, and is, another phrase for the Americanization of the Catholic Church. Part of the brilliance of Luce and *Time,* was their ability to sum up an entire dynamic in a single word or phrase, and this brilliance shone forth during the days of Vatican II.

Second, the Americans were savvy enough, and had good enough intelligence, to know the existence of an organizational dynamic within at the Council pitting the edges against the center. The bishoprics in the field were depicted as being at odds with a reactionary, authoritarian center, represented by the Curia. This division was used to advance the American agenda with the bishoprics in large measure depicted as representing American ideas and ideals. In reality, many of the bishoprics in America and Northern Europe, particularly the Germans, were infected with Americanism. In the case of the Germans and other Northern European episcopates, this was the result of the social re-engineering by the Americans that followed World War II.

The success of that campaign was documented in a number of reports gathered by the Merritts in two great studies from 1970 and

1980. The success of American psychological warfare on the German populace, particularly among the more affluent and more educated, had serious ramifications for the Catholic Church in general and for the Vatican Council in particular. The German theologians who had been re-engineered after the war found common cause with those infected with the same spirit in France, which harbored the intellectual virus of Americanism ever since Thomas Paine showed up there during the French Revolution.

The main psychological battleground during the Cold War was Germany, especially during the period of 1945 to 1955 when John McCloy and his social engineers[4] unleashed "heavy barrages of propaganda, aimed both at improving the image of the United States and sullying that of the Soviet Union. The 'Voice of America,' the information centers, and the American-controlled mass media saw to this latter task. And it is remarkable how receptive AMZON [American Zone of Occupation] Germans were to publications decrying Soviet policies."[5] The Germans took sides in an increasingly polarized world that required Europeans to choose either the Americans or the Soviet Communists.[6] American psychological warfare played a key role in this decision.

American psychological warfare changed the way Germans looked at themselves. Over time, the Germans changed their view on the reason for the start of World War II. In late 1949, about one third of the Germans thought the fault for World War II lay either exclusively with foreign countries or the fault should be shared by Germany and foreign countries, and about 41 percent blamed Hitler, the Nazis, and/or Germany. By early 1956, Germany was viewed by 47 percent as the cause of the war and foreign countries were viewed by about 23 percent as having responsibility for the war. Interestingly enough, a brave few "attributed the war to international capitalism." Similarly, the cause of German defeat shifted increasingly from the treason of Germans to Germany's lack of material resources as compared with the abundance of the material resources of their opponents.[7]

The Germans were aware of what was happening to them, as the American occupiers found out. In July, 1952 a third of the German population either approved, disapproved, or expressed no opinion about American propaganda. However, by December, 1952 about 80 percent of those interviewed held the view America's propaganda was "more to the FRG's [Federal Republic of Germany or West Germany] advantage than disadvantage." As the Merritts noted, "Whatever ambivalence West Germans felt about an American information program in general, they were quite receptive to its specific aspects." Roughly 78 percent of those interviewed who accepted "the appropriateness of an American information program also believed that such ideas and views would have a lasting effect in West Germany particularly in strengthening democratic tendencies."[8]

With the strengthening of so-called democratic tendencies, the philosophy known as Liberalism took root in German society and began to remake Germany in the image of her American conquerors.

American media—and Time, Inc., in particular—had a proven track record of successfully changing the viewpoints of targeted populations. Two examples of the singular power of *Time* were the overthrow of the Iranian President, Mohammed Mossadegh in 1953, and the overthrow of Guatemala's president Jacobo Arbenz Guzman in 1954. *Time* played a crucial role in the CIA-led coup in Guatemala by publishing "regularly for two years... stories concerning Arbenz's government dedicated to making it look vicious and ridiculous." *Time* articles, with the most notable being the article entitled "Oh, Come to the Fair!" from the November 2, 1953 edition: "celebrated a major moment of orchestrated mayhem: `To lure U.S. tourists scared off by its growing reputation as the center of Communist influence, Guatemala this year decided to stage a lavish international fair...a gambling casino, horse races, Miami-style dog racing, Ferris wheels, a roller coaster and a brand new bull ring.'"[9]

Difficulties arose, work went incomplete, a riot occurred, and "`soon many choice ringside seats...had barefoot occupants...'" Thousands of ticket-holders could not get in, the bullfight was cancelled, garbage littered the landscape, toilets were broken, and many were hurt. As *Time* reported, "Toriello's casino attracted little betting, his dog races were put off because of construction fights, and his fellow businessmen showed no interest in the fair's industrial pavilions....And to top it all the...crowds of U.S. tourists failed to show."[10]

When it came to the world at large, *Time* was quick to "give currency" to new terms and concepts like "modern man." *Time* did so by making use of Protestant Theologians like Reinhold Niebuhr, who were supposed to make sense of everything for the "modern man" who "knows almost nothing about the nature of God, almost never thinks about it, and is complacently unaware that there may be any reason to." Another word for *Time's* version of "modern man" was the American Protestant Male, an ideological, cultural, and occasionally biological, descendant of the Calvinists of old, much like Henry Luce. Educated, but without wisdom, modern man lived "Under the bland influence of the idea of progress . . . supposing himself more and more to be the measure of all things," he:

"achieved a singularly easy conscience and an almost hermetically smug optimism. The idea that man is sinful and needs redemption was subtly changed into the idea that man is by nature good and hence capable of indefinite perfectibility. This perfectibility is being achieved through technology, science, politics, social reform, education. Man is essentially good, says 20th Century liberalism, because he is rational, and his rationality is (if the speaker happens to be a liberal Protestant) divine, or (if he happens to be religious unattached) at least benign."[11]

The Germans were re-engineered according to the American image. Now, with the Vatican Council about to convene, it was the Catholics' turn to submit.

CHAPTER 85
CD JACKSON STUDIES THE CHURCH
BEFORE THE COUNCIL

C D Jackson traveled to Rome during the Summer of 1962, on the eve of Vatican II. His trip showed the importance of the upcoming ecumenical council to the Americans. During his involvement with political warfare operations during the 1950s, Jackson came to understand the crucial role that the Catholic Church played in keeping Communist governments at bay in places like Hungary and in Poland. Both Luce and Jackson appreciated the power of the institutional Church in Eastern Europe. When John XXIII announced the ecumenical council, Luce and CD Jackson saw an opportunity.

In 1958, the year Pius XII died, RCA in Italy did a study on "The Policy of the Catholic Church in the Selection and Training of Her Leaders," which contained was the following paragraph: "The Church appears to the world as the most complex of enterprises, inasmusch as she manages to coordinate the most heterogenous of efforts as regards cultural backgrounds and territorial dispersion without the resort to force; no other group at the moment has her extension nor employs so much human energy over such a wide area without any continuity or possibility of physical control."[1]

As CD Jackson read this passage, he must have come to understand the effectiveness of the Church in all sorts of cultures. The Church could surmount cultural barriers quite effectively, a most useful ability as the Americans were looking to reorganize societies all over the globe. Such ability comported with the American effort, as Dr. Possony indicated, to leverage technology for the American advantage. Such a proven ability was valuable to advance the capitalist spirit which always sought to reduce, or destroy, barriers not of the making of the capitalists. The Church and the Americans could be fellow travelers after all since they both sought to eliminate barriers not of their making, and the Americans could borrow or use Church techniques for doing so.

The Church's secret was an ethic of self-abnegation, something which contradicted America's business ethic but which did "appeal to a higher realm of human hopes" thereby tapping into an inchoate human desire for improvement. The study went on to describe how young men were selected for the priesthood, the importance of seminaries as its "nerve-centres," and the division of Church governance into the parochial, the episcopal and the Pontifical spheres. The religious vocation was a "tremendous draining away of intellectual energy from the field of economic competition" but it was in search of "ideals and satisfaction," and that is what the American ideology also had to offer. The study noted "The Church will permit dissent in certain intellectual questions but not disunity on the operational plane."[2]

At around the same time, the American financial elites also expressed an interest in using the Catholic Church as an asset to spread the American gospel. In an article appearing shortly before the 1960 presidential election, *The Wall Street Journal* commented on the "universality and autonomy" of the Catholic Church, praising her ability to manage so many people in a global effort that would "tax the brain power of an army of business executives." The article, which also discussed the "big growth" of Catholics in the US,[3] showed the financial powers had both motive and means, as proven by the recent successes of the CIA's doctrinal warfare campaign and

Madison Avenue advertising, to incorporate the Church into their efforts at world domination. The Vatican Council gave them a unique opportunity in this regard, and CD Jackson traveled to Rome to make sure that the opportunity was not wasted. While there, Jackson sent Luce a report on the situation, which predicted that Italy would become "the dominant business nation around the Africa and Middle Eastern rim of the Mediterranean, extending all the way into Somaliland and even Ethiopia."[4] Good relations with the Church were essential for that reason alone, but the Church was valuable for other reasons as well. Jackson described the Church as *"that tremendous mechanism all over the world."* The Church had a worldwide organization that could put people and ideas on the ground almost anywhere. The change in pontiffs added value to this dynamic and offered the Americans an opening to use the pope against his own people, the Catholics. Pope John could be depicted as progressive and pro-American simply by dint of his personality. Unlike Pius XII, whom Jackson described as "awesome, aloof, austere, intellectual," John XXIII was "a very human being, the friend, sort of the uncle, of everyone in the church." The current pope's "dogma may be impeccable," Jackson wrote, "but his method of communicating it are frequently unusual and must be the despair of the monsignor assigned to watch over him." The Pope "is strictly un-Orthodox in his behavior" and so CD could "see why the ultra conservatives are alarmed, the ultra conservatives both within the Church and among the laity."[5] John XXIII "knows how to talk to people, to get them on his side, to understand the ideas he wishes to promulgate. Conversely, if any monsignor had the responsibility of preparing the text or the notes for what the Pope was expected to say, his blood must have run cold a number of times over what he undoubtedly considered dangerous ad-libbing on the part of His Holiness."[6]

Using his clout as a member of the board of Pro Deo, Jackson obtained two audiences with Pope John and described the second, private audience in close detail:

"My second audience was in a smallish, private room in the Vatican. There were actually a whole series of rooms strung out one after the other of different sizes and depending upon the size of the room there was a different size group. I was able to notice this because I had to go through the entire series of rooms in order to get to the leading one, the small one, with not more than ten or a dozen people. But as I went through the others I was able to see the size of the groups. The Pope's interpreter is a Monsignor Ryan, six-feet-four, 250 pounds, no fat, and a wonderful brogue. He was the one who did the interpreting into English in St. Peter's. Monsignor Ryan warns you in advance that you are not supposed to ask questions but simply to follow along with the conversation that will be initiated by the Pope, who has been briefed in advance as to who you are, why you are there and what your main interests are.

"As you stand around against the wall in the room, all of a sudden another monsignor comes in and following him appears the Pope. He is a small, slightly round-shouldered, rather heavy man, with a very benevolent face and the biggest ears I have ever seen. He goes up, shakes hands, says a few words, listens in a friendly way and then moves on to the next person.

"When he came to me, he started talking in Italian. At a pause, Monsignor Ryan, who was next to him, broke in to tell the Pope that I spoke French, at which the Pope, in the most natural way in the world, said 'Bene' and started off in French, very good French but as I said before, with an Italian accent.

"He talked briefly about the importance of journalism in the modern world, with all the forces for good and evil that are at work; he mentioned 'Pro Deo' as an organization that he was all for and he then moved on to the next person in the most natural and friendly way imaginable."[7]

As a result of this brief encounter and the studies he had done leading up to it, CD Jackson perceived both a sea change in the Vatican and an opportunity. In making the transition from the austere Pius XII to the avuncular John XXIII, Catholic leadership became worldly and more open to advancing America's materialistic Revolution of Expectations. "Of course," Jackson continued:

"what is at stake is something far deeper and far more important and in a sense far more dangerous than just the difference between the personalities of two different Popes, John XXIII as I have described him, warm, human, friendly, relaxed, preferring to be with people and his predecessor Pius XII, intellectual, aloof, austere, aristocratic, aesthetic and vastly preferring things of the mind to things of human content and contact.

"As a non-Catholic, may I utter a vast over-simplification when I say that what is at stake is a decision by the present Pope and his close Vatican advisors that the traditional Catholic Church approach to human misery, unhappiness, poverty, of resignation on earth to whatever fate has decreed in order to achieve salvation through faith is no longer enough.

"As far as the Church is concerned, the old approach will no longer suffice as a way of preserving the spiritual, mental and moral allegiance of Catholics all over the world. Stated a different way, it means that today's priest, today's monsignor, today's bishop and archbishop, today's cardinals, today's pope must not only have his doctorate in theology but also in the social sciences in order to be a dynamic part of the lives of Catholics all over the world who are suddenly emerging from agriculture into a neo-industrialization and urbanization and all that that implies.

"Latin America is an example. The new African nations are another. The Vatican appreciates that the traditional approach is no longer good enough. Thanks to communications and the rise of industrialization, these people will all be jumping several centuries in one decade. Their standards of living will be improved, their political consciousness will go from zero to a fairly high point very, very quickly.

"Their social consciousness is being worked upon by the Communists, and the Vatican understands that unless it is an active participant in the process of this social, economic, political and industrial awakening it will no longer be able to hold the souls of these people after they are awake.

"The dangers inherent in this tremendous decision are quite obvious. It is impossible for the Catholic Church to participate sociologically, to participate in the development of the social sciences in these countries without at the same time becoming heavily involved politically. This is supposed to be what they are not supposed to be doing. But they are going to be doing it, and on the side of the angels."[8]

The Church's shift to social action was a direct result of the US-USSR struggle and was part of the "Revolution of Expectations" which both the Americans and the Soviets created. The fact the Church decided to enter "in the titanic struggle between the free world and international aggressive Communism" represented "a tremendous weapon on the side of Freedom" and a golden opportunity for the Americans. "The big question" in CD Jackson's mind was whether the Church could "overcome political suspicions in the various countries in which it works in order to ally itself with the right kind of regimes." This meant, could the Church effectively ally itself with the Americans by endorsing American-style capitalism against the domestic, authoritarian, and often Catholic, elites of various countries around the world? The authoritarian system was characterized by an economic situation that "was represented by twenty-five or fifty or one hundred and fifty or five hundred families and everybody else starved." That younger generation now realized that that form of capitalism "was not working. The question is whether the Church will be able to ally itself with these people as well as with the right political regimes in order to create what might be called a freedom front to counter the inevitably forming popular fronts behind which or in front of which are always to be seen the Communists."[9] The coming Ecumenical Council offered the Americans a way to remove barriers between the religions thereby allowing the advance of what Fanfani called the "capitalist spirit" in the name of "Freedom." Jackson sensed change was in the air at the Vatican. Whereas previous ecumenical efforts involved bringing:

"the Greek and Russian Orthodox Church back into the fold. The thinking and planning for the coming Council goes way beyond this. Conceivably, it would be willing to go the full length of the road with Protestants and Jews. When I say the full length of the road, I do not mean that the Catholic Church proposes to abandon any of its basic doctrine. I simply mean that they are wholeheartedly prepared to explore with other faiths those areas and those techniques where they can work together, not only for the brotherhood of man and the fatherhood of God, but the freedom of people."[10]

Because of the upcoming council, Rome had eclipsed London, Paris, and Bonn as the most important city in Europe, "from which may emerge an element, a factor, a technique, a dynamic of tremendous value to all of us. Watch Italy."[11] Like Paul Blanshard fifteen years earlier in the US, CD Jackson believed that the crucial area in Italy was the doctrinal issue of church and state. "None of this is going to be easy," Jackson continued. If the Americans played their cards right, and if the Vatican moved in the right direction, and did not *take one step too many too fast*" so that *"the hue and cry for the separation of Church and State might assume such proportions that the Catholic efforts in the social area might be largely vitiated. . . .* this ancient country may" become "the ally that we are all looking for. So I repeat, don't overlook Italy."[12]

Continuing his reports to Luce from Saigon, where he also had an opportunity to observe the Catholics in South Vietnam, CD Jackson addressed the struggle in the Church between the good guys, or "liberals," and the bad guys, or the "reactionaries." He wrote "the reactionary elements among the Catholics in Italy, the reactionary elements within the Vatican itself, may triumph over the present elements which are in the ascendency and, which for want of a better label, have to be called liberal."[13]

If the Americans could mobilize the "liberal" forces within the Church, it could use its vast, international resources as a way to monitor, create and support movements that could support American interests or the "freedom front," which atomized society the better to exploit it economically and politically. The Vatican, according to Jackson, recognized the so-called traditional Catholic approach to society was no longer adequate in places like Latin America, where "the equation for a Catholic country in Latin America went about as follows: Agriculture plus poverty plus illiteracy equals a Catholic country. The same can be said of a number of the new African nations. The Vatican appreciates that this equation is no longer good enough."[14]

In September, 1962, Jackson commissioned Miss Iride Cerabona to undertake a thorough study of the organizational and functional structure of the hierarchy of the Catholic Church. The study explained in twelve pages of diagrams and text the organization of the Church's "Central Sphere" with emphasis on the Curia. It also explained each of the Church's "Regional Spheres," which consisted of the various diocesan bishops, as well as the power and functions of each of the various agencies and organizations within the Church.[15]

On September 24, Jackson, fresh from his trip to Rome, wrote a letter to Monsignore Egino Cardinale, Chief of Protocol for the Vatican Secretary of State, asking that Cardinale "would make special provision for putting one LIFE photographer inside St. Peters, on the official photographers' stand, for the opening day ceremonies on Oct. 11 and for other important `open sessions of the Council."[16] In exchange for the privilege, *Life* would "portray this event in its full majesty and impact for the benefit of the Council and the edification of the world." Since *Life* was "without peer in the field of photographic journalism" admitting a *Life* photographer to the opening session was "as much in your interest as in LIFE's." [17] The fact that Monsignor Cardinale was not put off by Jackson's cocky, condescending tone goes a long way toward explaining how and why Time, Inc., and the Americans, were so successful in their characterization of the Council as an American morality play. The Americans were cocky, assured and confident, and so the Catholics were seduced.

CHAPTER 86
THE VATICAN PRESS VERSUS TIME, INC

Archbishop Pericle Felici was the head of the Council's "ecumenical press center" which issued the official communiqués on the progress of the Council. The Vatican attempted to control the public perception by these communiqués. The idea was a sincere one, like so many others from the Vatican, but the American media had an agenda. A personal letter from a confrere to Fr. Connell summed up the situation early in the Council: "The religious press continues fine. But the Secular Press is sadly slanted stressing disagreements in the Ecumenical Council, touching and hinting at 'revolts' and some 'Cardinals bolting'....What Nonsense!" The confrere then quoted a report from the *Baltimore Catholic News*: "Archbishop Shehan reports that Redemptorist Father Francis J Connell held seminars for 52 Bishops and prelates and priests on the Voyage. All were inspired by Fr. Connell...(there's an understatement)."[1]

In order to facilitate the dissemination of news on the council, the US bishops established a press panel that consisted of ten priests, including Connell, who articulated the norms by which the Press Panel was to operate:

"1. The group is not official and the meetings, though regular, are informal. They are not spokesmen, but friendly experts. 2. Our experts are available to offer facts connected with, or background to, matters set forth in official press releases; they will be eager to define words or phrases; they can relate to historical precedents or parallels; they can cite relevant Church law; they can identify persons. 3. They should avoid and watch for opportunities to eliminate phrases with tendentious 'political' or 'partisan' overtones, analogies to the political order like conservative, liberal, progressive. 4. They should be prompt and categorical in distinguishing between reports and rumors – and should decline to comment in any way on latter. 5. They should be available as a group at a specific time and place at a defined time following each meeting."[2]

The purpose of the press panel, as established by Bishop Albert Zuroweste of the NCWC Press Department, and as directed by William Fanning of the *Catholic News* from New York, was to follow those regulations. The panel was to "assist the representatives of the United States press and communications media to the extent possible, through definition, clarifications, and backgrounding [sic] on the subject matter of the day's official press communiqué from the secretariat of the second Vatican Council." [3]

After the first session, Fr. Edward L Heston from South Bend, Indiana, had a sense of "great pride" in the way the American press covered the council. Heston "was particularly impressed by the faithfulness with which top ranking correspondents attended the sessions. It was inspiring to see how hard they were willing to work to insure accuracy in their reports." Unlike the press agencies of other nations, the American press did not concern itself with "pettiness" or "small-minded gossip."

As *periti* who had taken an oath of secrecy, the members of press panel could not discuss the council's deliberations; however, some periti had no qualms about talking to the press, including Gustave Weigel, SJ (non-Catholic observers), Archbishop John Hallinan (liturgy), and even Hans Kung (Church unity).[4]

Heston's "pride" in the American press was not shared by the journalists who complained that "the lack of specific information in the communiqués made it impossible for them to do a serious job of reporting the council since their vagueness tended to obscure rather than enlighten."[5] Nor was Heston's pride shared by Fenton, who had been apprised of the press's intentions two years before the council began by someone who felt that "the so-called 'American Interpretation' is being given wide publicity throughout the world and is liable to make trouble for the Holy See in other countries as well as here."[6]

Fenton knew the power of the American press in general and the power of *Time* in particular. In an article which appeared in September, 1962 entitled "The Council and Father Kung," Fenton concluded that any book taken seriously by *Time* would be considered "a genuinely influential work," which "will be read and will be taken seriously by many of our people, and, in particular, by our young priests and seminarians." The fact *Our Sunday Visitor* gave a book a positive review was evidence of, and amplification of, this reality.[7] Hans Kung may have been a German but his demands for change in the Church were supported by the Americans and, if followed, would lead to re-making the Church in the image of America. Kung summarized "'a vague, undefined discontent' with the Catholic Church, its doctrines, and its activities." He came up with a laundry list: "Hopeless preaching and religious instruction – nonsense or rigidity in the liturgy – the Index – Roman centralism – Episcopal bureaucracy – all the things wrong with the training of priests – convent and monastic education – political conformism – moral theology, especially on atom bombs and sex – Latin in the liturgy – scandals in the clergy – the fussing over organization and congresses in Catholic societies – Thomism – rationalism – Marianism – the pilgrimage racket."[8]

The explanation for this was simple enough: Kung was a German who had been subjected during his formative years to the social re-engineering which American had inflicted on Germany after the war. It was hardly coincidental that Kung sounded like an American or that *Time* used its review of Kung's book, *The Council, Reform and Reunion* to point out where the Catholic Church was wrong and where it needed to change. In particular the "conservative" and "clerical" elements were at fault for keeping the Church, and especially the laity, in the dark all these years and not allowing them to become more American. Nor was it surprising *Time* titled its review "A Second Reformation, For Both Catholics and Protestants" when it appeared in the June 8, 1962 edition. Sheed & Ward, the publishing house started with financial assistance and backing from the Luces, published Kung's book and also Murray's *We Hold These Truths*. Kung's book was praised for its "liberal, ecumenical spirit" by key Protestants Henry Pitney Van Dusen, President of the Union Theological Seminary, and Episcopal Bishop James A Pike, American apologists.[9]

Kung, according to *Time*, "admits that his church has been guilty of `a spurious, self-righteous "splendid isolation"' from the intellectual currents of the age. He "expressed sympathy for many modern men who are exasperated by `the lack of any openness among the Church's leaders towards new problems and insights, new forms and values.' In displaying her claim of infallibility before the world, for example, the Catholic Church has refused to admit, `in all honesty and humility, that errors had occurred even in cases where she was perfectly capable of error and in simple fact has erred.'"[10]

By overstating the Church's claim to infallibility, Kung and *Time* proceeded to depict the Church as overreaching, overbearing, and elitist, something bound to turn Catholics against their own Church as they were saturated with American ideas of freedom, equality, and democracy. Kung and *Time* then set out some of the terms by which the Church leadership, and the laity themselves, could bring the Church into compliance with American standards. First, the Church needed to issue "A doctrinal statement on the role of the episcopacy that would restore the office of bishop `to its full value' and limit the tendency to `Roman centralism.'" It needed to implement "Liturgical reform that would allow bishops and diocesan councils wide liberty to create rites suitable to local needs." Third, the Church needed to "reform" or even abolish "the Index of Prohibited Books," even though the Index, Kung added sarcastically, "ensures 'to any book placed upon it the widest possible circulation.'" Fourth, it should issue "A declaration of principle on the role of laymen in the church, and restoration to the laity of the use of the chalice at Holy Communion on certain occasions. Finally, the Church needed to make "A declaration of repentance. 'We in the Church,' says Kung, 'are none of us guiltless of the world's unhappy state today, and the guilt of our fathers lies heavy upon us. It would be a truly Christian act if the Pope and the Council were to express this truth: forgive us our sins! Forgive us our sins, and in particular our share in the sin of schism!"[11]

Time effectively depicted the Church and Catholicism as failing. Evidence of this is found in the preface of a book written by Joseph Ratzinger, published in 2012. Ratzinger, a German peritus at the Council for Josef Cardinal Frings of Cologne, explained how, on the eve of the Council:

"Christianity. . . *appeared* weary and it *looked* as if the future would be determined by other spiritual forces. The *sense* of this loss of the present on the part of Christianity, and of the task following on from that, was well summed up in the word 'aggiornamento' (updating). Christianity must be in the present if it is to be able to form the future. So that it might once again be a force to shape the future, John XXIII had convoked the Council without indicating to it any specific problems or programmes. This was the greatness and at the same time the difficulty of the task that was set before the ecclesial assembly."[12]

Catholics like Kung and Ratzinger felt bad because they were Germans, Catholic, and not American enough. Their perceptions of reality were shaped by *Time,* by Americanists like Kung, and by US psychological warfare operations. By "modernizing" the Church, the "liberal" German Catholics were going to deconstruct the Church and re-make it like America in its worldview and policies, if not also in its principles of organization. In that way, the Church could no longer be the teacher of nations but it would be just another interest group with another agenda in a society created by Liberalism to serve the plutocrats.

There was still more work to be done. On October 5, 1962, *Time* presented the criteria whereby its readers could judge the success or failure of the council in an article entitled "Religion: Council of Renewal." Fenton referred to this and other articles in his diaries as establishing in the minds of the episcopacy the belief great results could be expected of the Council.[13] These great results required the Church adopt the American worldview, accepted American social organization as the ideal, and, in essence, become like America, which, as the narrative explained, was good and right. The Catholic Church had to modernize and knock down its barriers to others, or else, as the story line went, it would weaken and disappear because it could not satisfy the desires of the people and "keep up with the times." This all meant the Catholics had to accept as true what America said as the best and truest model for operating in this world, something that became clear in the first paragraph, when *Time* claimed that the purpose of the council was "aggiornamento," which they translated as "modernization."[14] The very premise that it had to modernize cast the Church in a negative light, and immediately put it on the defensive in the arena of public opinion, while confusing and dividing Catholics.

This image presented the Church as the cause for religious disunity. In order to remedy the situation, the Church had to change. *Time,* which was famous for publishing articles without "by-lines" and for attributing statements to unnamed persons, then put these sentiments into the mouths of "one group of missionaries," who supposedly said: "We must bestir ourselves and not rest until we have overcome our old habits of thought, our prejudices and the use of expressions that are anything but courteous, so as to create a climate favorable to the reconciliation we look forward to." Adding emphasis, Pope John "never stopped talking about Christian unity as the aim of the council."[15]

According to Archbishop Lorenz Jaeger of Paderborn, a man *Time* described as "one of Germany's most articulate advocates of change in the church," said Catholicism must "think in universal terms and abandon a number of concepts that governed its past. Among these are the belief that the alliance of temporal and spiritual powers is 'natural,' the rigid juridical view of the church derived from Roman law, the unduly abstract understanding of man's nature derived from scholastic thought, the acceptance of Western social and economic forms as practical ideal."[16] The Germans, recently conquered by the Americans, were used to bring the Catholics into captivity.

Time then listed the items "a new generation of theologically educated laymen" were demanding from the Church. One was "a proper share in running the affairs of the Church." Under the leadership of "scholars in France and Germany – notably Dominican Yves Congar" the "rigid scholasticism of 19th century Catholicism has given way to a more open form of Thomism, capable of incorporating insights from Freud, Dewey, Sartre and even Marx." Catholic Bible scholars were catching up with the Protestants, and Teilhard de Chardin was praised as trying to "bridge the wall between modern science and traditional faith." The Vatican was abandoning the "rigid anti-Communist stand of Pius XII." Catholics and Protestants were growing closer with Bea's efforts assisting in that regard. The "ecumenical revolution" was resulting in the Protestants being viewed as "separated brethren" and not "heretics" or "schismatics."[17] The Council was sure to address a number of "challenging issues," including episcopal infallibility, the structure of dioceses, priests and religious, the liturgy, the Church and non-Catholics, marriage, the laity, a married deaconate, decentralization, dogma, and religious liberty. In discussing the topic of dogma, *Time*, employing its penchant for non-attribution, quoted an unnamed "associate of the Pope" to emphasize an Americanist approach: "it is not necessary to propose new doctrines which might disturb Protestants and Eastern Christians."[18]

Time mentioned religious liberty in almost every article it did on the Council and presented the US bishops as the force for change by claiming: "At the strong urging of U.S. bishops, the council may adopt a formal statement that all men in all countries have an inherent right to worship God as they believe. The declaration will be strongly opposed by many prelates in Spain, Italy and Latin America, who are still reluctant to give full freedom to Protestant missions." According to the US bishops, while the "Church teaches that 'error has no rights,' it also teaches that erring men…do have inalienable privileges." [19] *Time* painted the Pope as a positive force, a modernizer, and hence a friend of the Americans, if not also an Americanist himself, when it wrote "many of the new directions within Catholicism are either tolerated or openly encouraged by the smiling old man," John XXIII "made the papacy into a different kind of job. 'He is not intellectual and only an indifferent theologian,' says one close friend. 'But he is a man with a great pastoral bent, and overwhelming charity.'" Quite a change from his predecessor Pius XII described in negative terms as "the ascetic, mystical descendant of Roman aristocracy…an intellectual who applied Catholic teaching to nearly every modern problem, from nuclear war to euthanasia…."[20]

Writing for an American audience, *Time* portrayed the Council as a contest against bad guys, epitomized by authoritarian, conservative, Italians who did not want change, and who did not want to modernize thereby thwarting good Pope John. *Time* confected a narrative, in which the forces of conservatism and reaction were lead by "such impressive figures as Alfredo Cardinal Ottaviani of the Holy Office, Ernesto Cardinal Ruffini of Palermo and Giuseppe Cardinal Siri of Genoa, the 'integralists'" who also included "nearly every bishop in Italy and Spain, a majority of the prelates from the U.S. and Latin America."[21] *Time* and America's psychological warriors described the "bad guys" at the council as enemies of "internal renewal of the Catholic Church," who were most frequently encountered among the "standpat conservatives as the cardinals of the Curia and the bishops of Italy and Spain." The upcoming fight showed that, as one anonymous "Irish cleric in Rome" said, even "'The Holy Ghost has his back up against the wall.'"[22]

Opposed to the conservatives were the liberals, or good guys, who believed "that the church should discard nonessentials that harm its mission, seek to make it, without sacrificing doctrine, more accessible as a home for modern man." They were lead by Bea, one of the few prelates in the "Vatican Curia" who gained *Time's* approval. Outside of the Vatican the list of good guys included: "Tanganyika's Laurean Cardinal Rugambwa, Utrecht's Bernard Jan Cardinal Alfrink, Montreal's Cardinal Leger, Munich's Julius Cardinal Dopfner, a clear majority of the bishops in France, The Netherlands, Germany, Austria, Africa and Asia."[23] The Council, according to *Time's* reading came down to a fight between the Americanists, especially from northern European countries, on one side and the Catholics on the other, a dichotomy which perdured for years after the Council ended. This was the essence of the struggle at Vatican II and within the Church for years afterwards though it has been termed, thanks largely to *Time,* liberal versus orthodox or liberal versus conservative.

The quintessential good guy at the Council, according to *Time,* was Pope John, who held traits Americans and their allies, the Americanists, could harken to because he was "aware of the mood of the Church" and hence open to democratic reform.[24] Pope John made appointments that "neatly balanced the claims of liberals and conservatives" thereby showing fairness, another American trait.[25] Another indication the Pope was on the side of the good guys, or liberals, was he "made it clear that hierarchical reformers would have plenty of opportunity to make their cases."[26] When he called Pope Pius IX "an admirable shepherd" and hoped to beatify him, Pope John could not shake the good guy label as he was said to be in touch with the Catholic's past.[27] Anyone else would have been excoriated.

Cardinal Bea was another good guy, who was described in almost Christ-like terms as the "son of a carpenter" who owed a "debt to Protestant scholarship." He was in addition a "supreme realist"[28] as well as a "wise old Jesuit" who could "avoid the diplomatic fiasco" which occurred at the first Vatican Council and who had "spent long hours conferring with Protestant and Orthodox churchmen." Bea was doing the American "thing" by inviting those who wanted to be there such as the World Council of Churches, the Lutheran World Federation, and the World Presbyterian Alliance[29] to bring about unity of the religions.

Time used the venerable American paradigm of the people rising up against the tyrant as the lens through which it viewed the Council. This is the same paradigm the Americans have used throughout their history to de-stabilize regimes not approved by the American elites, and it did so by appealing to material self-interest as some type of higher morality. In the case of the Catholic Church in 1962 and during the Council, the struggle was depicted as liberal versus conservative, laity versus the clerics. The conservatives and the clerics were authoritarian and reactionary, and the laity and the liberals were democratic and progressive. The former were bad guys, the latter were good guys. The bad guys were negative and downbeat, and the good guys were positive and smiling. The power of the Curia where the bad guys were "holed up" had to be broken, and that was to be one of the goals of the Council according to *Time,* which opined that: "the College of Cardinals and the Curia it operates have come in for sharp criticism from some Catholics, and suggestions for a bureaucratic reform have been sent in by non-Italian bishops for inclusion on the agenda of the Vatican Council. One of the most common requests: more freedom for diocesan bishops to adapt church practices to the needs of their people...."[30]

Just as the Germans had their role to play in this scenario, *Time* selected the leaders of the "long-passive Catholic laity," who were "beginning to rebel," according to certain criteria. They had to be Catholic, young, and trained at the best American institutions, which signified the high quality of thought and their loyal adherence to the American ideology. One of the lay leaders which *Time* annointed was "Harvard-educated Daniel Callahan, 32, an associate editor of the magazine [Commonweal] and co-editor of a scholarly collection of Protestant-Catholic ecumenical studies, Christianity Divided." He said"The Church is in the midst of a revolution with which it does not have the means, juridical or theological, to cope." *Time* continued this train of though: "Popes and contemporary theologians alike have exhorted the layman to become more active in the service of the Church; the new breed of well-educated, spiritually alert layman is eager to do so. Yet, thanks to centuries of lay inertia and clerical imperialism, the 'Church's organizational and institutional life has been the sole responsibility of the clergy; from the teaching office of the Church down to the most remote parish everything of importance has been in the hands of the clergy.'"[31] The situation was dire. If the Council did not accede to their demands, Callahan said, then "the whole lay apostolate could simply wither away to a feeble, insignificant movement...."[32]

Because both *Time* and the American Imperium whose interests it represented were at the peak of their power, they were able to frame the discussion in terms most Catholics themselves found persuasive. *Time* magazine could flatter, cajole, deceive, and impress its way into the Council to insure the right spin was put on the whole affair. Robert Blair Kaiser was the first correspondent assigned to cover the event, and he did so during the first and second sessions which lasted from 1962 to 1963. Years later, he confirmed that writers at *Time* were encouraged to take sides, and the best side to take was the one that Luce projected which supported *aggiornamento* and the modernization of the Catholic Church.[33]

Kaiser regularly met with Murray at the Council on Sunday evenings and he also had week-day breakfast and lunch interviews,[34] during which Murray would break his oath of secrecy and leak information on what had transpired at the Council. Murray was a source to *Time* and CD Jackson, Luce, and the CIA. When it came to shaping the views of Catholics towards their own leadership and the Council itself, *Time* and its people were the experts. The Catholic in the pew was being fed a narrative that gave rise to unrealistic expectations from the Council. The Church leadership had to deliver, and *Time* was there to make sure that they delivered the right thing. If Church leadership did not deliver, *Time* won as well because the subsequent disillusionment spread division in the Church which the Americans were trying to subdue. The editors at *Time* established themselves as the disinterested, truth-telling, narrator in the minds of their reading audience. In doing so, they won a great battle because the Catholics, separated from their own leadership came to trust strangers who could then separate Catholics from their history, their tradition, their best interests, and their fellow Catholics.

CHAPTER 87

"THE END OF THE CATHOLIC RELIGION AS WE HAVE KNOWN IT"

While CD Jackson was gathering intelligence about the Pope and the Vatican, Msgr. Fenton was invoking the aid of the Holy Spirit for the upcoming Council. In an August, 1962 article in *American Ecclesiastical Review* entitled "The Holy Ghost in the Ecumenical Council," Fenton emphasized the need for the Council to make expressions in "proper, rather than in metaphorical, terminology." Fenton continued, "God has promised the Church, within which the council speaks with the highest authority, that He would not allow it to be misled in matters of faith and morals."[1]

As Msgr. Fenton prepared to embark on his seventeenth journey to Rome, where he was to serve as a council peritus at the invitation of the Holy Office,[2] he brooded gloomily on the four secretly condemned errors that Cicognani had sent to him and Fr. Connell in the Autumn of 1954. "There has never been anything less effective in the Church than a secret condemnation of an error,"[3] Fenton confided to his diary. If he needed further proof of the ineffectiveness of the Holy Office's secret condemnation, he could read *Time*'s coverage of the Council, which "expects and wants a change in the Church."[4] Other media outlets were picking up *Time*'s

178

message. In a diary entry from the same day, Fenton noted "The Rome American carried an article about the council, prophesying that it would change the Church."[5]

The bishops were concerned about this sort of publicity, but they seemed oblivious to the doctrinal issues needing resolution before they could quiet the calls for change. The bishops failed to discern the publicity was a form of psychological warfare. Fenton

"found all the bishops, especially Bishop Weldon, quite worried. They have no doctrinal problems at all. Indeed, they act as if there were no doctrinal problems at all. They are concerned with the over-advertism of the Council, to which many of them have contributed. They know that the people of the world, and especially the American people, expect some miraculous result from the council. And they do not see how these are going to come about."[6]

At around the same time, Fr. Connell was quoted as saying "papal pronouncements in the past emphasized that the Roman Catholic Church was obliged to allow all religions to function, even in Catholic countries, for the common good of all. He added that should Roman Catholics ever become the majority in the United States, full liberty would be given to all faiths to worship as they please."[7] The Americanists could certainly use this though Connell did not intend his words to be used by them. The critical issue, anyway, was for every society to follow the Divine Positive Law, regardless of how it treated non-Catholic sects. The Americans did not miss a single opportunity to advance their agenda, and unfortunately the Council provided them with opportunities because the Church had disarmed itself before the Council began by not requiring the anti-modernist oath.[8]

The council began inauspiciously enough on October 11, 1962 with rain, but when the sun came out that afternoon, Fenton remarked that "I shall never forget the splendor of that opening." In his opening address, Pope John stated clearly that the doctrine of the Church would not be changed. "The greatest concern of the ecumenical council is this: that the sacred deposit of Christian doctrine should be guarded and taught more efficaciously," and "presented in exceptional form to all men." The purpose of the Council was not to be "a discussion of one article or another of the fundamental doctrine of the Church....which is presumed to be well known and familiar to all." Rather, the Council was to take "into great consideration...everything being measured in the forms and proportions of a magisterium which is predominantly pastoral in character." Instead of condemning erroneous propositions, the Church would use the "medicine of mercy rather than that of severity." The Church will meet the "needs of the present day. . . by demonstrating the validity of her teaching rather than by condemnations." This, according to the Pope, was sufficient because errors are "so obviously in contrast with the right norm of honesty, and have produced such lethal fruits, that by now it would seem that men of themselves are inclined to condemn them, particularly those ways of life which despise God and His law or place excessive confidence in technical progress and a well-being based exclusively on the comforts of life."[9]

Ignoring the Pope's condemnation of "excessive confidence in technical progress," *Time*'s coverage of the opening emphasized the fact that technology, specifically the satellite Telstar, "brought the pomp and pageantry, and even a searching closeup of the Pope's joyful if weary expression" to people around the globe. After mentioning that under the Communists, "Josef Cardinal Mindszenty languished through his sixth year of asylum in an upstairs room of the U.S. legation in Budapest" and that prelates from China were not allowed to attend the Council, *Time* got down to the business of falsifying what the Pope said, when it reported that "he...invited a new interpretation of doctrine" resulting from the use of recent Biblical scholarship. Once it made clear doctrine was on the table at the Council, *Time* described the "liberals" were a force which to be reckoned with and the "liberal minority was not going to be dominated by the Italian Curia." The liberal minority then "demonstrated its parliamentary ability" when Cardinal Lienart asked about the 16 Curial nominees to serve on the first ten commissions. At that point, Cardinal Frings of Cologne, sympathetic to the liberals, adjourned the meeting, stopped the proceedings thereby disrupting the Curia's plans.[10]

Fenton described Leinart's maneuvering from his front row seat: "Suddenly, Lienart arose and proposed that the voting be delayed until Tuesday the 16th. Frings backed him up. It was a real blow. The Americans did not understand at all. They all thought it was a good thing. Ottaviani was almost in tears."[11] This was rebellion, pure and simple, and *Time* was there to encourage it, cover it, and inflame it.

Ottaviani was not doing well. Fenton met Ottaviani the morning after the Council's opening and "was shocked to see the poor man. He told me he was `*mezzo morti*.'"[12] Fenton held out hope that the Pope would assist Ottaviani even if the "Pope may have to make a stand and lose his popularity with the liberals"[13] by doing it. The US bishops lost their moral standing among their peers "by living in the best hotels and spending so much money." That conceded the field to the Church leaders from "France, Germany Belgium, and Holland," who were out to hurt the Roman Curia. Fenton's initial fears about the Council were now coming true: "I had always thought that this council was dangerous. It was started for no sufficient reason. There was too much talk about what it was supposed to accomplish. Now I am afraid that real trouble is on the way."[14] Ottaviani understood the dynamic. Fenton wrote "Ottaviani is bewailing the Franco-German `bloc.' I told that to others this morning and they would not see it. The boss is going to try to get 8 names who can be shoved in ahead of the candidates of the Blocco. I hope he succeeds. The Pope may have to make a stand and lose his popularity with the Jebbies."[15]

It was a tense time all around. The burgeoning Cuban Missile Crisis added to it all. Catholic US President Kennedy was staring down Soviet Premier Kruschev over the presence of nuclear missiles in Fidel Castro's Cuba, and Henry Luce was in regular communications with JFK and his advisors about the military and political situation.[16]

Reports from US intelligence and Time, Inc. confirmed that the revolt in Rome came from the French, who harbored Americanism for a very long time, and from the Germans, who since 1945 were subject to intense American social engineering. Dohrn, Lovestone, Time, Inc. and the CIA were watching the Council closely. Dohrn advised Lovestone in letters that he was going to Rome prior to the Council to study the situation, and he would return for the start of the Council, where he "might be busy in Rome for the next couple of weeks or so."[17]

"Rome, needless to say, is very interesting these days," Dohrn wrote to Lovestone on October 16, 1962. "The council started with a real assertion of democratic spirit inside the Church." Dohrn's first report to Lovestone revealed that things started well for the Americans and that the Americanist spirit was infusing the entire event. According to Dohrn, "The 'palace revolt' was sparked by... close liaison between the French and the German hierarchy – so the 'alliance cordiale' works in this field as well. It is a good thing the German hierarchy spearheads the movement for ecclesiastical reforms....tactfully...while in other countries the supporters of such reforms are often prone to ...illusions about Communism – leftist deviations politically as well as ecclesiastically, I am sorry to say. Such illusions reach far up into the closest circles of the Pope himself....."[18]

According to Dohrn the "German bishops find their position greatly reinforced (to their own surprise) by a) the many...prelates of German descent b.) the impression their tremendous financial help to underdeveloped countries in general and South America in particular has made and the prestige all this has given them, particularly to Cardinal Frings of Cologne, who emerges as one of the leading figures of the council."[19]

Lovestone welcomed the reforms but feared the Church could tilt away from the Americans: "I was much interested in your all too brief comments on Rome. However, welcome as the mood for reforms is, let me tell you that the dangers are great. One of the worst demagogues and most dangerous characters around Ben Bella, to whom I am vigorously opposed in every sense of the word, is a gentleman of the cloth...."[20]

Fenton completed his work for the Commission on the same day as Dohrn's first report. In conversations with Romeo and Dulac, it became clear Fenton's work, viewed as integrist or anti-modernist and criticized by Congar, garnered much interest. A number of attendees at the Council wanted to meet with him and tell him "that I was being calumniated here in Rome."[21] Such concerned him less at the moment than the "bad theology" he was seeing in the drafts of documents coming out of the Council.[22]

The rebellion spread quickly. Within a few days, Fenton heard the French wanted a pastoral Council, a move Fenton described in his diary as an apostasy from the top of the Church. It was now time to "face the facts":

"Since the death of St. Pius X, the Church has been directed by weak and liberal popes who have flooded the hierarchy with unworthy and stupid men. The present conciliar set up makes this all the more apparent. Ed Hanahoe the only intelligent and faithful member of Beas secretariat has been left off the list of the periti. Such idiots as Quinn and the sneak McManus have been put on. Tavard is there as an American, God help us. From surface appearances it would seem that the Lord Christ is abandoning His Church. The thoughts of many are being revealed."[23]

The thoughts of the American bishops were revealed on October 18, when "the sneak McManus" announced Msgr. Fenton did "not represent American Catholic thought nor even the thought at CU."[24] The Catholics were losing to the Liberals, who, one such priest confided to Fenton, had been favored in Rome for decades.[25] The first casualty was going to be the Church, which "is going to be very badly hurt by this council. The opposition between the believers and the loyal Catholics has been brought out into the open."[26] By October 31, Fenton's diary entries were becoming increasingly dire. The Council was going to be an "entirely liberal" affair, and Fenton was anxious to get home because:

"I am afraid that there is nothing at all that I can do here....Being in this counsel is, of course the great experience of my life. But, at the same time, it has been a frightful disappointment. I never thought that the episcopate was so liberal. This is going to mark the end of the catholic religion as we have known it. There will be vernacular masses, and worse still, there will be some wretched theology in the constitution. ....I meet dozens of bishops I know. But I realize that I am all alone."[27]

Ottaviani, badly shaken by the rebellion and by the tenor of the discussions at the Council,[28] put Fenton to work reviewing the commentaries on a proposed doctrinal constitution. One commentator wrote "'These proposals are not an attempt to voice what some particular theologian champions, but to express the already tried and tested new tendency in theology, omitting strongly personal new insights.'" Fenton remarked how this was not in accord with the purpose of a conciliar doctrinal constitution. Citing the First Vatican Council, Fenton noted that council proposed doctrine "to be believed and held by all the faithful according to the ancient and constant faith of the universal Church." This one could hardly do anything different.[29]

When the Doctrinal Commission met the first time on November 13, Ottaviani commented "the people who are trying to reject the schema...favor the new theology." The French, especially Cardinal Leger, who personally attacked Ottaviani, were hostile to Ottaviani's remarks and attacked the schema. Tromp came to its defense saying "a pastoral council should not be non-doctrinal." A second, and more "frightful" schema would be offered if this schema were rejected, and the authors of the second schema were not members of the theological commission but were consultors. The first two days of the doctrinal commission's meeting were the most notable, though they continued to meet for several more days.[30]

On November 14, Ottaviani mounted a "magnificent" counter-attack by insisting that "they must consider this schema," that "pastoral and doctrinal are not opposed" and that "we should not have the new theology." In response, Cardinal Lienart of France, who along with Cardinal Alfrink of Utrecht were leaders of the "liberal" faction, gave a talk that crystallized in many ways the mood of the "liberals." He was opposed to the schema Ottaviani offered, which was the one that had been worked out in the years leading to the opening of the council. After listening to his presentation, Fenton noted that Lienart, who was "obviously not a scholar. . . takes no cognizance of the fact that this has been the language of Catholic theology since Trent. He imagines that the language is 'cold.' He uses the 'separated brethren' as a lousy theologian. They love our Lord as much as we do. Certainly most of them love Him more than Lienart."[31]

Frings then picked up where Lienart left off. He was against the Ottaviani preliminary documents because the language was "too scholarly" and because it "offends the separated brethren." That was Frings' "real argument" because he was "against doctrine on inspiration not inerrancy" and "against the truth of the Bible....."[32]

Cardinal Bea was also against the schema because it "does not answer or correspond to purpose of the Pope. We are supposed to please all who seek God. We must bring Catholic doctrine as a whole up to date." Some were for the schema such as the bishops of Indonesia and the Spanish bishops. Cardinal Siri spoke out for the schema rebuking Lienart and Frings. Siri also said, according to Fenton, the schema was "necessary and useful and should be submitted to the council as it is." It should also "mention the heresy of the Modernists. It is fitting that the doctrine of St. Pius X should be set forth positively. The faithful are troubled."[33] The obscure language fueled Fenton's sense of unease.

The discussions ended on November 21, 1962 with the Pope's intervention to discard the schema on the Church which had been so laboriously put together over the course of two years. Fenton recorded his shock and disappointment when Cosgrove called with the "bad news": "At the Pope's own order the rules were changed and the schema was thrown out. A new commission was set up including Cardinals Meyer, Alfrinks, and Lienart. On the same day, *Time* magazine came out with a dirty personal attack against Ottaviani...."[34]

Ottaviani was devastated. "I went up to see the old man in the afternoon," Fenton wrote. He continued "He is angry, and he talks about more action from our side. He is not going to get it with the bunch he has now. As I left Paul Philippe was going in. He was crying. And he said that this was the time of the devils.

"It was the 21st, and I went to the Canadian College for the reception. Rog was there and I talked with him. Leger was floating on air. I honestly believe that the poor fellow is out of his mind. He had a nervous breakdown a few months ago, and he does not seem to have recovered. He was always a venomous person....

"They plan to leave off this television nonsense in a day or two, and then take up the Church unity thing. That will be a disaster. If I did not believe God, I would be convinced that the Catholic Church was about to end."[35]

In an attempt to understand what was going on, Fenton read a book by a Tedeschi. The book "simply shows that some other people believe what I have thought for several months. Namely, that John XXIII is definitely a lefty. This nonsense to the effect that he is deceived or *mal servite* is disgraceful. He is the boss. In the light of what Tedeschi has written, it is easy to see why O has taken such a bad beating in the council and from the Pope."[36] A few days later, a Milan newspaper report made "him look like a real Modernist at heart. He probably is."[37]

Time's attack on Ottaviani infuriated Bishop Fulton Sheen, who criticized the press "for treating the council as a political convention" as well as "the `spirit of tension, conflict, opposition and disdain for truth' that seemed, to him at least, to characterize coverage of the counsel." *Time* was quick to counterattack by quoting Harold Fey, editor of *The Christian Century,* who opined "Bishop Sheen seems not to understand that the `council is necessarily political as well as religious.'"[38]

The press coverage of the council was more than political; it was a form of covert warfare which targeted Ottaviani and anyone else who dared to oppose the American agenda. *Time* depicted Ottaviani as a dark, authoritarian character who "diligently searched out those whom he considers modernists and heretics." Ottaviani "once opposed the idea of holding the council," he "opposed reform," and his motto was "Semper Idem," which, meaning "always the same," meant that Ottaviani was espousing "a hopeless cause."[39]

Time was intent on showing just how hopeless Ottaviani's cause was by bringing to light three incidents that were supposed to indicate Ottaviani's declining influence. One was the rebuff he suffered after voicing concern that the "schema proposing changes in Catholic liturgy bordered on heresy." The schema he opposed ultimately passed by a vote of 2,162 to 46, wrote *Time*. The approved proposal made "the Mass `more vital and informative for the faithful in accordance with present pastoral requirements.'" A second defeat of the "conservative" forces, according to *Time,* involved Ottaviani's attempt to get Fr. Carl Rahner out of Rome and to censure the Jesuits' Biblical Institute. Third, *Time* reported that Ottaviani suffered a defeat on the "draft constitution on Scripture and tradition proposed by the commission" he chaired. He proposed Scripture must be read under "ecclesiastical guidance," but Ritter from St. Louis said the proposal had a "`pessimistic, negative tone'". Bea said Ottaviani's proposal "would close the door to intellectual Europe and the outstretched hands of friendship in the old and new world." The other proposal made tradition and scripture "`like two arcs in the same searchlight'" and would "delight Protestants," wrote *Time*. All of this gave the impression Ottaviani and those like Ruffini and Siri, who stood by him, had little control and power. To add insult to injury, *Time* quoted an unnamed Irish bishop who said "We have had a mistaken idea that Cardinal Ottaviani represents the Holy See. We'll have to revise our definition of what the Holy See is."[40]

The Council was restructured after the Pope's November 21 intervention. There were five subcommissions. These met in intensive sessions on November 27 and 28, and during those meetings Cardinal Leger emphasized the material "should be presented in a positive manner." Ottaviani struggled through the remaining days of the First Session to present a schema that was satisfactory.[41]

As the first session ended, Connell presented a short talk on its results, which kept the situation from deteriorating faster than it might have done otherwise. He recognized many people were wondering just what had been accomplished so far. He said bishops from all over the world met to gain knowledge of the "state of the Church today." Every bishop "is expected to labor for the welfare of the universal Church as well as for the benefit of his particular diocese." Secondly, the bishops "had an opportunity to discuss common matters pertaining to Catholic faith, ecclesiastical administration, liturgy, the use of radio, television, the press, etc, as means of promoting the Church's mission. Many different views have been expressed on these topics, all with the sincere desire to extend the kingdom of Christ in some particular way. The decisions on these matters can be left to subsequent sessions, when they will be passed with the aid of the Holy Spirit. The bishops do not have to act hastily, as if there was danger that the Church would perish unless they act at once. The Church will continue to exist and function until the end of time; hence it can be slow in making decisions. How much longer the Council will last is very uncertain. But whether this be a space of several months or of many years, the final result will be a strengthening of Catholic life and a more effective invitation to those not of the household of the faith to study seriously the Catholic Church's claim to be the one true Church of Jesus Christ."[42] Connell's cool head and mild disposition was needed.

PART XIX

VATICAN II – 1963

CHAPTER 88
AMERICAN MEDIA BARRAGE

T he sessions of the Council ended in the late Autumn of
each year, and immediately thereafter, the American media
barrage began. The stories critiqued the previous session,
presented the American media's view of the state of the Church,
discussed the events and their significance in American terms, and
depicted the various personalities in terms of "good guys" and "bad
guys." The good guys were those who thought like Americans, and
the bad guys were those who thought like Catholics. Reports on the
Council were often sensationalized or supplemented by leaks from
insiders at the Council. One of the more notable leakers was Francis
Murphy, a Redemptorist priest who used the pseudonym of Xavier
Rhynne for the articles he wrote for *The New York Times*. Before the
Council began, Fr. Connell asked Murphy to obtain lodging and
had every reason to trust Murphy. When Connell asked him
whether he was Xavier Rhynne, Murphy lied and said no. [1]

SPINNING THE FIRST SESSION

As the First Session ended in December, 1962, the American press
and segments of the American Catholic press exclaimed in unison

that the "liberals" had been given a chance to regroup. "Recess an Aid to Catholic Liberals," is how *The Washington Post* framed it in a headline in its December 16 edition. Written by Leo Wollemberg, an Italian of Jewish descent, the article highlighted significant portions with bold black letters. The first such highlighted paragraph indicated that change was afoot amongst the Church leadership, which was opening up to the "modern world." Wollemborg wrote: **"Vastly more significant, however, is the evidence offered during two months of meetings of a new spirit among the council fathers as they review the church's relationship with the modern world and other Christian bodies."**[2]

Like *Time*, *The Washington Post* portrayed the Council as a battle between the reformers or the progressives (good guys) on one side, and the traditionalist forces (bad guys) on the other. This distinction was important enough to merit a passage in bold type:

"The first test came over the makeup of the council's commissions which will give final form to the bishops' decisions before they are submitted to the Pope. The majority of the council fathers, spearheaded by the well-organized and liberal minded episcopates from central and northern Europe, refused to be railroaded into approving a list of nominees reportedly drafted at the behest of the Curia. The roster of those vital commissions, as it has emerged from the free vote of the assembly, can be said to reflect accurately both the international character of the council and the strength and determination of the modern-minded elements."[3]

The "new spirit" which the media celebrated at the council was Americanism as refracted through the lens of the northern and central European episcopates. It put a premium on better relations with other churches, implying the Church had been unreasonable in the past. The breakdown of an authoritarian hierarchical Church was presented as a good thing, which might happen "by Christmas of next year," and would "tend to favor decentralization." The article ended with a number of bullet comments emphasizing trends enjoying the approval of the American media. First, there was the "emergence of the national episcopal conferences" and their growing influence. The media never tired of celebrating the "increasingly vocal and significant role played by the bishops from the new nations of Asia and Africa." There was the "remarkable display of organizational strength and doctrinal preparation offered by the reform-minded forces" lead by the northern and central European bishops. The media also celebrated a "new, moderate and constructive approach to the relations between the church and the state" though "it must be said that there is no real evidence as yet of a new look" in matters concerning the "relations with the press." Catholic prelates' attitudes towards "other Christian churches" were changing, and "above all, there is the clear-cut evidence that a majority of the council fathers fully back the forward-looking approach of Pope John, keyed to those twin goals of renewal and reunion."[4]

The Catholic press simply repeated the American line change was coming in the Church, and a "revolution in Catholic life" was underway. Typical of the stance of the Catholic press was the editor of *Catholic World,* Fr. John B. Sheerin, CSP., an advisor to the US Catholic Bishops. In a talk he gave at Wayne State University, Sheerin opined the "Church is recovering from forgotten wars and battles of long ago" and Church leaders were applying "'ecumenical criteria' in their evaluations of the worth of various proposals submitted for discussion." Sheerin addressed the issue of Church and State relations and religious liberty with an endorsement of Murray. He said "Certainly, the Pope's words do not give comfort to theologians who hold that an official Catholic state should suppress the rights of religious minorities." Dissenters could now speak out without the fear of sanctions as Sheerin repeated the Pope's opening statement at the Council that "the Church…prefers to make use of the medicine of mercy rather than of severity."[5] Sheerin adopted the American viewpoint on every issue before the Council. As a result, he became "a major interpreter of the Church reforms at the Second Vatican Council." His actions spoke as loud as his words in echoing the American point of view for he had attended the World Council of Churches convention, he supported the civil rights movement, and he participated in Catholic-Jewish "dialogue."[6]

CHAPTER 89
THE CATHOLICS ARE OUTRAGED

In the battle of perceptions, the sides were unevenly matched. On one side were the Americans, led primarily by *Time, The New York Times,* and increasingly the Catholic press parroting the American views. On the other side was Fenton with *American Ecclesiastical Review* and a few contributors at his disposal. When viewed globally, the odds were a little better because the Spanish and Italian press was largely loyal to the Church. However, they came nowhere near the scope of the American media in world reach and influence. Since America was the leader of the free world, it determined how the world thought. How America went, so went the world, since America was the leader.

In early 1963, Fenton read one of Xavier Rynne's *New Yorker* articles and commented on it in his diary: "Yesterday, the new issue of the *New Yorker* with an article by `Rynne' (Murphy CSSR) was brought to my attention. Murphy blames me (and Leo, Bobie, Ciappi, and others) for misinforming O[ttaviani]. The January issue, with my article defending O should be interesting. I hope I can do a lot of writing this year. My next for AER is `the Roman curia and the ecumenical council.'"[1]

The "Rynne" article galvanized Fenton into action, and Fenton authored two articles early in the same year which dealt with the value of perceptions. He identified a coalition of Catholicism's opponents beginning with "the Communist papers of Italy [which] never halted their drum-fire of journalistic attacks against the Cardinal…the professional anti-clerical press, particularly by Rome's *L'Espresso,* which, on Dec. 2, announced in three and a quarter inch headlines that it carried an article explaining `*La Sconfitta [defeat] di Ottaviani.*'…And, as might have been expected, our own *Time* and *Newsweek* joined in the shrill chorus of disapproval…."[2]

Fenton understood the kind of war the magazines were waging on the Church, as it was a war of perception and psychological pressure. The "vigorous anti-Catholic press," Fenton correctly observed, "would still like to see the Catholic Church change its basic teaching and its fundamental attitude toward other religious organizations…." An effort was afoot to show "in some way or another the Catholic Church might be said to be on the way towards a repudiation of the stand set forth in *Lamentabili sane exitu,* in the *Pascendi dominici gregis,* or in the *Oath against the Errors of Modernism.*"[3]

Whether it was classically anti-clerical magazines like *L'Espresso* or nuanced versions of the same view like *Time,* the objective was always the same: "Journals of this sort are always quite ready to applaud the men within the Church whom they believe to share their sentiments. And, of course, they are always ready to turn the engines of publicity against a man whom they consider as standing in the way of the attainment of their objectives…. During the time that passes between the ending of the first portion of the council and its reopening next September, it is to be expected that the press will try to influence its readers to believe that the cause of the men who are depicted as opposing Cardinal Ottaviani is the cause that will triumph and which deserves to triumph."[4]

Fenton, mentioning Wallemborg's December 16 editorial in *The Washington Post,* remarked how there were still others who "never miss a chance to praise the men it believes to be ready to change

Catholic doctrine or to abandon some portion of it, and will never miss a chance to place the defenders of the purity and the integrity of the Catholic faith in what they consider and hope to be an unfavorable light."[5]

The power of the press to distort the truth was not lost on Ottaviani either. Radio Bavaria interviewed him on December 16 after the conclusion of the first session, and the text of the interview was published in *Civilta Cattolica* on January 19. The NCWC News Service picked up the story on January 28. The interviewer mentioned public opinion, something Pius IX discussed nearly a century earlier. He taught without truth, everything breaks down to public opinion, which is based on perceptions subject to manipulation.[6]

Ottaviani dealt with his own public perception in the media and took the opportunity to defend Catholic doctrine. When told public opinion views the Holy Office as "a sinister, menacing and medieval institution'," the Cardinal responded "'public opinion is not well informed, possibly because 'many confuse the old Inquisition with the Holy Office of today.'" The discussion began with Ottaviani's role in the Council's Theological Commission, the Preparatory Theological Commission, and the Holy Office and then moved on to rumors of change of the Index of Forbidden Books. Ottaviani's answer foreshadowed the conciliar document, *Inter Mirifica*, especially when he said "An effective solution of the problem (of the Index), should also include the other instruments of social communication: films, radio and television. These last means can serve good as well as evil, especially in what concerns morals." Further, "It would be fitting to study other measures which our Mother the Church can and should take to protect her children, and especially the inexperienced, against the often hidden poison which today's audio-visual media spread among men." The "Index is ineffective, mainly because of the disproportion between the means of protection and the flood of publications."[7]

In discussing his duties at the Holy Office, Ottaviani explained he was the "man who has, from the nature of his office, the duty to keep the deposit of the Faith intact and who, at the same time, must leave full freedom to the progress which is necessary to better clarify, understand and expose Catholic teaching." He made clear that something new may not be "true and good." Rather, there "are some new opinions in theology today which are, if not false, at least debatable. In this situation, it is a completely positive action to defend the basic data of Holy Scripture and of Tradition, to avoid permitting some truths of the Faith to be obscured, under the pretext of progress and adaptation."[8]

Pope John joined with Fenton and Ottaviani in criticizing the press. On January 27, 1963, the Pope exhorted the Catholic press to "honor its special ministry, which is the exalted service of truth." One reporter responded "This cuts two ways. For before we can follow the Pope's precept, we must not only know the facts but what is behind them. All responsible reporters take pride in the accuracy of their stories. But you can't tell what you don't know."[9]

The NCWC News Service did cover important dynamics of the Council. In one story, it mentioned "a very prominent and able American priest said....'that the pope's act in setting up a special committee to coordinate revisional [sic]work during the council's long recess "means that a counter-reformation theology won't be able to exert influence on the schemata." The "counter-reformation theology" which the reformers so bitterly opposed held "there are some truths which the Church proposes to us to be received with the assent of divine and Catholic faith, and which are not contained in any way, implicitly or explicitly, obscurely or clearly, within the books of Holy Scripture." These truths were the "Catholic Church is the one and only true Church of Jesus Christ, and that outside of this one and only true Church man cannot attain to his eternal salvation."[10]

The opposition to this idea came from non-Catholics, and Catholics who wanted the Church to change its teachings, either from those Catholics who either believed "that a solemn enunciation of these theses by an ecumenical council would serve no good ecumenical purpose at the present time" or from those who believed it "would be unwise to set them forth at the present time because much more study and investigation are needed." Ottaviani held these truths should be announced as being revealed even if non-Catholics did not want to accept them, and even if further study could be possible or profitable. According to Fenton, there was no reason for the Church not to announce these counter-reformation theological principles because they were already part of the magisterium.[11]

The response to Fenton's defense of Ottaviani was overwhelmingly favorable. After the article appeared in the January issue, Fenton "received about twenty letters of congratulations," prompting him to conclude that his Ottaviani article was "the second most popular article in the 19 years I have been editor of AER....All the correspondence on the Ottaviani article has been favorable."[12]

Many in the Church hierarchy agreed with Fenton and echoed a growing concern about the American media. During the annual Clergy Day meeting of the Nashville Serra Club on February 19, Bishop William L. Adrian of Nashville said "Slanted writing in secular publications is giving Catholics a false impression of the Second Vatican Council.... The. . . accounts of the council in such magazines as *Time, Newsweek* and *the New Yorker* have given Catholics an incorrect impression of what goes on at the council." Bishop Adrian also defended Cardinal Ottaviani, saying "Good Catholics should not be scandalized by the recent attacks on Cardinal Ottaviani and the Roman Curia by certain segments of the press." Adrian corrected the misperception about the purpose of the Council: "The first objective of the council is not the conversion of non-Catholics but rather `to bring back the spirit of Christ to the Church."[13]

RHETORICAL AMMUNITION FOR THE AMERICANS

Many Catholic prelates from Northern Europe and the US provided the material the Americans used against them to spread Americanism through the episcopacies of the Third World. The Catholic press, in an NCWC News Service story by Manfred Wenzel dated March 11, 1963, quoted Cardinal Frings: "The majority of bishops share a moderate progressive tendency, and it appears that they will have the two-thirds' majority against the more conservative minority." The article attributed to Frings the idea Pope John supported the "moderate progressive" tendency of the Council. Frings was quoted as saying "the council Fathers are aware of the special encouragement Pope John gave them when he said that 'old truths must be preached to an entirely changed world with new methods and in a new language.'"[14]

The NCWC reported Frings said "The 'moderate progressive' bishops of the world are such a majority that they will probably have the two-thirds' vote necessary to put reform legislation through the Second Vatican Council."[15] The Catholic Press, far from trying to tell the Council story from a Catholic point of view, simply accepted the categories established by secular American outlets like *Time*, thereby increasing the ideological division among Catholics. Frings' claim that "the council has given the bishops a new awareness of the responsibility they bear the whole Church as successors of the Apostles"[16] was another way of saying the northern Europeans succumbed to the psychological warfare campaign the Americans had been waging on them since the end of World War II. With the collocation of so many bishops at one place for a period of time, solidarity threatened to result in an extension of American influence. This was something Bishop Francis J Green of Tucson, Arizona adverted to when he said "in two months, there has been a solidifying of ideas. We have gotten to know each other." Bishop Sheen observed the same as well as the Third World dynamic when he said the "council brought meetings and exchanges between the bishops of prosperous countries and the bishops of underprivileged countries."[17]

Unlike Cardinal Ottaviani, Cardinal Bea could always count on favorable press, and he reciprocated by issuing statements compatible with the Americanst agenda, as when he said: "The only thing that matters is to contribute toward union as much as possible through prayers and through work, performed with dedication and confidence."[18] Richard Cardinal Cushing of Boston spouted unity talk upon his return from the first session, claiming that the "council `may mark a decisive stage toward Christian reunification,'" adding "We hope to create a wonderful climate of unity of all believers in the Supreme Being."[19] Gustave Weigel, SJ, Murray's good friend if not also alter ego, provided a seriously defective definition of "ecumenism," seized upon by the Americans and their sympathizers, including the NCWC News Service, which quoted him as saying that ecumenism was "a movement to bring Christian churches into friendship, primarily manifested by conversation. It is not the purpose of ecumenical action to make a single, organic church. Rather it is the hope of those engaged in the conversation that their work might, if it so please the Lord, bring about some kind of unity."[20] Archbishop Denis E. Hurley, O.M.I., of Durban, South Africa articulated who the bad guys were in this drama by referring to the Curia as "geared to the implementation of `the Tridentine policy of fortress Catholicism'" which had heavily influenced the drafts that were presented to the bishops and which the bishops then rejected.[21] This was precisely the kind of talk the enemies of the Church wanted to hear coming from the mouth of a Catholic bishop.

CHAPTER 90
CATHOLICS PLAN TO FIX THE
AMERICAN MEDIA

C atholic criticism of the American media did not fall on deaf ears. The Council Fathers moved quickly to establish norms of behavior for the press. In an interview published in the February 28, 1963 edition of the *Long Island Catholic*, Archbishop Martin J. O'Connor, Rector of the North American College in Rome, leader of the Pontifical Commission for Movies, Radio and Television since 1947, member of the Council's Commission for the Lay Apostolate and Communications Media, and native of Scranton, Pennsylvania, remarked on the importance of the media, saying the "problems of mass media are not new to the Catholic Church." However, for the first time in Church history, the collective leadership decided to hammer out a statement on the matter. A study session at the Council on November 23, 24, and 26, 1962 determined "'all the Fathers without exception,' had a 'favorable opinion' of the project and some of them gave it 'great praise.'" In response, the Council Fathers expanded the mandate of the Pontifical Commission for Movies Radio and Television to include the press and called for a document.[1] O'Connor said his secretariat dealt with two problems in examining the doctrinal aspects of mass communications:

"First, there is the matter of the Church's duty and right to use the new mass communications to preach the Gospel and spread Christian educates as well as the question of the limitations of this right to concrete circumstances within the framework of modern laws.' In the second place...the secretariat was concerned with 'general use of mass communications in a world on the basis of Christian morality and on the basis of natural law: the first being of specific interest to the Catholic community; the second applying to all society."[2]

Archbishop Rene Stourm of Sens, France explained the moral aspect of the media in light of Christ's command to teach all nations: "It is precisely in her quality as mother that the Church is concerned that this entertainment should be harmful neither to the mind, nor the conscience, nor to the dignity of man. Communications media are never, in fact, indifferent on the moral plane, considered either as a means of entertainment or as a means by which ideas and culture are communicated."[3]

O'Connor recognized that the problem had a pastoral dimension when he wrote:

"The main problem is to determine how to use mass media for Christian purposes. Secondly, there is the question of how to help Christian people –viewers and listeners – to profit better from mass media and how to help them defend themselves in the world of mass media.... In fact, it is a question of how man can preserve sanctifying grace in the face of the effects of mass media.... the pagan concept of life which is so widespread in our times has its origin in great part in entertainment.... Catholics living in a pluralistic society must choose from among the programs and newspapers circulated in their country which do not offend their faith."[4]

Technical training had to be matched by intensive spiritual training O'Connor said.[5]

Echoing O'Connor's call to produce "good results" in terms of protecting the morals of the people of a society, Pope John told the

Italian Press Association and the Foreign Press Association that journalism must be subordinate to God:

"Your profession, my dear gentlemen, would imply not only interpreting events but sometimes anticipating their course...Even when vested with great authority, when expert in knowledge and gifted with virtues, man cannot fail to bow before divine wisdom and tremble at the tremendous contribution required of him in cooperating in the spread of truth of love, in cooperating in the education of his brothers who possess an immortal soul, toward the government of the world and of the individual institutions which form the social body. This relation between the Creator and the creature is called religion, and is an obligation for all.... It is my sincere conviction that for enlightened and honest people a positive exposition is the most persuasive reminder that the pen must not become the instrument of lies, of the systematic alienation of brothers or the corruption of morals."[6]

The Pope spoke of the media's power and its duty: "Always bear in mind the influences which the written word has on minds, particularly on the weaker ones.... To know how to wait and impose upon oneself the discipline of refraining from spreading sensational news, prepares practically always the triumph of truth and wisdom."[7]

The pope concluded by reminding journalists their actions had eternal consequences:

"Dear sirs: the time comes for every man when he must prepare himself to leave a place, or certainly his earthly dwelling, and give account of his actions. May each one of you be able to say: I did no [sic] not dig furrows of division and of diffidence, I did not sadden immortal souls with suspicion or with fear; I was frank, loyal, trustful; I looked with brotherly sympathy into the eyes even of those people who did not share my ideals, in order to allow the fulfillment in its own time of the great design of Providence which, even slowly, will have to achieve the divine teaching and commandment of Jesus: *unum sint*."[8]

CHAPTER 91
COMBATING AMERICAN MISINFORMATION

In the March edition of *American Ecclesiastical Review,* Fenton described the German theologian Hans Kung as "a young priest who seems hopelessly addicted to the practice of giving press conferences." *The New York Times* covered a press conference Kung gave in December, 1962 in which he said the Curia may regain some lost prestige pending the restart of the council on September 8, 1963. *Our Sunday Visitor* gave a version of a Kung press conference that was more critical of the Curia, prompting Fenton to note that "It has become fashionable to deride and to attack the Roman Curia." Criticism like this:

"tends to lead gullible people to disregard, or even to oppose, the directives which come to us from the Holy Office and from the other departments of the Curia. It tends to bring confusion and opposition in the Church of God, wherein God Himself wills that there should be order and love. It tends to turn Catholic against Catholic, at least in part on the grounds of a negative nationalism, and to influence some members of the Church to dislike others by reason of the fact that they are members of one race or citizens of one country."[1]

Bishops criticized the coverage they received and let that be known through their NCWC News Service. Archbishop Leo Binz of St. Paul, Minnesota complained of "much exaggeration" in the "accounts of differences of opinion among the council Fathers." Archbishop Gerald T. Bergan of Omaha contended the accounts of conflicts between the bishops gave the "idea that some bishops were wearing guns on their hips." Bishop Sylvester W. Treinen of Boise, Idaho cautioned the faithful to be careful in "reading some accounts about the result of the council" because of "chaff of uncertainty or assumption" in the articles. Bishop Robert E. Tracy of Baton Rouge, Louisiana said the labels of "conservative" and "liberal" were inaccurate.[2]

Msgr. John Tucek of the Rome Bureau of the NCWC News Service, a member of the press panel set up by the US Bishops, and later a biographer of Pope John, wrote a special report in early 1963 that indicted "rumor, gossip and plain `scuttlebut' in several influential and widely disseminated publications, chiefly magazines," claiming "innuendo and assumption" caused "real damage" to the reader.[3] Tucek correctly identified the phenomena used to attack and divide the Church as the "creation of villains and heroes." Labels, he observed, led to "the point of misinformation."[4] Misinformation, or disinformation, was exactly what the Americans pioneered with the OSS during World War II, and perfected during the Cold War. Ottaviani was the "favorite target" because "his office and its history make him a natural `villain.'" [5]

Tucek then proceeded to "set. . . the record straight" and spelled out in detail the errors, if not outright lies, of the press, which included *Time*. First, the press predicted that Ottaviani, Ruffini, and Siri would lead the "integralists" who supposedly consisted of nearly every bishop in Italy, Spain, and a majority from Latin America and the US. However, the "record of the first session of the council, both official and unofficial, has shown that this bit of crystalballing misfired."[6] Second, Pope John was reported as having called the Second Vatican Council "in spite of the internal opposition hidden behind the outward acquiescence" of Tardini, who "died of chagrin at being unable to change the Pope's mind." The Pope contradicted this account at a public audience in May, 1962 at which he said that Tardini's "agreement was immediate and exultant." Tardini, according to an aide, died as a result of his health breaking as a consequence of assisting for the preparation of *Mater et Magistra.* Third, Tucek wrote in his investigation he did not find any indication of opposition to the council from at least a dozen important prelates from the Church's administration.[7] Fourth, press reports claimed that the "council press office communiqué was often written in advance of the news it was reporting." Tucek, who was "directly engaged in composing the communiqués" said "no `news' was ever written in advance" though rosters of speakers for the following day were prepared. Fifth, the report that Cardinal Alfrink cut off Ottaviani's microphone after ten minutes was refuted by Ottaviani himself, who recounted how Alfrink politely told Ottaviani of a ten minute limit. Despite reports of the auditorium breaking into applause when Ottaviani's microphone was cut off, the only applause was "at the junior end" and it was quite localized.[8] Sixth, the claim floated by *Time* Ottaviani asked the Pope to order Fr. Karl Rahner, SJ to leave Rome was also false. Seventh, it was false to claim "only `safe men were chosen as council experts." Eighth, concerning reports that criticized the Holy Office for never justifying its activities in condemning books and professors, Ottaviani explained condemning books or writings, "no explanation is required. The book is its own evidence for its condemnation."[9]

Finally, speaking about the "problems of the Catholic press," Ottaviani said the roles of the Holy Office and the Catholic press were different, as are their means, but "their ultimate end must be the same....The Holy Office and the Catholic press are instituted to defend the truth. The Catholic press would demean its function if it concerned itself too much with petty gossip, scandal and sensationalism."[10]

CHAPTER 92
"MAY GOD PROTECT HIS CHURCH"

W hen Fenton arrived back in Rome for the second session, he discovered the Pope changed the rules for conducting the work of the Council. In an address to each of the fathers of the Second Vatican Ecumenical Council, the Pope emphasized four main points. First, a new Coordinating Commission of Cardinals under the presidency of Amleto Cardinal Cicognani, the Secretary of State was created to coordinate the work of the various commissions of the Council. Second, in accordance with a general theme of "relations between council headquarters and Fathers residing throughout the world," the Pope instructed the "Supreme Pontiff must approve the decrees in official and final form, as they acquire from his apostolic authority the quality and force of law." The Council Fathers were to "propose, discuss, prepare, in due form, the sacred deliberations" and then assemble them for review by the Pope. The bishops were to be present "at the forthcoming meetings," maintain "close spiritual union" with their brethren, and reply "in writing without delay" when requested. The bishops were allowed to "employ, as a complement to their own work, the assistance of priests from each ecclesiastical district who are outstanding in doctrine and virtue." However, these assistants must be "capable of maintaining the secrecy of the council scrupulously." Third, the Pontiff noted the unity of clergy and laity in contributing to the work of the Council.[1] Finally, Catholics should not concern themselves with just themselves, as there were objectives of the council relative to Christianity and the entire human family," for to do so would not be a proper response to the nature of Christ, as the "Divine Saviour Light of mankind." Pope John hoped the Council might "call up within the Church...abundant spiritual energy and open wide a vast field for the Catholic apostolate, so that men, led by the Bride of Christ, may attain those lofty and most desired goals that have not yet been reached. A great hope that interests the Church and the entire human family!"[2]

The doctrinal commission on which Msgr. Fenton served met a total of six times: on February 21, 22, 23, 25, and on March 1 and 4. By the time the second meeting concluded, Fenton was dismayed by the long speeches of the participants, whose "verbosity. . . has been the ruination of the entire meeting." In spite of all the talk, there was no vote on the five propositions presented. Fenton characterized the third meeting as "tragic." On February 13, Fenton confided to his diary "The other group (Bea's) is working to dilute the teaching as much as possible."[3] Ottaviani, who along with Bea was one of the presidents of the meeting that day, suggested a vote on the issue of revelation being more than what is in scripture. During a recess, Ottaviani left the meeting, and the meeting resumed without him. After becoming de facto president of the meeting, Bea pushed through a vote on an issue proposed by DeSmedt "to the effect that it is inopportune to say anything about the tradition being more extensive than...scripture." DeSmedt's motion carried with nine voting against it, and the two from the US voting with DeSmedt. At the fourth meeting, Ottaviani claimed the vote was invalid and he charged Bea, "for all intents and purposes," with "treachery."[4]

By March 4, Ottaviani and his allies were in retreat. A 4:30 meeting of the mixed commission approved the first chapter. of the constitution on scripture, which was such "a poor thing" that all the exasperated Fenton could exclaim was "May God protect his

Church."[5] Fenton felt that Ottaviani was no longer an effective leader of the Catholic forces because he was being subverted by his own secretariat, something that "is becoming more and more obvious." Fenton felt "Tromp has been trying to run the whole show from the beginning. The results are apparent. Parente, in a nice way (for once), pointed this out in his report."[6]

Rumors began circulating. Dearden and Griffiths told Fenton "the rumor is going around that O[ttaviani] is getting fed up with the situation, and that he is going to allow anything to go."[7] Fenton could only concur, confiding to his diary "O seems to show a great deal of weakness."[8] Fenton was also growing irritated at Ottaviani's failure to respond to the deteriorating situation in America. Kung was going to speak at Georgetown; Davis had just attacked Fenton in America; and all that Ottaviani could say was "I should pay no attention to it." Fenton was by now "sick of the 'let them hit you again' attitude of the Romans – and even of uncle. Believe me, if I could, I would withdraw the March AER article."[9] Fenton concluded by claiming "O's leadership this time has been pathetic. He has really lost the touch or maybe he is just fed up with the whole mess."[10]

In late February, 1963, Fenton heard "that the Pope will die in May or June. If he does this will be lost effort."[11] By the Spring of 1963 Fenton concluded "The thing is hopeless. O seems not to care." Bishop Mark Hurley commiserated with Fenton over supper: "We agreed that no one over here seems to care."[12]

CHAPTER 93

TIME FIGHTS FOR ACADEMIC FREEDOM

In early Spring,1963, controversy erupted at the Catholic University of America when it barred Murray, Weigel, Fr. Godfrey Diekmann, SJ, and Kung from speaking on campus. In an article entitled "Universities: Crisis at Catholic U." published in its March 29, 1963 edition, *Time* complained these "liberals" theologians had been excluded by "conservative," authoritarian men who were bent on suppressing the truth. The article, which attacked the rector of Catholic University, Monsignor William J. McDonald, viewed as acting out of timidity and not out of principle, placed academic freedom – a positive and American sounding term – as being on the side of the "liberals":

"Catholic University in Washington, D.C., has a high aim -- `to search out truth scientifically, to safeguard it, and to apply it' – qualified in practice by a timid feeling that now and then some of the truth has to be suppressed. The newest case of suppression has the school's faculty in revolt and deeply worries many of the 239 Roman Catholic bishops in the U.S., who are C.U.'s guardians…..
Monsignor William J. McDonald…giving a forum to these scholars might seem to place his school on the liberal side in debate at the council…and he did not want the school to be on any

side....Catholics have long thought of C.U. as a model of academic freedom – subject to neither `the hand of an order' nor the pressure of a state legislature. Even in student rules, it is unusually liberal for a Catholic campus (no `lights out,' no supervised study).

Yet in recent years, notably under Irish-born Rector McDonald, who took over in 1957, the faculty has increasingly complained of academic timidity at the top."[1]

By not allowing Murray, Kung, Weigel and Diekmann to speak at CUA, the university became a "citadel of mediocrity." *Time* cited Monsignor John Tracy Ellis, who "went on to charge that `for nearly a decade, this type of suppression has been going on constantly at this university.'"[2] The American Catholic prelates were for the most part in favor of the liberals. *Time* published "More than 200 of the university's 350 faculty members appealed McDonald's `speaker ban' to the 40-man board of trustees, which consists of all U.S. cardinals and archbishops, plus five bishops and six laymen." Bea, another American darling, spoke the following month at CUA as a result of this protest, *Time* concluded.[3]

Kung was allowed to speak at CUA and he urged the Church to become like America, because "Kung readily admits that there are superficial parallels between Catholic authoritarianism and Communist dogmatism, and that `even today the spirit of the Inquisition and unfreedom [sic] has not died out' in his church. Nonetheless, he argues that Catholicism by its nature is a free society. This freedom is often imperfectly realized and must be won over and over again...."[4]

Time followed Kung in his triumphal progress across American, visiting Catholic institutions like the University of Notre Dame where he drew a capacity crowd of 3,000, which gave him a standing ovation when he appeared on stage at the Stepan Center, which was built the year before and named after the donor who was the owner of an international chemical company. "Another 3,000," according to *Time*, "heard him speak at Boston College, and 5,000 showed up in Chicago for his contribution to a lecture series that has never drawn more than 500 listeners. The enthusiasm was understandable: Kung's message to the U.S. is a fresh, provocative discussion of the place of freedom in the Catholic Church....The church, he argues, should: `Publicly admit the right of all men to worship as they please – and put this doctrine into action in such places as Spain.'"5

Shortly before Kung spoke at Notre Dame, the Church took a step towards implementing what he said. In February, 1963, Fernando Maria Castiella y Maiz, Spain's Foreign Minister, along with "Malaga's reform-minded Bishop Angel Herrera" petitioned the Vatican for approval of a law to "grant freedoms to Protestants." This meant granting the Protestant churches "legal standing" which would put them on a par, or equal footing, with Catholicism. According to *Time*, "at a secret meeting in Madrid, Spain's Metropolitan Council – composed of 15 ranking prelates, including four cardinals – approved in principle Castiella's `statute for non-Catholic religions.'" The law denied the Protestants the right to proselytize but their churches would have legal status as religious groups and they could operate their own schools, seminaries, hospitals, cemeteries, and distribute Bibles. Additionally, the "proposed law even affirms the right of all Spaniards to hold every civic office but that of chief of state, who must be a Catholic...." Pope John was depicted as supporting change in Spain after he was asked: "`Is it better for these people to spend their Sundays cavorting on the beaches, or worshiping God in their own way?' Answered the Pope: `You are right my son. Leave the draft with me.'" The implication was that one religion was as good as another in keeping people on the "straight and narrow." Such an approach was endorsed by *Time* as "a more ecumenical attitude toward the country's Protestants." The truth of the Protestant endeavor in Spain actually became clearer in the pages of *Time,* when it explained that "Spanish laws theoretically grant the country's tiny (30,000) Protestant minority the right to the unhampered private exercise of their faith. But Protestant churches have no legal standing, and must operate as `foreign commercial firms.'" 6

The Catholic Church was being recruited to become a torchbearer for the crusade to spread an essential principle of the American ideology—religious liberty—around the world. During Cardinal Bea's visit to Harvard, *Time* touted his Americanism.[7] Two months later, in a piece on the death Pope John, *Time* gave their definition of a good Catholic as someone who was "pastoral" and would work to eliminate barriers between Catholics and Protestants This modernization was a good thing in the eyes of *Time*:

"John XXIII was, in the best possible sense, a revolutionary – a Pope of modernization....It was left to John XXIII – neither intellectual nor theologian – to throw open the windows and doors of Catholicism to the breeze of change. To John, it was more than just a catechism statement that heaven was opened to Protestants – it was a fact that called out for man to work for Christian unity..... Christ's injunctions to his Apostles were not memories but living commands that had political consequences, such as that a wholly defensive and intransient 'church of silence' was no true witness for human beings behind the Iron Curtain. Thanks to his charismatic warmth and pliancy, the Roman Catholic Church seemed to change from wariness of new trends in the secular world to acceptance of them. It is not odd, considering the scope and influence of a Pope, that one man who seemed to be responsible for it all. What is extraordinary is that the change was visible in the space of one year: 1962.... John did nothing to remove the great doctrinal obstacles that bar the way to ecumenical unity; but by his example of love he encouraged church leaders and scholars to join in discovering how much of the Christian faith they shared. Says Dr. Willem Visser Hooft, general secretary of the World Council: "He changed the history of church relations."[8]

The problem, according to *Time,* was always the Catholic Church. John got the Church to start thinking right. With modernization, went *Time's* reasoning, the Church no longer would have enemies. This was not lost on the Catholic laity who were avid readers and believers of the *Time*, and hence, American, worldview. This was driven home by statements such as "When he first summoned the council, John declared that its purpose would be the renewal of the church, and ultimately, the unity of Christians."[9] Murray was quoted as the expert on the matter:

"But far from being the caretaker that the church expected, John created an atmosphere in which says Jesuit Theologian John Courtney Murray, 'a lot of things came unstuck – old patterns of thought, behavior, feeling. They were not challenged or refuted, but just sort of dropped.' In place of the dogmatic answer, John asked questions, and encouraged others to join him in finding out whether old forms were still right forms, customary methods were effective methods. Says Father Murray: 'He gave rise to a whole new "problematic": What is the problem? How do we somehow alter the state of the problem? These questions are his heritage.'"[10]

Pope John's practice of assuming sincerity and transparency of others, whether friend or foe, became the modus operandi of Catholic prelates after he died. *Time* reinforced this:

"When he was editing Pacem in Terris and came to a sentence that noted how both sides in the cold war had entered the nuclear arms race for defensive purposes, John added: 'And there is no reason to disbelieve them.' Did he mean that? 'No,' answers monsignor Pietro Pavan, the Vatican scholar who drafted the encyclical. 'This was a strategic statement of the Holy Father, He said "Who really knows? And anyway, I cannot posit bad faith on the part of either party. If I did, the dialogue would be over and the doors would be closed."[11]

CHAPTER 94
DEFINING LIBERAL CATHOLICISM

Fenton tried to make sense of was going on at the Council before returning to Rome in May, 1963. While resting in Rochester, New York in a guest room of the Bishop's House, he collected his thoughts for an upcoming lecture by delineating the Council's goals: while the purpose of the Council was spiritual, it involved teaching and also legislation, and the "object of this legislation is to direct the people of God so that their faith may be protected and may become more intense, and so that they may love God and each other more effectively."[1]

The issue of most interest to Catholics was the "Conservative-Liberal question." "Liberal Catholicism," he wrote, "represented" the teaching of the Catholic Church:

"as compatible with the maxims that guided the French Revolution. In practice, the men who advanced the doctrines of separation of Church and State etc. as these have been condemned by the Popes since Leo XII, are called liberal Catholics. The term was not considered respectable...until . . . a few years ago. . . . Practically the men . . . who are designated as liberals by the press, are those who seek a 'pastoral' rather than a 'scholastic' approach to the teaching and the legislation of the council."[2]

The danger lurking beneath the surface of the "pastoral" approach was Americanism. In presenting its doctrine and dogma in a new way, the Church ran the danger of running afoul of the prohibitions set forth by Leo XIII in *Testem Benevolentiae*. Those who sought to gain others to the Catholic fold, Leo taught, often ended up downplaying certain doctrines and emphasizing others, which resulted in confusion. Many of the periti who formulated or wrote the documents were certainly motivated by a desire to be pleasing to non-Catholics. This, in turn, led to a new, and as of today, still unresolved theological issue. That issue was whether the Holy Spirit's protection extended from doctrinal or substantive error to the way in which the issue was formulated? Fenton's answer was "no." The issue of interpretation implicit in Fenton's formulation of the problem would become crucial after the Council, as Council documents got deliberately twisted to conform to an agenda or just plan misunderstood. During the Summer of 1963, as Fenton grew increasingly ill, it didn't look as if he were going to be around to fight that battle. He suffered two heart attacks. The first was on July 12 during the course of the meetings of the Theological Commission. The second was the morning of September 8 and resulted in his receiving the Sacrament of Extreme Unction.[3]

CHAPTER 95
MURRAY TO THE RESCUE

I n August, 1963, the US Catholic bishops gathered at an "informal meeting" at which they issued a public statement claiming they "intended to support fully the document on religious liberty." After their meeting, these bishops sent Cardinal Spellman "quietly" to Pope Paul to begin the process of finalizing the document.[1] None of this would have happened without the efforts of John Courtney Murray, who became a peritus at the council thanks to Spellman's efforts. Murray sent a strategy paper to Bishop Lawrence Shehan, Archbishop of Baltimore, proposing a plan of action for attacking Ottaviani and bringing religious liberty to the forefront of the discussion at the upcoming session of the Ecumenical Council.[2] The goal was a doctrinal change which would approve in principle the American system of Church and state relations and put it on the same theological footing as that in Spain. To achieve this, Murray sought first to attack the terminology used by Ottaviani which consisted of "thesis" and "hypothesis." With that out of the way, then the idea of the Catholic State as the ideal would fall and the American view of Church and state, as good in principle, would prevail. The Church could then exert pressure on countries like Spain which would allow the American system to supplant the current status quo:

"Ottaviani's `two standard' theory (what I call the disjunctive theory) will remain on the books, untouched, as the essential and pure Catholic doctrine (he holds that it is *proxima fidei,* and Ruffini agrees). And the Council's `practical' statements will look like sheer concessions to `today's circumstance' – a matter of expediency, or, in a word, the thing called `hypothesis,' again affirmed, to the joy of the curial Right, who will have triumphed in what will have been in effect no more than an affirmation by the Council of their own doctrine. Is this what the American bishops want?"[3]

Murray answered his own question brazenly: "I am inclined to think – I hope not unjustly – that many American bishops really believe in their own minds that the American constitutional situation is no more than `hypothesis' in the Ottaviani sense – a situation to be consented to only on grounds of expediency, because in the practical order it works well, even though it cannot really be defended in principle."[4]

Murray personalized the fight so that principles were not the only motivator of the bishops. The position of the "Curial right" as Murray called it, was upheld by sheer force ("only by the power of the Holy Office") he argued to Shehan, and hence, it was bound to fall.[5] Murray claimed the categories of thesis and hypothesis had appeared in the previsou century were "not imbedded in the tradition. They are not to be found textually even in Leo XIII. There is no valid reason why one should be obliged to think in terms of them. And as long as one does, there is no getting on with the real problem of today....Grant Ottaviani the eternal validity of these categories (and the doctrinal validity of the concept that supports them, scil., the `Catholic state'), and we are forever sunk."[6]

· · ·

With that characterization gone, then "its supporting concept, the 'Catholic state,'" becomes "a time conditioned disjunction, involved in the relativities of history."[7]

In the "Notes," Murray framed the terms of the debate and, in doing so, handed both *Time* and the American bishops a potent rhetorical weapon they could wield against their opponents in the Church. The categories:

"(a)Libertas Ecclesiae seu Populi Dei [freedom of the Church or of the people of God], and (b) Libertas societatis seu Populi Temporalis [freedom of society and of the temporal people]". . . represent a transposition into terms at once contemporary and traditional of the ancient doctrine of the 'Two Powers,' only now in the form of the 'Two Freedoms.' This, I think, is aggiornamento. And it is a correction of the clericalist intention and tendency of the 'two-standards' theory, in that it brings into emphatic focus the Peoples, not the Powers." [8]

Murray concluded his notes with the flattering claim American bishops were submitting "to the Council a genuinely magisterial document – and not a diffident 'practical' one."[9]

Murray's change in Church teaching was based on four principles. First, the "concept of the 'state'" was evolving. Second, "society" and the "state" were distinguished from each other which, according to Murray, was a good thing because Leo XIII confused the two "because of his polemic preoccupations." Third, there were at least two kinds of "separation of Church and State" – that presented by "Continental Liberalism" and the other being "American constitutionalism." Fourth, the "'pragmatic test' – the experience of the American Church" should be corrected to reflect that the "American Constitution is not good because it works; it works because it is good." Murray admitted three of the foregoing points are "indeed matters of…political theory," and in the "American tradition…both separation and freedom of religion derive from the same political and legal principle, scil., limited government. Government limits itself to the protection of freedom of religion, not of religion itself. So too government limits itself to the sphere of the secular, public, terrestrial common good." With emphasis he added "recognition of freedom of religion" cannot depend "only on sheer fact. This again is expediency."[10]

In arguing Catholic societies around the world would do well to imitate America, Murray turned to John XXIII's *Pacem In Terris* for help by claiming the Pope "firmly embraces the juridical theory of the state, not the ethical theory that is predominant in Leo XIII and in the canonical manuals." This to Murray "marks a long stride forward in the thinking of the Church – a development that can lead to further development." Perhaps most ominously, Murray wrote the document "also affirms that freedom is the political method. And freedom of conscience is situated in the context of this affirmation."[11]

Murray understood the Church had to accept his notion of freedom as well as his essentially undefined concept of natural law before the Church could be persuaded to accept The American Proposition, and, more importantly, before the Church could be used to implement and disseminate The American Proposition to the Catholic faithful throughout the world. The existing state of Canon law, specifically canons 752 and 1351 provided for "freedom of conscience" but "only in the private forum" and hence were insufficient for achieving this goal. Murray explained Canon Law set out "a pertinent principle…but one which does not by itself put a footing under the First Amendment. The principle is purely theological. Other principles of the political and legal order have to be adduced before there is a case." Finally, the "next step – which is easy," is to demonstrate that the Church possesses a "stable condition" and "full independence." These possessions had to be present in a "constitutional situation in which the powers of government are limited by law (a) to the secular concerns of society and (b) to the protection of a universal civil right to the free exercise of religion." Murray explained such an arrangement should take the place of Concordats, which he denigrated by a veiled reference to Pius XI's Concordat with Italy in 1929.[12]

In providing doctrinal support for the First Amendment as a good in itself, Murray was bringing to completion the work that he pledged to do at the Biltmore conference in April, 1948.

CHAPTER 96

POPE PAUL IS CONCERNED ABOUT
DOCTRINE

While in Rome waiting for the Council to begin, Fenton read two books on Modernism given him by a good friend, and former student, the eulogist at Fenton's funeral years later, Fr. Edward Hanahoe. Fenton found "the teaching in the first chapter of the new schema on the Church and the language are those of Tyrrell. May God preserve His Church from that chapter. If it passes, it will be a great evil. I must pray and act."[1]

Act he did. He explained this reality to Bishop Fearne, Archbishop Staffa, and Cardinal Ottaviani all of whom expressed surprise. Meanwhile a number of periti wrote a "Latin letter to the individual bishops, warning them about the 'new theology.'"[2] Later, Ruffini used the same information provided by Fenton to great effect.[3]

Fenton's efforts were having an impact in resisting Modernism and Americanism while keeping the Council focused on the truth. Fenton explained Paul VI's own concern with doctrinal liberties by some at the Council: "At Holy Office, I saw O and Parente. All is going well. All of them were disgusted with Murphy and Kaiser. O was very grateful for my research on Tyrrell. He had just seen the

Pope, and he reported that the Pope is concerned with the doctrinal issue."[4]

Not only was the new Pope concerned about doctrinal matters, but he was incensed by the antics of Redemptorist priest Murphy. Fenton wrote "Then I saw Cecchetti and Romeo....It seems that the Pope knows about M[urphy] and is quite disturbed, or at least so Piolanti says."[5]

Before session two began, Pope Paul reiterated the "preeminence of the pastoral nature of this council." It was to benefit the Catholic Church, the Apostolic See, hasten the "union of separated brothers with the Catholic Church," and promote peace and "spiritual prosperity of humanity throughout the world."[6]

PLEADING FOR REFORM

Before the second session of the Council began on September 29, Kung's book *The Council in Action,* was published by Sheed & Ward and, of course, praised by *Time.* The Americans again had an opportunity to depict as good the reformers who pointed out the problems with the Church, and to castigate those who opposed such "intellectuals" and progressive modernizers. All of these reformers had at one time or another been censured for the views that they expressed as these views were considered by higher authority to be against the teaching of the Church. Each one of these "intellectuals" or "reformers" was someone who advocated a position or a view that was favored by the Americans because it would result in a weakening of the Church and its authority as well as the effectiveness of its doctrine. *Time* put well in reviewing Kung's book:

"The Council in Action . . . pleads for such reforms as internalization of the Roman Curia, reduction of its power, greater authority for regional councils of bishops. He speaks of 'reactionary doctrinaire tendencies' in certain council fathers, and dismisses the agenda items drawn up for the council by the Curia dominated preparatory commission as 'ill-prepared, partisan schemata.' Not one of these views is heretical, although some Catholics feel that

Kung shows excessive zeal in pointing out the defects of the church. Kung is still listed as one of the council's theological experts, but there are rumors of an instruction pending in Rome that might restrict his freedom to publish or give public speeches. If so, Kung would join a long list of distinguished Catholic thinkers who have been silenced, at least temporarily, by Curia officials." [7]

Time turned censure by the Holy Office into a badge of honor:

"The great Jesuit paleontologist Pierre Teilhard de Chardin was forbidden to publish his non-technical works during his lifetime. In recent years, three of France's finest theologians—Jesuit Henri de Lubac and Dominicans Yves Congar and M. D. Chenu—have been temporarily relieved from teaching posts and forced to submit their writings to the Holy Office for special censorship. Last year Austrian Jesuit Karl Rahner was required to submit all future writings to his superior in Rome for clearance, a restriction since lifted; Father John Courtney Murray of the U.S. was advised not to write any more in his special field of study, church-state relations. `In the Catholic Church of the 20[th] century, a U.S. priest dryly explains, `the grace of martyrdom has been given to the intellectual.'"[8]

Those who attacked, or "martyred" these "intellectuals," were intellectually mediocre. After Kung received an honorary doctorate at St Louis University, Archbishop Dino Staffa of the said Sacred Congregation tightened the rules for honorary degrees. *Time's* heading ridiculed Staffa: "Speaking of Stupidities…Staffa argued…."[9]

Connell fought against the divisions created by the media at the Council and among Catholics by explaining to seminarians and others that the "division of all the bishops into conservatives and progressives, like Republicans and Democrats, or two baseball teams, is absurd." He refuted erroneous ideas of the Council put there undoubtedly by *Time* when he said the "main purpose of the Council is to…improve the religious life of Catholics," not "begin some form of union with non-Catholics."[10]

All of the periti at the Council took an oath of secrecy. Connell and Fenton upheld theirs, Murray did not, thereby giving the dissenters a distinct advantage in promoting their views. One of his routines was to meet or lunch regularly with *Time's* Robert Blair Kaiser every ten to fourteen days while the Council was in session.[11] Another routine was to share the secret drafts of Council documents with the Luces and then solicit comments on issues of concern to them which could then be later added to the Council document. After sending Clare a draft of the document on the role of the laity, Murray asked Clare, who was particularly concerned about the role of women, to "Shoot me back a couple of sentences, just making points that you think necessary. These conciliar texts cannot be essays. They also tend to be rather gneeral [sic], since they are supposed to apply throughout the world.]"[12] Murray also sent secret drafts to Harry, one of which highlighted the statement: "The Government may not undertake those initiatives for the common good which can be achieved by the free forces of individuals and of private organizations. This principle of subsidiarity applies not only to the economic-social but also to the religious-social forces because without risks there is no virtue, as there is no economic-social progress without risk and incentive."[13] So much for the papal admonition of secrecy applying to Murray.

CHAPTER 97
THE BATTLE OVER RELIGIOUS LIBERTY AT SESSION TWO

T he Protestant observers at the Council were pushing for consideration and approval of a declaration on religious liberty. Robert McAfee Brown of the Union Theological Seminary mentioned that there was "no more important matter" than religious liberty. Dr. Ludwig Fischer of the World Council of Churches said "it would be wrong to regard national religious unity a good that could impose limits on religious liberty." John Courtney Murray expressed support for Fischer's comments as the Council Fathers moved towards a discussion of the topic.[1]

When the second session began in the Autumn of 1963, the battle over religious liberty, which had been brewing for a long time, broke out in earnest. Ottaviani blocked any attempt to address the matter for more than a year, but Summer, 1962 saw a duel ensuing between Ottaviani's Theological Commission and Bea's Secretariat. Each submitted draft documents on the topic, and Pope John created a commission to reconcile the two. Negotiations lasted for a while but broke down in August. That is where things remained until November, 1963 when Cardinal Spellman demanded in a letter to Cardinal Cicognani, President of the Council, that the issue of religious liberty be discussed.[2]

Pope Paul ordered Ottaviani to convene his commission to discuss the issue of religious liberty and to consider the draft from Bea's Secretariat.[3] A special subcommission led by Cardinal Leger of Montreal, Bishop John J. Wright of Pittsburgh, an Italian bishop and a Spanish bishop met to prepare a report for the plenary session meeting.[4]

A meeting was held November 11 at 4:30 p.m. as Fenton recorded in his diary: "M shows up for 1st time. It would be interesting to know if he was invited."[5] Perhaps because of Father Murray's presence, the meeting was "pretty tense from beginning to end," and resulted in a resolution by the Commission to consider the issue of religious liberty.[6] According to Novak, Archbishop Pietro Parente who was a member of both the theological commission and the Holy Office "delivered himself that evening of an almost hysterical defense of the doctrine that error has no rights." Murray, on the other hand, according to Novak, spoke "clearly and very well indeed.'" After a secret vote, "Bishop Wright's report stood approved by a vote of 18 to 5 with one null. Cardinal Bea's statement on religious liberty, therefore, was free for presentation to the Council."[7]

On November 18, Murray wrote to Spellman explaining the arguments for "an intervention in defense of the American Constitutional system and its guarantee of `the free exercise of religion.'" Murray based his argument on three grounds. First, the US Constitution guaranteed "all citizens freedom from governmental interference" in professing and practicing their religion. Second, the US constitutional system was based on "sound moral and political doctrine." In support of this point, Murray stated that government's functions were "limited to the temporal and terrestrial affairs of men" and that government was "incompetent in the field of religion." Government only had to protect and promote freedom of the "Church and of the churches and of all citizens," and the "primary purpose of government and law is to protect the rights of the human person." Finally, Murray argued "American bishops and the American faithful positively approve and support the First Amendment and its provision for the free exercise of religion." The American Catholics believe it is in accord with *Pacem in terris.*[8] Under the American arrangement, the institutional Church received material prosperity, and the societal powers kept the Church and other religious groups out of matters of public policy by the Church. Murray presented the American system as promoting the freedom of the Church, when in fact it worked against the church fulfilling its proper role by confining it to the private sphere. In practice it operated against the churches and religion. The precious diarchy Murray touted was another monism like Continental Liberalism or, more relevant to his day, the Soviet Constitution which guaranteed religious freedom much like the Americans' First Amendment.

The following day, November 19, De Smedt gave four main reasons for a religious liberty declaration, all of which amounted to an endorsement of America vis a vis the Soviets. De Smedt, speaking in "an eloquent and powerful manner which arrested the attention of the bishops," according to Novak, said the Church needed to proclaim:

"the truth about the right to religious liberty; the defense of this right, against atheistic materialism, in our time; the need of a peaceful social life in a time when men must live together, despite varying religious convictions; and Christian unity, since many non-Catholics suspect the Church of a kind of Machiavellianism, which seems to demand full exercise of religion when Catholics are in a minority, and to suppress religious liberty when Catholics are in a majority."[9]

De Smedt explained what religious liberty was not: it was not religious indifferentism, laicism, doctrinal relativism, or dilletantistic pessimism. "Positively, religious liberty is the right of the human person to the free exercise of religion according to the dictates of his conscience. Negatively, it is immunity from all external force in his personal relations with God...." The decree was a practical approach and it removed the question from "the world of abstractions which was so dear to the 19th century." The decree sought to "meet 'real man in his real dealings with other men, in contemporary human and civil societies.'" The justification was that "life is more complex than logic."[10]

De Smedt set out rules "by which Catholics ought to conduct themselves toward men who do not share their faith." First, Catholics should by prayer, penance, witness and "evangelizing in the Holy Spirit" bring "their non-believing brothers to the blessings of the Gospels." Second, there must not be any direct or indirect coercion as all must follow the "dictates of their own conscience," and if one "'errs in good faith'" then so be it for faith is a gift given by the Holy Spirit. Third, Catholics must help "their non-Catholic brothers in their human needs."[11]

In claiming "the man who sincerely obeys his own conscience intends to obey God himself, although at times confusedly and unknowingly and is to be considered worthy of esteem," De Smedt was articulating the rules by which Catholics were to accommodate themselves to pluralistic societies like America. The Church should take up the cause of religious liberty around the world, he urged, by having the Council "'solemnly demand religious liberty for the whole human family, for all religious groups, for each human person whether his conscience be sincere and true, or sincere and false concerning faith, provided only that he sincerely follow the dictate of conscience.'"[12]

This religious liberty was "'fruitless and empty'" unless men could carry out the "'dictate of their conscience in external acts'" in private and public. Citing to John XXIII's *Pacem in Terris*, and using it as authority for a claim that public authority is to accommodate religious liberty, De Smedt said that the rights of all should be safeguarded and people should not be hindered in the fulfillment of their duties." The bishop also claimed *Pacem In Terris* explained how the doctrine of religious liberty had developed over time in accordance with the "law of continuity." The doctrine of religious liberty, he said, could be founded in Scripture because man was made in the image of God but under the "law of nature" as well, where a person has "the right to the free exercise of religion in society according to the dictates of a sincere conscience" regardless of whether the conscience is "true, or captive either of error or of inadequate knowledge of truth and sacred things." De Smedt distinguished the teachings of Popes Pius IX, Leo XIII, and Pius XI so as to justify the schema claiming that their teachings were either historically limited to the events of their day or dealt with motivations and ideologies that were not present in or motivating the schema on religious liberty. With approval, De Smedt quoted Pius XII's radio message of June 1, 1941 in which he said "The chief duty of any public authority is to safeguard the inviolable rights that are proper to men and so to provide that each one might more easily fulfill his duties," and John XXIII's *Pacem in Terris.*[13]

De Smedt concluded by assuring his audience the document he endorsed was:

"not a dogmatic treatise, but a pastoral decree directed to men of our time. The whole world is waiting for this decree. The voice of the Church on religious liberty is being waited for in universities, in national and international organizations, in Christian and non-Christian communities, in the papers, and in public opinion – and it is being waited for with urgent expectancy. We hope that it will be possible to complete the discussion and the approbation of this very brief, but very important, decree before the end of this second session. How fruitful our work would appear to the world if the conciliar Fathers, with the voice of Peter's successor, could announce this liberating doctrine on religious liberty!"[14]

As the applause thundered through the hall, Novak claimed that, "John Courtney Murray may have been smiling, and perhaps recognizing 'one or two' of the phrases,"[15] if not also his ideas and argument. When the applause died down, the pope decided to delay the question on religious liberty because "well-placed cardinals believe...that the doctrine on religious liberty is heretical." Some thought that with this heretical doctrine the poorly educated would be allowed to vote Communist in some Catholic countries and to oppose the clergy. Others thought that the reason was due to financial concerns in that certain Curial cardinals would suffer financial loss.[16]

Fenton wrote a ditty to Ottaviani summing up the essence of the fight between the Catholic and the American factions:

> There are Weigel and Rahner and Kung
> Whose praises are everywhere sung
> But some fine domain
> Old Ottaviani
> Will see that they're properly hung.
>
> Old Suenens dislikes segregatio
> So he spoke out in full congregatio
> The bishops are churls
> So let's bring in the girls
> In spite of the world's admiration.
>
> Hanahoe, Fenton, and King
> Their names have a militant ring
> They argue for Rome
> But were silenced at home
> It was, perhaps, a very good thing.[17]

CHAPTER 98
INTER MIRIFICA

On December 4, 1963, Pope Paul VI promulgated the first two documents of the Vatican II Council: *Sacrosanctum Concilium,* or The Constitution on the Sacred Liturgy, and *Inter Mirifica,* the Decree on the Means of Social Communication. Unlike other documents from the Council, *Inter Mirifica* had an urgency about it which indicated that the warnings of Fenton, Connell, and others, as well as lessons of the past several years, had not been lost on the Church leadership, who knew that they had to act quickly.

Inter Mirifica went directly to the heart of psychological warfare as the source of the power of the societal elites, and it called the Catholic media and arts to loyalty towards the Church and Christ. It called the Americans to a moral responsibility that they refused to accept for to do so would be to give up a great weapon. The relatively short Decree dealt with "the press, the cinema, radio, television and others of a like nature." These were the chief avenues of the most effective communication, "directly" touched "man's spirit," and "opened up new avenues of easy communication of all kinds of news, of ideas and orientations." These "means of social communication" had the ability by "their nature" to "reach and influence not merely single individuals but the very masses and even the whole of human society."[1]

The Council recognized the beneficial nature of these means of social communication if "properly used." The Church knew "man can use them in ways that are contrary to the Creator's design and damaging to himself." In Chapter I, the Church taught pastors had a responsibility of "instructing and directing the faithful how to use these media in a way that will insure their own salvation and perfection and that of all mankind." Laymen were to "animate these media...in accordance with God's plan." This required all who "use them [the media] know the principles of the moral order and apply them faithfully in this domain." This meant that one should take account of the circumstances in which the content is communicated – the purpose...the people, the place, the time, etc." These "circumstances could modify and even totally alter the morality of a production." The Council knew that "the manner in which any given medium achieves its effect" is to be given importance and cognizance.[2]

The Council fathers put the means of communication in their proper transcendental context: "the content of the communication [must] be true and – within the limits set by justice and charity – complete," and this meant that "in the gathering and in the publication of news the moral law and the legitimate rights and dignity of man should be upheld."[3]

Moral evil could be depicted as a "suitable dramatization" that would "lead to a deeper knowledge and analysis of man and to a manifestation of the true and the good in all their splendor." In this, also, the "moral law must be rigorously observed."[4] Public opinion was recognized as having "enormous influence nowadays over the lives, private or public, of all citizens." Therefore, justice and charity demanded that he means of social communication be used in the "formation and diffusion of sound public opinion."[5]

The consumers ("readers, viewers, audiences") of the means of social communication had duties also. These were a responsibility to be selective in their viewing or consumption, to properly form their consciences, to inform themselves about "assessments arrived at by the authorities with competence in this sphere," to conform to assessments in accord with a "right conscience," and to "resist less wholesome influences and profit more fully from the good." The consumers of the media, "especially the young, should learn moderation and discipline in their use" of the media, and parents had a duty to "see that entertainments and publications which might endanger faith and morals do not enter their houses and that their children are not exposed to them elsewhere."[6]

The media had important duties:

"A special responsibility for the proper use of the means of social communication rests on journalists, writers, actors, designers, producers, exhibitors, distributors, operators, sellers, critics – all those, in a word, who are involved in the making and transmission of communications in any way whatever. It is clear that a very great responsibility rests on all of these people in today's world: they have power to direct mankind along a good path or an evil path by the information they impart and the pressure they exert. It will be for them to regulate economic, political and artistic values in a way that will not conflict with the common good. To achieve this result more surely, they will do well to form professional organizations capable of imposing on their members – if necessary by a formal pledge to observe a moral code – a respect for the moral law in the problems they encounter and in their activities. [7]

The duty of these people to the young and to the proper presentation of religious matters was specifically mentioned.[8] The civil authorities had specific responsibilities "because of the common good, toward which these media are oriented." The civil authorities were "to defend and safeguard – especially in relation to the press – a true and just freedom of information…." The civil authorities were to act positively in protecting the "well-being of the citizens," and they were "bound to ensure, equitably and vigilantly, that public morality and social progress are not gravely endangered through the issue of these media. This they can achieve by promulgating laws and tirelessly enforcing them. The liberty of individuals and groups is not in the least compromised by such vigilance...."[9]

The Council recognized that the "influence of the means of social communication extends beyond national frontiers" and that all the various national projects should coordinate their efforts at the international level through an organization approved by the Holy See. The Council also "invites all men of good will, especially those who control the media, to use them solely for the good of humanity, for its fate becomes more and more dependent on their right use." The proper use of the media would not cause people to "suffer damage" but rather, "like salt and light, add savor to the earth and light to the world."[10]

Inter Mirifica is a decree, and in paragraph 6 it put forth one of Fr. Connell's key positions in the battle with Murray and the Americanists: "The Council proclaims that all must accept the absolute primacy of the objective moral order. It alone is superior to and is capable of harmonizing all forms of human activity, not excepting art, no matter how noble in themselves. Only the moral order touches man in the totality of his being as Gods rational creature, called to a supernatural destiny. If the moral order is fully and faithfully observed, it leads man to full perfection and happiness." [11]

The Divine Positive Law is to form the basis of all actions by the civil authorities and the Vatican II Council decreed that position in full vindication of Fr. Connell's efforts. Murray argued it was only the natural law to which societies had to adhere, and his effort, which formed the major thrust of his theology, was denied in *Inter Mirifica*. The most important issue of the debates over the last two decades was determined in the favor of Fr. Connell and the Catholics. Much of what followed was just the side show Murray and the Americans tried to use to change Catholic doctrine.

THE SCREECHES OF SATAN

Recognizing it struck at the heart of American power, the opposition to *Inter Mirifica* was intense. Perhaps they knew they lost the most important battle, and Murray should have realized it. But if he did, he certainly did not let on, at least not right away. The Americans focused on the obvious and the immediate. The American sympathizers were, most notably, John Cogley, Michael Novak who replaced Robert Blair Kaiser as *Time's* correspondent at the Council, and Murray, led the attack. Cogley objected that the document subjected those working in the media to the moral order and the teachings of the Church. *Inter Mirifica*, he claimed:

"puts people working in the communications field – let us say a man who works for the NBC, CBS, *Time*, or the New York Times – in an impossible situation. . . . It means that he just simply can't work. These secular magazines and means of communications will not permit a man to work for them if he must clear everything through somebody else." [12]

Cogley objected to the requirement legislation insure morality and truth-telling by the media, claiming such a requirement was "a very dangerous thing in itself – politically dangerous. It is also contrary to the First Amendment of the Constitution of the United States....we have found from experience that it is much better if there be severe limitations on government regarding the press and means of communication." [13] Cogley objected to the requirement "one should read the Catholic press in order to find out what the natural law position and the Christian position is on issues of the day" because "it suggests that there is an easy way to find what is the Christian solution to a given problem." Finally, Cogley objected because the Declaration "oversimplifies completely the problem of the artist who has to be true on the one hand to morals, and on the other hand to his own vision, to his own art and all the rest that goes on with it." The decree suggested that "the artist, whether he be novelist or a painter, should have as his primary objective to edify the faithful and somehow to give witness, in a very direct and uncomplicated way, to his religion and all that goes with it. It seems to us that this was a complete oversimplification of the whole problem of art and prudence."[14]

As the Decree was being considered, Cogley signed a statement objecting to it in general and specific portions in particular. Michael Novak and Robert Kaiser joined the protest, along with Murray, Jean Danielou SJ, Fr. Jorge Mejia, and Redemptorist Fr. Bernard Haring, all of whom claimed that the document "seems to give the state…an authority over mass media which is dangerous to political liberty everywhere and which in some countries like the United States is proscribed by constitutional law." This, they said, was a "threat to the integrity of the media." Once again, the US Constitution was evoked to guide the Church, rather than having the Church guide the Constitution. As such the protestors portrayed the document as "a classic example of how the Second Vatican Ecumenical Council failed to come to grips with the world around it."[15]

Before long, the real dynamics behind the protest became clear: the "liberals" wanted the subordination of Church teaching to the powerful, who held that power largely through their control of the media. In the end, the protest of the Americans and their arguments for freedom had no effect on the final document. All the Americanists could do from that point on was to excoriate the Pope for doing what he did. And then ignore the decree, declare victory after losing and act like victors. The same sort of thing the Americans did in 1973 with the end of the Vietnam War.

CHAPTER 99
A VACUUM AT THE TOP

The Americans were dissatisfied with Paul VI. Not only was he not moving fast enough on the things that mattered to them, but he affirmatively moved against them with the promulgation of *Inter Mirifica*. *Time* harshly wrote "Last week the council railroaded through without discussion a schema on communications that tolerates states censorship of mass media, suggesting civil authorities prevent 'harm to the morals and progress of society through the bad use of these instruments.'"[1] The use of "railroaded" gave away the American opposition to this decree that threatened their power.

Pope Paul had been the Americans' darling for much of Autumn, 1963, but by the time the Council adjourned, he was painted as weak. In an October 4, 1963 article, "Roman Catholics: Readiness for Reform," the Americans started touting a number of "reforms" of the Curia which were needed because the Curia was "out of tune", "subject to much criticism", and "old, less suited to the times." Paul seemed to be pushing for action and they were lavish in their praise of him when he did. They wrote he "seems to be displaying the artful sovereignty of a Prospero and the action-now dash of Henry V" as well as "a notable zeal for carrying out the renewal of Catholicism planned by John XXIII."[2]

The same article mentioned the discussion of the schema entitled *De Ecclesia* and noted it emphasized the teaching and governing role of bishops, who stood to gain power at the expense of the Pope. *Time* presented a number of suggestions that might lead to spiritual renewal including trading in the golden pectoral crosses for wooden ones, elimination of titles such as "excellency" or "eminence," and, as Bishop Sheen was quoted, requiring laymen and parish priests to take vows of poverty like monks and nuns. But the magazine made sure to depict the prelates of the Church as living like princes, separated from the workers and the poor.[3]

Paul VI remained strongly in the liberal camp, or so *Time* said. The magazine wrote "It was Pope Paul's intention to make the Vatican Council as democratic as possible" explained the magazine which proceeded to present Ottaviani as the leader of the forces opposing democracy and Cardinal Suenens as the "leader of the progressive forces." Collegiality was favored and "papolatry," a word coined to signify the power of the pope, was disfavored.[4]

The magazine did not discuss the religious liberty issue with much optimism. Towards the end of the Second Session, *Time* explained religious liberty was an issue that concerned the "relationship of Catholicism to other faiths" and was one of two "landmarks in the history of the 20th century church." The other landmark dealt with "a strong denunciation of anti-Semitism." When it came to religious liberty, the schema faced "bitter opposition from Italian and Spanish conservatives at the council," even thought it "declares that every man has the right to worship as his conscience dictates, and that all men, as well as the state, are duty-bound to respect this right. Says U.S. Jesuit John Courtney Murray: 'This hits right at the heart of the old Roman thesis that freedom of religion is only tolerated when Catholics are in the minority, and disappears when Catholics are in the majority.'"[5]

Murray presented Catholic doctrine as contingent, or changing, and not based on unchanging principle. The article depicted Catholics as divided, an important objective if the Catholics were to be subjugated.

The American media did not think the Church was moving fast enough with "modernization of the church." This meant it was not reorganizing itself in accordance with American principles of organization which in turn meant adopting as church policy the advancement of America, and things American, as the ideal. John XXIII was the "inspiration" of a "council that promised to bring about a sweeping inner renewal of Roman Catholicism." At the end of the Second Session, the Council had "become a parliament of stalemate, compromise and delay" and there existed a "vacuum" at the top. The man who a few weeks earlier had been lauded was criticized for having "failed to intervene when intervention was called for," "sometimes settled for half-measures when he did act," and did not sweep away the "roadblocking Curia officials" when he should have as asked by the progressives. Troubling to the Americans was the reported comment from the Pope to a visitor that "'I fear that the bishops are rushing toward the brink of schism.'" More troubling still was that the schema on religious liberty was not only stalled but would undergo review by the arch-enemies of America: "The Theological Commission and its president, Alfredo Cardinal Ottaviani, who is dead set against Murray's ideas on liberty of conscience."[6]

A final article for the year re-emphasized that the Catholic Church had been wrong all of these years and the Protestants were right. In choosing to "modernize" the Mass by putting it in the vernacular, and by making other changes, the "Roman Mass of the future will bear a much greater outward resemblance to the Anglican and Lutheran Communion services developed by the Reformation fathers 400 years ago."[7] The American media assault on the Church was relentless, and continuous.

CHAPTER 100

FILLING THE VACUUM: THE POSITIONING OF CARDINAL CUSHING

Everybody remembers where they were and what they were doing when they got word President Kennedy had been shot. Walter Cronkite in his characteristic laconic tone made it clear that JFK was dead at 1 p.m. central time, November 22, 1963.

By 8 a.m. the following morning, two secret service men and *Life* editor, Richard Stolley, were standing on the doorstep of "58 year old amateur film buff" and Jewish clothing merchant Abraham Zapruder to buy the film showing JFK choking and his head exploding from the bullets of the assassins. How Stolley and the Secret Service were able to identify Zapruder and ascertain the existence of his film so quickly was never made clear in a supposed "Stolley tells all" aired November, 2014 and published by Time/Life.[1] This dearth of critical information only serves to lend legitimacy to the allegations that JFK's assassination was planned, if not also conducted by, someone other than Lee Harvey Oswald.

There were a lot of people who wanted JFK dead. The traditional suspects were Cuban Communists or Soviet Communists or the Mob. But the Israelis also came to figure into the picture with the revelations of Jewish nuclear scientist turned Christian Mordechai Vanunu who said in July 2004 upon his release from eleven years of solitary confinement and 7 more years of Israeli imprisonment that the Mossad targeted JFK because he opposed David Ben Gurion's efforts to arm Israel with nuclear weapons. Catholic Michael Collins Piper provided over 700 pages of documentation to support these claims with his book *Final Judgment: The Missing Link in the JFK Assassination Conspiracy.*[2] But there could have been others.

JFK had made an enemy of David Rockefeller by the Summer of 1962, even though Henry Luce, who had incredible access to the White House even to the point of sitting in on national security briefings, put a friendly, cooperative, positive face on the matter by publishing in *Life* magazine "A Businessman's Letter to J.F.K. and His Reply." The magazine printed a letter from Rockefeller to JFK and JFK's response, and the subject of the exchange was the US economic, monetary, and tax policy in light of a growing trade deficit and gold flight from the US. Rockefeller's main point was "tax reform" to allow greater investments by lowering the "corporate income tax rate," which translated into letting private money flow out of the country to buy up foreign assets to maximize the return on investments for the monied classes. JFK was not keen to that idea, and he did not want to devalue the dollar, either. Instead, he proposed a more cooperative stance with foreign economies, and one in which American business remained loyal to Americans while the US Government cared for all the people entrusted to its care. This infuriated Rockefeller and the monied elites who ran America. Henry Luce said as much when interviewed on November 11, 1965 by historiographer John L. Steele. Luce explained the dynamic: "The President had made a speech again in which he had said there ought to be more dialogue between the government and business. For whatever reasons this speech was, on the whole, not well received by the business community." [3]

Luce agreed with Steele that JFK was talking about "old myths and new realities" which signified curbing the appetites of the financial elites: "Oh, yes, he got off into some of perhaps Galbraith's [John Kenneth Galbraith] language. At any rate, this talk about myths and old realities, or new, at any rate in general it did not go down well with the business community. However, he spoke about a dialogue. Now it just happened that very soon after that I had occasion to see Mr. David Rockefeller of Chase National Bank, and in discussing this general topic he told me that he had written confidentially a letter to the President on the subject and so I said to David, 'Why don't you let me have that letter and let me ask the President if he will permit its publication in *Life* with his reply to it.' And the President instantly agreed to that, so we had, as you say, rather than unusual story."[4]

If the plutocrats do not like you or your policies, then you have a real problem, because plutocrats by their nature use the system for their benefit. With JFK's assassination, Lyndon Baines Johnson became the 36th President of the United States of America and he commenced his work to advance civil rights, medicare, and a tax cut.[5]

JFK's assassination also provided an opportunity for the Americans to fill the vacuum at the top of the Church since Paul VI was so disappointing. The guy to fill that vacuum was Richard Cardinal Cushing who celebrated the Requiem Mass for JFK in Washington's St. Matthew's Cathedral. Attended by world leaders, dignitaries, heads of state, and royalty, the mass provided Cushing with a podium to be the face of Catholicism and earned him great support for the work the Americans wanted him to accomplish at the Council. This dynamic was reinforced with Cushing delivering the televised eulogy for JFK on November 24, 1963. Expressing sorrow for the Kennedy family while extolling Jack, Cushing ended the moving talk with a blessing "in the name of the Father and the Son and the Holy Ghost, amen," but not before setting out the American Catholic truth and solidifying his own role as a leader of the Church in the days to come at the Council: "John F. Kennedy, 35th President of the United States of America, has fought the good fight for the

God-given rights of his fellow man and for a world where peace and freedom shall prevail."[6] Cushing got the job of leading the Catholics for America because plutocrats like David Rockefeller who benefitted so well from the American ideology badly needed the Church to carry The American Proposition around the world.

CHAPTER 101
THE CATHOLIC PRESS TURNS

A s the second session wound down, the Catholic media was turning more and more Americanist in its reporting on the Vatican Council. An ill-defined freedom was the most important issue of the day, and Murray was an important figure in that regard. The Catholic press was playing along with the American ideological warfare plans of stressing freedom and America as goods in themselves. Tied to this dynamic was the "vindication" of Murray, who became the great American liberator of the Catholic Church.

On November 22, 1963, the Oklahoma *Courier* carried a story by Michael Novak entitled "Council Meeting Vindicates Long Harassed U. S. Jesuit." It described the November 11 plenary meeting of the full Theological Commission as a victory for freedom. "The Nov. 11 vote," Novak opined, "showed that freedom, open discussion, and convincing reflection can win an overwhelming victory even in the theological commission, as well as on the council floor. The vote was a sign of how great an evening it was, not only for Father Murray but for the Church."[1]

Novak described how Bishop John J Wright guided the "statement on religious liberty which Cardinal Bea's Secretariat for Christian

Unity has prepared for presentation to the Council" under the watchful gaze of Father Murray, whom Wright had invited as his peritus. Also present "in the room" were those who "had harassed" Murray, including Cardinal Ottaviani and Archibishop Pietro Parente both of the Holy Office, which had worked hard to prevent the publication of Murray's views in book form, thereby placing "America's greatest theologian" and his "life's work…under a cloud."[2] Although Murray could only speak for a few moments and then only in Latin, "America's greatest theologian" acquitted himself well, and the Theological Commission passed the report of the subcommittee by a vote of 18 to 5, with credit going to Bishop Wright for bringing about this success.[3]

One month later, Msgr. Vincent A Yzermans weighed in with a report for the *St Cloud Visitor* entitled "Conversation at the Council" based on an October 28 meeting with four "distinguished theologians"—Murray, Weigel, Fr. Godfrey Diekmann, OSB and Hans Kung—who "came together to engage in an informal conversation" on the ecumenical trend, the liturgy constitution, the Church and the episcopacy, and "church and society."[4] Murray led off by urging trashing all books on public ecclesiastical law because "you do not find any good political philosophy in the books on public ecclesiastical law." The "problem of Church and society is an enormously complicated one, but it basically has to be conceived in terms of theology first and good political philosophy secondly [sic]" said Murray. The extant books did not frame the "genuine nature of the political relationship" properly. Rather, they presented a paternalistic or absolutist view based on a ruler to the ruled relationship instead of the "democratic development" in which the "citizen…is himself a bearer of political power." Murray stated Leo XIII tried to "change the position of the problem by employing the terms Church and human society," but this effort was "ruined and distorted" by the training manuals which dealt with laicism in Europe. These training manuals took no cognizance of the situation in America, which is different.[5] In the same edition of the *St Cloud Visitor* Father Weigel was quoted as expressing his admiration for the American bishops because "they stood for freedom."[6]

The Rev. John B Sheerin, CSP, Editor of *The Catholic World,* wrote a short editorial entitled "Council Experts Vindicated" in the Baltimore *Catholic Review* which also mentioned Murray's victory in the Theological Commission session on November 11. As a result of that victory, Murray was now "emerging as one of the towering figures of the Council," was much admired in Europe and America, "played a large role in the framing of the document," and, most importantly, was "roundly applauded" at the Commission meeting. Sheerin reminded the readers Murray had been "under a cloud" for a "period of more than 10 years," and forbidden to write on religious liberty, but that was clearly all in the past because "the Church is on the march and time marches on."[7] The fact the last phrase in Sheerin's article was taken from Luce's media machine that created the video news slips called "Time Marches On" betrayed the depth of Americanist penetration of Catholic thought. Murray had moved from censured priest to the designated peritus for the American episcopate which was "greatly pleased that the issue of religious liberty has finally appeared on the agenda of the Council, notwithstanding many efforts to block discussion of it."[8]

Eager to capitalize on his de facto rehabilitation at the hands of the American bishops, Murray wrote an article for *America* magazine entitled "On Religious Liberty: Freedom Is the Most Distinctively American Issue Before the Council," which was widely discussed in the Catholic press. The Catholic press wondered whether the "Roman Catholic Church should assume a universal, active patronage of the freedom of the human person, according to a leading Jesuit theologian." The American Catholic press took pride in the fact religious liberty was "the most distinctively American issue at the Council" and Murray was the guy most responsible for addressing it.[9] In his article, Murray credited Cardinal Spellman's "strong intervention, demanding that the issue be presented to the conciliar Fathers"[10] as carrying the day in Rome.

At this stage in the Council, two documents, or versions, existed of a statement on religious liberty. One was Chapter Five of the Decree on Ecumenism entitled "On Religious Freedom" and the second was

Belgian Bishop De Smedt's *relatio,* which Murray termed "more important" because of its discussion of the "rationale of the decree." The crux of the matter, according to Murray, revolved around two crucial points: First, "every man by right of nature…has the right to the free exercise of religion in society according to the dictates of his personal conscience" and this "right belongs essentially to the dignity of the human person as such." Second, this translates into "an obligation…on other men in society, and upon the state in particular, to acknowledge this personal right, to respect it in practice, and to promote its free exercise."[11] Murray derived "this doctrine" from "the concrete situation of the world today." In other words, the reasons for adopting it were historical rather than theological. First, "it is necessary today to state the true doctrine of the Church with regard to religious freedom in society" as clarified by "theological reflection, and also by political experience, over the past few generations." Second, the Church must necessarily "assume a universal patronage of the dignity of the human person and of man's essential freedoms, in an age in which totalitarian tyranny has imposed itself upon nearly half of the human race." Third, it was the age of the "religiously pluralist society" when men of "all religions and of no religion must live together in conditions of justice, peace and civic friendship, under equitable laws that protect the whole range of human rights, notably…the right to religious freedom." The Church therefore had to "show the way to justice and peace in society, by espousing the cause of human freedom, which is, as John XXIII taught, both an essential end of organized society and also the essential method and style of political life." Finally, "we are living in an age in which a great ecumenical hope has been born" and the "goal of Christian unity lies…beyond the horizons of our present vision." The "path to this far goal can lie only along the road to freedom: social, civil, political and religious freedom. Hence the Church must assist in the work of creating conditions of freedom in human society" for this was "integral to the spiritual mission of the Church, which is to be herself the spiritual unity of mankind and to assist all men in finding this unity."[12]

In other words, history, or what Hegel would have called the Zeitgeist, consorted with the American Spirit, and the two together gave birth to a new Catholic principle. This was a far cry from "*Semper idem*": it corresponded to the textbook definition of modernism.

Murray concluded his article with an emotional allusion to the need for pastoral and ecumenical action to counter the implied Soviet Communist threat. "The human person, who was created by God as his image," Murray wrote in unabashedly theological terms, "who was redeemed by the blood of Christ . . . stands today under a massive threat to everything that human dignity and personal freedom mean." The only question was whether the Church, which he said had always fought for the freedom of Catholics, would now extend this fight to "fellow Christians and toward all men" by joining with America in the anti-Communist crusade. Coercion was a bad thing as it contravened the "essential law of the divine economy of salvation" which was that men must freely accept the gift of God's grace if at all.[13] However, like so much else in Murray's writings, "coercion" was never defined and would go on to wreak havoc in the years following the Council. Man's "essential freedom requires that he should be governed, in the end, only by the will of God." Therefore, Man "has a right to be free from all manner of coercion or compulsion that might be brought to bear on him by other men." De Smedt's *relatio* provided the formula of "religious freedom within the Christian vocabulary" so as to allow "general agreement among all Christians, Catholic and non-Catholics" while rejecting indifferentism and the "ideology of the `outlaw conscience'" which asserted divine laws do not govern the human conscience.[14] It was a step towards expanding the meaning of Leo XIII's reference to religion to mean all religions, not just Catholicism, and to do so Murray lifted language right from the American Founder Thomas Jefferson.

There were problems though with the *relatio* in that it discussed limiting the right to religious liberty, and this could allow for abuse. One means to limit the freedom was by invoking the "common good" and another was to invoke protection of the "rights of others," both Catholic ideas used to protect the Catholic majorities in some countries. The latter could become a "veiled invocation of the rights of a majority, which again is dangerous doctrine." Therefore, it was a good first step to define the common good as including a number of rights including the right to religious liberty, which if infringed, violates the common good. Murray, speaking as an American, said "the Anglo-American tradition of politics, law and jurisprudence" was the way to insure the protection of religious liberty from the power of the state:

"The American constitutional system is based squarely on two fundamental principles: first, man is endowed by his Creator with certain inalienable rights, second, government and the order of law exist primarily for the protection and promotion of these rights. These principles were clearly affirmed by Pius XII and John XXIII. However, the American system also enshrines another principle, namely, the incompetence of government as judge or arbiter in the field of religious truth, as also, for instance, in the field of art and science."[15]

Murray then launched into an exposition of the role of the government which was consistent with his writings in the 1950s and with the beliefs of the American Founders. However, it contradicted Catholic teaching, especially as he maintained "Government is a secular authority whose competence is limited to the temporal and terrestrial affairs of men who must live together in justice, peace and freedom…Government would be acting . . . *ultra vires* if it were to enforce upon citizens, by the medium of law, any kind of technological judgment; if, that is, it were to assert by law that a particular religion – say, the Catholic religion – ought to be the religion of the national community." Murray claimed it asserted the competence of the secular authority in the field of religion. Even Leo XIII "made it quite clear that political authority has no part whatsoever in the care of souls…or in the control of the minds of men."[16]

Murray backtracked a bit claiming: "It is, of course, true that this political principle was obscured in Europe for centuries, largely in consequence of the rise of royal absolutism and the `Union of Throne and Altar.'" Then he made a fantastical claim: "The true tradition was. . . preserved in the American constitutional system. Absolutism never set foot in America, much to the joy, both of the Church and of the American people. Together with my fellow countrymen, both Catholic and non-Catholic, I should like to see this principle asserted in the final conciliar text on religious freedom. It is, I think, essential to the case for religious freedom in society. It completes the theological and ethical arguments by adding to them a sound political argument. And this political principle, namely, that political authority is incompetent in the field of religion, needs particularly to be invoked when there is question of legal limitations to be imposed on the free exercise of religion in society."[17]

Murray asserted "theological development" to avoid conviction for holding views "directly contrary" to "certain utterances of the Church in the 19th century, which seem to have denied this right." Thankfully, the *relatio* recognized "a problem of true and genuine development, both in the doctrine of the Church and in her pastoral solicitude: for the dignity and freedom of man."[18]

Murray's claims went unanswered largely because Father Fenton was incapacitated by a heart attack while on the ship sailing to the second session of the Council.[19] The one Catholic publication in the US consistently true to the Magisterium was about to go silent at a critical time.

PART XX
VATICAN II – 1964

CHAPTER 102

BAD NEWS FOR THE AMERICANS

The new year started off badly for the Americans and their allies in the Church. Gustave Weigel, Murray's alter ego, died of a heart attack in early January, 1964, age 57. Weigel was praised as having a "ready wit," explaining things so they could be understood by reporters, and possessing a powerful theological mind.[1] *Time* counted him a real hero, who had: "played a major role in the 1960 Kennedy campaign with a speech stating that the church would not interfere with a Catholic president, acted as informal press secretary at the Vatican's Ecumenical Council, was widely hailed for his understanding of other religions, winning a 1962 honorary degree from Yale as one 'who had broken through the Reformation wall and pioneered Catholic-Protestant dialogue.'"[2]

The New York Times' obituary for Weigel praised him as a leader in the ecumenical movement of the past decade, who had a cordial relationship with Jews, and was "a central figure in the liberal wing of Catholic theology." Weigel's most notable accomplishment, according to the *Times*, was:

"His speech in Washington in September, 1960, clarifying the Catholic position on church-state relations, [which] was regarded as an important factor in reducing the religious controversy over the Presidential candidacy of Senator John F. Kennedy [as well as] an authoritative exposition of the Roman Catholic hierarchy's views on church-state relations. He said that the Catholic Church would not attempt to interfere with the political activities of a Catholic President nor would a Catholic President be bound by Catholic morality in deciding public issues."[3]

Murray himself suffered a heart attack during the same month in which Weigel died. For fear of upsetting Clare, Dorothy Farmer, her secretary, kept the news from Clare until after she gave an important speech.[4]

REFORM AND ECUMENISM

Time's articles for early 1964 emphasized ecumenism and the idea the Church was being reformed as it was behind the times. One story covered a talk given by Julius Cardinal Dopfner of Munich, West Germany, who was described as a young prelate (Dopfner was actually 51 at the time of the talk) and was immediately counted among the good guys in the great American drama. "[O]ne excited Lutheran churchman" said this was "'the first time anyone so high up in the Catholic hierarchy has made a speech quite so daring.'"[5]

Using language reminiscent of John Tracy Ellis' attack on Catholic higher education in the '50s, *Time* went on to quote Dopfner as saying that: "Masses of the faithful have been lost" because to many the Catholic Church appeared as "'an institution that enslaved freedom' and as a 'superannuated souvenir from a past age.'" The Church, *Time* continued, "spoke to man in an ancient tongue, through incomprehensible rituals, in preaching concepts that have no relation to current life. Instead of penetrating the world, the church seemed to sit 'in a self-imposed ghetto, trying to build its own small world adjoining the big world.'" The way to solve all of this was for the Church to repudiate Catholicism's apparent rejection of "ideological pluralism, political democracy and modern technology." This, the Cardinal said, was why Pope

John called the Council, and the Church was "a church ever in need of reform."[6]

Throughout 1964, *Time* kept up the drumbeat for all of its favorite causes, arguing not only for intercredal cooperation but for changes in doctrine as well. It was eager to showcase prelates who promoted their agenda. Leo Josef Cardinal Suenens was a particular favorite, not only because he was "debonair and witty," but because he stressed the need to make more of "practical collaboration notably in the social and humanitarian field" and determine "new applications of the church's teaching on birth control" due to "new medical research."[7] As if to emulate Henry Luce's magazine, the NCWC highlighted American favorites and American themes. Redemptorist Priest Bernard Haering said unless the "Second Vatican Council... stiffens the resolve of Christians, they may again become mute spectators at the slaughter of Jews."[8]

But no matter how diverse the issues the good guys promoted, the fundamental issue remained religious liberty. C. Stanley Lowell, associate director of Protestants and Other Americans United for Separation of Church and State (POAU), said ecumenism was the Church's "new strategy" because "killing Protestants off" or "walling them off" or trying to convert them did not work. He made clear that "while we're all appreciative of the Roman Church's new friendliness we must have serious reservations. I can't imagine a worse fate for Christians than to be under one tent." What the Protestants wanted was a statement on religious liberty which "would be of tremendous significance. But it wasn't considered, it wasn't passed."[9] Archbishop Denis E Hurley of Durban, South Africa criticized keeping the schemata secret. He urged passing clear rules of procedure concerning voting and carrying on the business of the Council, a proposal the "Anglo-Saxon world" would appreciate. Schemata on holiness and education could be omitted according to Hurley who predicted the religious liberty schemata being soundly approved in Autumn, 1964 by a vote of four to one.[10] In *America,* Bishop Robert Tracy of Baton Rouge, Louisiana blamed "delays, frustrations and disappointments" on "obstructionists" and "antiquated and inefficient procedures." Paul VI was different than John by "temperament and training" and he moved slower than his predecessor.[11] Nonetheless, Tracey saw religious liberty coming to a vote during the third session. Archbishop Robert Lucey of San Antonio was wary but optimistic and urged the US bishops to take the lead at the Council to "obtain adoption of a decree proclaiming authentic and universal freedom of religion." At the Eighteenth Annual Convention of the Archdiocesan Council of Catholic Women, he adopted Murray's line when he said: "The world is waiting for the Second Vatican Council to dispel once for all the suspicion that we preach two gospels of human rights according to circumstances; namely, that where Roman Catholics are a minority, we proclaim religious liberty as something sacred, but where we are a majority, we are not greatly concerned about the consciences of sincere and earnest believers of other faiths." [12]

Lucey continued with "liberty of conscience does not mean that a man may willfully ignore God or consider falsehood as equal to truth. Intelligent creatures have some obligation prudently to inform themselves regarding the existence of the Creator and His intervention in human affairs."[13]

Cardinal Cushing created more drama when he claimed that without a statement on religious liberty the "ecumenical movement will fall on its face" because "if there is no statement, then we cannot be considered sincere."[14]

CHAPTER 103
TIME IS EXCORIATED FOR DISTORTIONS

Recognizing the American media was running the show, Pope Paul issued norms which limited the ability of *periti* to discuss the ongoing work of the council. Henceforth, the *periti*: "1)…should answer with knowledge, prudence and objectivity the questions which the commissions have proposed to them. 2). They are forbidden to organize currents of opinions or ideas, to hold interviews or to defend publicly their personal ideas about the council. 3). They should not criticize the council, nor communicate to outsiders news about the activities of the commissions, observing always in this regard the decree o the Holy Father about the secret to be observed concerning conciliar matters."[1]

In his final article as editor of *American Ecclesiastical Review* published in December, 1963, Fenton claimed those who disregarded the orders to remain silent towards outsiders concerning activities of the Council were doing evil. The article was entitled "A Letter from Rome," and it was directed at the writings of Xavier Rynne, the pseudonym of Father Francis X. Murphy, a Redemptorist priest, who Fenton alluded to as "M, the Mixer, or the Master of the Midrash." Fenton explained M's "A Letter from Vatican City" articles published in the *New Yorker* and M's subsequent book, *Letters from Vatican City*, were just so much inflammatory rubbish.[2]

Fenton accurately described how M had "set himself to the task of forming attitudes rather than of presenting truth." The "purpose of his writing was to influence those readers who might be gullible enough to take him seriously." Murphy "sought to mislead people into imagining that whatever and whoever might be designated as 'conservative' within the Catholic Church should be opposed and repudiated, and the Church stood in need of practically unlimited change." As a result of doing this work, M received financial rewards and notoriety.[3]

M's writings faithfully mirrored "the point of view of the more venomous among the lay adversaries of Cardinal Ottaviani and the Roman Curia in general." Their purpose was to express "what these people wanted others to believe, during the spring and summer of 1963." Fenton in his long article went about the work of refuting the stories told about Ottaviani, Ruffini, Pizzardo, and the Apostolic Delegates. He denounced the alleged division within the Curia, and the attacks on a number of theologians as well as the teachings of the pontiffs for the last two centuries.[4]

Perhaps the strongest rebuke to the American media, particularly *Time* magazine, came from Bishop Albert R. Zuroweste of Belleville, Illinois, who criticized *Time*'s December 6, 1963 roundup of the Council in a letter to the editor of the magazine which was subsequently printed in its entirety by the NCWC News Service on January 11, 1964.

Zuroweste began by expressing "Sincere sympathy to TIME readers who at best got an incomplete and distorted account of the Council," saying that it was "abnormal for a writer to ignore or misrepresent facts in order to convey his views." Zuroweste listed misrepresentations *Time*'s reporter made in support of a "campaign against his favorite 'bad guys,'"[5] including such things as: "there 'is no such thing as a "stand-pat schemata"'"; 2) never was a schema "proposed by the conservative Roman Curia"; 3) neither Pope John nor Paul were "ever called upon to 'mediate a dispute' or 'to intervene'"; 4) the schema on Communications "was not 'railroaded through without discussion'"; 5) Curial officials "have no direct or indirect involvement in the Council" and hence it was false to refer to "'the roadblocking Curia officials'"; 6) there are only 10 council commissions and not twelve; and 7) the procedure concerning the religious liberty declaration was improperly explained." [6]

EXPANDING ON THE LAST POINT, ZUROWESTE CHARGED

"Your reporter alleges that the chapter on religious liberty was composed in party [sic] by a U.S. Jesuit, and that 'Pope Paul intends to have it revised by the Theological omission and its president,….who is dead set against….(the Jesuits') ideas on liberty of conscience.' The fact is that the initial draft of the chapter was prepared by the Secretariat for Christian Unity, and was then discussed and revised by a joint Commission consisting of members of both the Secretariat and the Theological Commission, and was then voted out of the Theological Commission for submission to the Council Fathers."[7]

After Zuroweste's letter appeared, Fr. Connell wrote a letter congratulating him: "I was very glad to read in the NCWC news your letter to TIME magazine. I hope it will do Bob Kaiser some good."[8] Zuroweste's remarks may or may not have helped Bob Kaiser, but they opened the floodgates of episcopal criticism of the American media. Bishop Albert L. Fletcher of the Diocese of Little Rock, Arkansas flatly denied the American accounts that there are "'practically two "armed camps" in the Council – in one…the reactionaries or conservatives, and in the other the progressives or liberals!'" The Bishop mentioned a litany of problems of perception caused by outsiders. He noted the Council Fathers "were not disagreeing on defined matters of faith and morals" but were discussing pastoral matters, which was the reason that the Council was called. He told Catholics they should not be "confused by 'strange ideas' which he said are being widely circulated" largely as a result of what is "in articles written even by some Catholic authors both clerical and lay....'You would think from what these people write and say that the Church is an "old fogy," outdated and in a rut.'" Also, these same writers seemed

"anxious to blame the Church in the past for what they consider the mistakes of some ecclesiastics in handling problems of their times. They consider it broadminded to call on the Church to confess her guilt in judging heretics rashly and in treating them harshly. They offer what they say not as an opinion or for consideration, but as a conclusion which is self-evident. They are very intolerant of anyone who does not agree with them. They seem to consider it sufficient to brand those who disagree with them as reactionaries, ultra-conservatives, old-fashioned; as ignorant of the "new look" the Church needs."9

While claiming to follow St. Thomas, Bishop Fletcher continued, these people "seldom define what they mean – their thinking is fuzzy and nebulous....When they run into a teaching of the Church contrary to their ideas, they very superiorly state that we should 're-think' this teaching in the atmosphere of our enlightened modern times." To further show the intellectual inferiority, if not dishonesty of this group, Bishop Fletcher said "'As a result of not distinguishing between truth and knowledge, they talk very glibly about the "development of truth as though eternal truths can change. Some of these Catholic writers and would-be scholars, who have based their thinking on false premises, have arrived at some strange conclusions regarding the obligation of obedience to authority....The very strangeness of these ideas and the fact that the writers themselves are Catholics come to most Catholic readers as a shock. It is easy to understand why many Catholics wonder what is happening in the Church.'" These ideas were causing "pain and suffering to the faithful." At the root was the work of "the Devil, through man's pride and egoism," for at this time "the Church, God's instrument of salvation on earth, is on the threshold of a great victory."10

CHAPTER 104
THE CATHOLICS SELL HISTORY

At the urging of CD Jackson, Henry Luce resigned as Chairman of the CIP which was responsible for funding Morlion's Pro Deo project. It was not an entirely unexpected move as Luce earlier in 1964 started to divest himself of his duties and responsibilities in the running of Time, Inc. by handing over to Hedley Donovan the role of editor in chief of *Time*.[1] In a letter to Luce who was residing mostly in his Phoenix, Arizona home, CD mentioned the Pro Deo project was no longer "high priority." The Catholics, lead by J. Peter Grace, were supposed to be raising funds for Morlion, but that never really seemed to work out. CD remarked how things were changing:

"The American Jewish Committee, the only one of the three religious groups that has a real ax to grind, is becoming more and more conspiratorial, and I suspect is maneuvering for a near-total takeover....What will probably happen is that the grandiose schemes will fade away, and the American committee will kick along on very much reduced steam, conceivably with an annual budget as low as fifteen or twenty thousand dollars, under the chairmanship of some fat cat from the AJC which will underwrite occasional projects in return for an occasional rewrite of history by the Curia."[2]

This was an interesting thing to say to Luce who became Chairman of the Board of the CIP in 1962,[3] and which was founded and supported by Catholics, Protestants and Jews. The three religions were not really "pulling together" despite all the rhetoric and Luce's promotion of unity. As Chairman, one of Luce's more notable achievements was to publicly honor Cardinal Bea who was billed as someone working to "promote civic unity and peace in freedom under God,"[4] the very theme which was the hallmark of the Pro Deo endeavor. Bea was honored at a banquet on April 1, 1963 in New York, and the title of his presentation was "Civic Unity and Freedom under God." Described as a scholar, Bea said the "greatest challenge to our generation is the problem of group antagonism...how to build peace with love...understanding and respecting him whom we love and therefore his opinions as well."[5] Bea was involved with improving relations with Protestants and Jews as part of an effort by the Catholic Church leadership, and he represented an important trend in the Catholic Church intent on eliminating barriers which were not the making of the financial elites. An important assistant of Bea's was the Jesuit Malachi Martin who at the Council kept close relations with the AJC as it strove to maximize its position and get a declaration benefitting the Jews.[6]

By the time the Council began, Pro Deo was having a big impact on the Catholic world. A. L. Lederer, President of the International committee of Scientific Management or *Comite international de l'organisation scientifique* (CIOS), reported on the efforts of Pro Deo in Latin America in a letter to Luce dated October 17, 1961. He wrote "In Venezuela, under the influence of Pro Deo...a plan has been almost completed in the private sector of the economy to produce 80,000 new productive jobs a year for the next ten years." Lederer commented on the importance of the Jesuits in Peru, Costa Rica, and Guatemala in assisting with the development of "economic action" programs, "economic development," programs that would "produce political stability," and programs to "make an accelerated transition from 19th Century economic thinking to 20th Century economic purpose." He wrote the "Jesuit Fathers in three of the countries...are bestirring themselves to provide universities with

Schools of Education and Management because the present classical institutions do not respond to the needs of the countries. They are not only backed by local interests but also by some of the Jesuit sections in the United States...."[7]

Professors instructing at Pro Deo and shaping the curricula were Professor Charles Dechert, a research analyst for the US Army and for Johns Hopkins University as well as a professor at the Catholic University of America, Peter Drucker (New York University), Eli Ginsberg (Columbia), C. Hildebrand (U of California) and from Harvard O. Williams.[8] Guest lecturers were always welcome and Morlion asked Luce and CD Jackson to lecture at Pro Deo campuses in Europe about leadership.[9]

Pro Deo was still engaged in a process to obtain legitimacy and accreditation by the time Luce resigned. This effort was helped by the ascension of John XXIII to the papacy. CD wrote that "the new regime, convinced that sociological activity and identification must parallel its efforts to save souls" and so was approving of Pro Deo and its phenomenal growth in the late 1950s to include about 1,800 students from 30 plus countries. Three important juridical matters had been reached to help with Pro Deo's legitimacy and accreditation. These were an agreement with the Italian government to recognize Pro Deo under Italian civil law; an accommodation with the Church under Canon Law so as not to be found in violation of Church tradition; and an arrangement with the Vatican State that "legitimizes Pro Deo's international activities."[10]

Even after Luce's official withdrawal from CIP and Pro Deo, Morlion continued to communicate with Luce. In late April, 1964 he contacted CD who relayed information to Luce. Morlion had "a special Pro Deo audience with the Pope, and…he has matters of importance to communicate to you…Conceivably you may want to hear what he has to say regarding his conversation with Paul VI."[11]

Morlion revealed he was funneling information to Luce on the topic of religious liberty discussed at the Council. He suggested Luce use this information for "a history making series of articles, as you organized on the national purpose and for other important cases." Morlion suggested that "I will also bring with me an important article of Card. Bea, and we could get Pitney, van Dusen, U-Thant, etc. to develop their ideas expressed at the Agape along the same lines."[12] Paul VI directed the international headquarters of Pro Deo be moved to Rome, which Morlion said indicated the importance of Pro Deo.[13]

CHAPTER 105
SATANISMO IN THE CHURCH

While Luce was contemplating withdrawal from Pro Deo, Connell and other *periti* were studying schemata to identify any "theological problems and theological assertions as they appear in each of the schemata." This was in preparation of a meeting of the US *periti* in June at the Catholic Theological Society of America. Connell wrote to "suggest that the theological problem of freedom of conscience be thoroughly discussed at the meeting of the `periti.'"[1]

Connell continued to raise concern about the so-called right for people to profess whatever religion they wanted. He wrote to Bishop John J. Garner of Pretoria, South Africa to make this point: "As Your Excellency knows, there are some (especially from our land) who want the Council to declare that everyone has a real right to profess whatever religion he sincerely accepts, without making any distinction between objective and subjective right. I trust Your Excellency will do your part toward making this correction if this fifth chapter when the Schema on Ecumenism comes to the floor."[2]

The Second Session did not arrive at a decision on the issue of religious liberty. More work was needed, and so Murray took charge of organizing the forces for a statement on religious liberty during the Third Session. He started the organizing process with an article entitled "On Religious Liberty" in *America* published at the end of November, 1963 and which "termed religious liberty `*the* American issue at the Council.'" He praised the US bishops who tried to advance the issue, and he attacked those engaged in the "many efforts to block discussion" of it.[3]

Murray's heart attack delayed his preparations for the Third Session. There were various comments to the religious liberty schema presented the previous Autumn, but these had to wait. In the meantime, Archbishop Vagnozzi, the Apostolic Delegate to the United States, issued the norms for the *periti* which had been promulgated by Cicognani. These norms restricted the activities of the periti, who could answer questions but were not to "defend publicly their personal ideas," nor criticize the Council, nor communicate with outsiders concerning the Council. Murray rebelled against this exercise of legitimate authority because it threatened to weaken the influence of the Americans at the Council. In a letter from May, 1964 to his Jesuit Provincial, Murray complained Vagnozzi had no jurisdiction in these things, and Vagnozzi was now Murray's "personal enemy." Spellman, Murray wrote, would set Vagnozzi straight as the former, according to Murray, was "my patron" and approved of an article by Murray in *America*.[4] Murray would not obey, though Connell did.

Fenton, due to ill health, left as editor of *American Ecclesiastical Review* at the end of 1963. In his final "Letter from Rome," Fenton described the assault against the Church that Xavier Rynne and others launched during the Council. Rynne was a Modernist Fenton concluded and had acted like Blanshard in accusing the Curia of using "fear-inspired tactics" and "thought control," the very things which the Americans used. Fenton continued to serve as a *peritus* during the Council, but a reading of his diaries makes clear that his involvement diminished and that he worked with reduced energy for the last two sessions.[5] His comments on the schema on Revelation explained how so much confusion could arise after the Council. The statements in the documents were correct, but they were also deficient. After perusing the schema on Revelation, he explained on June 4, 1964 that:

"There is nothing erroneous in the material we have passed. But there is a great deal that is incomplete and misleading. I am sorry to have left the University since I am one of the very few who know the background of this schema and the one on the Church. Francis again attacks the attempts made by the progressives to sneak in scripture alone as a norm."[6]

In what amounted to a foreshadowing of Pope Paul's famous speech years later about the "smoke of Satan" entering the Church, Fenton mentioned that Msgr. "Romeo keeps talking about `satanismo' in the Church."[7]

Time continued to target those who objected to the American and Americanist agenda and continued to praise those who were willing to advance it. Deemed a conservative, Los Angeles' James Francis Cardinal McIntyre was attacked in the pages of *Time*. McIntyre was one of the few cardinals who criticized the change of the liturgy at the Mass and who also criticized the "technique of form criticism, devised by German Protestant theologians" which many Catholic Bible scholars implemented. As archbishop of the Archdiocese of Los Angeles, the "ascetic and humble" McIntyre had doubled the size of his California flock in less than 15 years, but in doing so ran afoul of the Americans, who viewed his resistance to racial politics as a problem. McIntyre denounced and helped defeat a California anti-discrimination law in 1947, insisting that "`there is no racial problem in Los Angeles.'" With that kind of a record, he was, as *Time* put it, "a wide-open target for critics, both in and out of the church." He was labeled as someone who had "failed to seize the moral leadership that many of his flock had expected of him."[8]

Time continued to praise those who opposed church teaching and who advanced the American agenda. Jesuit Archbishop Thomas D'Esterre Roberts was a case in point. At 71, he was depicted as "an independent spirit who feels free to put churchly propositions up to the measure of his own reason" and "has no use for pomp." *Time* felt Roberts had just the right amount of American irreverence as reported when he would "discourage people from kissing his Episcopal ring" by joking that "'I carry it in my back pocket.'" Even better, Roberts was in favor of changing church teaching on birth control to be in line with the Protestants, expediting marriage annulment procedures while supporting the "ban-the-bomb movement," and a "bigger voice for the laity in church affairs."[9]

Throughout Summer of 1964, *Time* kept up a barrage of stories that supported radical change in the Church designed to turn it into a Protestant Church and, hence, colonizers of the world for capitalism. The issues were birth control, married priests, approval of mixed marriages, and, in particular, ecumenism as a code word for melding the doctrine and practice of various sects. *Time's* message was that change was inevitable, and the magazine continued to use Church leaders to make that statement. On the topic of married priests, Cardinal Cushing was quoted as saying "change in the church's attitude 'will come in the future.'"[10]

Time convincingly and powerfully promoted better relations between Catholics and Jews, depicting Cardinal Cushing of Boston as a hero of progress and leader of the forces who "have indicated that they will fight for a strong declaration [on the Jews] at the third session." The term "strong declaration" was *Time's* code word for removal of the "reference to conversion" that remained in the statement on anti-Semitism as it stood after the Second Session. Seeking conversions was bad for it would "foster reciprocal distrust as well as bitterness and resentment" said Rabbi Abraham Joshua Heschel, who was a professor at the Jewish Theological Seminary in Manhattan and a "good friend of Cardinal Bea." Raising the specter of the last war in an emotional bid to force the Catholics to change the draft statement, the article quoted a rabbi who said "'As I have repeatedly stated to leading personalities of the Vatican, I am ready to go to Auschwitz any time, if faced with the alternative of conversion or death.'"[11]

Time targeted other barriers to fall. "Next to papal infallibility, the biggest barrier to Catholic-Protestant unity is the humble Jewish girl who gave birth to Jesus of Nazareth." In order to remove obstacles separating Catholics and Protestants, the "bishops voted to reject a separate schema on Mary and instead incorporate it into a schema on the church" because "[r]ecent Popes have warned against excessive devotion to Mary that obscures the uniqueness of Christ, and many Catholic thinkers are earnestly seeking to relate their church's Marian doctrines to Biblical theology."[12]

To their credit, many prelates fought back. Bishop John Wright of Pittsburgh mentioned the press coverage gave the impression there were three councils occurring simultaneously in Rome. He said one would be the approximately 2,300 bishops in St Peter's which was "'a rather drab affair.'" Then there was a second council composed of the "council experts who sat in the galleries, dreaming about what the Bishops should do." The third council "was made up of the press panel and writers. 'Every now and then, we had the feeling that some writers were there not so much to report the news as to make the news – to make interventions.'" The media and its ability to utilize modern communications made the Council "a kind of neighborhood forum" but at the same time "projected an image of the council that often was 'very imprecise and bewildering.'"[13]

Bishop Cornelius Lucey of Cork and Ross in Ireland blamed the "experts" "who through their tendentious press releases, special reporters and spicy 'inside the council' publications generally use their position to lobby and make propaganda for their view of what the council should do. It is the slanted writing of these publicists, a mixture of rumor, gossip quips, propaganda, and truth that has given the word the distorted picture it has of the council and its proceedings. They it is who have done the sinister labeling. They it is who have divided the council into 'camps' and 'cliques', into 'progressives' or 'liberals' and 'reactionaries' and 'conservatives' into those crusading for the Gospel and those 'intriguing for the letter of the law.'"[14]

Different viewpoints among the bishops dealt with incidentals, he said, and not essentials, and votes are inspired by the Holy Spirit for unity.[15]

Even the Bishop of Rome joined in. In early May, 1964, Pope Paul VI said during his mid-week press conference: "The Church and the Papacy can and must love one another...This is perhaps the lesson, which many moderns who yet call themselves Catholics, do not understand, intent as they are and almost passionately looking for faults in the Church and in the Roman curia...." He made clear these "moderns" formulated criticisms which were neither true nor helpful.[16]

In a talk during a CCD Workshop at the Catholic University of America, Connell explained the attack on the Church and the misleading nature of the liberal/conservative dichotomy which Time used to explain it, by saying

"Frequently we read in the newspapers and news magazines that the Conciliar Fathers were divided into two parties, designated as conservatives and progressives, or reactionaries and liberals. Actually, this division was largely due to the exaggeration of reporters....every bishop at the Council was in some respects conservative and in other respects progressive. He had to be conservative because as a Catholic he knew that no change of the Church's solemn teachings can be possible; he had to be progressive, because both Pope John and Pope Paul had called for some elements of modernization in the Church. But there were various shades of difference between these two attitudes. I do not hesitate to say that no two bishops at the Council were exactly alike in their leanings toward conservatism and progressivism."[17]

Quoting one of the Council Fathers to explain the point further, Connell said:

"In his Lenten pastoral letter, Bishop Fletcher of Little Rock denied that there are `practically two armed camps in the Council, in one the reactionaries or conservatives, and in the other the progressives or liberals. Of course, there were differences of opinion among the

Council Fathers, but they were no disagreements on defined matters of faith and morals The Council was called by the Holy Father to discuss pastoral problems....It would have been very strange if all the Bishops had the same ideas.'"[18]

Connell described Cardinal Ottaviani as "much maligned" and presented the following rebuttal to the *Time* story, which claimed

"he had asked the Pope to order Father Karl Rahner, SJ a German theologian with advanced ideas, to leave Rome. An American priest in Rome, Msgr. Tucek, approached the Cardinal and asked him about the matter. Cardinal Ottaviani answered: 'This is completely false. This whole matter was completely unknown to me until I heard others speak of it. Neither I nor anyone else in the Holy Office, either directly or indirectly suggested that Father Rahner should leave Rome. Quite the contrary. Twice I invited Father Rahner to address the members of the preparatory Commission on Theology."[19]

Connell quoted Michael Novak, who was forced to admit in *The Open Church:* "'Without question, Cardinal Ottaviani is one of the great figures of the Second Vatican Council, faithful to his lights, courageous, frank, an urbane an devoted man. He is a greater man than many of his critics.'"[20]

Connell dispelled errors about the Church's position on religious liberty:

"A person has an objective right to practice only the one true religion, but he can have a subjective right (which can bind him in conscience) to practice a religion that is objectively false. And the Catholic Church looks on all forms of non-Catholic religion as objectively false. At any rate, if we take the Church's legislation it is difficult to see that she looks on everyone as having a right to follow his conscience, even when it is sincere. For example, if a baptized non-Catholic marries his second cousin, even though he himself believes he is permitted to do so, and his church allows him, the Catholic Church declares the marriage null and void."[21]

Connell also dispelled the expectations which the media, and *Time* in particular, had created in the mind of the public on the role of the laity, which would not change and was to remain what it had always been, which is to proclaim the faith, uphold moral values, and serve as examples of Christian virtue. They had a right to receive "from their clergy the means necessary or useful for their salvation…and they also have the right to make known their ideas toward the benefit of the Church to the clergy." The laity is to cooperate with, revere, and render obedience to the hierarchy. However, the laity is not "called to holiness of life" by practicing the evangelical counsels.[22]

In his own understated way, Connell explained the Curia was under an attack which the Council Fathers could no longer ignore. The Church was in the process of debating issues of Church governance to decide things such as whether the bishops or the Curia should be the "direct counselors of the Pope." There was a reorganization of the Curia under way to allow in non-Italian prelates, but the Pope had as recently as April 29 of that year praised the Curia and condemned those who criticized the Curia.[23] Church leadership was rousing itself in defense of the faith and to counter the attacks against the institutions needed to propagate it.

CHAPTER 106
CUSHING IS CHOSEN

War was brewing in Southeast Asia with the Gulf of Tonkin incident in early August. The USS Maddox was attacked by three North Vietnamese torpedo boats causing some damage to an American aircraft sent in to help. Shortly thereafter, the US Congress passed the Gulf of Tonkin Resolution which authorized LBJ to use military force to repel Communist aggression. The Vietnam War was on.

Half way around the world, the Americans planned their aggression to achieve a declaration on religious liberty for the Third Session of the Council. To that end, they needed a leader, an army, and weapons. Cardinal Cushing was to lead the effort, the army was the US Bishops, and Murray provided the weapons in the form of ideas.

Time selected Cushing as leader of the campaign because they considered him a personification of the "Catholicism of tomorrow,"[1] and made him the subject of a cover story in the August 21, 1964 edition of *Time,* which was juxtaposed to one on the Pope in that same issue. *Time* depicted the Pope in a negative light as weak but presented Cushing as the face of love itself, the best the Church had to offer. He was "in tune with the times," and he "personally illustrates the stirring of that placid giant of Roman Catholicism, the church in the U.S." Cushing was glowingly presented as helping the poor of Peru by pouring milk into the bowls of orphans and blessing new churches in slums.[2]

The same article which lauded Cushing criticized McIntyre and served to endorse a pro-American view within the Church. According to *Time:*

"the American Catholic renewal can be credited to spiritual fallout from the Vatican Council and the church-wide modernization unleashed by Pope John. Signs of change, in the case of the American Catholic church, are also signs of maturation.....The truest sign of American Catholic maturity is the development and vociferous presence of something that has been rather grandly called "the renewal elite." It includes bishops, priests, seminarians and sisters, but its driving force is a young, college-trained laity that accepts the church's essential mysteries and matters of faith while questioning the authoritarian way moral theologians reduce these dogmas to terms of practical behavior. As one California Jesuit puts it, "The catechism answers don't satisfy any more – thank God."[3]

"Layman Michael Novak" as *Time* called him at the time, was quoted as an authority on the changes in the Church:

"In parish life, renewal means a comprehensible liturgy with parishioner participation instead of novenas, family study groups instead of membership in the Holy Name Society (an organization formed in part to cut down profanity). It means the displacement of what Layman Michael Novak calls 'nonhistorical orthodoxy' – the abstract, rationalistic theology that has dominated Catholic thinking since the Council of Trent – by a Gospel-centered Catholicism that is open to accept the insights of Freud, Camus, and even Marx."[4]

"To the renewal elite," *Time* said: "the church is not only a juridical institution governed by the Pope and the bishops, but also the 'people of God.' Such Catholics feel free to challenge betrayals of the moral law – segregation or political expedience – even when they are tolerated by priests and bishops on grounds of prudence."[5]

Those who rejected this "church renewal" were labeled "conservative," "ecclesiastical conservatives," "born-and-bred bead-sayers for whom faith is simply a comfortably furnished apartment of the mind," and called "Bapto-Catholics" by *Time*. Their fears though were accurately described by *Time* when it interviewed a "Denver housewife" who said "I left the Baptist Church for Roman Catholicism, and now it is being dismantled all around me. At the rate they are going, it will look like the Baptist Church before long."[6]

As Session Three approached, most of the Catholic prelates were wary of change and criticized because of it. Bishops were ranked on their willingness to go along with *Time's* agenda, from McIntyre of Los Angeles who "openly supports the status quo" to Spellman of New York who "objects to 'change for change's sake,' and classifies most change as just that" to Meyer of Chicago who "is regarded as a moderate who promotes liturgical reform" to Ritter of St. Louis who "is a proponent of change." Cushing was the one who "most actively supported" what *Time* called "church renewal." While he was depicted as a "doer rather than an original thinker," he gained the approval of *Time* and the Americans by demonstrating acceptance of the American spirit. Cushing was lauded for being a "life member of the N.A.A.C.P.," calling his clerical robes "glad rags," and having "little use for the trappings of his office." In addition, he was quoted as saying that his prayer at the JFK inauguration in 1961 "'didn't seem to do any good'," depicted as fostering "good will…among men of other faiths," and being a "product of South Boston's melting pot ghetto."[7]

Cushing was, by *Time's* own estimation, a typical American Catholic prelate: "a tireless fundraiser out of the mold of brick-and-mortar prelates." Indeed, "some laymen complain he thinks of nothing else," but the money went to a number of projects both in and out of his Archdiocese that was growing. Several of these projects were the renovation of cathedrals and churches overseas in places like Formosa, Tanganyika, and the birthplace of Pope John, but an offer to pay for a "simultaneous translation system for the Ecumenical

Council" was declined by the Pope. Cushing was presented as a positive, progressive, and sympathetic American figure motivated to help others, growing his Archdiocese and suffering from various ailments at the same time.[8]

That, according to *Time,* was the result of the efforts of John XXIII in calling the Council in the first place. Cushing called him "good Pope John," and Cushing had "its spirit," referring to Vatican II. Consistent with this image was Cushing's disregard for canon law and his inability to understand Latin or moral theology. He favored the liturgy translated into English, the laity involved in church affairs, older vocations for men, and ordination of at least one married man who was a former Episcopal priest. He outlawed racial segregation from Boston's Catholic institutions declaring he would "accept a Negro as an auxiliary bishop."[9]

At this point, the discussion in *Time* allowed William Storey, then a professor at Pittsburgh's Duquesne University, to introduce the trajectory of all of the so-called reforms of the Church. Storey said "Cushing fits in with the new spirit, but I wonder if he realizes that the whole process must go a lot farther."

Time explained where "a lot farther" went:

"Going a lot farther would include approval of married deacons, lay election of bishops, general adoption of civilian dress in place of clerical black and Roman collars, the abolition of such medieval practices as ring kissing and ermine-trimmed robes for cardinals, the right of Catholics to contract mixed marriages before Protestant ministers. Perhaps the greatest possibility is that of a person-centered theology of marriage that owes more to Martin Buber's I-Thou relationship than to canon law – and thus might resolve the most troubling moral issue that faces U.S. Catholics today: birth control."[10]

Cushing was not the "originator, rebel, theologian, theoretician or organizer of the change" as the magazine explained. He was the one who gave "renewal" a push, or in other words, lead the Church to eliminate "aspects of unfreedom," as another *Time* darling, Hans Kung, said.[11]

MICHAEL NOVAK

Michael Novak was one of those "young, college-trained" members of the laity that *Time* extolled. In 1958 he earned an STB from the Pontifical Gregorian University in Rome, and then obtained a Master's in Theology from Harvard. By the Summer of 1964, he published his first book, *The Open Church.* Robert Blair Kaiser, the *Time* correspondent who covered the First Session and was the author of *Pope, Council and the World,* asked fellow ex-seminarian Novak to write a book on the Second Session, because "troubles developing in his own life that necessitated his departure from Rome" prevented Kaiser from completing the contract on the book. Novak was at the time a free-lance reporter for *Commonweal* and the *National Catholic Reporter* covering the Second Session of the Council. He accepted Kaiser's offer, and Novak covered the Third Session for *Time.*[12]

Novak's second book, *A New Generation: American and Catholic,* also came out in 1964. Both of his books characterized the Council's dynamics in a way which allowed for doctrinal or policy change. In *A New Generation: American and Catholic,* Novak set out to reconcile two incompatible theologies by calling one Catholic and the other American or Protestant. This provided a modus vivendi "to be an American and a Catholic in the present generation."[13] Novak claimed "The Catholic of our generation is – by virtue of the very air he breathes – indebted to the Protestant inheritance; he too benefits (not, though as if all has been gain) by gains won seemingly in the teeth of his own inheritance."[14] There was a "Catholic conscience now, quite different from that of the Catholic generations closer to peasant, paternalistic Europe." Even though Catholics intellectually found their "best expression in Europe in men like Kung, Geiselmann, Rahner, Danielou, and others," American Catholics were to be the decisive agents of change because, as Novak put it: "the millions of

Catholic graduates of the United States" were "the most sophisticated, religiously educated laity the church has ever known" and "will one day prove a more important voice."[15] Novak's second book came out just in time to exhort the US bishops to action at the Council.

Novak repeated the idea, first floated by John Tracy Ellis nearly a decade earlier, that the Catholic Church was somehow isolated:

"A thick crust had formed on the Church over the centuries, massive walls had been put up, blocking off the freedom of the Church, and inhibiting her movement: walls of isolation, defense, fear. Above all, the Church has seemed to be afraid of her own gift: freedom.... The Second Vatican Council began to show the Church the way to a new order, through orderly renewal."[16]

The problem was isolation. In fact, the "greatest weakness of the Catholic educational system, then, is its isolation; and such a weakness among Catholics harms Americans as a whole. Moreover, there is no need for this isolation to continue indefinitely."[17] Young Catholics held the key to helping the Church break out of this isolation: "The future depends on the young, who do not wait for their elders; the world their elders leave them is not admirable."[18]

In his first book, *The Open Church: Vatican II, Act II,* Novak put his own spin on the Second Session. Recognizing the American press divided the "'parties' at the Council" into "liberal" and "conservative" in accordance with their own "doctrinaire" agenda,[19] he wrote the Council was founded on "the principle of historical development and the principle of concrete reality."[20] Novak claimed both of these principles denied truth as something unchanging. "Both principles," Novak wrote:

"insist that the man who uses them must enter the stream of history and work from within it, conscious that his words and his concepts are conditioned by it (the principle of development), and that his theories must meet the test of concrete facts, movements, and events (principle of concrete reality). The first principle is aimed against the idea that words have meaning outside of their historical context, or are unconditioned by their origins. The second is directed against the idea that ideology is 'pure' and should be judged only in the light of logic; it insists on judgment of institutions, men, and events as they appear in fact as well as in theory. Both principles deny the man who uses them the right to claim that he or his ideas are uninfluenced by history, or that he need not undertake the work of brining this ideas and methods to the bar of concrete reality."[21]

Opposed to this was the entrenched view of "non-historical orthodoxy" which held "truth is unchanging." The fundamental struggle at the Council was between Ottaviani's "Semper idem" and "other theologies"[22] which meant Novak's promotion of Modernism with its relative Americanism.

CHAPTER 107
MURRAY PROVIDES THE ARGUMENTS

In the same issue of *Time* that chose Cushing to lead the Americanist charge, *Time* tagged the Pope with ambiguity as one who "frequently has difficulty in making up his mind." With his first encyclical, *Ecclesium Suam*, he "kept the ambivalences dancing" when it came to conservatives and progressives. While Paul was depicted as still being for aggiornamento, he wrote things the Americans found troubling. For instance, he wrote, "Naturally it will be for the Council to suggest what reforms are to be introduced" but "the reform cannot concern either the essential conception of the church or its basic structure." Pope Paul wrote "the Church will rediscover her renewed youthfulness not so much by changing her exterior laws as by interiorly assimilating her true spirit of obedience to Christ." This defined modernization as something of the spirit to bring Catholics closer to Christ. With statements like "'Without the Pope, the Catholic Church would no longer be Catholic'," the likelihood of reducing barriers between Protestants and Catholics seemed distant.[1] Pope Paul was disappointing the Americans who had held such high hopes for him when he was Msgr. Montini.

As the commencement of Session Three drew near, and after a month's vacation for medical reasons, Murray wrote a letter to Archbishop

Alter. He confirmed sending an "essay in clarification" to all the US bishops at the request of Archbishop Sheehan and Bishops Primeau and Helmsing, and three to the Secretariat for Christian Unity. [2] It also went to Rome and the "Dutch documentation center" for "translation and distribution to the conciliar Fathers." Murray sent copies around the world.[3] This was a violation of the instructions issued by the Vatican, but Murray was helped and encouraged by Archbishops Alter, Shehan, Helmsing and Primeau and the Secretariat of Christian Unity.

Murray's essay appeared in the December issue of *Theological Studies* and discussed "two views": the Catholic state as the ideal and the American system of church and state relations as well as the shortcomings of the text on religious liberty at that point. Msgr. Pavan and Murray agreed the extant text (De Smedt's) lacked a consideration of the "political and legal aspects of the problem," and so Murray asked Alter to prepare an intervention to address the political and legal aspects of religious liberty. Murray and Pavan agreed that the "political-legal aspects are coordinate with, not subordinate to, the theological-ethical aspects." Murray believed "a new clarification" of the competence of the public powers in re religiosa"[4] was needed. This need, explained Murray, arose as a result of a meeting he had had with a few *periti* and a number of Spanish bishops before the end of the second session. The Spanish were "very friendly and open to discussion, and anxious to reach a Catholic consensus," Murray told Alter, but:

"They don't want to stand up and be counted as being against religious freedom. But they do want to hold on to their doctrine on the religious prerogative of government – their theory of `el Estado catolico' as an `ideal' – according to which government has far more extensive powers in re religiosa than we are inclined to acknowledge. They want, in effect, to make government the servant of the religious unity of the nation, as the leading element of the common good of the people." [5]

Murray had no intention of giving the Spanish what they wanted, which meant allowing the Catholic State to remain as an ideal. "I fully agree with you," he told Alter, "that the solution of the issue must be sought along pragmatic lines, under consideration of existent historical situations. At the same time, I feel strongly that this pragmatic solution must be so conceived and stated, and so undergirded by considerations of principle, that it will in effect disallow the contention that the Spanish system is 'the Catholic ideal.'

"If this notion of a Catholic 'ideal' is not disallowed, we are back where we were, and no progress will have been made. The thesis-hypothesis disjunction will still stand as Catholic doctrine. And the American system will be only hypothesis, a pragmatic solution reached for reasons of expediency, but at variance with the 'ideal.' The 'ideal' will continue to be obligatory, wherever possible, scil., under conditions of a Catholic majority. And American Catholics will remain under the ancient suspicion."[6]

Murray's solution was to relativize the traditional teaching by reducing the Spanish system to "suitable to their historical situation" but in no way the ideal. "I am not willing to let them qualify it as 'the Catholic ideal,'" he told Alter, "as the 'thesis.' The question will be how to disallow the 'ideal,' without seeming to condemn the Spanish system as valid in situ (this last thing is what the Spaniards are afraid of, and will resist)." Murray concluded by advising Alter he would "put together some ideas about the intervention for your consideration."[7]

Archbishop Alter responded by endorsing Murray's views:

"In my mind, a clear, precise, and comprehensive definition of what we mean by 'Free Exercise of Religion' and 'Freedom of Conscience' is absolutely necessary to avoid confusion and futile debate. Secondly, that our problem concerning 'Religious Liberty' is primarily a pragmatic one; that it cannot be solved apart from the existing historical situation and hence that the Church's doctrine on the subject admits legitimate development without contradiction of previous essential teaching'"[8]

Murray had not yet won the day. Many bishops attacked Murray's position as being "too 'juridical,'" too dependent on the "Anglo-

American constitutional tradition," and too dependent on the "American experience under the First Amendment to the United States Constitution." The argument was not sufficiently theological. Murray responded to Alter by elevating the political-legal aspects to the same level as the theological. He held the "public powers" were not competent in religious matters, a position that ignored Catholic teaching on the responsibility and competence of public powers to determine the true religion. The basis of religious liberty could not be just theological, it also had to be founded on a "political philosophy which carefully defined the limited functions of government....Juridical and constitutional principles were consequently essential to the discussion."[9]

The argument was invariably based on historical premises. This "contemporary man" demanded freedom of religion. "Contemporary man" had somehow gained a "deeper insight into the needs of the human person than possessed earlier generations," and so "perceived the necessity for new dimensions of freedom." A "personal and political consciousness" demanded religious freedom. In making these demands, "contemporary man" was essentially a throwback. His demands were in accordance with natural law, and not the law of Christ. Murray claimed that "The common consciousness of men today considers the demand for personal, social and political freedom to be an exigency that rises from the depths of the human person. It is the expression of a sense of right approved by reason. It is therefore a demand of natural law in the present moment of history." Human rights "evolve in history and emerge gradually into men's consciousness" as these rights "spring from their basic needs and that what is required for the proper development of human nature changes in the course of time." The right to religious liberty was therefore situated "in the context of history."[10]

The NCWC helped Murray spread his views and set out reasons for the need for religious liberty which included a reference to atheistic totalitarianism, the need for men of "diverse...and...no religious faith" to "live together in civic peace," for pastoral and ecumenical reasons, and finally because the Church had to modernize, or achieve aggiornamento. The NCWC's Rome office issued a statement entitled "The Council and the Issue of the Free Exercise of Religion: The Urgency of the Issue" in support of Murray's view of the declaration. The NCWC urged a statement on religious liberty which said there is a "widespread conviction that it is altogether necessary for the Council to make a clear and firm statement with regard to the right of the human person to the free exercise of religion according to the dictates of the personal conscience. This conviction obtains in many countries of the world." [11]

The NCWC then cited *Pacem in Terris* endorsing Murray's views: "the principle of constitutional government, that is, government whose powers are limited in the first and crucial instance by the order of human rights whose roots are in the human person, and also limited by the principle of the consent of the governed, whose awareness of their dignity of human persons requires that they be given a voice in affairs of public law and administration." The encyclical "clearly recognized that the day of centralized, personal, and paternal rule has passed." The "government should endeavor to assist the creation of those political and social conditions which will make it possible for citizens to exercise their rights in the spiritual order with ease and to the fullest extent." Supposedly sections 75, 76 and 79 of the encyclical supported this claim. [12]

A review of those sections does not support the NCWC interpretation that Catholic doctrine approved the US political and constitutional theory. [13] In claiming "the present-day situation," is validly "confirmed both by reason and by political experience (not least in the United States)," the NCWC concluded the Spanish system was discarded. *Pacem In Terris* "recognizes, that this form of government [that is, the "paternalistic form" of government] no longer existed," [14] but in doing so the NCWC distorted the meaning of *Pacem In Terris* and used it to justify the US political system and supporting American ideology as good in principle.

CONNELL'S COMMENTS

Vagnozzi asked Connell to provide a critique of the religious liberty schema being considered by the bishops. Earlier that year, the ever prolific Connell, wrote a book answering the pressing questions of the day, including the use of contraception and procurement of abortion and why they were immoral. The book, consisting of a series of 236 questions, devoted much of Chapter I to issues of church and state relations and religious liberty. Connell explained that Catholic officials and Catholic citizens are to act in accordance with a properly formed conscience and so obey the divine laws, and that legislation in a democracy like the US should not violate a law of God. In response to question 15, Connell made clear, as set out in Canon Law and Holy Scripture, that the Church "has the right and the duty of teaching the evangelical doctrine to all nations, independently of every civil power; and all are bound by divine law to learn this doctrine and to embrace the true Church of God." All men have an objective duty to "investigate the claims of the Church," to "pray for divine light and guidance," and to become Catholics. However, the Church did not approve of "any form of coercion," and Connell quoted Leo XIII's *Immortale Dei* in which that Pontiff wrote "The Church is accustomed to take very great care that no one shall be unwillingly forced to embrace the Catholic faith."[15]

Question 17 asked "Has error any rights?" a phrase Murray and the Americanist press ridiculed over and over. Taking on the Americanists, Connell said, in a way that was both brilliant and disarming: "It is difficult to see how any intelligent person can object to this principle," because according to that "figure of speech. . . . a person has no real right, as far as God's law is concerned to hold as true what is objectively false, or to propagate it or to base his actions on it." Even though a person may sincerely hold erroneous or immoral beliefs as good, or act immorally out of a sincere belief that what he is doing is right or good, the person has "no *real* right to accept in good faith what is erroneous." The "*real* right" is objective and is based on objective truth, and not one that is based on "*his honest conscience."* Instead of a real right "based on the objective relations of things," such a person has a "deemed right."[16]

That subjective right, Connell explained, does not give an "unrestricted claim" to the person to "put his ideas into practice, particularly when others will thereby be injured." Therefore, a "Catholic government—that is, the government of a nation that has been thoroughly Catholic in population and customs for centuries – may sometimes forbid non-Catholic propaganda on the ground that this is harmful to the spiritual welfare of the Catholic citizens...." Expediency dictates when a Catholic government may put such a policy into effect. By expediency, Connell distinguished between its primary and oftentimes positive sense, "suited to the circumstances or the occasion" instead of its secondary and oftentimes negative sense which is "based on advantage rather than on what is right and just." The guiding principle of such a policy, which is a policy of tolerance, is to "produce more good or prevent greater evil than the policy of restrictions." Some of the evil that could be produced included spiritual evil as a result of insincere conversions. Connell noted Pius XII's position in *Ci Riesce* in 1953 was the same Connell set out in 1944 which was that religious toleration promoting a greater good is a policy that is not "inconsistent with any principle of...faith." Connell emphasized "this does not meant that, *as far as God's law is concerned,* a person would have the right *to spread an erroneous doctrine....* But, in the circumstances described, a person would have a right *not to be impeded from spreading false doctrine."*[17]

Regrettably, towards the end of the answer to question 17, Connell signaled a lack of Catholic fortitude when he wrote that a "policy of perfect religious equality for all" had existed in the U.S. since the creation of the Bill of Rights in 1791. Catholics accepted this "wholeheartedly" and they "certainly have no intention of modifying" this policy. He even suggested that Catholics employ rhetorical tricks to strengthen support for this policy if asked whether they would change the policy should the Church grow strong enough.[18]

Question 18 dealt with relations between the Church and the State. Connell explained Catholic doctrine holds Jesus Christ "granted His Church certain prerogatives and immunities that *per se* (considered by themselves) should be recognized by civil governments, even though this implies some limitation and restriction of the authority which civil rulers would possess if they were subject merely to the natural law." This recognition of immunities involves compliance with Divine Positive Law and renders the Church "independent of every civil jurisdiction."[19]

Connell did not receive the same help as Murray in circulating his comments to the US bishops. In fact, he had to write to Apostolic Delegate asking for help just to get the document to the US bishops: "If the services of the NCWC were afforded to him for the publication and transmission of his [Murray's] document, justice demands that my brochure receive the same cooperation."

Connell could not rely on Murray to give an honest rendering of opposing views. In fact, Murray:

"makes no mention of the objections and difficulties to his view which I bring up. If several bishops procured the services of the NCWC for him, I believe that some would do the same for me. I feel that Archbishop McGucken and perhaps Bishop Ahr would sponsor my efforts. I am sure that the expenses would be met by my Congregation, if necessary, but I would not know how to go about the matter, and the time of departure of many bishops is drawing near. It is possible that my commentary could be sent to the Bishops from the Rome Office of the NCWC, so that they would have it when the matter is brought up.....I leave the matter in Your Excellency's hands."[20]

Connell's "Comments on the Declaration on Religious Liberty" was typically concise and clear. He began by endorsing the idea of an "honest, logical declaration." He recognized "Americans particularly are anxious to have a declaration on religious liberty" because the "Church has prospered in the United States under the policy of complete religious freedom." Catholics in the US were "convinced that we actually enjoy greater liberty than do the Catholics of some nations where the Church is recognized as the true Church and restrictions are put on the religious activities of non-Catholics." Connell acknowledged the proposed declaration was a call to every government to adopt "the policy of religious freedom such as we have it in the United States." Such a policy, he believed helped to make the Church "more effective in its mission nowadays." At the same time, a "world-wide policy of religious liberty, adduces as an argument the promotion of peaceful relations and concord throughout the human race." This was "quite in accord with the statements of Pope Pius XII in Ci riesce."[21]

Connell recognized such a declaration had to "be theologically correct, in full conformity with the teachings of the Catholic Church," which meant that "We cannot conceal or modify the revealed truths that Jesus Christ established only one religion and one Church that He commanded all human beings to join that Church and that the Catholic Church of today is the same Church that was established by the Son of God two thousand years ago." These truths were in the present declaration and should be retained because if omitted the "impression will be given that the Catholic Church no longer holds them."[22]

Connell noted two statements were deleted from the previous draft. These deletions were prudent as they were the "chief stumbling blocks to the acceptance of the previous declaration on the part of many bishops." These two statements were a "person has a true and proper right to exercise his religion privately and publicly – evidently even an objectively false religion" and "that the state (res publica) is incapable of determining which is the true religion." The basis of religious liberty under the provisions of the present draft was the "dignity possessed by every human being." Each person has "the right to be immune from all coercion and limitation from the civil power in the practice of his religion." This does not include the "right to practice a false religion," but only the "right to be free from any coercion on the part of the civil authority if one does practice a false religion (provided there is no violation of public order)."[23]

Connell continued by explaining "acceptance of faith is physically free because man has the power to reject it. But it is not morally free because man has not the right to reject it, since Christ imposed on all mankind the obligation to accept His doctrine under penalty of eternal damnation (Mark, 16:16)." Second, Connell stressed the "declaration should be confined to religious liberty with respect to civil power." It should not include the denial of "the Church's claim to use coercive measures toward those subject to its jurisdiction in their religious activities" nor should it be used to prevent a father from using "coercive measures in regard to his children in religious matters." The phrase "human power" should be replaced by the phrase "civil power."[24] Third, Connell objected to the statement "that there is an absolute moral principle forbidding one to be forced to do anything against his conscience." It was too broad. The civil authority may force someone to act or not act against their erroneous conscience. He suggested the declaration be improved by omitting "the word absolute, and…add the sentence `unless it is opposed to public order.'" Fourth, the statement that "Our Lord never used any coercion to induce people to accept" the Gospel was erroneous. Indeed, "He threatened eternal damnation to those who would not believe (Mark, 16:16). He uttered stern threats against those who would not receive the preaching of the disciples, and said their punishment would be greater than that of Sodom. He explicitly said of Capharnaum, which rejected Him: `Thou shalt be thrust down to hell.' (Luke, 10:10-15)."[25]

CHAPTER 108
THE AMERICANIST ATTACK

E xpectations ran high when the Third Session of the Second Vatican Council began on September 14, 1964. "Too high," John Courtney Murray commented "People are expecting too much and there is not going to be that much coming out of the council. It is a very slow growth."[1] John Cogley, Director of the Center of Democratic Studies, was less optimistic when interviewd for *Columbia* magazine by Fr. Vincent A. Yzermans, Director of the NCWC Bureau of Information. Cogley said the Council was trying to remedy a "cold war between the priest and the laity and the cold war between the Church and the churches." He hoped for a "changed relationship between Catholicism and modern culture... the end of a number of cold wars that have been going on" and "a greater relevance between religion and life at the end of the Council." The "proper means" was "dialogue" for dealing with differences and not what he claimed the Church had been doing, namely: "subversion and hatred and talking to oneself and all the rest."[2]

Murray organized the attack to get the Church to adopt in principle the American view of Church and State relations and religious liberty as an intrinsic good (and not something to be just tolerated) by affirming the First Amendment, and American political and social theory. The notion that civil authorities need only follow a vague natural law and not the Divine Positive Law was already lost with the Decree of *Inter Mirifica.* Murray prepared a number of interventions for Archbishop Shehan, Bishop Primeau, Bishop Carberry, Archbishop O'Boyle and Cardinal Cushing. Shehan was to lead off by claiming the American system of separation of church and state was grounded in both scripture and theology. Murray told Shehan to say that:

"religious freedom is indeed formally a juridical notion developed through historical experience, and presently affirmed by the rational consciousness of mankind, personal and political. However, it has its remote roots in certain scriptural texts, and, what is more important, in general scriptural doctrine (1) on the ways of God with men (God's free 'descent' to man; His refusal to coerce, etc.), and (2) on the condition of man before God (man is free, but he stands under the judgment of God for the use of his freedom). The Church models her dealings with men on God's own way with men. A fortiori, all secular powers must respect the freedom of man, especially in matters of man's relation to God."[3]

The freedom of the Church was *jure divino,* and the Church's freedom was consistent with the other religions' call for freedom. [4] It was an echo from the Protestants who attacked Catholicism over the course of the past twenty years.

Primeau was to make the connection between "internal freedom of religious decision, which is freedom of conscience; and external freedom of religious expression in worship, observance, witness, teaching, which is free exercise of religion." At the same time, he was to couple this with the Church's view that not "all men are equally empowered by God, or conscience, to practice any religion they choose."[5] This was designed to quiet the concerns of those prelates who thought the Catholic Faith was not being sufficiently defended as the one, true faith.

Carberry and O'Boyle were to address the "competence of government in religious affairs." This meant making a distinction between the state and society and government, and it meant endorsing as good the U.S. theory of a government of limited powers. "The free exercise of religion in society," Murray explained, "is to be immune from governmental or legal inhibition, unless it results in serious disturbance of the public order, either by disturbance of the public peace, or by violation of common standards of morality and health, or by injury done to the rights of others."[6]

Msgr. Shea was critical. He saw Murray's position as eliminating the state's concern for the common good and contradicting papal teaching. He also felt that the Spanish system would accomodate the American system of religious liberty but not vice versa. Finally, Shea pointed out that private and social religious practice were two different things, and the latter could be prohibited on ethical grounds.[7] Murray's theological argument emphasized freedom over truth, justice, and duty to Christ the King. He sought, as a minimum, the creation of a policy at odds with Catholic doctrine.

TIME *TELLS THE CATHOLICS TO HURRY UP*

Time's coverage of the Third Session began with a nudge to the Catholics to quicken the pace. In two articles, one entitled "The Vatican Council: Speedup," and another "Roman Catholics: Not to Herself, but to God," the magazine discussed how the Council could finish its business quicker. The Council officials got the message and closed the various coffee shops until two hours after the Council began daily.[8] Fenton noted even with this prohibition "More than half of the occupants of the hall leave their places to go to one of the bars or to talk to one another in the corridors." He observed "In a paper over the weekend George Higgins was quoted as saying that no one was going to the bars this session.... But, as I have seen for myself, there is more crowding at the bars now than there has been since the council started 2 years ago."[9]

The bishops seemed intent on speeding things up as demanded by *Time*. Fenton wrote:

"Philips is running the meeting….The fifth chapter of the schema on the church is being steam-rollered through. The relator (Philips) has insisted on hurrying up the affairs time after time. He does not allow the discussion of what some would think important points. He has just broken into a discussion on this plan of the religious and gone on to another point. And they seem to love it."[10]

Pope Paul VI, according to *Time*, was acting "with prudent change," most significantly, by promoting the internal changes the Americans favored: "Many Catholics believe that the council has already completed its essential job, in giving its imprimatur to worldwide currents of church renewal and in opening the doors to further free debate about still unseen change." The matters pending before the Council were "the nature of the church, ecumenism, the duties of bishops, divine revelation, and…marriage and the church in the modern world." The US hierarchy was strongly backing "1) a ringing affirmation of every man's right to worship as his conscience dictates, and 2) a somewhat less than forthright condemnation of anti-Semitism."[11]

THE ATTACK

The opening of the Autumn campaign for religious liberty began on September 17 when Murray addressed the assembled US bishops at the North American College. The talk laid out the outline for what ultimately became much of the Declaration of Religious Liberty. Murray directly attacked Leo XIII's teaching that the state is supposed to protect and give pre-eminence to the Catholic religion and simply ignored important segments of Leo's writings, especially paragraph 6 of *Longinqua Oceani Nostrae*. The duty of society was the central issue, but Murray avoided it and emphasized freedom, a popular concept during the Cold War:

"The concrete practical and doctrinal question being asked by the world today is, whether the Church accepts in principle, and gives positive approbation to, religious freedom as a human right and a legal institution, universally valid in all countries. In other terms, the question being asked today is, whether the Church will finally give a forthright answer to the age-old constitutional question with regard to the care of religion (cura religionis) by government, as this question arises in the contemporary world, in which men are becoming more and more conscious of their personal and political dignity (cf. Pacem in terris)."[12]

Murray's "The Schema on Religious Freedom: Critical Comments" proposed five "criteria of judgment" as the proposed structure for the statement on religious liberty. First, the world expected the Church to make a pronouncement on the "validity of the legal institution of religious freedom as it is found in the contemporary world" and so there was a "concrete practical and doctrinal problem today." The Church should respond to that demand by saying that religious liberty American-style was a good thing in principle and as such should be so endorsed by the Church. Second, the "concept of religious freedom" means "immunity from coercion" whether that be "legal or extra-legal, in the personal or social practice of religion." Religious freedom is a civil right, "independent of the state of the personal or collective conscience, whether it be true or erroneous, in good faith or in bad faith" since "neither government nor society... has any way of discerning the state of conscience." Murray distinguished religious freedom as a civil right from "civil tolerance, which [was] a moral attitude adopted by a person or a community."[13]

In addition, the "competence of government in the order of religion" had to be defined as meaning that the government had limited powers. True to the philosophy of Thomas Paine and James Madison, he said that the "competence of government" and the "reach of public law" are concerned only with and limited by the "care of religious freedom" which is "bound on the principle of the civil equality of all citizens." Directly contradicting the teaching of Leo XIII, Murray claimed "it is not, in principle, the function of government to defend or promote the good of the Church. The function of government is limited, in principle, to the recognition and protection of the freedom of the Church to defend and promote her own good." This is based on the "theological principle" of "Libertas Ecclesiae," he claimed.[14]

Finally, religious freedom is not "absolute, illimitable in its exercise." To address this, Murray claimed a distinction had to be made between society and the state ("or, in the American idiom, between the people and government") as well as between the "comprehensive common good of the people" and "that limited area of the common good which is called public order." The limited common good is "the public order" and is "committed to the powers of government" which uses the "coercive discipline of law." The public order has three elements: the "political good which is public peace, the moral good which is that measure of public morality which is necessary for social life, and the juridical good which is social harmony in the exercise of civil rights through peaceful settlement of conflicts." The idea of the "common good" means only the "temporal and terrestrial, secular and civil common good" and while religion and "religious unity" are "integral elements of the common good of the people…it does not follow that they are to be protected or promoted by coercive means."[15]

In dealing with methodology, Murray distinguished between the French version of religious liberty, which was based on "theological and ethical principles," and the English/Italian version, which based religious freedom "both on theological and ethical principles and also on political and legal principles" as both are of equal importance. The key question for Murray was "which structure of argument is the more solid… less vulnerable to attack, more convincing in its appeal to the contemporary mind, whether Catholic, non-Catholic, or secular…." The first version of the schema adopted the theological or ethical argument. The second had "diplomatic value" and an argument couched in those terms was "more likely to win acceptance" as it focused the entire controversy on the "competence of the public powers in re religiosa," meaning religious freedom as an "immunity from legal or extra-legal coercion."[16]

Murray criticized the first version (i.e. French) of the religious liberty schema because it repeated the premise that man has a "duty to follow the will of God according to the dictate of conscience." This meant religious liberty applied to the "right and true conscience" and not to the "man of erroneous conscience." The latter would be denied "empowerment to act in the public order" and denied "immunity from the repressive action of the public power, employed in the interest of the common good." The way to overcome this objection was to limit religious freedom to an immunity, which meant religious freedom is an "endowment of the human person" and is both "internal and external." The "moral state of conscience is irrelevant to the issue of religious freedom as a civil right," and the government had no power to use coercion to violate the immunity of the person in this regard. The French version denies a man "public freedom…in the face of the public power, when he publicly" manifests false convictions. Murray claimed one cannot argue that something is a right because it is a good.[17] The revised schema overreached because it saw religious freedom as a "genuine empowerment." This led to charges of indifferentism which could be avoided "only by adhering closely to the understanding of religious freedom as strictly a rightful claim to immunity from coercion in religious matters."[18]

The first schema failed, according to Murray, because the norm for limiting religious liberty was "too broad." Murray also objected to the first schema because it suggested "paternalism" in that someone decided what the good of society was, and not the people or whatever he was proposing.[19] The first schema lacked "precision" on the "competence of government in the order of religion" and what it provided "is not abreast of contemporary constitutional theory and practice, as approved by Pacem in Terris." As an essential point, Murray commented that a "personalist" conception of government that mentions "what the 'rulers' should do" was archaic in that the "constitutional government" of today is a "government of laws and not of men." Since the "competence of government (the public powers) is limited to the temporal, and terrestrial, secular and civil order of human life," then government's competence is "limited to the care of that civil and secular good which is public order in its threefold aspect." This in turn "furnishes the norm for governmental limitation of the free exercise of religion" and provides the answer to the question of at what point does "a particular activity gravely damage…the civil good which is public order"? The question becomes "whether the human power which is legitimate political authority has a right to restrain a man from acting, when his conscience is erroneous."[20]

Murray further criticized the first schema because it did not give "the necessary clear and unequivocal answer to the question being asked today…." Religious freedom had to "be furnished with a juridical guarantee and thus legally affirmed as a civil right. This should be explicitly stated." The schema should vindicate the right to religious freedom for the atheist. The issue of an erroneous conscience is irrelevant in the discussion about religious freedom as a civil right. The Catholic Church's claim to religious freedom is based on "the pregnant phrase, `*libertas Ecclesiae*,' in which `Church' means both authority' and `community….'" meaning the Church is a "divine institution." As to all other religious bodies, the Church claims religious freedom on the "nature of political society in its contemporary state of development, in which the principle of equal civil liberties must obtain, as a matter of political truth, justice, civic friendship, and freedom." Murray disagreed, naturally, with the view the "Catholic government…has the duty and right to see that public and social life are kept purely Catholic by the repression, wherever possible, of heretical views and activities" because of the limits on the "competence of government."[21]

Murray said "In principle, the Church does not claim legal or social privilege, or any right to use the coercive force of government to serve her spiritual purposes. She is the missionary Church, in the service of the peoples of the world. She is the `poor' Church, relying only on the spiritual resources with which she was endorsed by Christ her Lord."[22]

Murray proposed a three part declaration[23] he hoped would change church teaching and bring the Catholic Church more in line with the role Protestant denominations played in the United States. The American bishops were continuing the "liberating" efforts contained in FDR's "Four Freedoms" speech and Henry Luce's "American Century." During an age of freedom and rights, America was the shining city on the hill leading the Church out of darkness. Murray tapped into this sentiment with great success.

Because Murray spoke for an hour, Fr. Connell and Msgr. Shea were limited to a few minutes each, and Fenton didn't speak at all. What they said was irrelevant because the US bishops had already decided how they were going to vote on the Church state issue. They were intent on carrying the Spirit of '76 into the heart of the Church, where it later became known as the Spirit of Vatican II. Fenton described the events of the day in his diary:

"Murray spoke for an hour. Connell and Shea for a few minutes apiece. I was not called.... As soon as Shea had finished his few words, Meyer charged up to the front, thanked M (but not Connell or Shea) and set about organizing the bishops to present M's 'arguments' to the Council. There was no trace of any discussion and no trace of any desire for debate or discussion. Connell & Shea walked out in disgust. I stayed until the end. . . . After the party Boland came up and apologized. He said he did not know I was there. He never took the trouble to ask, and even if he had, Meyer did not give him a chance to do anything. I told him I was disgusted with the whole thing. . . .10:40 A.M. – M has just come in to see the triumph of his false doctrine."[24]

Connell wrote a letter to Apostolic Delegate Vagnozzi explaining what happened:

"Yesterday (Sept 17) the American Bishops had a meeting to discuss the schema DE LIBERTATE RELIGIOSA. Fr. Murray had been invited to present his side. I heard of it, and requested that I be allowed to speak; and so I was invited. Fr. Murray spoke for an hour, although it had been announced that the entire meeting would be ended in an hour. I spoke only five minutes, because of the lateness of the hour. I emphasized especially the difficulty of saying that everyone is free to practice his religion without hindrance in view of the fact that the Church imposes certain laws (especially matrimonial impediments) on baptized non-Catholics. At the end the bishops decided almost unanimously to uphold the schema. At the same time several spoke to me today, and said that they had been affected by my statement, and believed that my ideas should be considered. I hope I did some good. I foresee many difficulties if the present schema is accepted as it stand."[25]

Connell received a note from Bishop William G. Connare thanking him "for the gracious words of warning you gave us today on the danger in the question of religious liberty! I am sure that the Bishops generally appreciated the basic theological position which you stressed so clearly. We need these reminders constantly, so that we will not lose sight of the roots upon which all sound conciliar statements must thrive."[26]

"The US bishops," Fenton confided to his diary, "have timidly mouthed M's nonsense, as they have been told to do by Meyer. Yesterday and especially today the UPI articles in the Rome American….praise the US bishops as champions of religious liberty and attack the 'conservatives' and especially O as enemies of religious liberty. Today's article, and a wholly uncalled for editorial in the Roman American, concentrates on O. Thus through the obstinate ignorance of M and of Meyer, and by the childlike weakness of the US episcopate, the people are being told that the 'sanior pano' of the Catholic episcopate is opposed to religious freedom."[27]

When the document finally went to the floor of the Council for debate, Ruffini attacked it "for its tendency toward subjectivism and religious indifferentism." The US bishops, led by Cushing, Meyer, Ritter, and Alter counterattacked. Suenens called for a vote to end the debate, which promptly occurred. Murray with Pavan,

Willebrands, Hamer, and De Smedt then rewrote the draft based on the various comments.[28] In listening to the various speeches by the bishops, Fenton made a telling observation:

"10:30 – Johnny Wright has just finished one of the 'faceless man' speeches. He was trying to prove that religious freedom was requisite for the 'bonum commune.' Considering that Johnny did not seem to know what the common good is, except that it is ethical and demands religious faith, he did well. Some colored fellow from Africa is now following Johnny. They do not want a 'merely pragmatic' statement. There will be a lot of indifferentism out of this one."[29]

Shea observed Wright brought out the issue of the responsibility of each society to give "fundamental obedience to divine and positive moral law" and this "must be present in" the Declaration.[30] At a press conference sponsored by the US bishops, Murray explained the events of the day. He stated there "was a group of Spanish bishops who visited De Smedt to assure him they were for the schema." The hierarchy of Spain, according to Murray, wanted the "question of religious liberty to be settled this session" because "conditions in Spain need this."[31] More discussions were held. Bishop Biagio D'Agostino from Italy observed "today's society is naturalistic."[32] De Smedt, the relator of one of the versions of the Declaration, gave a talk in which he told the Council Fathers "modern man needs liberty" because "people today do not want to be dealt with as children."[33]

CHAPTER 109
MORE BAD NEWS FOR THE AMERICANS

As the American and Americanist attack was raging in Rome, Charles Douglas Jackson, C. D. Jackson, died from cancer at the age of 62 on September 18, 1964. In "A Letter from the Publisher: Sep. 25, 1964," *Time* told the world a little something about this man who knew so much about so much for so long. Condolences poured in from a former President, a former CIA director, and the conductor of the Boston Symphony, among others.[1] CD and his wife Gracie both were excellent piano players and he was a pilot as well as a journalist, which *Time* said held his "strongest loyalty." His "confidential reports" on his meetings with world leaders "delighted his editorial colleagues with their vividness and clarity" and at Time Inc. he dealt with the most difficult publishing problems. [2] Jackson spent many years in service to the US Government, too. He held a basic "conviction that freedom would win out – but that its victory required idealism aided by salesmanship." He was enthusiastic and idealistic.[3]

The five short paragraphs were just that – a little something – about a man whose influence and involvement reached across the US and across the world as he did the bidding of Henry R. Luce and the powerful interests he in turn served.

Time could have written about CD Jackson's involvement with the Bilderberg Group which came to signify the world economic and financial elites who bent world leaders to do their will. In 1952, Dr. Joseph Retinger, a colleague of Prince Bernhard, the consort to Queen Juliana of the Netherlands, contacted the likes of Averell Harriman, David Rockefeller and General Walter Bedell Smith with the idea of forming a group of the "leaders of opinion" together to present a critique of the Americans.[4] Dr. Retinger was the secretary general of the European Movement which was a "coalition of institutions dedicated to promoting European political and economic unity."[5] The European Movement received nearly half of its funding from the American Committee for a United Europe, which itself was funded by the CIA, with which Jackson was associated.[6]

There was a lot more. But *Time* didn't tell of those things, and many more. That was part of Luce's power and the power of American media – people were told what was important and what was not important by the stories that were covered, and by how these stories were covered. After all, civil society was good to borrow from Thomas Paine and who better to represent civil society than the privately owned and operated main stream media?

CHAPTER 110
THE SPIRIT OF VATICAN II

Time was encouraged by the tone the Council took at the opening of the Third Session. Its optimism found expression in an article that began with the trademark American phrase found in the Declaration of Independence, "A Decent Respect." It strongly endorsed the efforts of Murray and the US bishops in urging the Council to hold the course in promoting religious liberty:

"which affirms the right of every man, Catholic and atheist alike, to worship or not as his conscience dictates. It is a proposal that has little appeal to prelates from such strongly Catholic countries as Spain, Italy and Ireland. But their objections seemed halfhearted, questioning, almost resigned to defeat – and council watchers believe that the declaration will be approved by at least 85% of the bishops. Alfredo Cardinal Ottaviani of the Holy Office upheld the traditional view that `a man in error should not be entitled to honor'; yet even he did not condemn the declaration outright. The traditionalist arguments were forcefully answered by American cardinals. Chicago Albert Meyer said: `We must give to others what we claim for ourselves.' Boston's Richard Cardinal Cushing, in a speech written partly by Jesuit Theologian John Courtney Murray, principal author of the declaration, argued that the religious-liberty statement was 'something that the Catholic world and the non-Catholics alike have been waiting for' – admission by the church that it has 'a decent respect for the opinion of mankind.' It was Cushing's first speech in three sessions of the council; he was greeted by a torrent of forbidden applause when he sat down."[1]

Murray wrote to *Time* claiming he was "a bit disturbed by the TIME story that said that I was the 'principal author of the declaration' on religious freedom [Oct. 2]. This is not true. I had nothing to do with the text that was submitted at the session, though I did write a formidable set of footnotes for it."[2]

Time launched into an attack on Pope Paul VI, describing him, via an anonymous bishop," as "afraid," "so sensitive," "in need of our help." "Let's face it," said one Australian bishop, "He's weak."[3]

On October 9, the Secretary General of the Council, Cardinal Felici, appointed a mixed commission to examine and revise the document on religious liberty. The members of the commission—Cardinal Browned, Father Fernandez who was the Master General of the Dominicans, Archbishop Lefebvre, and Bishop Colombo of Milan —were not acceptable to the Americans because of their "opposition to the very idea of religious liberty." Bishops Ritter, Meyer and Cardinal Frings responded with a letter to the Pope "deploring the underhanded tactics and decisions reached contrary to Council rules."[4]

True to form, *Time* depicted the struggle between Felici and the Americans as conservative versus progressive:

"Time and again throughout the Second Vatican Council, a few conservative officials of the Roman Curia have tried to block the bishops' ambitious efforts to reform and renew the Catholic Church. Time and again, the progressive minded majority has suffered these tactics in silence and indecision. Last week, goaded by the most serious curial threat so far to the spirit of Vatican II, the bishops openly rebelled."[5]

Time criticized Felici's proposals that the "somewhat lackluster declaration on anti-Semitism...should be reduced to a short chapter in the schema...On the Church" and that "a declaration on religious liberty be rewritten" by a committee of four bishops. Other "repressive curial moves" included a "threat to end the council at the end of the current third session and an attempt to water down the passage in *De Ecclesia* defining the authority of the bishops over the church."[6]

Felici was protrayed as a bad guy as was Cardinal Cicognani, who suggested Felici's proposals. The good guys were the "seven progressive cardinals" who met at the residence of Cologne's Cardinal Frings to draft a memorandum entitled "Cum Magno Dolore" that was sent to the Pope and ultimately signed by fifteen prelates. The tactic worked. According to *Time,* "Paul VI agreed the Christian Unity office would bear the major responsibility for revising the two declarations" and he also allowed the bishops to decide if they wanted a fourth session.[7]

The Americans were emboldened to push for more concessions, or, as *Time* put it: "the bishops continued to approve aspects of reform unforeseeable a decade ago – and to demand still more." These "reforms" included allowing Catholics to receive communion from Orthodox priests, and to participate in common prayer services with Protestants. Further efforts were under way to strengthen the power of the laity in the Church by attacking a "schema on the priesthood that woodenly emphasized obedience and duty rather than clerical rights."[8]

By the third session, Michael Novak had replaced Robert Blair Kaiser as *Time's* Vatican correspondent, and it was on his watch—in its October 23, 1964 edition of the magazine, to be precise—when the infamous term "spirit of Vatican II" first reared its ugly head. It would prove next to impossible to exorcise this spirit once it appeared. The term came to represent in one neat, psychologically debilitating phrase the essence of the Americanization of the Church, which continues to this day. Since Novak previously mentioned in his writings the existence of a spirit surrounding this event, one may surmise that he, in conjunction with *Time's* editors, coined this infamous phrase.[9]

Ambitious young Catholics who were avid to advance their careers by advancing Americanism in the Church could have consulted Novak's article in the October, 1964 edition of *U. S. Catholic,* entitled "Will the Council Build the Bridge?" as their guidebook. Novak explained the importance of words at the Council: "At every stage, the Council fathers must make compromises about which words to use."[10] Compromise was necessary because there was no unity. American Catholics and those from Northern Europe were different from Latin Catholics. "Italian theology," he wrote:

"has been able to continue largely unchanged for several generations. But in northern Europe and, to some extent, in the United States, the discoveries of the secular world and of the Protestant world have forced theologians to look upon the Scriptures and upon history from a new perspective. New questions are asked. More difficult and more complex theological methods are required. Wider knowledge – of psychology, linguistics, archeology, literary forms, historical researches – is demanded. Such contemporary theology has thus had to think out the meaning of the Gospels in a new intellectual context, not less worthy than the intellectual context of 19th-century Italy and Ireland, for example."[11]

Every Novak piece in *Time* went out of its way to discredit the Church. "Churchmen," he wrote, "are well aware that the Church is not the spiritual leader of modern society. Some of them seem to be eating the bitter grapes of envy when they speak of the modern world." Without educated young gadflies egging it on, the Church ran the danger of "coaxing the world *back* to where it was, rather than at joining the struggles forward into a new civilization." Because Catholics "feel alien from modern philosophy, modern art, and the modern political and social revolutions," the Church had to become like the world, or, more exactly, like the prince of the world, America. This meant

"The fourth aim of the Council is to end our isolation and to construct a bridge to the world in which we live. To be Catholic is to share in the life, love, and good will of God toward men. It is to cherish every human value, to work harder than any at constructing a just and free and inquiring civilization. To be Catholic is to be open to the uniqueness and importance of every man one meets. It is to be catholic with a small 'c,' eager for all that is good, a force for unity among men of all cultures, temperaments, and dispositions. It is to live in hope rather than in fear."[12]

The same edition of *U.S. Catholic* featured an article entitled "Protestants and the Council: What Protestants expect from the Council is one thing. What they want is another." The Protestant leadership was pleased with the developments but they knew "it could go another way – backward. I believe it will move forward, but I do not believe it will do so automatically. It will do so only as the progressive forces marshal their resources and determine their line of action. And if we Protestants cannot directly help them in this noble endeavor, we can at least reinforce them with our prayers."[13]

The Protestant leaders saw the Catholic Church taking down its barriers to the Protestants and acting as though Catholic and Protestant were friends. The Protestants did not want the union of the Churches – "I don't want Catholics to become Protestants" – but they were encouraged by things such as liturgical changes, collegiality of the bishops, ecumenism, the church as "the people of God," freedom (meaning freedom of conscience and church-state separation among others), possibly even changes in birth control, the reorganization of the Holy Office, and the elimination of the Index of Forbidden Books. The main issue was religious freedom because that meant the state would remain secular:

"All branches of Christianity....must find some way to reconcile the essential freedom of conscience of the individual, liberty of church from state and of state from church, and the proper authority of both church and state. It will mean withdrawal of the institutional churches from political, economic, and social power in the world –

and active involvement of 'the people of god' in secular society and all its urgent human problems."[14]

Throughout Autumn, 1964, *Time* reported that Pius IX's *Syllabus of Errors*, which taught the Church should not accommodate itself to the modern era, was in the crosshairs of Schema 13, "The Church in the Modern World." According to *Time* and Edward Schillebeeckx, Catholics had to chose between "'whether the institutional church considers herself the be-all and end-all, or whether she deems herself an instrument in the hands of Christ at the service of all mankind.'" Schema 13 called Catholics to "be of service in the renewal of the world" and approved the renunciation of "ancient rights when new circumstances demanded" the pursuit of "dialogue with all men of good will" to "achieve justice on earth."[15]

Time praised the Schema's "discussion of major world problems" which "follows the tone and spirit of Pope John's encyclicals." It held out hope that part of improving the quality of life that occurs with marriage included "church acceptance of some form of birth control."[16] The reasoning on the purpose of marriage as proposed by Cardinal Leger advanced the acceptance of birth control as a good. Marriage, according to Leger, was "'the intimate union of the marriage partners finds its end in love as well as procreation." Suenens and Maximos IV, the Melchite Patriarch of Antioch were quoted as supporting a revision of Church teaching on birth control especially in light of changes in medical science. Cardinal Suenens urged his brother bishops to:

"'avoid a new Galileo case – one is certainly enough in the history of the church.' Even more explicit was Maximos IV Saigh, the Melchite Patriarch of Antioch. Speaking, as always, in French rather than the Council's official Latin, the Patriarch admitted that 'the immense majority' of Catholics did not practice what the church teaches on birth control. 'Shouldn't the official position of the church in the matter be revised in the light of modern science?' he asked."[17]

The more the progressives and liberals articulated their agenda, the more paradoxical it became. Christianity should have no part in governing states, but the Church should involve itself with the issues of the day, most of which issues developed in states under the control of anti-Christian forces in the name of secularism. *Time* portrayed the Church's capitulation to worldly power as being:

"in the interest of greater realism rather than Romanism, clarity rather than cliché. Challenging the schema on religious orders last week, Belgium's Leo Josef Cardinal Suenens attacked the `ridiculous complications' of nuns' flowing habits, `which gives the impression that the church is growing old rather than trying to renew itself in order to meet the needs of the day.'…Archbishop George Andrew Beck of Liverpool argued that the schemas said too much about banning the bomb and too little about disarmament controls….`To turn the other cheek is a counsel of perfection addressed to individuals, not to governments that have a grave duty to defend the citizens entrusted to their authority.' The schema was sent back for rewriting."[18]

CHAPTER 111
"THE POPE RUNS THE CHURCH"

T he Secretariat unanimously approved Murray's revised draft on October 24, and three days later the draft received the approval of four members of the Theological Commission. De Smedt wrote a text that was rejected. By November 16, the text was ready for distribution and the following day it was distributed to the Council. De Smedt made introductory remarks on the 19th. Everything seemed to be going smoothly until Cardinal Tisserant announced a preliminary vote would be postponed until the Fourth Session, and then all hell broke loose. Undeterred by the clamor, the Pope rebuffed an appeal by Meyer, Leger, and Ritter and upheld Tisserant's decision.[1]

In spite of the unanimous support of the Americans, many Council Fathers remained troubled by the document on religious liberty. First, there "was still a strong minority insisting that the Declaration uphold the classical theory of tolerance" which was a reaction to "progress in doctrine that an affirmation of religious freedom necessarily entails." Second, there was conflict between those who saw religious freedom as based on ethical and theological grounds which led to the juridical notion, and those who saw religious liberty as primarily legal and political and sought to find the theological basis to support it. Third, there was a fear that the authority of the Church would be undermined. Murray complained that the Church had still not come to grips with the principle of religious liberty, when it had long been accepted in principle by the "common consciousness of men and civilized nations." The Church's problem was the "deeper issue of the effective presence of the Church in the world today" Murray said.[2]

Fenton and Connell, unsurprisingly, had a different view. True, Shea appeared "gloomy as ever," but Fenton reassured him: "We are much better off now than we were towards the end of the 1st & 2nd sessions."[3] Fenton felt optimistic because the Pope finally asserted his authority over the Council in an allocution the first week of November."[4]

Connell felt the same way. "The Pope," he wrote to a fellow priest at the Divine Word Seminary, "did a very noble and brave act when he delayed action on this decree until the next session. It shows that he is alert to the needs of the Church.... Our Lord is still watching over the Church." Connell added: "I assure you that the decree on religious liberty has bee [sic] carefully checked and the principal objectionable features have been removed."[5]

Time, needless to say, was not happy and ran an attack on the Pope for not letting the progressive prelates have their way. "Pope Paul VI," the article began:

"last week coldly and dramatically reaffirmed that it is the Pope, and not the bishops of the Vatican Council who really runs the Roman Catholic Church. Just as the third session of the council was ending, Pope Paul – siding with conservative cardinals of the Roman Curia – took a major decision out of the hands of the progressive majority of prelates. Thereby, he raised doubts whether he essentially favors the aggiornamento begun by John XXIII and whether he intends to give anything more than lip service to collegiality – the doctrine, approved by the bishops, that they, as descendants of the Apostles, share ruling authority over the church with the Pope."[6]

The outraged Americanist prelates "quickly drafted a petition to the Pope that 'urgently, very urgently and most urgently' requested him to overrule the president, 'lest the confidence of the world, both Christian and non-Christian, be lost.'" De Smedt was quoted as saying with tears in his eyes that "'religious liberty is demanded by human dignity itself'." De Smedt was "rewarded with applause that rolled on and on, the moderator powerless to stop it."[7]

In spite of De Smedt's tears, the Pope was siding with the Curial "bad guys," and this created "fears for the future." The bishops left the Council "far more disturbed about the future of the council than they had been at the end of the stalemated Second Session. The Pope's final actions at the Council made it clear that collegiality was largely an ideal, not an ecclesiastical fact. His support of the Curia's maneuvering left many bishops resentful, their faith shaken in his progressive intentions."[8]

Making matters worse, Paul VI acted on two other matters dear to the progressive bishops, by making 19 changes in the final draft of the schema on Christian unity that "had already been accepted by the council in chapter-by-chapter votes." Some of these changes "clearly modified the ecumenical intentions of the prelates" wrote *Time*. Then, the Pope proclaimed Mary the "Mother of the Church," when the bishops had decided not to give this title to her.[9]

After serious attacks from within and without, the Church seemed to be holding firm, and Connell's Divine World confrere, Joseph Busch was encouraged:

"How happy I am that the Council did not issue a decree on this matter but postponed it until the next session. People will be completely misled, I think, if the wording of the decree is not very exact. The same applies to what Pope Paul called the problem when he spoke to the cardinals last June. So much has been written on birth control that the faithful are confused more and more. Take for example, the article by Father Curran in Jubilee, August 1964, page 8, Christian Marriage and Family Planning. Little wonder that Pope Paul cautioned the American Hierarchy in an audience on Nov. 16

to correct false rumors of what is being done in Rome in regard to family limitation."[10]

The World Council of Churches condemned the Pope's action. The WCC stated "One had thought when a notable majority had manifested its views on this topic favorably that the time had come for a solution to one of the most delicate problems concerning relations between the Roman Catholic Church and other churches."[11]

Key cardinals weighed in. Cardinal Ritter on his return said the Pope told him "the religious liberty statement before the Vatican Council has faults in it." Ritter stated "The Holy Father told us, 'We don't want a faulty statement – we want a statement based on sound principle,'…He said there were some parts of the statement that he had doubts about. I, of course, never had any doubts about it at all." Ritter described the emotion at the Council: "It would be impossible to mark the disappointment of the council Fathers at the failure to record even a preliminary vote on religious liberty… Our feeling of frustration at being balked a the threshold of a first vote on the subject was heightened by the conviction that we were stalled by the delaying tactics of a very small minority. Indeed, subsequent events showed how small a minority is opposed….We were very angry about it. We can't face the world much longer without making a decision of this kind…." However, he "predicted a strong statement on religious liberty" was to be forthcoming, even "inevitable." In the meantime, the most effective instrument in the renewal of the Church – which is the proper purpose of the council" was the dogmatic constitution on the Church which was promulgated during the Third Session.[12]

Archbishop O'Boyle in a December 15 address, prepared largely by Connell and given to about 400 members of the John Carroll Society explained aggiornamento in a way that discarded false notions. He provided an update on the religious liberty document, recounting its history and the concern the "Church must avoid the error of indifferentism, the idea that all religions are equally good." The Church "teaches and believes that, objectively, there is only one true religion and that is the Catholic religion" though "anyone who honestly and sincerely follows the dictates of his conscience is pleasing to God and can be saved." However, good reasons exist to grant "all religions…full freedom, even in the most Catholic country."[13]

The third draft improved on the first two drafts because it based the "need of religious liberty on the dignity of the human person – even though he may be in honest error." O'Boyle said that even Murray "The American who has been working for years to promote a declaration on religious liberty" said that "I am inclined to think the decision was wise" and "more mature reflection" will win people over. Despite the protestations of about 800 bishops who wanted the matter voted on November 19, the Pope "stayed with the rules of procedure" which allowed for the postponement of the vote when the "group of twelve cardinals known as the presidency agreed….to postpone the voting on this declaration until the next session."[14]

O'Boyle said the third draft avoided the danger of promoting indifferentism because it "explicitly asserts that 'every man is not free to follow in his religious life whatever opinion he may choose, but that there is one true religion which God and the Father of our Lord Jesus Christ revealed through His Incarnate Son and committed to the Church to be guarded and preached to all men, and men have the grave duty to seek truth in the matter of religion and to follow it when they recognize it.'" Men "should not be hindered by the civil power from practicing the religion of their choice, as long as they do not thereby interfere with the rights of others or disturb the public order."[15]

O'Boyle urged all concerned to "exercise discretion in what you read about the Council when it next meets and realize that the printed accounts are sometimes misleading. Above all, be convinced that there can be no change in those matters which the Church has previously proclaimed as true, either by the solemn definitions or by the universal teaching of Pope and bishops. Those truths, however, can be further developed and their application to the problems of the day can be declared more clearly."[16]

In his own comments on the Third Session, Connell showed concern the media distortion of the Council was creating division in the Church. Connell portrayed the media depiction of the delayed vote as "a kind of rebellion or revolt against the Pope" as "sheer nonsense" and "not the only instance of the misrepresentation of the news by the press":

"Indeed, from the beginning of the Council the newspapers gave the impression that all the bishops were divided into two opposing camps, the conservatives and the liberals, who were constantly at war with each other on every issue. The conservatives were presented as narrow-minded, scheming old men, hostile to every new movement in the Church, and the liberals or progressives as brilliant, broad-minded persons who will give a new look to the old Church. The truth is that every bishop was to some extent a conservative and to some extent a liberal. And there were numerous degrees of difference among them, inasmuch as they manifested a tendence [sic] to be conservative or liberal on the different issues. Another point that the press could not understand is that this assembly was not a political convention, in which each member tries to have his party win the most issues, but was an ecumenical Council in which the Fathers were all trying, not to gain any personal advantage, but to preset the Catholic faith in the clearest and most accurate manner and to pass legislation best adapted to give glory to God and the Church of Christ and to bring salvation to the souls of men. . . . Catholics must remember therefore that the Council is a supernatural gathering, made up of bishops to whom Christ has given the task of teaching and ruling His Church and assisted in their deliberations by the guidance of the Holy Spirit of God."[17]

O'Boyle and Connell were not alone in their criticism of the press coverage. After being demonized for years by *Time*, Archbishop Felici, secretary of the ecumenical council, "lashed out at 'untrue inexact and incomplete' press reports regarding the third session's uproar over the religious liberty schema" at a special conference for diplomats and ecclesiastics held on November 27, 1964. According to the NCWC account, Felici "Without naming names . . . drew a bead on 'certain parasites' who express ideas which are 'far from serving truth, foster confusion and insubordination.'" The Archbishop criticized the reporting of the "emotional exchanges in the council" when the document on religious freedom was denied a vote. Felici said that the deplorable reporting was "by certain press services which do not have, particularly as regards the secretariat general, the necessary serenity of judgment."[18]

Felici explained that the document on religious liberty, and a few others, could have been given approval had the session been extended to December 8. However, as it was, with the ending of the session on November 21, and the presentation of the final draft to the secretariat on the evening of November 11, the earliest the document could be distributed was November 17 with a vote two days later. "Any reflection," he said "will be a help to everyone because in the end even those who wanted the schema on religious liberty approved at this session would have disliked haste."[19]

CHAPTER 112
SOMETHING FOR EVERYONE

As 1964 wound down, life was good in America. LBJ handily defeated Arizona Senator Barry Goldwater who seemed willing to wage nuclear war with the Soviets to the destruction of everything. The Great Society was beginning, there was plenty for everyone, Blacks were gaining Civil Rights, and Vietnam was only an occasional mention in the news. Confident, proud and righteous described the American psyche at the time, and the American Catholic press shared that pride and righteousness at being first and foremost American.

The diocesan papers, almost without exception, echoed the American media, especially *Time,* in terms of their endorsement of America as good in principle, and so the American Catholic press wrote approvingly of the "spirit of Vatican II" and the Americanist agenda sweeping the Council. These papers even went so far as to copy American techniques of printing certain sentences in bold to emphasize their point, and in positioning articles for maximum reinforcement of the Americanist message. The NCWC News Service stoked the fires of rebellion in the Church, notably with an article by a Benedictine with the curious name of Placid Jordan who wrote the Council was showing "progress toward true freedom in the

Church."[1] The *Boston Pilot*, the official Catholic paper for the Boston Archdiocese, or Cardinal Cushing's, was perhaps the most Americanist, as it assumed a certain pride of place given Cushing's role at the Council. It was therefore more effective in advancing America as a good thing. The paper strongly responded to the actions of Pope Paul who acted with great wisdom in tabling discussion on religious liberty in November, 1964. As Boston was a center of the American Revolution in 1776, it was the center of the revolution that made the Catholic Church a satrap of America in the 1960s.

On one prominent page of *The Pilot* for Saturday, December 5, 1964, the Rev. Charles K. Von Euw, a peritus for Cardinal Cushing, published an article entitled "Council's Candor: Sure Sign of Church Renewal." Von Euw presented an image of the Church changing with the clear implication that it had been wrong for too long, and that the nations of the world taught the Church. The bishops came to the Council one way but things changed as the "problems of the 20th century world" broke the Church's "counter-Reformation mentality" and "isolationism" to show "their universal pastoral responsibility." One sign of such progress was the "ecclesiological consciousness," and the second sign was the "quality of candor or openness or frankness which has come about as the Church has examined itself." The First Session's secrecy was gone, and "Fresh air has indeed entered the Church....the Second Vatican Council has shown itself unafraid to open the 20th Century Church. There is a new candor and Christlike guilelessness abroad in the Church...."[2]

Fr. R. J. Sennott in an article "Council's Productivity Amazes" offered that the Council would change, or update, Catholic theology as he wrote "The Council is not a mere debate; it is not an advanced school of theology...no abstract process of reasoning" but it "serves as a great university in which the bishops exchange theological thoughts and in which all are theologically updated."[3] Next to Sennott's article was one concerning the observations of Methodist minister Dean Walter G. Muelder of the Boston University School of Theology who wrote his attendance as an observer at the Council was like "sitting in the middle of a quiet revolution." Dean Muelder "said that one of the important results of the Council would undoubtedly be greater Christian unity but that this was only a by-product of the sessions."[4] Catholic Auxiliary Bishop Thomas J. Riley spoke of a nebulous "commandment of love" in an article emphasizing certain parts of the "Dogmatic Constitution On the Church" by using the bolded black type method to point out the need for the laity to participate in the priesthood and prophetic nature of Christ's office.[5] Other articles emphasized, again with boldface, the ecumenism, unity, and the brotherhood of all that called themselves Christian, and at the same time these articles divided the concepts of truth and love as though the two were antithetical.[6]

John Cogley was featured prominently especially as he was a willing and revered servant of the American elites, so he criticized and attacked Ottaviani and the ever ominous Curia in Cushing's Archdiocesan newspaper. He kept alive the false images of the Council condemned by so many prelates, except by Cushing. Recalling frustration, gloom, and pessimism at the end of the Second Session, Cogley wrote that "Again, at the end of this year's session there were dark hours after the Council Presidents' decision not to call even for a preliminary vote on religious liberty." A "spirit of defeat" seemed to infuse the Council fathers who were being frustrated by a bureaucracy and "conservative managers." "American bishops" such as the "sober, prudent, circumspect prelates" like Cardinal Meyer of Chicago lead 1,400 of the fathers to insist on such a vote, Cogley claimed. This depiction of events put pressure on both the Pope and the "conservatives." In boldface, Cogley stated "Pope Paul remains an enigmatic figure…he is inevitably subject to misunderstanding, misinterpretation and that special misery of the father who has to head a family of divided children." This conveyed the displeasure of the Americans with the Pope's decision to prevent a preliminary vote on the religious liberty document. The majority of the Council was progressive, he wrote, intent on change, and exhibiting success in doing so. There were some defeats such as the decree on communications, *Inter Mirifica,* which Cogley, like other

Americans, condemned. He wrote "With the exception of the slap-dash communications decree published in the last session, the pronouncements have been forward-looking and profound. And the progressives have only themselves to blame for letting the mediocre communications decree slip by them." However, "The three pronouncements issuing from the third session, along with the liturgical constitution of the second, will change the face of Catholicism." Cogley stated that the most urgent "theological need" of the Church was a "Self-Understanding." The documents coming out of the Council were positive in that regard. The "right-wing clericalist press" portrayed Pope John and those around him as villains, and some in the Curia threatened revolt against that Pope. Paul was the "first pontiff of this new era."[7]

For the theologically minded, or those who were not the hoi polloi sitting in the pews every Sunday and working to make a living for themselves and their families, the Catholic press provided "an even more profound and significant insight into the ecclesiastical revolution now going on" in the pages of the December, 1964 edition of *Theological Studies,* Murray's magazine. Barrett McGurn, a Fordham graduate, writer for the Army, the *New York Herald Tribune,* and later State Department official in Italy,[8] endorsed Murray, who did "original thinking," in his article, "The Problem of Religious Freedom at the Council" found in *The Boston Sunday Globe* dated December 6, 1964. [9]

Murray's very influential paper containing the arguments for the American attack was published in the December issue of *Theological Studies.* Originally entitled "Right of the Human Person to Liberty on Matters of Religion," it was renamed "The Problem of Religious Freedom at the Council," and it impacted the intellectuals and the shepherds in the Church especially those attending the Council. It was perhaps the most important document in advancing the cause for a declaration on religious liberty at the Council as it indicated "what became pivotal for the Council's Declaration on Religious Freedom."[10]

Monsignor George Shea read Murray's article, and debunked it, though the American Catholic press did not give Shea a voice. In his typically thorough and categorical approach he disputed and questioned, paragraph by paragraph, almost statement by statement, Murray's position. Reflecting on Murray's position and the latter's comments about public opinion and pressure, Shea wrote the Conciliar Fathers should be "all the more circumspect lest they [be] guilty of bowing to…non-Catholic – public opinion." Indeed, "non-Catholic opinion has never been regarded as a locus theologicus for Cath. Doctrine, as a norm…for determining truth of a teaching." Any sensus fidelium must include the bishops, but the bishops were divided on the issue of religious liberty, Shea wrote. Murray's reliance on Biblical passages to support his view of religious freedom indicated to Shea this was tantamount to holding that Leo XIII taught contrary to the Bible. The Church's due for religious liberty comes from the fact she is a divine institution and the State must recognize such. Murray's claim of universal recognition of a right to religious liberty was suspect in itself, but further suspect was his claim it arose from the natural law. After all, Shea asked, if it came from the natural law why was it so "late in coming?" Shea made clear religious unity is part of the common good.[11]

PART XXI

VATICAN II – 1965

CHAPTER 113
GETTING RID OF TERRIBLE
LIMITATIONS

After spending the Christmas, 1964 and the New Year with the Luces and Murray at the Luces' home in Arizona, Gerald Heard, the self-proclaimed "psychedelic psychopomp" for a new humanity, wrote a glowing letter to William Mullendore, the Chairman of the Board of the Southern California Edison Company. Mullendore was a promoter of a number of conservative, or libertarian, economic causes and served as a trustee of the Foundation for Economic Education that garnered the support of national business leaders. Aside from being a powerful business executive and supporter of libertarianism in economics, he was also a supporter of a libertarian social philosophy, and hence of Heard's writings and thoughts. An avid fan of Heard's mysticism, Mullendore took psychedelic journeys to gain spiritual insights.[1] Mullendore, along with Heard, Mullendore's son-in-law, Louis D.T. Dehmlow, and Congregationalist minister Norman Ream formed a group known as "Spiritual Anonymous." He also spent time with James C. Ingebretsen's Spiritual Mobilization group ("Faith and Freedom Circle") which seemed to comport nicely with economic libertarianism.[2]

After mentioning the book *Swan on a Black Sea* in his letter, Heard shared information that he received from Murray, who had shared his experiences at the Council during his stay with the Luces in Arizona. Heard was stunned at "The speed at which the R.C. church is getting rid of its terrible limitations, its attachment to scholasticism and its fear of critical examination is to me quite amazing. Where it will stop no one can say. But those on its thinking edge are ready to go considerably further."[3]

It was 1965, and *Time* pushed the Catholics to revolt against the hierarchy. The key moment in this regard occurred with the March 19, 1965 edition of the magazine in an article entitled "Roman Catholics: Authority Under Fire." This article was the signal for Americanists and American sympathizers in the Church to rise up against all authority in the Church. The rebellion, festering for years, was now in the open, and from that point it would only grow in intensity.

Time trotted out Hans Kung to sound the battle cry. "The real problem" Kung opined, "is how soon and how widely the spirit of the council is accepted throughout the church." This spirit was most evident in the article entitled "Quitting the Seminaries," *Time* attempted to foment rebellion in religious orders by reporting on that rebellion as if it were already a fact. Or as *Time* put it: "Increasingly, priests and laymen disobey the orders of an immediate superior in the name of obedience to `the mind of the church.'" All of this was closely tied to a "restructuring of authority" and a change "from a religion of paternalism to a religion of personal responsibility," as Robert Hoyt, layman and editor of the *National Catholic Reporter,* said.[4]

Fr. Joseph Gallagher of the Archdiocese of Baltimore said there was a "`crisis of obedience in the church'" and the reason resided in the fact "members of the church are also citizens of the world.....They are unavoidably influenced by the spirit of their own time in history." That spirit, *Time* reported, was of the "modern world of free men." Bishop Bernard Topel of Spokane, Washington said "1964 will go down in the history of the Catholic press as a year of shame.

Not only were certain publications guilty of attacking bishops by name, but, claimed the prelate, they called into question 'the obligation of the laity to accept the teaching of bishops.'"[5] This was to be expected since the US hierarchy was itself rebelling against Rome.

Time explained how the Vatican II Council released and enabled an American spirit to take over the Church: "Moreover, the council's decree on the nature of the church marks the triumph of a revolution in theological thinking about what Catholicism is. It not only restores to bishops collegial rule that was theirs in the early church; it also justifies freedom of action and thought by the laity, who, the decree says, are 'permitted and sometimes even obliged to express their opinions on those things which concern the good of the church.'" Part of that good included "the new spirit of questioning" which was evident in "such lay-edited Catholic journals as *Commonweal, Ramparts Jubilee,* and the *National Catholic Reporter,* which have sharply criticized such authoritarians as James Francis Cardinal McIntyre, and have given plenty of space to speculative proposals for further Catholic reforms in clerical celibacy and the theology of marriage."[6]

The message from *Time* was that the "Roman Catholic Church" as "an authoritarian, hierarchal institution whose Pope and bishops claim to govern by divine right as descendants of Christ's Apostles" is "now undergoing widespread scrutiny, criticism and questioning."[7] Statements like this put psychological pressure on the bishops, who found themselves incapable of responding when the rebellion broke out into the open on such a massive scale. The rebellion spread American ideas throughout the world. The Spirit of Vatican II was another name for the Spirit of '76, and both came from the Americans.

CHAPTER 114
MURRAY EXPLAINS AGGIORNAMENTO

The work on the document concerning religious liberty started with the submission of written interventions in December and continued through February. There were two versions of the proposal (known as the second and the third), and the Council Fathers were considering both of them. The bishops solicited Fr. Connell's help in private letters, and he voiced his support for version three for very important reasons. In response to Cardinals Ritter and Meyer, who were promoting the second version of the document, Connell told Bishop William T. McCarthy:[1]

"I beg of you not to approve the change back to the second text on religious liberty. It will, however, revive heated controversy and perhaps be thrown out. The third text is substantially satisfactory, although among the notes you sent me (enclosed) I definitely oppose leaving out the paragraph on page six, which asserts that there is only one true religion. This truth must ever be emphasized; if it is left out for ecumenical reasons, we are not giving an honest picture. I am enclosing also some notes on the third text which I have written for one of the prelates in Rome. Things are certainly becoming very confused over here. Today's news from the NCWC stated that a `possible Catholic-Episcopal Mass of the future is being demonstrated in Pueblo, California.' What are we coming to!"[2]

Connell stressed the need to keep language in the document that referred to the Catholic Church as the one true church. "I have heard," he told Bishop Richard H. Ackerman:

"that an attempt is being made by some to have the second schema on religious liberty accepted instead of the third. I would regret very much if that were done. The second schema contains statements that cannot be reconciled with traditional Catholic doctrine. Besides, there would be a long controversy on the floor and it might be rejected again, to the detriment of all concerned. I think that the third is substantially acceptable. But even that is being attacked in one of its most important paragraphs, the statement that there is only one true religion. Some wish to suppress this. I do not see how we can get an honest statement on religious liberty without bringing in this truth."[3]

After receiving a number of interventions, the Secretariat for Christian Unity secluded itself at Monte Mario outside of Rome to consider them. Murray tried to get as many Council Fathers as possible to approve the American position, and the tide finally turned when Yves Congar gave his support to Murray's American position.[4]

Murray received opposition from De Smedt, and he tried to smooth it over before the Preparatory Commission met. In a letter dated a couple of days before he and Cardinal Designate Shehan traveled to Italy for the conferences, Murray told De Smedt "that the historical record of the Church has been so bad, and needs to be corrected." The traditional position, which calls for the Catholic state as the ideal "cum intolerance," "is a juridical theory, which must be repudiated; otherwise no one will listen to anything else we have to say. Besides, there is a plethora of Spanish literature extolling the Spanish juridical situation as the only 'Catholic' one." Even though the Church "in papal documents from Gregory XVI to and through Pius XII" has given "a clear defense of the rights of the Catholic conscience; there is no clear defense of a universal right of religious freedom in the face of the state. Even John XXIII is not... unambiguous.....I should think that the conciliar Declaration must situate itself with relation to this whole line of papal thought – and mark a new beginning, precisely with regard to the juridical aspect of the problem."[5]

From February 18 to 28, the consultants reviewed the various proposals received. Murray mentioned the "social aspect" of the document should not be neglected. It should "repudiate social as well as legal discrimination on grounds of religion." He was of the view that the social problem came about as a result of the "problem of 'tolerance' than of 'religious freedom'...." While stating he was opposed to a police state, Murray said the US was headed to a "Kulturstaat" but his main concern was to deal with "a privileged human right" and the role of the state in regards to it was "minimal" – "the efficacious defense of an immunity."[6]

Murray dismissed various objections to his position. One was confusion amongst the various Protestant and Catholic experts between "libertas religiosa," "libertas evangelica" or "Christiana." Murray's concern with the French view on religious liberty was its principled stance – the assertion "that the condition of man in the face of the ultimate questions of human existence is a condition of freedom."[7] This was different from the Americans who left questions such as these to the individual and who sought mainly practical accommodations.

In describing the deliberations over the religious liberty document in February, 1965, Yves Congar expressed misgivings about Murray and the influence he was having on the document. "Fr. Murray," Congar mentioned in his diary, "is less precise than I thought, and has no gift at all for elegant expressions. He is dry and brief. A certain imprecision reigns over our work. In my view, it would have been preferable if a single person had conceived the text as a whole, and we had made that our starting point."[8]

On Thursday, February 25, the Commission agreed "the drafting should be done by Murray, with advice from Feiner and myself. . . . But Msgr De Smedt was not happy with this last decision. He said so to Hamer. In general, De Smedt does not like Murray's intervention very much. For him, Murray is the one who transformed the first text (De Smedt) in the textus emendates; he is also and this is true, a man of a dry and too juridical style; he sees things from a rather individualistic angle. De Smedt, for his part would have wanted to do the drafting doubtless going back as much as possible to his original text. But in the group there was some fear (especially from Willebrands), of his brisk and rather peremptory manner of intervening. In the afternoon it was said: Murray and Feiner (for the drafting)."[9]

Two days later, Congar was praising Murray's "lovely ability to make welcome the questions of others, which implies an interior humility and an authentic intellectual code of ethics. He also brings to his response a serenity characterize by a composure and a courteous distinction more British, even Oxonian, than American."[10]

While these discussions were taking place, *Time* published an article extolling Pope John and *Pacem In Terris* as an endorsement of "the fundamental of Western democracy, government by constitution." This meant "rejecting government by coercion" and it "endorsed the explicit definition of the rights and duties of governments and citizens in every nation's basic law, including a charter of fundamental human rights" which came from "the design of the Creator." Man knew God's design, not by the Church, but by "man's instinctive but God-given knowledge of right and wrong. It is the law of nature, he argued, that man has the right to life, education, private property and has the duty to cooperate with others in building an orderly world."[11] This was The American Proposition and if the Catholic Church accepted it as good, the Church became irrelevant as a mere echo chamber of the plutocrats.

Congar's concerns proved to be accurate. Murray gave Clare an update from Piesso Lago Albano, explaining that *aggiornamento* meant acceptance of the American political and social principles.

Murray found the deliberations "Completely exhausting," but was encouraged by "good results on the whole, by and large, give or take a paragraph or two. And we have to come back in May for the last go-around. I wish I could come directly to Arizona and collapse for a bit. But no such good fortune. At that, it has been sufficiently absorbing – even though I am utterly bored with the whole subject of religious freedom."[12]

Murray let the Americanist cat out of the bag: "Aggiornamento means getting the Church of 1965 up to where the U. S. Constitution was in 1789."[13]

During the deliberations which took place during the Spring of 1965, Congar became aware of the real problem. The document on religious liberty:

"runs the risk of being interpreted as a charter of freedom WITHIN THE CHURCH, with regard to the Church (on this point, Mgr Willebrands, who seems to me to have got it from somewhere else, told me that this fear is not unrelated to the crisis concerning the Young Christian Students movement in France. Since the beginning of this crisis I foresaw and said that this case would have some repercussions on us and even on some steps taken by the Council....)"[14]

Congar's concerns proved to be an accurate prediction of what happened three years later when Paul VI issued *Humanae Vitae* and the revolution in the church broke out in earnest.

COMPARING THE SECOND AND THE THIRD VERSIONS

The third version of the declaration was substantially ready and it was sent with an introductory report to the Council Fathers in June.[15] Version three held religious liberty referred to immunity from coercion by "individuals or social groups or...any human authority" from acting contrary to conscience or being impeded from acting in accordance with conscience in private or public, "within due limits." While version two was silent on the matter, version three claimed that "this right must be so recognized in the juridical structure of society as to become a civil right".[16]

Importantly, version three contained the following language: "This matter of religious liberty therefore leaves intact catholic doctrine regarding the one true religion and the one Church of Christ." Both versions mentioned that the "supreme norm of human conduct is the divine law, eternal and absolute...." Both versions also discussed in essentially equal terms that man has a duty and right to "seek out the truth" in a "human way, that is, by free inquiry and by a personal assent." Version three added a requirement that once the truth was arrived at by the individual, "he must adhere to it firmly, that is, by a personal assent to it."[17]

The actions by authority were circumscribed differently by the two versions. Version two prohibited "especially...civil authorities" from "acting in religious matters in accordance with his own conscience." Version three prohibited the use of force by "individuals or by social groups or by the government" to prevent one from acting in conformance with one's conscience. Version three made more explicit that the "free exercise of religion," or external acts of religion, not be prohibited. Both versions recognized that the "competence of civil authority is limited to the terrestrial and temporal order" though they explained this differently. Version three defined this as "civil authority must...be regarded as going beyond its bounds, when it interposes itself in matters which have to do with man's directing himself towards God." Civil authority must restrict itself to "the things of this world" and not prevent a person from acting "according to his own conscience both in private and public, within due limits." Version two held that if "civil authority injects itself in any way into a regimenting of minds or in the case of souls, it is going far beyond its bounds." Human dignity was the reason for this restriction according to both versions.[18]

Version three allowed the government the right to protect civil society against abuses of religious liberty based on the "needs of public order." Public order was defined as "that good of society which requires the adequate maintenance of public peace, the proper preservation of public morality, a peaceful accommodation of the equal rights of all the people, and the effective protection of those rights." Version 2 gave a different definition of public order as being that "essential part of the common good that is entrusted to civil authority, to be protected by it especially by means of the coercive power of law." The same version prohibited invoking the coercive power of the civil authority unless the abuses were "gravely injurious to public order" which would be either "disturbance of public peace…a violation of public morality…an injury to the civil rights of others."[19]

Both versions expressed either an "earnest desire" (version two) or a "fervent wish" (version three) that the right of "religious freedom be recognized and "made secure by effective juridical safeguards". However, version three added the following paragraph not in the previous version:

"This policy of religious liberty, however, does not prevent the granting of special recognition, in the constitutional law of a state, for some one religious body, when the historical circumstances of the people warrant it. But this should be allowed only with the understanding that at the same time the right of all people and of all religious bodies to freedom in matters of religion is duly recognized and observed in practice."[20]

When it came to religious bodies, again another term that was not defined in the documents, they were to be all afforded the same rights. Based on the "social nature of man" and the social nature of religion itself, they were to be allowed to govern themselves by their own laws, engage in public worship, assist fellows in carrying out religious life or practices, "nourish" their "fellow members" with "their religious doctrine," and "promote those institutions in which their members" cooperate or may cooperate in "ordering their lives in accordance with their religious principles." Both versions held the "religious bodies" were not to be impeded by administrative action of either the state (version two) or the government (version three) in the selection and training of ministers, communications with "religious authorities in other parts of the world," and in the "acquiring and use of property." Both versions held that "religious bodies" were not to be impeded in "publicly teaching" or "in giving witness" to their faith. These "religious bodies" were not to engage in practices that would "savor of coercion or of harmful or undue influence" (both versions) especially, as concerns the "poorly educated" and the "needy" (version three).[21]

When it came to the family, version three was far more demanding of government. It explained the phrase, also held in version two which was that "no unjust burdens are to be imposed upon them [families]" by adding the following: "Government therefore violates the rights of parents, if it makes obligatory a single system of education, from which all religious training is excluded."[22]

The two versions presented two different views on religious liberty. Version two noted that the Church lends her support to a policy of religious liberty, and encourages it out of "her pastoral concern for human freedom." Version three stated that the Church "Is following the way of Christ and the Apostles, when she recognizes the principle of religious liberty as in accord with human dignity, and encourages such liberty."[23] Both versions confirmed that religious liberty is good for the Church and the faithful and hence "a harmony…exists" between what the Church claims for herself and all men.[24]

Both versions lacked definitions of key terms. This allowed for ambiguities and hindered agreement on proper understanding. This was the kind of situation that the Americanists and Americans could exploit to their advantage.

CHAPTER 115
SUMMER, 1965

American technology dazzled and was on display as the Summer began. Astronaut Edward White made the first American space walk with Gemini 4, and *Life* was there to cover it in "16 Pages of Fantastic Color." The cover of the June 18 issue showed Astronaut White floating "120 miles up...over Lower California" and in the background one could see the globe with the outline of Baja California.[1] The photos showing White in a variety of positions outside of the space capsule and suspended over the earth were stunning and fueled the imagination of not only the Americans, but the entire world. America really was the ideal, the dream, the greatest, and technology and science the way to achieve it all. Man's mind was sufficient. Anything was possible, even great evil.

Evil like the breakdown of LBJ's Great Society and a major defeat in his War on Poverty both of which represented the efforts of the mind of man alone. In August, Los Angeles exploded in fire and mayhem in what has come to be called the Watts' Riots. Over a thousand buildings were destroyed, damage to property reached into the tens of millions of dollars while 4,000 were arrested, over 1,000 injured, and 34 killed.[2] The National Guard had to be called in as the weeklong rampage continued in the Black ghetto. It was the beginning of a period of rioting and social unrest around the country. Every year, especially in the summers when the weather got too hot, people rioted and cities burned. It was racial unrest, poverty, and eventually growing opposition to the Vietnam War that brought all this on. Things looked great in outer space, but that was not the situation back on earth – where you could get "high".

The growing drug culture promoted by Luce, Heard, and Time, Inc. magazines caused the young to follow the advice of LSD guru Timothy Leary to "turn on, tune in, drop out." The irony, or perhaps the planned trajectory of this, was that Luce and his magazines promoted LSD and drug use in the 1950s before he, Clare and Murray started indulging. In 1954, *Time* first dealt with LSD as a tool to aid psychotherapy in "Dream Stuff," and then J P Morgan VP R. Gordon Wasson's positive encounters with hallucinogens were recounted in "Seeking the Magic Mushroom." In 1960, *Time* published "The Psyche in 3-D" which used celebrities to promote the taking of LSD under a doctor's supervision. As late as 1966, *Time* and *Life* were blaming psychoses as the reason for problems with the drug and were urging regulation of LSD, not its prohibition.[3] All of this was expected given that Heard was a close friend of the Luces and promoted by them. This was real power Henry Luce held – the power to build up and the power to tear down the very people who read his magazines.

Time was doing the same thing to the Catholics it was doing to the youth of America. The extent to which the Council was being used to undermine the teaching of the Church was nowhere more obvious than in the battle over the Eucharist and the idea of transubstantiation. According to *Time,* the "medieval Scholastics" were "static, mechanistic," and their teaching was full of "inadequacies," especially with regard to the doctrine of transubstantiation, which held that the substance of the bread and wine became Christ and the accidents were "the shape and texture of the host, the taste and color of the wine." The "new Eucharistic thinking" was fueled by ecumenical concerns and consisted in a "new way of looking at the Real Presence." That viewpoint was based on a "dissatisfaction with the medieval way of stating the doctrine" in that it "overemphasizes a magical change in the bread and wine." The scholastic view, according to Dominican priest Edward Schilebeeckx, "'has been philosophically untenable since Kant.'" Schilebeeckx proposed instead the new doctrine of "transignification" which held "through the host" the Lord "offers me his reality, his body." Just in case the meaning of this change in Catholic doctrine was lost on the reader, *Time* gave the last word in its article to one of the proponents of transignification who said with transignification "Now it is possible to be a Catholic in the modern world."[4]

Birth control was another important area of conflict. In a review of his book *Contraception*, *Time* described author John Noonan as a "Notre Dame Law Professor John T. Noonan Jr., 38," who "produced a magisterially documented history of church teaching on birth control, from Genesis to genetics." In reviewing Noonan's book, *Time* turned the tables and made the Church the aggressor: "'The church's attack on contraception, Noonan says, must be seen in its historic context, as a response to a particular challenge." The article then traced, in accordance with Noonan's position, the "development" of church doctrine from sex and marriage only for children (St. Justin Martyr said "'We Christians marry only to produce children'") to sex and marriage as a "personal action, which…effects the union 'in one flesh alone.'"[5]

The issue was whether the Church would grow. Growth, according to *Time*, meant "progress," and progress meant becoming like America, where contraception use was left to the discretion of the individual whose desires and wants were the measure of all things. Noonan could find "no valid reason why the church cannot move with the times. Already it has come a long way toward acceptance of the principle that other personal values can take primacy in marriage over childbearing." After all, Noonan and *Time* argued, the Church had "long since abandoned the medieval view that sexual intercourse during menstruation and pregnancy is a sin equal to that of contraception."[6]

Time attacked every aspect of the Catholic Church. It even ran stories concerning indulgences, and subtly endorsed a change in the sacrament of confession, endorsing general confession[7] confirming Fenton's long-held suspicion that Catholic doctrine was under attack, and *Time* waged the major assaults.

Responding to attacks on doctrine and requests from the episcopacy was the seemingly indefatigable Fr. Connell who at 77 years of age kept a rigorous work schedule. Apostolic Delegate Vagnozzi asked Connell's comments on a book that supposedly explained current events, but hid the reality of the American and Americanist assault on doctrine. It was entitled *What's Happening in the Church?* Connell pointed out the author's errors and explained that the religious liberty discussed in the schema "does not imply that a human being may equally esteem false and true."[8]

In response to increasing attacks on the Church's teaching on contraception, Connell sent Archbishop O'Boyle a lengthy memorandum explaining that "it would be a great blow to the Church in the United States if any mitigation of the traditional doctrine was permitted by the Holy Father."[9] Citing *Casti Connubii,* Connell concluded with the quote that "No difficulty can arise that justifies the putting aside of the law of God which forbids all acts intrinsically evil."[10]

In a letter to John Cogley, who was now working for the *New York Times*, Connell took issue with Murray's claim "that contraception is a private act. It is an occult act, it is true, but it has the repercussions on society, and hence it is public. Hence, per se it can be forbidden by civil law, as in Connecticut, until recently. But I admit that such a law is unrealistic, because it cannot be enforced. But the distribution of literature favoring contraception, contraceptives, etc., comes within the scope of civil law."[11]

Meanwhile, Murray was explaining his views on religious liberty, and other matters, to key churchmen who needed to get results on the religious liberty question during what many thought would be the final session of the Council. In a memo to Cardinal Cushing, Murray explained the schema on religious liberty was needed because it was a "pastoral necessity of the first order" that is "solidly founded and altogether Catholic."[12] The "foundation of the right to religious freedom is a truth" about the "dignity of the human person." That dignity means "a man should set on his own judgment and responsibility, that he should set freely out of a sense of duty, and not as one driven by coercion from without." The "foundation of all human rights"[13] was freedom, which was the "primary good... It is good for the human person not to be compelled to act against conscience. It is good for the human person not to be obstructed by others, even by government, when he is acting in accord with conscience."[14]

The pastoral aspect was also important. The "Gospel of freedom":

"needs to be preached more emphatically today on account of the historical fact that was noted by John XXIII. The fact is that in many quarters of the world dictatorial governments are imposing excessive restrictions on human freedom, especially on religious freedom....When the human right to religious freedom is denied, it customarily happens that many other of his civil rights are likewise denied. And when these civil rights are denied or too sharply limited in their exercise, society itself ceases to be human, since it becomes impossible for men in it to lead lives worthy of a man."[15]

So, Murray wrote, while the "Church does not hide the truth of the Gospel...in these our days, the Church must also proclaim in the spirit of Paul the Apostle, and indeed in the spirit of our beloved Pope Paul, 'I do not fear the Gospel, the Gospel of freedom.'..."[16]

In conclusion, Murray told Cushing :

"Whether we like it or not, the word that falls most gratefully on the ears of the man of today is the word 'freedom.' The value and the good which the man of today is anxiously seeking is the good of freedom and its value in human life. It is therefore our pastoral duty to preach the whole Gospel of the freedom of Christ. This Declaration of ours on religious freedom makes a beginning in the preaching of this Gospel to the whole world. May God grant that the proclamation of this human freedom may everywhere stir in the hearts of men the beginnings of faith in the Gospel of truth that comes to us through Christ our Lord."[17]

By stressing freedom, an idea Henry Luce stressed to the US Senate in 1960 and throughout his career, an essential part of The American Proposition and hence the US Government's Doctrinal Warfare Program was advanced. Murray provided a portal through which the social engineers could enter the Church and turn it into an agent promoting the American ideology at the expense of the Gospel of Jesus Christ.

CHAPTER 116
SESSION FOUR

T ime followed the progress of the religious liberty document closely during the Fourth Session and pressured the prelates to pass it. Recognizing that Paul was the "key to the direction and drama of the fourth session – and after,"[1] *Time* painted the Pope as a tortured and conflicted personality who could not be trusted. This depiction weakened the hierarchy while at the same time inflaming the fires of rebellion among the laity. In "The Papacy: Reluctant Revolutionary," Paul VI appeared as a disappointing, and ambivalent figure. On one hand he "shares something of the modern world's aversion to certainty and pontification," and on the other hand he was the author of the encyclical *Mysterium Fidei*. That encyclical defended the Church's traditional teaching on the Eucharist and appeared aimed at several Dutch theologians who held a different theory and therefore warned "theologians to stay away from far-out speculation on other doctrinal issues." As a result, while being described as a "puzzle, an enigma," Paul was believed to have "deliberately sided all along with the conservative Curia." Others criticized his leadership because he was "an intellectual perpetually saying 'but, but, but'" and "wavers when faced with a many-sided problem."[2]

Time cited Paul's encyclical *Ecclesiam Suam* as evidence that he was operating as a "brake on the progressive majority." He prevented a vote on religious liberty at the end of the Third Session. In August, 1965 he warned against "'strange and confused voices' even among the bishops who have been questioning 'principles, laws and traditions to which the church is firmly bound.'"[3] But *Time* kept revolutionary hope alive when it wrote that the "impetus to complete the reformation is already there in the records of Vatican II, waiting for another council, or another John. Or another Luther."[4]

IT STARTS

The fourth and final session commenced on September 14, and on the next day the schema on religious freedom was the first item for discussion. Bishop De Smedt gave the opening remarks followed by a parade of American bishops, which prompted the opposition to it as a "mere American political document aimed at easing pressures from a pluralistic community back home, no matter the cost to Catholics in other countries."[5] During the comments, which lasted for five days, the divide separating the Americans from everyone else became more apparent. Cardinal Spellman praised the document because "Many persons today do not know that the Catholic Church approves those modern societies which grant religious freedom and political equality to the followers of every religion."[6]

Cardinal Ruffini of Palermo, Italy demurred, claiming:

"It is necessary to distinguish physical or psychological freedom from moral freedom, which alone is concerned with truth. We may not separate religious liberty from the truth. There can be only one true religion, which per se has a right to freedom. In this life with its temptations, errors, and sins, civil authorities must permit various kinds of divine worship for the sake of public order and the common good. But it is not proper to omit the above mentioned distinction, lest the Council appear to demand of the State nothing more than the observance of Articles 18, 19, and 20 of the Universal

Declaration of Human Rights adopted by the UN in 1948, which is praiseworthy for its effort to preserve civil harmony among men of different religions but smacks of agnostic indifferentism. Moreover, in the schema (p. 9) the civil authority is exempted from any religious duty; it is true that its competence is limited to the temporal order, but it is still obliged to worship God and to protect and aid religion, for civil authority cannot act as if God did not exist."

Ruffini was dismayed fearing "the complete separation of the Church from the civil authority" would give confidence to the enemies of the Church, like the Communists, who "even now . . . object that we use undue persuasion on the ignorant and the poor. . . . I dare to state that this Declaration will have the most serious consequences and that therefore the schema should be revised in a more accurate way."[7]

Cardinal Siri of Genoa, Italy joined with Ruffini in attacking the schema because it:

"affirms religious freedom for all religious communities, and also for those which deviate from natural truth, and even for immoral and sanguinary ones. But God only tolerates and promises to punish such abuse of freedom. We cannot defend what God only tolerates, and we cannot tolerate beyond certain limits, e.g., beyond the limits of the common good. But the schema indiscriminately defends the religious freedom of everyone. It is more important to defend the divine law than freedom. Whether the schema really accords with the teaching on religious freedom found in theological sources and Popes should be more deeply explored. If we change this doctrine and don't treat rather of the RIGHT religion, right at least by reason of natural law, we will undermine theological and our own authority."[8]

Supporting his Italian confreres, Bishop De Arriba y Castro from Tarragona, Spain, said

"only the Catholic Church has the right and duty to preach the Gospel. Therefore, proselytism on the part of non-Catholics among

Catholics is unlawful, and insofar as the common good requires, must be impeded not only by the Church but also by the State. The Council should be careful not to bring about the ruin of the Catholic religion in nations where that religion is practically the only one. There are many who say that all religions are the same. This leads to indifferentism. It is a mistake to think that freedom for non-Catholic proselytism will aid the spread of the Gospel. Only the private practice of non-Catholic religions can be free; no religion, however, should be forced upon any man.[9]

The schema's defenders appealed to freedom and the Zeitgeist as reasons to approve it. Giovanni Cardinal Urbani speaking for 32 Italian bishops defended the schema as "opportune," because at this historic moment, men of different origins and opinions live within the same boundaries." Cardinal Cushing defended the schema because it:

"teaches that the foundation of the right of religious liberty is the truth of the dignity of the human person which demands that man ought to act on his own judgment and responsibility, and that he should act freely out of a sense of duty and not out of mere external coercion. The same truth is also the foundation of the entire social order. . . . To the pastoral office pertains especially the preaching of the Gospel, not only of truth, but also of liberty. . . .In many places today dictatorial government restricts human liberty especially in religious matters."[10]

Cardinal Paul Peter Meouchi of Lebanon said "The terminology used in the schema should be derived, not from our philosophic and theological systems, but from the concrete existence of modern man whose cultural, social, historical, etcetera, evolution has often adapted new meanings to these same terms….."[11]

Bishop Marcel Lefebvre complained

"The concept of religious liberty contained in this schema, as the relator himself admits (p. 43), came into existence in the eighteenth century, and indeed outside the Church, among the philosphes who tried to destroy the church. In the nineteenth century, the Liberal

Catholics (such as Lamennais) who attempted to reconcile the concept with Catholic doctrine were condemned by Pius IX. Leo XIII condemned it in Immortale Dei as contrary to sane philosophy, Scripture and Tradition.....Since the Catholic Church alone possesses the divine law and has received the command to teach it, the Catholic Church alone has a real right or religious liberty...."[12]

At the US bishops' press panel on the evening of September 16, Murray explained the idea of the "public order" limiting the exercise of religion as consonant with the teaching of Pius XII. He also mentioned the schema would deal with religious liberty only in society, and the Catholic Church was free to censure who they wanted. Most notably, though, Murray made it clear that in societies that have established religions, the schema was to "avoid canonizing the religion of the state." This was to be part of the document, which was to be an "authentic declaration" which Murray said "we want... to get through as a doctrinal statement." In response to a question from a reporter from the *New York Post* as to whether the document would be binding on Spain, Murray said simply, "Yes. In a sense this document is binding on all mankind."[13] Murray went on to state that the schema was doctrinal, but not a matter of faith. It was "based on reason, a philosophical document." It was a "development of doctrine which has come to clarification" because "what we have had are archaistic, time-conditioned views."[14]

Four days later, the press conference led to a heated exchange between Murray and Connell. When Murray mentioned the Council was "trying to make a case for religious freedom" by adopting the US First Amendment as good in principle, Connell asked: "If this passes, will the rulers of Catholic countries be bound to accept it?"

"Murray: It is a doctrinal document, and I presume that all Catholics, whether rulers or not, would be called on to accept it.

Connell: The Schema says rulers have no competence to judge regarding religious matters. Would that apply to Catholic countries too? Why would they have to accept it?

Murray: What the document actually says is that the ruler must govern according to constitutional principles, that human rights warrant the protection of government.

Connell: I see a real difficulty here.

Murray: The doctrine of the schema. It is a doctrine issued to the whole world. It is a rational doctrine which we hope Russia will accept.

Connell: But they would not be acting as Catholics? Would not be bound???

Murray: I think the objection can be solved by distinguishing between reasons and motivation; the latter, his being a Catholic; the reasons being the reasonableness of the doctrine."[15]

Connell got Murray to acknowledge the entire effort for a statement on religious liberty was about sanctifying the US system of political organization as good in principle.

As the prelates were talking, *Time* issued a progress report quoting Josef Cardinal Beran of Czechoslovakia as saying that failure to recognize religious liberty was the reason "the church is suffering today in expiation for its past sins against religious liberty – such as the burning of the 15th century heretic, Jan Hus." The Church, according to *Time,* wrongly condemned and burned this heretic. Bishop Emile De Smedt explained that the "statement on liberty was a necessary way for the church to advance with the times."[16]

Time said the "…declaration affirms that man's right to religious liberty is based on both divine revelation and the 'very dignity of human nature,' and that in religious affairs no one can be forced to act against his conscience. It states further that the state must protect this human right, and that governments can neither impose any religion on an individual nor prevent him from joining or leaving any religious group."[17]

Time's formulation endorsed Murray's position which in turn was an endorsement of American, Anglo-American constitutional principles, the American ideology, and Liberalism, the center of which was a rejection of Christ. *Time* was repeating Thomas Paine's ideas from *Common Sense* and Madison's views from his *Remonstrance* both of which relegated religion to a private matter without any claim on public policy.

On September 21, the last day of discussion, Enrico Cardinal Dante of the Curia pointed out:

"a serious equivocation in this schema, which proposes the liberal doctrine of Lamennais, echoed in the tenth declaration on the rights of men: 'No one should be troubled because of his opinions, even his religious ones, as long as their manifestation does not disturb the public order, established by law.' The precise equivocation is this: that the State establishes the limits (peace, public morality, etc.) beyond which the exercise of religion cannot go. It follows: If the state is Christian, it will propose limits which more or less conform to the natural law. If the state is pagan, these limits may prescind from natural law and may become a weapon against the one true religion. If the State is Communist, such limits will go against natural law. Thus the declaration on religious freedom will obtain the very opposite effect if it does not rectify such limits."[18]

De Smedt as the Relator said in "revising the text, all suggestions will be carefully weighed." "The schema," he said, "will be re-reamended in keeping with your observations with the hope of obtaining moral unanimity in the final vote."[19]

At the end of the discussions, Bishop Robert Emmett Tracy of Baton Rouge counted a total of 55 speakers with 22 against the schema and 33 for it. He wrote as "the U.S. speakers rose, one after another, a bishop beside me observed: 'The voices are the voices of U.S. bishops, but the thoughts are the thoughts of John Courtney Murray.'"[20] Murray suffered another heart attack after the speeches and was sidelined for weeks. The debate on the schema ended and the text was "in possession" with final edits being done by the Secretariat for Christian Unity. These were De Smedt, Willebrands, A. Ancel, Carlo Colombo, Pavan, Hamer, Congar, Benoit, and others. Various changes and revisions were considered in October. The final text was completed November 9 with approval on the 19th and the final voice vote in December.[21]

Time was cautiously optimistic despite the "strain of compromise and revision" and an "added paragraph asserts that God has indicated to all men the way of salvation, which is through membership in the Catholic Church, and that all men have a 'sacred duty' to join it once they perceive the truth of the church's faith." American Theologian George Tavard complained that this was "A very annoying thing." Then there came a "host of amendments seeking to emphasize the truth of Catholic thinking and the error of other views" which were submitted by Italian Bishop Luigi Carli of Segni.[22]

Fenton was in Rome during the debate, but his notes were few and far between. Fenton described Ottaviani as having "lost a lot of his energy. I think that he has wasted a lot of his life and has canceled out a great deal of his value to the Church by reason of his attachment to a political group."[23] The last meeting of the mixed commission in November was "entirely in the hands of the bishops, which is to say, entirely in the hands of the ruling clique. We discussed number 13. It is a mess."[24] On the evening of November 24, Fenton had dinner with Ottaviani, during which "I found that the Pope had written to O about 13. I saw the letter. It is a great mistake to let that one, the one on religious liberty, and the one on non-Christian religions, get by the council."[25] When *Dignitatis Humanae* was promulgated by Pope Paul VI on December 7, 1965, a weapon was put in the hands of the Americans and their allies in the Church, the Americanists. The US bishops had been instrumental in making that happen, just as they did with the declaration on non-Christian religions, as *Time* proudly observed.[26]

CHAPTER 117

A "STEADY DRIVE FORWARD" – SPINNING OF THE DOCUMENTS

T he documents produced by the Vatican II Council did not change Catholic doctrine, but they gave something the enemies of Catholicism would use as a weapon. Mischief was done in the interpretation of the documents and the hermeneutic for that interpretation was not the Catholic Faith, but the American ideology, and the American experience.

Rev. Lukas Vischer, an observer at the council from the World Council of Churches (WCC), issued a report two months after the council's closing saying that the work of the council was not yet done and that there needed to be a "steady drive forward" in the development of the Church's positions on a number of matters. His explanation of how the documents were to be spun was given wide distribution by the US Catholic bishops through the NCWC News Service:

"The texts which were promulgated make up a stately volume...But the fact that the council is not yet finished is related precisely to this fact. In several cases, many more questions were raised than were really answered. The texts present the problems; they *require further interpretation.* The theological and practical conclusions remain to be drawn…The…impulses radiating from the council are only partially expressed in the texts. They are more comprehensive, deeper and also more complicated than the promulgated works."[1]

Vischer asked crucial questions: "Thus we are faced with a hermeneutical problem which is not easy to solve. How are the texts of the council to be explained? Must we keep strictly to what has been laid down in them? Or can we allow ourselves to be guided by the general directions which found expression in the context of the council, and use these as the criteria of what is to be judged as more and what as less important?"[2]

When it came to the all important Declaration on Religious Liberty, Vischer stated the erroneous and American interpretation of the document as he wrote the Church decided to support "religious liberty as a principle" which "changes at its very foundations the attitude of the Roman Catholic Church toward the world" since "The Church no longer sees those who do not confess the truth as erring ones, to be tolerated and indulged, but acknowledges them in the liberty given them by God….For this reason, the declaration is the prerequisite for dialogue, both in the broader and in the narrower sense of the word. For genuine dialogue can only take place if the partner is taken seriously in this liberty."[3]

Most importantly, "The idea of the confessional state is—if not explicitly, at least implicitly –given up."[4] Spain, Italy, and any other country thinking of building their societies on Catholic unity and Catholicism no longer had that right. If there was any question as to the authoritative voice on the meaning of *Dignitatis Humanae,* that was to be Murray, and if there was any question on the hermeneutic to be used to interpret the documents, that was resolved in favor of the Americans by Father General of the Society of Jesus, Pedro Arrupe who was arrested the day after the attack on Pearl Harbor by the Japanese as a spy and who was a survivor of the American nuclear bombing of Hiroshima on August 6, 1945. Singing paens to America as the teacher of the Church, a reversal of Christ's statement in Matthew 28:19-20 that the Church was to teach the nations, he claimed human dignity and freedom were Christian values and that:

"the Church has also proven her capacity to learn....More particularly, she has learned from that school to which the contemporary world owes so much: the American experience. For without the American democratic experiment...without the American experience of religious pluralism how much longer would we have had to wait for the recent Council's Constitution on Religious Liberty? That document is highly regarded, and with a fraternal pride...I salute with you the role of that patient, strong and courageous thinker we have with us here today, Father John Courtney Murray. It really represents the peculiar contribution of the entire American people: it puts the seal on a central strand of experience itself."[5]

An important part of Murray's work was after the Council concluded, and that was to interpret *Dignitatis Humanae* in an American hermeneutic thereby insuring Catholic support for The American Proposition and turning the Church into a vast dispenser of the American ideology. His opportunity came when another Jesuit, Walter M. Abbott, assembled a work called *The Documents of Vatican II* published in 1966 and billed as "a New and Definitive Translation with Commentaries and Notes by Catholic, Protestant and Orthodox Authorities."[6]

Murray wrote a gloss for the Declaration and lengthy footnotes throughout the document, particularly Chapter I. The gloss was significant for it established in the reader's mind that he was an authority especially as he had been involved in the process that lead to the consideration and passage or adoption of the Declaration by the Council. This in turn gave credence to him as an authority on the document thereby giving his thoughts contained in the footnotes more authority as the definitive interpretation of the document. To reinforce what Murray wrote, if such was needed, was "A Response" written by Methodist minister and "Protestant scholar" Franklin Littell, defender of the theological right of Israel to exist and an early proponent of creating the cult of the Jewish Holocaust.[7] In Abbott's volume he endorsed the ideas that the Church was approving of American political philosophy and societal organization as good in itself, objectives of Murray's work also: "The American experience of religious freedom is not only an advance in Church history; it is also an important breakthrough in government."[8]

Murray claimed that the Declaration was a doctrinal development, and not just a pragmatic statement, in that it "declared" the following three tenets: "the ethical doctrine of religious freedom as a human right (personal and collective); a political doctrine with regard to the functions and limits of government in matters religious; and the theological doctrine of the freedom of the Church as the fundamental principle in what concerns the relations between the Church and the socio-political order."[9]

Just what kind of doctrinal development it was, Murray never made clear. The reader should have been alerted to a problem when Murray, considered to be a pre-eminent theologian, wrote "The Course of the development between the *Syllabus of Errors* (1864) and *Dignitatis Humanae Personae* (1965) still remains to be explained by theologians. But the Council formally sanctioned the validity of the development itself; and this was a doctrinal event of high importance for theological thought in many other areas."[10]

Sounding a note from Vischer's report and stating Catholic doctrine was up for debate with and formation by non-Catholics, Murray wrote more work was needed to develop the "certain lines or elements of argument" present in *Dignitatis Humanae*. This work had to be done by "scholars of the Church, working in ecumenical spirit with scholars of other religious communities." In footnote 7, Murray said the scholars should agree with "American theorists" who "are generally disposed to relate religious freedom to a general theory of constitutional government, limited by the rights of man, and to the concept of civic equality."[11]

Murray stressed in footnotes 7, 21, and 22 that the "principle of freedom is paramount" [12] in the "relationship between the people and government and between man and man," and that freedom meant "freedom from coercion." [13] In footnote 51 he explained that it extended even to the Church which was to repudiate "all means and measures of coercion in matters religious."[14] This freedom, or "liberation of the human person," was the fourth principle upon which society is to be based, in addition to truth, justice and charity, was set out in *Pacem In Terris* by John XXIII and constituted a "renewal of the tradition." Responsible freedom "implies a rightful response to legitimate authority" he wrote in footnote 22 and in the following footnote set out that "religious freedom is not an end in itself, but a means for the fulfillment of the higher purposes of man" rising "out of a consciousness of human dignity." [15]

Murray emphasized the point that *Dignitatis Humanae* was in harmony with the First Amendment, and hence the American view of religious liberty and church state relations was approved as good in principle if not also being the ideal. In footnote 5 he wrote:

"It is further to be noted that, in assigning a negative content to the right to religious freedom (that is, in assigning a negative content to the right to religious freedom...in making it formally a `freedom from' and not a `freedom for'), the Declaration is in harmony with the sense of the First Amendment to the American Constitution. In guaranteeing the free exercise of religion, the First Amendment guarantees to the American citizen immunity from all coercion in matters religious. Neither the Declaration nor the American constitution affirms that a man has a right to believe what is false or to do what is wrong. This would be moral nonsense....It is, however, true and good that a man should enjoy freedom from coercion in matters religious."[16]

The First Amendment was the example for the world to follow as Murray stated in footnote 24 that "Both as a principle and as a legal institution, religious freedom is less than two hundred years old. The First Amendment may claim the honor of having first clearly formulated the principle and established the institution...." even though the council held that religious liberty "has its `roots in divine revelation'."[17] Human dignity justified religious liberty and the American model of "limited government" protected human dignity.[18] God-given rights, and the "dignity of man" were concepts advanced by the US ideological warfare program, but Murray did not write that, instead he claimed in footnote 4 that Pius XII and John XXIII approved these ideas which were "at once new and also in harmony with traditional teaching."[19]

In footnote 14, Murray stated Catholic doctrine approved of the limitation of government's powers so as to secure the "common welfare," a new term, which consisted of the protection of rights and the performance of duties of the individual.[20] The common good consisted of "the care of the rights of man – devolves upon government" which is:

"forbidden to assume the care of religious truth as such, or jurisdiction over religious worship or practice, or the task of judging the truth or value of religious propaganda. Otherwise it would exceed its competence, which is confined to affairs of the temporal and terrestrial order. On the other hand, government is likewise forbidden to adopt toward religion an attitude of indifference or skepticism, much less hostility."[21]

Curiously, Murray made no mention of perhaps the most significant passage of the Declaration: "Religious freedom…leaves untouched traditional Catholic doctrine on the moral duty of men and societies toward the true religion and toward the one Church of Christ."[22] In addition, he never stated societies had a duty to follow the Divine Positive Law which meant they were to give the Church and the Faith pre-eminence. Instead, in footnote 9 (and reiterated in footnote 14) he wrote the Church wanted nothing special for itself that it did not want for other religions. This was quite a change from the teachings of the pontiffs of the previous 150 years.[23] *Dignitatis Humanae* ended a double standard thereby bringing the Church, at least in Murray's formulation: "A long-standing ambiguity has finally been cleared up. The Church does not deal with the secular order in terms of a double standard – freedom for the Church when Catholics are a minority, privilege for the Church and intolerance for others when Catholics are a majority."[24]

Allied with this was the jettisoning of the Catholic goal to create confessional states all in the interest of advancing "ecumenical relationships."[25] The idea of the confessional state, or the established Church, was reduced to an historical anomaly or aberration, and was not a theological necessity Murray wrote borrowing language from the Declaration of Independence. In footnote 17 he wrote the "Council did not wish to canonize the institution" [26] though "A respectable opinion holds that establishment is always a threat to religious freedom. Furthermore, the Council wished to insinuate that establishment, at least from the Catholic point of view, is a matter of historical circumstance, not of theological doctrine. For all these reasons the text deals with the issue in conditional terms."[27]

It would not be Murray, and it would not be the Cold War if Communism was not attacked, so in footnote 19, which explained section 6 of *Dignitatis Humanae,* Murray wrote the Council condemned religious persecution but did so by couching the condemnation "in temperate terms and without naming the guilty. However, the reference to totalitarian regimes of Communist inspiration is unmistakable."[28]

Murray encapsulated his efforts in a short phrase written in an article in the December, 1966 issue of *Theological Studies* and entitled "The Issue of Church and State at Vatican Council II." He wrote "In any event, the statements in *Gaudium et spes,* like those in *Dignitatis humanae,* represent *aggiornamento*. And they are programmatic for the future. From now on, the Church defines her mission in the temporal order in terms of the realization of human dignity, the promotion of the rights of man, the growth of the human family towards unity, and the sanctification of the secular activities of this world." [29]

"Sanctification of the secular activities of the world" did not mean changing them to be in accord with the law of God, but instead it meant approving of them if they were American. This was the main thrust of the rest of his article in which he rehashed the arguments he made over the years such as: Leo XIII only dealt with the Liberalism of Continental Europe; that historical contingencies lead to the "religiously pluralist society" and that freedom of the Church was the essential principle of Catholic doctrine that became clear in light of this historical development; that the confessional state was merely a "matter of historical circumstances, and not a matter....of doctrine"; that the meaning of "religion" in the various papal encyclicals of Leo XIII meant all religions and not just the Catholic religion; that secular governments of the day did not have to power to make judgments in "matters of theological truth"; and that Pius XII set out a political doctrine that supported or endorsed constitutional and limited government.[30]

However, as Murray admitted, Pius XII spoke of constitutional systems providing "protection and promotion of the rights of man and the facilitation of the performance of man's native duties."[31] The pope recognized that man had rights and duties, and it was this important concept that was present in *Dignitatis Humanae* and served to preserve in reality Catholic doctrine on the necessity of the confessional state. Murray would have none of that, and the boldness of his statements carried the day for a long while influencing the comments of Pope Benedict XVI nearly 40 years later, who as Joseph Ratzinger was a peritus at the Council. The Church took a step towards eliminating the American hermeneutic and lessening Murray's influence with the publication of Dominican Austin Flannery's book containing the documents of the Vatican II Council, but that took another nine years during a very crucial period when the so-called reforms of the Council were implemented throughout the Church. The Preface of the volume, which received the *Imprimatur* of Bishop Walter Kellenberg, was penned by John Cardinal Wright. He stressed the necessity of the Flannery book as initial versions of the Conciliar documents suffered from "hasty" translations, "frequent infelicities," "inaccuracies," and contained "the journalistic touch." The Flannery version had an "air of permanence, completeness and academic thoroughness" which came about as a result of "sober second thoughts and carefully measured words." Unlike the earlier translations, the Flannery volume did not contain "commentary or reactions" that were "frequently irrelevant and even confusing to one seeking to learn exactly what the Council *said* rather than what someone outside the Council *thought* about the matter." The Flannery version was "*the* collection of Council documents and their authentic interpretation that is indispensable for the serious student" as well as scholars and it was long "overdue."[32]

CHAPTER 118
DIGNITATIS HUMANAE

" **A**mericans Defeated at Vatican II," "Frankie Connell Beats Murray, the New York Honk," or, "Error Loses to the Holy Ghost, or the Holy Spirit as He is Known These Days." Those could have been the headlines of any newspaper after the Vatican II Council ended on December 8, 1965, which was the day after *Dignitatis Humanae* was promulgated by Pope Paul VI. They would have conveyed the truth of what happened at the Council. After about twenty years of a global ideological conflict between the Americans with their massive media and governmental apparatus against a few faithful Catholic souls with the help of the Holy Spirit and Truth, the Catholics won. They won on three crucial points.

DIVINE POSITIVE LAW, NOT THE NATURAL LAW

The first point was an issue of doctrine and went to the heart of the question of the proper basis of organization of society and the proper basis of public policy in a society. The Council decided that civil authorities had to comply with the divine positive law and not just the natural law. Murray had since 1948, argued that the state or civil authorities or government had only to comply with the natural law. The American Proposition was based on a vague notion of the natural law. Fr. Francis "Frankie" Connell, who never grew gloomy or lost his cool and who ever kept the Faith, presented Catholic doctrine as set out in papal encyclicals, tradition and the Scriptures that the state or civil authorities or government had to comply with the divine positive law. The Council Fathers made clear that all civil authorities had to follow the divine positive law, and they clearly did so in two documents. The first was in the Decree[1] on the Means of Social Communications or *Inter Mirifica,* where in paragraph 6 the Council proclaimed the following:

"The Council proclaims that all must accept the absolute primacy of the objective moral order. It alone is superior to and is capable of harmonizing all forms of human activity....Only the moral order touches man in the totality of his being as God's rational creature, called to a supernatural destiny. If the moral order is fully and faithfully observed, it leads man to full perfection and happiness."[2]

The second instance was found in the Declaration[3] on Religious Liberty, or *Dignitatis Humanae* in which it was stated the truth that "the highest norm of human life is the divine law itself – eternal, objective and universal, by which God orders, directs and governs the whole world and the ways of the human community according to a plan conceived in his wisdom and love."[4]

Fr. Connell asked Rome for a statement to this effect in July, 1959[5] in response to Cardinal Tardini's inquiry of topics for the upcoming council. He sent letters to Cardinal Ottaviani and Apostolic Nuncio Vagnozzi over the years for a public condemnation of Murray's false doctrine, and in August, 1964, while Murray had the full weight of the American media and US bishops behind him, Connell again made sure to tell Vagnozzi there needed to be made mention of the need for the civil authorities to conform to the divine positive law in the schema on religious liberty. His steady, faithful work bore fruit.

Gus Weigel's September 27, 1960 "double life" speech,[6] essential for Catholics to serve the plutocrats without bringing the divine positive law to bear on their decisions and the policies of the state, was repudiated. Catholics were to bring the divine positive law to public policy as that was part of their life if they chose to serve in government. *Dignitatis Humanae* said all who embrace the "Christian faith…give it practical expression in every sphere of their lives."[7] And in reference to Scripture, the Declaration said "At the same time they were not afraid to speak out against public authority when it opposed God's holy will: `We must obey God rather than men'…This is the path which innumerable martyrs and faithful have followed through the centuries all over the world.[8]

AMERICA AND LIBERAL SOCIETIES REJECTED AS THE IDEAL

Secondly, the Council rejected America, and all Liberal societies, as the ideal of social organization, and with that rejection came the rejection of religious liberty (both in its practical application and in its theoretical or theological foundations) as defined by America and Liberal societies.

This was a natural consequence of the first point set out above, and it was a vindication of the Four Erroneous Propositions given to Msgr. Fenton and Fr. Connell in October, 1954.[9] The state is to recognize or establish the Catholic Church in law as the preferred Church of the society, and the state is to protect the faith and the Church from harm. The Catholic confessional state is the goal or the ideal for social organization, and it arises from a society's commitment to the divine positive law. The teachings of Pope Leo XIII set out in *Immortale Dei, Libertas,* paragraph 6 of *Longinqua Oceani,* and the requirements placed on societies by virtue of the doctrine of Christ the King which was presented by the teachings of Pius XI were endorsed as the ideal. *Dignitatis Humanae* made this clear: "religious freedom…leaves intact the traditional Catholic teaching on the moral duty of individuals and of societies towards the true religion and the one Church of Christ."[10]

That true religion and the one Church of Christ was the Catholic Faith: "God himself has made known to the human race how men by serving him can be saved and reach happiness in Christ. We believe that this one true religion continues to exist in the Catholic and Apostolic Church, to which the Lord Jesus entrusted the task of spreading it among all men when he said to the apostles: 'Go therefore and make disciples of all nations baptizing them in the name of the Father and of the Son and of the Holy Spirit, teaching them to observe all that I have commanded you' (Mt. 18[sic: 28]:19-20)."[11]

It was on this second major point, this second victory for the Catholics, that much of *Dignitatis Humanae* dwells. The Council recognized that they were doing their work at a period in history when most if not all of the societies of the world were organized in accordance with basic laws or constitutions. The US, the USSR, the People's Republic of China all had constitutions that essentially said similar things and that these things came from some vision of the nature of humanity and from some variation of the philosophy of the Enlightenment. The Council therefore sought a principled way of establishing Catholic doctrine in the variety individual societies that existed in the world. Many of those societies were pluralistic.

The Council Fathers explained this situation by writing that "contemporary man" was demanding "freedom in human society" as he was "becoming increasingly conscious of the dignity of the human person" and that "more and more people are demanding that men should exercise fully their own judgment and a responsible freedom."[12] The Church was addressing the historical situation, one which the American media and the US Government played no small role in making known, if not also creating. However, the Council made clear in the area of religious liberty that man had not only rights, but that he had rights and duties, which was something the American Declaration of Independence and First Amendment did not recognize. Religious freedom, as understood by Catholicism (and not by the Americans), received constitutional protection to enable humans to exercise rights and duties. This included seeking and attaining truth and then implementing it within society. It also meant protecting the common good as discussed herein.[13] Constitutionally protected religious freedom was supposed to advance the "highest of man's rights and duties – to lead a religious life."[14]

Catholic religious liberty is different from American religious liberty, and *Dignitatis Humanae* explained that difference. Given the state of the world, it was time to explain that difference. The Declaration's stated purpose was to "develop the teaching of recent popes on the inviolable rights of the human person and on the constitutional order of society."[15] There were three aspects to this. The first was the relation of the Church to the state. The second was the individual person's freedom from being impeded or compelled in doing certain religious acts. The third was freedom from meddling by the government in the internal governance and determination of doctrine of religious groups. It was a balancing of the various interests to permit a greater good – the protection and advancement of the common good – to be advanced in societies around the globe. The common good was defined[16] in cI, s6, p1 with the key terms being a "fuller measure of perfection with greater ease" thereby signifying those conditions which help one to seek truth, which is a duty under the Declaration, and to live truth, which is another duty established by the Declaration. Therefore, individual rights and freedoms were not absolute and the greater good – the common good – was superior, as discussed herein.

Dignitatis Humanae was a restatement, with greater detail, of the Catholic historical policies set forth by Cardinal Ottaviani to the assembled diplomats in his March, 1953 speech. Ottaviani addressed the issue of the Church's two different policies: one for when the Catholics were in the majority in a society and the other when they were not. The former called for the confessional state with a duty to protect only Catholicism, and the latter advocated a right to tolerance or "equality of cults." He explained a multiplicity of cults is a situation that arose as a result of "free thinkers," "multiple religious professions" as well as the pre-eminence of private judgment. In such a situation where "the exclusiveness of its mission is not recognized," or the rights of God are ignored, the Church speaks of toleration, equality, and the rights of man. In all other situations, it speaks of God's rights.[17]

Dignitatis Humanae defined religious freedom: "the human person has a right to religious freedom. Freedom of this kind means that all men should be immune from coercion on the part of individuals, social groups and every human power so that, within due limits, nobody is forced to act against his convictions, nor is anyone to be restrained from acting in accordance with this convictions in religious matters in private or in public, alone or in associations with others."[18]

The Catholic understanding of religious freedom is that it is an immunity from coercion by the state, or civil authority, or any other human being, "in civil society" (that excludes "within the Church" or by Christ who said those who do not believe are damned, a very important distinction). It does not confer a moral right on persons to believe and act as they please as Fr. Connell repeatedly explained to the prelates. Fr. Connell's voice can be heard again in *Dignitatis Humanae* where it is written "the right to religious freedom has its foundation not in the subjective attitude of the individual but in his very nature."[19] Man has the right to be free from this kind of coercion, but he is to use that freedom responsibly to seek the truth, and once finding it to adhere to the truth.

Sections 3, 4, and 5 discussed specifics. The Council set forth the meaning of religious freedom when it came to the individual (section 3), the religious / faith group (section 4), the family (section 5), and then society at large (section 6). The discussions in sections 3, 4, 5, 6 are merely a more detailed discussion of what the Church has always held which is that the civil authorities do not have the right to meddle in religious matters (e.g., matters of doctrine, matters of church governance) nor do they have the right to compel belief or acceptance of religious tenets (e.g., forced conversions, oaths rejecting certain beliefs or duties) nor to impede one's decisions in the religious realm nor to interfere with a family's religious training by that family.

Specific acts are approved and specific acts are disapproved, therefore all in the interest of protecting society which is a creation of the natural law if not also the divine law, and therefore all in the interest of protecting the faithful which is in the interest of the divine law. Certain acts of the individual pursuit of truth are recognized as acceptable and these are "free enquiry with the help of teaching or instruction, communication and dialogue" (cI, s3, p2) and certain "private and public acts of religion" are in keeping with man's social nature are allowable. (cI, s3, p4) Religious communities could therefore publicly teach and bear witness to "their beliefs by the spoken or written word" (cI, s4, p4), demonstrate the "special value of their teachings for the organization of society and the inspiration of human activity" (cI, s4, p5) and "hold meetings" of "educational cultural, charitable and social organizations." (cI, s4, p5) However, they may not do things that "suggest coercion" or are "dishonest or unworthy persuasion especially when dealing with the uneducated or the poor." (cI, s4, p4) The exercise of religious freedom, is subject to review as comporting with the common good and with the concept of the public order which is more fully explained in cI, s7, p3.

Section 7 sets out the limits of religious freedom so as to protect society from its abuse. There are limits: "In availing of any freedom men must respect the general moral principle of personal and social responsibility: in exercising their rights individual men and social groups are bound by the moral law to have regard for the rights of others, their own duties to others and the common good of all."[20]

Knowing that the Catholic Faith and the Catholic Church are established by Christ, men cannot threaten or shake that faith as held by others, nor can they harm the church or the existence of both in society. To do so would be to harm all of society. The common good is what is at stake and that is "the sum total of those conditions of social life which enable men to achieve a fuller measure of perfection with greater ease."[21] Since the Council Fathers at the start of *Dignitatis Humanae* reaffirmed "traditional Catholic teaching on the moral duty" of individuals and societies to the Catholic Church and the Faith, these restrictions on religious liberty are personally in accord with Catholic doctrine or teachings and cannot be contrary to such. And, most importantly, Catholics were called to work for, institute, and defend the confessional state.

The Council subtly re-iterated that all societies are to be organized on the divine positive law, which is Catholic doctrine, and that other viewpoints on organizing society could be considered, but were not to be given equal weight though they could be considered: "The right of religious groups not to be prevented from freely demonstrating the special value of their teaching for the organization of society and the inspiration of all human activity."[22]

Chapter II of the Declaration set forth the theological basis for religious freedom. Religious freedom, unlike the American and Liberal understanding of the term, was not based on a subjective intent of the individual. It was something that was granted theologically for the purpose of the individual to find and live truth freely and purely.

Chapter II restated Church doctrine that forced conversions were not allowed. It also made clear, in accordance with Fr. Connell's advice to Vagnozzi in an August, 1964 letter that the right being protected by the state was a physical right not a moral right, ended up in the document:

"God calls men to serve him in spirit and in truth. Consequently they are bound to him in conscience but not coerced....For Christ... [did] not...coerce....He did indeed denounce the unbelief of his listeners but he left vengeance to God until the day of judgment. When he sent his apostles into the world he said to them: 'He who believes and is baptized will be saved; he who does not believe will be condemned.' (Mk. 16:16)."[23]

The Declaration set forth Church policies based on Catholic doctrine and proper theology defining religious liberty in the Catholic understanding of the term: "In consequence, the principle of religious freedom makes no small contribution to the creation of an environment in which men can without hindrance be invited to the Christian faith, embrace it of their own free will, and profess it effectively in their whole manner of life."[24]

Fr. Connell saw a declaration on religious liberty as good policy, provided, he told Vagnozzi in an August 20, 1964 letter, that the policy or declaration: "be theologically correct, in full conformity with the teachings of the Catholic Church…We cannot conceal or modify the revealed truths Jesus Christ established only one religion and one Church that He commanded all human beings to join that church and that the Catholic Church of today is the same Church that was established by the Son of God two thousand years ago."[25]

Fr. Connell understood that policy must always protect doctrine, and that policy can change over time as the situation changes. That is the very nature of a policy and that is the very definition, as alluded to above, of a "Declaration". Fr. Connell saw a benefit to adopting this policy as he said that such a policy would make the Church "more effective in it mission nowadays" and a "world-wide policy of religious liberty, adduces as an argument the promotion of peaceful relations and concord throughout the human race" as Pius XII suggested in *Ci riesce*.[26] Fr. Connell had good reason for holding to this and the episcopacy had high hopes too given that the Church in 1964 was still strong given the large number of "baby-boomers" in the US and its notable presence in so many countries of the world.

The Council Fathers adopted Fr. Connell's view. The Declaration's statement on religious freedom had a "further purpose and aim, namely, that men may come to act with greater responsibility in fulfilling their duties in community life."[27] They held "it is necessary that religious freedom be everywhere provided with an effective constitutional guarantee and that respect be shown for the high duty and right of man freely to lead his religious life in society."[28] It was a moral means to a moral end, and it was in accordance with the natural law, the divine positive law, Church history, and Church doctrine. The Church in America appeared strong even as late as 1965, and so the thought was that by accepting a policy of religious liberty as set out in the Declaration, which was not inconsistent with American style religious liberty, the Church would benefit. It was a reasonable belief at the time, but the times changed quickly and the entire society became toxic very quickly.

One final point on this major victory for the Catholics. The reference to "circumstances of a particular people" giving "special civil recognition…to one religious community [i.e., church] in the constitutional organization of a State"[29] whether it is taken to refer to Catholic states or not, certainly also applies to Protestant countries such as England and the Scandinavian countries with their state established Churches. In any event, there was not a call for the disestablishment of the established church. There was simply a call for the religious freedom for other groups as expressly explained in the Declaration. Further, this reference does not abrogate any duties of Catholics to comply with the common good and to order society in accordance with the divine positive law, the latter which would result in the establishment of the Catholic Church and the Catholic religion as the state's religion as discussed above and more fully set forth in the papal encyclicals as previously discussed.

REJECTION OF ANGLO-AMERICAN POLITICAL PHILOSOPHY

The third Catholic victory was that the Anglo-American political philosophy Murray and the Americans wanted the Council to canonize so badly was rejected, condemned by the Council. Points one and two as discussed above made sure of that, and the Council elsewhere made sure to refute the errors contained in the First Amendment with its ideas that government must be limited to allow powerful private interests to govern society through inordinate influence.

Inter Mirifica clearly set forth the role of the state or civil authorities in making sure that the moral order, or the divine positive law, was followed by the practitioners of the means of social communication.[30] *Gaudium Et Spes,* the "Pastoral Constitution[31] on the Church in the Modern World," placed affirmative duties on the state when it came to protecting the culture:

"...culture must be subordinated to the integral development of the human person, to the good of the community and of the whole of mankind. Therefore one must aim at encouraging the human spirit to develop its faculties of wonder, of understanding, of contemplation, of forming personal judgments and cultivating a religious, moral and social sense....

"All this demands that man, provided he respects the moral order and the common interest, is entitled to seek after truth, express and make known his opinions....

"The scope of public authority extends, not to determining the proper nature of cultural forms, but to building up the environment and the provision of assistance favorable to the development of culture...one must avoid at all costs distorting culture from its proper purposes and its exploitation by political or economical forces."[32]

The civil authorities had to keep the plutocrats from determining culture and that meant a system of organization different than the First Amendment's free speech and free press.

IN SUM

Murray, Americanists, and the American media blatantly lied about what transpired at the Vatican II Council. They lied about the meaning of *Dignitatis Humanae* and they hid the significance of *Inter Mirifica* as well as of other relevant Council documents. Claims by Catholics that *Dignitatis Humanae* is a break with Catholic tradition and the Catholic Faith is a failure to understand or is a failure of faith. Since the documents of the Council were in epideictic style, since they relied on people understanding the fullness of the Faith to begin with so as to properly understand the documents, since the documents were not clear statements of the faith, and since many people simply did not have as deep an understanding of the Faith as they needed to understand these documents, there was much room for misunderstanding and manipulation.

These things serve to fuel division in the Church, a perennial aim of its enemies. Many Catholics simply have not studied the documents of the Council and do not know about *Inter Mirifica* with the larger issues that are involved. Part of that is due to the machinations of some to focus on points of disagreement for their own purposes, and part of it is due to the conscious and continuing efforts of the Americanists to serve the plutocrats. To a certain extent, they were aided in this regard by the use of language that, at least in the English translations, could be spun to support arguments or meanings in contravention of those intended by the Council Fathers. And, in large measure, the study of theology was corrupted in large measure so it did not serve the bishops and the Church but instead it served the desires of the plutocrats, and still does.

Unfortunately, a great deal of blame is to be placed at the feet of the leadership of the Church, and that means the episcopacy. They did not correct Murray and his misinterpretation of *Dignitatis Humanae* nor did they correct the errors and the willful ignorance of many others in leadership roles in the Church. If you ask a bishop today if he has heard of *Inter Mirifica,* you are likely to get a blank stare. The prelates and priests do not know their own documents from the Council. As a result, the laity and others were mislead, confused, and given over to error and its spirit, "the Spirit of Vatican II". The laity and the peoples of societies around the globe suffered for all of this while the Church leadership was able to avoid suffering – at least for a while.

From *Inter Mirifica, Gaudium et Spes,* and *Dignitatis Humanae,* one can see the Council Fathers decisively discredited the idea that the First Amendment of the US Constitution set the ideal of social organization. The Council Fathers did not approve of as good in principle the political philosophy underlying the US, nor did it approve of the American ideology underlying that society and represented in The American Proposition. The Council did not mandate Catholic societies and countries conform themselves to America. Indeed, the Council reiterated the Church's condemnation of Liberalism or the ideology underlying America.

Catholics have not been properly catechized about their faith, the significance and real meaning of the Council, and the context in which all of this happened. It is here in the pages of this book that for the first time Catholics, and the peoples of the world, can come to a better understanding of the context and issues addressed by the Vatican II Council. In the pages of this book, we can begin to understand the importance and necessity of properly organizing society to give the Triune God His rights.

PART XXII
AFTER VATICAN II

CHAPTER 119
THE CHURCH DESCENDS INTO ANARCHY

Msgr. George A. Kelly described in his book, *The Battle for the American Church,* the situation in the Catholic Church after Vatican II. Writing less than twenty years after the end of the Council, Kelly's observations led him to conclude Catholics came to accept the "stereotypes about the Church that were first invented by the Church's enemies." This in turn led to the formation of "political parties" within the Church that rallied "for or against the values favored or ridiculed by the stereotypes." The natural consequence of this was division within the Church that was made plain for all to see, and also legitimacy was given to the "public debate about the meaning and finality of Catholic doctrine."[1] Kelly effectively described the absorption of the Catholic Church into the American Empire. The Church became American.

INTERNAL STRIFE

The Catholic Church started the descent into anarchy before the end of Vatican II. After the Council, the process picked up speed notwithstanding the statement of Pope Paul VI on January 12, 1966

377

that the "Council…avoided any extraordinary statements of dogmas endowed with the note of infallibility" as it was "of the pastoral nature." The "mind of the Council" pertained to certain "aims of each document" and the faithful were to accept the "authority of the Ordinary Magisterium…with docility."[2]

In January, 1965, *Time* declared the Protestants were gaining ground in Italy. The 1929 Concordat between the Vatican and Mussolini's Italy reduced Protestant growth in Italy, but things were changing a generation later. The magazine remarked on how the unification of Italy brought in Baptists and Methodists, while the Cold War campaigns against the Communists lead to the excommunication of Catholics who then joined the Protestant ranks. *Time* stated that "Nowadays, Protestants face nothing worse than occasional bureaucratic delays in getting permission to build churches."[3]

France was in turmoil due to anxieties roused among conservative Roman Catholics by the "current reforms." The French "church has been sharply divided into progressive and conservative wings since the Revolution." The *integristes* and the "reforming spirit" of the council were at odds. *Time* claimed that the *integristes* were against Communism and so viewed the likes of Congar as a Marxist. Many *integristes* were threatening to leave the church "rather than accept the liberal definitions of religious liberty and the church in the modern world that the Vatican Council will probably approve this fall." Indeed, it was reported that a "silent schism" was ongoing in the Church.[4]

In "How Vatican II Turned the Church Toward the World," *Time* assessed the Council and its effect on achieving the American objective of making the Church like America sociologically while having the Church leadership endorse American principles. The political, almost American democracy like discussions and struggles between the bishops from the various parts of the world representing constituencies with different interests and needs produced a wide range of documents. The assessment was mixed with "substandard" and "mediocre" decrees and declarations. One of the "worst is a decree on mass communications [*Inter Mirifica*] which implies the right of governments to censor the press; hardly better is the declaration On Christian Education which is little more than a cliché-ridden defense of parochial schools." *Time* found the Declaration On Religious Liberty disappointing because of language that "insists that all men have a duty to embrace Catholicism once they recognize its truthful claims, and argues that the church has always professed liberty of conscience – which ignores several centuries of the Inquisition." The Declaration on Non-Christian Religions was also disappointing because it "omits what might have given it maximum moral impact – a phrase acknowledging the church's role in fostering anti-Semitism in previous centuries."

Finally, Catholics, according to *Time,* were disappointed that Vatican II "did not settle pressing ethical issues – most notably, birth control.[5]

However, there still existed the potential for changes in Church teaching and in the Church itself. The seed of this hope for the Americans was the "theology, dominated by a textbook scholasticism" seemed to be on retreat and the churchmen had "found fresh, nontraditional language that escaped from what Italian Bishop Jolando Nuzzi calls 'the Western mortgage' on scholastic theology." Perhaps of great significance was the "atmosphere and attitudes" had changed drastically in the Church. The decree "On Ecumenism" committed Catholics to working for Christian unity and "for the first time acknowledges Protestant bodies as churches that share God's grace and favor." Also, *Dignitatis Humanae* said religious liberty was "the right of all men to freedom of conscience in worship" while anti-semitism was condemned in another decree.[6]

The greatest hope for the Americans and their allies in the Church lay with the future. The language of some of the various documents, most notably the document known as *On Divine Revelation*, "tries to avoid any uncertain declaration, and thus leaves room for further research and dialogue" according to German Redemptorist Bernard Haring. A "new understanding of the nature of the Church" emerged from the Council. This new understanding, according to Archbishop Eugene D'Souza as quoted by *Time,* was largely a new approach to the world. That new approach "is one of sincere admiration, not of dominating it but of serving it, not of despising it but of appreciating it, not of condemning it but of strengthening and saving it." There was a "positive appreciation of terrestrial values in themselves." According to Bishop Joseph Blomjous of Tanzania, the Church was to enter into a "permanent state of dialogue – dialogue with itself for a continuous renewal; dialogue with our Christian brothers in order to restore the visible unity of the body of Jesus Christ; dialogue, finally, with today's world, addressed to every man of good will."[7]

The proponents of change in the Church were going to wait out their opponents who had tried to limit or stop the spirit of rebellion. Quoting "Jesuit Scholar John McKenzie," *Time* held that there "will be little reform until the death of the present incumbent" in many dioceses. And "the council's impact will not be felt until a reform of church seminaries and schools produces a new generation of priests and laymen." As if to warn Catholics not to return to the ways and attitudes that the Council changed, *Time* commented that since the Reformation "the church reacted badly to the loss of its claim to be God's only spokesman and clung to its shrunken patrimony of power in ways that justified the exasperation of those who stood outside it." So "the church returns in spirit to the unfettered simplicity of the Gospel from which it sprang, the more likely it is that its voice will be heeded again by the world."[8]

The first and most important country to begin to feel the effects of Vatican II was Spain. *Time* called it "The Awakening Land" and credited "affluence and mobility" for changes to "the Spaniard's habits." These changed economic conditions were the result of "thousands of new enterprises" and foreign investment pouring into the country thereby ending its "long years of isolation and decay." All of this started in July, 1959 when Commerce Minister Alberto Ullastres "announced a sweeping stabilization plan. Credit was tightened, the budget slashed, the peseta devalued to a realistic 60 to the dollar. With the aid of a $400 million international loan, Ullastres threw open Spain's doors to imports necessary to rebuild its economy. And over the howls of government protectionists, he pushed through a series of measures to encourage foreign investors to enter Spain." The result was to make Spain the "fastest-growing nation in Europe" which was "rapidly changing the structure of its society" at a time that "coincided with a vast surge in the living standards of the rest of Western Europe."[9]

Concurrently, the Spanish government was involved in pushing through legislation that would "grant religious freedom and end censorship." *Time* editorialized not surprisingly by noting "Both, if passed, will be a step in the right direction" but both bills were being slowed down in ministries and committees. "The religion bill, pushed by Foreign Minister Fernando Maria Castiella to wipe away the image of religious intolerance that has hurt Spain since the Inquisition, would permit the nation's tiny non-Catholic minority (5,000 Jews and 30,000 Protestants) to build their own houses of worship – which in practice, they are already doing." Spain wanted to keep its economy expanding, *Time* wrote, and to "restore itself as Latin America's godfather." Spanish relations with Latin American countries were strong despite Communism, and the Spaniards serviced the "growing Latin American market".[10] The message sent was, jettison the confessional state and live well.

Time turned the Church against the government of Spain by citing Vatican II and targeting the youth. In May, 1966 a "bloody police attack on 120 black-robed priests in Barcelona…. erupted when the priests staged a march protesting alleged police brutality in connection with anti-government student unrest at Barcelona University." *Time* quoted a Father Laurel who said "We are now aware that to follow the principles of the Gospel and of the Vatican Council to their utmost meaning in our country, one may come under the definition of 'unlawfulness.' But this does not frighten us. Jesus Christ was the first to go against the law – against the law of the Caesars, of the Jews and of occupying powers."[11]

This was all indicative, according to *Time*, of a far deeper problem: "the roots of the trouble went far deeper – to the core of the Catholic Church in Spain." This core struggle was "between a rising new generation of social-minded priests and the elderly, hidebound church hierarchy bent on maintaining a cautious and comfortable status quo." *Time* inserted the idea into the Catholic mind that "over the years the Spanish church – in the pay and shadow of the Franco government – has drifted out of touch with almost everything it stands for. Its religion has become one that is imposed rather than preached." The Church in Spain therefore strove to "identify ourselves with the people, their frustrations and their fulfillment."[12]

BEING NICE

The Holy Office accepted John XXIII's command to use the "medicine of mercy" and not condemn. Shortly after the end of the Council, Ottaviani had a discussion with Fr. Rosendo Roig, SJ, of *Ya* magazine, the Madrid Catholic Daily. He said "Catholics – priests and laymen – who feel themselves called to the apostolate of criticism are carrying out a dismal mission, indeed an anti-Christian one." When asked by Roig if the two of them had a dialogue, Ottaviani would say "Yes, yes, yes...dialogue, a beautiful word. I like it. State the truth in the press. Say we had a dialogue." When asked about Spain he said that "it can contribute toward the progressive idea of the Church, as it is `a great Catholic nation, a rue hope and reality of the Church.'"[13]

A couple of days later Ottaviani was interviewed by Msgr. S. J. Adamo of the *Catholic Star Herald* of Camden, New Jersey. When asked if he thought that the Council would "push the Church forward," Ottaviani replied "Yes." Adamo reported that Ottaviani was pleased with the schema on the Church and the priesthood but he was concerned about the growing boldness of laity as they may overreach to dominate the clergy. He also said that as to ecumenism "care would have to exercised lest it lead to indifferentism."[14]

In the Spring of 1966, Ottaviani presented a more positive view of the Church with the establishment of the Doctrinal Congregation. It "represented...the abolition of the inquisitorial and repressive character" of the Holy Office, which it replaced. And, "Indeed, the

Doctrinal congregation assumes a propelling character, because his job is to promote studies, discussions and cultural works concerning Catholic doctrine."[15]

This dynamic was part of a change in tone from the Catholic Church. During the course of the discussions at the Council, the main emphasis was on the pastoral by the so-called progressives. That meant presenting things a certain way, a different way, than how Catholic teachings may have been presented in the past. The pastoral came to mean a change in genre. However, as Ottaviani said, the "pastoral could not be separated from doctrinal."[16] It involved a "new style of discourse" that was

"best exemplified in the four constitutions of the council....The genre can be precisely identified. It was a genre known and practiced in many cultures from time immemorial, but it was clearly analyzed and its features carefully codified by classical authors like Aristotle, Cicero, and Quintilian. It is the panegyric, that is, the painting of an idealized portrait in order to excite admiration and appropriating. An old genre in the rhetorical tradition of the West, it was used extensively by the fathers of the Church in their homilies and other writings. It derives from neither the legal tradition of classical antiquity nor the philosophical/dialectical but from the humanistic or literary."[17]

The genre of the Council documents was epideictic which "changed the ethos, purpose, and content of preaching there, moving it from its medieval and Scholastic form to something quite different. The appropriation of the epideictic genre redefined what a sermon was supposed to do: rather than proving points it was now to touch hearts and move hearers to action for their fellow human beings. Like any good oration, these, of course, 'taught,' but in a different mode than did the Scholastic sermons." The style of the Vatican II documents was to "heighten appreciation for a person, an event, an institution, and to excite emulation of an ideal," and they were "not so much to clarify concepts."[18]

Ottaviani failed to understand how the epideictic style served American purposes and advanced the American ideology. With terms not clarified, one could read into the documents whatever one wanted or found pleasing. Since not everyone operated in good faith, the enemies of the Church had valuable weapons to use on Catholics and the Church. The documents were twisted to assume an American worldview. Catholics came to believe they had to adapt to the modern world to keep their message relevant. This was a sure sign of the Americanism condemned by Leo XIII. The evidence of this was the drastic loss of the faithful and of vocations since 1965.

CONTRACEPTION, CONCESSIONS, CONFUSION

Fr. Gregory Baum, OSA, was a theologian and peritus at the Council who wrote an article on how the Church was changing its positions on several points. With "crucial and vital"[19] change in the doctrine of religious liberty came the belief that the Church could change in other areas, and theologians and churchmen started to push for changes. This dynamic was exacerbated by the evident weakness of the episcopacy and the complicity of the Catholic press in fanning the flames of dissent. "From my rather desultory reading of the Catholic press," Fenton wrote to Msgr. Shea, "I would say that our leadership is somewhat weak. Gregory Baum is sounding off at will, and to the disedification of any who are silly enough to take him seriously...."[20]

Fr. Connell fought for years to maintain the Catholic position on contraception, beginning with an October, 1939 article in *The Atlantic Monthly*.[21] Ten years later, Connell repeated these key arguments in talks that he gave to adults about the need to properly instruct their children.[22] Fr. John A O'Brien was one of many priests leading the charge for change. He wrote an article in *Look* magazine in 1961 entitled "Let's Take Birth Control Out of Politics." Connell critiqued O'Brien's position and sent the critique to Archbishop Vagnozzi, the Apostolic Delegate, with a cover letter in which Connell advised Vagnozzi of his knowledge of and friendliness towards O'Brien, who Connell said was "very zealous and devoted" and "done much good in the field of convert-making." However, Connell did not hold back in writing that O'Brien "is not familiar with the fine points of theology, and is inclined to make concessions on important matters, with a view to winning the good will of non-Catholics." As a result of a controversy regarding the "nature and the eternity of hell" years earlier, O'Brien had to retract "by ecclesiastical authority" his views. That was in August, 1935, "the last time," according to Connell "an American priest was required to make a public retractation [sic] for publishing error regarding faith or morals."[23]

Connell wrote he was "convinced that in the United States today there are many erroneous or ambiguous statements being made in regard to faith and morals, and I fear even that the way is being opened to heresy or schism." Connell's criticism of the O'Brien article consisted of several points. First, O'Brien used "freedom of conscience" and "rights of conscience" in a way "different from Catholic usage" by placing an erroneous conscience on the "same plane with a true conscience." Second, O'Brien was in error when he argued that laws against contraception are "beyond the competence of the civil authorities because contraception is a <u>private</u> sin" and that because "contraception is a <u>private</u> sin it cannot be a <u>public</u> crime." Third, O'Brien's claim that "legislation intended to prevent contraception <u>imposes</u> the religious views of some citizens on others; and he implies that this is wrong" must also fail. Connell explained the American form of government was based on the idea that the will of the majority was imposed on the minority and so O'Brien was criticizing the American system. O'Brien seemed to imply that the opposition to contraception came from the Church, and not from God's law. Fourth, O'Brien stated the "moral consensus" of the people may uphold certain bans on contraceptive availability. Connell pointed out O'Brien was advocating "that the consent of the people, not the law of God, determines morality, and that when the consensus changes there is a change in morality."[24]

Connell sent a copy of his critique to Bishop Leo Pursley, of the Diocese of Fort Wayne-South Bend. However, he did not intend it to be "a formal charge against Dr. O'Brien.....but he is not familiar with the fine points of theology, and I fear that at times in his desire to show charity toward non-Catholics, he is likely to make doctrinal concessions."[25] Pursley provided the following amazing response:

"I have known Father O'Brien for the past thirty-four years. When I was appointed Ordinary in 1956 I undertook to clarify his status in this diocese. He was indignant when I requested a copy of his papers of excardination from his native see and of his incardination in this diocese. We had nothing at all in our Chancery files concerning these matters. He was 'de facto' incardinated by my predecessor twenty years ago but he has operated in his own chosen field with almost total independence of his own bishop and with little or no indication that he has any obligation to his diocese. He is apparently not even aware of any irregularity in the situation. You will understand readily that, at this late date, there is little I can do to correct..... Father O'Brien leans heavily on his own sincerity and good intentions and this habit obviously shuts out of his view a number of other important considerations, canonical and otherwise."[26]

O'Brien reappeared the following year writing an article that stressed the need for unity, of the false ecumenical type. O'Brien was billed as a "research professor of theology at Notre Dame, a cochairman in the National Conference of Christians and Jews, and the author of more than a dozen books on theology, philosophy and science." He authored an article entitled "Can Christians Unite?" which was called "a question that has become more urgent than ever before in history." His article was consistent with the American effort to get Catholics to oppose Communism. "With Communism striving to complete its conquest of the world by pulling the remaining free nations behind its Iron Curtain," he wrote, "the need for Christians to unite is imperative. Unable to present a united front, we are losing one battle after another in the underdeveloped countries."[27]

During the Vatican Council, Connell corresponded with Fr. John Ford, SJ expressing great concern surrounding the push for a change in the Catholic position on birth control. In one letter Connell expressed concern: "You have probably learned from the papers the events of the Council in recent days. The impression has been given – and I fear with reason – that some are pushing for a radical change in the Church's stand on birth-control. That was apparently implicit in the speeches of Suenens, Leger and Maximos…..I respect the Pope's conscience, but I pray that he will soon speak firmly."[28]

Murray's efforts contributed to the Catholic prelates' public retreat on contraception because his work furthered the belief that there was something called public morality that could be separate from the moral law. He held that as long as the State did not positively affirm evil and did not positively restrict good, then Catholics should not have any objection to its laws. Hence, restrictions against contraception and abortion could be removed without Catholic protest because the State did not positively affirm these evils. Initially, Cushing fought the efforts to legalize, or at least, decriminalize, the selling of contraceptives. By the 1960s, he was no longer interested in maintaining the fight. Murray provided him in early 1965 with the necessary intellectual cover to justify Cushing's support for contraception or at least the Catholic surrender on the issue.

Murray's rationale for not opposing contraception consisted of two parts as his memorandum to Cushing shows. First, and primarily, Murray claimed that there was a distinction between public morality and private morality, and that public law was only to serve a "minimum of public morality" as such was a "social necessity." The extent of the public law was determined by the popular will, not by truth. "The people whose good is at stake," Murray wrote, "have a right of judgment with regard to the measure of public virtue that is to be enforced on them, and with regard to the manner of public evils that are to be repressed."[29]

A "minimum of public morality is a social necessity." Law exists to "safeguard the social order" and punish an "act or practice" that "seriously undermines the foundations of society or gravely damages the moral life of the community as such." Murray argued that "there must be a reasonable correspondence between the moral standards generally recognized by the conscience of the community and the legal statutes concerning public morality" so as to avoid making the laws "unenforceable and ineffective." This avoided creating resentment as "undue restrictions on civil or personal freedom." Sometimes, as in the racial equality laws, the "law may be 'ahead' of the public conscience," but in the "field of sex morality the public educative value of law seems to be almost nil" as it was "useless to attempt to suppress fornication, or even adultery, by law."[30]

In his quest to justify the conclusion sought and not in the quest for truth and goodness, Murray proceeded under the first point to justify why "public morality" should permit of the use and sale of contraceptives. First, Catholics were themselves divided on the issue. Second, the use of contraceptives is so widespread that "so many people do not consider it to be wrong." Third, the practice has received "official sanction by many religious groups within the community" who view it as being "undertaken in the interests of 'responsible parenthood.'" Therefore "numerous religious leaders approve as morally right" the use of contraceptives, and so to Murray this was "decisive from the point of view of law and jurisprudence." In the areas of law and jurisprudence the norm of "'generally accepted standards' is controlling." Finally, to Murray, even though contraception "raises an issue of public morality because it has public consequences," law cannot control these consequences, and any law attempting to do so would result in "other social evils."[31]

The second main argument that Murray presented dealt with religious freedom. Murray wrote that the "laws in restraint of the practice [of contraception] are in restraint of religious freedom." The use of contraception is a matter of private morality, Murray told Cushing. To outlaw or restrict the use of contraception is a violation of conscience: "a man may not be coercively constrained to act against his conscience. Second, a man may not be coercively restrained from acting according to his conscience, unless the action involves a civil offense – against the public peace, against public morality, or against the rights of others."[32]

As far as the Church's public position on the pending legislation permitting the sale and use of contraception, Murray instructed Cushing that "issues of prudence" dictated the law "should be put through with as little public agitation as possible." He opposed anything that "stirs popular passions, raises false issues of power and prestige, and divides the community on a moral issue when it should be united on an issue of law and civil freedom." Instead, Catholics should make known "the grounds of their approval" which were "they, like all citizens are bound on the principles of law, jurisprudence, and religious freedom." Finally, Murray said that while contraception involves public morality, Catholics are to live by Church teaching in their private lives, and their decision to live in accordance with Church teaching is "adopted freely, out of personal conviction and in intelligent loyalty" to the Church.[33]

Publicly, according to Murray, the Church should exhort Catholics to "lift the standards of public morality...not by appealing to law and police action, but by the integrity of their Christian lives" while approving of the civil law permitting contraception as "a matter of civic conscience". Murray explained to Cushing the Church should make clear "from the standpoint of morality Catholics maintain contraception to be morally wrong." However, from their "understanding of religious freedom Catholics repudiate in principle a resort to the coercive instrument of law to enforce upon the whole community moral standards that the community itself does not commonly accept."[34] Murray sounded Catholic while gutting the Church's stance. It was a proven ability he had acquired and allowed the prelates to accept his positions which were essentially that might makes right.

As time went on, Murray lent more credence to the efforts to legalize contraception and change Church doctrine on it. In the *Catholic Chronicle* from May 5, 1967, Murray, billed as "a Vatican II expert," was quoted as saying "The Church reached for too much certainty too soon, went too far. Certainty was reached in the absence of any adequate understanding of marriage. This, many would hold – I would hold – is today no longer theologically tenable...It's also psychologically untenable. We're seeing a new systemization. The other was only theology; it wasn't dogma. It was system, not faith."[35]

Murray criticized the Church itself by saying that in the area of birth control prohibition "There was a little too much exuberance for a Church whose dynamism was not within the Christian faith itself but in classicism which had infiltrated into Christian faith. In itself it is not Christian but Platonic." But, like the "liturgy and obedience-authority," which at one point were viewed as "unquestioned," birth control could also be questioned, and changed, Murray intimated.[36]

Murray presented the Church's position on the immorality of birth control as something that the Church, as apart from God, was advocating. So, he said "'The problem of the world today is the problem of God....The Church is not the focus of interest today – but the issues of God, faith, revelation, belief, unbelief.'" This suggested there was a higher, and better, understanding of the issue than what the Catholic Church had to offer.[37]

Following his usual approach, Murray first claimed tradition could be maintained while allowing progress. Then he said that the majority wanted progress and the majority should rule as the majority is the determiner of what is right or wrong. He encouraged "reconciliation" or "discourse" which translated to surrender. Those who held birth control as immoral were "classicists" to Murray. The classicists infiltrated the Church and gutted the Christian faith. "There was a little too much exuberance for a Church whose dynamism was not within the Christian faith itself but in classicism which had infiltrated into Christian faith," he wrote. In fact the defenders were not "Christian but Platonic."[38]

Murray leaned towards legalizing abortion. In a June 21, 1967 letter written to answer a question posed by a Mrs. James Moran as to "what a baby is," Murray wrote the following incredible response: "The question that you ask – what is a baby – is certainly a valid one. But I am not one to judge what the answer should be."[39] Fred McDonald, Director of The Joseph Kennedy Jr. Foundation, invited Murray to the International Conference to be held September 6, 7, and 8, 1967. Sponsored by the Foundation and the Harvard Divinity School, the conference was, according to the Foundation, "to explore the impact of abortion on children and parents, particularly with reference to mental retardation." Dr. Samuel H Miller gave three reasons for Harvard's participation: "First, the ethical aspects of abortion have not yet been a sufficient part of the public discussions. Second, the complexity of the issue requires the cooperation of scholars from medicine, sociology, ethics, psychology, religion and law. Third, our ecumenical responsibilities require us to discuss all disagreements until we find mutually acceptable solution." Clergy, physicians, educators, legislators, members of the press, parents and civic group representatives were invited. Also a panel of public figures would "participate in the conference to correlate the academic discussion to current trends and attitudes. Among those planning to attend are John D. Rockefeller III, Whitney Young, Mitchell Ginsberg, Justice Abe Fortas, Carl Kaysen and Erwin Nathaniel Griswold."[40]

ASSESSMENTS

About the same time as Msgr. Kelly's assessment, Malachi Martin, summed up the state of the Catholic Church. He wrote "The Roman Catholic Church which used to present itself as the One, Holy, Catholic and Apostolic Church, appears now as a pluralistic, permissive, ecumenical, and evolutionary ecclesial group."[41] He described the result of the efforts of Murray, Luce, a number of Jesuits, and Phil Scharper, all of whom believed, or said they believed, that "both America and American Catholicism are built on the same beliefs, principles of natural law...."[42] America had conquered the Catholic Church. The Church came to see the world through American eyes as the "spirit of Vatican II" infused its leadership.

To the everyday Catholic, the noted dissident priest, Charles Curran, presented it quite well when he wrote that: "Catholics who hold that individual human life is present from conception could also argue against opposing *Roe v Wade*. Given the deep division in public opinion on the question of abortion, one could legitimately give the benefit of the doubt to individual freedom."[43] Freedom had come to exist on a par with truth and duty as a result of the Murray's work on *Dignitatis Humanae.* The theologians, as Curran admitted, had in fact "brought the Church up to date" (*aggiornamento*) which meant adopting the values of the dominant culture, America. [44] They used *ressourcement* to effectuate the break with the Faith and Catholic history.

America's elites were still working to make sure the Church lost all influence in society, too. An example was an article by J. Howard Pew in the May 1966 issue of the widely read *Reader's Digest.* Pew was the board chairman of Sun Oil Company and previously the president of the General Assembly of the United Presbyterian Foundation and chair of National Lay Committee of the National Council of Churches. He was clear and adamant that "Christ... refused to enmesh himself or his followers in the economic, social and political problems of the day." Authority for that was a misreading of Christ's admonition to the Pharisees to give to Caesar what is Caesar and to God what is God's.[45]

At around this time, Murray started to have doubts about the American experiment, in spite of the all of years he had spent arguing in its favor. "The thing we have not yet proved in the U.S.," wrote Murray to Wolf, "is that the social consensus, as at least moral, can be maintained in the absence of religious unity, sc., in the presence of radical divisions. There are signs that the consensus is eroding."[46]

CHAPTER 120

MURRAY CONTINUES ADVANCING AMERICAN INTERESTS

L ess than two years after the end of the Vatican II Council, Murray was being lionized by the Americanists, and yet had a sense of pessimism. "We have done something and time will tell the effects."[1] In a letter to Fr. Robert Tucci, SJ, editor of *Civilta Cattolica* in Rome in May, 1967, he wrote that "There is no doubt that we are all in trouble, but I courageously hope that it is a good kind of trouble."[2] The trouble was the bad kind of trouble. In advancing American objectives, Murray had spread chaos in the Church.

Murray lived to witness the unraveling of his own Jesuit institution all as part of that desire for "freedom in the Church" that he mentioned to Clare.[3] Gary Wills in a *Worldview* article explained the significance of the defeat of Murray's efforts to move Woodstock Theological School to Yale. After Murray lost that battle "all of Woodstock's academic apparatus was moved piecemeal into New York – faculty, students, library, and *Theological Studies* (old forum for the Murray thesis throughout a hot decade of liberal debate). In general the liberals were losing; radical young men took their old causes into the streets, turned their distinctions into protests, their carefully guarded praise of the secular into active politicking. They had brought it on themselves."[4]

Wills destroyed Murray's carefully created media image of himself as an academic and thinker and replaced it with a picture of Murray as servant of the plutocrats willing and eager to do their bidding:

"Prophets are not summoned; they come unbidden – and so they irrupted into Murray's postwar liberal world. These young disturbers of the ecclesiastical peace, once they began to doubt their liberal elders, found much to object to in their elders' world. Catholics, indeed, repeated the experiences of secular radicals, who discovered that much of their parents' liberal ventures had been financed by the CIA, or by interlocking elites from government, the academy, and foundations. 'Establishment' no longer meant for them, a State-endorsed Church, but this secular caste of 'clerks,' with the shared belief that American standards of 'self-determination' should be imposed on the rest of the world by coaxing or by judicious coercion.....Father Murray himself, often on call to deliver papers at foundation meetings, was this kind of cold warrior."[5]

Wills continued noting that "Much of youth's disillusionment in the late sixties came from the discovery that liberals were only the left wing of the Establishment, and that they conceived of no position leftward of their own as legitimate; and Catholic liberalism was even less venturesome than the nonreligious kinds.....It is no wonder that Father Murray's last pupils at Woodstock thought his brand of liberalism simply obsolete or irrelevant."[6]

The fires of Americanism were burning in the Catholic Church in the United States, and these fires soon spread around the globe. *Time* explained Americanism's tidal wave by quoting "Philosopher Michael Novak of Stanford," who said "the council 'demythologized' the Church." The Church "'was brought down to human size and seen in the context of real life'" by the media. The "evidence of elderly bishops openly challenging hallowed traditions inspired lay Catholics, young and old, to re-examine their faith on their own. In brief, the spirit of the council made membership in the church a matter of choice rather than inheritance." Added to that was the harsh reality of unfulfilled "too-high hopes for change in the church."[7]

The consequence was a "take-it-or-leave-it attitude toward church doctrine and discipline" as "more and more young members of the church are deciding for themselves whether or not a teaching is valid for them." *Time* wrote "Unlike the time before the council, when an alienated Catholic felt that his choices were to still his doubts or defect, many Catholics today feel free to deny or ignore doctrines and yet also count themselves good members of the church." *Time* proclaimed the birth of the cafeteria Catholic as one could be a good Catholic and hold a questioning attitude to "virtually every area of the church's life and discipline" including meat on Fridays and birth control.[8]

BREAKING DOWN BARRIERS

Towards the end of the Council in 1965, the American Unitarians gave Murray an award for "conspicuous service in the cause of religious liberty," a most "incongruous" award.[9] In 1966, Murray became a member of the Fordham Board of Trustees, and he became Director of the John LaFarge Institute. He grew more involved with dialogue between Catholics on one side and atheists and Marxists on the other.[10]

In a December 23, 1966 talk to the Religious Education Association in Chicago, entitled "The Ecumenical Revolution: Genesis, Challenge, Response," Murray said the ecumenical movement "was born again – in 1964, in consequence of the Vatican Council Decree on Ecumenism, Unitatis redintegratio. The movement now has a new scope, a new depth, an added seriousness, in consequence of... Roman Catholic commitment...."[11]

Murray discussed how ecumenism caused the Church to examine the relation with the Jews, the religions of the East and the atheists. Dialogue, which was always emphasized but never clearly defined, included the "affirmation that the proclamation of the Gospel today must be made from within history, not from above it, and must therefore be made in dialogue – in dialogue within the Church, among the Christian churches, between the Church and the Synagogue, between the People of God and the world which is increasingly choosing to be without God."[12] The "future of theological education lies with an ecumenical community of scholars – teachers and students," and the "ecumenical community must somehow become a presence in the secular university" given that society has become "secular."[13]

A meeting was held at the residence of John Dearden, Archbishop of Detroit on December 29, 1966 to discuss ecumenism. Murray met with Fr. Avery Dulles, SJ, Fr. Daniel J O'Hanlon SJ, Fr. Norris Clarke SJ, Fr. Patrick Reid OP, Fr. Richard Butler OP, and Msgr. William Baum executive director of the Bishops' Committee for Ecumenical and Interreligious affairs. (Fr. Ernan McMullen of the University of Notre Dame could not attend.) The group was to discuss "the possibility of initiating some program in the United States and to discuss the relationship of this program with the Bishops' Committee for Ecumenical and Interreligous Affairs."[14]

Murray attended a meeting in Rome three months earlier to discuss the plan or directorium on relations with non-believers, but the Americans were unhappy with the document.[15] The group did not like the term "non-believers" thinking that it was an "unhappy one" and so they would find another term after consulting with some of the "non-believers." The dialogue with the "non-believers" would be carried on at a level higher than the diocesan level, and should be "sponsored at the national level and should be restricted to participants to acknowledged competence." Murray supported that idea and all agreed that participants had to have more than just "good will." The group, according to Murray, should be "very flexible" and the American secretariat of the group should have the role of not only "gathering and providing information" but of "planning for some financial support."[16]

The Archbishop expressed the importance of involving the scientific community in the discussions and that a "great many research scientists are employed by industrial corporations rather than by universities, and that many of them are deeply interested in the relationship between religion and science." Murray, in the most notable moment, said "many business and industrial leaders are also deeply interested in these questions."[17]

Murray mentioned that there were a "number of non-believers who are engaged in the communications media, and especially…the phenomenon of the 'deracinated' Jew who retains a concern for ethical and religious values." The Archbishop's response was "we must go to these people where they live and work."[18]

The group agreed on a letter to Bishop John Carberry, Chairman of the Committee on Ecumenical and Interreligious Affairs, and Murray agreed to draft it.Murray placed both himself and the LaFarge Institute in a position of taking leadership of the dialogue with others, and this would require remuneration for the Institute.[19]

1967

In early 1967, the Episcopalians asked Murray to take part in Bishop Pike's heresy trial. The Presiding Bishop of the Episcopal Church wrote to Murray and asked "What is heresy? How should the Church define, detect and deal with it?" Murray wrote back that "the dynamism of…progress…is…freedom and not authority….The first function of authority is to foster the freedom of theological inquiry. This has not always been well understood in my own beloved Church."[20] As a result of putting freedom ahead of doctrine, Pike was cleared, and the Episcopalians discarded the idea of heresy.

Murray tried to clean up his legacy. In May,1967, Mrs. J. M. DeWine, writing a graduate thesis on JFK for Miami University, was analyzing JFK's Houston speech and noted that Theodore Sorensen's book on JFK "mentions your name in connection with his preparation of this speech. He says that he read the speech over the phone to you for your opinion," prompting DeWine to ask:

"Did you suggest any changes in the speech? Why? What was your opinion of the speech when you first heard it? To your knowledge, did any one else help Sorensen write this speech? What do you feel was the effect of this speech? Did it help Kennedy win the election? Do you feel it changed any of the minds of the people about Kennedy's religious influences? Did Kennedy say anything in this speech that might have offended the Catholic Church?"[21]

Murray responded in a letter dated two weeks later:

"I am afraid that I cannot be of much help to you. It is true that Sorensen did read to me over the phone the speech that President Kennedy gave in Houston. But it is so long ago that I do not remember any of the details. It may be that I did suggest some changes but I cannot remember what they were. I told Sorensen at the time that it was unfair to ask me for an opinion just on hearing the speech on the phone, but he was standing by the side of a plane just about to take off for Houston. My impression is that Sorensen wrote the speech himself. Undoubtedly it had an effect on its immediate audience and on others and was of assistance to Kennedy. At that, I should say that Kennedy was far more of a `separationist' that I am. In this connection you might look up William Buckley's review of a book by a man named Fuchs in a recent *New York Times* Sunday Book Review Section. He compares my views with Kennedy's on the school question."[22]

Fr. Hesburgh of Notre Dame invited Murray to participate in the 125th Anniversary celebration of the University in December, 1967. Murray was asked to give a paper during the symposium on "The University in a Developing World Society." The symposium was to be a discussion of "the role that knowledge must and will play in the development of a world society, the university and the life of the student, and the university as a major social institution in a developing world society." Hesburgh expressed hope LBJ would give an address. He concluded with the statement that "you will find Notre Dame a beautiful, vigorous, and congenial university" and that Murray's participation would insure the success of the celebration.[23] Murray declined the offer, explaining that "a hospital check-up…revealed that a heart condition of several years standing has begun to show some signs of deterioration. It is not serious, but the doctor has strongly advised me to curtail activities as much as possible."[24] Murray was wrong, it was serious, and Murray was dead within two months of the doctor's diagnosis.

CHAPTER 121
LUCE DIES, THE TRINITY DISSOLVES

"Oh, Jesus!" screamed Henry Luce as he slid to the floor in his bathroom at St Joseph's Hospital in Phoenix, Arizona. By the time the nurse got to him, he was dead. It was just after 3 a.m. on the morning of February 28, 1967.[1] Coincidentally, Luce's partner, Britton Hadden, who helped found Time, Inc. died on the same day thirty-eight years earlier. And even more coincidentally so, February 28 was the day in which the first issue of *Time* magazine started hitting the streets in 1923.

The first obituary came from *The New York Times,* which had always been Luce's competitor and which earlier in February broke the story of CIA covert operations involving a number of front organizations that for years looked as though they were legitimate operations by concerned American citizens.[2] The *Times* started running a series of stories, and this could only have worried Luce whose own *Time* magazine had for years worked closely with the intelligence agency, oftentimes doing things like providing CIA officers with journalistic credentials, propping up other magazines not doing so well, sharing information, and generally working hand-in-glove with the CIA.[3] This investigative reporting threatened to prove quite embarrassing to Luce, who two days before his death said he was too sick to play a round of golf – something unheard of for him.[4]

Alden Whitman, who prided himself on writing personalized obituaries, was the man who wrote Luce's obituary for *The New York Times*. Appearing the day after Luce died, Whitman hailed him as the creator of "the modern news magazine" and "restyled pictorial reporting." Luce as a result of his work "rose to a position of vast and pervasive economic, political and social influence and helped shape the reading habits, political attitudes and cultural tastes of millions" though he lived inconspicuously. The causes he espoused were "righteous" and the US had a "constitutional dependency on God."[5]

Time magazine did better, placing a stylized visage of Luce on the cover of its March 10, 1967 edition, the first time ever he made the cover. The editors wrote that from his missionary parents Luce "absorbed the Calvinist faith and the love of his homeland that were to influence his whole life." Tied closely with this patriotism and Calvinism was the document that has proven to be the tool of subjugation of societies through the reordering of these societies to Mammon – the US Constitution, and in particular the First Amendment. Luce "later said that he could never remember a time when he did not know all about the U.S. Constitution."[6]

The fabulous growth and reach of Luce's magazines – *Time, Fortune, Life, Sports Illustrated* – were recounted. *Time* was "full of innovations in journalism" while *Fortune* presented business as "drama, personalities and technology" because according to Luce, "America's great achievement has been business." *Life* came about to "see life" Luce said and to "be instructed," and what became known in shorthand as *SI* had the "largest initial circulation…in magazine history." [7]

In Luce, patriotism and journalism were joined. *Time* remarked how: "Between the founding of TIME and the day that its 2,295[th] issue appeared on the newsstands, Henry Luce built the world's largest, most influential publishing enterprise. `The magazines that bear his stamp,' said Lyndon Johnson last week, `are an authentic part of life in America.' As hundreds of tributes from the U.S. and foreign countries attested, the publications that Luce created and nurtured have also become a valued and trusted voice of America throughout the free world." [8]

Both the American Century and the American Proposition were not just promoting a political system but a "moral and spiritual undertaking based on universal principles and relevant to all mankind." [9] Luce's positions, and influence, on the course of history were summarized. The Depression was a result of "lack of business confidence" and so he broke with FDR's reforms which were directed at the working man and his family. Luce was an "interventionist" who with his article "The American Century," urged "full entry into the war" after which the US would "assume worldwide responsibilities." The Cold War was Luce's too as both *Time* and *Life* before the end of World War II "were warning their readers that the Russians were not to be trusted." Luce was "well-versed in theology" and was "comfortable with the works and ideas of Teilhard de Chardin, Bonhoeffer, Barth, Kung and Tillich." While a Presbyterian, he "frequently attended Mass," and "one of his closest friends was Jesuit John Courtney Murray." [10]

Murray gave a short eulogy for his deceased benefactor and friend, which showed his "deep devotion to Harry." [11] No records of that eulogy remain in Murray's papers. After a memorial service in the Madison Avenue Presbyterian Church that was piped to a number of locations for the benefit of the Time/Life workers, Harry was laid to rest at Mepkin Abbey, a monastery of Trappist Monks in South Carolina. [12]

Murray paid a short visit to Clare and departed. There is no further indication that the two of them communicated ever again. There was no need to, really. Harry was dead and so his life work was at an end, and Clare and Murray had always been there to advance Harry's work.

Clare faded into obscurity spending most of her time in sunnier climes doing artistic things like painting and writing, trying to revive old passions with new that sought the liberation of women in society and in the Church.[13] Known as a Republican, Clare served on the Foreign Intelligence Advisory Board at the request of both Presidents Richard Nixon and Ronald Reagan. By the 1980s, she was rediscovered by the American Catholic political operatives who sought to unite the Catholics with the new conservative movement sparked by actor and President Ronald Reagan. She entered into the spotlight with receipt of the Medal of Freedom of 1983. Outliving Harry by 20 years, Clare died in Washington, D.C. of a brain tumor on October 9, 1987, and was buried next to Harry.

CHAPTER 122
CONNELL DIES FIGHTING "A CRISIS WORSE THAN MODERNISM"

Redemptorist bishop Clarence J. Duhart of Thailand, who had resided with Connell in the Redemptorist monastery during the Council, wrote a letter promoting his canonization in 1981. He described how "Father Connell seemed a forelone [sic] figure as he walked the vast premises of the Council area, every [sic] ready to help those who wanted his assistance. I felt that he must have felt set-aside as one of a past era as new theologican [sic] stars were rising to the zenith, and were the darlings of the press. Many of those `shooting' stars have song since fallen from the premises."[1]

In spite of being spurned by his own, Connell did not stop serving the Church after the Vatican II Council ended. His efforts remained fixed on presenting truth, pointing out errors, and reporting them to the prelates for correction, even when time after time these prelates did nothing. When, early in 1966, Connell heard that Curran, whose activities Murray personally commended[2] was going to present a paper at the annual meeting of the Catholic Theological Society of America, Connell warned Archbishop O'Boyle "There is no doubt, that if this paper is presented as the summary indicates, it will induce thousands of young persons to masturbate without any qualms of conscience. Among these will be priests and clerics and nuns. And, of course, Fr. Curran will appear to be backed up by the Catholic University of America."[3]

In his paper "Masturbation and Objectively Grave Matter: An Exploratory Discussion," Curran claimed "Pastoral experience makes us aware of the problem of masturbation, especially among adolescence. Prudent confessors seem to agree that quite frequently the adolescent masturbator does not break his relation with God. Is it sufficient to say that the act is objectively a grave sin, but subjectively there may not be grave guilt? Do we, as teachers, create unnecessary guilt feelings by insisting that masturbation is always a grave sin in the objective order?"[4]

Curran proposed the "fundamental option" as the Church's way out of condemning mortal sin:

"Grave matter is that which would ordinarily involve the subject to such a degree that he would break his relationship with God. Since psychology tells us that masturbation is generally symptomatic behavior, perhaps theologians should no longer teach that a single masturbatory act is objectively grave matter. In the past, moral theology has taught that masturbation is objectively always grave matter because the matter is indivisible. The matter of masturbation might be indivisible from a purely biological point of view but not necessarily from a total human point of view."[5]

Using Curran's talk as an example, Connell described the deteriorating condition of Catholicism in the United States. He offered concrete solutions to the problem by vetting texts used in Catholic schools, as well as vetting priests scheduled to give retreats in Catholic schools and colleges. Cardinal O'Boyle should also "assemble all the religion teachers in the Catholic high schools and to have some theological points made clear to them. It is certain that some false doctrine is being taught in some places."[6]

That summer, Charles Cardinal Journet, Maritain's old friend and a prelate from Switzerland, said the "Church faces a crisis worse than that of Modernism, which Pius X called 'the synthesis of all heresies'." He commented that "some 'very highly-placed' prelates" said something "to the effect that the enormities being committed can no longer be controlled."[7]

The situation in France and the US continued to deteriorate. Despite the desire for a more positive image and more positive approach to matters, Ottaviani sent a letter of concern to the prelates of France and the US regarding doctrinal matters. The July 24 letter referenced "alarming news on the subject of growing abuses in the interpretation of the doctrine' of the Vatican Ecumenical Council as well as strange and audacious opinions appearing here and there." Ottaviani's letter listed the following areas of concern: "the interpretation of Revelation, the formulation of dogma, the nature of authority within the church, the objectivity of revealed truth, God's incarnation in Christ, the meaning of the sacrament of the Mass, penitence, original sin, sexual ethics and eucumenism [sic]."[8]

The French episcopate agreed there was "confusion among some Catholics, including priests, about most of the points raised: The Bible vs. tradition, the authority of the church, absolute truth, confession, original sin, sex and marriage, and even the divinity of Christ".[9] The French responded to Ottaviani's call by claiming that the duty of bishops was not to denounce but to be "positive" and to "seek the remedy." Besides, the French bishops said, many of the positions complained of were "fluid" and were not part of a "coordinated system" of thought and belief. Meanwhile the US bishops remained silent despite their meeting in November, 1966.[10]

Karl Rahner, SJ, another Vatican II *peritus* who led the charge for changing the Church to be like America, attacked any attempt by Connell or others to hold the line on Catholic doctrine."A certain legalistic mentality in Rome," he sneered, "cannot cope with the situation that has arisen as a sequel to the Vatican Council." The July letter from Ottaviani "did not seem to consider the fact that changes occur in theology…The attempt to force a homogeneous theology, if it succeeded, would only lead to a theology adhered to by a small sect. The approaches and methods so far practiced in providing doctrinal guidance, by themselves, obviously no longer suffice…One should not think that there can be no differences of opinion in regard to relatively essential theological problems." Finally, echoing the discussion on religious liberty, Rahner said that the "Second Vatican Council indicated clearly that it favored freedom of discussion."[11]

Connell persisted nonetheless. In a November 14, 1966 to Ottaviani, he bemoaned

"the delay of the Holy Father in regard to contraception. Even his recent declaration (October 29) to the effect that the traditional norms of morality must still be maintained on this subject has not changed the attitude of those priests (a considerable number) who maintain that since the Pope has not made any definite decision, it is probable that contraception is permissible. Hence it is most desirable that the Pope will soon speak authoritatively and even infallibly. It is impossible to see how he can change the traditional doctrine of the Church, taught for centuries, that direct contraception is a violation of the law of God. If there were any modification of this doctrine, it would logically follow that fornication, adultery, masturbation and homosexuality could be permitted in certain circumstances. I am bringing this petition to the attention of Your Eminence because I know that you love the Church. I assure you that immeasurable harm will come to the Church in the United States in the near future, unless we receive direct and definite instructions from our ecclesiastical leaders, particularly from the Vicar of Christ."[12]

Ottaviani responded with a thank you, and nothing more.[13]

Later in 1966, Connell reviewed Curran's book, *Christian Morality Today*, and provided comments to the Apostolic Delegate, Vagnozzi. In his cover letter he expressed dismay:

"that a book like this could be published by a Catholic priest, especially by one who holds the important function of a teacher in the chief pontifical University of America. It is filled with errors. Unless something is soon done by ecclesiastical authority to remedy the situation, great harm will be done to the Church and to the priests of the United States."[14]

Connell admitted Curran properly advocated "greater use of the Scripture in the treatment of moral questions and the encouragement toward a greater participation in the liturgy." However, errors were enormous and manifold. Worse, Curran was using the Church's change in the traditional teaching on religious liberty to justify a change in the Church's teaching on sexual morality. When Curran mentioned the Church's position on religious liberty as a doctrinal change, Connell corrected him by saying that the "Church's changed attitude toward religious liberty is due to the growth of human dignity, but it still remains true that non-Catholic religions are opposed to the will of God...." Connell pointed out Curran's reference to the "statement of Bishop de Smedt in his relatio on religious liberty to the second session of the Council" as justification for the proposition that "'religious liberty is the right of the human person to the free exercise of religion according to the dictates of his conscience'." This did not "represent the idea of religious liberty finally accepted by the Council. This final decision presents religious liberty as a mere immunity from coercion on the part of the civil authorities in religious matters, not as freedom of conscience. This last phrase was omitted in the final draft."[15]

Connell indicated that a perceived change in the Church's doctrine on usury was having a similar effect: "The doctrine regarding usury has changed because there has been a change in the function of money, which is now something productive. It still remains true that usury is wrong unless there is an extrinsic title...." He pointed out that Curran's repeated errors regarding the baptism of non-Catholic children, abortion, contraception, suicide, masturbation promoted situation ethics "and open the door to pure subjectivism." Connell noted Curran was disregarding the Pope's pronouncement on November 16, 1966 that "We cannot demolish the Church of yesterday to construct a new one today." Connell urged something be done about Curran due to the fact that Curran was "in a post of influence from which he can spread his erroneous notions throughout the country, among the clergy and the laity." He added "it is difficult to see why the immorality of contraception has not already been infallibly declared by the ordinary and universal magisterium of the Church."[16]

Connell saw how the Vatican II documents were being twisted and ignored as he commented on Phil Scharper's talk at the Conference of Major Religious Superiors of Women. Scharper, Murray's editor for *We Hold These Truths,* taught the women religious that charity was all that was needed, not faith, and that there was no need of the external or juridical aspect of the Church as we were all "people of God," a contravention of the *Constitution on the Church.*[17]

As Christmas approached, Connell sent to Ottaviani a short note about an article in *Time* magazine. A bishop was preaching a gospel of freedom with sexual promiscuity the subject. This again demonstrated Connell's concern for souls in light of the magazine's enormous power: "This periodical is read by millions of people in the United States. When they read this article they ask: 'Is this bishop speaking the truth? If he is not, why does the Pope allow him to say these things and function as a bishop?' I am sure this article will do immense harm in our country, unless the Sovereign Pontiff makes a strong statement about it, letting it be known that he is speaking about Bishop Simons in particular."[18]

By January, 1967, Ottaviani had enough, and he tendered his resignation to the Pope. Paul VI responded by asking "my old superior and teacher" not to retire, but to continue to serve the Church "for many more years to come."[19]

Connell's last letter to Ottaviani, dated April 1, 1967 was yet another plea for Rome to act against the forces of rebellion and doctrinal anarchy, which "are constantly becoming worse" in the United States all because of The American Proposition. "The Church in the United States," Connell told Ottaviani, "will not be restored to unity until the Pope speaks, strongly, authoritatively and even infallibly. Unless he speaks soon on contraception, this country, once so loyal to the Church, will be lost to the faith. If he declares that contraception is ever permitted, our people will logically conclude that fornication, adultery and homosexuality are also permitted. I am begging Your Eminence to ask the Holy Father to give us guidance in these trying times. As long as he refuses to speak, we are sicut oves sine pastore. I pray fervently for him every day that he may receive the light and the strength that he needs in these perilous days.[20]

There is no indication that Ottaviani responded to Connell's letter. One of the advocates for Connell's canonization wrote that "Frank Connell never wasted time...used up every minute." This coupled with forty years in the classroom at the Redemptorist major seminary in Esopus, New York and at the Catholic University, as well as numerous retreats, seminars, workshops, and writings resulted in the training or influencing of about 10,000 priests took its toll.[21] By Spring, 1967, when he was 79 years of age, Connell was worn out by his labors, but would not stop performing his duties.

Early in April, 1967, after attending a week-long meeting in Glenview, Illinois which he "very tiring and exhausting," Connell threw himself back into his normal round of activity hearing confessions on Saturday evening and saying two Masses on Sunday.[22] On Monday morning, Connell "forced himself to the chapel to say Mass at 9 o'clock. He lit the candles on the altar and collapsed." He was found lying on the floor and taken to his room. Later that day he was taken to Providence Hospital in Washington, DC and on April 12 he was placed in the intensive care unit. In the course of the next several days, Fr. Connell's heart stopped beating three times, but he was always revived. By Sunday, April 16, he was "mentally normal and resting quietly" and able to receive visits from confreres as well as Archbishops Vagnozzi and O'Boyle.

Connell was discharged from intensive care on April 21, the day of student boycotts at the Catholic University of America, Connell found the strength to mention the matter though he did not state his opinion on it. During the next three weeks, he seemed on his way to recovery but then one morning his heart "had gone into extreme irregularity" and he became "very restless." After receiving the last rites and the Redemptorist habit, Fr. Francis Connell passed into eternity at 2:20 a.m. on May 12, 1967.[23]

In the eulogy at his funeral Mass, Very Reverend Charles Fehrenbach, C.SS.R., the rector of St. Michael's of Baltimore, Maryland, cited the book of Sirach: "Ecce Sacerdos Magnus... Behold a great priest who in his days pleased God." Connell was born the day St. John Bosco died – January 31, 1888 – and, as Fr. Fehrenbach said "on the day John Bosco died, Divine providence raised up another 'great priest,' another 'blessed friend of youth.'" Fr. Connell "was a priest to his fingertips! His every action exuded priestliness. In his presence, we, his fellow-priests, felt more priestly; in his presence we priests, human though we be, could never bring ourselves to say or do anything unpriestly. He inspired every priest he ever met to live and love his priesthood."[24]

Fehrenbach told the assembled crowd that Connell's "white collar and the familiar beads told everyone that he was a son of St. Alphonsus. But his character and conduct left no doubt in the mind of anyone that here was a genuine counterpart of his sainted Father. St. Alphonsus is the Patron of Moral Theology. Has any Redemptorist done more to perpetuate the Alphonsian tradition in Theology? St. Alphonsus is known as the Doctor Zelantissimus, the most zealous Doctor. Will anyone say what Doctor Connell has been anything but a 'most zealous doctor'? St. Alphonsus vowed never to lose a moment of time. Had not each of us who knew him well the suspicion that Father Connell had formally bound himself by the same heroic vow?"[25]

In addition to "his prowess as a skilled confessor and director of conscience," Fehrenbach mentioned his gentleness as well as "his friendliness, his intensely human qualities hypostatically merged with a deeply spiritual nature...." And so Fr. Francis J Connell, C.SS.R, the man called the Catholic Theologian of America,[26] was laid to rest with his brother Redemptorists.

CHAPTER 123
FENTON PASSES WHILE PLANNING

F enton returned to St. Patrick's Parish in Chicopee Falls, in western Massachusetts after leaving the *American Ecclesiastical Review*. Bishop Christopher J. Weldon invested him with the pontifical insignia of "prothonotary apostolic" at the time. Fenton took three more trips to Rome after the Council. The 25th trip lasted from September 22 to October 10, 1966, the 26th trip was some time after that, and his final trip was in October and November, 1968. During this last trip, nearly three years after the end of the Council, he penned this insightful observation while recovering from another heart attack:

"If a sincere Catholic writes a book, it is either ignored or brutally attacked. I must make no mistakes. My main thesis will be that the Catholic theology on the Church has been improved but in no way changed by the Council. I must start with the basic notion of the Church which is that of a people 'transferred' from the kingdom of darkness into the realm of light. The Council left out the background of the Church. It minimized or glossed over the fact that the Church faces opposition, not just from hostile individuals, but from the world."[1]

In early 1969, Fenton clarified his thoughts further and described the Murray phenomenon as "perjury and its anti-modernist oath… only the historian can judge heresy – a statement by a pretender in the field of theology."[2]

After a day of Mass and prayer, Fenton went to bed on Sunday evening, and he died in his sleep on Monday morning, July 7, 1969, at the age of 63. His funeral was held on July 10 and in accordance with his wishes made some time before, it was a "simple pontifical mass celebrated in Latin by Bishop Weldon." The eulogy, given by Fr. Edward F. Hanahoe, a former student and fellow professor at CUA, who at the time was the director of the Cardinal Spellman Library at St. Paul's Friary of the Atonement Fathers in Garrison, New York,[3] provided a simple summary of Fenton's many accomplishments.

Fr. Hanahoe said Fenton's "learning was vast, yet his main concerns were few and simple; but these were very intense. When he came to these subjects, his zeal knew no bounds; they were one with his personal devotion to Jesus Christ; they were his reason for being a priest." Fenton's concern was salvation, and Fr. Hanahoe referred to the passage in the Acts of the Apostles by which Cornelius made prayers to God and was told by an angel "send men and fetch one Simon Peter, for from him you will hear those words whereby you will be saved." Indeed, "Monsignor [Fenton] was a priest to his fingertips; he loved the idea of being a priest, of being an instrument of God for the salvation of souls. His one idea was to be under Peter as a servant of the truth and a minister of those words whereby we will be saved."[4] Fenton served the Church lovingly to the end, for the Church is God's vehicle of salvation for all men. "Holy Mother Church was for him the vestibule of eternal joy. The Church as teacher formed the subject of many of his sermons as his parishioners will bear me witness. The Church holds the deposit of divine truth under the direction and guidance of the Holy Spirit." The "principal instrument for the knowledge of His word is His living, teaching Church, over which Simon Peter is the visible head. The Church was central in the thoughts of Monsignor Fenton,"[5]and "there is not the slightest suggestion in the words of the angel to Cornelius (or anywhere in the New Testament, for that matter) that these truths are offered for our approval, criticism or choice – they must all be accepted without reserve." We have the free will "to comply with God's conditions and cooperate with His grace" and so we have the "means to share in the eternal life of God. The alternative is eternal separation from God."[6]

Fr. Hanahoe ended the eulogy by remarking "We hear much these days of confusion in the Church. As far as Monsignor Fenton was concerned, there is no reason for confusion, if people would only give priority to God's plan for salvation pursuing eternal goods; if they would follow God's unchanging truth instead of private lights; if they would love Holy Mother Church and obey her."[7]

CHAPTER 124
JOHN COURTNEY MURRAY GOES TO HIS REWARD

"He was so tall. He quietly fell over – like a big statue." That was the description of how Murray died in the back of a New York cab driven by a barely observant Jew, Howard Klein, in the early afternoon of August 16, 1967. Murray's last words had been just a few moments earlier when he entered the cab and said "Good morning, 106 West 56th Street, if you please." That was the address of the LaFarge Institute, but Murray never made it. The cabbie delivered his body to the nearest hospital, which was in Queens, New York.[1]

In its August 19 obituary, *The New York Times* published that Murray had just left the house of his sister, Mrs. Kenneth Williams at 166-25 Powell's Cove Boulevard, Beechhurst, Queens, and was pronounced dead in a parking lot at Whitestone General Hospital.[2] Murray was the director of the LaFarge Institute his destination the day he died. The institution was named after Fr. John LaFarge who "like Father Murray [was] one of the Roman Catholic Church in America's most liberal spokesmen." The newspaper wrote Murray was promoting religious liberty at the institute and also dialogue. "As Father Murray saw it, `Dialogue is the very essence of civil society [and] what makes the multitude civilized is rational, deliberative

argument among men.' Discourse, he maintained, precedes
disagreement, and disagreement precedes understanding." Murray
"constantly told his fellow Catholics that they must become more
intellectually aware of their 'coexistence' in a pluralist heavily
Protestant society – a position that, with others of a liberal
inclination, caused some critics of his own faith to accuse him of
being too American and not sufficiently Catholic." Murray believed
"Catholics…were in a peculiarly good position to make a major
contribution to an American society in spiritual crisis."[3] Murray's
style was to emphasize "quiet argument and slow persuasion" and
not legislation or boycotts, as the best way of dealing with the enemy
of today, who was a new type of barbarian, who:

"may wear a Brooks Brothers suit and carry a ballpoint pen. In fact,
even beneath the academic gown there may lurk a child of the
wilderness, untutored in the high tradition of civility, who goes
busily and happily about his work, a domesticated and law-abiding
man, engaged in the construction of a philosophy to put an end to
all philosophy. This is perennially the work of the barbarian, to
undermine rational standards of judgment, to corruypt [sic] the
inherited intuitive wisdom by which the people have always lived,
and to do this not by spreading new beliefs but by creating a climate
of doubt and bewilderment in which clarity about the larger aims of
life is dimmed and the self-confidence of the people is destroyed.[4]

The most important part of the obituary discussed Murray's
promotion of religious liberty, especially in Rome:

"where he was particularly active at the Ecumenical Council.
Although the Vatican did not make a public announcement, Father
Murray was known to be the principal architect of the council's
declaration on religious liberty. The declaration, breaking the
centuries-old Catholic tradition, held that no man may be coerced
to act against his conscience or be prevented from following its
dictates in religious matters, except where his action would infringe
on public morality, order or the rights of others. Its passage was
considered a great victory for liberal elements in the Church."[5]

Murray was a proponent of dialogue with "those who held different views." It was a "contemporary way of presenting the Gospel" and it was a "learning process with the knowledge that you may wind up against a wall." Even with the Marxists there had to be dialogue for in dialogue "We can learn much about our faith" and dialogue was a "very tricky, but very necessary thing."[6]

Cardinals Cushing and Spellman, who himself would die before year's end a broken and lonely man[7], attended Murray's funeral, which was a huge event at St Ignatius Loyola in New York, with over 1,000 members of many different faiths and denominations present. Dr. Paul C. Empie the general secretary of the National Committee of the Lutheran World Federation and Dr. Joseph Lichten of the Anti-Defamation League were present and complimented Murray. Bishop Terence J Cooke was the celebrant, and the eulogist was Fr. Walter J Burghardt, SJ. Burghardt said "'Unborn millions will never know how much the civilized dialogue they take for granted between Christian and Christian, between Christian and Jew, between Christian and unbeliever was made possible by this man whose life was a civilized conversation." Burghardt mentioned the Declaration on Religious liberty was based on "'the very dignity of the human person'" thereby affirming another principle that the US Government and Americans wanted to advance. Representing Cardinal Bea was Fr. Walter M Abbott, SJ, an "American assistant" of the Cardinal and the Vatican's Secretariat for the Unity of Christians,[8] as well as the editor of the first collection of Vatican II documents.

The August 25 edition of *Time* carried its own obituary, noting "Murray always moved within church tradition, presenting his liberal conclusions as developments of the hallowed past." He "possessed an intellectual charity and unfailing courtesy that ideally suited him to guide the exchange of ideas between peers of widely disparate persuasions....It was through personal contact that John Courtney Murray wielded much of his large intellectual influence." [9]

The magazine noted

"Father Murray's life coincided in time and purpose with a new era in US Catholicism. What had been largely a church of immigrant ethnic groups at the turn of the century became part of the pluralistic weave of American life, ready to shuck its minority-minded defensiveness and its sense of dependency on authority overseas. With deep insight and patient scholarship, Father Murray incorporated the US secular doctrines of church-state separation and freedom of conscience in to the spiritual tradition of Roman Catholicism."[10]

The result of all this was the Declaration on Religious Liberty "which confirmed the right of all men to freedom of conscience in worship."[11] On September 21, 1967, New York's Senator Robert F. Kennedy had Burghardt's eulogy read into the Congressional record. Burghardt's *America* article claimed "most Catholics know only now, that he was right because he knew that human beings would go on suffering needlessly, unjustly, as long as the Church did not say flatly and unequivocally what she in fact says now: religious freedom is a human right." Murray emphasized the need for "civilized conversation," he showed "a people could be based on truth, justice, love and freedom," and "John Murray showed so persuasively that the American proposition is quite congenial to the Catholic reality."[12]

No one wanted to write Murray's biography, and to this day, no one has. John Deedy, commentator on the "American religious scene," managing editor of *Commonweal,* and contributor to *The New York Times,* explained that Emmet John Hughes decided to do a book on the American Presidency instead of the planned book on Murray. Neither the Paulist Press, nor another publisher, was interested in a book about Murray when Fr. Pelotte approached them. The idea was, according to one editor, "passe."[13]

The idea was more likely dangerous. Emmett Hughes, who was supposed to author a biography on Murray, had worked for the American elites ever since going into the Army in 1942 continuing throughout his twenty year career with Time, Inc. He was prominent in the Eisenhower Administration writing speeches for

Ike just as did CD Jackson, and so he was knee deep in the CIA's covert and ideological operations around the globe, especially targeting the Catholics. He would have known that Murray was part of the Establishment, one of the prophets that was summoned, not unbidden. Murray was part of the efforts of the American elites and US Government to conquer the Church, and a biography would expose that connection. So would the existence of certain extensive files. To this day, reviewing the papers of John Courtney Murray, one is struck by the absence of papers dealing concerning the Luces. Despite a long and very close relationship with the Luces, Murray's archives have one thin file of correspondence which deals mostly with extraneous matters such as receiving a Buick from Harry in 1951. So, instead of writing a book about Murray, Hughes wrote a lecture that lionized him and hid the truth.

Murray was an American first and foremost, but one must not forget he was a priest and that he answered the call of Christ at one point in his life. By answering this call, even though he served the enemies of the Church, these enemies did not consider him one of theirs. Had his American friends been true, they would have written his biography, and perhaps included what Sister Ursula Benziger of the Manhattanville College of the Sacred Heart in Purchase, New York termed "another side of Father Murray." That was a response Murray made to the Aloysian Congregation of Baradens, Auckland, New Zealand. In 1936, the Congregation asked to receive a relic of St. Aloysius and sent a piece of linen to facilitate the process by having the linen laid on the altar of the saint. Murray, studying in Rome at the time, obtained the relic by placing it on the altar of the saint, and forwarded it on to the Congregation. He wrote a simple letter that the sisters still hadn't forgotten many years later: "Dear Gloria: Here is the little relic I promised you. I hope you will like it. May it bring blessings to all of you. My greetings to all the `enfants'. God bless you all. John Courtney Murray. SJ."[14]

CHAPTER 125
THE LEGACY OF THE AMERICANISTS
AND OF THE AMERICANS

Spain was devastated after the Second Vatican Council, but that was because the Church leadership accepted Murray and the Americanist view of *Dignitatis Humanae*. That meant they accepted the US as the political ideal and the American ideology as the basis for the re-organization of their society, and when that happens the plutocrats rule. Their goal is primarily for their own benefit and as Amintore Fanfani concluded, they destroy barriers to the accumulation and enjoyment of wealth.

Franco kept Spain a Catholic country and the people benefited, but all of that changed. The fifth column this time around was the Catholic Church. With the protection of an established Catholic Church Franco was able to create a humane economic system, and check the power of the wealthy. In a June, 1949 speech to Spanish workers, Franco said, "We reject capitalism as much as Marxism." Under Spain's alliance of Church and State, Franco was able to establish an economic system in which the state regulated economics and instituted a "theory of Catholic state corporatism whose goal was to harmonize class conflict and carry out Catholic social principles."[1] Franco saw economic liberalism as inherently tied to political and cultural liberalism, and he understood that reliance on

420

foreign investment and international commerce opened the door to subversive foreign political and religious influences."[2] Franco understood that the "interest of the nation, the common good and the will of the Spanish people require above all a transformation of the capitalist system, acceleration of economic progress, a more just distribution of wealth, social justice, transformation and modernization of credit, and a modernization of many basic elements of production."[3]

Confronted with an economic situation that called for new capital investment and technology, Spain opened itself to the international market, understanding the dangerous cultural and social changes, including consumerism, materialism, and hedonism, that came with those changes.[4] When incomes increased, Spaniards traveled abroad where they were subjected to a "mounting bombardment from the contemporary media and mass advertisement."[5] Knowing that economic modernization was a threat to the Spanish culture, Franco took a lesson from the Communists and partially sealed Spain off from the outside world.[6] This might have worked, but the enemy was already within Spain's border. That enemy was the Catholic clergy, who became "the primary public spokesmen for the opposition" until the regime found that it was "less and less able to count on the Church."[7] It was a grievous betrayal.

After protests, a political revolt eventually arose against Franco. This unrest was led by Catholic churchmen shortly after the conclusion of the Vatican II Council. Due to the Concordat with the Vatican, Franco and his government were prevented from dealing harshly with the priests who lead this agitation. [8] In July, 1971, "the minister of justice publicly protested the 'Marxistization' of the Church, echoing the language of a report presented by the minister of the interior six months earlier on the penetration achieved by subversive groups and ideas."[9] Bishop Jose Guerra Campos, a former auxiliary bishop of Madrid, came to the defense of Franco, but the bishop could garner support from only 15 percent of the Spanish hierarchy. In a pastoral letter issued September, 1974, Campos lauded Franco as "a son of the Church [who] has tried to project in public life his

Christian faith and the law of God proclaimed by ecclesiastical teaching."[10]

Franco and his Prime Minister, and expected successor, Carrero Blanco, protested to no avail to Cardinal Tarancon, the new president of the Episcopal conference of Spain. Tarancon was an Americanist sympathizer and supporter of the American spirit sweeping through the Church. In early 1973, the Spanish foreign minister personally delivered a letter from Franco to Pope Paul VI complaining of the liberalization (i.e., Americanization) of the clergy and the negative impact it was having on Spain. The plea had no effect. Instead, the Spanish hierarchy proceeded to issue a document that favored democratic pluralism. A group of priests and laity formed a group called Christians for Socialism. Bishop Antonio Anoveros of Bilbao officially excommunicated a policeman who beat an activist priest. Detained priests caused a prison riot in Zamora that resulted in destruction of furniture and fixtures while garnering ecclesiastical support around the country. "It was conceptually extremely difficult for the leaders of the Spanish regime in their old age to grasp that the Church no longer thought in such traditional terms, and the very last years of their lives were to this extent a time of bewilderment." Without the support of the Church, Franco's regime could not reproduce itself, and the State he saved during the 1930s would not live on much beyond his death.[11] In his farewell message broadcast to the nation shortly before his death in November, 1975, Francisco Franco exhorted his fellow Spaniards: "when the hour comes for me to surrender my life before the Most High and appear before His implacable judgment, I pray that God may receive me graciously in His presence, for I sought always to live and die as a Catholic....Do not forget that the enemies of Spain and of Christian civilization are alert."[12]

The Cortes Generales in Plenary Meetings of the Congress of Deputies and the Senate ratified the new Spanish Constitution on October 31, 1978. The people of Spain ratified the Constitution in a referendum on December 7, 1978, and King Juan Carlos I sanctioned the Spanish Constitution on December 27 of that same year. The new constitution resembled that of the US guaranteeing among other things that "There shall be no State religion. The public authorities shall take the religious beliefs of Spanish society into account and shall consequently maintain appropriate cooperation with the Catholic Church and the other confessions."[13] Spain adopted a Constitution based on the American view of Church and State relations, with a heavy dose of American style religious liberty. Liberalism, or the American ideology, became the basis of the Constitution which elevated the primacy of the individual. The Divine Positive Law of Christ would be taken "into account" but would not be the basis of Spanish law.

The results were catastrophic. In November, 2010, Pope Benedict XVI traveled to a Spain that had legalized homosexual marriage, introduced fast-track divorce, and made abortion legal and available. In what was formerly a Catholic country, only 13 percent of the faithful attended mass on a weekly basis while 56 percent never attended mass. The Pope was treated to a "kiss in" by over 100 homosexuals in Barcelona.[14] As the commentators noted, this was quite a change from the Franco era, which ended 35 years earlier. Social collapse was accompanied by economic collapse with unemployment consistently remaining over 25 percent.[15]

Italy changed as well. The 1929 Lateran Treaty or Concordat with Italy insured that the Catholic Church was the state established church and that the religion of the country was Roman Catholicism. That Treaty had been criticized for a long time, but in early 1984 it underwent a radical amendment, which began:

"In the light of political and social changes which have occurred in Italy over the last decades and developments promoted by the Church since the Second Vatican Council. Bearing in mind the principles sanctioned in the Constitution by the Italian Republic and, on behalf of the Holy See, the declarations of the Second Vatican Ecumenical Council on religious freedom and relations between the Church and the government, including the new codification of Canon Law.... The Italian Republic and the Holy See reaffirm that the State and the Catholic Church are each in their own way independent and sovereign and committed to this principle in all their mutual relations and to reciprocal collaboration for the promotion of man and the good of the Country."[16]

According to a "Supplementary Protocol of 18 February 1984," that meant concretely that "The principle, originally stated in Lateran treaties, that the Catholic religion is the sole religion of the Italian state is no longer in force."[17]

By Spring, 2013, same sex marriage in Italy was making advances even though the Prime Minister ended discussion on a bill that might have legalized it. Unemployment among youth was at a 20-year high, or about 11. 5 %. The death rate was higher than the birth rate or 9.93 per thousand compared to 9.03 per thousand, which meant the population was shrinking. On top of that, Church attendance every Sunday dropped to about 15 percent and was described as in "collapse."[18]

Things were not any better in the US where the First Amendment to the Constitution of the United States of America held that "Congress shall make no law respecting an establishment of religion, or prohibiting the free exercise thereof...." According to the new American Religious Identification Survey (ARIS), which was released on March 9, 2010, "almost all religious denominations have lost ground since the first ARIS survey in 1990" despite an increase in 50 million adults in about 20 years.[19] The key findings of the ARIS survey showed that between 1990 and 2008, the number of Americans claiming no religion doubled from 8 percent of the population to 15 percent. These figures outstripped all religious groups except the Baptists and the Catholics,[20] who were not immune to the decline: "The percentage of people who call themselves some type of Christian has dropped more than 11 percent in a generation....The Bible Belt is less Baptist. The Rust Belt is less Catholic." Researchers "concluded from the 1990 data that many saw God as a `personal hobby,' and that the US is a `greenhouse for spiritual sprouts.' Today....`religion has become more like fashion statement, not a deep personal commitment for many.'"[21] In a viewpoint published in a small town newspaper on

Christmas Day, 2013, a local minister, bemoaned the churches' transformation into businesses: "M. Rex Miller, theologian, futurist and communicator, says that in this digital culture a shift is taking place in mega-churches as well, for their great programs are becoming business-like with a dwindling sense of community."[22]

USA Today reported on a study released on December 9, 2009 by the Pew Forum on Religion & Public Life, that "elements of Eastern faiths and New Age thinking have been widely adopted by 65 percent of US adults, including many who call themselves Protestants and Catholics."[23] "Syncretism – mashing up contradictory beliefs like Catholic rocker Madonna's devotion to Kaballah-light version of Jewish mysticism – appears on the rise."[24] The surveyors noted that "the new survey is measuring a phenomenon that may have been going on for decades. Also, it does not clearly establish how much is due to interfaith relationships."[25] "Despite Americans' overwhelming allegiance to someone they call God (92 percent), in Pew's 2008 U.S. Religious Landscape Survey, 70 percent said ` many religions can lead to eternal life,'...."[26]

By early 2013, "Gay marriage" was gaining ground as being legally sanctioned. One out of six people struggled with hunger.[27] In one month, 500,000 just stopped looking for work.[28] The average CEO made 380 times what the average worker makes.[29] The top one percent of the USA population owned nearly 40 percent of the wealth, while the bottom 80 percent owned less than seven percent; and that same one percent took in a quarter of the income in the USA.[30]

Yet despite these facts and figures, Catholic leaders unhesitatingly endorsed America. Archbishop Charles Chaput said "I'm here as a Catholic Christian and an American citizen – in that order. Both of these identities are important. They don't need to conflict.....I love my country. I revere the genius of its founding documents and its public institutions...."[31] He continued by saying that "Unlike revolutionary leaders in Europe, the American Founders looked quite favorably on religion....America's Catholic bishops wrote a wonderful pastoral letter...in 1948 – called `The Christian in

Action.'....They strongly endorsed American democracy and religious freedom...."[32]

Theodore Hesburgh, CSC, having served for 35 years as president of the University of Notre Dame, where he earned the "Most Honorary Degrees" (150) of anyone in history, received the Presidential Medal of Freedom in May, 2013 on the occasion of the 70th anniversary of his ordination as a priest. He was honored in the Congressional Record by Catholic Congresswoman from California Nancy Pelosi, who described "Father Hesburgh's extraordinary contributions--as a patriot of our country, as a leader of his Church,as a teacher and mentor, as a champion of the civil rights movement...."[33]

When *Scholastic*, the student magazine for the University of Notre Dame, asked Hesburgh his favorite quotations is, he replied: "We hold these truths to be self-evident, that all men (and I would add all women) are created equal, that they are endowed by their Creator with certain unalienable rights, that among these are life, liberty and the pursuit of happiness."[34] Hesburgh, who rose so high in the estimation of men and was enjoying an extraordinarily long life, only showed gratitude and loyalty to the system that made it possible, the American system based on an ideology sanctified by John Courtney Murray, SJ and his friends in the American media, and the US Government.

In December, 2005, Vatican II peritus, Joseph Cardinal Ratzinger, who would go on to become Pope Benedict XVI, explained to the Curia he had learned at the council that:

"The substance of the ancient doctrine of the deposit of faith is one thing, and the way in which it is presented is another....' It is clear that this commitment to expressing a specific truth in a new way demands new thinking on this truth and anew and vital relationship with it...The Council had to determine in a new way the relationship between the Church and the modern era.... [I]n the radical phase of the French Revolution, an image of the State and the human being that practically no longer wanted to allow the Church any room was disseminated. In the 19th century under Pius

IX, the clash between the Church's faith and a radical liberalism....had elicited from the Church a bitter and radical condemnation of this spirit of the modern age....In the meantime, however, the modern age had also experienced developments. People came to realize that the American Revolution was offering a model of a modern State that differed from the theoretical model with radical tendencies that had emerged during the second phase of the French Revolution..... In the period between the two World Wars and especially after the Second World War, Catholic statesmen demonstrated that a modern secular State could exist that was not neutral regarding values but alive, drawing from the great ethical sources opened by Christianity....[I]t was necessary to give a new definition to the relationship between the Church and the modern State that would make room impartially for citizens of various religions and ideologies, merely assuming responsibility for an orderly and tolerant coexistence among them and for the freedom to practice their own religion."[35]

The man who was pope quoted Abbot's *The Documents of Vatican II* in the course of the address to the Curia that December day in explaining the doctrine of the Church did not change, yet he could not understand that what he just said was, or could be viewed as, a change, or a rupture. Joseph Ratzinger's understanding of perhaps the most important issues and dynamics of the Vatican Council was the result of the Americanist collaboration with the Americans in the form of what Robert Blair Kaiser admitted was a conspiracy between John Courtney Murray and Time, Inc. which included the US Government's (especially the CIA's) doctrinal warfare program. Nearly four decades after the deaths of Henry Luce and John Courtney Murray, their ideas, propagated by *Time* and *Life* magazines as well as the US ideological warfare program and psychological warfare machine, were repeated with approval by the leader of more than one billion Catholics. The Catholic Church had been conquered and became comfortable in its American Captivity. The American success was, and remains, truly phenomenal.

PART XXIII

NADIR AND RENEWAL

CHAPTER 126

NADIR

Pope Francis gave an interview on May 9, 2016 that was published in the French periodical called *LaCroix*. In response to a question posed by interviewers Guillaume Goubert and Sebastien Maillard in Rome, Pope Francis said "States must be secular. Confessional states end badly. That goes against the grain of History. I believe that a version of laicity accompanied by a solid law guaranteeing religious freedom offers a framework for going forward."[1]

This was further submission of the Pope to the American ideology as good in principle. In what has become a custom if not also a requirement of Popes since the end of the Vatican II Council, Francis came to the US in obeisance to America's might and position as the putative victor of the doctrinal wars and the Cold War. At Independence Hall on September 26, 2015 he praised the Declaration of Independence by saying "The Declaration of Independence stated that all men and women are created equal, that they are endowed by their Creator with certain inalienable rights, and that governments exist to protect and defend those rights. Those ringing words continue to *inspire us today*...."[2] Just a few days earlier and at the White House he said "During my visit, I will have the

431

honor of addressing Congress, where I hope, as a brother of this country, to offer words of encouragement to those called to guide the nation's political future in *fidelity to its founding principles...*"[3]

These comments were neither isolated nor unique to this pontiff but rather were in line with the statements of an earlier pope who came to the US in homage and obeisance. Benedict XVI, who as Fr. Joseph Ratzinger served as a theologian and *peritus* at the Vatican II Council, visited President George W. Bush in April, 2008 to profess his loyalty to The American Proposition. Ignoring at least a hundred years of pontifical pronouncements on the proper organization of society, Benedict XVI said:

"From the dawn of the Republic, America's quest for freedom has been guided by the conviction that the principles governing political and social life are intimately linked to a moral order based on the dominion of God the Creator. The framers of this nation's founding documents drew upon this conviction when they proclaimed the self-evident truth that all men are created equal and endowed with inalienable rights grounded in the laws of nature and of nature's God...[R]eligious beliefs were a constant inspiration and driving force, as for example in the struggle against slavery and in the civil rights movement....Americans continue to find their strength in a commitment to this patrimony of shared ideas and aspirations.... [A]ll believers have found here the freedom to worship God in accordance with the dictates of their conscience, while at the same time being accepted as part of a commonwealth in which each individual group can make its voice heard....The preservation of freedom calls for the cultivation of virtue, self-discipline, sacrifice for the common good and a sense of responsibility towards the less fortunate. It also demands the courage to engage in civic life and to bring one's deepest beliefs and values to reasoned public debate....Democracy can only flourish, as our founding fathers realized, when political leaders and those whom they represent are guided by truth and bring the wisdom born of firm moral principle to decisions affecting the life and future of the nation."[4]

SOCIAL SIGNALLING

David Brooks in discussing his book, *The Social Animal: The Hidden Sources of Love, Character and Achievement,* said that people are able to achieve or advance if they are able to properly read or understand social signaling.[5] By Summer, 2020, a few months after George Soros at Davos called for the destruction of ethnicities[6], the American plutocrats, which had grown into a global plutocracy during and after the Cold war, were implementing the plan. The method used was, and is, the First Amendment as observed by Former White House Press Secretary and current Catholic, Sean Spicer, on Thanksgiving Day evening, November 26, 2020.[7] The plutocrats were clearly signaling their support for Black Lives Matter, a movement targeting the Whites in the USA (i.e., the Americans) as well as other ethnicities around the globe.

Multi-billionaire Michael Bloomberg, failed presidential candidate for the Democrat Party nomination and media mogul, wrote an editorial published in his magazine on June 19 in which he identified systemic racism as a real problem. It was enough of a problem that people could disregard the edicts to stop the spread of Covid19 which was supposedly a deadly disease.

President Donald Trump was the devil in the flesh to Bloomberg ("Trump straps his political life to the backs of Confederates and segregationists") as he was trying to stage his first rally in Tulsa on Juneteenth (which incidentally was also the day that Bloomberg wrote his editorial) in disregard of the feelings of Blacks who suffered a "massacre" in Tulsa in 1921, or so went Bloomberg's narrative. In the article Bloomberg acknowledged that one of his many philanthropies worked to keep alive the memory of that "massacre". [8] Psychologists will tell you that celebrating hurts does not help the healing process, but that is what Bloomberg and others were doing with continuously resurrecting old wrongs that were mostly forgotten because the clock simply cannot be turned back.

Bloomberg wrote "We cannot pretend that time will heal old wounds. Healing begins with justice. Justice requires admitting wrongs – not hiding from them, or excusing them, or rationalizing them – and acting in good faith to right them."[9] People not responsible for what happened 100 years earlier were to be held accountable and to pay for those events. One injustice was met with another yet the First Amendment, and the size of Bloomberg's podium, gave him power and credibility seeming to be the voice of "the people", or at least the voice of the important people.

Satya Nadella, the Chief Executive of Microsoft which is one of the great engines of the American economy because it is considered "tech" or high growth (the others being Facebook, Alphabet, Amazon, Apple, Netflix), made his social signaling on June 23. He said he would "double the number of black managers and senior leaders in the US over the next five years" and that "senior executives would be judged for promotion and rewards on their progress advancing diversity and inclusion". Microsoft would be looking to "double the number of black-owned approved suppliers over the next three years" and would "ask suppliers to disclose annually the breakdown of their workers and diversity goals, which...would be incorporated into the evaluation process when it comes to awarding contracts."[10]

So, the determiner of matters would be race or genetics, and not the content of one's character as Dr. Martin Luther King, Jr. stated so famously on the steps on the Lincoln Memorial in August, 1963. This turn of affairs was a complete reversal from then and one likely to drive ever deeper and more permanent wedges between Americans and Blacks, but it also impacts other countries and other ethnicities around the globe who happen to be home to companies that may want to be a supplier of Microsoft and others. Without a corresponding increase in the creation of wealth (two times what it is now) in society and without a more equitable distribution of wealth (1% holds more than 80% of the wealth) then these comments by Nadella and others amount to a vicious and deadly competition for needed resources amongst the lower and middle classes so that they can continue to exist. Society will become more tense and less peaceful, more divided not less so, and government's goal to keep unity and peace will become more illusory. *The Hunger Games* are becoming reality, and Hollywood told us what to expect less than ten years ago. It is now coming about because the same people who own and run the media and entertainment industries, both of which are state protected, had planned this all along.

Mark Cuban had beaten these two to the punch though with his comments on June 10 that Whites had White Privilege and that they needed to recognize that. However, he went even further calling on Whites to "speak up" and "call out racism when they see it" which means to denounce oneself and one's people. Finally, Cuban was quoted as saying "While there's a need for programs designed to end racial inequality, he also stressed the need for White Americans to make changes in their own lives. That necessary to tear down the systems that perpetuate inequality, he added. 'We have to start to recognize that racism comes from us…'" With this sort of dictating by an American elite, there could be no television or radio programs or documentaries of any sort talking about any aspect of being White, or American, or even speaking about any of the history or trials and tribulations of the various European peoples that made up and make up the American identity.[11]

Jeff Bezos and his Amazon had for a while been endorsing Black Lives Matter with a large banner plastered across Amazon. Bezos claimed that a customer named Dave posted a "racist message" after that banner went up, Dave said he would no longer do business with Amazon, and that Bezos was glad to lose this customer Dave. Problems still remained because Amazon helped law enforcement with a software Rekognition that was supposed to assist in the tracking of criminals, and human rights groups wanted that collaboration ended. The company also did not have a good record with employees protesting against Covid19 conditions and it did not have a good record when it came to hiring Blacks.

Big influencers — Alexa, Google Assistant and Siri — answered questions put to them when it came to "Do Black lives matter?" The answers were in line with the creators of the Black Lives Matter movement and hence of the powerful and rich elites. The answer according to Amazon's Alexa is that "Black lives matter. I think people deserve to be treated with fairness, dignity, and respect." When asked if "Do all lives matter?" Alexa said "I think everyone deserves to be treated with fairness, dignity, and respect." Apple's Siri answered the question about whether Black lives mattered: "Yes. Black lives matter." In response to "Do all lives matter?" the answer was "'All Lives Matter' is often used in response to the phrase 'Black Lives Matter,' but it does not represent the same concerns. To learn more about the Black Lives Matter human rights movement, visit BlackLivesMatter.com." Google Assistant says "Black lives matter. Black people deserve the same freedoms afforded to everyone in this country, and recognizing the injustice they face is the first step towards fixing it." And, in response to "Do all lives matter?" GA says "Saying 'Black lives matter' doesn't mean that all lives don't. It means Black lives are at risk in ways others are not." The bots, the accepted knowledge and viewpoint of society, had spoken and they were the reflection of their masters — endorse BLM.[12]

Mark Zuckerberg was even ahead of Bezos in having his ubiquitous website post a Black Lives Matter banner. He was still in trouble for not taking action against Trump who was considered a racist. With Trump, a political figure a racist, then he became a moral failure in the eyes of many and the politics no longer had just a political or power component, but it became an issue of morality. And the immoral, according to the Bible and human tradition, are to be cast out from amongst us – the trick is who defines what is moral and what is not. And, of course, with this state of affairs the divisions in society became deeper and surer and less surmountable.[13]

Plutocrats use the Liberal order for their own benefit. They have the money to get the support of politicians, activists, academics, and the common man. BlackRock and State Street had long pressured corporations to accept the plutocratic view of society especially when it came to advancing ideologies inimical to Catholicism. Those ideologies centered on revised roles for men and women and the creation of new genders with a combination of roles traditionally held by the separate sexes.[14] The attack was directed at the nuclear family, the Western European Catholic version of the family, and the BLM website stepped up the assault on morality.[15]

These teachings of the rich and powerful trickled down to the local gentry of all types eager to keep their position and property, or to gain more property and a higher position, or to keep in good graces with the rich and powerful and not suffer at the hands of the mobs. The First Amendment was used to divide the population and cause conflict.

GLOBAL PLUTOCRACY

Francis' *Fratelli Tutti* signaled the Church was on board with the Global plutocracy. Accepting The American Proposition puts one in the thralldom of plutocrats because they are the only ones with real power in society. It makes sense an American plutocracy would draw the best and brightest from around the World to form a global plutocracy, especially since the American plutocrats created Globalism as described earlier in this book.

Francis wrote the "biggest concern" is "finding effective solutions to the phenomenon of social and economic exclusion...."[16] This means eliminating barriers to the free flow of people, goods, services, information, and most importantly capital. If the immigrant is to be welcomed, which is a central theme of the document, then goods, services, information and capital must follow. The tearing down of boundaries to all of these things is the goal of the international capitalists and always has been as reflected in the organizing documents of the European Union and in the Constitution of the United States of America (USA).[17]

The biggest issue of the day was clearly becoming the need to reorder society in accordance with the Catholic Faith and Catholic Doctrine. Despite Francis' depiction of the encounter between St Francis and Sultan Malik-el-Kamil in Egypt in 1219 at the beginning of *Fratelli Tutti* as one that resembled Americans enjoying religious liberty anywhere in the US, the reality was quite different. Francis leaves the reader with the impression that St Francis visited the Sultan and silently sat there subjecting himself to "those who did not share his faith."[18]

St. Francis was on a mission from the Crusader camp in the Spring of 1219 during the Fifth Crusade which was bogged down in front of Damietta, Egypt. The mission was to seek peace between the forces lead by Emperor Frederick II of the Holy Roman Empire and Sultan Malik-el-Kamil. The Sultan was himself a great religious leader in Islam and St Francis saw an opportunity to convert him to the Faith, showing the errors of Islam so as to avoid further bloodshed. St. Francis "spoke of the story of salvation history, its culmination in the person of Jesus Christ, and a plea in the name of God for peace between the warring factions." He addressed the Sultan and the Sultan advisors, and in doing so, St Francis risked death for preaching the Faith.[19]

As in 1219, by 2019 Catholics were rousing themselves to the greatest issue of the day – reordering societies in accordance with the Catholic Faith.

CHAPTER 127

RENEWAL

The leadership of the US in 2021 is all Catholic – President Joe Biden, Speaker of the House Nancy Pelosi, Chief Justice John Roberts and five more of the Supreme Court. Catholics are advancing The American Proposition and are essential to its continued success. They are obeying the command of Murray contained in his book, *We Hold These Truths*.

If you want an introduction to error, as goes the saying, ask an American Catholic. They should know better but seem to hold the most tenaciously to the doctrinal systems opposed to their own religion. Part of the reason is that such offers a way to material success. A podcast episode of the *Tom Woods Show* entitled "Did America Have a Christian Founding?" and posted November 27, 2019 had Thomas Woods, considered to be a pre-eminent American Catholic economic thinker, defending the American foundational principles as Catholic. Woods has some fame as an author of twelve books, and was co-editor of *The Latin Mass* magazine. In Episode 1543, Woods interviewed Dr. Mark David Hall who is the Herbert Hoover Distinguished Professor of Politics as well as a Faculty Fellow in the William Penn Honors Program at George Fox University. He has authored or edited at least twelve books, and his latest work, *Did*

America Have a Christian Founding? Separating Myth from Historical Truth, was the topic of the interview. If America had a Christian[1] founding, then of course America was a good thing, it was organized on Christian principles, and Catholics should support it and they should especially support the Constitution as originally intended which means that Catholics should get involved in the political system as it is and lend their might to the GOP and the conservative cause. Dr Hall, an Evangelical Christian, concluded America is based on Christianity. To arrive at that point, Dr Hall said that the founders were Christians and not Deists so therefore, the argument is suggested, what they created was Christian. According to Dr Hall, the disestablishment clause of the First Amendment allows Christianity to flourish (which means have a lot of real estate and buildings and institutions) and the prohibition against religious tests in Article VI, clause three is, according to Woods, a way to keep people and religions from becoming hypocrites. Woods also said that separation of church and state and disestablishment of the Church keeps the Church from being corrupted. Both authors agreed that the religions and the state can cooperate though they are separate, but the history of America shows little support for this proposition especially for the last seventy plus years. It was Murray, Americanism and The American Proposition for the most part.

Some Catholics are starting to disagree. They are saying the Faith should be applied to the organization of society. Some Catholics, influencers at that, are starting to articulate Catholicism, or integralism, as the basis of society. The plutocrats were taking notice by late 2019. *On The Media* is a podcast that airs Saturday mornings, and on the morning of December 7, 2019 "Making Sense of the Illiberal Right: How the Conservative Conversation about Democracy is Shifting" aired.[2] The host was Brooke Gladstone as she interviewed Matthew Sitman, co-host of Know Your Enemy blog site, and associate editor of Commonweal Magazine. The very title of the episode pigeonholed the efforts to reorder America as something concocted by the conservatives.

The key events that were the focus of the Gladstone Sitman discussion were a manifesto published on March 21, 2019 in *First Things* entitled "Against the Dead Consensus"[3] and then a September 5, 2019 debate between Sohrab Ahmari of the *New York Post* and David French, professor, lawyer and one of the staff writers of the *National Review.* Both events were viewed as an attempt by some to redefine conservatism as being something that was opposed to democracy. "Democracy" is code for a system that lends itself to manipulation by the plutocrats. Its opposite is Authoritarianism because that means a strong government capable of checking the plutocrats. The plutocrats generally do not like authoritarianism.

According to Sitman and other liberals, the position offered by the Ahmari and the *First Things* crowd, as well as the (apparently first of its kind) National Conservatism Conference held in July, 2019 in Washington D.C., is one in which the highest good comes to define the goal of the political system, and perhaps more importantly, "traditional authoritarianism" becomes resurgent. The illiberals consist of nationalists who approved the return to the nation state and the Catholic integralists who saw society based on the laws of God. These ideas threaten Liberalism which is due process, constitutional government, individual rights, equality, the rule of law, and limited government.

The September, 2019 debate between French and Ahmari at the Catholic University of America was troubling to the Liberals as the editorialized journalism a result of Luce's "newspeak" revealed.[4] French, 50 years of age and an evangelical Christian, is a Harvard graduate and law professor as well as constitutional lawyer. Asked to oppose Donald Trump for the Presidency in 2016, French defended the fusionist camp – the joining of the free market business class with the traditional social values and traditional family value crowd with it the First Amendment which "allowed Christian groups to flourish"[5] even if it did permit Drag Queen Story Hours in the Sacramento, California library.

Ahmari, an Iranian by birth fled the Ayatollah more than twenty years ago, obtained a law degree from Northeastern University, worked in London for two years. At 34 years of age, he was a recent convert to Catholicism who decried the Drag Queen Story Hours as demonic, and calls himself post-fusionist. With Matthew Schmitz, an editor at *First Things* and another recent Catholic convert like Ahmari, explained the fusion between "social traditionalists and economic free-marketers" which defined Reagan era conservatism was dead. Ahmari called for a "public square re-ordered to the common good and ultimately the Highest Good."[6] They made mention of a changed historical fact – the Cold War that spawned The American Proposition and during which the Vatican II Council was held had ended: "defeating Communism in the last century, by promoting prosperity at home and the expansion of rules-based international order...defended the natural rights of Americans and the `transcendant dignity of the human person....' Against the depredations of totalitarian regimes."[7] Taking Murray's own argument from sixty years earlier, the time was right to consider other means by which to morally order society and The American Proposition was up for debate.

Professor Michael Hanby critiqued Robert Reilly's defense of America aptly entitled *America on Trial: A Defense of the Founding.* Reilly, who had a history of working for agencies that promoted The American Proposition, argued the "American founding was based on natural law principles rooted in the premodern Catholic tradition." Hanby debunked that view of history and Reilly's entire defense by writing that there was a "radical transformation of that tradition at every level – theological, metaphysical, natural scientific, ecclesiastical, cultural and sociological." This radical transformation gutted terminology and even ideas of their original meaning and substituted in an entirely different, and alien, worldview that bore no semblance to Catholic tradition.[8]

Professor Patrick Deneen of the University of Notre Dame critiqued Michael Sandel's *The Tyranny of Merit: What's Become of the Common Good?* Deneen argued that the system of political philosophy used to establish the American institutions came from John Locke and provided not for the common good but rather for the promotion of the interests of the few. One could advance in this meritocracy for it was merit that was promoted, and not virtue, and certainly not a common good.[9]

Meanwhile, integralism was on the rise with the creation of an association of Catholic intellectuals who published their work on *The Josias* website around 2016. That term, as defined by Edmund Waldstein, O.Cist., is "Catholic Integralism is a tradition of thought that, rejecting eh liberal separation of politics from concern with the end of human life, holds that political rule must order man to his final goal. Since, however, man has both a temporal and an eternal end, integralism holds that there are two powers that rule him: a temporal power and a spiritual power. And since man's temporal end is subordinated to his eternal end, the temporal power must be subordinated to the spiritual power." In other words, what counts is not the form of government but the basis on which the laws are made.

Big guns were needed to defend The American Proposition. So George Weigel was called in. The 69 year old authored a definitive work on Pope St John Paul II and other books, is a Distinguished Senior Fellow and Chair of Catholic Studies at the Ethics and Public Policy Center in Washington, DC, has a column that runs regularly in Catholic publications, is married, has three children and in short is a Super Catholic. He wrote

"…I was pondering one of the strangest phenomena in this season of many discontents: the emergence of anew 'Catholic integralism' that (in the words of an advocate) promotes the notion that 'the state should recognize Catholicism as true and unite with the Church as body to her soul.' The proponents of a confessionally Catholic state as the optimum form of government are small in number. But they've demonstrated an impressive ability to rile up the debate about the current American political situation, and about Catholic social doctrine generally….."[10]

Weigel raised the specter of Fascist Italy and National Socialist Germany as though somehow integralism or the Catholic confessional state (two terms that he equated with each other) lead to dictatorships of recent memory or alliances with Stalin's Soviet Union. Obviously, there was no intellectual discussion here, just fear mongering.

Weigel's argument rested on the phrase "we hold these truths," the same phrase used by Murray to name his book in support of The American Proposition. He could not explain how the Supreme Court of the United States (SCOTUS) could decide *Obergefell v. Hodges* 576 US 644 (2015) and establish a constitutionally protected right to marry someone of the same sex. He just said it was the result of a "complex causal chain."[11]

All we needed to do, he said, was to follow the advice of John Paul II and Benedict XVI and get involved because they

"Emphasiz[ed]…the crucial importance to democracy of a vibrant, truth-based, public moral culture, they correctly diagnosed the deepest causes of today's political distortions and dysfunctions. Teaching that the church's public role is to shape the public moral culture by forming citizens who live in the truth, they set Catholic social doctrine in the context of the New Evangelization and defended the Church's liberty to be itself. Stressing the theological incompetence of the state, they helped strengthen the barriers to any new form of authoritarianism, left or right."

That was the same failed plan and the same deceitful rhetoric that got everyone into the worsening mess that we find ourselves because the plutocrats remain in control and power with the Anglo-American political philosophy and the protections of the First Amendment.

Professor Thomas Pink of King's College London wrote an article about two weeks before Weigel's piece. Pink's article entitled "Integralism, Political Philosophy, and the State" appearing in *Public Discourse* on May 9, he presented a reasoned and accurate disputation of the conflict between Liberalism and integralism. He explained integralism is natural law and in conformance with the Roman Catholic Faith. Integralism is supposed to use reason, build consensus, and it uses the law to teach. Catholic integralism includes the grace to help one deal with those times when reason is blocked for any of a number of different reasons. He explained that *Dignitatis Humanae* condemned the secular state's use of power to force belief because it is an exercise of power without jurisdiction. In a secular state such as the United States, the rules increasingly are turning against the natural law and liberty represents freedom from everything.[12]

Intellectuals were advancing integralism or the Catholic Confessional State – and drawing fire – for a while. Ross Gregory Douthat, is an American conservative political analyst, blogger, author and a columnist for *The New York Times*. He was a senior editor of *The Atlantic* and Douthat is perhaps responsible for starting a lot of the discussion on the emerging desire for the Confessional State or the integralist society. In October, 2016 he penned "Among the Post-Liberals" an op-ed in *The New York Times*. He caused a firestorm that echoes to this day. In his article he wrote that Liberalism attenuates basic natural human urges – for tribe, family and religion which equates to honor, community and metaphysical hope. The backlash against the secular state or Liberalism is seen in the angry nationalism that lead to Brexit and was sweeping Donald Trump into office. John Zmirak responded ten months later (July, 2017) to Douthat in "Catholics Reject Freedom at their own Peril," published in *The Stream*. It set the tone for all of those who attacked the integralist position – fear, tyranny, darkness. It was all very reminiscent of the American tactics demonizing the Soviet Union.[13]

But truth and faith drives out fear.

The *Catechism of the Catholic Church* (CCC), the revised version of which was published in 1992, provided the doctrinal basis for the Catholic confessional state, and justified Fr. Connell's position that the divine positive law is to form the basis of public policy. The reasoning is simple. Man is called to beatitude, or holiness, and that is his vocation. (CCC 825, 1694, 1716-1729, 2012-2029). Society and the civil authorities must therefore promote virtue (CCC 1895). Error has no rights, and there is no right to hold to error. (CCC

2108.) "Freedom" to be and do anything, is error. (CCC 1738, 1747.)

The tools are in place, the foundation is laid for the renewal. The workers and warriors are gathering. A leader is needed. The Catholics are on the march.

APPENDIX A
AMINTORE FANFANI EXPLAINS THE CAPITALIST SPIRIT AND RELIGIOUS LIBERTY

The issue of church and state, with its corollary of religious liberty, implicates economics, theology, philosophy, and politics for we are dealing with social organization. One of the most helpful guides in gaining an insight into this relationship was an Italian. Amintore Fanfani, named after one of the leaders of the Italian Risorgimento, was one of the founders of "the little professors," a group of Catholic academics formed into a "semi-monastic political group" that was "intense in their Catholicism and militant in their reformism."[1] These "little professors" lived in monastic cells and walked barefoot.[2]

Fanfani was born north of Rome in Arezzo Province in 1908 into a very religious Catholic family. His father was an attorney and member of Partito Popolare. His mother, a very devout woman, was the only person who scared him he admitted later.[3] Short in stature at 5 foot 3 inches, Fanfani was a mental giant.[4] He began advanced schooling at the Catholic University of the Sacred Heart in Milan where he did well in mathematics and physics, but later decided to study political economy in which he earned his doctorate at the age of 24, in 1932.[5]

Fanfani's thesis was published in 1935 as *Catholicism Protestantism and Capitalism,*[6] and after that he was hired to teach economics and economic history at the Catholic University of Milan where he taught with only one interruption, until 1955.[7] He also taught at the University of Venice from 1938 to 1943.[8] After 1955, he was a member of the faculty of the University of Rome, where he was known affectionately as "il professorino," until 1983.[9] During his career as a professor, he wrote 16 books on politics and economics, and with the "little professors" he formed the nucleus of what came to be known as the "Democratic Initiative" that grew into an anti-communist wing of the Christian Democratic Party.[10]

Fanfani's involvement with politics came during the Mussolini era when he participated in the Federazione Universitaria Cattolica Italiana ("FUCI" or University Federation of Italian Catholics) and the Laureati (Catholic University graduates). Mussolini, who had removed Fanfani's father from Parliament for being too liberal,[11] was himself removed from power in 1943 at about the same time Fanfani fled to Switzerland where he taught Italians interned in Lausanne and Geneva.[12]

Within two years of returning to Italy, Fanfani ran for and was elected to the constituent assembly in 1946 as a member of the Christian Democrats, whose leader, Alcide De Gasperi, was viewed as his mentor. One of the chief tasks facing the Italian government was the creation of a new constitution. Fanfani's greatest contribution to this effort was the drafting of the following provision explaining the nature of the Italian government: "Italy is a democratic republic founded on work." This contrasted sharply with the Communist proposal (which was "Italy is a democratic republic of workers") and it reflected much of Fanfani's view on economics and politics.[13]

In 1948, Fanfani was elected to the Chamber of Deputies, and was a member of De Gasperi's cabinets.[14] From 1947 to 1950, he was the minister of labor and social welfare, and during that time he instituted a program to build housing for workers by contributions from government, employers, and workers.[15] Within several years, about 7,700 of the homes were built.[16] As minister of agriculture and forestry in 1951, he expedited land reforms and put to work 200,000 of the unemployed in a reforestation program.[17] In 1953, he became minister of the interior.[18]

With the death in 1954 of DeGasperi, Fanfani became the party leader, or secretary-general of the party until 1959, a position that he again held from 1973 to 1975. As party secretary-general, Fanfani's political power was at its peak until the mid-1960s. During that time he served as Premier or Prime Minister in a number of different governments. His longest term was from July, 1960 to May 1963, and during his terms of office he successfully pursued policy initiatives the Americans did not like. These initiatives included focusing Italian foreign policy on the Mediterranean and commencing a pro-Arab foreign policy. His greatest accomplishment, with the help of fellow party member Aldo Moro, was to forge a Center-Left coalition with the Communists in the early 1960s. The coalition resulted in increased participation by the masses in the political system, the democratization of the educational system, the expansion of regional governments, nationalization of the electrical industry, and an easing of East-West tensions.[19]

Defeated in his bids in 1964 and 1971 to become President of Italy, he served as Foreign Minister (1965-1966), President of the United Nations General Assembly (1965), and President of the Senate (1968-1973; 1976 – 1982; 1985 -- 1987).[20] Fanfani was senator for life as of 1972 and in 1987 served 11 days as Prime Minister upon the request of the President.[21] He lived to the ripe age of 91, passing away in 1999.

Catholicism inspired Fanfani's politics and, along with his scrupulous honesty, he was able to bring together Italy's divided political word.[22] Commentators wrote that he "was a Catholic corporatist committed to finding a `third way' between collectivist communism and the free market."[23] Fanfani believed that "`private economic initiative' was justifiable only if harnessed to the common good," and he used the public sector developed by Mussolini to serve as an instrument of political rule and employment for when the private sector failed.[24] He knew the power of television and with his friend Ettore Bernabei, Fanfani kept mass communications under the control of the Christian Democrats.[25]

Ambassador Clare Boothe Luce kept her eyes on Fanfani as the Americans were never comfortable with him. Clare wrote to CD Jackson, who at that moment was back at his desk in Time, Inc., a letter dated September 29, 1954. She told him

"My hunch is that the politico who has to be watched (and worked over) most carefully is Fanfani. Mr. Fanfani has never been to America. He does not have America in his heart, mind, or imagination. A product of Fascism, in which he played a small but useful role as a young man, he now acts and reacts only in a European context. Today, that means a context in which ever European politico feels himself forced to seek domestic power through compromise with the pro-Cominform Left, and in which Russia (not the USA) is the nearest and most powerful neighbor. Fanfani may well be Italy's Mendes-France. Indeed, he is reputed already to have begun to talk privately with Nenni."[26]

Clare was of the view the Soviets were working behind the scenes to "release" Nenni to Fanfani who would pursue a neutralist approach towards international matters, thereby making Fanfani the Italian Kerensky. Clare based this on a number of "straws in the wind" which were the publication by Valletta's *La Stampa* of a number of neutralist editorials, Fanfani's support among "big industrialists," and the release of Mendez-France's memoirs for publication in Nenni's publication.[27]

Fanfani was the subject of a study by the United States Information Service (USIS). The purpose of the study was to "ascertain prof. Fanfani's views with regard to any particular system of economies and to the American system in particular." The Americans termed Fanfani as a "neovoluntarist." A neovoluntarist was one who believed that an "economy is like a brainless and purposeless body requiring the agency of the human will; but it is capable of resisting the human will and frequently, to the very utmost, it is this possible resistance that must be accounted for by the human will both in aiming at a given purpose and in leading the way toward it."[28]

When it came to America, Fanfani, according to the USIS, was critical of the American economists who failed to define man's "well-being." Fanfani ascribed to the view of leading a good life, or "good living," and this view "is now part and parcel of the Christian social current of opinion, the `integral neo-voluntarist current'."[29] This "integralistic theory" is responsible for the position that holds there is:

"no rational solution of the economic problem [that] can be reached except through an `all-comprehensive view embracing both economic and non-economic life on the one side, and both natural and supernatural on the other....While an economist is a technician of human well-beings, a politician instead must aim at achieving `the common good, namely, such conditions as will consent every individual his rightful measure of good living, including those rights that are inherent to his social position as an individual."[30]

The "policy of good living together with the economy of well-being is nothing but `one human activity whose object consists in allowing society to correct the inadequacies and the errors of the individual in order to bring about those conditions which will permit everyone to avail himself of all means to develop all his personal talents while enjoying all those rights that are inherent to his social position as an individual." Society must "provide `a plan for the education, the reeducation and the reclamation,' of the individual by a plan made necessary by the continued effects of original sin – so that economy of well-being may be practiced in conjunction with a policy of good living."[31]

When Italy was faced with the possibility of a referendum to abolish the new divorce laws in 1974, Fanfani energetically threw himself into the fight even though it is reported the Church reluctantly backed him.[32] He famously said "Divorce will hurl the nation into ruin…How will you like it when your wife leaves to marry your best friend's wife, or runs away with the chambermaid?"[33]

Catholicism Protestantism and Capitalism explained the main dynamic behind the last 500 years of the history of the West. As a foundational principle, Fanfani posited "since every derivative human attitude is the result of a fundamental principle, the economic spirit of a given age is necessarily inseparable from the current idea of wealth and its ends."[34] The economic principle that grew in power and influence over the years is capitalism. Capitalism, Fanfani explained, is an "economic mode of life as led by man and by society." It is characterized by the capitalist who governs "impulses and resolutions to action, determines the creation of new means and new institutions or the modification of those already in existence." One's view of wealth is linked to one's view of the universe, and so "Modern man, who is capitalistic, regards wealth as the best means for an ever more complete satisfaction of every conceivable need; he also regards [sic] as the best means for improving his own position." The capitalist spirit has two central components: "the unlimited use of all means of acquiring wealth that are held to be morally lawful and economically useful…. [and]….an individual and utilitarian conception of the use of wealth." Capitalists "break down the barriers that civil and ecclesiastical legislation set to their action."[35]

Throughout the course of several hundred years, the capitalist spirit grew. Mercantilism came about during a time when a non-capitalist spirit informed social institutions which in turn fostered agencies that were informed by the capitalist spirit.[36] Making hidden reference to the American Revolution, Fanfani wrote:

"When towards the end of the eighteenth century an outcry is raised against the mercantile system – not through any aggravation of its burdens, but through the growing vigour of the aspirations of those on whom they fell – the struggle between the politico-social pre-capitalism of the State and the capitalism of individuals would be openly renewed; the capitalist spirit would make its last and most successful attempt to gain possession of the whole of society….Thus the development of the capitalist spirit occupies nearly ten centuries, from the ninth to the eighteenth, in the course of which it passes from the stage of timid and sporadic appearances in isolated individuals to that in which it is firmly established in nearly the whole of the ruling classes, in doctrines, in society, and in all social institutions."[37]

Amongst institutions and societies where the pre-capitalist spirit reigned, circumstances "of a spiritual order…directly draw man away from the pre-capitalist spirit and indirectly lead him to approach the capitalistic mode of thought…" Declining faith lead man to a reorientation of his views towards the world around him as well as to the role of economics in life, and so the very reasoning for the old economic order weakened. Material and spiritual circumstances, sometimes working separately or other times working in combination, explained how people can come to break from the pre-capitalist mode of thinking in which moral and religious concerns limit or direct economic activity and to accept the capitalist mode of thinking or spirit, which is a spiritual phenomenon that "transformed the life of men and the structure of society."[38]

This transformation ultimately occurred in the public life of the society, which meant that "culture, the State, and public and private activities harmonized one with the other and supported one another in the work of construction." The state had to be captured and public life had to be rationalized in accordance with the capitalist spirit. Madame C. proclaimed in 1764 that England would "become `a democratic republic in which commerce is God'."[39]

Commerce requires money, and money begs the creation of banks. Those who control the banks, therefore, control the money. With the control of the money comes the control of the economy, and with that comes the control over society.[40]

The state became the protector of economic activity and then later it became the "guarantor of its liberty." The State did this in three ways: by "guaranteeing security"; by education; and by establishing "freedom, so that the economic machine, as transformed and to be transformed still further by the individual, may so function as to achieve the maximum economic rationalization that will mark the triumph of the capitalist spirit." The State was urged to "political colonial expansion, as a platform for economic colonial expansion."[41]

Thomas Paine, along with James Madison and Adam Smith, presented a view of society based on individuals whose only connection came about as a result of "accident, interest and circumstances" in the pursuit of their respective livelihoods. Government was to serve only as a referee and it had no positive duty to "promote justice or virtue."[42]

Such a view was the view of Liberalism which made "freedom" a principal value. Liberalism, and Enlightenment philosophy in general, served to create good conditions for the growth of the capitalist spirit. These philosophies provided justification to allow the private, monied interests to pursue their objectives lessening interference from the government. The view of society and human nature that underlay these philosophies permitted the atomization of society. This in turn gave the monied interests greater power over their fellow citizens, and inordinate government influence.

Catholicism presents a world view, organization of society, and purpose of material things, particularly wealth that is basically at odds with Liberalism, including the American ideology. Catholicism looks at all things as they relate to God, and capitalism does not. In other words, the "Catholic order is a supernatural order, the capitalistic order is a rational order in the sense of the Enlightenment."[43] Catholicism teaches:

"earthly goods are a means, and as means man not only may desire them, but he must take possession of them for his corporal sustenance and for the relief of his neighbour. Wealth, says Orlich, becomes an evil when, instead of a means it becomes an end and absorbs human activity at the expense of the attainment of his eternal goal. For temporal goods `are subjected to man that he may use them according to his needs, not that he may place his end in them.[44]

This was essentially the position of St. Thomas Aquinas.

A society imbued with a capitalist spirit is opposed to Catholicism in three crucial areas. First, such a society adopts the "economic criterion as the criterion of order." Second, such a society fails to "consider third persons," and finally such a society exalts "a quest for purely individual profit." All of this is because the "capitalistic conception of life is founded on a separation of human aims. It fixes its gaze on natural and in particular on economic goals; it precludes supernatural religious goals."[45]

Catholic theology sets out a view for society and the state that keeps in mind man's ultimate end. That ultimate end is to be union with God when this life ends. This is therefore a threat to the capitalist spirit and must be overthrown, or its influence lessened. The one with the capitalist spirit seeks to free the state from the influence of religious standards or beliefs. He proclaims and demands "freedom of conscience," a "spirit of toleration," and "religious liberty." Once these so-called freedoms are established, then the State, "no longer guardian of religious ends as the supreme ends of society, became the guardian of its own, political ends" and the State became secular.[46]

These political ends change with the economic purposes and goals of the capitalist. The State serves capitalism in a number of key ways. The first is by unifying a national market by "establishing uniformity of law" and thereby satisfying capitalism's demand for a vast market. Another is the "establishment of uniform weights and measures." A third is improved communications meaning roads and what is now known as infrastructure or critical infrastructure.[47]

Since there are certain things that private industry, or individual capitalists cannot do well or profitably on a large scale, the State becomes the means by which to encourage the expansion of capitalism by defining public needs, and proceeding to satisfy these. One need is the "needs of defence" in which the government exercised a "perceptible and beneficial influence on industrial activity." The State's involvement in public works and education was important. In the former case it "lessens the risks of producers, and almost plays the part of an insurance system" by creating demands when private demand diminishes. In the latter case, education "facilitates business inasmuch as it means the spread of culture, indispensable for economic progress." Finally, the State has an "increasing need of financial resources" which means "compensating and regularizing the demand for money on the market." Public finance is regulated in "accordance with economic rather than political criteria" while fulfilling those "economic functions that private individuals would not be able to compass."[48]

Catholics and Catholic societies succumb to the capitalist spirit, according to Fanfani, when faith fails. The result is that the "world is judged by purely worldly criteria." A person then seeks "goods because he no longer believes in a faith that bounded his desires, and he no longer believes because he has experienced the pleasures of possession and influence."[49] Such a person no longer believes in divine penalties and rewards, nor does such a person believe in the purpose of life as taught by generations of Catholics.

The "humanist conception of life" strengthened the capitalist spirit because it detached the "conception of wealth from its moral setting, and withdrawing the acquisition and use of goods from the influence of the rules and restrictions of religious morality." With the rise of Protestantism's many sects, States faced the issue of freedom of conscience which removed another obstacle to the capitalist spirit. Fanfani explained:

"Protestantism destroyed the unity of the State in the religious sphere and made its restoration impossible, so that King and subjects were faced with the problem of shelving the religious question in order to obtain such unity. Protestantism thus obliged the States to face the problem of freedom of conscience, which, advocated by authoritative Protestants, once solved, meant the removal of an obstacle to economic life and encouraged the tendency to count the religious question among problems that could be left out of reckoning. From that time forth the State became more favourably disposed towards capitalism; it had no longer a creed to defend, but only interests, and in this sphere it was not hard to reach an understanding."[50]

Economic life could therefore become organized solely along criteria of utility that rested with economic or monetary value. The Protestant missionaries were important foot soldiers in this effort set forth in this book. They worked closely with America's plutocrats to Americanize the Church.

APPENDIX B
BISHOP JOSEPH FESSLER EXPLAINS "HEATHEN CAESARISM"

Bishop Dr. Joseph Fessler, Secretary General of the First Vatican Council authored a document entitled "The True and the False Infallibility of the Popes: A Controversial Reply to Dr. Schulte." A copy of it was given to Clare Boothe Luce by Bishop John Noll in 1948. The article, published in 1875 after the Bishop's death, set forth reasons behind the Church's teachings in the realm of Church and Civil Society, and it explained the proper relationship between the two societies based on their purposes or ends. Bishop Fessler set out several assertions to "satisfy all but Caesarists." These assertions were first that "civil society of men has God for its Founder" as its creation occurred "potentially in the creation of man." This included the view that "The human family contains the first principles and laws of authority, obedience and order. These three conditions of society are of Divine origin, and they are the constructive laws of all civil or political society."[1]

Second, Fessler explained that "supreme authority is given immediately by God" to Civil Society and mediately "to the person or person to whom society may commit its custody and its exercise." Regardless of the form of the Civil Government, those who are part of that Government hold a "Divine sanction and a Divine authority" and it has the "power of life and death…for self defense. It passes to society at large, which likewise has the right of self defense. It is committed by society to its chief executive." Society has "no power to revoke its act" provided the "Civil Ruler does not deviate from the end of his existence." Therefore it follows that "just resistance to an unjust prince is not rebellion" especially if the "Civil Ruler…should make war upon the people" for the "right of self-defense would justify resistance" as that "right is undeniable."[2]

Third, the "laws of such society are the laws of nature. It is bound by the natural morality written on the conscience and on the heart." Fessler wrote that "Politics are but the collective morals of society…..The Civil ruler may bind all subjects by an oath of allegiance. He may call on all to bear arms for the safety of the State." Fourth, the end of the State is "not only the safety of person and property, but in its fullest sense, the temporal happiness of man….." Bishop Fessler cited to Romans 13:1-5 in which St. Paul teaches that everyone "should be subject to higher powers: for there is no power but from God; and those that are, are ordained of God…..For he is God's minister to thee for good…."[3]

While the State is a perfect society and is supreme within its own sphere, it "is not the highest end of man, so the State is not the highest society among men; nor is it, beyond its own sphere and end, supreme." God is the source of the institution of the Civil Society. The "laws of the order of nature are from God" so therefore "[i]t is mere shallowness to say that between the Civil authority, as Divinely founded in nature, and the spiritual authority of the Church there can be opposition." Provided that a "sovereign power" "exercises his domestic authority according to the law of God, no other authority can intervene to control or to hinder his government."[4]

The Church is the other society and it has for its end "the eternal happiness of mankind" for it has "God for its Founder, and that immediately." The Church is therefore of "an order higher than the society which aims only at the natural happiness of man." The "temporal and the eternal happiness of man are both ordered by

Divine laws, these two societies are, of necessity, in essential conformity and harmony with each other" unless either should deviate from their respective laws. The natural or civil society "aims directly at the temporal happiness of its subjects, but indirectly it aims also at their eternal happiness." The Church, or "the supernatural society aims directly at their eternal happiness, and indirectly at their temporal happiness, but always in so far only as their temporal happiness is conducive to their eternal end." From this flow a number of corollaries. The first is "the higher or supernatural society is supreme because it has no other society… with an end higher than its own." The "office of the supernatural society is to aid, direct, and perfect the natural society." The action of the supernatural society "is always in aedificationem non in destructionem" for "it is governed by the same Divine Lawgiver, and it is directed to an end which includes and ensures the end of the natural society also."[5]

The Bishop wrote Jesus Christ gave the Catholic Church "supreme doctrinal authority, and a supreme judicial office, in respect to the moral law, over all nations, and over all persons, both governors and governed." This was made clear in Matthew 14:19 in which He said "To thee I will give the keys of the Kingdom of Heaven. And whatsoever thou shalt bind on earth shall be bound also in heaven, and whatsoever thou shat loose on earth shall be loosed also in heaven." And again in Matthew 28:18-20 Christ said "all power is given to me in heaven and in earth. Going, therefore, teach all nations…teaching them to observe all things whatsoever I have commanded you." Provided "Princes and their laws are in conformity with the Christian law", the authority and the office of the Church are "directive and perceptive." The authority becomes judicial ("ratione peccati") "by reason of sin" whenever there is a deviation from this by these earthly powers.[6]

"Heathen Caesarism" denied these principles and held that princes have "no superior but the law of God." Fessler held that such is to "play with words" for a "law is no superior without an authority to judge and to apply it." The will of the Civil Society is above that of the King. However, "this doctrine, unless it be tempered by vigorous restraint is chronic revolution" and "what adequate restraint is there but in a divine authority higher than the natural society of man?"[7]

There are limits to this doctrine. The first is that the "Supreme Judicial Power of the Church has no jurisdiction over those that are not Christian." All the Church can do with "such a people…both individually and socially outside the Divine jurisdiction of the Church" is to "convert it to Christianity." If it applied any authority at all, the Church would use it to "confirm the natural rights of sovereignty and to enforce the natural duty of allegiance." There is an order of nature to which even the heathen sovereigns are subject. The Church does not come to destroy such or to depose such a sovereign as the principle set forth in 1 Cor. 5:12 states: "What have I to do to judge those that are without?" The duty of the church is to convert such a society to Christianity, and it has no power of enforcement of God's laws.[8]

In the case of "Christian Princes and their laws," the Church is to "confirm, consecrate, and enforce the sanctions of religion and of conscience, of doctrine and of discipline, the whole code of natural and political morality and all laws that are made in conformity with the same." The Church has the power and authority from God to enforce corrections from the deviations or departures from justice.[9]

In response to the question of which of the two powers – the State or the Church – has the competence to judge or decide "what does and what does not fall within" the respective spheres, it is the Church which holds that power and not the State. This is so because the Church is the repository of Christian Revelation and it can fix the limits of its own jurisdiction. Since the Church is the highest society and so independent of all other societies it is supreme over them when it comes to the eternal happiness of men. Therefore, two consequences follow. First, in things purely temporal that lie "extra finen Ecclesiae, outside of the end of the Church" it does not have jurisdiction nor does it claim such. Second, the Church has power to judge and to enforce all things which promote or hinder the eternal happiness of man.[10]

Bishop Fessler set out five propositions for the relation between the Church and State when pressed by his opponents who argued the Bishop was claiming for the Church supreme temporal authority. First, "so long as Princes and their laws are in conformity to the law of God, the Church has no power or jurisdiction against them, nor over them." Second, should "Princes and their laws deviate from the law of God, the Church has authority from God to judge of that deviation, and to oblige to its correction." Third, the Church's authority is spiritual and comes from God. Fourth, the Church's authority "indirectly condemns and declares not binding on the conscience such temporal laws as deviate from the law of God, and therefore impede or render impossible the attainment of the eternal happiness of man." Finally, the Church's spiritual authority in this regard is "inherent in the Divine constitution and commission of the Church." Its "exercise in the world depends on certain moral and material conditions, by which alone its exercise is rendered either possible or just."[11]

From this discussion, it became clear Catholic teaching was that the civil authorities had the responsibility to conform their actions to the Divine Positive Law. The Church insured compliance with the Divine Positive Law. The First Amendment kept that from happening in America because it disestablished the Catholic Church, and other churches, all in the name of religious liberty. From that point on, the Government, or State, had greater power than the churches, had control over the churches, and used them to advance the purposes and goals of the powerful private interests in society. The plutocrats gained power over culture, Civil Society, and the Church all for the benefit of the plutocrats. This is exactly what the Cold War and the American victory in the Cold War demonstrated.

Clare Boothe Luce knew all of this when Bishop John Noll of the Diocese of Fort Wayne, Indiana handed her Bishop Dr. Joseph Fessler's "The True and the False Infallibility of the Popes: A Controversial Reply to Dr. Schulte" back in 1948. She chose to serve Harry and the plutocrats.

APPENDIX C
"THE TWO VIEWS"

Murray's paper containing the arguments for the American attack was published in the December, 1964 issue of *Theological Studies*. Originally entitled "Right of the Human Person to Liberty on Matters of Religion," it was renamed "The Problem of Religious Freedom at the Council." It was perhaps the most important document in advancing the cause for a declaration on religious liberty at the council as it indicated "what became pivotal for the Council's Declaration on Religious Freedom."[1]

Disclaiming any intent to present his own views, Murray just wanted to "further the conciliar dialogue, in so far as a theologian may make a modest effort to do this." Murray wrote there were two views on religious freedom. The "central question that is in dispute between the two Views...concerns the cura-religionis by the public powers." The "care of religion" goes back to when the Church "first emerged into public existence within the Roman Empire." The issue was political, juridical, theological ("because it touches doctrines of faith, chiefly in ecclesiology"), and moral ("because it raises the issue of conscience"). It was also constitutional because "nowadays an answer to the question of cura-religionis is customarily provided...in the constitutional law of organized political communities."[2]

Murray started the paper with a reference to a talk by Paul VI and then the identification of the twin themes of American doctrinal war: the goodness of America, and the evil of Communism. Religious freedom was integral to the "Catholic experience in the United States" while the Church encountered difficulties in "countries under Communist domination." A doctrinal change, or development was required, but such could come about because the material for such are already in Catholic doctrine.[3]

The "First View" was the position advanced and defended by Ottaviani, Fenton, Connell and Shea. The "Second View" was the position that he, DeSmedt, and the US bishops were advancing. There were two methodologies in the "Second View" with one being De Smedt's, or the French, and the other being his or the Anglo-American. The First View was based on a simple principle: "that only the truth has rights, whereas error has no rights, within the public sector of society." This "abstract and simple" principle determined both the moral question of conscience rights and the "constitutional question." The First View made a "distinction between thesis and hypothesis. The thesis states the ideal – the cura religionis (care of religion) that constitutional law ought to provide, per se and in principle. The hypothesis states the concessions that may have to be made to circumstances – the cura religionis that constitutional law may provide, per accidens and in view of circumstances." The "state is bound not only on the natural law but also on the positive divine law whereby the Church was established." The state therefore has a duty "per se and in principle, to recognize by constitutional law" the Church as "a perfect society," the only one with a right to "public existence and action," and it "ought to be, by constitutional law, the one religion of the state."[4]

Murray described this situation in negative and inflammatory terms. The First View called for the extermination of "all false religions" which meant the "legal institution of intolerance." Religious error can be "repressed by law or by the police action of the State" and it "ought to be repressed by the state." The reasons for this repression were first that "error and evil are...contrary to the rational and moral nature of man"; that error and evil are "contrary to the common good of society, which is constituted by what is true and good"; that error and evil are "injurious to the rights of others, especially their right to be protected from error and evil and to be left undisturbed in the profession of truth and in the practice of the good"; and finally that error and evil are "scandal, an occasion of moral wrongdoing and of defection from the truth."[5]

The "quaestio facti" was when the thesis (confessional state) applied versus when the hypothesis (non-confessional state) applied. The thesis applied when the majority of citizens of a nation are Catholic, the nation "historically reached the social consciousness of Catholic truth," or the nation has a tradition of "Catholic religious unity." In societies that are not Catholic, or are pluralistic, or the Catholics are a minority, or where "Catholicism has not permeated the national consciousness," then the hypothesis applies "as a matter of fact." The Church, he wrote, "foregoes her right to legal establishment as the one religion of the state, with its juridical consequence, legal intolerance. The Church, however, gives no positive approval to the resultant constitutional situation. Per se the situation is an evil, but it may be regarded as a lesser evil….Therefore it may be tolerated…."[6]

The First View "is declared to be the doctrine of the Church, supported by magisterial authority." That authority was found first and foremost in Pius XII's *Ci Riesce* and also in the writings of Leo XIII going back to Gregory XVI. However, the First View was itself a development of doctrine in that it rejected "certain conceptions of cura religionis that were prevalent in former eras." The First View clarified "traditional principles – in particular, the distinction between the religious order and the political order, and the limitations of political sovereignty in the order of religion." Since Leo XIII, the Church saw religious freedom "as a personal right and as a legal institution" representing "decadence, not progress" that created more evils.[7]

John XXIII's *Pacem In Terris* engaged in a discussion of human and civil rights "commanded by the historical consciousness" and by a "sense of man's `spiritual aspirations'." Man desired personal, political and social freedom from "legal coercion and constraint, except in so far these are necessary." This desire came from the "depths of the human person" and was the expression of a "sense of right approved by reason" as well as the "demand of natural law in the present moment of history." The demand is for the "goods of the human spirit" which include the "search for truth, the free expression and dissemination of opinion, the cultivation of the arts and sciences, free access to information about public events, adequate opportunities for the development of personal talents and for progress in knowledge and culture...."[8]

With these developments, the "ancient question concerning cura religionis has been altered...." The new questions he posited were, first, what does "religious freedom mean in the common consciousness today," and second, "why religious freedom, in the sense of the common consciousness, is to receive the authoritative approval of the Church. The Second View addresses itself to the question in its new historical and doctrinal state." There are two methods of setting forth the Second View with one being De Smedt's and the other being Murray's. DeSmedt's method was "theological-moral" with the emphasis primarily on religious liberty as a juridical concept founded in principles of "theology, ethics, political philosophy, and jurisprudence." DeSmedt arrived at his position by "abstract argument" carried on in a "vacuum of historical, political, and juridical experience." His position raised the "legal institution of religious freedom" as an ideal of constitutional law when it came to the care of religion. Murray's method was more attuned to the times, or the "historical consciousness," in that it held religious freedom as "a human and civil right." The definition of religious freedom is important, and is determined by "contemporary historical experience."[9]

Religious freedom was first, an "immunity that attaches to the human person within society, and it has its guarantee in civil law." It is a human and civil right and consists of freedom of conscience and the free exercise of religion. Freedom of conscience means the person is immune from all "external coercion in his search for God, in the investigation of religious truth, in the acceptance or rejection of religious faith, in the living of his interior religious or non-religious life…it is the freedom of personal religious decision." While it is personal, it is also social and a man has a right to be free of all "manner of compulsion, constraint, and restraint, whether legal or extra-legal" and "society and all its institutions are obliged to respect this right and to refrain from coercion." Social discrimination, economic disadvantage, civil disabilities, psychological pressure such as brainwashing and massive propaganda are all condemned and prohibited.[10]

Freedom of religious expression includes an autonomy that consisted of freedom to associate in religious groups and be free from government interference in conducting the affairs of the group. This included immunity from intervention by the "public powers" when it came to the society's existence, determination of its doctrines, its internal discipline and self-government, and communications with other communities. This included "immunity from coercion in what concerns the public worship of God, public religious observances and practice, the public proclamation of religious faith, and the public declaration of the implications of religion and morality for the temporal affairs of the community and for the action of the public powers." Murray concluded his definition of religious freedom was "substantially in accord with the understanding contained in the pertinent declarations of the World Council of Churches," and important in the "ecumenical dialogue."[11]

The term "constitutional government" had to be defined since religious freedom arose in that context. A government based on these four political truths is based on truth: 1) "the distinction between the sacred and the secular orders of human life"; 2) the "distinction between society and state"; 3) the "distinction between the common good and public order"; and 4) the "principle and rule of 'freedom under law'." The common good, Murray noted, included "all the social goods, spiritual and moral as well as material" which man "pursues here on earth in accord with the demands of his personal and social nature." The "public order" which "devolves upon the state" to provide, consists of three goods the state can achieve through its "coercive discipline of public law." These three goods are public peace, the "highest political good," public morality "determined by moral standards commonly accepted among the people," and justice which consists of freedoms. The state is responsible for public order, but not the common good according to Murray, as the latter is the responsibility of society at-large. As to "freedom under law," Murray explained that the "higher purpose of the juridical order" is the freedom of the people and that freedom is the "political method per excellentiam" which also "sets limits to the power of government."[12]

Murray did not see the state as a moral actor other than to guarantee freedoms which were of greater importance than truth. It was a justification of the American system of social-political organization and it ignored the ultimate end of the person. It was also a justification of the American ideology or the American Proposition, and served US doctrinal warfare purposes. Of note, Murray's foundations for religious liberty illustrated the characteristic of American activities, which is the primacy of manipulation and not theory or principle. DeSmedt's view reflected the European characteristic of the primacy of principle or theory in fashioning structures.

There were limits to religious freedom. Public authorities may "inhibit forms of religious expression...only when such forms of public expression seriously violate either the public peace or commonly accepted standards of public morality, or the rights of other citizens." A violation must be "really serious" and legal intervention "really necessary" as religious freedom should have a "privileged character." Society should have a "spirit of tolerance" as well as "reverence and respect for others." He condemned "proselytism" which he defined as representing "an un-christian use of force in religious matters" such that it "does not stand at the door and knock; it rushes rudely into the house."[13]

After this discussion, Murray engaged in an admittedly brief sketch of the history of "cura religionis" as a "theological, ethical, political, legal and jurisprudential problem" from the Roman Empire to the present. He characterized the comments of the various pontiffs from Leo XIII through Pius XII. However, the key event in history was the creation of the US Constitution and Bill of Rights which altered the "state of the historic question." No longer was the issue to be the "political and legal support of the exclusive rights of truth, with consequent intolerance of error." Instead, "religious freedom – personal, ecclesial, associational, practical" was the "question" when it came to the care of religion. The result was the "the restoration, in a new form adapted to new circumstances, of ancient and medieval constitutionalism." Religious freedom was established by the First Amendment as an institution that could operate in harmony with the political idea of a government of limited powers. Cura religionis became cura libertatis religiosae. The Church did not "reckon with the new development" Murray wrote because there were only 30,000 Catholics in the US at the time, and the Church was involved in Europe in a conflict with the French Revolution and its different idea of religious freedom. Murray concluded the Church's attention, "from Pius VI to Pius IX" was "totally engaged in the condemnation and containment of the new European revolutionary ideology." [14] With that turn of phrase, Murray was able to avoid such teachings as the *Syllabus* and *Quanta Cura* issued by Blessed Pius IX and so destructive to Murray's arguments.

Leo XIII responded not to the Anglo-American constitutional systems but to European constitutional systems which Murray termed totalitarian ideologies creating a totalitarian state ("totalitarian democracy") which was atheist. Religion was a private matter, churches were voluntary associations, the state gave existence to the churches, and all religions were considered "equally true as equal expressions of the individual outlaw conscience." The state held to "autonomous individual reason" and was "the supreme arbiter of religious truth and church polity." This was the "lineal progenitor of the people's democracy of contemporary Communist theory" which removed religion from the public domain. [15]

Leo's position was designed to defend the "status quo ante" and was based on historical circumstances of the day. However, Leo opened the door to doctrinal development in at least a couple of important areas. First, Leo engaged or utilized a "ressourcement, a creative return to the sources of the tradition, a review of traditional doctrine within a new perspective created by history." Second, Leo changed the understanding of the diarchy, or the two powers, to include "two societies, two orders of law, and two powers." This formed the heart of Leo's "doctrine on constitutionalism." The Church was a transcendent spiritual authority ruled by God's law as revealed in Christ, and there existed an autonomous "People Temporal, who are ruled by a civil law, under a government whose powers are limited by a higher order of law not of its own making." Leo's teaching resulted in the restoration "to its proper centrality" of the Gregorian doctrine of the freedom of the Church.[16]

However, Murray wrote that Leo's greatest contribution and achievement was the idea of Libertas Ecclesiae. The "first property" of the Church is freedom Leo taught, and Proposition 39 of the *Syllabus* (scil., "The State, as being the origin and source of all rights, is endowed with a certain right not circumscribed by any limits"[17]) destroyed the Church's freedom. The same Proposition 39 was at the same time the destruction of the "essential dignity of man, which resides in his freedom." Leo did not focus on human dignity because "it did not lie within his historical problematic."[18]

Pius XI referenced the "freedom of the human person." This freedom was in accord with the "law of nature." Pius XII contributed to doctrinal development at a time when Communist totalitarianism was a "threat...not simply to the freedom of the Church in the traditionally Catholic nations of Europe" but was a threat to the "freedom of the people everywhere." Communism "rejected and denied the rights, the dignity, and the freedom of the human person," and the mission of the Church had to be the "vindication of the 'dignity of man'." With the rise of Communism, people were desirous of a "system of government that will be more in accord with the dignity and freedom of the citizenry."[19]

Pius XII was supportive of the American conception of government and the relationship of Church and state. Pius XII broke with Leo XIII by abandoning the idea government was paternal and familial, substituting instead the idea that government was political and society was to be built not from the top down but built from the bottom up. The state was an agent of the society, and Pius, rejecting Leo's conception of the society-state, held the state was juridical, owed its roots to Christian inspiration, and, along with society, was built on a "concrete conception of the human person in the present historical moment." Government's primary function was to "protect the inviolable rights that are proper to man, and to have a care that everyone may more readily discharge his duties." Government was limited in regards to the common good.[20]

Pius XII addressed the question of the cura religionis most notably in *Ci Riesce*. While both the First View and the Second View laid claim to the allocution as supporting their respective positions, Murray held the document's "major doctrinal intention" was to "clarify an issue of jurisprudence with regard to the legal institution of intolerance" in the circumstance of the modern world as an international juridical community was being formed. Murray claimed four principles may be derived from the allocution. Most importantly, Pius XII denied both the premise and the conclusion that held the norm of action of the state was to repress religious and moral error. The "possibility of legal repression of error and evil is not the juridical criterion that justifies such repression." While error and immorality have no objective right to existence, dissemination or action, one may not "draw from this ethical axiom the jurisprudential conclusion that, whenever the state can repress error and evil, it ought to repress them, as a matter of primary and ultimate duty." That was because there were limits on the state's competence in matters of religion that required dialogue between the Church and jurists though jurists are competent to determine the "common good of the Church and of the public order of society in given circumstances."[21]

Murray concluded Pius XII's work supported the Second View theologically, ethically, politically, juridically, and jurisprudentially. This meant the question about the "care of religion as the care for the exclusive rights of truth and for the consequent extermination of error" were "archaistic." The next proper inquiry was the widening of the question from "its Gregorian form, cura libertatis Ecclesiae" to "cura libertatis religiosae." This is where John XXIII came along, and extended the state's care of religion to all religions thereby granting all of them liberty.[22]

Pope John endorsed the Second View with a 1962 radio message to the world, and with the encyclical *Pacem in Terris*. John XXIII not only "reiterated the triad – truth, justice, and love" for society as set out by Leo XIII and Pius XII, but he added a fourth spiritual force to "sustain human society." That fourth force, freedom, was "coequally essential" with the other three forces. The freedom mentioned was freedom of the church and of the people, the "two freedoms," and it allowed society to reach its "highest good, which is their own unity as a people" while allowing one to "live a life worthy of a man." With all of this, Pope John was "quietly bidding goodbye to both thesis and hypothesis....Now the Church positively affirms the validity of the institution of religious freedom. It embodies a civil and human right, personal and corporate....immune from restriction by any legal or extralegal force."[23]

Murray's analysis was faulty. Pope John defined the meaning of the "common good" and it included a person's spiritual welfare, a definition Murray declined to accept. The spiritual welfare of persons necessarily means protecting and advancing the truth and that truth is found in the Catholic Faith. John XXIII explained in paragraphs 57 through 59 of *Pacem In Terris*:

"57....the common good touches the whole man, the needs both of his body and of his soul. Hence it follows that the civil authorities must undertake to effect the common good by ways and means that are proper to them; that is, while respecting the hierarchy of values, they should promote simultaneously both the material and the spiritual welfare of the citizens. 58. These principles are clearly contained in the doctrine stated in Our Encyclical, *Mater et Magistra*...59. Men, however, composed as they are of bodies and immortal souls, can never in this mortal life succeed in satisfying all their needs or in attaining perfect happiness. Therefore the common good is to be procured by such ways and means which not only are not detrimental to man's eternal salvation but which positively contribute to it."[24]

Murray's analysis was faulty for a second reason. The Pope was remarking on the situation of the day. This dynamic infused the entire discussion in *Pacem In Terris*, with reference to several key passages in sections 75, 76, and 79. The Pope was not setting forth doctrine, he was describing the situation in the world. But Murray had an agenda, and that was to serve the Americans so facts and proper perspectives did not matter.

The final quarter of Murray's article dealt with what he called "The Dialogue and the Issues." This was in essence a summary to advance the American view of religious liberty, and hence to advance the American system of societal organization. The two views "represent the contemporary clash between the classical mentality and the historical consciousness." The First View accused the Second View of doctrinal errors such as Liberalism, neo-liberalism, subjectivism, relativism, indifferentism, Rousseauism, laicism, social and juridical modernism, humanistic personalism, existentialism, situation ethics, false irenicism. The Second View claimed the First View held to theological fallacies such as fixism ("the fallacy which maintains that the Church's understanding and manner of statement of her faith, and of doctrines of reason related to faith, can and ought to be halted in some particular stage, under denial of the possibility and legitimacy of further development"), archaism ("the rejection, on principle, of the more recent synthesis or systematization, and in the effort to adhere or return to the synthesis or systematization of a prior age, which is judged to be simpler and more pure"), and "misplaced abstractness" ("the fallacy that creates ideologies").[25]

At this point, Murray, endorsed the Second View. He wrote "if the First View stands as the immutable formulation of Catholic

doctrine, the whole dialogue ad extra is cut off before it can begin."
Murray did not outright condemn the Catholic state. He just wrote
there were various manifestations of it through history.[26]

Murray ended with a series of questions on twelve interrelated topics
presenting the issues in controversy between the two views. He
included a discussion of "the ideal" as a "red herring across the trail"
that should not be discussed. He concluded with an emphasis on
evangelism and the "contemporary need for ecumenical dialogue on
the issue of religious freedom." The Church needed a doctrine on
religious liberty that "can be made intelligible to the contemporary
man of good will."[27]

Monsignor George Shea read Murray's article. In his typically
thorough and categorical approach he disputed and questioned,
paragraph by paragraph, almost statement by statement, Murray's
position. Reflecting on Murray's position and the latter's comments
about public opinion and pressure, Shea wrote the Conciliar Fathers
should be "all the more circumspect lest they [be] guilty of bowing
to…non-Catholic – public opinion." Indeed, "non-Catholic opinion
has never been regarded as a locus theologicus for Cath. Doctrine, as
a norm…for determining truth of a teaching." Any sensus fidelium
must include the bishops, but the bishops were divided on the issue
of religious liberty, Shea wrote. Murray's reliance on Biblical passages
to support his view of religious freedom indicated to Shea this was
tantamount to holding that Leo XIII taught contrary to the Bible.
The Church's due for religious liberty comes from the fact she is a
divine institution and the State must recognize such. Murray's claim
of universal recognition of a right to religious liberty was suspect in
itself, but further suspect was his claim it arose from the natural law.
After all, Shea asked, if it came from the natural law why was it so
"late in coming?" Finally, Shea made clear religious unity is part of
the common good.[28]

BIBLIOGRAPHY
ARCHIVES

Americanism Collection. Archives of the University of Notre Dame, Notre Dame, IN.

Billings, John Shaw, Papers. South Caroliniana Library, University of South Carolina, Columbia, SC.

Blanshard, Paul, Collection. Bentley Historical Library, University of Michigan, Ann Arbor, MI.

Catholic Theological Society of America Collection. Catholic University of America, Washington, D.C.

Cogley, John, Papers. Archives of the University of Notre Dame, Notre Dame, IN.

Connell, Francis J., Papers. Redemptorist House Archives, Province of New York, Brooklyn, NY.

Deardan, John F., Papers. Archives of the University of Notre Dame, Notre Dame, IN.

Emmett, Christopher, Papers. Hoover Institution on War, Revolution and Peace, Stanford, CA.

Fenton, Joseph Clifford, Papers. Catholic University of America, Washington, D.C.

Fenton, Joseph Clifford, Papers. Elms College, Chicopee, MA.

Harry S. Truman Presidential Library, Independence, MO.

Heard, Gerald, Papers. John V. Cody, Ph.D. Collection, Berkeley, CA.

Hesburgh, Theodore Martin, Papers. Archives of the University of Notre Dame, Notre Dame, IN.

Jackson, Charles Douglas, Papers. Dwight D. Eisenhower Presidential Library, Abilene, KS.

Jackson, Charles Douglas, Records. Dwight D. Eisenhower Presidential Library, Abilene, KS.

John F. Kennedy Presidential Library and Museum, Boston, MA.

Lilly, Edward P., Papers. Dwight D. Eisenhower Presidential Library, Abilene, KS.

Lindbeck, George, Papers. Special Collections. Yale Divinity School Library, New Haven, CT.

Lippmann, Walter, Papers (MS 326). Yale University Library, Manuscripts and Archives, New Haven, CT.

Lovestone, Jay, Papers. Hoover Institution on Revolution War and Peace, Stanford, CA.

Luce, Clare Boothe, Papers. Clare Boothe Luce Papers, Library of Congress, Washington, D.C.

Luce, Henry R., Papers. Henry R. Luce Papers, Library of Congress, Washington, D.C.

Luce, Harry Winters, Family Papers. Special Collections, Yale Divinity School Library, New Haven, CT.

Murray, John Courtney, Papers. Georgetown University Library, Special Collections Division, Washington, D.C.

Murray, John Courtney, Papers. Archives of the New York Province of the Society of Jesus. Baltimore, MD.

Nelson Rockefeller Personal Archives. Rockefeller Archive Center, Sleepy Hollow, New York, NY.

Rockefeller Brothers Fund Archives. Rockefeller Archive Center, Sleepy Hollow, New York, NY.

Scharper, Phil, Papers. Archives of the University of Notre Dame, Notre Dame, IN.

Sealantic Fund Archives. Rockefeller Archive Center, Sleepy Hollow, New York, NY.

Shea, George Papers. Monsignor William Noe Field Archives & Special Collections Center, Seton Hall University, South Orange, NJ.

Sheed and Ward Family Papers. Archives of the University of Notre Dame, Notre Dame, IN.

Shuster, George N., Papers. Archives of the University of Notre Dame, Notre Dame, IN.

Stritch, Samuel Cardinal Papers. Archdiocese of Chicago's Joseph Cardinal Bernardin Archives and Record Center, Chicago, IL.

Weigel, Gustave, Papers. Archives of the New York Province of the Society of Jesus, Baltimore, MD.

Weigel, Gustave, Papers. Georgetown University Library, Special Collections Division, Washington, D.C.

White House Office, National Security Council Staff: Papers, 1948-61, Dwight D. Eisenhower Library, Abilene, Kansas.

--NSC Registry Series, 1947-1962. ("NSC Registry")

--OCB Central File Series. ("OCB Central Files Series")

--OCB Secretariat Series. ("OCB Secretariat Series")

White House Office, National Security Council Staff: Papers 1953-61, Dwight D.

Eisenhower Library, Abilene, Kansas.

--Psychological Strategy Board (PSB) Central Files Series. ("PSB Central Files Series")

ORAL HISTORIES

Billings, John Shaw. Parts I, II, and III on January 16, 1966 and March 4, 1966. John Shaw Billings Papers. South Caroliniana Library, University of South Carolina, Columbia, SC.

Cushman, General Robert. Interviewed by Dr. Thomas Soapes on March 4, 1977. Dwight D Eisenhower Presidential Library, Abilene, KS.

Gray, Gordon. Interviewed by Maclyn P. Burg on June 25, 1975. Dwight D. Eisenhower Presidential Library, Abilene, KS.

Lilly, Edward P. Interviewed by Neil M. Johnson on September 20, 1988. Harry S Truman Presidential Library and Museum, Independence, MO.

Luce, Henry R. Interviewed by John L. Steele on November 11, 1965. John F. Kennedy Presidential Library, Boston, MA.

Luce, Henry III. Interviewed by Mack Teasley on July 26, 2000. Dwight D Eisenhower Presidential Library, Abilene, KS.

McCrum, Marie. Interviewed by David Horrocks on May 15, 1975. Dwight D. Eisenhower Presidential Library, Abilene, KS.

Toner, Albert P. Interviewed by Dr. Burg on November 19, 1974. Dwight D. Eisenhower Presidential Library, Abilene, KS.

Yost, Charles. Interviewed by Dr. Thomas Soapes on September 13, 1978. Dwight D Eisenhower Presidential Library, Abilene, KS.

INTERVIEWS

Fr. Carl Hoegerl, C.Ss.R., interviewed by author, Brooklyn, NY, May, 2010.

Robert Blair Kaiser, interviewed by author, via telephone, July 2009 and July 2010.

Msgr. Francis Seymour, interviewed by author, via telephone, August, 2013.

AZ (who wishes to remain anonymous), interviewed by author, via telephone, December, 2009.

BOOKS AND ARTICLES

A

Abbott, Walter M., S.J., ed. *The Documents of Vatican II: In a New and Definitive Translation With Commentaries and Notes By Catholic, Protestant and Orthodox Authorities.* New York: Herder and Herder Association Press, 1966.

Adams, John. *Papers of John Adams.* Edited by Gregg L. Lint, C. James Taylor, Hobson Woodward, Margaret A. Hogan, Mary T. Claffey, Sara B. Sikes, Judith S. Graham. Vol. 9, 13, 14. Cambridge, Massachusetts: The Belknap Press, 1996.

America. "Religious Liberty In Spain." May 24, 1952.

America. "Puerto Rican Pastoral." November 5, 1960.

"Amintore Fanfani." *Encyclopedia of World Biography.* 2004 ed. Encyclopedia.com. http://www.encyclopedia.com/doc/1G2-3404702090.html (accessed July 10, 2011).

An, Daechun. "Content Analysis of Advertising Visuals in the Magazine Advertisements: The Roaring Twenties and the Great Depression." *WJMCR* 6:3 June 2003. http://www.scripps.ohiou.edu/

wjmcr/vol06/6-3a-b.htm (accessed May 13, 2010).

Anderson, Floyd, ed. *Council Daybook: Vatican II Session 1, October 11 through December 8, 1962 and Session 2 September 29 to December 4, 1963.* Washington, DC: National Catholic Welfare Conference, 1965.

Anderson, Walter Truett. *The Upstart Spring: Esalen and the Human Potential Movement: The First Twenty Years.* Lincoln, Nebraska: iUniverse, Inc., 2004.

Aquinas, St. Thomas. *Summa Contra Gentiles.* First Book. New York: Benziger Brothers, 1924.

Aquinas, St. Thomas. *Summa Contra Gentiles.* Second Book. London, England: Burns Oates & Washbourne LTD, 1923.

Aquinas, St. Thomas. *Summa Theologica.* Great Books of the Western World Series. Ed.

Mortimer Adler. William Benton Publisher, Encyclopedia Britannica, 1952.

Aquinas, St. Thomas. *On Kingship: To the King of Cyprus.* Toronto, Canada: The Pontifical Institute of Mediaeval Studies, 1949.

Aradi, Msgr. Zsolt, James I Tucek, James C. O'Neill. *Pope John XXIII: An Authoritative Biography.* New York: Farrar, Straus and Cudahy, 1959.

Arlington National Cemetery Website, "Byron K Enyart Colonel United States Air Force." Arlington National Cemetery Website. www.arlingtoncemetery.net/bkenyart.html (accessed January 18, 2013).

Auchincloss, Douglas. "City of God and Man." *Time,* December 12, 1960.

Avella, Steven M. *This Confident Church: Catholic Leadership and Life in Chicago, 1940-1965.* Notre Dame, Indiana: University of Notre Dame Press, 1992.

B

Bailyn, Bernard. *The Ideological Origins of the American Revolution.* Cambridge, Massachusetts: Belknap Press of Harvard University Press, 1967.

Bancroft, Mary. *Autobiography of a Spy: Debutante, Writer, Confidante, Secret Agent.* New York: William Morrow and Company, 1983.

Barnet, Richard J. and Ronald E. Muller. *Global Reach: The Power of the Multinational Corporations.* New York: Simon and Schuster, 1974.

Baughman, James L. *Henry R. Luce and the Rise of the American News Media.* Baltimore, Maryland: The Johns Hopkins University Press, 2001.

Beard, Charles Austin. *An Economic Interpretation of the Constitution of the United States.* General Books Publication, 2010.

Belloc, Hillaire. *The Free Press.* Norfolk, Virginia: IHS Press, 2002.

Benigni, Mario and Goffredo Zanchi. *John XXIII: The Official Biography.* Translated by Elvira DiFabio. Boston, Massachusetts: Pauline Books & Media, 2000.

Berard, Aram S.J., tr. *Preparatory Reports: Second Vatican Council.* Philadelphia, Pennsylvania: The Westminster Press, 1965.

Bernays, Edward. *Propaganda.* New York: Ig Publishing, 2005.

Bernstein, Adam. "Martin Quigley, who used film work as cover for World War II espionage, dies." *The Washington Post.* February 11, 2011. http://www.washingtonpost.com/wp-dyn/content/article/2011/02/11/AR2011021106050_pf... (accessed May 7, 2013).

Billington, Ray Allen. *The Protestant Crusade 1800-1860: A Study of the Origins of American Nativism.* Chicago, Illinois: Quadrangle Books, 1964.

Bird, Kai. *The Chairman John J. McCloy: The Making of the American Establishment.* New York: Simon & Schuster, 1992.

Blackstock, Paul W. *The Strategy of Subversion: Manipulating the Politics of Other Nations.* Chicago, Illinois: Quadrangle Books, 1964.

Blake, Eugene Carson and G. Bromley Oxnam. "A Protestant view of a Catholic for President." *Look,* May 10, 1960.

Blanshard, Paul. *American Freedom and Catholic Power.* Boston, Massachusetts: The Beacon Press, 1949.

Blanshard, Paul. "The Catholic Church and Fascism." *The Nation,* April 17, 1948.

Blanshard, Paul. *Personal and Controversial: An Autobiography.* Boston, Massachusetts: Beacon Press, 1973.

Blum, William. *Killing Hope: U.S. Military and CIA Interventions Since World War II.* Monroe, Maine: Common Courage Press, 1995.

Blum, William. *Rogue State: A Guide to the World's Only Superpower.* Monroe, Maine: Common Courage Press, 2000.

Bokenkotter, Thomas. *A Concise History of the Catholic Church.* New York: Doubleday, 2005.

Bowie, Dean Walter Russell. "Protestant Concern Over Catholicism." *The American Mercury,* September, 1949.

Brinkley, Alan. *The Publisher: Henry Luce and His American Century.* New York: Alfred A. Knopf, 2010.

Brown, Anthony Cave. *The Last Hero: Wild Bill Donovan.* New York: Times Books, 1982.

Brown, Charles C. *Niebuhr and His Age: Reinhold Niebuhr's Prophetic Role and Legacy.* Harrisburg, Pennsylvania: Trinity Press International, 2002.

C

Caldwell, Mary Gwendoline. "The Catholic University of America: The Heritage of CUA." Catholic University of America. http://alumni.cua.edu/heritage/biographies/marycaldwell.cfm (accessed July 23, 2011).

Catechism of the Catholic Church. New York: Doubleday, 1995.

"Catholic Position is Reiterated." *The Catholic Transcript,* September 29, 1960.

Cody, John V. *Gerald Heard Timeline and Chronology.* Compiled and annotated by John V. Cody, Ph.D. 1999.

Cody, John V. *Glossary of Names Related to Gerald Heard.* Compiled and annotated by John V. Cody, Ph.D. 1999.

Coleman, Peter. *The Liberal Conspiracy: The Congress for Cultural Freedom and the Struggle for the Mind of Postwar Europe.* New York: The Free Press, A Division of Macmillan, Inc., 1989.

"The 1929 Concordat Between the Kingdom of Italy and The Holy See." Concordat Watch. http://www.concordatwatch.eu/topic-39251.843 (accessed August 27, 2013).

Congar, Yves. *Mon Journal du Concile.* Paris: Les Editions Du Cerf, 2002.

Congar, Yves. *My Journal of the Council.* Collegeville, Minnesota: Liturgical Press, 2012.

Connell, Francis J. "Christ the King of Civil Rulers". *American Ecclesiastical Review* CXIX (October 1948): 244-253.

Connell, Francis J. "Radio and the Red Curtain: The Morality of Psychological Warfare." *Catholic Men* (June-July 1954): 6-7.

Connell, Francis J. "Reply to Father Murray." *American Ecclesiastical Review* CXXVI (January 1952): 49-59.

Connell, Francis J. "The Theory of the `Lay State'." *American Ecclesiastical Review* CXXV (July 1951): 7-18.

Connell, Francis J. "Paul Blanshard: American Freedom and Catholic Power." *Cornell Law Quarterly* 35 (Spring 1950): 678-684.

Connell, Francis J. *Morals In Politics and Professions: A Guide For Catholics in Public Life.* Westminster, Maryland: The Newman Bookshop, 1946.

Connell, Francis J. *More Answers to Today's Moral Problems.* Ed. By Fr. Eugene J. Weitzel. Washington, D.C.: The Catholic University of America Press, 1965.

Conway, Edward J. "Pius XII on `The Community of Peoples'." *America,* December 26, 1953.

Cook, Blanche Wiesen. "First Comes the Lie: CD Jackson and Political Warfare." *Radical History Review* 31 (1984): 42-70.

Cooney, John. *The American Pope: The Life and Times of Francis Cardinal Spellman.* New York: Dell, 1984.

Coughlan, Robert. "The Religious Issue: An Un-American Heritage A Long Tradition of Bias in Politics Is Being Challenged by A New Outlook." *Life,* July 4, 1960.

Covert Action Information Bulletin. "Nazis, the Vatican, and CIA." Winter 1986.

Curran, Charles E. *Loyal Dissent: Memoir of a Catholic Theologian.* Washington, D.C.: Georgetown University Press, 2006.

D

Davies, Michael. *The Second Vatican Council and Religious Liberty.* Long Prairie, Minnesota: The Neumann Press, 1992.

"Declaration of Independence," July 4, 1776. www.archives.gov (accessed June 19, 2011).

"Declaration of the Causes and Necessity of Taking Up Arms." July 6, 1775. www.federalist.com (accessed December 30, 2000).

Deedy, John. *Seven American Catholics.* Chicago, Illinois: The Thomas More Press, 1978.

De Tocqueville, Alexis. *Democracy in America.* Translated by Henry Reeve. New York: Schocken Books, 1970.

De Volder, Jan. *The Spirit of Fr. Damien: The Leper Priest A Saint for Our Times.* San Francisco, California: Ignatius Press, 2010.

DiMeglio, Giuseppe. "*Ci Riesce* and Cardinal Ottaviani's Discourse" *American Ecclesiastical Review* CXXX (June, 1954): 384-387.

Dorrien, Gary. "Communitarianism, Christian Realism, and the Crisis of Progressive Christianity." *Cross Currents,* Fall 1997.

The Dunwoodie Review. "History." The Dunwoodie Review. http://dunwoodiereview.org/History (accessed September 15, 2012).

Dzuback, Mary Ann. *Robert M. Hutchins: Portrait of an Educator.* Chicago, Illinois: The University of Chicago Press, 1991.

E

Egnal, Marc and Joseph A. Ernst. "An Economic Interpretation of the American Revolution." *The William and Mary Quarterly* 29 (Jan., 1972): 3-32.

Elliott, Lawrence. *I Will Be Called John: A Biography of Pope John XXIII.* New York: Reader's Digest Press, E. P. Dutton & Co., Inc., 1973.

Ellis, John Tracy, ed. *Documents of American Catholic History.* Milwaukee, Wisconsin: The Bruce Publishing Company, 1956.

Ellis, John Tracy, ed. *Documents of American Catholic History.* Milwaukee, Wisconsin: The Bruce Publishing Company, 1962.

Ellis, Joseph J. *American Creation: Triumphs and Tragedies At the Founding of the Republic.* New York: Alfred A. Knopf, 2007.

Engel, Randy. *The McHugh Chronicles.* Export, Pennsylvania: New Engel Publishing, 1997.

Engel, Randy. *The Rite of Sodomy: Homosexuality and the Roman Catholic Church.* Export, Pennsylvania: New Engel Publishing, 2006.

F

Falby, Alison. *Between the Pigeonholes: Gerald Heard 1889-1971.* Newcastle, United Kingdom: Cambridge Scholars Publishing, 2008.

Falconi, Carlo. *Pope John and His Council: A Diary of the Second Vatican Council, September – December 1962.* Translated by Muriel Grindrod. London: Weidenfeld and Nicolson, 1964.

Fanfani, Amintore. *Catholicism Protestantism and Capitalism.* Norfolk, Virginia: IHS Press, 2003.

Fenton, Joseph Clifford. "A Letter From Rome." *American Ecclesiastical Review* CXLIX (December 1963): 392-430.

Fenton, Joseph Clifford. "Appraisal in Sacred Theology." *American Ecclesiastical Review* CXXXIV (January 1956): 24-36.

Fenton, Joseph Clifford. "Brotherhood in Catholic Theology." *American Ecclesiastical Review* CXXXII (March, 1955): 191-203.

Fenton, Joseph Clifford. "Cardinal Ottaviani and the Council." *American Ecclesiastical Review* CXLVIII, no. 1 (January 1963): 44-53.

Fenton, Joseph. "The Catholic Church and Freedom of Religion." *American Ecclesiastical Review* CXV (October 1946): 286-301.

Fenton, Joseph Clifford. "Catholic Polemic and Doctrinal Accuracy." *American Ecclesiastical Review* CXXXII (February 1955): 107-117.

Fenton, Joseph Clifford. "The Components of Liberal Catholicism." *American Ecclesiastical Review* CXXXIX, no. 1 (July 1958): 36-53.

Fenton, Joseph Clifford. "The Council and Father Kung." *American Ecclesiastical Review* CXLVII (September 1962): 178-200.

Fenton, Joseph Clifford. "The Doctrinal Authority of Papal Allocutions." *American Ecclesiastical Review* CXXXIV, no. 2 (February 1956): 109-117.

Fenton, Joseph Clifford. "Doctrine and Tactic in Catholic Pronouncements on Church and State." *American Ecclesiastical Review* CXLV, no. 4 (October 1961): 266-276.

Fenton, Joseph Clifford. "The Holy Father's Statement on Relations Between the Church and the State." *American Ecclesiastical Review* CXXXIII (November 1955): 323-331.

Fenton, Joseph Clifford. "The Influence of the Holy Ghost in the Ecumenical Council." *American Ecclesiastical Review* CXLVII (August 1962): 116-127.

Fenton, Joseph Clifford. "Intellectual Standards Among American Catholics." *American Ecclesiastical Review* CXXXV, no. 5 (November 1956): 323-336.

Fenton, Joseph Clifford. "Pope Benedict XV and the Rules for Theological Discussion." *American Ecclesiastical Review* CXXXV, no. 1 (July 1956): 39-53.

Fenton, Joseph Clifford. "Pope Pius XII and the Theological Treatise on the Church." *American Ecclesiastical Review* CXXXIX, no. 6 (December 1958): 407-419.

Fenton, Joseph. "Principles Underling Traditional Church-State Doctrine" *American Ecclesiastical Review* CXXVI (June 1952): 452-462.

Fenton, Joseph Clifford. "Religion and Charity In Our Lady's Contribution to the Apostolate." *American Ecclesiastical Review* CXXXIX, no. 4 (October, 1958): 261-275.

Fenton, Joseph Clifford. "Revolutions in Catholic Attitudes." *American Ecclesiastical Review* CXLV, no. 2 (August 1961): 120-129.

Fenton, Joseph Clifford. "The Roman Curia and the Ecumenical Council." *American Ecclesiastical Review* CXLVIII, no. 3 (March 1963): 185-198.

Fenton, Joseph Clifford. "Rome and the Status of Catholic Theology." *American Ecclesiastical Review* CXLIII, no. 6 (December 1960): 395-417.

Fenton, Joseph. "Some Recent Writings in Fundamental Dogmatic Theology. Part I" *American Ecclesiastical Review* CXXXIV, no. 4 (April 1956): 255-272.

Fenton, Joseph. "The Teachings of the *Ci Riesce.*" *American Ecclesiastical Review* CXXX (February 1954): 114-123.

Fenton, Joseph. "*Time* and Pope Leo." *American Ecclesiastical Review* CXIV (May 1946): 369-375.

Fenton, Joseph. "Toleration and Church-State Controversy." *American Ecclesiastical Review* CXXX (May 1954): 330-343.

Filipowicz, Joseph. "The Sad Story of Thomism in North America." *Culture Wars* 31, 5 (April 2012): 34-47.

Finney, John W. "Jesuit rules out church control over a president: Says religious law would not apply to public act of an elected official." *The New York Times,* September 28, 1960.

Flannery, Austin OP, General Editor. *Vatican Council II: The Conciliar and Post-Conciliar Documents.* Northport, New York: Costello Publishing Company, 1992.

Fogarty, Gerald P. *The Vatican and the Americanist Crisis: Denis J. O'Connell American Agent In Rome 1885-1903.* Roma: Universita Gregoriana, 1974.

Foot, Michael and Isaac Kramnick, editors. *The Thomas Paine Reader.* London, England: Penguin Books, 1987.

Freedman, Benjamin. *Hidden Tyranny: A True Story.* Liberty Bell Publications.

G

Galbraith, John Kenneth. *American Capitalism.* Boston: Houghton Mifflin Company, 1956.

Garrigou-Lagrange, Reginald OP. *The Three Ages of the Interior Life.* Rockford, Illinois: TAN, 1989.

Gay Marriage Watch Italy. "Europe: New Rainbow Map Shows How Gay Friendly (or Not) European Countries Are." *Gay Marriage Watch Italy,* May 16, 2013. http://purpleunions.com/bog/tag/italy (accessed May 19, 2013).

Georgetown University Library. "The Rev. Gustave A. Weigel, SJ Papers." http://www.library.georgetown.edu/dept/speccoll/c165.htm (accessed May 15, 2012).

Gibbons, James Cardinal. *The Faith of Our Fathers: Being a Plain Explanation and Vindication of The Church Founded by Our Lord Jesus Christ.* New York: John Murphy Company, 1905.

Graham, Billy. *Just As I Am: The Autobiography of Billy Graham.* San Francisco, California: Zondervan, 1997.

Griffin, G. Edward. *The Creature from Jekyll Island: A Second Look at the Federal Reserve.* 4th ed. Westlake Village, California: American Media, 2002.

The Guardian. "Amintore Fanfani: He held every political office in Italy but the one he craved most – president of the Republic." 22 November 1999. www.guardian.co.uk (accessed July 10, 2011).

Gurian, Waldemar and M. A. Fitzsimons, M.A. *The Catholic Church in World Affairs.* Notre Dame, Indiana: University of Notre Dame Press, 1954.

H

Haag, A. (1912). "Syllabus." *In the Catholic Encyclopedia*. New York: Robert Appleton Company. Retrieved July 11, 2011 from New Advent: http://www.newadent.org/cathen/14368b.htm

Halberstam, David. *The Powers That Be*. Chicago, Illinois: University of Illinois Press, 2000.

Hall, Mark David. *Roger Sherman and the Creation of the American Republic*. New York: Oxford University Press, 2013.

Hamilton, Alexander. *The Papers of Alexander Hamilton*. Edited by Harold C. Syrett, Jacob E. Cooke. Volume IV, "January 1787 to May 1788." New York: Columbia University Press, 1962.

Handy, Robert T. *A History of Union Theological Seminary in New York*. New York: Columbia University Press, 1987.

Hanley, John. "In Memoriam William Ross Adey, MD Professor of Anatomy and Physiology Los Angeles (1922-2004)." University of California. http://www.universityofcalifornia.edu/senate/ inmemoriam/williamrossadey.htm (accessed July 17, 2012).

Harr, John Ensor and Peter J. Johnson *The Rockefeller Century*. New York: Charles Scribner's Sons, 1988.

Hassard, John. *Life of the Most Reverend John Hughes, D.D., First Archbishop of New York*. New York: D. Appleton and Company, 1866.

Hatch, Alden. *Ambassador Extraordinary Clare Boothe Luce*. New York: Henry Holt and Company, 1956.

Hayes, P. (1910). "John Hughes." In The Catholic Encyclopedia. New York: Robert Appleton Company. Retrieved May 31, 2013 from New Advent: http://www.newadvent.org/cathen/07516a.htm

Hawke, David Freeman. *Paine*. New York: Harper & Row, 1974

Heard, Gerald. *The Five Ages of Man: The Psychology of Human History.* New York: Julian Press, Inc. Publishers, 1963.

Heard, Gerald. *Letters from the Growing Edge 1960-1962: Training Techniques for a Life of Growth: How to Generate Powers of Apt Force in a Small Group.* Edited by John V. Cody, Ph.D. Berkeley, California, 1999.

Heideking, Jurgen and Christof Mauch, ed. *American Intelligence and the German Resistance to Hitler: A Documentary History.* Boulder, Colorado: Westview Press, 1996.

Heinrichs, Waldo H. *American Ambassador: Joseph C. Grew and the Development of the United States Diplomatic Tradition.* New York: Oxford University Press, 1986.

Helland, Peter. "Calvin the Judaizer." *Culture Wars* 32, 2 (January 2013): 42-49.

Hendershott, Anne. "How Support for Abortion Became Kennedy Dogma." *The Wall Street Journal,* January 2, 2009. http://online.wsj. com/article/SB123086375678148323.html (accessed August 29, 2013).

Herrera, R. A. *Donoso Cortes: Cassandra of the Age.* Grand Rapids, Michigan: William B. Eerdmans Publishing Company, 1995.

Hersh, Burton. *The American Elite and the Origins of the CIA.* New York: Charles Scribner's Sons, 1992.

Hesburgh, Theodore M. *God, Country, Notre Dame.* Notre Dame, Indiana: University of Notre Dame Press, 1999.

"History and Development." International Law Institute. http://www.ili. org/about/history.html (accessed July 14, 2012).

Hitler, Adolf. *Mein Kampf.* Translated by Ralph Manheim. Boston, Massachusetts: Houghton Mifflin Company, 1971.

Hitler.org. "Programme of the NSDAP, 24 February 1920." Hitler.org. http://www.hitler.org/writings/programme/ (accessed February 23, 2003).

Hoeflich, M. H. "Gelasius I and Roman Law: One Further Word" *Journal of Theological Studies* 26 no. 1 (April 1975): 115.

Houston, Jean. *Life Force: The Psycho-Historical Recovery of the Self.* Wheaton, Illinois: Quest Books, 1993.

Hoyt, Robert. "Opinion Worth Noting." *America,* November 5, 1960.

Hudson, Michael. *Super Imperialism: The Origin and Fundamentals of U.S. World Dominance.* New York, New York: Pluto Press, 2003.

Hudson, Michael. *Trade, Development and Foreign Debt: A History of Theories of Polarisation and Convergence in the International Economy.* London, England: Pluto Press, 1992.

Huertas, Thomas F. "Can Banking And Commerce Mix?" *Cato Journal* 7, no. 3 (Winter 1988): 743-769.

I

Ignotus, Auctor. *AE: The Open Persuader.* Los Angeles, California: One Incorporated, 1969.

Index Mundi. "Italy Death rate –Demographics." http://www.indexmundi.com/italy/death_rate.html (accessed May 19, 2013).

Isaacs, Jeremy and Taylor Downing. *Cold War: An Illustrated History, 1945-1991.* Boston, Massachusetts: Little Brown and Company, 1998.

The Independent. "Obituary: Amintore Fanfani." 22 November 1999. www.independent.co.uk (accessed July 10, 2011).

J

Jewish Telegraph Agency. "J.D.B. News Letter," March 21, 1928. http://www.jta.org/1928/03/21/archive/j-d-b-news-letter-101 (accessed May 14, 2013).

Johnson, Douglas. "Obituary: Fr Raymond Bruckberger." *The Independent.* January 9, 1998. http://www.independent.co.uk/news/ obituaries/obituary-fr-raymond-bruckberger-1137571 (accessed June 24, 2012).

Jones, E. Michael. *Libido Dominandi: Sexual Liberation and Political Control.* South Bend, Indiana: St. Augustine's Press, 2000.

Jones, E. Michael. *The Slaughter of Cities: Urban Renewal as Ethnic Cleansing.* South Bend, Indiana: St. Augustine's Press, 2004.

Joseph, Sister Miriam. *The Trivium: The Liberal Arts of Logic, Grammar, and Rhetoric.* Philadelphia, Pennsylvania: Paul Dry Books, 2002.

"'The Problem of Religious Freedom,' by John Courtney Murray," *Journal of Church and State* (1966) 8:(3) 475-477.

Journet, Charles. *Journet Maritain Correspondence.* Paris, France: Editions Saint-Paul, 1996.

K

Kaiser, Robert Blair. *Clerical Error: A True Story.* New York: Continuum, 2002.

Kaiser, Robert Blair. *Pope, Council and World: The Story of Vatican II.* New York: The Macmillan Company, 1963.

Kelly, Msgr. George A. *The Battle for the American Church.* Garden City, New York: Image Books, 1981.

Kennan, George. "George Kennan's 'Long Telegram.'" George Washington University. http://www.gwu.edu/~nsarchiv/coldwar/documents/episode-1/kennan.htm (accessed July 14, 2013).

Kerwin, Jerome G. *Catholic Viewpoint on Church and State.* Garden City, New York: Hanover House, 1960.

Kilcullen, John, "Medieval Political Philosophy." *The Stanford Encyclopedia of Philosophy (Spring 2012 Edition).* Edward N. Zalta, ed. Stanford University. http://plato.stanford.edu/archives/spr2012/entries/medieval-political/ (accessed April 25, 2012).

Knebel, Fletcher. "The Bishops vs. Kennedy." *Look,* May 23, 1961.

L

Lambert, Bruce. "Msgr. John Tracy Ellis, 87, Dies; Dean of US Catholic Historians." *The New York Times.* October 17, 1992. http://www.nytimes.com/1992/10/17/us/msgr-john-tracy-ellis-87-dies-dean-of-us-catholic...... (accessed July 12, 2012).

Lamont, John. "Determining the Content and degree of Authority of Church Teachings" *The Thomist* 72 (2008): 371-407;

Lamont, John. "The historical conditioning of Church doctrine" *The Thomist* 60 (1996): 511-535.

Langan, Jeffrey J. *The Influence of the French Revolution on the Lives and Thought of John Adams, Thomas Jefferson, Edmund Burke, Mary Wollstonecraft, Immanuel Kant, and Pius VI: The End of Conservatism.* Lewiston, New York: The Edwin Mellon Press, 2012.

Leary, William M., ed. *The Central Intelligence Agency: History and Documents.* University, Alabama: University of Alabama Press, 1984.

Lee, Martin A. and Bruce Shlain. *Acid Dreams: The Complete Social History of LSD: The CIA, the Sixties, and Beyond.* Grove Press, 1985.

Luce, Henry. *The Ideas of Henry Luce.* Edited by John K. Jessup. New York: Atheneum, 1969.

Lernoux, Penny. *In Banks We Trust.* Garden City, New York: Anchor Press/Doubleday, 1984.

Lewin, Leonard C., ed. *Report from Iron Mountain on the Possibility and Desirability of Peace.* New York: The Dial Press, Inc., 1967.

Lewis, Michael. *The Money Culture.* New York: W. W. Norton & Company, 1991.

Lippmann, Walter. *Public Opinion.* Radford, Virginia: Wilder Publications, 2010.

Lippmann, Walter. *Essays in the Public Philosophy.* Boston, Massachusetts: Little, Brown and Company, 1955.

Locke, John. *Two Treatises of Government.* Mark Goldie, ed. London, England: J. M. Dent, 1993.

M

MacDonogh, Giles. *After the Reich: The Brutal History of the Allied Occupation.* New York: Basic Books, 2007.

McConnell, Campbell R. *Economics Principles, Problems, and Policies.* 9th Ed. New York: McGraw-Hill Book Company, 1984.

McDonald, Forrest. *We The People: The Economic Origins of the Constitution.* Chicago, Illinois: University of Chicago Press, 1958.

McNeill, William H. *Hutchins' University: A Memoir of the University of Chicago 1929-1950.* Chicago, Illinois: University of Chicago Press, 1991.

McPherson, James M. *Battle Cry of Freedom: The Civil War Era.* New York: Bantam Books, 1989.

Machiavelli, Niccolo. *The Prince.* George Bull, tr. London, England: Penguin Classics, 1995.

Madison, James, Alexander Hamilton, John Jay. *The Federalist Papers*. Isaac Kramnick, ed. London, England: Penguin Classics, 1988.

Martin, Douglas. "William F. Buckley Jr Is Dead at 82." *The New York Times*. February 27, 2008. http://www.nytimes.com/2008/02/27/business/media/27cnd-buckley.html?pagewanted=all&_r=0 (accessed June 15, 2013).

Martin, Malachi. *The Jesuits: The Society of Jesus and the Betrayal of the Roman Catholic Church*. New York: The Linden Press, Simon and Schuster, 1987.

Martin, Ralph G. *Henry & Clare: An Intimate Portrait of the Luces*. New York: Putnam's Perigee Books, 1991.

May, Gary. *Un-American Activities: The Trials of William Remington*. New York: Oxford University Press, 1994.

Mayer, Milton. *Robert Maynard Hutchins: A Memoir*. John H. Hicks, ed. Berkeley, California: University of California Press, 1993.

Meade, David. "Protestants and the Council: What Protestants Expect from the Council Is One Thing. What They Want Is Another." *U.S. Catholic*, October, 1964.

Merritt, Anna J. and Richard L. Merritt, editors. *Public Opinion in Occupied Germany: The OMGUS Surveys, 1945-1949*. Urbana, Illinois: University of Illinois Press, 1970.

Merritt, Anna J. and Richard L. Merritt, editors. *Public Opinion in Semi-sovereign Germany: The HICOG Surveys, 1949-1955*. Urbana, Illinois: University of Illinois Press, 1980.

Metzger, John Mackay. *The Hand and the Road: The Life and Times of John A. Mackay*. Louisville, Kentucky: Westminster John Knox Press, 2010.

Miller, Merle. *Plain Speaking: An Oral Biography of Harry S. Truman*. New York: Tess Press, 2004.

Mitteis, Heinrich. *The State in the Middle Ages: A Comparative Constitutional History of Feudal Europe.* Amsterdam, the Netherlands: North-Holland Publishing Company, 1975.

"Modern Times at Darlington," Seton Hall University, New Jersey. http://www.shu.edu/academics/theology/sesquicentennial/modern-darlington.cfm (accessed August 31, 2013)

"Modifications to the Lateran Concordat (1984): text." *Concordat Watch.* http://www.concordatwatch.eu/showtopic.php?org_id=878&b_header_id=39221 (accessed May 19, 2013).

Moran, Robert Paul SS. "Reflections on America" *American Ecclesiastical Review*139 (October 1958): 282-283.

Morgan, Ted. *A Covert Life: Jay Lovestone: Communist, Anti-Communist, and Spymaster.* New York: Random House, 1999.

Morris, John D. "Catholic Laymen Uphold Kennedy: 165 Sign Statement Backing Church-State Separation – A Protestant Replies." *The New York Times,* October 6 1960 as retrieved from FJC Papers in Redemptorist Archives, Brooklyn, NY.

Morris, Sylvia Jukes. *Rage for Fame: The Ascent of Clare Boothe Luce.* New York: Random House, 1997.

Moynihan, James H. *The Life of Archbishop John Ireland.* New York: Harper & Brothers, 1953.

Munoz, Vincent Phillip. *God and the Founders: Madison, Washington and Jefferson.* New York: Cambridge University Press, 2009.

Murphy, Paul I. *La Popessa.* New York: Warner Books, 1983.

Murray, John Courtney. "A Memorable Man," from *One of a Kind: Essays in Tribute to Gustave Weigel,* 11–22. Wilkes-Barre, PA: Dimension Books, 1967. http://woodstock.georgetown.edu/library/Murray/1967e.htm (accessed January 3, 2010).

Murray, John Courtney. "The Bad Arguments Intelligent Men Make." *America*, November 3, 1956. http://woodstock.georgetown. edu/library/Murray/1956A.htm (accessed June 10, 2012).

Murray, John Courtney. "The Construction of a Christian Culture, I. Portrait of a Christian; II. Personality and the Community; III. The Humanism of God." Abridged, and republished in *Bridging the Sacred and the Secular*, 101–23. Three talks given in February 1940 at St. Joseph's College. Murray Archives, file 6–422. http:// woodstock.georgetown.edu/library/Murray/1940A.htm. (accessed December 21, 2008).

Murray, John Courtney. "Contemporary Orientations of Catholic Thought on Church and State in the Light of History." *Theological Studies* 10 (June 1949): 177-234. http://woodstock.georgetown.edu/ library/Murray/1949b.htm (accessed April 24, 2012).

Murray, John Courtney. "A Crisis in the History of Trent." *Thought* 7 (December 1932): 463-473. http://woodstock.georgetown.edu/ Murray/1932.htm (accessed December 21, 2008).

Murray, John Courtney. "Current Theology: Co-operation: Some Further Views." *Theological Studies* 4 (March 1943): 100-111. http:// woodstock.georgetown.edu/library/murray/1943a.htm (accessed February 12, 2012).

Murray, John Courtney "Current Theology: Intercredal Co-operation: Its Theory and Its Organization." *Theological Studies* 4 (June, 1943): 257-286. http://woodstock.georgetown.edu/library/ murray/1943b.htm (accessed February 12, 2012).

Murray, John Courtney. "Current Theology Christian Cooperation." *Theological Studies*, 3 (September 1942): 413-431. http://woodstock- .georgetown.edu/library/murray/1942b.htm (accessed February 12, 2012).

Murray, John Courtney. "Current Theology on Religious Freedom." *Theological Studies*, 10 (September 1949): 409-432. http://woodstock. georgetown.edu/library/Murray/1949c.htm (accessed April 24, 2012).

Murray, John Courtney. "For the Freedom and Transcendence of the Church." *American Ecclesiastical Review* CXXVI (January 1952): 28-48. http://woodstock.georgetown.edu/library/Murray/1952b.htm (accessed April 21, 2012).

Murray, John Courtney. "Freedom of Religion I. The Ethical Problem." *Theological Studies* 6 (June, 1945): 229-286. http://wodstock.georgetown.edu/library/murray/1945b.htm (accessed February 12, 2012).

Murray, John Courtney. "Governmental Repression of Heresy." http://woodstock.georgetown.edu/library/murray/1948c.htm (accessed January 20, 2011).

Murray, John Courtney. "The Issue of Church and State at Vatican Council II." *Theological Studies* 27 (December 1966): 580-606. http://woodstock.georgetown.edu/library/Murray/1966h.htm (accessed November 11, 2012).

Murray, John Courtney. "The Natural Law." In *Great Expressions of Human Rights*. Edited by Robert M. MacIver. New York: Harper, 69–104. http://woodstock.georgetown.edu/library/Murray/whtt_c13_1950a.htm (accessed April 24, 2012).

Murray, John Courtney. "Necessary Adjustments to Overcoming Practical Difficulties." *Man and Modern Secularism: Essays on the Conflict of the Two Cultures*, edited by National Catholic Alumni Federation. New York, NY: National Catholic Alumni Federation, 1940: 152–57. http://woodstock.georgetown.edu/library/Murray/1940b.htm (accessed December 21, 2008).

Murray, John Courtney. "On the Problem of Co-operation: Some Clarifications." *American Ecclesiastical Review* CXII (March 1945): 194-214. http://woodstock.georgetown.edu/library/murray/1945f.htm (accessed February 12, 2012).

Murray, John Courtney. "The Problem of the 'Religion of the State'." *American Ecclesiastical Review* CXXIV (May 1951): 327-351. http://woodstock.georgetown.edu/library/murray/1951b.htm (accessed April 21, 2012).

Murray, John Courtney. "The Problem of Religious Freedom at the Council," University of Notre Dame Archives, Archbishop John Deardan Papers Box 6 File 9; and http://woodstock.georgetown.edu/library/Murray/1964e.htm (accessed March 7, 1963).

Murray, John Courtney. "Religious Liberty: The Concern of All." *America,* February 7, 1948. http://woodstock.georgetown.edu/library/murray/1948e.htm (accessed February 12, 2012.)

Murray, John Courtney. "On Religious Liberty: Freedom is the most distinctively American issue before the Council." *America,* November, 1963. http://woodstock.georgetown.edu/library/Murray/1963j.htm (accessed March 3, 2013).

Murray, John Courtney. "Separation of Church and State." *America,* December 7, 1946. http://woodstock.georgetown.edu/library/murray/1946e.htm (accessed February 12, 2012).

Murray, John Courtney SJ. "Special Catholic Challenges." *Life,* December 26, 1955.

Murray, John Courtney. "The Court Upholds Religious Freedom." *America,* March 8, 1947. http://woodstock.georgetown.edu/library/murray/1947b.htm (retrieved February 12 2012).

Murray, John Courtney. "On the Structure of the Church-State Problem." In *The Catholic Church In World Affairs,* edited by Waldemar Gurian and M. A. Fitzsimons, 11-32. Notre Dame, Indiana: University of Notre Dame Press, 1954.

Murray, John Courtney. *We Hold These Truths: Catholic Reflections on the American Proposition.* New York: Rowman and Littlefield Publishers, Inc., 2005.

N

National Catholic Reporter. "Debate surfaces over origins of the `Serenity Prayer'." July 25, 2008.

National Conference of Christians and Jews. "Historical Note." National Conference of Christians and Jews.http://special.lib.umn. edu/findaid/xml/sw0092.xml (accessed May 14, 2013).

NCWC News Releases.

--"Ottaviani" Editorial Information NCWC News Service June 12, 1959 FJC Papers at Redemptorist Archives, Brooklyn, NY.

-- James C O'Neill "Cardinal Ottaviani Lauds Church in U.S. On Return from Visit; Cites Growth" NCWC News Service (Foreign) June 29 1959 FJC Papers at Redemptorist Archives, Brooklyn, NY.

The New York Times. "Aims to Harmonize National Groups; Conference outlines a wide campaign of good will among all class; plans educational drive; fosters communal movements and spirit of understanding among the young." December 11, 1927

The New York Times. "Archer Says Vatican Denies US Freedom." July 23, 1953.

The New York Times. "Jesuit Sees Shift in Political Era: Editor of Catholic Weekly finds more tolerance for Non-Protestant President." February 28, 1960.

The New York Times. "Martin S. Quigley." February 8, 2011. http:// legacy.com/obituarites/nytimes/obituary-print.aspx?n=martin-s-quigley&pid=14..... (accessed May 7, 2013).

The New York Times. "Pope's Envoy Hails U.S. Church Liberty." March 20, 1960.

Novak, Michael. *A New Generation: American and Catholic.* New York: Herder and Herder, 1964.

Novak, Michael. "Introduction to The Open Church (Millennium Edition)." American Enterprise Institute, November 24, 2003. http://www.aei.org/print/introduction-to-the-open-church-millennium-edition (accessed October 23, 2013).

Novak, Michael. *The Open Church: Vatican II, Act II.* New York: The MacMillan Company, 1964.

Novak, Michael. "Will the Council Build the Bridge?" *U.S. Catholic,* October, 1964.

Nuti, Leopoldo. "The United States, Italy, and the Opening to the Left, 1953-1963," *Journal of Cold War Studies,* Vol. 4 (Summer 2002), 3: 36-55.

O

O'Connell, Marvin R. *John Ireland and the American Catholic Church.* St. Paul, Minnesota: Minnesota Historical Society Press, 1988.

O'Donovan, L. (1908). "John Carroll." *In The Catholic Encyclopedia.* New York: Robert Appleton Company. Retrieved July 3, 2011 from New Advent: http://www.newadvent.org/cathen/03381b.htm.

O'Daniel, V. (1910). John of Paris. In The Catholic Encyclopedia. New York: Robert Appleton Company. Retrieved April 25, 2012 from New Advent: http://www.newadvent.org/cathen/08475b.htm.)

O'Malley, John W. SJ. "Vatican II: Did Anything Happen?" *Theological Studies.* 67 (2006): 3-33.

Oakes, Edward T. "The Irony of American History, Revisited." *America,* May 30, 1992.

"Obituaries: Barrett McGurn." *The Washington Post,* July 8, 2010. http://www.washingtonpost.com/wp-dyn/content/article/2010/07/07/AR2010070705112.html (accessed March 18, 2013).

Ottaviani, Alfredo Cardinal. trans. Fr. Denis Fahey "Duties of the Catholic State in Regard to Religion." Translated by Fr. Denis Fahey. 2nd ed. Kansas City, Missouri: Angelus Press, 1993.

Ottaviani, Alfredo Cardinal. Trans. "Church and State: Some Present Problems n the Light of the Teaching of Pope Pius XII."

Translated by Msgr. Joseph Fenton. *American Ecclesiastical Review* CXXVIII (May, 1953): 321-334.

Our Sunday Visitor's Catholic Almanac 2005. Ed. Matthew Bunson. Huntington, Indiana: Our Sunday Visitor, Inc., 2005.

Our Sunday Visitor's Catholic Almanac 2005 Edition. Ed. Greg Erlandson. Huntington, Indiana: Our Sunday Visitor Publishing Division, 2004.

P

Pace, Eric. "NY Times Obituary: Raymond-Leopold Bruckberger, Priest and Author, Dies at 90". *The New York Times,* January 12, 1998.   http://dominicanhisory.blogspot.com/2011/07/raymond-leopold-bruckberger-op-1907.html (accessed June 24, 2012).

Paddock, Alfred H. Jr. *U.S. Army Special Warfare: Its Origins Psychological and Unconventional Warfare 1941-1952.* Fort Lesley J. McNair, Washington DC: National Defense University Press, 1982.

Paine, Thomas. *Common Sense.* Mineola, New York: Dover Publications, Inc., 1997.

Paine, Thomas. *The Thomas Paine Reader.* Edited by Michael Foot and Isaac Kramnick. London, England: Penguin Books, 1987.

Parry-Giles, Shawn J. *The Rhetorical Presidency, Propaganda, and the Cold War 1945-1955.* Westport, Connecticut: Praeger, 2002.

Paterson, Thomas G. and Robert J. McMahon, editors. *The Origins of the Cold War, Third Edition.* Lexington, Massachusetts: D.C. Heath and Company, 1991.

Payne, Stanley G. *The Franco Regime 1936-1975.* Madison, Wisconsin: The University of Wisconsin Press, 1987.

Pelotte, Donald E. SSS. *John Courtney Murray: Theologian in Conflict.* New York: Paulist Press, 1976.

Pike, James A. "Should A Catholic Be President?" *Life,* December 21, 1959.

Piper, John F. Jr. *Robert E. Speer: Prophet of the American Church.* Louisville, Kentucky: Geneva Press, 2000.

Plank, Geoffrey. *Rebellion and Savagery: The Jacobite Rising of 1745 and the Rise of the British Empire.* Philadelphia, Pennsylvania: University of Pennsylvania Press, 2006.

Pollen, J.H. (1912). "The Suppression of the Jesuits (1750-1773)." *In the Catholic Encyclopedia.* New York: Robert Appleton Company. Retrieved July 3, 2011 from New Advent: http://www.newadent. org/cathen/14096a.htm.

Pope Gregory XVI. *Mirari Vos.* www.papalencyclicals.net (accessed January 2, 2010).

Pope John XXIII. *Mater et Magistra.* www.papalencyclicals.com (accessed November 7, 2006).

Pope John XXIII. *Peace on Earth.* NCWC Translation. Boston, Massachusettes: Pauline Books & Media.

Pope Leo XIII. *Diuturnum.* http://www.vatican.va/holy_father/leo_xiii/encyclicals/documents/hf_1-xiii-enc-29061881... (accessed July 11, 2011).

Pope Leo XIII. *The Great Encyclical Letters of Pope Leo XIII Plus Other Documents.* Rockford, Illinois: Tan Books and Publishers, Inc., 1995.

Pope Leo XIII. "Testem Benevolentiae Nostrae." *The Great Encyclical Letters of Pope Leo XIII Plus Other Documents* (Tan Books and Publishers, Inc. 1995), 441-453.

Pope Leo XIII. *Humanum Genus.* http://www.vatican.va/holy_father/leo_xiii/encyclicals/documents/hf_1-xiii_enc_18840420... (accessed December 24, 2004).

Pope Leo XIII. *Immortale Dei.* http://www.vatican.va/holy_father/leo_xiii/encyclicals/documents/hf_1-xiii_enc_01111885... (accessed July 11, 2010).

Pope Leo XIII. *Inscrutabili Dei Consilio.* http://www.vatican.va/holy_father/leo_xiii/encyclicals/documents/hf_1-xiii-enc-21041878... (accessed July 19, 2011).

Pope Leo XIII. *Libertas.* In *The Papal Encyclicals 1740-1878,* edited by Claudia Carlen. Wilmington, North Carolina: McGrath Publishing Co., 1981.

Pope Leo XIII. *Libertas.* http://www.vatican.va/holy_father/leo_xiii/encyclicals/documents/hf_1-xiii_enc_20061888... (accessed December 28, 2004).

Pope Leo XIII. *Longinqua Oceani.* http://www.vatican.va/holy_father/leo_xiii/encyclicals/documents/hf_1-xiii_enc_06011895... (accessed January 17, 2010).

Pope Pius VII. *Diu Satis.* http://www.papalencyclicals.net/Pius07/p7diusat.htm (accessed July 3, 2011).

Pope Pius IX. *Quanto Conficiamur Moerore.* www.papalencyclicals.net (accessed November 7, 2006).

Pope Pius IX. *Quanta Cura.* www.papalencyclicals.net (accessed November 7, 2006).

Pope Pius IX. *Qui Pluribus.* www.papalencyclicals.net (accessed April 3, 2006).

Pope Pius IX. *The Syllabus of Errors Condemned by Pius IX.* www.papalencyclicals.net (accessed November 7, 2006).

Pope Pius IX. *Ubi Primum.* www.papalencyclicals.net (accessed April 3, 2006).

Pope Pius XI. *Ubi Arcano Dei Consilio.* http://www.vatican.va/hoy_father/pius_xi/encyclicals/documents/hf_p-xi_enc_23121922_... (accessed January 12, 2011).

Pope Pius XII, *Humani Generis*. http://www.vatican.va/holy_father/ pius_xii/encyclicals/documents/hf_p-xii_enc_12081950...(accessed January 18, 2010).

Pope Pius XII. *Ci Riesce.* http://www.ewtn.com/library/ PAPALDOC/P12CIRI.HTM (accessed August 15, 2010).

"Position Paper." *The Free Dictionary by Farlex.* www. thefreedictionary.com (accessed May 16, 2013).

Possony, Stefan T, Jerry E Pournelle, Col Francis X Kane. *The Strategy of Technology.* Publication Informitiona, 1997. http://baen. com/sot/sot_1.htm (accessed January 29 2013).

Powers, Richard Gid. *Not Without Honor: The History of American Anticommunism.* New York: The Free Press, 1995.

Preparata, Guido. *Conjuring Hitler: How Britain and America Made the Third Reich.* Ann Arbor, Michigan: Pluto Press, 2005.

Q

Quigley, Carroll. *The Anglo-American Establishment From Rhodes to Cliveden.* New York: Books in Focus, 1981.

Quigley, Carroll. *Tragedy and Hope: A History of the World in our Time.* New York: The MacMillan Company, 1966.

Quigley, Martin. *A U.S. Spy In Ireland.* Dublin, Ireland: Marino Books, 1999.

Quigley, Martin. *Peace Without Hiroshima: Secret Action at the Vatican in the Spring of 1945.* New York: Madison Books, 1991.

Quigley, Martin. *Magic Shadows: The Story of the Origin of Motion Pictures.* New York: Biblo and Tannen, 1969.

Quigley, Martin and Msgr. Edward M. Connors. *Catholic Action in Practice: Family Life, Education, International Life.* New York: Random House, 1963.

R

Rashkover, Randi. "Editorial." *Crosscurrents,* Summer 2005: 148-150.

Rasmussen, Frederick N. "George W. Constable Sr., 90 Partner in Law firm served on area boards," *The Baltimore Sun,* January 29, 2002. http://articles.baltimoresun.com/2002-01-29/news/0201290060_1_constable-dame-of-maryland-college-of-notre (accessed July 14, 2012).

Rifat, Tim. "Microwave and Mind Control." http://www.whale.to/b/rifat.html (accessed July 17, 2012).

Roazen, Paul. Introduction. In *The Public Philosophy.* New Brunswick, USA: Transaction Publishers, 1989.

Rock, P.M.J. (1908). Pontifical Decorations. In The Catholic Encyclopedia. New York: Robert Appleton Company. Retrieved May 26, 2012 from New Advent: http://www.newadvent.org/cathen/04667a.htm.

Rockefeller, David. *Memoirs.* New York: Random House, 2002.

Rockefeller Panel Reports. *Prospect for America: The problems and opportunities confronting American democracy – in foreign policy, in military preparedness, in education, in social and economic affairs.* Garden City, New York: Doubleday Press, 1961.

Roosevelt, Franklin Delano. "Four Freedoms Speech." University of Sand Diego. http://history.sandiego.edu/gen/text/us/fdr1941.html (accessed May 29, 2010).

Ross, Gaylon, Sr. *Who's Who of the Elite Members of the: Bilderbergs Council on Foreign Relations & Trilateral Commission.* Spicewood, Texas: RIE, 2000.

Rosswurm, Steve. *The FBI and the Catholic Church 1935-1962.* Boston, Massachusetts: University of Massachusetts Press, 2009.

Ryan, John A. and Moorhouse F. X. Millar, ed. *The State and the Church*. New York: The MacMillan Company, 1930.

S

Santelli, Anthony. "Money, Oil, Blood, Death." *Culture Wars* 32, 4 (March 2013): 12-22.

Scholastic: University of Notre Dame's Student Magazine Since 1867. "Exit Interview," November 12, 2009.

Schroth, Raymond A. *The American Jesuits: A History*. New York: New York University Press, 2007.

Schultz, Kevin M. *Tri-Faith America: How Catholics and Jews Held Postwar America To Its Protestant Promise*. New York: Oxford University Press, 2011.

Severo, Richard. "Henry A. Grunwald, Editor Who Directed Shift in Time Magazine, Is Dead at 82." *The New York Times*, February 27, 2005. http://www.nytimes.com/2005/02/27/obituaries/27grunwald.html?pagewanted=print&posit (accessed June 29, 2012)

Shadegg, Stephen. *Clare Boothe Luce*. New York: Simon and Schuster, 1970.

Shavit, David. *The United States in Asia: An Historical Dictionary*. New York: Greenwood Press, 1990.

Shea, George W. "Catholic Doctrine and 'The Religion of the State'." *American Ecclesiastical Review* CXXIII (September 1950): 161-174.

Shea, George W. "Orientations on Church and State." *American Ecclesiastical Review* CXXV (December 1951): 405-416.

Shea, George W. "Spain and Religious Freedom," *American Ecclesiastical Review* CXXVII (September 1952): 161-172.

Sheed, Wilfrid. *Clare Boothe Luce*. New York: Berkley Books, 1982.

Sheed, Wilfrid. *Frank and Maisie: A Memoir with Parents.* London, United Kingdom: Chatto & Windus, 1986.

Sheen, Fulton J. *Treasure in Clay: The Autobiography of Fulton J. Sheen.* Garden City, New York: Image Books, 1982.

Shelley, Thomas J. "John Tracy Ellis and Catholic Intellectual Life." *America,* June 3, 1995. http://www.americamagazine.org/content/article.cfm?article_id=10705 (accessed July 12, 2012).

Short, Philip. *Mao: A Life.* New York: Henry Holt and Company, 2000.

Simpson, Christopher. *Science of Coercion: Communication Research & Psychological Warfare 1945-1960.* New York: Oxford University Press, 1994

Singer, C. Gregg. *The Unholy Alliance.* New Rochelle, New York: Arlington House Publishers, 1975.

Smith, Adam. *The Wealth of Nations.* Edwin Cannan, ed. New York: Bantam Classic, 2003.

Smith, Roy C. *Adam Smith and the Origins of American Enterprise: How the Founding Fathers Turned to a Great Economist's Writings and Created the American Economy.* New York: Truman Talley Books, 2004.

Smith, M.P. (1910). "Isaac Thomas Hecker". In *The Catholic Encyclopedia.* New York: Robert Appleton Company. Retrieved August 2, 2011 from New Advent: http://www.newadvent.org/cathen/07186a.htm.

Smith, William B. "Selected Methodological Questions in the Fundamental Moral Theology of Francis J. Connell, C.SS.R." A Dissertation Submitted to the Faculty of the School of Sacred Theology of the Catholic University of America In Partial Fulfillment of the Requirements for the Degree Doctor of Sacred Theology. Washington, D.C., 1971.

"Spanish Decry U.S. Catholic View; Religious Freedom Labeled 'Error'." *New York Times,* May 12, 1952.

Speaight, Robert. *The Life of Teilhard De Chardin.* New York: Harper & Row Publishers, 1967.

Steinfels, Peter. "Rev. John B Sheerin dies at 85; A Catholic editor and columnist." *The New York Times,* January 15, 1992. http://www.nytimes.com/1992/01/15/nyregion/rev-john-b-sheerin-dies-at-85-a-catholic-editor-and-columnist.html (accessed March 17, 2013).

Stern, John Allen. *C. D. Jackson: Cold War Propagandist for Democracy and Globalism.* New York: University Press of America,® Inc., 2012.

Stone, Ronald H. *Professor Reinhold Niebuhr: A Mentor To The Twentieth Century.* Louisville, Kentucky: Westminster/John Knox Press, 1992.

Sutton, Antony C. *The Best Enemy Money Can Buy.* Billings, Montana: Liberty House Press, 1986.

Swanberg, W. A. *Luce and His Empire.* New York: Scribner, 1972.

T

Time. "A Second Reformation, For Both Catholics & Protestants." June 8, 1962. http://www.time.com/time/subscriber/printout/0,8816,896321,00.html (accessed October 13, 2012).

"Books: Hope of the World." July 13, 1959. http://www.time.com/time/subscriber/printout/0,8816,869183,00.html (accessed June 24, 2012).

"Christians and Jews: Combatting Contempt." May 29, 1964. http://www.time.com/subscriber/printout/0,8816,940460,00.html (accessed October 21, 2012).

"Christianity: The Servant Church." December 25, 1964. http://www.time.com/time/subscriber/printout/0,8816,830969,00.html (accessed October 21, 2012).

"Churches: Ecumen In." March 13, 1964. http://www.time.com/time/subscriber/printout/0,8816,828258,00.html (accessed October 21, 2012).

"Ecumenism: A Seed Planted." January 17, 1964. http://www.time.com/time/subscriber/printout/0,8816,875590,00.html (accessed October 21, 2012).

"Ecumenism: Toward Easier Mixed Marriage." July 17, 1964. http://www.time.com/time/subscriber/printout/0,8816,875971,00.html (accessed October 21, 2012).

"Ecumenism: What Catholics Think About Jews." September 11, 1964. http://www.time.com/time/subscriber/printout/0,8816,830659,00.html (accessed October 21, 2012).

"Education: For Yale, a Thomist." August 13, 1951. http://www.time.com/time/printout/0,8816,889191,00.html (accessed December 31, 2009).

"Education: The Absentees." July 8, 1957. http://www.time.com/time/printout/0,8816,825113,00.html (accessed January 1, 2010).

"How Vatican II Turned The Church Toward the World." December 17, 1965. http://www.time.com/time/subscriber/printout/0,8816,834774,00.html (accessed November 11, 2012).

"Italy: Distensione." May 23, 1955. http://www.time.com/time/prntout/0,8816,891210.00.html (accessed January 2, 2011).

"Italy: The Little Professor." January 25, 1954. www.time.com (accessed July 10, 2011).

"The Lasting Vision of Pope John." February 26, 1965. http://www.time.com/time/subscriber/printout/0,8816,833488,00.html (accessed November 11, 2012).

"Letters: Oct. 16, 1964" October 16, 1964. http://www.time.com/time/subscriber/printout/0,8816,876221,00.html (accessed October 21, 2012).

"Milestones: Jan. 10, 1964." January 10, 1964. http://time.com/time/subscriber/printout/0,8816,875544,00.html (accessed October 23, 2012).

"The Papacy: The Pilgrim." October 15, 1965. http://www.time.com/time/subscriber/printout/0,8816,834512,00.html (accessed November 11, 2012).

"The Papacy: Reluctant Revolutionary." September 24, 1965. http://www.time.com/time/subscriber/printout/0,8816,834370,00.html (accessed November 11, 2012).

"The Papacy: Vatican Revolutionary." June 7, 1963. http://www.time.com/time/subscriber/printout/0,8816,874758,00.html (accessed October 13, 2012).

"The Press: The Prelates & the Press." November 16, 1962. http://www.time.com/time/subscriber/printout/0,8816,829416,00.html (accessed October 13, 2012.

"Protestantism: Emancipation in Spain." February 8, 1963. http://www.time.com/time/subscriber/prntout/0,8816,829837,00.html (accessed October 13, 2012).

"Protestants: Getting Ahead In Italy." January 4, 1965. http://www.time.com/time/subscriber/printout/0,8816,898354,00.html (accessed November 11, 2012).

"Religion: The 21st Council." February 9, 1959. http://www.time.com/time/subscriber/printout/0,8816,892187,00.html (accessed October 13, 2012).

"Religion: A Life on the Brink." September 12, 1969. http://www.time.com/time/subscriber/printout/0,8816,901405,00.html (accessed July 29, 2012).

"Religion: America in Rome." February 25, 1946. http://www.time.com/time/subscriber/printout/0,8816,852693,00.html (accessed April 29, 2012).

"Religion: Best Seats in the House." October 26, 1962. http://www.time.com/time/subscriber/printout/0,8816,874538,00.html (accessed October 13, 2012).

"Religion: Birth Control and Catholics." September 15, 1961. http://www.time.com/time/subscriber/article/0,33009,938765-1,00.html (accessed February 18, 2013).

"Religion: The Bishops' Agenda." September 24, 1965. http://www.time.com/time/subscriber/printout/0,8816,834371,00.html (accessed November 11, 2012).

"Religion: The Cardinal's Setback." November 23, 1962. http://www.time.com/time/subscriber/printout/0,8816,82950,00.html (accessed October 13, 2012).

"Religion: Catholics and Tolerance." August 3, 1953. http://www.time.com/time/subscriber/printout/0,8816,822913,00.html (accessed May 19, 2012).

"Religion: Cheeky Reporter." November 19, 1965. http://www.time.com/time/subscriber/printout/0,8816,834677,00.html (accessed November 11, 2012).

Religion: The Council Opens." October 19, 1962. http://www.time.com/time/subscriber/printout/0,8816,827893,00.html (accessed October 13, 2012).

"Religion: The Council's Prospects." September 14, 1962. http://www.time.com/time/subscriber/printout/0,8816,874481,00.html (accessed October 13, 2012).

"Religion: Council of Renewal." October 5, 1962. http://www.time.com/time/subscriber/printout/0,8816,829210,00.html (accessed October 13, 2012).

"Religion: Death in the Wilderness." September 12, 1969. http://www.time.com/time/subscriber/printout/0,8816,901404,00.html (accessed July 29, 2012).

"Religion: Faith for a Lenten Age." March 8, 1948. http://www.time.com/time/printout/0,8816,853293,00.html (accessed April 23, 2011).

"Religion: Four Centuries Late." April 7, 1952. {as retrieved from the Connell Papers at the Redemptorist Archives.}

"Religion: The Lowly Catholic Layman." August 17, 1962. http://www.time.com/time/subscriber/printout/0,8816,870050,00.html (accessed October 13, 2012).

"Religion: Offer In Error." July 9, 1956. http://www.time.com/time/magazine/article/0,9171,893473,00.html (accessed December 31, 2009).

"Religion: On the Roads to Rome." February 18, 1946. http://www.time.com/time/subscriber/printout/0,8816,792623,00.html (accessed April 29, 2012).

"Religion: The Princes of the Church." March 30, 1962. http://www.time.com/time/subscriber/printout/0,8816,895979,00.html (accessed October 13, 2012).

"Religion: R.S.V.P." July 20, 1962. http://www.time.com/time/subscriber/printout/0,8816, 896383,00.html (accessed October 13, 2012).

"Religion: The Supreme Realist." July 6, 1962. http://www.time.com/time/subscriber/printout/0,8816,940032,00.html (accessed October 13, 2012).

"Religion: St. Pius IX?" August 31, 1962. http://www.time.com/time/subscriber/printout/0,8816,938909,00.html (accessed October 13, 2012).

"Religion: Toleration in Seville." March 17, 1952. http://www.time.com/time/subscriber/printout/0,8816,816,816129,00.html (accessed May 12, 2012).

"Religion: Yes & No." July 29, 1946. http://www.time.com/time/subscriber/printout/0,8816,776965,00.html (accessed April 29, 2012).

Roman Catholics: Answer on the Way." July 3, 1964. as retrieved October 21, 2012 from http://www.time.com/time/subscriber/printout/0,8816,873935,00.html (accessed October 21, 2012).

"Roman Catholics: Authority Under Fire." March 19, 1965. http://www.time.com/time/subscriber/printout/0,8816,833583,00.html (accessed November 11, 2012).

"Roman Catholics: Beyond Transubstantiation: New Theory of the Real Presence." July 2, 1965. http://www.time.com/time/subscriberprintout/0,8816,833876,00.html (accessed November 11, 2012).

"Roman Catholics: The Bravest Schema." October 30, 1964. http://www.time.com/time/subscriber/printout/0,8816,876333,00.html (accessed October 21, 2012).

"Roman Catholics: The Case Against celibacy." August 28, 1964. http://www.time.com/time/subscriber/printout/0,8816,876117,00.html (accessed October 21, 2012).

"Roman Catholics: Clear It with the Vatican." September 20, 1963. http://www.time.com/time/subscriber/printout/0,8816,870552,00.html (accessed October 13, 2012).

"Roman Catholics: Confession: Public or Private?" August 6, 1965. http://www.time.com/time/subscriber/printout/0,8816,834152,00.html (accessed November 11, 2012).

"Roman Catholics: Council on the Move." November 8, 1963. http://www.time.com/time/subscriber/printout/0,8816,897019,00.html (accessed October 13, 2012).

"Roman Catholics: Cum Magno Dolore." October 23, 1964. http://www.time.com/time/subscriber/printout/0,8816,897340,00.html (accessed October 21, 2012).

"Roman Catholics: In Dutch with the Vatican." June 5, 1964. http://www.time.com/time/subscriber/printout/0,8816,938627,00.html (accessed October 21, 2012).

"Roman Catholics: Ecumenical Voices." April 5, 1963. http://www.time.com/time/subscriber/printout/0,8816,830066,00.html (accessed October 13, 2012).

"Roman Catholics: Eldest Daughter in Turmoil." June 11, 1965. http://www.time.com/time/subscriber/printout/0,8816,833719,00.html (accessed November 11, 2012).

"Roman Catholics: Flying Red Hats." May 22, 1964. http://www.time.com/time/subscriber/printout/0,8816,871117,00.html (accessed October 21, 2012).

"Roman Catholics: Gadfly." July 31, 1964. http://www.time.com/time/subscriber/printout/0,8816,874002,00.html (accessed October 21, 2012).

"Roman Catholics: Indulgences Made Easy." December 31, 1965. http://www.time.com/time/subscriber/printout/0,8816,842343,00.html (accessed November 11, 2012).

"Roman Catholics: The Married Priest." July 10, 1964. http://www.time.com/time/subscriber/printout/0,8816,871270,00.html (accessed October 21, 2012).

"Roman Catholics: Modernizing the Mass." December 13, 1963. http://www.time.com/time/subscriber/printout/0,8816,875469,00.html (accessed October 13, 2012).

"Roman Catholics: The Next Cardinal." June 25, 1965. http://www.time.com/time/subscriber/printout/0,8816,833806,00.html (accessed November 11, 2012).

"Roman Catholics: No More Galileos." November 6, 1964. http://www.time.com/time/subscriber/printout/0,8816,876412,00.html (accessed October 21, 2012).

"Roman Catholics: Not to Herself, but to God." September 25, 1964. http://www.time.com/time/subscriber/printout/0,8816,876193,00.html (accessed October 21, 2012).

"Roman Catholics: The Pope's Man in Recife." March 27, 1964. http://www.time.com/time/subscriber/printout/0,8816,938559,00.html (accessed October 21, 2012).

"Roman Catholics: Praying It in English." May 29, 1964. http://www.time.com/time/subscriber/printout/0,8816,940459,00.html (accessed October 21, 2012).

"Roman Catholics: A Question of Freedom." December 24, 1965. http://www.time.com/time/subscriber/printout/0,8816,834867,00.html (accessed November 11, 2012).

"Roman Catholics: A Question of Leadership." June 26, 1964. http://www.time.com/time/subscriber/printout/0,8816,898179,00.html (accessed October 21, 2012).

"Roman Catholics: Readiness for Reform." October 4, 1963. http://www.time.com/time/subscriber/printout/0,8816,875264,00.html (accessed October 13, 2012).

"Roman Catholics: Renewal Among the Jesuits." May 21, 1965. http://www.time.com/time/subscriber/printout/0,8816,901724,00.html (accessed November 11, 2012).

"Roman Catholics: The Right to Worship According to One's Conscience." October 2, 1964. http://www.time.com/time/subscriber/printout/0,8816,940522,00.html (accessed October 21, 2012).

"Roman Catholics: Selective Faith." September 16, 1966. http://www.time.com/time/subscriber/printout/0,8816,836376,00.html (accessed November 11, 2012).

"Roman Catholics: Toned-Down Consistory." March 5, 1965. http://www.time.com/time/subscriber/printout/ 0,8816,839311,00.html (accessed November 11, 2012).

"Roman Catholics: The Unfinished Reformation." February 7, 1964. http://www.time.com/time/subscriber/printout/ 0,8816,870689,00.html (accessed October 21, 2012).

"Roman Catholics: The Unlikely Cardinal." August 21, 1964. http:// www.time.com/time/subscriber/printout/0,8816,876036,00.html (accessed October 21, 2012).

"Roman Catholics: A Word to Outsiders." November 22, 1963. http://www.time.com/time/subscriber/printout/ 0,8816,898039,00.html (accessed October 13, 2012).

"Spain: The Awakening Land." January 21, 1966. http://www.time. com/time/subscriber/printout/0,8816,835066,00.html (accessed November 11, 2012).

"Spain: Warning from the Church." May 27, 1966. http://www. time.com/time/subscriber/printout/0,8816,835645,00.html (accessed November 11, 2012).

"The Vatican Council: What Went Wrong?" December 6, 1963. http://www.time.com/time/subscriber/printout/ 0,8816,898101,00.html (accessed October 13, 2012).

"Theology: Any God Will Do." March 19, 1965. http://www.time. com/time/subscriber/printout/0,8816,8633584,00.html (accessed November 11, 2012).

"Theology: Church & Birth Control: From Genesis to Genetics." July 16, 1965. http://www.time.com/time/subscriber/printout/ 0,8816,834007,00.html (as accessed November 11, 2012).

"Theology: What Mary Means to Protestants." September 11, 1964. http://www.time.com/time/subscriber/printout/ 0,8816,830660,00.html (accessed October 21, 2012).

"The Papacy: His Church." August 21, 1964. http://www.time.com/ time/subscriber/printout/0,8816,876035,00.html (accessed October 21, 2012).

"Universities: Crisis at Catholic U." March 29, 1963. http://www. time.com/time/subscriber/printout/0,8816,896755,00.html (accessed October 13 2012).

"The Vatican Council: A Blow for Liberty." October 1, 1965. http:// www.time.com/time/subscriber/printout/0,8816,834445,00.html (accessed November 11, 2012).

"The Vatican Council: The Fourth Session." September 10, 1965. http://www.time.com/time/subscriber/printout/ 0,8816,834306.html (accessed November 11, 2012).

"The Vatican Council: A Mind of its Own." November 20, 1964. http://www.time.com/time/subscriber/printout/ 0,8816,830822,00.html (accessed October 21, 2012).

"The Vatican Council: The Pope Runs the Church." November 27, 1964.   http://www.time.com/time/subscriber/printout/ 0,8816,871415,00.html (accessed October 21, 2012).

"The Vatican Council: Speedup." September 18, 1964. http://www. time.com/time/subscriber/printout/0,8816,830734,00.html (accessed October 21, 2012).

"Vatican Council: The Uses of Ambiguity." November 5, 1965. http://www.time.com/time/subscriber/printout/ 0,8816,901776,00.html (accessed November 11, 2012).

"The Vatican Council: A Vote Against Prejudice." October 22, 1965. http://www.time.com/time/subscriber/printout/ 0,8816,941409,00.html (accessed November 11, 2012).

Totaro, Lorenzo. "Italy Unemploymnt Rate Remains Close to 20-year-high amid slump." *Bloomberg,* April 30, 2013. http://www. bloomberg.comnews/print/2013-04-30italy-unemployment-rate-remains-clos... (accessed May 19, 2013).

Toy, Eckard V. "The Conservative Connection: The Chairman of the Board Took LSD Before Timothy Leary." *American Studies* 21 (Fall 1980): 65-77.

U

U. S. Congress. *Congressional Record.* May 23, 2013. Pelosi, Nancy, "Honoring Father Hesburgh." 113th Congress, 1st Session, Vol. 159, No. 74. http://beta.congress.gov/congressional-record/2013/05/23/ extensions-of-remarks-section/article/E729-1 (accessed June 15, 2013).

V

Vatican Radio. "Pope pens rare article on his inside view of Vatican II." October 10, 2012. http://en.radiovaticana.va/print_page.asp?c= 628717 (accessed October 12, 2012).

W

Weaver, Richard M. *Ideas Have Consequences.* Chicago, Illinois: University of Chicago Press, 1948.

Weber, David K. "Niebuhr's Legacy." *The Review of Politics* 64, (2002): 339-352.

Weigel, Gustave. "Religious toleration in a world society," *America,* January 9 1954.

White, Hilary. "Italy's Last Catholic Generation? Mass Attendance in 'Collapse' among Under-30s." *Life Site News,* August 9, 2010. http://www.lifesitenews.com/home/print_article/news/1979/ (accessed May 19, 2013).

Wilde, Melissa J., Kristin Geraty, Shelley L. Nelson, and Emily Bowman. "Religious Economy or Organizational Field? Predicting Bishops' Votes at the Second Vatican Council." *American Sociological Review* 75(4): 586-606. asr.sagepub.com (accessed August 11, 2010).

Wilford, Hugh. *The Mighty Wurlitzer: How the CIA Played America.* Cambridge, Massachusetts: Harvard University Press, 2008.

Will, Allen Sinclair. *Life of James Cardinal Gibbons.* New York: John Murphy Publishers, 1911.

Will, Allen Sinclair. *Life of Cardinal Gibbons Archbishop of Baltimore.* New York: E. P. Dutton & Company, 1922.

Wills, Garry. "Secular Incompetence and Catholic Confusion." *Worldview,* June, 1972.

Wills, Garry. *Why I Am A Catholic.* New York: Houghton Mifflin Company, 2002.

Winski, Norman. *Mysticism for the Millions.* Los Angeles, California: Sherbourne Press, Inc., 1965.

Wollemborg, Leo. "Recess an Aid to Catholic Liberals." *The Washington Post,* December 16, 1962.

Woodiwiss, Michael. *Organized Crime and American Power.* Toronto, Canada: University of Toronto Press, 2001.

Woods, Randall B. *Shadow Warrior: William Egan Colby and the CIA.* New York: Basic Books, 2013.

XYZ

Zimbalist, Efrem Jr. *My Dinner of Herbs.* New York: Limelight Editions, 2003.

MISCELLANEOUS MATERIALS

"The Current Situation in Italy," 10 October 1947, Central Intelligence Agency, Harry S. Truman Library. Papers of Harry S. Truman President's Secretary's file, http://www.foia.cia.gov/browse_-docs_full.asp (accessed May 8, 2010).

"Current Intelligence Weekly," Central Intelligence Agency Office of Current Intelligence dated 5 June 1953, http//www.foia.cia.-gov/browse_docs_full.asp (accessed May 8, 2010).

Intelligence Memorandum No. 250 dated 5 April 1950; Subject: Potentialities for Anti-Soviet Underground Resistance in the Event of War in 1950, http://www.foia.cia.gov/browse_docs_full.asp (accessed May 8, 2010).

Memorandum from Whitney H. Sheperdson, Subject: Harte Reports, dated January 27, 1945 containing Memorandum from Harte to Karl Brennan, dated January 4, 1945, http://www.foia.cia.-gov/browse_docs_full.asp (accessed May 8, 2010).

"Probable Developments in Italy," National Intelligence Estimate from the Central Intelligence Agency Published 31 March 1953, http://www.foia.cia.gov/browse_docs_full.asp (accessed May 8, 2010).

"Probable Developments in Italy," National Intelligence Estimate from the Central Intelligence Agency Published 16 November 1954, http//www.foia.cia.gov/browse_docs_full.asp (accessed May 8, 2010).

PSB D-33 June 29, 1953, "U.S. Doctrinal Program", Psychological Strategy Board.

"The University of South Caroliniana Society Programs," 38th Annual Meeting, University of South Carolina Thursday, April 26, 1974, Henry Savage, Jr. President, Presiding.

FREEDOM OF INFORMATION ACT REQUESTS

Documents provided by the FBI in a letter dated December 29, 2010 pursuant to a request under the Freedom of Information Act Subject: Luce, Clare Boothe / 1944-1957 Request No. 1150282-000.

CIA online Dr. Everett R. Clinchy to Allen Dulles Letter dated April 8, 1958 from a CIA online FOIA request.

PHOTOGRAPHS

*Charles Douglas ("CD") Jackson (1902-1964. CREDITS: Courtesy
of the* White House Staff Book 1953-1961 *and Dwight D.
Eisenhower Presidential Library and Museum*

Dr. Edward P. Lilly ca 1945. CREDITS: Courtesy of the Cullen Photo Company Of Washington, D.C. and Dwight D. Eisenhower Presidential Library and Museum

John Shaw Billings and Henry R. Luce ca. December, 1936. CREDITS: Courtesy Time, Inc./Life magazine and South Carolina Library, University of South Carolina

Fr. Francis J. Connell, C.Ss.R. (1888-1967) in his study.
CREDITS: Courtesy of the Redemptorist Archives, Philadelphia.

Clare Boothe Luce ca. November, 1949. CREDITS: Courtesy of
John Courtney Murray Papers Washington, DC

Fr. John Courtney Murray, SJ ca. May, 1962. CREDITS: Courtesy of John Courtney Murray Papers Georgetown University Library Special Collections Research Center Washington, DC

Henry R. Luce ca. May, 1962. CREDITS: Courtesy of John Courtney Murray Papers Georgetown University Library Special Collections Research Center Washington, DC

Fr. Gustave Weigel, SJ (1906-1964). CREDITS: Courtesy of John Courtney Murray Papers Georgetown University Library Special Collections Research Center Washington, DC and Woodstock Theological School (Fr. Leon Hooper, SJ)

Msgr. George Shea (1910-1990). CREDITS: Courtesy of Monsignor William Noe Field Archives & Special Collections Center, Seton Hall University

Msgr. Joseph C. Fenton (1906-1969). CREDITS: Courtesy of the Catholic University of America Washington, DC

Fr. Robert Leiber, SJ, (1887-1967) personal secretary of Eugenio Cardinal Pacelli (later Pope Pius XII), ca. 1929. CREDITS: Wikipedia -- Wilhelm Sandfuchs -- Public Domain

Pope John XXIII with Papal Nuncio to USA Archbishop Egidio Vagnozzi ca. 1959. CREDITS: Courtesy of Archdiocese of Chicago's Joseph Cardinal Bernardin Archives and Records Center Chicago, Illinois; photographer unknown

Pope Paul VI with (l tor) Cardinals John J. Carberry John F Dearden, Patrick J. O'Boyle, John P. Cody, John J. Wright, Terence J. Cooke ca. 1969. CREDITS: Courtesy of Archdiocese of Chicago's Joseph Cardinal Bernardin Archives and Records Center Chicago, Illinois and Religious News Service Photo (2-NY-5B-69-W)

531

WORLD WAR II BLESSING — Pope Pius XII in 1943 blesses his audience following one of his many radio broadcasts where he called for peace during World War II. Second from right is Msgr. Giovanni Battista Montini who later became Pope Paul VI. A Jesuit expert on the war years has reported in a magazine in Rome that the British had a "lie factory" which created rumors and false news reports unfavorable to Germany and Italy, many of which involved the Vatican. (NC Photo) (Horizontal 1-20-78) EDITORS: See story 13-1-19-78.

Pope Pius XII with Msgr. Giovanni Montini (2nd from right) ca. 1943. CREDITS: Courtesy of Archdiocese of Chicago's Joseph Cardinal Bernardin Archives and Records Center Chicago, Illinois; NC Photo

Francis Cardinal Spellman (1889-1967). CREDITS: Courtesy of Archdiocese of Chicago's Joseph Cardinal Bernardin Archives and Records Center Chicago, Illinois; photographer unknown

Alfredo Cardinal Ottaviani (1890-1979). CREDITS: Courtesy of Archdiocese of Chicago's Joseph Cardinal Bernardin Archives and Records Center Chicago, Illinois; photographer unknown

Samuel Cardinal Stritch (1887-1958). CREDITS: Courtesy of Archdiocese of Chicago's Joseph Cardinal Bernardin Archives and Records Center Chicago, Illinois; photographer unknown

President Dwight D. Eisenhower and Cardinal-designate Amleto Cicognani ca. 1959. CREDITS: Courtesy of Archdiocese of Chicago's Joseph Cardinal Bernardin Archives and Records Center Chicago, Illinois; and Religious News Service Photograph (SM-WASH-12B-58-JS)

Richard Cardinal Cushing on his 68th Birthday. CREDITS: Courtesy of Archdiocese of Chicago's Joseph Cardinal Bernardin Archives and Records Center Chicago, Illinois; and Religious News Service

INDEX

O

O'Boyle, Patrick Cardinal 98, 138, 283, 305-307, 331, 391-392, 397

O'Brien, Reverend John 46, 372-374

Office of Strategic Services (OSS) 19, 29, 197

Ottaviani, Alfredo Cardinal 30-35, 59, 67, 70-71, 84, 89-90, 99-106, 114-116, 119, 135, 165, 172-178

Our Sunday Visitor 122, 160, 196

Oxnam, Bishop Bromley 43-47, 61

P

Pacem In Terris (Encyclical) 206, 212, 219, 221-222, 276, 286, 288, 323, 346, 451, 457-458

Paine, Thomas 144, 147, 286, 294, 439

Pike, Albert 27-30

Pius IX, Pope 30-31, 46, 126, 166, 188, 221, 337, 413, 455

Pius X, Pope 99, 108, 122, 174, 176, 392

Pius XI, Pope 120, 133, 221, 352, 456

Pius XII, Pope 31, 40, 99, 116, 123, 126, 131-134, 150-154, 164-165, 241, 279, 321, 338, 346, 349, 358, 454, 456-458.

Pizzardo, Giuseppe Cardinal 33, 98, 250

Political Warfare 150

Protestants and Other Americans United for Separation of Church and State (POAU) 247

Psychological Warfare 144-147, 162, 170, 191, 224, 414

ABOUT THE AUTHOR

David Wemhoff received an AB in Government from the University of Notre Dame and a Juris Doctor from the University of the Pacific, McGeorge School of Law. He earned a Master of Laws (LLM) in international and comparative law from Indiana University. Mr. Wemhoff taught college level courses at two universities in Business Law, American Government, Constitutional Law, and State and Local Government. He is a member of the Society of Catholic Social Scientists. He resides in Granger, Indiana.

NOTES

SUMMARY OF PARTS XV THROUGH XXIII

1. John LaFarge to John Courtney Murray, Letter dated October 14, 1955, *John Courtney Murray Papers*: Box 1 Folder 134, Georgetown University Library, Special Collections Division, Washington, D.C.
2. Mario Benigni and Goffredo Zanchi, tr. Elvira DiFabio, *John XXIII: The Official Biography* (Boston, Massachusetts: Pauline Books & Media, 2000), 291-294.
3. Ibid.
4. Klaus Dohrn to CD Jackson, Memorandum undated, CD Jackson Papers: "Dohrn, Klaus, (2)," Dwight D. Eisenhower Library, Abilene, Kansas.
5. Klaus Dohrn to CD Jackson, Letter dated June 29, 1960, CD Jackson Papers: "Dohrn, Klaus (1)," Dwight D. Eisenhower Library, Abilene, Kansas.
6. "Text of Motu Proprio on Ecumenical Council," NCWC Special Service June 6, 1960, Francis J. Connell Papers, Rdemptorist House Archives, Baltimore Province, Brooklyn, New York.
7. "Editorial Information," from NCWC News Service dated November 21, 1960, from Francis J. Connell Papers, Redemptorist House Archives, Baltimore Province, Brooklyn, New York.
8. CD Jackson to Vittorio Vaccari, Letter dated January 29, 1963, CD Jackson Papers: Box 109 File "V-Misc (1)," Dwight D. Eisenhower Library, Abilene, Kansas.
9. Carlo Falconi wrote that Cardinal Montini was an "enigma" though considered an "exponent of progressive Catholicism" before rising to the Papacy. Falconi, *Pope John and His Council,* 96-97. "Progressive" denotes someone acceptable to the Americans.
10. Joseph Clifford Fenton, Entry for May 11, 1963, Diary
11. Falconi, *Pope John and His Council,* 173-174.
12. "Christianity: The Servant Church," *Time,* December 25, 1964. http://www.time.com/time/subscriber/printout/0,8816,830969,00.html (accessed October 21, 2012).
13. "Religious Liberty 1st on Council Agenda," *Camden Star Herald,* January 15, 1965.
14. Melissa J. Wilde, Kristin Geraty, Shelley L. Nelson, and Emily Bowman, "Religious Economy or Organizational Field? Predicting Bishops' Votes at the Second Vatican Council" *American Sociological Review* 75(4): 587, 599-600. Sage Journals website. asr.sagepub.com (accessed August 11, 2010).
15. Melissa J. Wilde, Kristin Geraty, Shelley L. Nelson, and Emily Bowman, "Religious Economy or Organizational Field? Predicting Bishops' Votes at the Second Vatican Council" *American Sociological Review* 75(4): 587. Sage Journals website. asr.sagepub.com (accessed August 11, 2010).
16. Melissa J. Wilde, Kristin Geraty, Shelley L. Nelson, and Emily Bowman, "Religious Economy or Organizational Field? Predicting Bishops' Votes at the

Second Vatican Council" *American Sociological Review* 75(4): 587, 599-600. Sage Journals website. asr.sagepub.com (accessed August 11, 2010).
17. Msgr. R. G. Bandas, "The Aims of the 21st Ecumenical Council," *The Wanderer,* August 26, 1965, Francis J Connell Papers, Redemptorist House Archives, Baltimore Province, Brooklyn, New York..

CHAPTER 65

1. John Courtney Murray to Clare Boothe Luce, Letter dated "July 31 [1960]," Clare Boothe Luce Papers: Box 766 Folder 11, Library of Congress, Washington, D.C.
2. John Courtney Murray to Clare Boothe Luce, Letter dated July 29, 1959, Clare Boothe Luce Papers: Box 795 Folder 10, Library of Congress, Washington, D.C.
3. Clare Boothe Luce, "By Love Possessed" dated September 8-10, 1959, Clare Boothe Luce Papers: Box 793 Foder 7, Library of Congress, Washington, D.C.
4. Clare Boothe Luce, "By Love Possessed."
5. Clare Boothe Luce, "By Love Possessed."
6. Clare Boothe Luce, "By Love Possessed."
7. "Conference between HRL and CBL Subject: Divorce," Clare Boothe Luce Journal, Clare Boothe Luce Papers: Box 793 File 8, Library of Congress, Washington, D.C.

CHAPTER 66

1. Wilfrid Sheed, *Clare Boothe Luce* (New York: Berkeley Books, 1982), 125-126.
2. Alison Falby, *Between the Pigeonholes: Gerald Heard 1889-1971*(Newcastle, United Kingdom: Cambridge Scholars Publishing, 2008), 148. In a letter dated June 26, 1951 Clare Boothe Luce told Heard "being with you, talking with you, listening to you, was the best of Hollywood." Clare Boothe Luce Papers,: Box 189 Folder 5, Library of Congress, Washington, D.C.
3. Jack Jones, telephone interview by John V. Cody, May 30, 1992, John V. Cody PhD Collection on Gerald Heard.
4. Jean Houston. *Life Force: The Psycho-Historical Recovery of the Self.* (Wheaton, Illinois: Quest Books, 1993), 275.
5. Ray Bradbury, telephone interview by John V Cody August 9, 1995, John V. Cody, PhD. Collection on Gerald Heard.
6. Keith Ditman and John V. Cody, telephone interview by John V. Cody September 16, 1998, John V. Cody, Ph.D. Collection on Gerald Heard.
7. Ditman and Cody telephone interview of September 16, 1998.
8. Jack Jones, telephone interview by John V. Cody May 27, 1992, John V. Cody, Ph.D. Collection on Gerald Heard.
9. Jones and Cody telephone interview of May 27, 1992; Jack Jones, telephone interview by John V. Cody May 30,1992, John V. Cody, Ph.D. Collection on Gerald Heard.
10. Houston, *Life Force: The Psycho-Historical Recovery of the Self,* 271-274.
11. Jim Kepner and John V. Cody, telephone interview by John V. Cody May 25,1992, John V. Cody, Ph.D. Collection on Gerald Heard.
12. John V. Cody, Ph.D., *Gerald Heard Timeline and Chronology* (1999), 40.
13. Falby, *Between the Pigeonholes: Gerald Heard 1889-1971,* 12.

14. Houston, *Life Force: The Psycho-Historical Recovery of the Self*, 274-275.

15. Falby, *Between the Pigeonholes: Gerald Heard 1889-1971*, 123.

16. Falby, *Between the Pigeonholes: Gerald Heard 1889-1971*, 137.

17. Gerald Heard to Clare Boothe Luce, Letter dated April 7, 1948, Clare Boothe Luce Papers: Box 760 Folder 6, Library of Congress, Washington, D.C.

18. Falby, *Between the Pigeonholes: Gerald Heard 1889-1971*, 122; Derek Bok, interview by John V. Cody, August 30, 1994, transcript, 10-11, John V. Cody PhD Collection on Gerald Heard.

19. Falby, *Between the Pigeonholes: Gerald Heard 1889-1971*, 137.

20. Gerald Heard to Clare Boothe Luce, Letter dated February 13 1960, Clare Boothe Luce Papers: Box 766 Folder 9, Library of Congress, Washington, D.C.

21. Gerald Heard to Clare Boote Luce, Letter dated March 12, 1960, Clare Boothe Luce Papers: Box 766 Folder 9, Library of Congress, Washington, D.C.

22. James C. Ingebretsen, *Apprentice to the Dawn* Manuscript John V. Cody, PhD Collection on Gerald Heard, 64.

23. Ingebretsen, *Apprentice to the Dawn,* 59-63.

24. John Courtney Murray, to Clare Boothe Luce, Letter dated "Sunday," Clare Boothe Luce Papers: Box 795 Folder 11, Library of Congress, Washington, D.C.

25. Steve Allen, interviewed by John V. Cody, June 3, 1993, John V. Cody PhD. Collection on Gerald Heard.

26. John Courtney Murray to Clare Boothe Luce, Letter dated "Sunday, 5th", Clare Boothe Luce Papers: Box 795 Folder 11, Library of Congress, Washington, D.C.

27. Sid Cohen to John Courtney Murray, Letter dated December 11, 1960, Clare Boothe Luce Papers: Box 795 Folder 3, Library of Congress, Washington, D.C.

28. Sid Cohen to Clare Boothe Luce, Letter dated December 12, 1960, Clare Boothe Luce Papers: Box 795 Folder 3, Library of Congress, Washington, D.C.

29. John Hanley, "In Memoriam William Ross Adey, MD Professor of Anatomy and Physiology Los Angeles (1922-2004)." http://www.universityofcalifornia.edu/senate/inmemoriam/williamrossadey.htm (accessed July 17, 2012).

30. Tim Rifat, "Microwave and Mind Control." http://www.whale.to/b/rifat.html (accessed July 17, 2012).

31. Martin A. Lee and Bruce Shlain, *Acid Dreams: The Complete Social History of LSD: The CIA, the Sixties, and Beyond* (Grove Press, 1985), 7-8.

32. Sid Cohen to Clare Boothe Luce, Letter dated December 14, 1960, Clare Boothe Luce Papers: Box 795 Folder 3, Library of Congress, Washington, D.C.

33. Ditman telephone interview by Cody September 16, 1998.

34. Ditman telephone interview by Cody September 16, 1998.

35. Notes of 3/11/1959,Clare Boothe Luce Papers: Box 793 Folder 4, Library of Congress, Washington, D.C.

36. Notes of 4/4/1959, Clare Boothe Luce Papers: Box 793 Folder 4, Library of Congress, Washington, D.C.

37. Notes of 5/16/1959,Clare Boothe Luce Papers: Box 56 Folder 12, Library of Congress, Washington, D.C.

38. Notes of 12/8/1959,Clare Boothe Luce Papers: Box 793 Folder 4, Library of Congress, Washington, D.C.

39. Undated notes, Clare Boothe Luce Papers: Box 793 Folder 4, Library of Congress, Washington, D.C.

40. Notes of 4/16/1960, Clare Boothe Luce Papers: Box 793 Folder 4, Library of Congress, Washington, D.C.

41. Notes of 8/8/1960, Clare Boothe Luce Papers: Box 793 Folder 4, Library of Congress, Washington, D.C.
42. Undated notes, Clare Boothe Luce Papers: Box 793 Folder 4, Library of Congress, Washington, D.C.
43. Notes of 1/8/1961, Clare Boothe Luce Papers: Box 793 Folder 4, Library of Congress, Washington, D.C.
44. Notes of 2/14/1961, Clare Boothe Luce Papers: Box 793 Folder 4, Library of Congress, Washington, D.C.
45. Notes of June, 1962, Clare Boothe Luce Papers: Box 793 Folder 4, Library of Congress, Washington, D.C.
46. Walter Truett Anderson, *The Upstart Spring: Esalen and the Human Potential Movement: The First Twenty Years* (Lincoln, Nebraska: iUniverse, Inc., 2004), 9-13.
47. Anderson, *The Upstart Spring: Esalen and the Human Potential Movement: The First Twenty Years,* 9-13, 111.
48. Anderson, *The Upstart Spring: Esalen and the Human Potential Movement: The First Twenty Years,* 111.
49. Robert Speaight, *The Life of Teilhard De Chardin* (New York: Harper & Row Publishers, 1967), 260-263.
50. Speaight, *The Life of Teilhard De Chardin,* 263.
51. Anderson, *The Upstart Spring: Esalen and the Human Potential Movement: The First Twenty Years,* 290.
52. Ingebretsen, *Apprentice to the Dawn,* 26-29.
53. Ingebretsen, *Apprentice to the Dawn,* 11-12.
54. Ingebretsen, *Apprentice to the Dawn,* 38-39.
55. Ingebretsen, *Apprentice to the Dawn,* 12, 56
56. Ingebretsen, *Apprentice to the Dawn,* 101-102.
57. Ingebretsen, *Apprentice to the Dawn,* 126-127.
58. Ingebretsen *Apprentice to the Dawn,* 56.
59. Derek Bok, telephone interview by John V. Cody, August 30, 1994, John V. Cody, PhD Collection on Gerald Heard, 18; Ingebretsen, *Apprentice to the Dawn,* 62.
60. Auctor Ignotus, *AE: The Open Persuader* (Los Angeles: One Incorporated, Inc., 1969), 96.
61. Ignotus, *AE: The Open Persuader,* 145.
62. Ignotus, *AE: The Open Persuader,* Forward.
63. Ignotus, *AE: The Open Persuader,* Forward.
64. Gerald Heard, *Some Notes on Dr. Evelyn Hooker's "Value-Conflict and Value-Congruence of a Homosexual Group in a Heterosexual Society,"* ed. by John V. Cody (1996), i through xii.
65. Houston, *Life Force: The Psycho-Historical Recovery of the Self,* 268-269.
66. Gerald Heard to Louis Dehmlow, Letter dated December 8, 1962, John V. Cody PhD Gerald Heard Collection.
67. Falby, *Between the Pigeonholes: Gerald Heard, 1889-1971,* 121.
68. Gerald Heard, "Business Leadership" Lecture given at Idyllwild, California August 16, 1956, John V. Cody Collection on Gerald Heard.
69. Gerald Heard, "Ethics in Business" Lecture given at Harvard, date unknown, John V. Cody PhD Collection on Gerald Heard, 1-2.
70. Heard, "Ethics in Business" Lecture, 1-2.
71. Heard, "Ethics in Business" Lecture, 2-3.
72. Heard, "Ethics in Business," Lecture, 13-15.
73. Falby, *Between the Pigeonholes: Gerald Heard 1889-1971,* 121-122, 148.

74. Jack Jones and John V. Cody, interview by John V. Cody July 19, 1995, John V. Cody, Ph.D. Collection on Gerald Heard.
75. John V. Cody, *Glossary of Names Related to Gerald Heard* (1999), 281.

CHAPTER 67

1. Clare Boothe Luce to John Courtney Murray, Letter dated March 1960, Clare Boothe Luce Papers: Box 795 Folder 11, Library of Congress, Washington, D.C.
2. Clare Boothe Luce to Murray, Letter dated March 1960.
3. Clare Boothe Luce to Murray, Letter dated March 1960.
4. Clare Boothe Luce to Murray, Letter dated March 1960.
5. Clare Boothe Luce to John Courtney Murray, Letter dated April 5, 1960, Clare Boothe Luce Papers: Box 795 Folder 11, Library of Congress, Washington, D.C.
6. "Conference between HRL and CBL Subject: Divorce," Clare Boothe Luce Journal, Clare Boothe Luce Papers: Box 793 File 8, Library of Congress, Washington, D.C.
7. "Conference between HRL and CBL Subject: Divorce."
8. "Conference between HRL and CBL Subject: Divorce"; Clare Boothe Luce, "A background review of 'The Situation' in the form of a questionnaire, for John Courtney Murray June 12, 1960," Clare Boothe Luce Papers: Box 793 Folder 6, Library of Congress, Washington, D.C.
9. Clare Boothe Luce, Journal dated July 11, 1960, Clare Boothe Luce Papers: Box 793 Folder 3, Library of Congress, Washington, D.C.
10. Clare Boothe Luce, "A background review of 'The Situation' in the form of a questionnaire, for John Courtney Murray June 12, 1960," Clare Boothe Luce Papers: Box 793 Folder 6, Library of Congress, Washington, D.C.
11. Clare Boothe Luce, "A background review of 'The Situation' in the form of a questionnaire, for John Courtney Murray June 12, 1960."
12. Clare Boothe Luce, "A background review of 'The Situation' in the form of a questionnaire, for John Courtney Murray June 12, 1960."
13. Clare Boothe Luce, "A background review of 'The Situation' in the form of a questionnaire, for John Courtney Murray June 12, 1960."
14. "Report of Honest Broker," undated, Clare Boothe Luce Papers: Box 795 Folder 11, Library of Congress, Washington, D.C.
15. "Report of Honest Broker."
16. Henry R. Luce to Clare Boothe Luce, Letter dated June 19, 1960, Clare Boothe Luce Papers: Box 795 Foder 11, Library of Congress, Washington, D.C.
17. Clare Boothe Luce to John Courtney Murray, Letter dated December 26, 1961, Clare Boothe Luce Papers: Box 795 Folder 11, Library of Congress, Washington, D.C.
18. John Courtney Murray to Clare Boothe Luce, Letter "Dec. 29 [1961]," Clare Boothe Luce Papers: Box 767 Folder 1, Library of Congress, Washington, D.C.

CHAPTER 68

1. James A Pike, "Should a Catholic Be President?" *Life,* December 21, 1959, 79.
2. "Religion: A Life on the Brink," *Time,* September 12, 1969. http://www.time.com/time/subscriber/printout/0,8816,901405,00.html (accessed July 29, 2012).

3. "Religion: A Life on the Brink," *Time,* September 12, 1969.

4. "Religion: A Life on the Brink," *Time,* September 12, 1969.

5. "Religion: A Life on the Brink," *Time,* September 12, 1969.; "Religion: Death in the Wilderness," *Time,* September 12, 1969. http://www.time.com/time/ subscriber/printout/0,8816,901404,00.html (accessed July 29, 2012).

6. "Purpose," Teleos Institute website. http://www.consciousnesswork.com/ abouteleos.htm#Purpose (accessed August 11, 2012).

7. Pike, "Should A Catholic Be President?" *Life,* December 21, 1959, 79.

8. Pike, "Should A Catholic Be President?" *Life,* December 21, 1959, 79-80.

9. Pike, "Should A Catholic Be President?" *Life,* December 21, 1959, 80-81.

10. Pike, "Should A Catholic Be President?" *Life,* December 21, 1959, 80-81.

11. Pike, "Should A Catholic Be President?" *Life,* December 21, 1959, 81.

12. Pike, "Should A Catholic Be President?" *Life,* December 21, 1959, 82-83.

13. Pike, "Should A Catholic Be President?" *Life,* December 21, 1959, 82-83.

14. Francis J. Connell to James Pike, Letter dated December 19, 1959, Francis J. Connell Papers, Redemptorist House Archives, Baltimore Province, Brooklyn, New York.

15. James Pike to Francis J. Connell, Letter dated December 21, 1959, Francis J. Connell Papers, Redemptorist House Archives, Baltimore Province, Brooklyn, New York.

16. Paul Hallatt to Francis J. Connell, Letter dated January 6, 1960, Francis J. Connell to Paul Hallatt, Letter dated January 12, 1960, both found at Francis J. Connell Papers, Redemptorist House Archives, Baltimore Province, Brooklyn, New York.

17. Francis J. Connell to Editor of *Life,* Letter dated December 21, 1959, Francis J. Connell Papers, Redemptorist House Archives, Baltimore Province, Brooklyn, New York.

18. Connell to Editor of *Life,* Letter dated December 21, 1959.

19. The Editors of *Life* to Francis J. Connell, Letter dated January 11 1960, Francis J. Connell Papers, Redemptorist House Archives, Baltimore Province, Brooklyn, New York.

20. "Pope Names Secretary to Vatican Holy Office," *The New York Times,* October 21, 1959.

21. "Ottaviani," Editorial Information, NCWC News Service dated June 12, 1959, Francis J. Connell Papers, Redemptorist House Archives, Baltimore Province, Brooklyn, New York.

22. "Ottaviani," Editorial Information, NCWC News Service dated June 12, 1959.

23. James C. O'Neill, "Cardinal Ottaviani Lauds Church in U.S. On Return from Visit; Cites Growth" NCWC News Service (Foreign) dated June 29 1959, Francis J. Connell Papers, Redemptorist House Archives, Baltimore Province, Brooklyn, New York.

24. O'Neill, "Cardinal Ottaviani Lauds Church in U.S. On Return from Visit; Cites Growth" NCWC News Service (Foreign) dated June 29 1959.

25. O'Neill, "Cardinal Ottaviani Lauds Church in U.S. On Return from Visit; Cites Growth" NCWC News Service (Foreign) dated June 29 1959.

26. Francis J. Connell to Alfredo Cardinal Ottaviani, Letter dated December 21, 1959, Francis J. Connell Papers, Redemptorist House Archives, Baltimore Province, Brooklyn, New York.

27. Francis J. Connell to Bishop Lawrence Shehan, Letter December 13, 1959, Francis J. Connell Papers, Redemptorist House Archives, Baltimore Province, Brooklyn,

New York.

28. Francis J. Connell to Ottaviani, Letter January 12, 1960, Francis J. Connell Papers, Redemptorist House Archives, Baltimore Province, Brooklyn, New York.

29. Francis J. Connell to Ottaviani, Letter February 13, 1960, Francis J. Connell Papers, Redemptorist House Archives, Baltimore Province, Brooklyn, New York.

30. Connell to Ottaviani, Letter February 13, 1960.

31. "Jesuit Sees Shift in Political Era: Editor of Catholic Weekly finds more tolerance for Non-Protestant President", *The New York Times,* February 28, 1960, in Francis J. Connell Papers, Redemptorist House Archives, Baltimore Province, Brooklyn, New York.

CHAPTER 69

1. Clare Boothe Luce, Journal undated, Clare Boothe Luce Papers: Box 315 Folder 13, Library of Congress, Washington, D.C.

2. Clare Boothe Luce, Journal dated July 11, 1960, Clare Boothe Luce Papers: Box 793 Folder 3, Library of Congress, Washington, D.C.

3. Clare Boothe Luce, Journal dated July 11, 1960.

4. Niccolo Machiavelli, *The Prince* (New York: Penguin Books, 1995), 31-32.

5. Martin Quigley, *Peace Without Hiroshima: Secret Action at the Vatican in the Spring of 1945* (New York: Madison Books, 1991), 3, 5, 11-14; Martin Quigley, *A U.S. Spy In Ireland.* (Dublin, Ireland: Marino Books,1999), 26-28,60-63; Adam Bernstein, "Martin Quigley, who used film work as cover for World War II espionage, dies," *The Washington Post,* February 11, 2011 under http://www. washingtonpost.com/wp-dyn/content/article/2011/02/11/ AR2011021106050_pf... (accessed May 7, 2013); "Martin S. Quigley" *The New York Times,* February 8 2011, under http://legacy.com/obituarites/nytimes/ obituary-print.aspx?n=martin-s-quigley&pid=14....." (accessed May 7, 2013).

6. "Pope's Envoy Hails U.S. Church Liberty," *The New York Times,* March 20, 1960, as found at Francis J. Connell Papers, Redemptorist House Archives, Baltimore Province, Brooklyn, New York.

7. "American Liberty," Francis J. Connell Papers, Redemptorist House Archives, Baltimore Province, Brooklyn, New York.

8. Francis J. Connell to Egidio Vagnozzi, Letter dated March 9, 1960 with "Pope Leo XIII and the Problem of Human Liberty," Francis J. Connell Papers, Redemptorist House Archives, Baltimore Province, Brooklyn, New York.

9. Connell to Vagnozzi, Letter dated March 9, 1960 with "Pope Leo XIII and the problem of human liberty."

10. Connell to Vagnozzi Letter dated March 9, 1960 with "Pope Leo XIII and the problem of human liberty."

11. Connell to Vagnozzi Letter dated March 9, 1960 with "Pope Leo XIII and the problem of human liberty."

12. Vagnozzi to Francis J. Connell, Letter dated March 22, 1960, Francis J. Connell Papers, Redemptorist House Archives, Baltimore Province, Brooklyn, New York.

13. Francis J. Connell to Egidio Vagnozzi, Letter dated April 18, 1960 with review of *Counseling the Catholic,* Francis J. Connell Papers, Redemptorist House Archives, Baltimore Province, Brooklyn, New York; Randy Engel, *McHugh Chronicles* (New Engel Publishing, 1997), 9-10.

CHAPTER 70

1. Eugene Carson Blake and G. Bromley Oxnam, "A Protestant view of a Catholic for President," *Look,* May 10, 1960, 31-34.
2. Blake and Oxnam, "A Protestant view of a Catholic for President," *Look.*
3. Blake and Oxnam, "A Protestant view of a Catholic for President," *Look* (emphasis present in original)
4. Blake and Oxnam, "A Protestant view of a Catholic for President," *Look*
5. Blake and Oxnam, "A Protestant view of a Catholic for President," *Look*
6. Blake and Oxnam, "A Protestant view of a Catholic for President," *Look*
7. Blake and Oxnam, "A Protestant view of a Catholic for President," *Look*
8. Blake and Oxnam, "A Protestant view of a Catholic for President," *Look*
9. Blake and Oxnam, "A Protestant view of a Catholic for President," *Look*
10. Blake and Oxnam, "A Protestant view of a Catholic for President," *Look*
11. Blake and Oxnam, "A Protestant view of a Catholic for President," *Look*
12. Blake and Oxnam, "A Protestant view of a Catholic for President," *Look*
13. Blake and Oxnam, "A Protestant view of a Catholic for President," *Look* (emphasis present)
14. Blake and Oxnam, "A Protestant view of a Catholic for President," *Look* (emphasis supplied)
15. Pelotte, *John Courtney Murray: Theologian in Conflict,* 76-77.
16. John Courtney Murray, *We Hold These Truths: Catholic Reflections on the American Proposition* (New York: Rowman & Littlefield Publishers, Inc., 2005), 56.
17. John de Menil to John Courtney Murray, Letter dated August 25, 1960; Paul Tishman to John Courtney Murray, Letter dated August 30, 1960; John De Menil to John Courtney Murray, Letter dated March 31, 1961; Pierre St. Olivier to John Courtney Murray, Letter dated April 3, 1961; Leonard F. Howard to John Courtney Murray, Letter dated November 20, 1961 with enclosures; all found *at John Courtney Murray Papers*: Box 28 Folder 1252, Georgetown University Library, Special Collections Division, Washington, D.C.
18. Luce, "National Purpose and Cold War," *The Ideas of Henry Luce,* ed. John K. Jessup, 131.
19. Luce, "National Purpose and Cold War," *The Ideas of Henry Luce,* ed. John K. Jessup, 131-132.
20. Luce, "National Purpose and Cold War," *The Ideas of Henry Luce,* ed. John K. Jessup, 121-123.
21. Luce, "National Purpose and Cold War," *The Ideas of Henry Luce,* ed. John K. Jessup, 132-133.
22. Luce, "National Purpose and Cold War," *The Ideas of Henry Luce,* ed. John K. Jessup, 133.

CHAPTER 71

1. Robert Coughlan, "The Religious Issue: An Un-American Heritage - A long tradition of bias in politics is being challenged by a new outlook," *Life,* July 4, 1960, 78-86.
2. Coughlan, "The Religious Issue: An Un-American Heritage - A long tradition of bias in politics is being challenged by a new outlook," *Life,* 78-79.

3. Coughlan, "The Religious Issue: An Un-American Heritage - A long tradition of bias in politics is being challenged by a new outlook," *Life*, 79-81.
4. Coughlan, "The Religious Issue: An Un-American Heritage - A long tradition of bias in politics is being challenged by a new outlook," *Life* , 81.
5. Coughlan, "The Religious Issue: An Un-American Heritage - A long tradition of bias in politics is being challenged by a new outlook," *Life*, 82, 84.
6. Coughlan, "The Religious Issue: An Un-American Heritage - A long tradition of bias in politics is being challenged by a new outlook," *Life*, 84, 86.
7. Francis J. Connell to Robert Coughlan, Letter dated July 7, 1960, Francis J. Connell Papers, Redemptorist House Archives, Baltimore Province, Brooklyn, New York.
8. Francisco De Luis, "Papal Ambassador to Spain Defends Church's Role There," NCWC News Service (Foreign) dated July 11, 1960, as found in Francis J. Connell Papers, Redemptorist House Archives, Baltimore Province, Brooklyn, New York.
9. De Luis, "Papal Ambassador to Spain Defends Church's Role There," NCWC News Service (Foreign) dated July 11, 1960.
10. "No Protestant problem in Spain, Spanish Foreign Minister tells Great Britain's House of Commons," NCWC News Service (Foreign) dated July 18, 1960, from Francis J. Connell Papers, Redemptorist House Archives, Baltimore Province, Brooklyn, New York.
11. "No Protestant problem in Spain, Spanish Foreign Minister tells Great Britain's House of Commons," NCWC News Service (Foreign) dated July 18, 1960.
12. John Cogley to Francis J. Connell, undated letter, Francis J. Connell Papers, Redemptorist House Archives, Baltimore Province, Brooklyn, New York.
13. Cogley to Connell undated letter.
14. Francis J. Connell to John Cogley, letter dated July 14, 1960, Francis J. Connell Papers, Redemptorist House Archives, Baltimore Province, Brooklyn, New York.
15. Connell to Cogley Letter dated July 14, 1960.
16. John Cogley to Francis J. Connell, Letter dated July 26, 1960, Francis J. Connell Papers, Redemptorist House Archives, Baltimore Province, Brooklyn, New York.
17. Cogley to Connell Letter dated July 26, 1960.
18. Cogley to Connell Letter dated July 26, 1960.
19. "No `interference' by Church in Republics with Catholics as President, Delegate says," NCWC News Service (Domestic), July 4 1960, as found in Francis J. Connell Papers at Redemptorist House Archives, Baltimore Province, Brooklyn, NY.

CHAPTER 72

1. "Cooperation between Christians necessary, German Cardinal says on visit to native see," NCWC News Service release dated August 15, 1960, Francis J. Connell Papers, Redemptorist House Archives, Baltimore Province, Brooklyn, New York.
2. Francis J Connell to Ottaviani, Letter dated August 20, 1960, Francis J. Connell Papers, Redemptorist House Archives, Baltimore Province, Brooklyn, New York.
3. "Editorial Information," NCWC News Service, September 9, 1960, from Francis J. Connell Papers, Redemptorist House Archives, Baltimore Province, Brooklyn, New York.

4. "Drs. Bennett, Niebuhr cite `blind prejudice' in Protestant charges," NCWC News Service Domestic September 12, 1960, from Francis J. Connell Papers, Redemptorist House Archives, Baltimore Province, Brooklyn, New York.

5. "Editorial Information," NCWC News Service, September 12, 1960, as contained in Francis J. Connell Papers, Redemptorist House Archives, Baltimore Province, Brooklyn, New York.

6. "Editorial Information," NCWC News Service, September 12, 1960.

7. "Editorial Information," NCWC News Service, September 12, 1960.

8. "Editorial Information," NCWC News Service, September 12, 1960.

9. "Editorial Information," NCWC News Service, September 12, 1960.

10. "Editorial Information," NCWC News Service, September 12, 1960; "100 Noted Churchmen, laymen ask Church groups to fight voting based on religion" NCWC News Service (Domestic) September 12, 1960, Francis J. Connell Papers, Redemptorist House Archives, Baltimore Province, Brooklyn, New York.

11. Pelotte, *John Courtney Murray: Theologian in Conflict*, 76-77.

12. John D. Morris, "Catholic Laymen Uphold Kennedy: 165 Sign Statement Backing Church-State Separation – A Protestant Replies", *The New York Times*, October 6 1960, as found in Francis J. Connell Papers, Redemptorist House Archives, Baltimore Province, Brooklyn, New York.

13. Morris, "Catholic Laymen Uphold Kennedy: 165 Sign Statement Backing Church-State Separation – A Protestant Replies," *The New York Times*, October 6, 1960.

14. Morris, "Catholic Laymen Uphold Kennedy: 165 Sign Statement Backing Church-State Separation – A Protestant Replies," *The New York Times*, October 6, 1960; "Layman denies existence of `official' Catholic dogma on Church-State relations," NCWC News Service (Domestic) October 10, 1960, Francis J. Connell Papers, Redemptorist House Archives, Baltimore Province, Brooklyn, New York.

15. "Layman denies existence of `official' Catholic dogma on Church-State relations," NCWC News Service (Domestic) October 10, 1960, Francis J. Connell Papers, Redemptorist House Archives, Baltimore Province, Brooklyn, New York.

16. "Church-State `Dogma' Is Labeled Misnomer" ["Denver Colorado"] October 16, 1960, as found in Francis J. Connell Papers, Redemptorist House Archives, Baltimore Province, Brooklyn, New York.

17. "Layman denies existence of `official' Catholic dogma on Church-State relations," NCWC News Service (Domestic) October 10, 1960, Francis J. Connell Papers, Redemptorist House Archives, Baltimore Province, Brooklyn, New York.

18. "Layman denies existence of `official' Catholic dogma on Church-State relations," NCWC News Service (Domestic) October 10, 1960.

19. "Layman denies existence of `official' Catholic dogma on Church-State relations," NCWC News Service (Domestic) October 10, 1960.

20. "Layman denies existence of `official' Catholic dogma on Church-State relations," NCWC News Service (Domestic) October 10, 1960.

21. "Pledge Nation's Catholics to Religious Freedom: 100 Lay Leaders Speak Out" article from San Francisco Archdiocesan paper dated October 7, 1960, Francis J. Connell Papers, Redemptorist House Archives, Baltimore Province, Brooklyn, New York; "Editorial Information" NCWC News Service dated October 4, 1960, Francis J. Connell Papers, Redemptorist House Archives, Baltimore Province, Brooklyn, New York.

CHAPTER 73

1. John W. Finney, "Jesuit Rules out church control over a president: Says religious law would not apply to public act of an elected official," *The New York Times,* September 28, 1960.
2. Finney, "Jesuit Rules out church control over a president: Says religious law would not apply to public act of an elected official."
3. Finney, "Jesuit Rules out church control over a president: Says religious law would not apply to public act of an elected official."
4. Finney, "Jesuit Rules out church control over a president: Says religious law would not apply to public act of an elected official."
5. Finney, "Jesuit Rules out church control over a president: Says religious law would not apply to public act of an elected official."
6. "Church-State Relations," NCWC News Service, dated September 27, 1960 from Francis J. Connell Papers, Redemptorist House Archives, Baltimore Province, Brooklyn, New York.
7. "Church-State Relations," NCWC News Service, dated September 27, 1960.
8. "Church-State Relations," NCWC News Service, dated September 27, 1960.
9. "Church-State Relations," NCWC News Service, dated September 27, 1960.
10. "Church-State Relations," NCWC News Service, dated September 27, 1960.
11. Francis J. Connell, *Morals in Politics and Professions: A Guide for Catholics in Public Life* (Westminster, Maryland: The Newman Bookshop, 1946), 1-2, 11-12.
12. Francis J. Connell to Ottaviani, Letter dated October 2, 1960, Francis J. Connell Papers, Redemptorist House Archives, Baltimore Province, Brooklyn, New York.
13. Connell to Ottaviani Letter dated October 2, 1960.
14. Connell to Ottaviani Letter dated October 2, 1960.
15. Connell to Ottaviani Letter dated October 2, 1960.
16. Connell to Ottaviani Letter dated October 2, 1960.

CHAPTER 74

1. "Layman denies existence of `official' Catholic dogma on Church-State relations," NCWC News Service (Domestic) October 10, 1960 in Francis J. Connell Papers, Redemptorist House Archives, Baltimore Province, Brooklyn, New York.
2. "Layman denies existence of `official' Catholic dogma on Church-State relations," NCWC News Service (Domestic) October 10, 1960.
3. "Layman denies existence of `official' Catholic dogma on Church-State relations," NCWC News Service (Domestic) October 10, 1960.
4. "Layman denies existence of `official' Catholic dogma on Church-State relations," NCWC News Service (Domestic) October 10, 1960.
5. "Church in US committed to religious freedoms, Father Murray declares," NCWC News Service (Domestic) October 17, 1960 as found in Francis J. Connell Papers, Redemptorist House Archives, Baltimore Province, Brooklyn, New York.
6. "Church in US committed to religious freedoms, Father Murray declares," NCWC News Service (Domestic) October 17, 1960.
7. "Church in US committed to religious freedoms, Father Murray declares," NCWC News Service (Domestic) October 17, 1960.

8. "Bishop Warns Catholics against compromises," NCWC News Service (Domestic) October 24, 1960, as found in Francis J. Connell Papers, Redemptorist House Archives, Baltimore Province, Brooklyn, New York.

9. Francis J. Connell to Bishop John King Mussio, Letter dated October 25, 1960, Francis J. Connell Papers, Redemptorist House Archives, Baltimore Province, Brooklyn, New York.

10. Francis J Connell to Vagnozzi, Letter dated October 20, 1960, Francis J. Connell Papers, Redemptorist House Archives, Baltimore Province, Brooklyn, New York.

11. Fletcher Knebel, "The Bishops vs. Kennedy," Look, May 23, 1961, 44.

12. David Lawrence, "Free Speech and Church Disputes: Prelate's Political Advice Held All Right Except Where Penalty is Threatened" dated October 25, 1960, found Francis J. Connell Papers, Redemptorist House Archives, Baltimore Province, Brooklyn, New York.

13. Francis J Connell to Bishop McManus, Letter undated, Francis J. Connell Papers, Redemptorist House Archives, Baltimore Province, Brooklyn, New York.

14. Luis Munoz Marin to Walter Lippmann, Telegram dated 1960 Oct 21 PM 4:46, Walter Lippmann Papers (MS 326): Reel 78 Box 88 Folder 1449, Yale University, New Haven, Connecticut.

15. Luis Munoz Marin to Walter Lippmann, Telegram dated 1960 Nov 14 PM 7:18, Walter Lippmann Papers (MS 326): Reel 78 Box 88 Folder 1449, Yale University, New Haven, Connecticut.

16. Walter Lippmann Papers (MS 326): Reel 78 Box 88 Folder 1449, Yale University, New Haven, Connecticut.

17. CD Jackson to Munoz-Marin, Letter dated April 12, 1963, CD Jackson Papers: Box 72, Dwight D. Eisenhower Library, Abilene, Kansas.

18. "Papal Delegate Sees No Voting Ban in US," Washington Post, October 28, 1960, at Francis J. Connell Papers, Redemptorist House Archives, Baltimore Province, Brooklyn, New York.

19. "Political decisions up to people, Cushing says," Washington Post, October 28, 1960, at Francis J. Connell Papers, Redemptorist House Archives, Baltimore Province, Brooklyn, New York..

20. "Church State violations denied in bishops' act," Washington Post October 28, 1960, at Francis J. Connell Papers, Redemptorist House Archives, Baltimore Province, Brooklyn, New York.

21. "Puerto Rican Pastoral," America, November 5, 1960, 163-164.

22. "Puerto Rican Pastoral," America, 164.

23. "Puerto Rican Pastoral," America, 164.

24. "Puerto Rican Pastoral," America, 165.

CHAPTER 75

1. Robert Hoyt, "Opinion Worth Noting," America, November 5, 1960, 172.

2. Hoyt, "Opinion Worth Noting," America, 172.

3. Hoyt, "Opinion Worth Noting," America, 173-174.

4. Hoyt, "Opinion Worth Noting," America, 174-175.

5. Hoyt, "Opinion Worth Noting," America, 174-175.

6. Hoyt, "Opinion Worth Noting," America, 175.

CHAPTER 76

1. "Press Comments see religion factor in election, salute vote as defeat for bigotry," NCWC News Service (Domestic), November 14, 1960.
2. "Press Comments see religion factor in election, salute vote as defeat for bigotry."
3. Francis J. Connell to JFK, Letter dated November 14, 1960, Francis J. Connell Papers, Redemptorist House Archives, Baltimore Province, Brooklyn, New York.
4. Francis J. Connell to Apostolic Delegate Egidio Vagnozzi, Letter dated November 25, 1960, Francis J. Connell Papers, Redemptorist House Archives, Baltimore Province, Brooklyn, New York.
5. Douglas Auchincloss, "City of God and Man," *Time,* December 12, 1960, 64, 65.
6. Auchincloss, "City of God and Man," *Time*, 64. As the Americans were, and are, wont to do, they put forth a veiled admission. In this article that veiled admission was how they were bringing the spiritual crisis on society at large and Catholics in particular: The "barbarian is involved in work to undermine rational standards of judgment, to corrupt the inherited intuitive wisdom by which the people have always lived, and to do this not by spreading new beliefs but by creating a climate of doubt and bewilderment in which clarity about the larger aims of life is dimmed and the self-confidence of the people is destroyed."
7. Auchincloss, "City of God and Man," *Time*, 64-65.
8. Auchincloss, "City of God and Man," *Time*, 65-66.
9. Auchincloss, "City of God and Man," *Time,* 66, 69.
10. Auchincloss, "City of God and Man," *Time*, 66, 69.
11. Auchincloss, "City of God and Man," *Time*, 69.
12. Auchincloss, "City of God and Man," *Time*, 69-70.
13. Auchincloss, "City of God and Man," *Time*, 70.
14. John Deedy, *Seven American Catholics* (Chicago, Illinois: The Thomas More Press, 1978), 142.
15. "Fr. Murray to be On Catholic Hour," *St. Louis Review, John Courtney Murray Papers:* Box 28 Folder 1268, Georgetown University Library, Special Collections Division, Washington, D.C.
16. "Religious Freedom in America to be Explored by Father Murray on `Catholic Hour,' Jan. 8" from the National Council of Catholic Men Jan. 8, 1961, *John Courtney Murray Papers:* Box 28 File 1268, Georgetown University Library, Special Collections Division, Washington, D.C.
17. "To Be Honored by Xavier HS," *New York Sunday News,* April 30, 1961, *John Courtney Murray Papers*: Box 28 Folder 1268 Georgetown University Library, Special Collections Division, Washington, D.C.
18. "Jesuit Theologian Named by Manhattan for Medal," *The Catholic News,* May 20, 1961, *John Courtney Murray Papers*: Box 28 Folder 1268 Georgetown University Library, Special Collections Division, Washington, D.C.
19. Joseph C. Fenton to Francis J Connell, Letter dated December 7, 1960, Francis J. Connell Papers, Redemptorist House Archives, Baltimore Province, Brooklyn, New York.
20. Joseph C. Fenton, Diary Entry for December 12, 1960, "Journal of my fourteenth trip to Rome", 194-196, Joseph C. Fenton Papers, Catholic University of America, Washington, D.C.
21. Joseph C. Fenton, Diary Entry for December 16, 1960, "The Continuation of the Chronicle of My Fourteenth Trip to Rome", 22, Joseph C. Fenton Papers,

Catholic University of America, Washington, D.C.

22. Joseph C. Fenton to Francis J. Connell, Letter dated January 23, 1961, Francis J. Connell Papers, Redemptorist House Archives, Baltimore Province, Brooklyn, New York.

23. Francis J Connell to Egidio Vagnozzi, Letter dated March 20, 1961, Francis J. Connell Papers, Redemptorist House Archives, Baltimore Province, Brooklyn, New York.

24. Francis J Connell, "Comments on We Hold These Truths" attached to letter dated March 20, 1961 to Egidio Vagnozzi, Francis J. Connell Papers, Redemptorist House Archives, Baltimore Province, Brooklyn, New York.

25. Connell, "Comments on We Hold These Truths" attached to Letter dated March 20, 1961.

26. Connell, "Comments on We Hold These Truths" attached to Letter dated March 20, 1961.

27. Connell, "Comments on We Hold These Truths" attached to Letter dated March 20, 1961.

28. Connell, "Comments on We Hold These Truths" attached to Letter dated March 20, 1961.

29. Connell, "Comments on We Hold These Truths" attached to Letter dated March 20, 1961.

30. Connell, "Comments on We Hold These Truths" attached to letter dated March 20, 1961.

31. Connell, "Comments on We Hold These Truths" attached to letter dated March 20, 1961.

32. Connell, "Comments on We Hold These Truths" attached to letter dated March 20, 1961.

33. Francis J. Connell to Emigdio Vagnozzi, Letter dated March 27, 1961, Francis J. Connell Papers, Redemptorist House Archives, Baltimore Province, Brooklyn, New York.

CHAPTER 77

1. Joseph Clifford Fenton, Diary Entry for October 25, 1960, "Journal of My Fourteenth Trip to Rome, October, 1960", 89-91, Joseph Clifford Fenton Papers, Catholic University of America, Washington, D.C.

2. Joseph Clifford Fenton, Diary Entry for October 25, 1960, "Journal of My Fourteenth Trip to Rome, October, 1960", 87, Joseph Clifford Fenton Papers, Catholic University of America, Washington, D.C.

3. Joseph Clifford Fenton, Diary Entry for July 18, 1960, "Journal of My Fourteenth Trip to Rome, October, 1960", 74-75, Joseph Clifford Fenton Papers, Catholic University of America, Washington, D.C.

4. Francis J Connell to Joseph C Fenton, Letter dated July 25, 1960, Francis J. Connell Papers, Redemptorist House Archives, Baltimore Province, Brooklyn, New York.

5. Msgr. James I Tucek, "Pope embarks on final preparations for council; commissions are created," NCWC News Service, June 6, 1960, Francis J. Connell Papers, Rdemptorist House Archives, Baltimore Province, Brooklyn, New York.

6. "Roster of Ecumenical Council's Preparatory Commissions filled; more than 40 Americans included," NCWC News Service October 3, 1960, Francis J. Connell

Papers, Redemptorist House Archives, Baltimore Province, Brooklyn, New York.

7. Fenton, "Journal of My Fourteenth Trip to Rome, October, 1960," 78.

8. Francis J Connell to Ottaviani, Letter dated February 13, 1960, Francis J. Connell Papers, Redemptorist House Archives, Baltimore Province, Brooklyn, New York.

9. Henry P Cosgrove to Francis J Connell, Letter dated February 23, 1960, Francis J. Connell Papers, Redemptorist House Archives, Baltimore Province, Brooklyn, New York.

10. Joseph Clifford Fenton, Diary Entry for November 1, 1960, "Journal of My Fourteenth Trip to Rome, October, 1960", 139-141, Joseph Clifford Fenton Papers, Catholic University of America, Washington, D.C.

11. Joseph C Fenton to Francis J Connell, Letter dated November 2, 1960, . Francis J. Connell Papers, Redemptorist House Archives, Baltimore Province, Brooklyn, New York.

12. Joseph Clifford Fenton, Diary Entry for November 5, 1960, "Journal of My Fourteenth Trip to Rome, October, 1960", 195-196, Joseph Clifford Fenton Papers, Catholic University of America, Washington, D.C.

13. Joseph Clifford Fenton, Diary Entry for November 5, 1960, "Journal of My Fourteenth Trip to Rome, October, 1960", 195-196, Joseph Clifford Fenton Papers, Catholic University of America, Washington, D.C.

14. Joseph Clifford Fenton, Diary Entry for November 10, 1960, "Journal of My Fourteenth Trip to Rome, October, 1960", 239-240, Joseph Clifford Fenton Papers, Catholic University of America, Washington, D.C.

15. Fr. Sebastiaan Tromp, SJ, a Dutch Jesuit who ghost-wrote much of *Mystici Corporis.*

16. Fenton, "Journal of My Fourteenth Trip to Rome, October, 1960," 240-242.

17. Fenton, "Journal of My Fourteenth Trip to Rome, October, 1960," 240-242.

18. Joseph Clifford Fenton, Diary Entry for November 15, 1960, "Journal of My Fourteenth Trip to Rome, October, 1960", 280-281, Joseph Clifford Fenton Papers, Catholic University of America, Washington, D.C.

19. Joseph Clifford Fenton, Diary Entry for November 16, 1960, "Journal of My Fourteenth Trip to Rome, October, 1960", 286-287, Joseph Clifford Fenton Papers, Catholic University of America, Washington, D.C.

20. Joseph Clifford Fenton, Entry for December 11, 1960, Diary 6, 194-196, Joseph Clifford Fenton, Catholic University of America, Washington, D.C.

21. Joseph Clifford Fenton, Diary 8 "The continuation of the Journal of my fourteenth stay in Rome (10/23/60 – 2/18/61)…Beginning of the journal of My fifteenth trip to Rome 9/6/61," 3-5, Joseph Clifford Fenton Papers, Catholic University of America, Washington, D.C.: Joseph Clifford Fenton, Diary 6 "Notes of my 14th Trip to Rome continued from the previous volume 11/18/60 Place of the Holy Office (11/18/60-12/18/60," 6-7, Joseph Clifford Fenton Papers, Catholic University of America, Washington, D.C.

22. Joseph Clifford Fenton, Entry for January 28, 1961, Diary 8, 5; Joseph Clifford Fenton, Entry for November 18, 1960, Diary 6, 7-8, Joseph Clifford Fenton, Catholic University of America, Washington, D.C.

23. Joseph Clifford Fenton, Entry for January 21, 1961 Diary 7, 281-283, Joseph Clifford Fenton, Catholic University of America, Washington, D.C.

CHAPTER 78

1. Fenton, Diary 7, December 24, 1960, 66-68.
2. Fenton, Diary 7, January 21, 1961, 293-294.
3. Fenton, Diary 7, December 24, 1960, 68.
4. Fenton, Diary 7, January 27, 1961, 338-340.
5. Fenton, Diary 6, November 14, 1960, 271.
6. Fenton, Diary 6, November 17, 1960, 308-309, 313.
7. Fenton, Diary 7, January 27, 1961, 340-342.
8. Fenton, Diary 7, 338-339.
9. Fenton, Diary 7, January 20, 1961, 288-290.
10. Fenton, Diary 7, January 26 1961, 323-324.
11. Joseph Clifford Fenton to Francis J Connell, Letter dated January 23, 1961, Francis J. Connell Papers, Redemptorist House Archives, Baltimore Province, Brooklyn, New York.
12. Fenton, Diary 7, January 10, 1961, 201-202.
13. Fenton, Diary 7, January 11, 1961, 217-219.
14. Fenton, Diary 6, November 17, 1960, 312, 314.
15. Fenton, Diary 8, September 15, 1961, 135-139.
16. Fenton, Diary 7, December 26, 1960, 83-85.
17. Fenton, Diary 7, December 25, 1960, 73-76.
18. Fenton, Diary 8, February 13 and 17, 1961, 96, 120.
19. Fenton, Diary 7, October 29, 1960, 130-131.
20. Fenton, Diary 7, January 18, 1961, 279.
21. Fenton, Diary 8, February 7, 1961, 59.
22. Fenton, Diary 7, January 18, 1961, 279-280.
23. Fenton, Diary 8, February 7, 1961, 62-65.
24. Fenton, Diary 8, 55-59.
25. Fenton, Diary 8, 55-59.

CHAPTER 79

1. Fenton, Diary 6, November 29, 1960, 94-101.
2. Fenton, Diary 6, November 16, 1960, 290.
3. Fenton, Diary 7, January 18, 1961, 276.
4. Fenton, Diary 7, November 13, 1960, 260-261.
5. Fenton, Diary 7, November 16, 1960, 290-292.
6. Fenton, Diary 6, November 8, 1960, 221.
7. Fenton, Diary 7, November 13, 1960, 261-263.
8. Fenton, Diary 7, November 16, 1960, 293-294.
9. Fenton, Diary 7, December 17, 1960, 29-30. (emphasis by Fenton)
10. Fenton, Diary 7, December 23, 1960, 59-63; Fenton, Diary 7, January 11, 1961, 223-224.
11. Fenton, Diary 7, January 11, 1961, 223-224.
12. Fenton, Diary 7, December 26, 1960, 83, 86-87 (emphasis by Fenton)
13. Fenton, Diary 7, January 15, 1961, 252-254.
14. Fenton, Diary 7, December 29, 1960, 98-102.
15. Fenton, Diary 7, December 29, 1960, 98-102.

16. Fenton, Diary 7, December 29, 1960, 103-104, 109.
17. Fenton, Diary 7, December 29, 1960, 103-104, 109,111.
18. Fenton, Diary 7, December 29, 1960, 111-112.
19. Fenton, Diary 8, February 17, 1961, 119.
20. Fenton, Diary 8, February 13, 1961, 102-103.
21. Fenton, Diary 8, February 13, 1961, 104.
22. Fenton, Diary 8, February 10, 1961, 79-80.
23. Joseph Clifford Fenton, "Rome and the Status of Catholic Theology," *American Ecclesiastical Review* 143 (December 1960), 404-408, 410-411.
24. Fenton, "Rome and the Status of Catholic Theology," *American Ecclesiastical Review,* 410-411.
25. Joseph C. Fenton to Francis J. Connell, Letter dated February 11, 1961, Francis J. Connell Papers, Redemptorist House Archives, Baltimore Province, Brooklyn, New York.
26. Aram Berard, SJ, "Introduction," *Preparatory Reports: Second Vatican Council* (Philadelphia, Pennsylvania: The Westminster Press, 1965), 22.
27. "Pope to council preparatory commission," NCWC News Service June 26, 1961, Francis J Connell Papers at Redemptorist House Archives, Baltimore Province, Brooklyn, New York.
28. "Pope to council commissions," NCWC News Service, June 29 1961.

CHAPTER 80

1. Douglas Martin, "William F. Buckley Jr Is Dead at 82," February 27, 2008, *The New York Times.* http://www.nytimes.com/2008/02/27/business/media/27cnd-buckley.html?pagewanted=all&_r=0 (accessed June 15, 2013).
2. Gary Wills, *Why I Am A Catholic* (New York: Houghton Mifflin, 2002), 46-47.
3. Pope John XXIII, *Mater et Magistra.* http://www.papalencyclicals.net/John23/j23mater.htm, para 1 (accessed November 7, 2006).
4. Pope John XXIII, *Mater et Magistra,* para. 42. (emphasis supplied)
5. Pope John XXIII, *Mater et Magistra,* para. 181, 253.
6. Pope John XXIII, *Mater et Magistra,* para. 11, 37, 52.
7. Pope John XXIII, *Mater et Magistra,* para. 11, 37, 52.
8. Pope John XXIII, *Mater et Magistra,* para. 11, 37, 52.
9. Pope John XXIII, *Mater et Magistra,* para. 217, 235.
10. Joseph Clifford Fenton, "Revolutions in Catholic Attitudes" *American Ecclesiastical Review* 145, 2 (August 1961), 120-121.
11. Fenton, "Revolutions in Catholic Attitudes," *American Ecclesiastical Review,* 120-121.
12. Fenton, "Revolutions in Catholic Attitudes," *American Ecclesiastical Review,* 120-121.
13. Fenton, "Revolutions in Catholic Attitudes," *American Ecclesiastical Review,* 122-124.
14. Fenton, "Revolutions in Catholic Attitudes," *American Ecclesiastical Review,* 124-125.
15. Fenton, "Revolutions in Catholic Attitudes," *American Ecclesiastical Review,* 125-128.
16. Fenton, "Revolutions in Catholic Attitudes," *American Ecclesiastical Review,* 128-129.

CHAPTER 81

1. Fenton, Diary 8, "Fifteenth Trip to Rome", 132-134.
2. Fenton, Diary 8, September 15, 16, 20, 1961, 140-144, 169.
3. Robert Blair Kaiser, *Pope, Council and World* (New York: The Macmillan Company, 1963), 160-161.
4. Fenton, Diary 8, September 16, 1961, 145-149.
5. Fenton, Diary 8, September 16, 1961, 145-149.
6. Fenton, Diary 8, September 16, 1961, 145-149.
7. Fenton, Diary 8, September 16, 1961, 145-149.
8. Fenton, Diary 8, September 16 and 17, 1961, 148-163.
9. Fenton, Diary 8, September 16 and 17, 1961, 156.
10. Fenton, Diary 8, September 16 and 17, 1961, 161-164.
11. Joseph C. Fenton, "Doctrine and Tactic in Catholic Pronouncements on Church and State," *American Ecclesiastical Review* CXLV, no. 4 (October 1961): 266-276.
12. Fenton, "Doctrine and Tactic in Catholic Pronouncements on Church and State," 266-269.
13. Fenton, "Doctrine and Tactic in Catholic Pronouncements on Church and State," 269-270.
14. Fenton, "Doctrine and Tactic in Catholic Pronouncements on Church and State," 270-272.
15. Fenton, "Doctrine and Tactic in Catholic Pronouncements on Church and State," 272-274.
16. Fenton, "Doctrine and Tactic in Catholic Pronouncements on Church and State," 274.
17. Fenton, "Doctrine and Tactic in Catholic Pronouncements on Church and State," 275-276.
18. Fenton, "Doctrine and Tactic in Catholic Pronouncements on Church and State," 275.
19. Seth Kantor, "Expect Opposition, Protestants Told; Cardinal Cites Action `In some instance'," *Dallas Times Herald,* December 1, 1961, A-5, from the Francis J Connell Papers at Redemptorist House Archives, Baltimore Province, Brooklyn, New York.
20. "Text of papal bull convoking 2nd Vatican Council for 1962," NCWC News Service December 25, 1961, Francis J Connell Papers at Redemptorist House Archives, Baltimore Province, Brooklyn, New York.
21. "Text of papal bull convoking 2nd Vatican Council for 1962."
22. "Text of papal bull convoking 2nd Vatican Council for 1962."

CHAPTER 82

1. Bishop McManus to Francis J. Connell, Letter dated January 29, 1962; Francis J. Connell to Fr. Henry Brogan C.SS.R, Letter dated March 13, 1962; Francis J. Connell to Fr. Francis X Murphy C.SS.R., undated letter; Francis Xavier Murphy to Francis J. Connell, Letter dated March 27, 1962; Superior General of Redemptorists to Francis J. Connell, Letter dated May 25, 1962, all at Francis J Connell Papers at Redemptorist House Archives, Baltimore Province, Brooklyn, New York..

2. Francis J. Connell, Text of Speech for the Serra Club of Miami, February 6, 1962, Francis J Connell Papers at Redemptorist House Archives, Baltimore Province, Brooklyn, New York.
3. "Vatican City daily is critical of suggestions for Church reform made by Fr. Lombardi in new book," NCWC News Service, January 15, 1962, Francis J Connell Papers at Redemptorist House Archives, Baltimore Province, Brooklyn, New York.
4. "Write on council with 'prudence, objectivity,' Pope asks: request recalls criticism of Fr. Lombardi," NCWC News Service, January 29, 1962, Francis J Connell Papers at Redemptorist House Archives, Baltimore Province, Brooklyn, New York.
5. "Free discussion will mark coming council; public will be informed by enlarged press office, pope says," NCWC News Service, May 14 1962, Francis J Connell Papers at Redemptorist House Archives, Baltimore Province, Brooklyn, New York.

CHAPTER 83

1. Aram Berard S.J., tr. *Preparatory Reports: Second Vatican Council* (Philadelphia, Pennsylvania: The Westminster Press, 1965), 50-52.
2. Berard, *Preparatory Reports: Second Vatican Council,* 128-129, 132-134.
3. Berard, *Preparatory Reports: Second Vatican Council,* 133-136.
4. Berard, *Preparatory Reports: Second Vatican Council,* 136-138.
5. Berard, *Preparatory Reports: Second Vatican Council,* 136-138.
6. Berard, *Preparatory Reports: Second Vatican Council,* 136-138.
7. Berard, *Preparatory Reports: Second Vatican Council,* 138-139.
8. Berard, *Preparatory Reports: Second Vatican Council,* 196.
9. Berard, *Preparatory Reports: Second Vatican Council,* 200-201.
10. Berard, *Preparatory Reports: Second Vatican Council,* 201.
11. Michael Davies, *The Second Vatican Council and Religious Liberty* (Long Prairie, Minnesota: The Neumann Press, 1992), 295-302.
12. Davies, *The Second Vatican Council and Religious Liberty*, 295-296.
13. Davies, *The Second Vatican Council and Religious Liberty,* 296-298.
14. Davies, *The Second Vatican Council and Religious Liberty,* 298-299.
15. Davies, *The Second Vatican Council and Religious Liberty*, 300-302.
16. Berard, *Preparatory Reports: Second Vatican Council,* 201-206.
17. "Pope asks all bishops to study council agenda; make final suggestions," NCWC News Service, June 25, 1962, Francis J Connell Papers at Redemptorist House Archives, Baltimore Province, Brooklyn, New York.
18. Msgr. James I. Tucek, "Proposed Agenda for Vatican Council contained in 119 booklets sent to bishops; preparation was thorough," NCWC News Service, July 16, 1962, at Francis J. Connell Papers at Redemptorist House Archives, Baltimore Province, Brooklyn, New York.
19. "Text of 'Statement on the Ecumenical Council' Issued by U.S. Bishops in 1962," NCWC News Service August 20, 1962, Francis J. Connell Papers at Redemptorist House Archives, Baltimore Province, Brooklyn, New York.
20. Philip M. Hannan to Francis J. Connell, Letter dated September 7, 1962, Francis J. Connell Papers at Redemptorist House Archives, Baltimore Province, Brooklyn, New York; Francis J. Connell, "Sermon Outline for the Sixteenth Sunday After Pentecost (September 30, 1962) The Ecumenical Council," Francis J. Connell Papers at Redemptorist House Archives, Baltimore Province, Brooklyn, New York.

21. Connell, "Sermon Outline for the Sixteenth Sunday After Pentecost (September 30, 1962) The Ecumenical Council."
22. Connell, "Sermon Outline for the Sixteenth Sunday After Pentecost (September 30, 1962) The Ecumenical Council." Connell also elaborated on Msgr. Tucek's discussion of the documents that may issue, and this indicated that Connell was aware the Council would probably not make any clarifying doctrinal statements as Fenton and others thought it should. Connell said "The Council may issue certain statements that are meant to be authoritative, but not infallible. These statements must be accepted by the faithful, not with an act of faith, but with the type of acquiescence known as religious assent."
23. Connell, "Sermon Outline for the Sixteenth Sunday After Pentecost (September 30, 1962) The Ecumenical Council."

CHAPTER 84

1. Robert Blair Kaiser in two telephone interviews by the author in July, 2010 and July, 2011.
2. Carlo Falconi, *Pope John and His Council: A Diary of the Second Vatican Council, September – December 1962*, tr. Muriel Grindrod (London: Weidenfeld and Nicolson, 1964), 9-11, 42-45.
3. Robert Blair Kaiser, *Pope, Council, and World: The Story of Vatican II* (New York: The Macmillan Company, 1963), 78.
4. Anna J. Merritt and Richard L. Merritt, editors, *Public Opinion in Occupied Germany: The OMGUS Surveys, 1945-1949* (Urbana, Illinois: University of Illinois Press, 1970), 51.
5. Merritt and Merritt, *Public Opinion in Occupied Germany: The OMGUS Surveys, 1945-1949*, 52-53.
6. Merritt and Merritt, *Public Opinion in Occupied Germany: The OMGUS Surveys 1945-1949*, 52.
7. Anna J. Merritt and Richard L. Merritt, editors, *Public Opinion in Semi-sovereign Germany: The HICOG Surveys, 1949-1955* (Urbana, Illinois: University of Illinois Press, 1980), 8-9.
8. Merritt and Merritt, *Public Opinion in Semi-sovereign Germany: The HICOG Surveys, 1949-1955.*, 37, 48.
9. Cook, "First Comes the Lie: C. D. Jackson and Political Warfare," 58-59.
10. Cook, "First Comes the Lie: C.D. Jackson and Political Warfare," 58-59.
11. "Religion: Faith for a Lenten Age," *Time,* March 8, 1948. http://www.time.com/time/printout/0,8816,853293,00.html (accessed April 23, 2011).

CHAPTER 85

1. Vittorio Vaccari to CD Jackson, Letter dated January 23, 1959 with "The Policy of the Catholic Church in the Selection and Training of Her Leaders," CD Jackson Papers: Box 109 File "Misc. (1)," Dwight D. Eisenhower Library, Abilene, Kansas.
2. Vaccari to Jackson, Letter dated January 23, 1959 with "The Policy of the Catholic Church in the Selection and Training of Her Leaders."
3. Ray Vicker, "The Catholic Church: How It Skillfully Manages Vast Religious, Social, Economic, and Diplomatic Complex; Vatican Allows Local Units Much

Autonomy; It Meets Fiscal, Personnel Problems" *The Wall Street Journal,* October 6, 1960.

4. CD Jackson, "Overseas Report (Confidential) # 4 From C.D. Jackson," dated August 7, 1962, CD Jackson Papers: Box 109 File "World Trip, Transcripts, Italy 1962," Dwight D. Eisenhower Library, Abilene, Kansas.
5. C.D. Jackson "Overseas Report (Confidential) # 4 from CD Jackson," dated August 7, 1962. (emphasis supplied.)
6. C.D. Jackson "Overseas Report (Confidential) # 4 from CD Jackson," dated August 7, 1962.
7. C.D. Jackson "Overseas Report (Confidential) # 4 from CD Jackson," dated August 7, 1962.
8. C.D. Jackson "Overseas Report (Confidential) # 4 from CD Jackson," dated August 7, 1962.
9. C.D. Jackson "Overseas Report (Confidential) # 4 from CD Jackson," dated August 7, 1962.
10. C.D. Jackson "Overseas Report (Confidential) # 4 from CD Jackson," dated August 7, 1962.
11. C.D. Jackson "Overseas Report (Confidential) # 4 from CD Jackson," dated August 7, 1962.
12. C.D. Jackson "Overseas Report (Confidential) # 4 from CD Jackson," dated August 7, 1962. (emphasis supplied)
13. CD Jackson, "Italy # 7 & 8" dated August 1, 1962, CD Jackson Papers: Box 109 Folder "World Trip, Transcripts, 1962," Dwight D. Eisenhower Library, Abilene, Kansas.
14. CD Jackson, "Italy # 5 & 6," dated as arrived in New York August 1, 1962, CD Jackson Papers: Box 109 Folder "World Trip, Transcripts, 1962," Dwight D. Eisenhower Library, Abilene, Kansas.
15. CD Jackson to Cerabona, Letter dated September 27, 1962 and attached report, CD Jackson Papers: Box 40, Folder "Catholic Church," Dwight D. Eisenhower Library, Abilene, Kansas.
16. Dora Jane Hamblin to CD Jackson, Letter dated September 18, 1962, CD Jackson Papers: Box 39, Folder "CA-Misc. (2)," Dwight D. Eisenhower Library, Abilene, Kansas.
17. CD Jackson to Msgr. Egino Cardinale, Letter dated September 24, 1962 and note from Dodie Hamblin dated October 3, 1962, CD Jackson Papers: Box 39, Folder "CA-Misc (2)," Dwight D. Eisenhower Library, Abilene, Kansas.

CHAPTER 86

1. Joe from St. Joseph's Rectory Belmont, Massachusetts to Francis J. Connell, Letter undated, Francis J Connell Papers at Redemptorist House Archives, Baltimore Province, Brooklyn, New York.
2. "Norms," undated memorandum, Francis J Connell Papers at Redemptorist House Archives, Baltimore Province, Brooklyn, New York. (emphasis in the original)
3. Anna Brady, "Behind the press Scene at Vatican Council II," *The Long Island Catholic,* Francis J Connell Papers at Redemptorist House Archives, Baltimore Province, Brooklyn, New York.
4. Brady, "Behind the press Scene at Vatican Council II," *The Long Island Catholic.*

5. Brady, "Behind the press Scene at Vatican Council II," *The Long Island Catholic.*
6. "Tom" to Joseph C. Fenton, Letter dated February 26, 1960, Joseph C. Fenton Papers, Elms College, Chicopee, Massachusetts.
7. Joseph C Fenton, "The Council and Father Kung" *American Ecclesiastical Review* 147, 9 (September 1962), 178.
8. Fenton, "The Council and Father Kung," *American Ecclesiastical Review,* 198-200.
9. "A Second Reformation, For Both Catholics & Protestants," *Time,* June 8, 1962. http://www.time.com/time/subscriber/printout/0,8816,896321,00.html (accessed October 13, 2012).
10. "A Second Reformation For Both Catholics & Protestants," *Time.*
11. "A Second Reformation For Both Catholics & Protestants," *Time.*
12. "Pope pens rare article on his inside view of Vatican II," *Vatican Radio,* October 10, 2012. http://en.radiovaticana.va/print_page.asp?c=628717 (accessed October 12, 2012). (emphasis supplied)
13. JCF, Entry for October 8, 1962, Diary from 17th Trip to Rome, 48-49; JCF, Entry for October 5, 1962, Diary from 17th Trip to Rome, 40.
14. "Religion: Council of Renewal," *Time,* October 5, 1962. http://www.time.com/time/subscriber/printout/0,8816,829210,00.html (accessed October 13, 2012).
15. "Religion: Council of Renewal," *Time,* October 5, 1962.
16. "Religion: Council of Renewal," *Time,* October 5, 1962
17. "Religion: Council of Renewal," *Time,* October 5, 1962
18. "Religion: Council of Renewal," *Time,* October 5, 1962
19. "Religion: Council of Renewal," *Time,* October 5, 1962
20. "Religion: Council of Renewal," *Time,* October 5, 1962
21. "Religion: Council of Renewal," *Time,* October 5, 1962
22. "Religion: The Council's Prospects," *Time,* September 14, 1962. http://www.time.com/time/subscriber/printout/0,8816,874481,00.html (accessed October 13, 2012).
23. "Religion: The Council's Prospects," *Time,* September 14, 1962.
24. "Religion: Council of Renewal," *Time,* October 5, 1962.
25. "Religion: The Council's Prospects," *Time,* September 14, 1962.
26. "Religion: The Council's Prospects," *Time,* September 14, 1962. "
27. "Religion: St. Pius IX?" *Time,* August 31, 1962. http://www.time.com/time/subscriber/printout/0,8816,938909,00.html (accessed October 13, 2012).
28. "Religion: The Supreme Realist," *Time,* July 6, 1962. http://www.time.com/time/subscriber/printout/0,8816,940032,00.html (accessed October 13, 2012).
29. "Religion: R.S.V.P." *Time,* July 20, 1962. http://www.time.com/time/subscriber/printout/0,8816, 896383,00.html (accessed October 13, 2012).
30. "Religion: The Princes of the Church," *Time,* March 30, 1962. http://www.time.com/time/subscriber/printout/0,8816,895979,00.html (as accessed October 13, 2012).
31. "Religion: The Lowly Catholic Layman," *Time,* August 17, 1962. http://www.time.com/time/subscriber/printout/0,8816,870050,00.html (accessed October 13, 2012).
32. "Religion: The Lowly Catholic Layman," *Time,* August 17, 1962. http://www.time.com/time/subscriber/printout/0,8816,870050,00.html (accessed October 13, 2012).
33. Robert Blair Kaiser, interviewed by author July 21, 2010.
34. Robert Blair Kaiser, interviewed by author July 21, 2010 and July 27, 2009; Calendar of John Courtney Murray from John Courtney Murray Papers,

Georgetown University Library, Special Collections, Division, Washington, D.C.

CHAPTER 87

1. Joseph C Fenton, "The Influence of the Holy Ghost in the Ecumenical Council" *American Ecclesiastical Review* 147, 8 (August 1962): 116, 125-127.
2. Fenton, Diary from 17th Trip, September 27, 1962, 22.
3. Fenton, Diary from 16th Trip, 19-21.
4. Fenton, Diary from 17th Trip, October 5, 1962, 40.
5. Fenton, Diary from 17th Trip, October 5, 1962, 41.
6. Fenton, Diary from 17th Trip, October 5, 1962, 48-49.
7. George Dugan, "Prelates Want to Wear Simple Garb at Council," *The New York Times,* October 24, 1962. Francis J Connell Papers at Redemptorist House Archives, Baltimore Province, Brooklyn, New York.
8. Fenton, Diary from 17th Trip, October 9, 1962, 51-52.
9. Floyd Anderson, Editor, *Council Daybook: Vatican II Session 1, October 11 through December 8, 1962 and Session 2 September 29 to December 4, 1963* (Washington D.C.: National Catholic Welfare Conference, 1965), 25-29.
10. "Religion: The Council Opens," *Time,* October 19, 1962. http://www.time.com/time/subscriber/printout/0,8816,827893,00.html (accessed October 13, 2012).
11. Fenton, Diary from 17th Trip, October 13, 1962, 57-59, 61-62.
12. Fenton, Diary from 17th Trip, October 13, 1962, 57-59.
13. Fenton, Diary from 17th Trip, October 13, 1962, 64.
14. Fenton, Diary from 17th Trip, October 13, 1962, 62-64.
15. Fenton, Diary from 17th Trip, October 13, 1962, 64.
16. Henry R Luce, recorded interview by John L. Steele, November 11, 1965, 31-35, John F Kennedy Library Oral History Program.
17. Klaus Dohrn to Jay Lovestone, Letters dated August 23, 1962 and October 5, 1962, Jay Lovestone Papers: Box 365 Folder "1962," Hoover Institution On War, Revolution and Peace, Stanford, California.
18. Klaus Dohrn to Jay Lovestone, Letter dated October 16, 1962, Jay Lovestone Papers:, Box 365 Folder "1962," Hoover Institution On War, Revolution and Peace, Stanford, California.
19. Dohrn to Lovestone Letter dated October 16, 1962.
20. Jay Lovestone to Klaus Dohrn, Letter dated October 22, 1962, Jay Lovestone Papers: Box 365 Folder "1962," Hoover Institution On War, Revolution and Peace, Stanford, California.
21. Fenton, Diary from 17th Trip, 70-71
22. Fenton, Diary from 17th Trip, 71-72.
23. Fenton, Diary from 17th Trip, October 19, 1962, 74-76.
24. Fenton, Diary from 17th Trip, October 19, 1962, 76.
25. Fenton, Diary from 17th Trip, October 19, 1962, 74-76.
26. Fenton, Diary from 17th Trip, October 27, 1962, 88.
27. Fenton, Diary from 17th Trip, October 31, 1962, 91-95.
28. Fenton, Diary from 17th Trip, November 1, 1962, 96.
29. Fenton, Diary from 17th Trip, November 1, 1962, 96-101.
30. Fenton, Diary from 17th Trip, November 13, 1962, 103-108.
31. Fenton, Diary from 17th Trip, November 14, 1962, 109-112.
32. Fenton, Diary from 17th Trip, November 14, 1962, 109-112.

33. Fenton, Diary from 17th Trip, November 14, 1962, 110-113.
34. Fenton, Diary from 17th Trip, November 23, 1962, 110-112.
35. Fenton, Diary from 17th Trip, November 23, 1962, 112-115.
36. Fenton, Diary from 17th Trip, November 23, 1962, 120-121.
37. Fenton, Diary from 17th Trip, November 26, 1962, 127-128.
38. "The Press: The Prelates & the Press," *Time,* November 16, 1962. http://www.time.com/time/subscriber/printout/0,8816,829416,00.html (accessed October 13, 2012).
39. "Religion: The Cardinal's Setback," *Time,* November 23, 1962. http://www.time.com/time/subscriber/printout/0,8816,82950,00.html (accessed October 13, 2012).
40. "Religion: The Cardinal's Setback," *Time,* November 23, 1962.
41. Fenton, Diary from 17th Trip, 122-143.
42. Francis J. Connell, "The Progress of the Council," Francis J. Connell Papers, Redemptorist House Archives, Baltimore Province, Brooklyn, New York.

CHAPTER 88

1. Francis J. Connell to Francis Murphy, Letter undated, Francis J. Connell Papers, Redemptorist House Archives, Baltimore Province, Brooklyn, New York.; Francis J. Connell to Rudolph G. Bandas, Letter dated March 22, 1963, Francis J. Connell Papers, Redemptorist House Archives, Baltimore Province, Brooklyn, New York.
2. Leo Wollemborg, "Recess an Aid to Catholic Liberals," *The Washington Post* Sunday, December 16, 1962, Francis J. Connell Papers, Redemptorist House Archives, Baltimore Province, Brooklyn, New York. Emphasis present in original.
3. Wollemborg, "Recess an Aid to Catholic Liberals," *The Washington Post* (Emphasis present in original.)
4. Wollemborg, "Recess an Aid to Catholic Liberals," *The Washington Post* (Emphasis present in original.)
5. "Council Bringing About 'Revolution' In Catholic Life, Observer Declares," NCWC News Service (Domestic), February 18, 1963, Francis J. Connell Papers, Redemptorist House Archives, Baltimore Province, Brooklyn, New York.
6. Peter Steinfels, "Rev. John B Sheerin dies at 85; A Catholic editor and columnist," *The New York Times,* January 15, 1992. http://www.nytimes.com/1992/01/15/nyregion/rev-john-b-sheerin-dies-at-85-a-catholic-editor-and-columnist.html (accessed March 17, 2013).

CHAPTER 89

1. Joseph Clifford Fenton, Entry for January 1, 1963, Diaries.
2. Joseph C Fenton, "Cardinal Ottaviani and the Council," *American Ecclesiastical Review* 148, 1 (January 1963), 44.
3. Fenton, "Cardinal Ottaviani and the Council," *American Ecclesiastical Review,* 45-47.
4. Fenton, "Cardinal Ottaviani and the Council," *American Ecclesiastical Review,* 47, 52.
5. Fenton, "Cardinal Ottaviani and the Council," *American Ecclesiastical Review,* 52.

6. "Cardinal Ottaviani Explains Position at Council, Calls His Hopes 'Delicate Question'," NCWC News Service, January 28, 1963, Francis J. Connell Papers, Redemptorist House Archives, Baltimore Province, Brooklyn, New York.
7. "Cardinal Ottaviani Explains Position at Council, Calls His Hopes 'Delicate Question'," NCWC News Service, January 28, 1963.
8. "Cardinal Ottaviani Explains Position at Council, Calls His Hopes 'Delicate Question'," NCWC News Service, January 28, 1963.
9. Anna Brady, "Behind the Press Scene at Vatican Council II", *The Long Island Catholic*, Francis J Connell Papers, Redemptorist House Archives, Baltimore Province, Brooklyn, New York.
10. Fenton, "Cardinal Ottaviani and the Council," *American Ecclesiastical Review*, 48-49.
11. Fenton, "Cardinal Ottaviani and the Council," 49-51.
12. Joseph Clifford Fenton, Entry of February 11, 1963, Diaries.
13. "Slanted Writing Giving False Impression of Council, Bishop Says," NCWC News Service (Domestic), February 18, 1963, as found in Francis J. Connell Papers, Redemptorist House Archives, Baltimore Province, Brooklyn, NY.
14. Manfred Wenzel "Progressive Bishops have two-thirds majority in Council, Cardinal holds," NCWC News Service, March 11, 1963, Francis J. Connell Papers, Redemptorist House Archives, Baltimore Province, Brooklyn, New York..
15. Wenzel, "Progressive Bishops have two-thirds majority in Council, Cardinal holds," NCWC News Service, March 11, 1963.
16. Wenzel, "Progressive Bishops have two-thirds majority in Council, Cardinal holds," NCWC News Service, March 11, 1963.
17. "Well begun, promising speedier action in next session, council will produce much good, Bishops say," NCWC News Service (Domestic), February 18, 1963, Francis J. Connell Papers, Redemptorist House Archives, Baltimore Province, Brooklyn, New York.
18. "Unity Obstacles 'Enormous' But should Spur Greater Faith – Cardinal Bea," NCWC News Service (Foreign), March 25, 1963, Francis J. Connell Papers, Redemptorist House Archives, Baltimore Province, Brooklyn, New York..
19. "Well Begun, Promising Speedier Action in Next Session, Council will produce much good, Bishops say," NCWC News Service (Domestic), February 18, 1963, Francis J. Connell Papers, Redemptorist House Archives, Baltimore Province, Brooklyn, New York..
20. "Council observers 'genuinely happy' with their treatment, repots translater [sic] for them," NCWC News Service, January 14, 1963, Francis J. Connell Papers, Redemptorist House Archives, Baltimore Province, Brooklyn, New York.
21. "Veto of Controversial draft Council's 'Supreme Event,' African prelate says," NCWC News Service (Foreign), February 11, 1963, Francis J. Connell Papers, Redemptorist House Archives, Baltimore Province, Brooklyn, New York.

CHAPTER 90

1. James C O'Neill, "Council Fathers Study Communications Media," *The Long Island Catholic*, February 28, 1963, found at Francis J. Connell Papers, Redemptorist House Archives, Baltimore Province, Brooklyn, New York.
2. O'Neill, "Council Fathers Study Communications Media," *The Long Island Catholic*, February 28, 1963.

3. O'Neill, "Council Fathers Study Communications Media," *The Long Island Catholic,* February 28, 1963.
4. O'Neill, "Council Fathers Study Communications Media," *The Long Island Catholic,* February 28, 1963.
5. O'Neill, "Council Fathers Study Communications Media," *The Long Island Catholic,* February 28, 1963.
6. "Pope to Journalists," NCWC News Service, February 28, 1963, Francis J. Connell Papers, Redemptorist House Archives, Baltimore Province, Brooklyn, New York.
7. "Pope to Journalists," NCWC News Service, February 28, 1963.
8. "Pope to Journalists," NCWC News Service, February 28, 1963.

CHAPTER 91

1. Joseph C Fenton, "The Roman Curia and the Ecumenical Council" *American Ecclesiastical Review* 148, 3 (March 1963), 185, 197.
2. "Well begun, promising speedier action in next session, council will produce much good, bishops say," NCWC News Service (Domestic), February 18, 1963, Francis J. Connell Papers, Redemptorist House Archives, Baltimore Province, Brooklyn, New York.
3. Msgr. James I Tucek, "Editorial Information," NCWC News Service, March 21, 1963, Francis J. Connell Papers, Redemptorist House Archives, Baltimore Province, Brooklyn, New York.
4. Tucek, "Editorial Information," NCWC News Service, March 21, 1963.
5. Tucek, "Editorial Information," NCWC News Service, March 21, 1963.
6. Tucek, "Editorial Information," NCWC News Service, March 21, 1963.
7. Tucek, "Editorial Information," NCWC News Service, March 21, 1963.
8. Tucek, "Editorial Information," NCWC News Service, March 21, 1963.
9. Tucek, "Editorial Information," NCWC News Service, March 21, 1963.
10. Tucek, "Editorial Information," NCWC News Service, March 21, 1963.

CHAPTER 92

1. "Pope to Council Fathers," NCWC News Service, February 14, 1963, at Francis J. Connell Papers, Redemptorist House Archives, Baltimore Province, Brooklyn, New York.
2. "Pope to Council Fathers," NCWC News Service, February 14, 1963.
3. Fenton, Diary, February 13, 1963.
4. Fenton, Diary 9, March 2, 1963, 159-164.
5. Fenton, Diary, March 4, 1963.
6. Fenton, Diary 9, February 21, 1963, 147-148.
7. Fenton, Diary 9, February 25, 1963, 153.
8. Fenton, Diary 9, March 2, 1963, 159-160.
9. Fenton, Diary 9, February 23, 1963, 150-152.
10. Fenton, Diary 9, March 2, 1963, 161.
11. Fenton, Diary, February 20, 1963.
12. Fenton, Diary, March 6, 1963.

CHAPTER 93

1. "Universities: Crisis at Catholic U," *Time,* March 29, 1963. http://www.time.com/time/subscriber/printout/0,8816,896755,00.html (accessed October 13, 2012).
2. "Universities: Crisis at Catholic U," *Time,* March 29, 1963.
3. "Universities: Crisis of Catholic U," *Time,* March 29, 1963.
4. "Roman Catholics: Ecumenical Voices," *Time,* April 5, 1963. http://www.time.com/time/subscriber/printout/0,8816,830066,00.html (accessed October 13, 2012).
5. "Roman Catholics: Ecumenical Voices," *Time,* April 5, 1963. Of note, *Time* also quoted Kung as saying that the Catholic hierarchy, as part of this push for freedom within the Church, should "Abolish the Index of Forbidden Books and the prepublication censorship of theological writings, a practice that was inaugurated by such unsavory Renaissance Popes as Alexander VI and Leo X. Do away with star-chamber techniques used by the Holy Office in resolving questions of heresy, since such methods 'offend not only against the Gospel but against the natural law, which is often quoted.' Grant its sons greater liberty of action and recognize that in certain circumstances 'a Christian has the right, sometimes the duty, to act, in a spirit of free obedience and obedient freedom against the literal sense of an order' by a superior." It was the formula by which rebellion in the Church was to take place in earnest by 1965.
6. "Protestantism: Emancipation in Spain," *Time,* February 8, 1963. http:///www.time.com/time/subscriber/printout/0,8816,829837,00.html (accessed October 13, 2012).
7. "Roman Catholics: Ecumenical Voices," *Time,* April 5, 1963. *Time* reported that Bea emphasized the need for scholarship in "finding new ways to state theological truths in language understood by modern man...."
8. "The Papacy: Vatican Revolutionary," *Time,* June 7, 1963. http://www.time.com/time/subscriber/printout/0,8816,874758,00.html (accessed October 13, 2012).
9. "The Papacy: Vatican Revolutionary," *Time,* June 7, 1963.
10. "The Papacy: Vatican Revolutionary," *Time,* June 7, 1963.
11. "The Papacy: Vatican Revolutionary," *Time,* June 7, 1963.

CHAPTER 94

1. Fenton, Diary, May 11, 1963.
2. Fenton, Diary, May 11, 1963.
3. Fenton, Diary of 20th Trip to Rome, September 24, 1963.

CHAPTER 95

1. Michael Novak, *The Open Church: Vatican II, Act II* (New York: MacMillan Company, 1964), 256.
2. "Milestones," *Time,* September 10, 1984. http://content.time.com/time/subscriber/printout/0,8816,95253,00.html (accessed October 20, 2013).
3. John Courtney Murray to Archbishop Shehan, Memorandum "Notes on the papers concerning the Church-State issue," from August, 1963, *John Courtney*

Murray Papers: Box 18 File 1008, Georgetown University Library, Special Collections Division, Washington, D.C.

4. Murray to Shehan Memorandum "Notes on the papers concerning the Church-State issue," from August, 1963.
5. Murray to Shehan Memorandum "Notes on the papers concerning the Church-State issue," from August, 1963.
6. Murray to Shehan Memorandum "Notes on the papers concerning the Church-State issue," from August, 1963.
7. Murray to Shehan Memorandum "Notes on the papers concerning the Church-State issue," from August, 1963.
8. Murray to Shehan Memorandum "Notes on the papers concerning the Church-State issue," from August, 1963.
9. Murray to Shehan Memorandum "Notes on the papers concerning the Church-State issue," from August, 1963.
10. Murray to Shehan Memorandum "Notes on the papers concerning the Church-State issue," from August, 1963.
11. Murray to Shehan Memorandum "Notes on the papers concerning the Church-State issue," from August, 1963.
12. Murray to Shehan Memorandum "Notes on the papers concerning the Church-State issue," from August, 1963.

CHAPTER 96

1. Joseph Clifford Fenton, Entry for September 24, 1963, Diary of 20th Trip to Rome.
2. Joseph Clifford Fenton, Entries for September 25 and 26, 1963, Diary of 20th Trip to Rome.
3. Joseph Clifford Fenton, Entry for October 1, 1963, Diary of 20th Trip to Rome.
4. Joseph Clifford Fenton, Entry for September 27, 1963, Diary of 20th Trip to Rome.
5. Joseph Clifford Fenton, Entry for September 28, 1963, Diary of 20th Trip to Rome.
6. "Pope Paul VI issues new regulations for 2nd council session," NCWC News Service (Foreign), September 16, 1963, Francis J. Connell Papers, Redemptorist House Archives, Baltimore Province, Brooklyn, New York.
7. "Roman Catholics: Clear it with the Vatican," *Time,* September 20, 1963. http://www.time.com/time/subscriber/printout/0,8816,870552,00.html (accessed October 13, 2012).
8. "Roman Catholics: Clear it with the Vatican," *Time,* September 20, 1963.
9. "Roman Catholics: Clear it with the Vatican," *Time,* September 20, 1963.
10. Francis J. Connell, "Lecture on the Ecumenical Council," Francis J. Connell Papers, Redemptorist House Archives, Baltimore Province, Brooklyn, New York. Connell also explained that the council "is endowed with infallibility, at least in its solemn pronouncements. However, this is not inspiration. It is a negative help, a preservation from error. It is absolutely possible for a Council to act imprudently by not saying something, or by not condemning errors."
11. John Courtney Murray, Calendars, *John Courtney Murray Papers,* Georgetown University Library, Special Collections Division, Washington, D.C.

12. John Courtney Murray, Memorandum dated August 15, 1963 attached to a note from "dcf" [Dorothy C Farmer] on Clare Boothe Luce stationary, Clare Boothe Luce Papers: Box 795 Folder 11, Library of Congress, Washington, D.C.
13. "Conclusion" undated, Henry R. Luce Papers, Box 83 Folder 11, Library of Congress, Washington, D.C.

CHAPTER 97

1. George W Shea notes from November 6, 1963, AND 0004.001 George Shea Papers Box 13, Monsignor William Noe Field Archives and Special Collections Center, Seton Hall University, South Orange, New Jersey.
2. Pelotte, *John Courtney Murray: Theologian in Conflict*, 81-82.
3. Pelotte, *John Courtney Murray: Theologian in Conflict*, 81-82.
4. Novak, *The Open Church: Vatican II, Act I*, 256-257.
5. Fenton, Diaries from 20th Trip, November 11, 1963.
6. Pelotte, *John Courtney Murray: Theologian in Conflict*, 82.
7. Novak, *The Open Church, Vatican II Act II*, 257-258.
8. Pelotte, *John Courtney Murray: Theologian in Conflict*, 83-84; John Courtney Murray to Cardinal Spellman, Letter dated November 18, *John Courtney Murray Papers:* Box 18 Folder 972, Georgetown University Library, Special Collections Division, Washington, D.C.
9. Novak, *The Open Church: Vatican II Act II*, 273, 275-276
10. Novak, *The Open Church: Vatican II Act II*, 276.
11. Novak, *The Open Church: Vatican II Act II*, 276-277.
12. Novak, *The Open Church: Vatican II Act II*, 277.
13. Novak, *The Open Church: Vatican II Act II*, 277-280.
14. Novak, *The Open Church: Vatican II Act II*, 277-281.
15. Novak, *The Open Church: Vatican II Act II*, 281.
16. Novak, *The Open Church: Vatican II Act II*, 299-300.
17. Fenton, Diary Book 10, November 25, 1963.

CHAPTER 98

1. *Inter Mirifica*, in *Vatican Council II The Conciliar and Post Conciliar Documents*, ed. Austin Flannery (Northport, New York: Costello Publishing company, 1992), 283.
2. *Inter Mirifica*, 284-285
3. *Inter Mirifica*, 285-286.
4. *Inter Mirifica*, 285-286
5. *Inter Mirifica*, 286-287.
6. *Inter Mirifica*, 286-287.
7. *Inter Mirifica*, 287-288.
8. *Inter Mirifica*, 287-288.
9. *Inter Mirifica*, 288.
10. *Inter Mirifica*, 291-292.
11. *Inter Mirifica*, 285-286.
12. John Cogley, "A Layman Reflects on the Council," *Columbia*, September, 1964, as found in the papers of Francis J. Connell, Redemptorist House Archives,

Baltimore Province, Brooklyn, New York.
13. Cogley, "A Layman Reflects on the Council," *Columbia,* September, 1964.
14. Cogley, "A Layman Reflects on the Council," *Columbia,* September, 1964.
15. Novak, *The Open Church: Vatican II, Act II,* 261-262.

CHAPTER 99

1. "The Vatican Council: What Went Wrong?" *Time,* December 6, 1963. http://www.time.com/time/subscriber/printout/0,8816,898101,00.html (accessed October 13, 2012).
2. "Roman Catholics: Readiness for Reform," *Time,* October 4, 1963. http://www.time.com/time/subscriber/printout/0,8816,875264,00.html (accessed October 13, 2012).
3. "Roman Catholics: Readiness for Reform," *Time,* October 4, 1963.
4. "Roman Catholics: Council on the Move," *Time,* November 8, 1963. http://www.time.com/time/subscriber/printout/0,8816,897019,00.html (accessed October 13, 2012).
5. "Roman Catholics: A Word to Outsiders," *Time,* November 22, 1963. http://www.time.com/time/subscriber/printout/0,8816,898039,00.html (accessed October 13, 2012).
6. "The Vatican Council: What Went Wrong?" *Time,* December 6, 1963. http://www.time.com/time/subscriber/printout/0,8816,898101,00.html (accessed October 13, 2012).
7. "Roman Catholics: Modernizing the Mass" *Time,* December 13, 1963. http://www.time.com/time/subscriber/printout/0,8816,875469,00.html (accessed October 13, 2012).

CHAPTER 100

1. Ben Cosgrove, "JFK's Assassination: How LIFE Brought the Zapruder Film to Light," Time/Life http://time.com/3491195/jfks-assassination-how-life-brought-the-zapruder-film-to-light/ accessed December 10, 2014.
2. Aaron Klein, "Spy Claims Israel Assassinated JFK," *World Net Daily,* July 25, 2004. http://www.wnd.com/2004/07/25751/ accessed December 11, 2014.
3. "A Businessman's Letter to J.F.K. and His Reply," *Life,* July 6, 1962; Henry R Luce, recorded interview by John L. Steele, November 11, 1965, 38-40, John F Kennedy Library Oral History Program.
4. "A Businessman's Letter to J.F.K. and His Reply," *Life,* July 6, 1962; Henry R Luce, recorded interview by John L. Steele, November 11, 1965, 38-40, John F Kennedy Library Oral History Program.
5. "The Presidency: The Government Still Lives," *Time,* November 29, 1963.
6. "Eulogy to John F. Kennedy by Richard Cardinal Cushing," http://www.copperas.com/jfk/cushing.htm accessed December 10, 2014; "The Presidency: The Government Still Lives," *Time,* November 29, 1963.

CHAPTER 101

1. Michael Novak, "Council Meeting Vindicates Long Harassed US Jesuit," *Oklahoma Courier*, November 22, 1963, found in *John Courtney Murray Papers*: Box 28 Folder 1269, Georgetown University Library, Special Collections Division, Washington, D.C.

2. Novak, "Council Meeting Vindicates Long Harassed US Jesuit," *Oklahoma Courier*, November 22, 1963.

3. Novak, "Council Meeting Vindicates Long Harassed US Jesuit," *Oklahoma Courier*, November 22, 1963.

4. Msgr. Vincent Yzermans, "Conversation at the Council," *St. Cloud Visitor*, December 22, 1963, found in *John Courtney Murray Papers*: Box 28 Folder 1268, Georgetown University Library, Special Collections Division, Washington, D.C.

5. Yzermans, "Conversation at the Council," *St. Cloud Visitor*, December 22, 1963.

6. "Bishop Hock and Father Weigel Review Work of Second Session," *St Cloud Visitor*, December 22, 1963, in *John Courtney Murray Papers*: Box 28 Folder 1268, Georgetown University Library, Special Collections Division, Washington, D.C.

7. Rev. John B Sheerin CSP, "Council Experts Vindicated," Baltimore *Catholic Review*. November 26, 1963, John *Courtney Murray Papers*: Box 28 Folder 1268, Georgetown University Library, Special Collections Division, Washington, D.C.

8. Weldon Wallace "Criticism of Council Text Seen: US Priest Makes Prediction about Religious liberty Paper," *The Baltimore Sun* November 21, 1963, *John Courtney Murray Papers*: Box 28 File 1268, Georgetown University Library, Special Collections Division, Washington, D.C.

9. "Fr. Murray Cites Question Posed by 'Liberty' Question," *Catholic Messenger*, November 28, 1963, *John Courtney Murray Papers* Box 28 Folder 1268, Georgetown University Library, Special Collections Division, Washington, D.C.

10. John Courtney Murray, "On Religious Liberty: Freedom is the most distinctively American issue before the Council," *America*, November 1963, 704-706. http://woodstock.georgetown.edu/library/Murray/1963i.htm (accessed March 3, 2013).

11. Murray, "On Religious Liberty: Freedom is the most distinctively American issue before the Council," *America*, November 1963.

12. Murray, "On Religious Liberty: Freedom is the most distinctively American issue before the Council," *America*, November 1963.

13. Murray, "On Religious Liberty: Freedom is the most distinctively American issue before the Council," *America*, November 1963.

14. Murray, "On Religious Liberty: Freedom is the most distinctively American issue before the Council," *America*, November 1963.

15. Murray, "On Religious Liberty: Freedom is the most distinctively American issue before the Council," *America*, November 1963.

16. Murray, "On Religious Liberty: Freedom is the most distinctively American issue before the Council," *America*, November 1963.

17. Murray, "On Religious Liberty: Freedom is the most distinctively American issue before the Council," *America*, November 1963.

18. Murray, "On Religious Liberty: Freedom is the most distinctively American issue before the Council," *America*, November 1963.

19. Francis J. Connell to Fr. Joseph Collins, Letter dated October 8, 1963, Francis J. Connell Papers, Redemptorist House Archives, Baltimore Province, Brooklyn, New York.

CHAPTER 102

1. "Father Weigel Dies: Catholic Theologian," *The New York Times,* January 4, 1964, as found in Francis J. Connell Papers, Redemptorist House Archives, Baltimore Province, Brooklyn, New York.
2. "Milestones: Jan. 10, 1964," *Time,* January 10, 1964 http://time.com/time/subscriber/printout/0,8816,875544,00.html (accessed October 23, 2012).
3. "Father Weigel Dies: Catholic Theologian," *The New York Times,* January 4, 1964.
4. Dorothy Farmer to Henry R. Luce, Letter dated January 15, 1964, Clare Boothe Luce Papers: Box 795 Folder 11, Library of Congress, Washington, D.C.
5. "Roman Catholics: The Unfinished Reformation," *Time,* February 7, 1964. http://www.time.com/time/subscriber/printout/0,8816,870689,00.html (accessed October 21, 2012).
6. "Roman Catholics: The Unfinished Reformation," *Time,* February 7, 1964.
7. "Roman Catholics: Flying Red Hats," *Time,* May 22, 1964. http://www.time.com/time/subscriber/printout/0,8816,871117,00.html (accessed October 21, 2012). Also see "Roman Catholics: The Pope's Man in Recife," *Time,* March 27, 1964 http://www.time.com/time/subscriber/printout/0,8816,938559,00.html (accessed October 21, 2012) and "Churches: Ecumen In," *Time,* March 13, 1964 http://www.time.com/time/subscriber/printout/0,8816,828258,00.html (accessed October 21, 2012).
8. "Theologian Sees Statement on Jews Urgent," NCWC News Service (Foreign), May 1, 1964, from Francis J. Connell Papers, Redemptorist House Archives, Baltimore Province, Brooklyn, New York.
9. "Council Observer Questions Church Motives," NCWC News Service (Domestic), April 20, 1964, from Francis J. Connell Papers, Redemptorist House Archives, Baltimore Province, Brooklyn, New York.
10. "Predicts 4 to 1 Council Approval of religious Liberty Text," NCWC News Service (Foreign), April 23, 1964, from Francis J Connell Papers, Redemptorist House Archives, Baltimore Province, Brooklyn, New York.
11. "Bishop `Disappointed' at Council's Pace," NCWC News Service (Domestic), January 28, 1964, from Francis J Connell Papers, Redemptorist House Archives, Baltimore Province, Brooklyn, New York.
12. "Asks U.S. Bishops Take Lead on Council Liberty Decree," NCWC News Service (Domestic), February 29, 1964, from Francis J Connell Papers, Redemptorist House Archives, Baltimore Province, Brooklyn, New York.
13. "Asks U.S. Bishops Take Lead on Council Liberty Decree," NCWC News Service (Domestic), February 29, 1964.
14. "Religious Liberty Statement Seen Essential," NCWC News Service (Domestic), February 29, 1964, from Francis J Connell Papers, Redemptorist House Archives, Baltimore Province, Brooklyn, New York.

CHAPTER 103

1. "Rules Govern Council Experts," NCWC New Service (Domestic), March 9, 1964, from Francis J. Connell Papers, Redemptorist House Archives, Baltimore Province, Brooklyn, New York.

2. Joseph Clifford Fenton, "A Letter from Rome" *American Ecclesiastical Review* CXLIX (December 1963): 392-393.
3. Fenton, "A Letter from Rome," *American Ecclesiastical Review,* December 1963.
4. Fenton, "A Letter from Rome," *American Ecclesiastical Review,* December 1963, 394.
5. "Bishop Critical of Magazine's Council Coverage," NCWC News Service, January 11, 1964, from Francis J. Connell Papers, Redemptorist House Archives, Baltimore Province, Brooklyn, New York.
6. "Bishop Critical of Magazine's Council Coverage," NCWC News Service, January 11, 1964.
7. "Bishop Critical of Magazine's Council Coverage," NCWC News Service, January 11, 1964.
8. Francis J. Connell to Bishop Zuroweste, Letter dated January 14, 1964, Francis J. Connell Papers, Redemptorist House Archives, Baltimore Province, Brooklyn, New York.
9. "Bishop Raps Distortions of Vatican Council; Urges Catholics Not To Become Confused," *The Wonderer,* from Francis J. Connell Papers, Redemptorist House Archives, Baltimore Province, Brooklyn, New York.
10. "Bishop Raps Distortions of Vatican Council; Urges Catholics Not To Become Confused," *The Wanderer.*

CHAPTER 104

1. Baughman, *Henry R. Luce and the Rise of the American News Media,* 188.
2. CD Jackson to Henry R. Luce, Letter and memorandum dated April 22, 1964, Henry R. Luce Papers Box 52 Folder 7, Library of Congress, Washington, D.C.
3. Henry R. Luce, Memorandum of November 27, 1962, Henry R. Luce Papers Box 52 Folder 7, Library of Congress, Washington, D.C.
4. Luce, Grace, Warburg to Cardinal Masella, Telegram dated June 4, 1963, Henry R. Luce Papers Box 52 Folder 7, Library of Congress, Washington, D.C..
5. Program for the event honoring Cardinal Bea on April 1, 1963, Henry R. Luce Papers Box 52 Box 7, Library of Congress, Washington, D.C.
6. E Michael Jones, *The Jewish Revolutionary Spirit and Its Impact on World History* (South Bend, Indiana: Fidelity Press, 2008), 918-919.
7. C D Jackson Memorandum dated May 2, 1962 C D Jackson Papers Box 69 Folder "1962-64", Dwight D. Eisenhower Library, Abilene, Kansas.
8. Jackson Memorandum dated May 2, 1962.
9. Felix Morlion to Henry R. Luce, Letter dated January 22, 1958, Henry R. Luce Papers Box 52 Folder 7, Library of Congress, Washington, D.C.
10. CD Jackson to Henry R. Luce, Letter dated April 19, 1960, Henry R. Luce Papers Box 52 Folder 7, Library of Congress, Washington, D.C.
11. CD Jackson to Henry R. Luce, Memorandum dated April 27, 1964, Henry R. Luce Papers Box 52 Folder 6, Library of Congress, Washington, D.C.
12. Felix Morlion to Henry R. Luce, Letter dated April 20, 1964, Henry R. Luce Papers Box 52 Folder 6, Library of Congress, Washington, D.C.
13. Morlion to Luce Letter dated April 20, 1964; Felix Morlion to Henry R. Luce, Letter dated April 22, 1964, Henry R. Luce Papers Box 52 Folder 6, Library of Congress, Washington, D.C.

CHAPTER 105

1. Fr. Thomas William Coyle, C.Ss.R. to Francis J. Connell, Letter dated March 13, 1964, and Francis J Connell to Fr. Coyle, Letter dated March 24, 1964, Francis J Connell Papers, Redemptorist House Archives, Baltimore Province, Brooklyn, New York.
2. Francis J. Connell to Bishop John J Garner, Letter undated, from Francis J Connell Papers, Redemptorist House Archives, Baltimore Province, Brooklyn, New York.
3. Pelotte, *John Courtney Murray: Theologian in Conflict*, 85
4. Pelotte, *John Courtney Murray: Theologian in Conflict*, 85-87.
5. Pelotte, *John Courtney Murray: Theologian in Conflict*, 87-88.
6. Fenton, Diary, June 4, 1964.
7. Fenton, Diary, June 21, 1964.
8. "Roman Catholics: A Question of Leadership," *Time,* June 26, 1964. http://www.time.com/time/subscriber/printout/0,8816,898179,00.html (accessed October 21, 2012).
9. "Roman Catholics: Gadfly," *Time,* July 31, 1964. http://www.time.com/time/subscriber/printout/0,8816,874002,00.html (accessed October 21, 2012).
10. "Roman Catholics: Answer on the Way," *Time,* July 3, 1964. http://www.time.com/time/subscriber/printout/0,8816,873935,00.html (accessed October 21, 2012).; "Roman Catholics: The Married Priest," *Time,* July 10, 1964. http://www.time.com/time/subscriber/printout/0,8816,871270,00.html (accessed October 21, 2012); "Ecumenism: Toward Easier Mixed Marriage," *Time.* July 17, 1964 http://www.time.com/time/subscriber/printout/0,8816,875971,00.html (accessed October 21, 2012); "Roman Catholics: The Case Against celibacy," *Time,* August 28, 1964. http://www.time.com/time/subscriber/printout/0,8816,876117,00.html (accessed October 21, 2012).
11. "Ecumenism: What Catholics Think About Jews," *Time,* September 11, 1964. http://www.time.com/time/subscriber/printout/0,8816,830659,00.html (accessed October 21, 2012); "Theology: What Mary Means to Protestants," *Time,* September 11, 1964. http://www.time.com/time/subscriber/printout/0,8816,830660,00.html (accessed October 21, 2012).
12. "Theology: What Mary Means to Protestants," *Time,* September 11, 1964. http://www.time.com/time/subscriber/printout/0,8816,830660,00.html (accessed October 21, 2012).
13. "Three `Councils' In Rome," *Denver Register,* May 9, 1964, from Francis J. Connell Papers, Redemptorist House Archives, Baltimore Province, Brooklyn, New York.
14. "Blames Publicists for Distorted Image of Council," NCWC News Service, May 16, 1964, from Francis J. Connell Papers, Redemptorist House Archives, Baltimore Province, Brooklyn, New York.
15. "Blames Publicists for Distorted Image of Council," NCWC News Service, May 16, 1964.
16. "Constant Critics of Church Government Get Papal Rebuke: Passionate fault finders are given lesson," *Denver Register,* May 10, 1964, from Francis J. Connell Papers, Redemptorist House Archives, Baltimore Province, Brooklyn, New York.
17. Francis J. Connell, "Nature of the Church – Vatican Council II," CCD Workshop, Catholic University, June 15, 1964, from Francis J. Connell Papers,

Redemptorist House Archives, Baltimore Province, Brooklyn, New York.
18. Connell, "Nature of the Church – Vatican Council II."
19. Connell, "Nature of the Church – Vatican Council II."
20. Connell, "Nature of the Church – Vatican Council II."
21. Connell, "Nature of the Church – Vatican Council II."
22. Connell, "Nature of the Church – Vatican Council II."
23. Connell, "Nature of the Church – Vatican Council II."

CHAPTER 106

1. Falconi, *Pope John and His Council*, 135.
2. "Roman Catholics: The Unlikely Cardinal," *Time,* August 21, 1964. http://www.time.com/time/subscriber/printout/0,8816,876036,00.html (accessed October 21, 2012).
3. "Roman Catholics: The Unlikely Cardinal," *Time,* August 21, 1964.
4. "Roman Catholics: The Unlikely Cardinal," *Time,* August 21, 1964.
5. "Roman Catholics: The Unlikely Cardinal," *Time,* August 21, 1964.
6. "Roman Catholics: The Unlikely Cardinal," *Time,* August 21, 1964.
7. "Roman Catholics: The Unlikely Cardinal," *Time,* August 21, 1964.
8. "Roman Catholics: The Unlikely Cardinal," *Time,* August 21, 1964.
9. "Roman Catholics: The Unlikely Cardinal," *Time,* August 21, 1964.
10. "Roman Catholics: The Unlikely Cardinal," *Time,* August 21, 1964.
11. "Roman Catholics: The Unlikely Cardinal," *Time,* August 21, 1964.
12. Michael Novak, "Introduction to The Open Church (Millennium Edition)," November 24, 2003. American Enterprise Institute website. http://www.aei.org/print/introduction-to-the-open-church-millennium-edition (accessed October 23 2012).
13. Michael Novak, *A New Generation: American and Catholic* (New York: Herder and Herder, 1964), 17. Novak also made clear that he believed that "The United States is the creative land of this century...."
14. Novak, *A New Generation: American and Catholic*, 28.
15. Novak, *A New Generation: American and Catholic*, 28.
16. Novak, *A New Generation: American and Catholic*, 21.
17. Novak, *A New Generation: American and Catholic*, 223.
18. Novak, *A New Generation: American and Catholic*, 249.
19. Novak, *The Open Church: Vatican II, Act I* (New York: The Macmillan Company, 1964), 9-10.
20. Novak, *The Open Church: Vatican II, Act I*, 35.
21. Novak, *The Open Church: Vatican II, Act I*, 35.
22. Novak, *The Open Church: Vatican II, Act I*, 66-67.

CHAPTER 107

1. "The Papacy: His Church," *Time,* August 21, 1964. http://www.time.com/time/subscriber/printout/0,8816,876035,00.html (accessed October 21, 2012).
2. John Courtney Murray to Archbishop Alter, Letter dated August 24, 1964, *John Courtney Murray Papers*: Box 18 Folder 986, Georgetown University Library, Special Collections Division, Washington, D.C.

3. Pelotte, *John Courtney Murray: Theologian in Conflict*, 88-90.
4. Murray to Alter Letter dated August 24, 1964.
5. Murray to Alter Letter dated August 24, 1964.
6. Murray to Alter Letter dated August 24, 1964.
7. Murray to Alter Letter dated August 24, 1964.
8. Pelotte, *John Courtney Murray: Theologian in Conflict*, 89-90.
9. Pelotte, *John Courtney Murray: Theologian in Conflict*, 90-92.
10. Pelotte, *John Courtney Murray: Theologian in Conflict*, 91-92.
11. "The Council and the Issue of the Free Exercise of Religion: The Urgency of the Issue," NCWC Rome Office, John F. Deardan Papers (DRD): Box 6 Folder 9, University of Notre Dame Archives (UNDA), Notre Dame, Indiana.
12. "The Council and the Issue of the Free Exercise of Religion: The Urgency of the Issue," NCWC Rome Office.
13. A review of those sections does not support the NCWC interpretation. First of all, these three referenced sections are drawn from a larger section entitled "Characteristics of the present day" which merely indicated that what follows is an observation of the political realities of the day and not an endorsement of any one system or form of government. Paragraph 75 states that "it becomes clear that in the juridical organization of states in our times" and then proceeds to set forth certain requisites that are in consonance with the nature of these states, the values or goods that they should be promoting, and how they are to do so given the nature of these states. This is reiterated in paragraph 79 which states an observation as to the reason for and nature of political societies of the day and not an endorsement of them: "The tendencies to which We have referred, however, do clearly show that the men of our time are becoming increasingly conscious of their dignity as human persons." Pope John XXIII, *Peace on Earth*, tr. NCWC (Boston, MA: Pauline Books & Media), 23-24.
14. NCWC Statement, "The Council and the Issue of the Free Exercise of Religion: The Urgency of the Issue."
15. Francis J. Connell, *More Answers to Today's Moral Problems* (Washington, D.C.: The Catholic University of America Press, 1965), 1-20.
16. Connell, *More Answers to Today's Moral Problems*, 21-22.
17. Connell, *More Answers to Today's Moral Problems*, 22-24.
18. Connell, *More Answers to Today's Moral Problems*, 24-25.
19. Connell, *More Answers to Today's Moral Problems*, 24-25.
20. Francis J. Connell to Vagnozzi, Letter dated August 20, 1964, from Francis J Connell Papers, Redemptorist House Archives, Baltimore Province, Brooklyn, New York.
21. Francis J. Connell, "Comments on the Declaration on Religious Liberty," from Francis J Connell Papers, Redemptorist House Archives, Baltimore Province, Brooklyn, New York.
22. Connell, "Comments on the Declaration on Religious Liberty."
23. Connell, "Comments on the Declaration on Religious Liberty."
24. Connell, "Comments on the Declaration on Religious Liberty"; Connell explained that people have physical freedom, or power to do an act but that they may not have moral freedom, or the right, to do the same act (he cited to blaspheming as an example). He noted the terms "freedom" or "free" were used without distinction in the draft docuement and "without sufficient explanation," thereby causing confusion to arise. The same applied with regards to the use of the word, "liberty." People have a physical liberty, or freedom, to do an act, but that does not

mean that they have a moral liberty, or freedom, to do the act. This means people have the power to do something for which they have no moral right to do. Closely connected with this discussion was a reference in the draft that "man is invited to accept and profess the faith freely." Again he pointed out the ambiguity extant because there was no distinguishing between physical and moral freedom.

25. Connell, "Comments on the Declaration on Religious Liberty."

CHAPTER 108

1. Pelotte, *John Courtney Murray: Theologian in Conflict,* 92.
2. "A Layman Reflects on the Council." *Columbia,* September 1964, 14, 37-38, from Francis J Connell Papers, Redemptorist House Archives, Baltimore Province, Brooklyn, New York.
3. Pelotte, *John Courtney Murray: Theologian in Conflict,* 93-94.
4. Pelotte, *John Courtney Murray: Theologian in Conflict,* 93-94.
5. Pelotte, *John Courtney Murray: Theologian in Conflict,* 93-94.
6. Pelotte, *John Courtney Murray: Theologian in Conflict,* 93-94.
7. George W Shea "Church and State Murray's Reply to Me," AND 0004.001 George Shea Papers Box 19, Monsignor William Noe Field Archives and Special Collections Center, Seton Hall University, South Orange, New Jersey
8. "Roman Catholics: Not to Herself, but to God," *Time,* September 25, 1964. http://www.time.com/time/subscriber/printout/0,8816,876193,00.html (accessed October 21, 2012).
9. Fenton, Diary, October 9, 1964 and October 12, 1964.
10. Fenton, Diary, November 4, 1964.
11. "The Vatican Council: Speedup," *Time,* September 18, 1964. http://www.time.com/time/subscriber/printout/0,8816,830734,00.html (accessed October 21, 2013).
12. John Courtney Murray, "The Schema on Religious Freedom: Critical Comments," *John Courtney Murray Papers:* Box 18 Folder 986, Georgetown University Library, Special Collections Division, Washington, D.C.
13. Murray, "The Schema on Religious Freedom: Critical Comments." Murray wrote that the "conciliar schema should do justice to the concept in its commonly accepted sense." Freedom of religion was broader than freedom of conscience and it is "an external social freedom which essentially includes what American legal idiom calls the 'free exercise of religion.'" That includes "all manner of external and public manifestations of religious faith, in worship, observance, witness, and teaching" as well as "freedom of religious association" which is freedom in their internal governance.
14. Murray, "The Schema on Religious Freedom: Critical Comments."
15. Murray, "The Schema on Religious Freedom: Critical Comments."
16. Murray, "The Schema on Religious Freedom: Critical Comments."
17. Murray, "The Schema on Religious Freedom: Critical Comments."
18. Murray, "The Schema on Religious Freedom: Critical Comments."
19. Murray, "The Schema on Religious Freedom: Critical Comments." Murray made it clear that government should never be present to help the Catholic Church. He wrote that the government could act, under the first schema, to advance an impermissible purpose for either the benefit of the state or the Church. For instance, if a "particular society includes a religious purpose, the maintenance of

Catholic religious unity" then it "falls to government to repress all religious activities that contravene this purpose." A "political crime out of religious dissidence" could occur if the common good were considered, as Catholic doctrine taught, to be that the "ensemble of social conditions necessary or helpful for the perfection of man includes the social unity of the people in the faith."

20. Murray, "The Schema on Religious Freedom: Critical Comments."
21. Murray, "The Schema on Religious Freedom: Critical Comments."
22. Murray, "The Schema on Religious Freedom: Critical Comments."
23. Murray, "The Schema on Religious Freedom: Critical Comments." Part I was to be entitled "The Freedom of the Church." Part II was to be entitled "Religious freedom in contemporary society." Part III was to be entitled "Final exhortation: religious freedom today."
24. Joseph Clifford Fenton, Entries for September 21 and 25, 1964, Diary.
25. Francis J. Connell to Vagnozzi, Letter dated September 18, 1964, Francis J. Connell Papers, Redemptorist House Archives, Baltimore Province, Brooklyn, New York.
26. Bishop William G Connare to Francis J. Connell, Letter dated September 17, 1964, from Francis J Connell Papers, Redemptorist House Archives, Baltimore Province, Brooklyn, New York.
27. Fenton, Diary, September 21, 1964.
28. Pelotte, *John Courtney Murray: Theologian in Conflict,* 94-95.
29. Joseph Clifford Fenton, Entry for September 28, 1964, Diary.
30. George W Shea notes from September 25, 1964, AND 0004.001 George Shea Papers Box 13, Monsignor William Noe Field Archives and Special Collections Center, Seton Hall University, South Orange, New Jersey.
31. George W Shea notes from September 25, 1964, AND 0004.001 George Shea Papers Box 13, Monsignor William Noe Field Archives and Special Collections Center, Seton Hall University, South Orange, New Jersey.
32. Shea notes from September 25, 1964.
33. Shea notes from September 25, 1964.

CHAPTER 109

1. "A Letter from the Publisher: Sep. 25, 1964," *Time,* September 25, 1964.
2. "A Letter from the Publisher: Sep. 25, 1964," *Time,* September 25, 1964.
3. "A Letter from the Publisher: Sep. 25, 1964," *Time,* September 25, 1964.
4. Bird, *The Chairman: John J. McCloy: The Making of the American Establishment,* 471.
5. Bird, *The Chairman: John J. McCloy: The Making of the American Establishment,* 471.
6. Bird, *The Chairman: John J. McCloy: The Making of the American Establishment,* 471.

CHAPTER 110

1. "Roman Catholics: The Right to Worship According to One's Conscience," *Time,* October 2, 1964. http://www.time.com/time/subscriber/printout/ 0,8816,940522,00.html (accessed October 21, 2012).

2. "Letters: Oct. 16, 1964," *Time*, October 16, 1964. http://www.time.com/time/subscriber/printout/0,8816,876221,00.html (accessed October 21, 2012).

3. "Roman Catholics: The Right to Worship According to One's Conscience," *Time*, October 2, 1964.

4. Pelotte, *John Courtney Murray: Theologian in Conflict*, 94-95. The Pope intervened to keep the document under the Secretariat's jurisdiction so as to allow it to be examined by a joint committee consisting of representatives from the Secretariat and form the Theological Commission.

5. "Roman Catholics: Cum Magno Dolore," *Time*, October 23, 1964. http://www.time.com/time/subscriber/printout/0,8816,897340,00.html (accessed October 21, 2012).

6. "Roman Catholics: Cum Magno Dolore," *Time*, October 23, 1964.

7. "Roman Catholics: Cum Magno Dolore," *Time*, October 23, 1964.

8. "Roman Catholics: Cum Magno Dolore," *Time*, October 23, 1964.

9. "Roman Catholics: Cum Magno Dolore," *Time*, October 23, 1964.

10. Michael Novak, "Will the Council Build the Bridge?" *U.S. Catholic*, October, 1964, 9 and 11. Novak set agreement as the highest good when he wrote "The Council is sometimes forced to work out statements upon which all can agree. This means that a richly developed theology will sometimes have to surrender some of the affirmation it would like to make, in order not to exceed the limitations of an underdeveloped theology. A more precise theology will acquiesce in a looser terminology, in order to accommodate another point of view…there must be, compromise about *how to express* the common faith…."

11. Novak, "Will the Council Build the Bridge?" *U.S. Catholic*, 10-11.

12. Novak, "Will the Council Build the Bridge?" *U.S. Catholic*, 13

13. David Meade, "Protestants and the Council: What Protestants expect from the Council is one thing. What they want is another," *U.S. Catholic*, October, 1964, 14-24.

14. Meade, "Protestants and the Council: What Protestants expect from the Council is one thing. What they want is another," *U.S. Catholic*, 14, 23. Dr. Joseph Jackson (National Baptist Convention USA Inc.) gave evidence of the way the pope's comments were used against the Church when he wrote "I think the principle of brotherhood of all men has already been established by the Pope's opening address."

15. "Roman Catholics: The Bravest Schema," *Time*, October 30, 1964. http://www.time.com/time/subscriber/printout/0,8816,876333,00.html (accessed October 21, 2012).

16. "Roman Catholics: The Bravest Schema," *Time*, October 30, 1964.

17. "Roman Catholics: No More Galileos," *Time*, November 6, 1964. http://www.time.com/time/subscriber/printout/0,8816,876412,00.html (accessed October 21, 2012).

18. "The Vatican Council: A Mind of its Own," *Time*, November 20, 1964. http://www.time.com/time/subscriber/printout/0,8816,830822,00.html (accessed October 21, 2012).

CHAPTER 111

1. Pelotte, *John Courtney Murray: Theologian in Conflict,* 95-96.
2. Pelotte, *John Courtney Murray: Theologian in Conflict,* 96.
3. Fenton, Diary, November 16, 1964.
4. Fenton, Diary, November 10, 1964.
5. Francis J. Connell to Fr. Joseph Busch SVD, Letter dated December 1, 1964, Francis J Connell Papers, Redemptorist House Archives, Baltimore Province, Brooklyn, New York.
6. "The Vatican Council: The Pope Runs the Church," *Time,* November 27, 1964. http://www.time.com/time/subscriber/printout/0,8816,871415,00.html (accessed October 21, 2012).
7. "The Vatican Council: The Pope Runs the Church," *Time,* November 27, 1964.
8. "The Vatican Council: The Pope Runs the Church," *Time,* November 27, 1964.
9. "The Vatican Council: The Pope Runs the Church," *Time,* November 27, 1964.
10. Joseph Busch SVD to Francis J. Connell, Letter dated November 26, 1964, Francis J Connell Papers, Redemptorist House Archives, Baltimore Province, Brooklyn, New York.
11. "WCC Statement on Council 'Religious Liberty' Action 11/18/64," NCWC News Service (Foreign), from Francis J Connell Papers, Redemptorist House Archives, Baltimore Province, Brooklyn, New York..
12. "Pope said to see 'Faults' in religious liberty statement," NCWC News Service (Domestic), November 27, 1964, from Francis J Connell Papers, Redemptorist House Archives, Baltimore Province, Brooklyn, New York. NY. Cardinal Ritter exhorted the US bishops in a letter dated December 29 to stand in support of the third text which was the one distributed on November 17 as "The Pope assured them that the schema on Religious Liberty would be addressed during the Fourth and final Session of the Council." Pelotte, *John Courtney Murray: Theologian in Conflict,* 96-97. The NCWC News Service reported that Cardinal Meyer was "disappointed" and Cardinal Leger was "confident" about a statement on religious liberty. "Cardinal Meyer 'Disappointed' on Liberty Issue," NCWC News Service (Domestic), November 24, 1964 and "Cardinal Leger is Confident about Liberty Statement," NCWC News Service (Domestic), November 27, 1964 both from Francis J Connell Papers, Redemptorist House Archives, Baltimore Province, Brooklyn, New York.
13. Archbishop O'Boyle, "Observations on the Third Session of Vatican Council II" to the John Carroll Society on December 15, 1964, from Francis J. Connell Papers, Redemptorist House Archives, Baltimore Province, Brooklyn, New York. The Archbishop gave an explanation of aggiornamento. He said that aggiornamento, or a bringing up to date, occurs when the Church "can lay greater stress on certain of her teachings to respond to the particular needs of the time."
14. O'Boyle, "Observations on the Third Session of Vatican Council II." O'Boyle said the Secretariat for Christian Unity noted that the changes of the third draft were substantial: "on the first 6 pages – the old text had 39 lines – the new one, 141 lines" and "not only had the general principles and practical applications been amplified, but even the very structure of the text had been changed."
15. O'Boyle, "Observations on the Third Session of Vatican Council II."
16. O'Boyle, "Observations on the Third Session of Vatican Council II."

17. Francis J. Connell, "The Second Vatican Council," Francis J Connell Papers, Redemptorist House Archives, Baltimore Province, Brooklyn, New York. Connell emphasized that the "bishops were within their rights in making this appeal, and it was done with all courtesy and reverence. And when the Pope decided not to grant their appeal they accepting his decision with full obedience. This was not the only instance of the misrepresentation of the news by the press."

18. Fr. John P Donnelly, "Council Official Deplores Press Reports," NCWC News Service (Foreign), November 28, 1964, from Francis J Connell Papers, Redemptorist House Archives, Baltimore Province, Brooklyn, New York.

19. Donnelly, "Council Official Deplores Press Reports."

CHAPTER 112

1. Fr. Placid Jordan, OSB, "Vatican Council Gives a New Image to the Church," NCWC News Service, December 3, 1964, from Francis J Connell Papers, Redemptorist House Archives, Baltimore Province, Brooklyn, New York.

2. Rev. Charles K. Von Euw, "Council's Candor: Sure Sign of Church Renewal," *The Pilot*, December 5, 1964, from Francis J Connell Papers, Redemptorist House Archives, Baltimore Province, Brooklyn, New York.

3. Rt Rev. R. J. Sennott, "Council's Productivity Amazes," *The Pilot*, Francis J Connell Papers, Redemptorist House Archives, Baltimore Province, Brooklyn, New York.

4. "B. U. Observer Witnesses Church's 'Quiet Revolution'," *The Pilot*, Francis J Connell Papers, Redemptorist House Archives, Baltimore Province, Brooklyn, New York.

5. "Interfaith Dialogue Only Cure for Ills of Pluralism," *The Pilot*, Francis J Connell Papers, Redemptorist House Archives, Baltimore Province, Brooklyn, New York; Patrick Riley, "Historic Church Schema Summarized," *The Pilot*, Francis J Connell Papers, Redemptorist House Archives, Baltimore Province, Brooklyn, New York.

6. "Unity Is Theme of Decree on Ecumenism," *The Pilot*; Rt. Rev. E. G. Murray, "Moving Toward a Brotherhood of 'Most Dear Fellow Christians'," *The Pilot* both from Francis J Connell Papers, Redemptorist House Archives, Baltimore Province, Brooklyn, New York.

7. John Cogley, "Steady Hand Guides Barque of St. Peter," *The Pilot*, November 28, 1964, Francis J Connell Papers, Redemptorist House Archives, Baltimore Province, Brooklyn, New York. Cogley ignored comments by those like Bishop Robert F. Joyce of Burlington, Vermont who approved of the Pope's actions and said that it was merely a decision not to intervene in the affairs of the council by overturning the decision by the Council's presidency; Archbishop Vicente Enrique y Tarancon of Oviedo, Spain, expressed "regret" that certain press reports blamed the Spanish and Italian prelates for the delay. "Papal Decision Praised by Bishop," NCWC News Service (Domestic), December 4, 1964, Francis J Connell Papers, Redemptorist House Archives, Baltimore Province, Brooklyn, New York; Manuel Mira, "Spaniards Amazed by Council's Non-Action on Liberty," NCWC News Service (Foreign), December 8, 1964, Francis J Connell Papers, Redemptorist House Archives, Baltimore Province, Brooklyn, New York.

8. "Obituaries: Barrett McGurn," *The Washington Post*, July 8, 2010. http://www.washingtonpost.com/wp-dyn/content/article/2010/07/07/AR2010070705112.html (accessed March 18, 2013).

9. Barrett McGurn, "Priests' Views on Birth Control Pill, Religious Liberty," *The Boston Sunday Globe,* December 6, 1964, Francis J Connell Papers, Redemptorist House Archives, Baltimore Province, Brooklyn, New York.

10. "'The Problem of Religious Freedom,' by John Courtney Murray," *Journal of Church and State* (1966) 8:(3) 475.

11. George W Shea's notes "The Problem of Religious Freedom at the Council" AND 0004.001 George Shea Papers Box 19, Monsignor William Noe Field Archives and Special Collections Center, Seton Hall University, South Orange, New Jersey.

CHAPTER 113

1. Gerald Heard, *Letters from the Growing Edge 1960-1962: Training Techniques for a Life of Growth: How to Generate Powers of Apt Force in a Small Group,* ed. by John V. Cody, Ph.D. (1999), iv-v; Eckard V. Toy, "The Conservative Connection: The Chairman of the Board Took LSD Before Timothy Leary." *American Studies* Vol. 21,No. 2 (Fall 1980): 65-77.

2. Heard, *Letters from the Growing Edge 1960-1962,* iii-iv.

3. Gerald Heard to William C. Mullendore, letter dated January 5, 1965, Gerald Heard Papers, John V Cody Ph.D. Collection, Berkeley, California.

4. "Roman Catholics: Authority Under Fire," *Time,* March 19, 1965. http://www.time.com/time/subscriber/printout/0,8816,833583,00.html (accessed November 11, 2012).

5. "Roman Catholics: Authority Under Fire," *Time,* March 19, 1965.

6. "Roman Catholics: Authority Under Fire," *Time,* March 19, 1965.

7. "Roman Catholics: Authority Under Fire," *Time,* March 19, 1965.

CHAPTER 114

1. Bp William J McCarty to Francis J. Connell, Letter dated January 12, 1965, Francis J Connell Papers, Redemptorist House Archives, Baltimore Province, Brooklyn, New York.

2. Francis J. Connell to Bishop McCarty, Letter dated January 16, 1965, Francis J Connell Papers, Redemptorist House Archives, Baltimore Province, Brooklyn, New York.

3. Francis J. Connell to Bishop Richard Ackerman, Letter dated January 16, 1965, Francis J Connell Papers, Redemptorist House Archives, Baltimore Province, Brooklyn, New York.

4. Pelotte, *John Courtney Murray: Theologian in Conflict,* 97-98.

5. John Courtney Murray to Bishop DeSmedt, Letter dated February 13, 1965, *John Courtney Murray Papers*: Box 18 Folder 1009, Georgetown University Library, Special Collections Division, Washington, D.C.

6. Murray to DeSmedt Letter dated February 13, 1965.

7. Murray to DeSmedt Letter dated February 13, 1965.

8. Yves Congar, *My Journal of the Council* (Collegeville, MN: Liturgical Press, 2012), 727, 731, 734, 736.

9. Congar, *My Journal of the Council,* 727, 731, 734, 736.

10. Congar, *My Journal of the Council,* 727, 731, 734,736.

11. "The Lasting Vision of Pope John," *Time,* February 26, 1965. http://www.time. com/time/subscriber/printout/0,8816,833488,00.html (accessed November 11, 2012).

12. John Courtney Murray to Clare Boothe Luce, Letter dated "Ariccia. March 5 [1965]," Clare Boothe Luce Papers: Box 212 Folder 9, Library of Congress, Washington, D.C.

13. Murray to Luce Letter dated "Ariccia. March 5 [1965]." Of interest, Murray remarked on the *Time* magazine article extolling *Pacem In Terris* as he told Clare "I feel completely cut off – not even a newspaper for two weeks. I am anxious to know how the Pacem in terris affair went in New York (a proper phenomenon – that a papal encyclical should command such universal attention....Shall call to hear news. Love and love, John. Best to Harry."

14. Congar, *My Journal of the Council,* 754, 761.

15. Pelotte, *John Courtney Murray: Theologian in Conflict,* 97.

16. "Schema of Declaration on Religious Liberty," *John Courtney Murray Papers:* Box 18 Folder 1012, Georgetown University Library, Special Collections Division, Washington, D.C.

17. "Schema of Declaration on Religious Liberty."

18. "Schema of Declaration on Religious Liberty."

19. "Schema of Declaration on Religious Liberty." Both version 2 and version 3 contained prohibitions against the imposition on people "by force or fear" the "profession or rejection of any religious creed" (version 3) or the "profession or rejection of any religion" (version 2). Both versions prohibited the use of force to "repress religion itself" and both recognized that the government (version 3) or civil authority (version 2) may not prevent a person from entering or leaving any/a "religious body."

20. "Schema of Declaration on Religious Liberty."

21. "Schema of Declaration on Religious Liberty."

22. "Schema of Declaration on Religious Liberty." Version 3 put the duty of insuring religious liberty upon Christians, whereas version 2 was silent on the matter (version 3 was a longer document in any event). Both versions placed the source of religious liberty in the "dignity of the" person (version 2) or "human person" (version 3) and divine revelation.

23. "Schema of Declaration on Religious Liberty." Both versions recognized the Catholic doctrine that one cannot be forced to embrace the faith. Both versions recognized the principle of freedom of the Church but version 3 seemed to limit freedom of the Church as being just one principle of many in its relations with the secular authorities, and that the Church's freedom was pretty much unlimited so as to save souls.

24. "Schema of Declaration on Religious Liberty." Both versions mentioned the Church had a "grave duty"/"grave obligation" toward the "truth of Christ" and hence to spread the Faith. Version 2 spoke of a "gentle approach" to those in error or ignorance and both stated the need to "deal lovingly, prudently and patiently" with those in error. Version 2 contained the following deleted from version 3: "Error must be rejected, truth must be proclaimed, the intellect enlightened, and the human person respected with all due reverence." Both versions held "this Sacred Council exhorts the Faithful and implores all men of our time to consider most attentively how necessary religious liberty is, especially in the present circumstances of human life" and required "world religious liberty be made secure

by effective legal safeguards and that due respect be had for the highest duties and rights of men to lead a religious life in society with freedom."

CHAPTER 115

1. "The Glorious Walk in the Cosmos," *Life*, June 18, 1965.
2. Isaacs and Downing, *Cold War: An Illustrated History 1945-1991*, 249-256.
3. Jack Shafer, "The Time and Life Acid Trip: How Henry R. Luce and Clare Boothe Luce helped turn America on to LSD," June 21, 2010, *Slate* http://slate.com/articles/news_and_politics/press_box/2010/06/the-time_and_life_a..... as accessed December 10, 2014.
4. "Roman Catholics: Beyond Transubstantiation: New Theory of the Real Presence," *Time*, July 2, 1965. http://www.time.com/time/subscriberprintout/ 0,8816,833876,00.html (accessed November 11, 2012).
5. "Theology: Church & Birth Control: From Genesis to Genetics" *Time*, July 16, 1965. http://www.time.com/time/subscriber/printout/0,8816,834007,00.html (accessed November 11, 2012).
6. "Theology: Church & Birth Control: From Genesis to Genetics," *Time*, July 16, 1965.
7. "Roman Catholics: Confession: Public or Private?" *Time*, August 6, 1965. http:// www.time.com/time/subscriber/printout/0,8816,834152,00.html (accessed November 11, 2012); "Roman Catholics: Indulgences Made Easy," *Time*, December 31, 1965. http://www.time.com/time/subscriber/printout/ 0,8816,842343,00.html (accessed November 11, 2012).
8. Francis J. Connell, "Comments on the Pamphlet 'What's Happening in the Church?'" Francis J. Connell Papers, Redemptorist House Archives, Baltimore Province, Brooklyn, New York.
9. Francis J. Connell to Archbishop O'Boyle, Letter dated February 17, 1965, Francis J Connell Papers, Redemptorist House Archives, Baltimore Province, Brooklyn, New York.
10. Francis J. Connell to Archbishop O'Boyle, Memorandum entitled "Some Comments on Contraception," Francis J Connell Papers, Redemptorist House Archives, Baltimore Province, Brooklyn, New York.
11. Francis J. Connell to John Cogley, Letter dated June 21, 1965, Francis J. Connell Papers, Redemptorist House Archives, Baltimore Province, Brooklyn, New York.
12. John Courtney Murray to Cardinal Cushing, Memorandum entitled "(Cushing = 1965)," *John Courtney Murray Papers:* Box 18 Folder 1001, Georgetown University Library, Special Collections Division, Washington, D.C.
13. Murray to Cushing Memorandum entitled "(Cushing=1965)".
14. Murray to Cushing Memorandum entitled "(Cushing=1965)".
15. Murray to Cushing Memorandum entitled "(Cushing=1965)".
16. Murray to Cushing Memorandum entitled "(Cushing=1965)". Murray also indicated to Cushing that freedom is "the enjoyment of immunity from coercion."
17. Murray to Cushing Memorandum entitled "(Cushing=1965)".

CHAPTER 116

1. "The Vatican Council: The Fourth Session," *Time,* September 10, 1965. http://www.time.com/time/subscriber/printout/0,8816,834306.html (accessed November 11, 2012).
2. "The Papacy: Reluctant Revolutionary," *Time,* September 24, 1965. http://www.time.com/time/subscriber/printout/0,8816,834370,00.html (accessed November 11 2012).
3. "The Papacy: Reluctant Revolutionary," *Time,* September 24, 1965.
4. "The Papacy: Reluctant Revolutionary," *Time,* September 24, 1965.
5. Pellotte, *John Courtney Murray: Theologian in Conflict,* 98.
6. "Council Digest," *John Courtney Murray Papers*: Box 18 Folder 1014, Georgetown University Library, Special Collections Division, Washington, D.C.
7. "Council Digest," *John Courtney Murray Papers:* Box 18 Folder 1014.
8. "Council Digest," *John Courtney Murray Papers:* Box 18 Folder 1014.
9. "Council Digest," *John Courtney Murray Papers:* Box 18 Folder 1014.
10. "Council Digest," *John Courtney Murray Papers:* Box 18 Folder 1014.
11. "Council Digest," *John Courtney Murray Papers:* Box 18 Folder 1014.
12. "Council Digest," *John Courtney Murray Papers*: Box 18 Folder 987, Georgetown University Library, Special Collections Division, Washington, D.C.
13. George W Shea notes from September 16, 1965, AND 0004.001 George Shea Papers Box 13, Monsignor William Noe Field Archives and Special Collections Center, Seton Hall University, South Orange, New Jersey.
14. George W Shea notes from September 16, 1965, AND 0004.001 George Shea Papers Box 13, Monsignor William Noe Field Archives and Special Collections Center, Seton Hall University, South Orange, New Jersey. The following day, Ottaviani gave a talk in which he was critical of the proposed Declaration as he said "this Declaration touches disputed questions and frequently decides them against the common teaching" while other documents produced by the Council did "abstain from entering into disputed questions" therefore resulting from the elimination of "commonly held doctrines…from other documents." He criticized the assertion in paragraph 3 that "truth and error, right and false consciences are put in the same plane even though, as Leo XIII taught, they are evils which at most can be tolerated for the sake of a greater good." While the foundation of the Declaration is the dignity of the human person, "it is very doubtful whether such dignity can be the basis for teaching falsehood…especially since the Declaration itself observes that human dignity requires that all, especially the less instructed and children, be protected from whatever militates against the achievement of ultimate human perfection…" Finally, Ottaviani insisted that a "clearer distinction…be drawn between physical and moral coercion…God obligates but does not coerce us" and the "treatment of relations between Church and State must be revised to conform with the teaching of Leo XIII and Pius XII." "Council Digest," *John Courtney Murray Papers*: Box 18 Folder 987.
15. George W Shea notes from September 20, 1965, AND 0004.001 George Shea Papers Box 13, Monsignor William Noe Field Archives and Special Collections Center, Seton Hall University, South Orange, New Jersey.
16. "The Vatican Council: A Blow for Liberty," *Time,* October 1, 1965. http://www.time.com/time/subscriber/printout/0,8816,834445,00.html (accessed November 11, 2012).

17. "The Vatican Council: A Blow for Liberty," *Time,* October 1, 1965.
18. "Council Digest," *John Courtney Murray Papers*: Box 18 Folder 1014, Georgetown University Library, Special Collections Division, Washington, D.C.
19. "Council Digest," *John Courtney Murray Papers:* Box 18 Folder 1014, Georgetown University Library, Special Collections Division, Washington, D.C. In particular, De Smedt referenced that "special attention" would be given to designating religious liberty as "civil and social" and key terms be "more accurately defined" so as to avoid "expressions which could lead to indifferentism or laicism." The reference to conscience would be eliminated and the Scriptural section "shorted and better ordered" while the "limits of religious freedom" receive "clearer expositions" to define what is meant by "public peace, public order and the common good." De Smedt also said that "with respect to the human person...the obligations of seeking the truth, worshiping God, and acknowledging the rights of the Church be more clearly set forth." Expressing a confidence that Catholicism could progress so as to understand the "problem of civil and social liberty" which "is a new one," he said that the "civil and social order must be distinguished from the moral order in which: 1) all men and communities are bound objectively and subjectively to seek after truth and not to favor error. 2) Must be acknowledged the duty and rights of the Church and the corresponding obligations of others, all of which flow from the mandate of Christ to preach the gospel. 3) All men are obliged to forma right conscience and to follow its dictates...." The following day Archbishop Karol Wojtyla of Krakow Poland said that "the text is pleasing" as he spoke "In the name of the Polish Bishops." The "subject matter is not a mere declaration, but the moral teaching of the church." However, the declaration should not only declare the right of the person but also "his responsibility toward God and society in the use of this right." Moral law – "the natural or divine law" -- limits religious freedom, not human positive law.
20. Robert Emmet Tracy, *America,* October 9, 1965, 397.
21. Pellotte, *John Courtney Murray: Theologian in Conflict,* 98-101.
22. "Vatican Council: The Uses of Ambiguity," *Time,* November 5, 1965. http://www.time.com/time/subscriber/printout/0,8816,901776,00.html (accessed November 11, 2012).
23. Fenton, Diary, October 28, 1965.
24. Fenton, Diary, November 26, 1965.
25. Fenton, Diary, November 26, 1965.
26. "The Vatican Council: A Vote Against Prejudice," *Time,* October 22, 1965. http://www.time.com/time/subscriber/printout/0,8816,941409,00.html (accessed November 11, 2012).

CHAPTER 117

1. "Dr. Vischer on the Council," NCWC Documentary Service, March 23, 1966, Francis J. Connell Papers, Redemptorist House Archives, Baltimore Province, Brooklyn, New York. (emphasis supplied). Robert McAfee Brown, UTS professor, Presbyterian minister, and observer at the Council was more blunt about it all as judging by the title of the article he wrote for *Commonweal.* In "Using Council Documents" he made clear the Protestants had a weapon to argue that Church doctrine had changed as the council pronouncements were a "whole haystack of 'official' pronouncements, with all the weight of solemn declarations by the

magisterium......For now we can point to authoritative documents...appeal to the specific statements of the sacred synod, rather than private opinions of a handful of north European theologians...." Robert McAfee Brown "Using Council Documents," *Commonweal,* May 20, 1966, 254-255.

2. "Dr. Vischer on the Council," NCWC Documentary Service, March 23, 1966.
3. "Dr. Vischer on the Council," NCWC Documentary Service, March 23, 1966.
4. "Dr. Vischer on the Council," NCWC Documentary Service, March 23, 1966.
5. Emmet Hughes, "A Man for Our Season," January 16, 1969, John Courtney Murray Papers: Box 28 Folder 1288, Georgetown University Library, Special Collections Division, Washington, D.C.
6. Walter M Abbott, SJ, General Editor, "Declaration on Religious Liberty," *The Documents of Vatican II: In a New and Definitive Translations With Commentaries and Notes by Catholic, Protestant and Orthodox Authorities* (New York: Herder and Herder, Association Press, 1966).
7. Douglas Martin, "Franklin Littell, Scholar of Holocaust, Dies at 91," *The New York Times,* May 30, 2009.
8. Abbott, "A Response," *The Documents of Vatican II,* 699.
9. Abbott, "Declaration on Religious Liberty," *The Documents of Vatican II,* 672-673, 680.
10. Abbott, "Declaration on Religious Liberty," *The Documents of Vatican II,* 673.
11. Abbott, "Declaration on Religious Liberty," *The Documents of Vatican II,* 680.
12. Abbott, "Declaration on Religious Liberty," *The Documents of Vatican II,* 676, 687.
13. Abbott, "Declaration on Religious Liberty," *The Documents of Vatican II,* 683.
14. Abbott, "Declaration on Religious Liberty," *The Documents of Vatican II,* 693.
15. Abbott, "Declaration on Religious Liberty," *The Documents of Vatican II,* 687-688.
16. Abbott, "Declaration on Religious Liberty," *The Documents of Vatican II,* 678.
17. Abbott, "Declaration on Religious Liberty," *The Documents of Vatican II,* 688-689.
18. Abbott, "Declaration on Religious Liberty," *The Documents of Vatican II,* 678-679.
19. Abbott, "Declaration on Religious Liberty," *The Documents of Vatican II,* 677-678.
20. Abbott, "Declaration on Religious Liberty," *The Documents of Vatican II,* 684
21. Abbott, "Declaration on Religious Liberty," *The Documents of Vatican II,* 684
22. Abbott, "Declaration on Religious Liberty," *The Documents of Vatican II,* 677.
23. Abbott, "Declaration on Religious Liberty," *The Documents of Vatican II,* 682.
24. Abbott, "Declaration on Religious Liberty," *The Documents of Vatican II,* 673.
25. Abbott, "Declaration on Religious Liberty," *The Documents of Vatican II,* 673.
26. Abbott, "Declaration on Religious Liberty," *The Documents of Vatican II,* 685
27. Abbott, "Declaration on Religious Liberty," *The Documents of Vatican II,* 685
28. Abbott, "Declaration on Religious Liberty," *The Documents of Vatican II,* 685
29. John Courtney Murray, "The Issue of Church and State at Vatican Council II," *Theological Studies* 27 (December 1966): 580-606. Woodstock Theological Center at Georgetown University. http://woodstock.georgetown.edu/library/Murray/1966h.htm (accessed November 11, 2012).
30. Murray, "The Issue of Church and State at Vatican Council II," *Theological Studies.*
31. Murray, "The Issue of Church and State at Vatican Council II," *Theological Studies.*
32. Austin Flannery, OP, editor *Vatican Council II: The Conciliar and Post Conciliar Documents* (Northport, New York: Costello Publishing Company, 1992), xxiii-xxiv.

CHAPTER 118

1. A decree is "an order or law made by a superior authority for the direction of others." Dunford, D. (1908). Decree. In The Catholic Encyclopedia. New York: Robert Appleton Company. Retrieved July 3, 2021 from New Advent: http://www.newadvent.org/cathen/04670a.htm
2. "Decree on the Means of Social Communications," or "Inter Mirifica" Chapter I, Section 3, ed. Austin Flannery, OP, *Vatican Council II: The Conciliar and Post Conciliar Documents* (Northport, New York: Costello Publishing Company, 1992), 286.
3. A "Declaration" is a statement of policy or a position paper. Greg Erlandson, Ed., *Our Sunday Visitor's Catholic Almanac 2005 Edition* (Huntington, Indiana: Our Sunday Visitor Publishing Division, 2004), 136; "Position Paper," *The Free Dictionary by Farlex*. www.thefreedictionary.com (accessed May 16, 2013).
4. "Declaration on Religious Liberty," or "Dignitatis Humanae" Chapter I, Section 3, Paragraph 1 ["cI, s3, p1"], ed. Austin Flannery, OP, *Vatican Council II: The Conciliar and Post Conciliar Documents* (Northport, New York: Costello Publishing Company, 1992), 801.
5. "4. De relatione Ecclesiam inter et statum civilem. Recenter quidam theology proposuerunt theoriam, juxta quam rectores civiles, qua tales, non suordinantur legi divino-positivae Christi, sed tantum legi naturali, ex qua thoria sequitur statum civilem non teneri agnoscere Ecclesium Catholicam noque ejus immunitates." Translation: 4. On the relation between the Church and the Civil State. Recently there have arisen certain theologies which propose theories that civil rulers, as such are not to be subordinated to the divine positive law of Christ, but only to the natural law. From this theory it follows that the civil state does not have to recognize the Catholic Church or recognize her immunities." Francis J Connell to Archibishop O'Boyle, Letter dated July 28, 1959, Francis J. Connell Papers, Redemptorist House Archives, Baltimore Province, Brooklyn, New York.
6. See Chapter 73.
7. "Declaration on Religious Liberty," cII, s10, *Vatican Council II: The Conciliar and Post Conciliar Documents,* 807.
8. "Declaration on Religious Liberty," cII, s11, p2, *Vatican Council II: The Conciliar and Post Conciliar Documents,* 809.
9. Repeated herein for ease of reference: a) The Catholic confessional State, professing itself as such, is not an ideal to which organized political society is universally obliged. b) Full religious liberty can be considered as a valid political ideal in a truly democratic State. c) The State organized on a genuinely democratic basis must be considered to have done its duty when it has guaranteed the freedom of the Church by a general guarantee of liberty of religion. d) It is true that Leo XIII had said: `...civitates...debent eum in colendo numine morem usurpare modumque quo coli se Deus ipse demonstravit velle' (Enc. Immortale Dei). [Translation: "...cities... are absolutely bound, in the worship of the Deity, to adopt that use and manner in which God himself has shown that he wills to be adored."] Words such as these can be understood as referring to the State considered as organized on a basis other than that of the perfectly democratic State but to this latter strictly speaking are not applicable.
10. "Declaration on Religious Liberty," s1, p3, *Vatican Council II: The Conciliar and Post Conciliar Documents,* 800.

11. "Declaration on Religious Liberty," s1, p2, *Vatican Council II: The Conciliar and Post Conciliar Documents,* 799.
12. "Declaration on Religious Liberty," s1, p1, *Vatican Council II: The Conciliar and Post Conciliar Documents,* 799.
13. "Declaration on Religious Liberty," cII, s15, p4, *Vatican Council II: The Conciliar and Post Conciliar Documents,* 812.
14. "Declaration on Religious Liberty," cII, s15, p4, *Vatican Council II: The Conciliar and Post Conciliar Documents,* 812.
15. "Declaration on Religious Liberty," s1, p3, *Vatican Council II: The Conciliar and Post Conciliar Documents,* 800.
16. "Declaration on Religious Liberty," cI, s6, p1, *Vatican Council II: The Conciliar and Post Conciliar Documents,* 803.
17. Ottaviani, "Church and State: Some Present Problems in the Light of the Teaching of Pope Pius XII," *American Ecclesiastical Review,* 329-330.
18. "Declaration on Religious Liberty," cI, s2, p1, *Vatican Council II: The Conciliar and Post Conciliar Documents,* 800
19. "Declaration on Religious Liberty," cI, s2, p2, *Vatican Council II: The Conciliar and Post Conciliar Documents,* 801.
20. "Declaration on Religious Liberty," cI, s7, p2, *Vatican Council II: The Conciliar and Post Conciliar Documents,* 805
21. "Declaration on Religious Liberty," cI, s6, p1, *Vatican Council II: The Conciliar and Post Conciliar Documents,* 803.
22. "Declaration on Religious Liberty," cI, s4, p5, *Vatican Council II: The Conciliar and Post Conciliar Documents,* 803.
23. "Declaration on Religious Liberty," cII, s11, p1, *Vatican Council II: The Conciliar and Post Conciliar Documents,* 807.
24. "Declaration on Religious Liberty," cII, s10, *Vatican Council II: The Conciliar and Post Conciliar Documents,* 807.
25. Connell to Vagnozzi Letter dated August 20, 1964 with "Comments on the Declaration on Religious Liberty," from Francis J. Connell Papers, Redemptorist House Archives, Baltimore Province, Brooklyn, New York.
26. Connell to Vagnozzi Letter dated August 20, 1964.
27. "Declaration on Religious Liberty," cI, s8, p3, *Vatican Council II: The Conciliar and Post Conciliar Documents,* 805.
28. "Declaration on Religious Liberty," cII, s15, p2, *Vatican Council II: The Conciliar and Post Conciliar Documents,* 812.
29. "Declaration on Religious Liberty," cI, s6, p3, *Vatican Council II: The Conciliar and Post Conciliar Documents,* 804.
30. See Chapter 98.
31. An Apostolic Constitution is binding as a matter of Canon Law and requires the assent of faith of the faithful. Gil Mechelini, "Vatican II Documents," http://gilmichelini.com/what-are-the-vatican-ii-documents/#fn1 accessed July 3, 2021.
32. "Pastoral Constitution on the Church in the Modern World," *Gaudium et Spes,* section 59, *Vatican Council II: The Conciliar and Post Conciliar Documents,* 963-964.

CHAPTER 119

1. Msgr. George A. Kelly, *The Battle for the American Church* (Garden City, New York: Image Books, 1981), 5-20.

2. Michael Davies, *The Second Vatican Council and Religious Liberty* (Long Prairie, Minnesota: The Neumann Press, 1992), 257.

3. "Protestants: Getting Ahead In Italy," *Time,* January 4, 1965. http://www.time. com/time/subscriber/printout/0,8816,898354,00.html (accessed November 11, 2012).

4. "Roman Catholics: Eldest Daughter in Turmoil," *Time,* June 11, 1965. http:// www.time.com/time/subscriber/printout/0,8816,833719,00.html (accessed November 11, 2012).

5. "How Vatican II Turned The Church Toward the World," *Time,* December 17, 1965. http://www.time.com/time/subscriber/printout/0,8816,834774,00.html (accessed November 11, 2012).

6. "How Vatican II Turned The Church Toward the World," *Time,* December 17, 1965.

7. "How Vatican II Turned The Church Toward the World," *Time,* December 17, 1965.

8. "How Vatican II Turned The Church Toward the World," *Time,* December 17, 1965.

9. "Spain: The Awakening Land," *Time,* January 21, 1966. http://www.time.com/ time/subscriber/printout/0,8816,835066,00.html (accessed November 11, 2012).

10. "Spain: The Awakening Land," *Time,* January 21, 1966.

11. "Spain: Warning From the Church," *Time,* May 27, 1966. http://www.time.com/ time/subscriber/printout/0,8816,835645,00.html (accessed November 11, 2012).

12. "Spain: Warning From the Church," *Time,* May 27, 1966.

13. "'Apostolate of Criticism' Called Anti-Christian," NCWC News Service (Foreign), December 14, 1965, Francis J. Connell Papers, Redemptorist House Archives, Baltimore Province, Brooklyn, New York.

14. Msgr. S. J. Adamo, "US Editor Luncheon Guest of Cardinal Ottaviani," NCWC News Service (Foreign), December 16, 1965, Francis J. Connell Papers, Redemptorist House Archives, Baltimore Province, Brooklyn, New York.

15. "Sees Birth Control Report by Summer," NCWC News Service (Foreign) April 7, 1966.

16. John W. O'Malley, SJ., "Vatican II: Did Anything Happen?" *Theological Studies* 67 (2006): 31.

17. O'Malley, "Vatican II: Did Anything Happen?", 23.

18. O'Malley, "Vatican II: Did Anything Happen?", 25.

19. Gregory Baum, "The Final Session: Off to a Good Start" *Commonweal,* October 15, 1965, 52.

20. Joseph C. Fenton to George W. Shea, letter dated January 28, 1966, AND 0004.001 George Shea Papers, Box 11, Monsignor William Noe Field Archives and Special Collections Center, Seton Hall University, South Orange, New Jersey.

21. Francis J. Connell, "Birth Control: The Case for the Catholic," *The Atlantic Monthly,* October 1939, Francis J. Connell Papers, Redemptorist House Archives, Baltimore Province, Brooklyn, New York.

22. Francis J. Connell, "Sex Education and Birth Control (Adult Education Group, Baltimore, May 18, 1949)," Francis J. Connell Papers, Redemptorist House

Archives, Baltimore Province, Brooklyn, New York

23. Francis J Connell to Vagnozzi, Letter dated October 5, 1961, Francis J. Connell Papers, Redemptorist House Archives, Baltimore Province, Brooklyn, New York.

24. Connell to Vagnozzi Letter dated October 5, 1961; Francis J. Connell, "Comments on Fr. John A. O'Brien's Article 'Let's Take Birth Control Out of Politics' (Appearing in LOOK, October 10, 1961)," Francis J. Connell Papers, Redemptorist House Archives, Baltimore Province, Brooklyn, New York.

25. Francis J. Connell to Bishop Leo Pursley, Letter dated October 13, 1961, Francis J. Connell Papers, Redemptorist House Archives, Baltimore Province, Brooklyn, New York.

26. Bishop Leo Pursley to Francis J. Connell, Letter dated October 17, 1961, Francis J. Connell Papers, Redemptorist House Archives, Baltimore Province, Brooklyn, New York.

27. John A O'Brien, "Can Christians Unite?", Francis J. Connell Papers, Redemptorist House Archives, Baltimore Province, Brooklyn, New York.

28. Francis J. Connell to Fr. John Ford SJ, Letter dated November 1, 1964, Francis J. Connell Papers, Redemptorist House Archives, Baltimore Province, Brooklyn, New York.

29. John Courtney Murray, "Memo /s Card. Cushing," undated, *John Courtney Murray Papers*: Box 1 Folder 43, Georgetown University Library, Special Collections Division, Washington, D.C.

30. Murray, "Memo /s Card. Cushing," undated.

31. Murray, "Memo /s Card. Cushing," undated.

32. Murray, "Memo /s Card. Cushing," undated.

33. Murray, "Memo /s Card. Cushing," undated.

34. Murray, "Memo /s Card. Cushing," undated.

35. "Birth report 'leak' called act of genius," *Catholic Chronicle,* May 5, 1967, *John Courtney Murray Papers*: Box 2 Folder 264, Georgetown University Library, Special Collections Division, Washington, D.C.

36. "Birth report 'leak' called act of genius," *Catholic Chronicle,* May 5, 1967.

37. "Birth report 'leak' called act of genius," *Catholic Chronicle,* May 5, 1967.

38. "Birth report 'leak' called act of genius," *Catholic Chronicle,* May 5, 1967.

39. John Courtney Murray to Mrs. James Moran, Letter dated June 21, 1967, *John Courtney Murray Papers*: Box 2 Folder 173, Georgetown University Library, Special Collections Division, Washington, D.C.

40. Fred McDonald to John Courtney Murray, Letter dated August 11, 1967 with Press Release, *John Courtney Murray Papers:* Box 2 Folder 231, Georgetown University Library, Special Collections Division, Washington, D.C.

41. Malachi Martin, *The Jesuits: The Society of Jesus and the Betrayal of the Roman Catholic Church* (New York: The Linden Press, Simon and Schuster, 1987), 329.

42. Raymond A. Schroth, *The American Jesuits: A History* (New York: New York University Press, 2007), 213.

43. Charles Curran, *Loyal Dissent: Memoir of a Catholic Theologian* (Washington DC: Georgetown University Press, 2006), 77.

44. Curran, *Loyal Dissent: Memoir of a Catholic Theologian*, 209-211.

45. J Howard Pew "Should the Church 'Meddle' in Civil Affairs?" *Reader's Digest,* May, 1966 as found in AND 0004.001 George Shea Papers Box 19, Monsignor William Noe Field Archives and Special Collections Center, Seton Hall University, South Orange, New Jersey

46. Pelotte, *John Courtney Murray: Theologian in Conflict,* 57 n 122, 71-72.

CHAPTER 120

1. AZ, interviewed by author, December 28, 2009.
2. Pelotte, *John Courtney Murray: Theologian in Conflict,* 104.
3. John Courtney Murray to Clare Boothe Luce, Letter dated "Sunday, 6th", Clare Boothe Luce Papers: Box 212 Folder 9, Library of Congress, Washington, D.C.
4. Garry Wills, "Secular Incompetence and Catholic Confusion," *Worldview* (June, 1972), 5-6, from *John Courtney Murray Papers*: Box 28 Folder 1281, Georgetown University Library, Special Collections Division, Washington D.C.
5. Wills, "Secular Incompetence and Catholic Confusion," 9-10.
6. Wills, "Secular Incompetence and Catholic Confusion," 9-10.
7. "Roman Catholics: Selective Faith," *Time,* September 16, 1966. http://www.time.com/time/subscriber/printout/0,8816,836376,00.html (accessed November 11, 2012).
8. "Roman Catholics: Selective Faith," *Time,* September 16, 1966.
9. Hughes, "A Man for Our Season," *John Courtney Murray Papers*: Box 28 Folder 1288, Georgetown University Library, Special Collections Division, Washington, D.C.
10. Hughes, "A Man for Our Season."
11. John Courtney Murray, "The Ecumenical Revolution: Genesis, Challenge, Response," and letter from Aileen Bacalman to Herman E Wornom dated December 19, 1966, *John Courtney Murray Papers:* Box 6 Folder 469, Georgetown University Library, Special Collections Division, Washington, D.C.
12. Murray, "The Ecumenical Revolution: Genesis, Challenge, Response," and Bacalman to Wornom Letter dated December 19, 1966.
13. Murray, "The Ecumenical Revolution: Genesis, Challenge, Response," and Bacalman to Wornom Letter dated December 19, 1966.
14. Untitled Document starting with "Minutes of Meeting....on December 29, 1966", John F. Dearden Papers (CDRD): Box 12 Folder 10, University of Notre Dame Archives (UNDA), Notre Dame, Indiana.
15. Untitled Document starting with "Minutes of Meeting...on December 29, 1966."
16. Untitled Document starting with "Minutes of Meeting...on December 29, 1966."
17. Untitled Document starting with "Minutes of Meeting...on December 29, 1966."
18. Ibid.
19. John Courtney Murray to Archbishop Deardan, Letter dated October 25, 1966, *John Courtney Murray Papers*: Box 2 Folder 149, Georgetown University Library, Special Collections Division, Washington, D.C.
20. Hughes, "A Man for Our Season"; John Courtney Murray, Memorandum undated in response to letter of February 13, 1957 from Stephen F. Bayne, Jr. to John Courtney Murray, *John Courtney Murray Papers*: Box 1 Folder 11, Georgetown University Library, Special Collections Division, Washington, D.C.
21. Sue De Wine to John Courtney Murray, Letter dated May 5, 1967, *John Courtney Murray Papers*: Box 1 Folder 50, Georgetown University Library, Special Collections Division, Washington, D.C.
22. John Courtney Murray to DeWine, Letter dated May 19, 1967, *John Courtney Murray Papers*: Box 1 Folder 50, Georgetown University Library, Special Collections Division, Washington, D.C.
23. Theodore Hesburgh to John Courtney Murray, Letter dated June 14, 1967, *John Courtney Murray Papers*: Box 1 Folder 106, Georgetown University Library, Special

Collections Division, Washington, D.C.

24. John Courtney Murray to Theodore Hesburgh, Letter dated June 21, 1967, *John Courtney Murray Papers*: Box 1 Folder 106, Georgetown University Library, Special Collections Division, Washington, D.C.

CHAPTER 121

1. Swanberg, *Luce and His Empire*, 675.
2. Wilford, *The Mighty Wurlitzer: How the CIA Played America*, 3-5.
3. Wilford, *The Mighty Wurlitzer: How the CIA Played America*, 231-232.
4. Swanberg, *Luce and His Empire*, 672-674.
5. Alden Whitman, "Henry R. Luce, Creator of Time-Life Magazine Empire, Dies in Phoenix at 68" *The New York Times* http://www.nytimes.com/learning/geenral/onthisday/bday/0403.html as accessed December 10, 2014.
6. "Nation: He Ran the Course," *Time,* March 10, 1967. http://www.time.com/time/printout/0,8816,836724,00.html (accessed December 31, 2009).
7. "Nation: He Ran the Course," *Time,* March 10, 1967.
8. "Nation: He Ran the Course," *Time,* March 10, 1967.
9. "Nation: He Ran the Course," *Time,* March 10, 1967.
10. "Nation: He Ran the Course," *Time,* March 10, 1967.
11. John Courtney Murray to Mrs. Maurice T Moore, Letter dated April 4, 1967, *John Courtney Murray Papers*: Box 2 Folder 173, Georgetown University Library, Special Collections Division, Washington, D.C.
12. Swanberg, *Luce and His Empire,* 676-677.
13. Sheed, *Clare Boothe Luce,* 164-176.

CHAPTER 122

1. Bishop Clarence J. Duhart, C.Ss.R. to Dr. Vincent Zamoyta, Letter dated April 28, 1981, Redemptorist House Archives, Baltimore Province, Brooklyn, New York.
2. Curran, *Loyal Dissent: Memoir of a Catholic Theologian,* 45.
3. Francis J. Connell to Archbishop O'Boyle, Letter dated April 16, 1966, Francis J. Connell Papers, Redemptorist House Archives, Baltimore Province, Brooklyn, New York.
4. Francis J. Connell to Archbishop O'Boyle, Letter dated April 16, 1966, Francis J. Connell Papers, Redemptorist House Archives, Baltimore Province, Brooklyn, New York.
5. Francis J. Connell to Archbishop O'Boyle, Letter dated April 16, 1966, Francis J. Connell Papers, Redemptorist House Archives, Baltimore Province, Brooklyn, New York.
6. Francis J. Connell to Archbishop O'Boyle, Letter dated April 16, 1966, Francis J. Connell Papers, Redemptorist House Archives, Baltimore Province, Brooklyn, New York.
7. "Roman Curia Worried…" article, undated, unattributed from Francis J. Connell Papers, Redemptorist House Archives, Baltimore Province, Brooklyn, New York.
8. Jon L. Hess, "France's Bishops Deplore Tone of Vatican Warning on Ferment," *The New York Times,* February 2, 1967, 1, 15.

9. Hess, "France's Bishops Deplore Tone of Vatican Warning on Ferment," *The New York Times,* February 2, 1967.

10. "French Bishops Answer Cardinal's Letter, " NCWC News Service (Foreign), February 4, 1967.

11. Fr. Placid Jordan OSB, "Jesuit Criticizes Attempts to 'Hush Up' Problems," NCWC News Service (Foreign), December 6, 1966.

12. Francis J. Connell to Ottaviani, Letter dated November 14, 1966, Francis J. Connell Papers, Redemptorist House Archives, Baltimore Province, Brooklyn, New York.

13. Ottaviani to Francis J. Connell, Letter dated November 22, 1966, Francis J. Connell Papers, Redemptorist House Archives, Baltimore Province, Brooklyn, New York.

14. Francis J. Connell to Vagnozzi, Letter dated December 1, 1966, Francis J. Connell Papers, Redemptorist House Archives, Baltimore Province, Brooklyn, New York.

15. Francis J. Connell to Vagnozzi, Letter dated December 1, 1966 with "Comments on Christian Morality Today by Rev. Charles E Curran," Francis J. Connell Papers, Redemptorist House Archives, Baltimore Province, Brooklyn, New York.

16. Connell to Vagnozzi Letter dated December 1, 1966 with "Comments on Christian Morality Today by Rev. Charles E. Curran."

17. Francis J. Connell, "Comments on Proceedings of the Annual Assembly, CMSW, 1966," Francis J. Connell Papers, Redemptorist House Archives, Baltimore Province, Brooklyn, New York.

18. Francis J. Connell to Ottaviani, Letter dated December 8, 1966, Francis J. Connell Papers, Redemptorist House Archives, Baltimore Province, Brooklyn, New York.

19. "Pope Asks Cardinal Ottaviani Not to Resign," NC News Service (Foreign), March 2, 1967.

20. Francis J. Connell to Ottaviani, Letter dated April 1, 1967, Francis J. Connell Papers, Redemptorist House Archives, Baltimore Province, Brooklyn, New York.

21. "Frank Connell" paper, undated, Folder "Cause of Francis J Connell & Francis J Connell I," Redemptorist House Archives, Baltimore Province, Brooklyn, New York.

22. "RP Francis J. Connell's Obituary," *C.SS.R. Chronicle,* November, 1967, 31, Francis J. Connell Papers, Redemptorist House Archives, Baltimore Province, Brooklyn, New York.

23. "RP Francis J. Connell's Obituary."

24. "Sermon delivered by Rev. Charles Fehrenbach, C.SS.R. at the Funeral of Very Rev. Francis J. Connell, C.SS.R.," May 16, 1967, Francis J. Connell Papers, Redemptorist House Archives, Baltimore Province, Brooklyn, New York.

25. "Sermon delivered by Rev. Charles Fehrenbach, C.SS.R at the Funeral of Very Rev. Francis J. Connell, C.SS.R.," May 16, 1967.

26. Fr. Titus, S.A., "Every Priest Is Appointed to Act for Men in Their Relationship with God," Francis J. Connell Papers, Redemptorist House Archives, Baltimore Province, Brooklyn, New York.

CHAPTER 123

1. Joseph Clifford Fenton, Entry from November 23, 1968, Diary, 24.
2. Joseph Clifford Fenton, Entry from February 27, 1969, Diary, 30-31.
3. "Obituary of Msgr Joseph Fenton," *The Catholic Observer* (Official Publication of the Diocese of Springfield, Mass.), July 11, 1969.
4. "Eulogy for Msgr. Fenton," *The Catholic Observer*, July 18, 1969.
5. "Eulogy for Msgr. Fenton," *The Catholic Observer*, July 18, 1969.
6. "Eulogy for Msgr. Fenton," *The Catholic Observer*, July 18, 1969.
7. "Eulogy for Msgr. Fenton," *The Catholic Observer*, July 18, 1969.

CHAPTER 124

1. Hughes, "A Man for Our Season," January 16, 1969, *John Courtney Murray Papers*: Box 28 Folder 1288, Georgetown University Library, Special Collections Division, Washington, D.C.
2. "Rev. John Courtney Murray, 63, Leading Jesuit Theologian, Dies; Was Expert on Church-State Relations and on Freedom Under Religious Rules," *The New York Times*, Saturday, August 19, 1967.
3. "Rev. John Courtney Murray, 63, Leading Jesuit Theologian, Dies; Was Expert on Church-State Relations and on Freedom Under Religious Rules," *The New York Times*, Saturday, August 19, 1967
4. "Rev. John Courtney Murray, 63, Leading Jesuit Theologian, Dies; Was Expert on Church-State Relations and on Freedom Under Religious Rules," *The New York Times*, Saturday, August 19, 1967
5. "Rev. John Courtney Murray, 63, Leading Jesuit Theologian, Dies; Was Expert on Church-State Relations and on Freedom Under Religious Rules," *The New York Times*, Saturday, August 19, 1967
6. "Rev. John Courtney Murray, 63, Leading Jesuit Theologian, Dies; Was Expert on Church-State Relations and on Freedom Under Religious Rules," *The New York Times*, Saturday, August 19, 1967
7. Cooney, *The American Pope: The Life and Times of Francis Cardinal Spellman*, 399-406.
8. "Cardinals Attend Mass for Murray: Spellman, Cushing at Rites for Jesuit Theologian," *The New York Times* August 22, 1967, from *John Courtney Murray Papers*: Box 28 Folder 1268, Georgetown University Library, Special Collections Division, Washington, D.C.
9. "Religion – Man of the City," *Time*, August 25, 1967, from *John Courtney Murray Papers*: Box 28 Folder 1265, Georgetown University Library, Special Collections Division, Washington D.C.
10. "Religion – Man of the City," *Time*, August 25, 1967, from *John Courtney Murray Papers*: Box 28 Folder 1265, Georgetown University Library, Special Collections Division, Washington D.C.
11. "Religion – Man of the City," *Time*, August 25, 1967, from *John Courtney Murray Papers*: Box 28 Folder 1265, Georgetown University Library, Special Collections Division, Washington D.C.
12. Robert F Kennedy, Letter of September 27, 1967 with copy of Congressional Record – Senate S13295-13296, *John Courtney Murray Papers*: Box 28 Folder

1264, Georgetown University Library, Special Collections Division, Washington, D.C.

13. John Deedy, *Seven American Catholics* (Chicago, Illinois: The Thomas More Press, 1978), 152-153.

14. Sister Ursula Benziger to Fr. Burghardt, Letter dated January 20, 1968 with attachment, *John Courtney Murray Papers:* Box 2 Folder 264, Georgetown University Library, Special Collections Division, Washington, D.C.

CHAPTER 125

1. Payne, *The Franco Regime: 1936-1975,* 392-393.
2. Payne, *The Franco Regime: 1936-1975,* 470.
3. Payne, *The Franco Regime: 1936-1975,* 470.
4. Payne, *The Franco Regime: 1936-1975,* 466.
5. Payne, *The Franco Regime: 1936-1975,* 492
6. Payne, *The Franco Regime: 1936-1975,* 625
7. Payne, *The Franco Regime: 1936-1975,* 493.
8. Payne, *The Franco Regime: 1936-1975,* 561.
9. Payne, *The Franco Regime: 1936-1975,* 561.
10. Payne, *The Franco Regime: 1936-1975,* 562-563
11. Payne, *The Franco Regime: 1936-1975,* 562-563.
12. Payne, *The Franco Regime: 1936-1975,* 620.
13. Spanish Constitution. http://www.lamoncloa.gob.es/IDIOMAS/9/Espana/LeyFundamental/index.htm (accessed April 27, 2014). "Human dignity" formed the basis of the "fundamental rights" to be protected. The Constitution states that "2. The principles relating to the fundamental rights and liberties recognized by the Constitution shall be interpreted in conformity with the Universal Declaration of Human Rights and the international treaties and agreements thereon ratified by Spain." Of these "rights and liberties" included ideological and religious freedom contained in Article 16: "1. Freedom of ideology, religion and worship of individuals and communities is guaranteed, with no other restriction on their expression than may be necessary to maintain public order as protected by law. 2. No one may be compelled to make statements regarding his religion, beliefs, or ideologies."
14. "Pope Leaves Spain, Urging it to Own Up to Christian Roots." M & C or Monsters and Critics. www.monstersandcritics.com (accessed November 7, 2010); "Fewer Spaniards say they are Catholic: study." AFP and Yahoo News. http://au.news.yahoo.com. (accessed July 30, 2010).
15. Paul Day, "Fragile Spanish Economy Limps Out of Recession," *Business and Financial News.* http://www.reuters.com/article/2013/10/30/us-spain-economy-idUSBRE99T0BH20131030 (accessed April 27, 2014).
16. "Modifications to the Lateran Concordat (1984): text." *Concordat Watch.* http://www.concordatwatch.eu/showtopic.php?org_id=878&b_header_id=39221 (accessed May 19, 2013).
17. "Modifications to the Lateran Concordat (1984): text." *Concordat Watch.* http://www.concordatwatch.eu/showtopic.php?org_id=878&b_header_id=39221 (accessed May 19, 2013).
18. "Europe: New Rainbow Map Shows How Gay Friendly (or Not) European Countries Are," *Gay Marriage Watch Italy,* May 16, 2013. http://purpleunions.

com/bog/tag/italy (accessed May 19, 2013); Lorenzo Totaro, "Italy Unemployment Rate Remains Close to 20-year-high amid slump," *Bloomberg,* April 30, 2013. http://www.bloomberg.comnews/print/2013-04-30italy-unemployment-rate-remains-clos... (accessed May 19, 2013); "Italy Death rate – Demographics," *Index Mundi.* http://www.indexmundi.com/italy/death_rate.html (accessed May 19, 2013); Hilary White, "Italy's Last Catholic Generation? Mass Attendance in `Collapse' among Under-30s," *Life Site News,* August 9 2010.http://www.lifesitenews.com/home/print_article/news/1979/ (accessed May 19, 2013).

19. Cathy Lynn Grossman, "Most Religious Groups in USA Have Lost Ground, Survey Finds," *USA Today*, updated March 17, 2009. http://usatoday30.usatoday.-com/news/religion/2009-03-09-american-religion-ARIS_N.htm (accessed April 30, 2013).

20. Grossman, "Most Religious Groups in USA Have Lost Ground, Survey Finds," *USA Today,* updated March 17, 2009.

21. "Mixing their religion," *USA Today,* December 10, 2009.

22. Rev. Leonard M. Jepson "Viewpoint: Consider World Change as Adventure," *South Bend Tribune,* December 25, 2013.

23. "Mixing their religion," *USA Today,* December 10, 2009.

24. "Mixing their religion," *USA Today,* December 10, 2009.

25. "Mixing their religion," *USA Today,* December 10, 2009.

26. "Mixing their religion," *USA Today,* December 10, 2009.

27. "Hunger Facts," *Feeding America.* http://feedingamerica.org/hunger-in-america/hunger-facts.aspx (accessed April 27, 2014).

28. Paul Davidson, "Drop In Labor Participation Rate is Distress Signal," *USA Today.* http://www.usatoday.com/story/money/business/2013/04/07/march-labor-force-participation/2057887/ (accessed April 27, 2014).

29. Jennifer Liberto, "CEO Pay Is 380 Times Average Worker's – AFL CIO," *CNN,* http://money.cnn.com/2012/04/19/news/economy/ceo-pay/ (accessed April 27, 2014).

30. Zaid Jilani, "How Unequal We Are: The Top Five Facts You Should Know About the Wealthiest One Percent of Americans." http://thinkprogress.org/economy/2011/10/03/334156/top-five-wealthiest-one-percent/ (accessed April 27, 2014).

31. Sandro Magister, "The Doctrine of the Catholic Kennedy? Worthless" containing the text of a talk given by Archbishop Charles J. Chaput entitled "The Vocation of Christians in American Public Life" given March 1, 2010 in Houston Texas. La Chiesea. http://chiesa.esperesso.repubblica.it/articolo/1342344?eng=y.

32. Magister, "The Doctrine of the Catholic Kennedy? Worthless."

33. "Exit Interview: Father Theodore Hesburgh," *Scholastic* Vol. 152 No. 4, 40; Hon. Nancy Pelosi, "Honoring Father Hesburgh" from the Congressional Record for May 23, 2013 from http://beta.congress.gov/congressional-record/2013/05/23/extensions-of-remarks-section/article/E729-1 (accessed June 15, 2013).

34. "Exit Interview: Father Theodore Hesburgh," *Scholastic,* Vol. 152 No. 4, 40.

35. Pope Benedict XVI, "Address of His Holiness Benedict XVI to the Roman Curia Offering Them His Christmas Blessing," Thursday, 22 December 2005, Vatican website. http://www.vatican.va/holy_father/benedict_xvi/speeches/2005/december/documents/hf_ben_xvi_spe_20051222_roman-curia_en.html (accessed July 21, 2013).

CHAPTER 126

1. Guillaume Goubert and Sebastien Maillard, "Interview Pope Francis," *LaCroix* posted May 17, 2016 and retrieved October 9, 2016 from http://www.la-croix.com/article/imprimer/Religion/Pape/Interview-Pope-Francis-2016....

2. Myles Snyder, "Read the pope's speech at Independence Hall," *abc27news*, published September 27, 2015. http://abc27.com/2015/09/27/read-the-popes-speech-at-independence-hall/ (accessed October 9, 2016) (emphasis added).

3. Ryan Teague Beckwith, "Read the Speech Pope Francis Gave at the White House," *Time,* published September 23, 2015. http://time.com/4045956/pope-francis-us-visit-white-house-transcript/. (accessed October 9, 2016) (emphasis added).

4. Pope Benedict XVI, "Address At the White House, April 16, 2008," *American Rhetoric* at https://www.americanrhetoric.com/speeches/popebenedictxvi-whitehouse.htm as retrieved July 5, 2021.

5. See, Kirsten Gilbert, Karyn Hall and R. Trent Codd, "Radically Open Dialectical Behavior Therapy: Social Signaling, Transdiagnostic Utility and Current Evidence," *Psychology Research and Behavior Management,* 8 January 2020 Volume 2020:13 Pages 19—28 **DOI** https://doi.org/10.2147/PRBM.S201848: " What truly makes RO DBT unique is that RO DBT builds on this compelling literature by being the first treatment to emphasize social signaling as a primary mechanism of change. It underscores the importance of targeting publicly observable behaviors (eg, social signals) to increase psychological connectedness with important others. A social signal is defined as any action or overt behavior, regardless of its form, intent, or the performer's awareness, that is carried out in the presence of another person. A social signal is a form of communication, such as an eye roll, the silent treatment, walking away, or a smile. RO DBT hypothesizes that the mechanism of change in treatment is that open expression of emotion leads to trust, which leads to social connection. Mechanisms of behavior change generally refer to the underlying basic psychological processes that drive change in therapy, and for RO DBT, the theorized critical process driving change in treatment is social signaling. As such, RO DBT aims to teach overcontrolled individuals how to modify their social signaling so as to openly express emotions and vulnerabilities, which results in increased social connectedness." Social signaling in this article refers to public actions that build trust and connectedness. It also implies social signaling is a way of leading with the initiator of the signal as the leader. This is the situation in society at large in which the rich and powerful show their support for something thereby authorizing others in society to join in that belief system.

6. David Dawkins, "Billionaire George Soros Pledges $ 1 Billion University Fund To Fight `Would-Be Dictators,'" January 24, 2020, *Forbes,* www.forbes.com.... as accessed June 14, 2020.

7. Sean Spicer, "Spicer & Company," *Newsmax,* November 26, 2020 at 6:49 p.m. ET.

8. Michael Bloomberg, "The Road to Racial Justice Runs Through Tulsa," June 19, 2020, *Bloomberg,* as accessed from https://www.bloomberg.com/opinion/articles/2020-06-19/mike-bloomberg-road-to-racial-justice-runs-through-tulsa?sref=JTYs6URC June 24, 2020.

9. Ibid.

10. Satya Nadella, "Addressing Racial Injustice," June 23, 2020, *Microsoft,* as accessed from https://blogs.microsoft.com/blog/2020/06/23/addressing-racial-injustice/ on June 29, 2020.
11. Callie Caplan, "Mark Cuban Calls Out Defensiveness About White Privilege As Mavericks Discuss Systemic Racism," *The Dallas Morning News,* June 10, 2020.
12. Author's test of the systems, June 29, 2020.
13. Jonathan Capriel, "Bezos Says Good Riddance to Racist Customers, While Amazon Is Sued Over Its Covid19 Practices," June 9, 2020, *Washington Business Journal.*
14. Saijel Kishan, "BlackRock to Push Companies on Racial Diversity in 2021," December 10, 2020, *Bloomberg;* Andrea Vittorio and Jeff Green, "State Street to Vote Against More Directors at Male Only Boards," September 27, 2018, *Bloomberg;* Jeff Kearns, "BlackRock and Vanguard Among Firms Democrats Ask About Diversity," March 18, 2021, *Bloomberg.*
15. "What We Believe," *Black Lives Matter,* as accessed from https://blacklivesmatter.com/what-we-believe June 29, 2020.
16. Pope Francis, *Fratelli Tutti,* October 3, 2020, para. 188.
17. As to the USA, of note one should review what is known as the interstate commerce clause as contained in Article I, Section 8, clause 3; the exclusive ability to coin money and issue securities in Article I, Section 8, clause 5; the Supremacy Clause in Article VI, clause 2.
18. Pope Francis, *Fratelli Tutti,* October 3, 2020, paras. 3 and 4.
19. The account that follows comes from Allyson Kenny's "The Sultan and the Saint," February 4, 2019, *Salt and Light Catholic Media.* It is one of many accounts that hold that St Francis was on a peace mission and actually engaged in extensive theological discussions with the Sultan who was himself a great spiritual leader amongst the Moslems.

CHAPTER 127

1. The term is never defined and has come to mean any of a number of different understandings and sects.
2. "Making Sense of the Illiberal Right: How theConservative Conversation about Democracy is Shifting," *On the Media,* December 6, 2019 https://www.wnycstudios.org/podcasts/otm/segments/making-sense-illiberal-right as accessed December 6, 2019.
3. "Against the Dead Consensus," March 21, 2019, *First Things,* https://www.firstthings.com/web-exclusives/2019/03/against-..... as accessed December 7, 2019. Signed by Sohrab Ahmari, Jeffrey Blehar, Patrick Deneen, Rod Dreher, Pascal-Emmanuel Gobry, Darel Paul, C.C. Pecknold, Matthew Peterson, James Poulos, Mark Regnerus, Matthew Schmitz, Kevin E. Stuart, David Upham, Matthew Walther, Julia Yost.
4. Benjamin Wallace-Wells, "David French, Sohrab Ahmari, and The Battle for the Future of Conservatism," September 12, 2019, *The New Yorker,* https://www.newyorker.com/news/the-political-scene/david-french-sohrab-ahmari.... as accessed December 18, 2019.
5. According to the Wallace-Wells article, French defined the flourishing of Christian groups (by virtue of the First Amendment), as consisting of their ability to organize in universities and public spaces.

NOTES

6. Wallace-Wells, ""David French, Sohrab Ahmari, and The Battle for the Future of Conservatism," *The New Yorker.*
7. Wallace-Wells, "David French, Sohrab Ahmari, and The Battle for the Future of Conservatism."
8. Michael Hanby, "The Birth of Liberal Order And the Death of God: A Reply to Robert Reilly's *America on Trial," New Polity,* February 26, 2021 accessed at https://newpolity.com/blog/the-birth-of-liberal-order as of February 27, 2021.
9. Patrick Deneen, "A Tyranny Without Tyrants," February 20, 2021, *American Affairs.*
10. George Weigel, "Games Intellectuals Play," May 20, 2020, *First Things.*
11. Ibid.
12. Thomas Pink, "Integralism, Political Philosophy, and the State," May 9, 2020, *Public Discourse.*
13. *See,* Antonio Spadaro, Marcelo Figuero, "Evangelical Fundamentalism and Catholic Integralism: A Surprising Ecumenism," July 13, 2017, *La Civilta Cattolica*; Joshua J. McElwee, "Italian Jesuit Magazine Criticizes Political Attitudes of Some US Catholics," July 13, 2017, *National Catholic Reporter*; Massimo Faggioli, "Why Should We Read Spadaro on `Catholic Integralism'?", *Commonweal.*

APPENDIX A

1. "Italy: The Little Professor," *Time,* January 25, 1954.
2. Ibid.; "Amintore Fanfani," *Encyclopedia of World Biography* 2004. http://www.encyclopedia.com/doc/1G2-3404702090.html (accessed July 10, 2011).
3. "Amintore Fanfani," *Encyclopedia of World Biography;* "Obituary: Amintore Fanfani," *The Independent,* 22 November, 1999. www.independent.co.uk (accessed July 10, 2011).
4. "Italy: The Little Professor."
5. "Amintore Fanfani," *Encyclopedia of World Biography*
6. "Amintore Fanfani," *Encyclopedia of World Biography*
7. "Italy: The Little Professor"; "Amintore Fanfani," *Encyclopedia of World Biography;* "Obituary: Amintore Fanfani";"Amintore Fanfani: He held every political office in Italy but the one he craved most – president of the Republic", *The Guardian,* 22 November 1999. www.guardian.co.uk (accessed July 10 2011.)
8. "Amintore Fanfani," Encyclopedia of World Biography.
9. "Amintore Fanfani," Encyclopedia of World Biography; "Obituary: Amintore Fanfani"
10. "Italy: The Little Professor," *Time.*
11. "Italy: The Little Professor"
12. "Amintore Fanfani," *Encyclopedia of World Biography.*
13. Amintore Fanfani," *Encyclopedia of World Biography*
14. Amintore Fanfani," *Encyclopedia of World Biography*
15. Amintore Fanfani," *Encyclopedia of World Biography*
16. "Italy: The Little Professor."
17. "Italy: The Little Professor"; "Amintore Fanfani," *Encyclopedia of World Biography.*
18. "Amintore Fanfani," *Encyclopedia of World Biography.*
19. Amintore Fanfani," *Encyclopedia of World Biography*

20. "Amintore Fanfani," *The Guardian*; "Amintore Fanfani," *Encyclopedia of World Biography*.
21. "Amintore Fanfani," *Encycopedia of World Biography*.
22. "Obituary: Amintore Fanfani," *The Independent*
23. "Amintore Fanfani," *The Guardian*.
24. "Amintore Fanfani," *The Guardian*.
25. "Obituary: Amintore Fanfani," *The Independent*.
26. Clare Boothe Luce to CD Jackson, Letter dated September 29, 1954, CD Jackson Papers Box 70 Folder "Luce, Henry R. & Clare, 1954 (1)", Dwight D. Eisenhower Library, Abilene, Kansas.
27. Luce to Jackson Letter dated September 29, 1954.
28. Frank Dennis, Memorandum dated February 1, 1954 entitled "Prof. Fanfani and the American Economy," Clare Boothe Luce Papers, Box 633, Library of Congress, Washington, D.C. , 1.
29. Dennis Memorandum dated February 1, 1954, 9-10.
30. Dennis Memorandum dated February 1, 1954, 10.
31. Dennis Memorandum dated February 1, 1954, 10.
32. "Amintore Fanfani," *The Guardian*.
33. "Obituary: Amintore Fanfani."
34. Amintore Fanfani, *Catholicism Protestantism and Capitalism,* (Norfolk, Virginia: IHS Press, 2003), 56.
35. Fanfani, *Catholicism Protestantism and Capitalism* (Norfolk, Virginia: IHS Press, 2003), 51, 56-57, 59-60, 64.
36. Fanfani, *Catholicism Protestantism and Capitalism,* 64.
37. Fanfani, *Catholicism Protestantism and Capitalism,* 64-65.
38. Fanfani, *Catholicism Protestantism and Capitalism,* 64-66.
39. Fanfani, *Catholicism Protestantism and Capitalism,* 90.
40. Huertas, Thomas F. "Can Banking And Commerce Mix?" *Cato Journal* 7, no. 3 (Winter 1988): 743-769.
41. Fanfani, *Catholicism Protestantism and Capitalism,* 70, 88.
42. Michael Foot and Isaac Kramnick, editors, *The Thomas Paine Reader* (London, England: Penguin Books, 1987), 22-25.
43. Fanfani, *Catholicism Protestantism and Capitalism,* 89.
44. Fanfani, *Catholicism Protestantism and Capitalism,* 108.
45. Fanfani, *Catholicism Protestantism and Capitalism,* 114, 135.
46. Fanfani, *Catholicism Protestantism and Capitalism,* 94-95.
47. Fanfani, *Catholicism Protestantism and Capitalism,* 100-101.
48. Fanfani, *Catholicism Protestantism and Capitalism,* 102-105.
49. Fanfani, *Catholicism Protestantism and Capitalism,* 137-138.
50. Ibid., 138, 142.

APPENDIX B

1. Dr. Joseph Fessler, Bishop of St. Polten, Austria, and Secretary General of the Vatican Council, "The True and the False Infallbility [sic] of the Popes: A Controversial Reply to Dr. Schulte," p. 1, Clare Boothe Luce Papers Box 699 Folder 3, Library of Congress, Washington, D.C.
2. Fessler, "The True and False Infallbility [sic] of the Popes: A Controversial Reply to Dr. Schulte," 1-2.

3. Fessler, "The True and False Infallbility [sic] of the Popes: A Controversial Reply to Dr. Schulte," 2.
4. Fessler, "The True and False Infallbility [sic] of the Popes: A Controversial Reply to Dr. Schulte," 2-3.
5. Fessler, "The True and False Infallbility [sic] of the Popes: A Controversial Reply to Dr. Schulte," 3-4.
6. Fessler, "The True and False Infallbility [sic] of the Popes: A Controversial Reply to Dr. Schulte," 4.
7. Fessler, "The True and False Infallbility [sic] of the Popes: A Controversial Reply to Dr. Schulte," 4-5.
8. Fessler, "The True and False Infallbility [sic] of the Popes: A Controversial Reply to Dr. Schulte," 5.
9. Fessler, "The True and False Infallbility [sic] of the Popes: A Controversial Reply to Dr. Schulte," 5-6.
10. Fessler, "The True and False Infallbility [sic] of the Popes: A Controversial Reply to Dr. Schulte," 6-7.
11. Fessler, "The True and False Infallbility [sic] of the Popes: A Controversial Reply to Dr. Schulte," 7-8.

APPENDIX C

1. "'The Problem of Religious Freedom,' by John Courtney Murray," *Journal of Church and State* (1966) 8:(3) 475.
2. John Courtney Murray "The Problem of Religious Freedom at the Council," *John F. Deardan Papers (DRD):* Box 6 Folder 9, 3-5, University of Notre Dame Archives (UNDA), Notre Dame, Indiana; and Woodstock Theological Center at Georgetown University. http://woodstock.georgetown.edu/library/Murray/1964e.htm (accessed March 7, 2013).
3. Murray, "The Problem of Religious Freedom at the Council," 3-5.
4. Murray, "The Problem of Religious Freedom at the Council," 3-5.
5. Murray, "The Problem of Religious Freedom at the Council," 3-5.
6. Murray, "The Problem of Religious Freedom at the Council," 5.
7. Murray, "The Problem of Religious Freedom at the Council," 6-8.
8. Murray, "The Problem of Religious Freedom at the Council," 8, 9, 39.
9. Murray, "The Problem of Religious Freedom at the Council," 8-10.
10. Murray, "The Problem of Religious Freedom at the Council," 11.
11. Murray, "The Problem of Religious Freedom at the Council," 12-13.
12. Murray, "The Problem of Religious Freedom at the Council," 13-14.
13. Murray, "The Problem of Religious Freedom at the Council," 20-21.
14. Murray, "The Problem of Religious Freedom at the Council," 24.
15. Murray, "The Problem of Religious Freedom at the Council," 24-26.
16. Murray, "The Problem of Religious Freedom at the Council," 26-28.
17. Pius IX, *Syllabus of Errors Condemned by Pius IX.* http://www.papalencyclicals.net/Pius09/p9syll.htm (accessed November 7, 2006).
18. John Courtney Murray, "The Problem of Religious Freedom at the Council," John F. Deardan Papers (DRD): Box 6 Folder 9, 28-30, University of Notre Dame Archives (UNDA), Notre Dame, Indiana; and Woodstock Theological Center at Georgetown University. http://woodstock.georgetown.edu/library/Murray/1964e.htm (accessed March 7, 2013).

19. Murray, "The Problem of Religious Freedom at the Council," 31-33.

20. Murray, "The Problem of Religious Freedom at the Council," 31-32.

21. Murray, "The Problem of Religious Freedom at the Council," 34-37.

22. Murray, "The Problem of Religious Freedom at the Council," 37.

23. Murray, "The Problem of Religious Freedom at the Council," 38-41.

24. Pope John XXIII, *Pacem In Terris,* paras. 57-59.

25. Pope John XXIII, *Pacem In Terris*, paras. 41-44.

26. Pope John XXIII, *Pacem In Terris*, paras. 44-46.

27. Pope John XXIII, *Pacem In Terris,* paras. 51-54.

28. George W Shea's notes "The Problem of Religious Freedom at the Council" AND 0004.001 George Shea Papers Box 19, Monsignor William Noe Field Archives and Special Collections Center, Seton Hall University, South Orange, New Jersey.

Made in the USA
Monee, IL
26 October 2022

16578845R30351